Twelve Good Men and True

Edited by
J. S. Cockburn and Thomas A. Green

Twelve Good Men and True
The Criminal Trial Jury in England, 1200–1800

Princeton University Press
Princeton, New Jersey

Published by Princeton University Press,
41 William Street,
Princeton, New Jersey 08540
In the United Kingdom:
Princeton University Press,
Guildford, Surrey

Library of Congress Cataloging in Publication Data
will be found on the last printed page of this book

ISBN 0–691–05511–4

This book has been composed in Trump Medieval

Clothbound editions of Princeton University Press books
are printed on acid-free paper, and binding materials
are chosen for strength and durability.
Paperbacks, although satisfactory for personal collections,
are not usually suitable for library rebinding

Printed in the United States of America
by Princeton University Press,
Princeton, New Jersey

Contents

List of Illustrations

List of Tables

Preface

This collection of essays on the English criminal trial jury originated in a panel held at the 1983 conference of the American Society for Legal History. On that occasion the editors and one of the contributors, John Beattie, addressed, *inter alia*, two closely related questions: Who were the jurors? and, How did the institution of the jury trial function? The second question commanded the greater interest—of both the panel and the audience—but it became clear that in order to answer that question fully, one had to know the answer to the first question.

Given the demands of such an undertaking, and possible variations in local experience, it seemed appropriate to commission from interested scholars a range of essays on jury composition and its implications for the nature of the criminal trial and the administration of the criminal law. The history of crime, the criminal law, and more broadly, the administration of criminal justice had already attracted the attention of English historians of all periods from the Middle Ages to modern times, and many of these scholars had, each for his own time and locale, mastered the kinds of records that can be made to reveal the status, wealth, residence, and degree of literacy (if any) of those called upon to serve as jurors in the criminal courts. It appeared likely that a sustained focus on these records would not only shed light on the changing contours of composition but would also illuminate some critical turning points in the administration of the criminal law. This has indeed turned out to be true.

Each of the essays collected here stands on its own. Together they form a kind of continuous history, although there are inevitable gaps, questions posed but left unanswered, and, at times, conflicting streams of emphasis or interpretation. A brief summary of their contents will aid selective readers who wish to know what is relevant to them as well as readers who are prepared to examine all the trees but who wonder in what forest they are wandering. The essays fall into three main periods: the medieval, the early modern, and the late seventeenth and eighteenth centuries. Individually, they may be epitomized as follows.

Roger Groot examines the manner in which the trial jury was formed about the year 1220, when, the ordeal having been abolished, the royal authorities required some new means of testing the presentments made to them at visitations of the shires. Bernard McLane discusses the sorting out by presenting and trial jurors of accusations made in response to the Crown's call for a special inquiry into the causes of disorder in early-fourteenth-century Lincolnshire. John Post analyzes late-fourteenth-century jury lists to determine what they reveal about jury composition and the nature of trial. Edward Powell, focusing on jury composition in several counties in the early fifteenth century, challenges the received wisdom on the degree to which self-informing dominated trial by jury in late medieval criminal cases.

Peter Lawson's study of assizes in Jacobean Hertfordshire combines an analysis of composition with an analysis of verdicts in an attempt to explain the social and economic role of the criminal trial jury. James Cockburn's essay ranges over the years from 1560 to 1670, examining several periods in the history of the jury's composition, its relationship to the bench, and its manifestations of dependence or independence. Stephen Roberts's focus on Devon quarter sessions provides insight into the local political and socio-economic concerns that conditioned the selection and behavior of jurors during the Interregnum and early Restoration years.

John Beattie establishes the economic and social status of London jurors in the late seventeenth century and suggests the ways in which England's leading metropolitan area either followed or led the provinces in the administration of criminal law. Peter King's analysis of eighteenth-century Essex jury composition broadens out into an assessment of the jury in practice and compares the jury's actual role with the rhetoric that contemporaries employed in describing the institution. Douglas Hay's study of jury composition in late-eighteenth-century Staffordshire and Northamptonshire similarly (but with different results) assesses the distance between, on the one hand, the status and interests of jurors, and, on the other, contemporary rhetoric regarding the institution of trial by jury.

Professor Green's history of the criminal trial jury appeared before the essays collected in this volume were completed. *Verdict Accord-*

ing to Conscience: Perspectives on the English Criminal Trial Jury, 1200–1800, published in 1985, is a study of the phenomenon known as jury nullification of rules of law, and it assesses the effects of such jury behavior on the administration of the law and on the way the English thought about the jury, the law, and criminal justice. In *Verdict According to Conscience* Professor Green made use of the few studies of composition then in print, but in the main he left the question of composition to others, daring—insofar as the issue of composition bears upon his own subject—to put the cart well ahead of the horse. His concluding essay in the present volume attempts to relate the essays to each other, to compose at least one version of the running story that they tell, and to relate them to those aspects of his own book that they touch upon. The other ten contributors had the relevant sections of Green's book to hand as they wrote. They worked to some extent within, and to some extent without and against, the framework provided in the institutional chapters of *Verdict According to Conscience*. Green's concluding essay carries the often-implicit debate a step further, highlighting the questions that remain regarding this important subject, about which so much has recently been learned but about which so little has been firmly settled.

The increasing interest in the history of crime and the administration of the criminal law reflects in part a shift of attention within the ranks of legal historians from a nearly exclusive concern with doctrinal and institutional history to a concern with social history. Studies of the development of private law actions have increasingly been complemented by studies of threats to public order and the response to those threats via the rules and institutions of the criminal law. Such studies have sought to ascertain, inter alia, the status and gender of criminals and their victims, the geographical distribution of offenses, the relationship between crime and the economy, and the place of the criminal law within the ongoing contest among groups competing for political dominance. The history of crime and punishment has, in short, proved to be an important source of insight into many aspects of English society over the past eight or nine hundred years. But the separation between scholars of private law and historians of crime and the criminal law has taken its toll. Institutions common to both private and criminal law have sometimes been studied as though they were entirely separate institutions, or have been studied in the context of one but not the other. The latter fate has befallen the jury, which has recently attracted the attention of historians of crime but has not yet been subjected to study by those whose work is on the private law side. This volume, we frankly admit, does not attempt an assessment of the degree to which the jury in criminal cases owed its development to the use of the jury in cases of trespass, or contract, or disputes over the ownership of real or personal property. Yet, surely the use of the jury in private litigation did influence, if only accidentally, its use in criminal cases (and vice versa). We hope that the limitations inevitably inherent in this particular artifact of our age of specialization will encourage others to test our perhaps parochial views by undertaking similar studies of the civil jury. In this as in other ways, the present volume will, we hope, pave the way for a unified study of one of the central institutions of Anglo-American culture.

J. S. Cockburn and Thomas A. Green
June 1987

Acknowledgments

The editors would like to thank Thomas Bowes, Sarah Harrison, and Lynne Taylor for their assistance.

Abbreviations

A J L H	*American Journal of Legal History.*
Beattie, *Crime and the Courts*	J. M. Beattie. *Crime and the Courts in England, 1660–1800.* Princeton, 1986.
B I H R	*Bulletin of the Institute of Historical Research.*
B L	British Library.
Add.	Additional Manuscript
Faust.	Faustinia Manuscript
Harl.	Harleian Manuscript
Lansd.	Lansdowne Manuscript
Cockburn, *Assizes*	J. S. Cockburn. *A History of English Assizes, 1558–1714.* Cambridge, 1972.
Cockburn, *Assize Introduction*	J. S. Cockburn. *Calendar of Assize Records: Home Circuit Indictments, Elizabeth and James I. Introduction.* 1985.
C P R	*Calendar of Patent Rolls.*
E H R	*English Historical Review.*
Green, *Verdict According to Conscience*	T. A. Green. *Verdict According to Conscience: Perspectives on the English Criminal Trial Jury, 1200–1800.* Chicago, 1985.
P R O	Public Record Office.
ASSI	Assizes
C	Chancery
E	Exchequer
JUST	Justices Itinerant
KB	King's Bench
SP	State Papers
STAC	Star Chamber
T R H S	*Transactions of the Royal Historical Society.*

Note

The place of publication of works cited in the notes, unless otherwise stated, is London.

Twelve Good Men and True

One

The Early-Thirteenth-Century Criminal Jury

Roger D. Groot

The most important event in the history of the criminal jury was the abolition of the ordeal by edict of the Roman church in 1215. That act removed the most common method of proof from the English criminal process and so necessitated a search for its successor. The trial jury was that successor.

My contribution to this volume is about the decision to use a jury verdict in place of the ordeal and about the problems faced and the solutions found in implementing that decision. Because the post-1215 events depended so heavily and directly upon the jury forms extant before the abolition of the ordeal, I begin with them. But because that material is examined in detail elsewhere, the treatment is cursory.

I break the succeeding period into three parts: the 1218–19 phase of the 1218–22 eyre, the 1219–21 interim, and the 1221–22 phase of the 1218–22 eyre. The first phase of the eyre is distinct because it was conducted without the ordeal and, I believe, without a true trial jury. But that phase is important to jury development because it used, for the first time, quasi-convicting verdicts as a basis for sanctions. These quasi-convicting verdicts, which demonstrated a new, stronger attitude about public harm from criminality, were one more step toward the convicting jury.

The true trial jury first appears at Westminster during the 1219–21 interim, specifically at the end of Hilary term 1220. It began in approvers' appeals, a specialized kind of prosecution with a specialized non-convicting jury procedure, the inquest *de fidelitate*. The first convicting juries grew out of this inquest. At this stage the convicting jury was limited by specialization and by the fact that the court at Westminster did not have juries readily available.

The first opportunity to use the new trial jury in general criminal prosecutions, and in courts with juries at hand, came in the second phase of the eyre of 1218–22. As that phase of the eyre moved from one session to the next, the justices, the juries, and the defendants, whose interests obviously conflicted, explored the limits of the new system. This caused its application at each session to vary from the last. Publicly prosecuted defendants were tried by jury at Worcester, and the trial jury was extended to appeals at Gloucester. But this extension of the final-verdict jury to appeals was an addition to procedure; it did not replace the older, non-convicting jury verdicts that had long been part of the process of appeals. By the end of the Gloucester session, the trial jury had developed the form it would have as long as the eyre system lasted: twelve hundredors and four vills. But the trial jury did not work well at Gloucester, because defendants regularly refused to put themselves upon it.

The judicial response, at Warwick, was an experiment with forced juries of the hundredors plus twenty-four knights. Because the jury might have been abandoned at that point, the decision to continue with some form of it indicates the depth of the commitment to the concept of lay judging. As a result of the Warwick experiment, defendants again began to accept trial by their communities—the hundredors and vills. This placed the power of judgment back in the hands of the visne (neighborhood)—commoners who could judge both the crime and the accused.

Before 1215

In the mid twelfth century, most criminal prosecutions were privately initiated. In their simplest form, these prosecutions—appeals—began with a formal complaint by the injured party. The accused—the appellee—denied the accusation. Proof was made by judicial combat between the appellor and the appellee.

The form of publicly initiated prosecutions at this time is still debated. Some data suggest that a form of communal accusation, a prehistoric jury, initiated prosecution of crimes not pursued by appeal.[1] More recent scholarship, however, argues strongly for the existence of prosecution initiated upon the complaint of a public official.[2] Which-

1. N. D. Hurnard, "The Jury of Presentment and the Assize of Clarendon," *EHR* 56 (1941): 374ff.

2. R. C. van Caenegem, "Public Prosecution of Crime in Twelfth-Century England," in *Church and Government in the Middle Ages . . . Essays Presented to C. R. Cheney*, ed. C.N.L. Brooke (Cambridge, 1976), 41ff.

ever was the case, Henry II reformed the public prosecution system in 1166, and the criminal jury can be traced from that date. King Henry ordained, in the Assize of Clarendon, that twelve lawful men of each hundred, and four of each vill, should report to the royal justices or sheriffs those persons reputed to have committed certain serious crimes.[3] The reported persons were to make proof by ordeal. Those who failed in their proof were to be mutilated; those who succeeded were nonetheless required to abjure England if the community reported most evilly about them.

We know that this assize was applied[4] and that it was strengthened by the Assize of Northampton in 1176,[5] but we know very little about the actual mechanics of its application. Glanvill, writing in the 1180s, discussed criminal prosecutions primarily in terms of appeals. To the extent that he discussed public prosecution, he seems to describe a variant of the Assizes of Clarendon and Northampton. He implies that the initial report of the jurors was scrutinized by the justices for substance so that the jurors were required first to report all of those reputed to be criminals and then to designate which of them the jurors themselves suspected.[6] The latter group was required to make proof by ordeal; the remainder were probably assigned an easier proof, compurgation, but this is not clear.[7]

From 1194 on we have an unbroken, although quite incomplete, set of judicial records. These records, because they were made contemporaneously with the hearing of the case, yield a clearer picture of procedure than do the earlier materials. At this time, felony prosecution was largely administered by the eyre, a periodic visitation of each county by the royal justices.[8] The sheriff was notified that an eyre was

3. William Stubbs, *Select Charters*, 9th ed. (Oxford, 1921), 143–46 (Latin); C. Stephenson and F. Marcham, *Sources of English Constitutional History*, rev. ed. (New York, 1972), 1:76–77 (English)

4. J. C. Holt, "The Assizes of Henry II: The Texts," in *A Study of Medieval Records: Essays in Honor of Kathleen Major*, ed. D. A. Bullough and R. L. Story (Oxford, 1971), 103ff.

5. Stubbs, *Select Charters*, 150–53 (Latin); Stephenson and Marcham, *Sources*, 1:80–82 (English).

6. G.D.G. Hall, ed., *The Treatise on the Law and Customs of England Commonly Called Glanvill* (1965), 173–74, 175. Glanvill's failure to refer more specifically to public prosecution in general and to the Assize of Clarendon in particular is odd, since as sheriff of Yorkshire he vigorously applied it. See Holt, "Assizes of Henry II," 103–4.

7. Hurnard, "Jury of Presentment," 390–91.

8. The material in the remainder of this section is a synopsis of R. D. Groot, "The Jury of Presentment before 1215," *AJLH* 26 (1982): 1; and idem, "The Jury in Private Criminal Prosecutions," *AJLH* 27 (1983): 113. For more detailed descriptions of the

imminent, and he was responsible for insuring that each hundred in his county was represented by twelve leading men and that each vill was represented by its reeve and four other men. When the justices arrived the hundred jurors were apprised of the articles of the eyre—the list of matters about which they were required to report to the justices. Felonies were always included.

The hundred jurors reported felonies in their hundred by delivering to the justices their *veredicta*, their responses to the articles. The veredicta reported felonies in two ways: a report of the felony itself, a presentment, or a report that an appeal, a private prosecution, had been made. A presentment that could actually be tried—one in which the hundred jury had reported a felony and named a defendant, and the defendant was present—could proceed directly to condemnation if the suspect had confessed before local officials or if the suspect was manifestly guilty.[9]

In all other cases the accused could and did deny. Proof, if there was to be any, would be by ordeal. But not all presented persons were awarded an ordeal. There are many instances of hundred juries presenting someone and then stating that the person was "not suspected"; there was no ordeal in such cases:

> Gilbert of Sausthorpe, accused of [burglary], offers himself and is not suspected by the jurors and therefore let him be under pledges.[10]

An ordeal was adjudged in two instances: first, when the hundred jurors alone brought forth supporting evidence:

> Andrew of Burwarton is suspected by the jurors of the death of a certain Hervey because he concealed himself on account of that death, and therefore let him purge himself by the judgment of water.[11]

and second, when the hundred jurors accused and were joined by four vills in suspecting the accused:

---

eyre, see the introductions to F. W. Maitland, ed., *Pleas of the Crown for the County of Gloucester, 1221* (1884) and C.A.F. Meekings, ed , *Crown Pleas of the Wiltshire Eyre, 1249*, Wiltshire Record Society, vol. 16 (1961).

9. *Curia Regis Rolls*, 5:237; 6:350 [F. W. Maitland, ed., *Select Pleas of the Crown* (1888), pl. 111]; 6:351 [*Select Pleas*, ed. Maitland, pl. 112].

10. D. M. Stenton, ed., *Earliest Lincolnshire Assize Rolls, AD 1202–1209* (Lincoln, 1926), pl. 588c.

11. G. Wrottesley, ed., *Staffordshire Suits: Collections for a History of Staffordshire* (1882), 3:94 [*Select Pleas*, ed. Maitland, pl. 66].

> William de Lusby and Robert Fitebant, accused of [burglary], are suspected of it by the jurors and the four neighboring vills. And therefore let William purge himself by the water; Robert is a clerk and a deacon. . . .[12]

The jurors' statement about Andrew's concealment may have been spontaneously reported or may have been discovered when the justices, after accusation and suspicion, inquired into the basis of the suspicion. If these inquiries did not produce supporting evidence, the four vills were consulted. If they joined the hundred jurors in suspecting the defendant, he, like William de Lusby, went to the ordeal. If they did not join in the hundredors' suspicion, the defendant avoided the ordeal.[13]

The ability of the jurors to accuse but not suspect, illustrated by the first example, is probably derived from the Assizes of Clarendon and Northampton. A duty to report crime can be and was rigorously enforced, but the assizes had also reinforced the principle that communal statements about defendants were important.[14] In particular, one cleared by the ordeal was to abjure if his evil reputation was attested by lawful men. It is implicit that such a person avoided abjuration if lawful men declared favorably about him. Between the assizes and the early thirteenth century, jurors apparently had learned that a favorable statement could precede the judgment awarding the ordeal. By the early 1200s, jurors could fully perform their reporting function, thus avoiding amercement, and yet spare the accused the ordeal; if hundredors were unwilling to do so, the vills still could. In fact, the favorable statement, "not suspected," from either source did more. Abjuration after purgation, introduced in the assizes, had become part of the general practice, so when a jury returned an accused as not suspected, he was spared both the ordeal and abjuration.

In sum, only when a hundred jury suspected and either produced extrinsic evidence or was joined in suspicion by the four vills did the defendant go to an ordeal. So by 1215 presenting juries were more than simply accusing juries. After accusing, these jurors decided which defendants should make proof by ordeal and which should not. This screening of defendants, ostensibly a statement about guilt or innocence, was just that when the hundredors produced evidence. When they did not but were joined in suspicion by the vills, the verdict was

12. *Lincolnshire Assize Rolls*, ed. Stenton, pl. 588d.

13. *Staffordshire Suits*, ed. Wrottesley, 42.

14. For the earlier history of the concept of the "unworthy man" and its relation to the assizes, see van Caenegem, "Public Prosecution of Crime," 48–49.

probably as much a statement about the defendant's character—about the likelihood that he would do what he was accused of—as about factual guilt or innocence. Nonetheless, an adverse verdict was medial only; it sent the defendant to the ordeal but did not convict.[15]

While presenting juries were acquiring this adjudicatory power, there was a simultaneous jury development in private criminal prosecutions—appeals. An appeal was an accusation made by the victim against the alleged perpetrator. The paradigmatic proof in an appeal was combat between the appellor and the appellee, but the ordeal was appropriate if either party was unable to fight. When an appellor formally pleaded his appeal in the county court, the appellee was attached to reappear before the itinerant royal justices. Generally the appeal would lie dormant in the county until an eyre, but occasionally appellors would remove appeals into the central royal courts. When an appeal was so removed, and the parties were present, a judgment awarding proof—combat or ordeal—could be granted. To avoid such a judgment, the appellee had somehow to challenge the appeal. From the time of the earliest records, an appellee could plead that the appeal had been made from hate and spite (*de odio et atia*) and buy a writ to have a jury decide the issue.[16] Upon plea and payment, the case could be remanded to await an eyre, or the sheriff could be ordered to bring a jury to Westminster or to hold the inquest and make a return. In this way an appellee could always defer a judgment awarding physical proof. A de odio verdict favorable to the appellee forestalled a judgment awarding proof; a verdict unfavorable to the appellee permitted that judgment. If the appeal was not removed to the central courts, it would be heard at the next eyre. At the eyre the appellee could plead the de odio issue and purchase a jury verdict. But at the eyre a jury was immediately available. The substantive possibilities upon a plea de odio were the same, but the outcome was immediate rather than deferred.

The de odio issue ostensibly asked whether the appeal was motivated by hate and spite, but it actually raised the essential question of guilt or innocence. Generally the issue was framed alternatively: Is this appeal made from hate and spite or from just cause? For example, in 1208 a central court writ ordered the sheriff of Sussex to inquire

15. I use the phrase *medial verdict* to denote a jury decision that sent the defendant to proof by ordeal. Of course, since an adverse verdict required abjuration after purgation, it did have a convicting—a sanction imposing—quality.

16. This procedure was in place by the 1180s. N. D. Hurnard, *The King's Pardon for Homicide before A.D. 1307* (Oxford, 1969), 339 and nn. 2, 3.

whether the appellee was in Chichester at the time of the crime (alibi), or the appeal was made from hate over certain land, or the appellee was guilty.[17] The issue framed for an eyre jury followed the same pattern. At Lincoln in 1202 an appellee purchased an inquest to inquire whether he was appealed from just cause or from hate and spite; the jury answered that he was appealed from hate and spite and unjustly.[18] Since the primary question in these de odio inquests, whether by writ or at eyre, was about guilt or innocence, a jury returning a verdict unfavorable to the appellee was saying that the crime had (probably) occurred and that the appellee was (probably) the perpetrator. These de odio juries screened defendants in the same way that the presenting juries did. Of course, an unfavorable de odio verdict was medial only; the appellee was still adjudged physical proof.

This is not the entire story of the pre-1215 jury, but it does cover the two major forms: the presenting jury reporting accusations and the de odio jury, whether specially formed pursuant to writ or at eyre. Every presented person, and every appellee who sought a jury, was spared physical proof until a jury had viewed the case and found against him. There are also scattered cases in which appellees who did not seek juries were put upon them by justices. The feature distinguishing them from apparently identical cases is not obvious, but at least these cases tell us that the justices had power *sua sponte* to ask for jury verdicts. Of course, these appellees generally would have gone to the ordeal if there had been no jury referral. The worst outcome of the referral was an unfavorable verdict, and that would simply place the appellee in his prior position. But there are instances of jury referral that increased the appellee's risk. Some appeals were concorded and some retracted; most often the appellor simply failed to appear at eyre to prosecute. Concords and retractions ordinarily acquitted the appellee, while failures to prosecute continued cases indefinitely. Nullified appeals were similar. Infrequently, for some reason not discernible from the cases, an appeal not actively prosecuted or a nullified appeal was referred to a jury. The starkest of these unsought inquest cases are those in which, in the usual course, the appellee would have been acquitted. When the justices referred such cases to the jury, the prosecution was exceeding its usual bounds. Of course, while these juries could almost acquit, they could not convict.

17. *Curia Regis Rolls*, 5:152–53.

18. *Lincolnshire Assize Rolls*, ed. Stenton, pl. 607.

The 1218–19 Phase

Judicial activity virtually ceased in 1214, and it resumed late in 1217 after the accession of Henry III. In the interim, Magna Carta had been granted, rescinded, and reissued. In addition, the Fourth Lateran Council had in 1215 forbidden the ordeal.[19] There was little in Magna Carta that directly affected the development of the jury.[20] The edict of the Church, however, meant that the only criminal cases that could go to conviction were instances of confession, manifest criminality, and appeals between able-bodied males.

In late 1218 a major nationwide eyre commenced. Instructions were sent to the justices during January 1219. These instructions, noting that the ordeal had been abolished and that an appropriate judicial response had not been determined before the eyre, provided that those accused of major crimes about which there was strong suspicion of guilt should be committed to prison for safekeeping; that those accused of medium crimes, for which the ordeal would have been appropriate, should be permitted to abjure the realm; and that those accused of minor crimes about which there was no strong suspicion should be placed under good-conduct pledges. Other cases were specifically left to the discretion of the justices.[21]

Four aspects of this order must be noted. First, it strongly implied that there had been discussions about the resolution of cases that no longer had proof. Second, since indefinite imprisonment of suspects would soon overload the prisons, those drafting the order must have known that it was only temporary. Third, the order provided only for the disposition of suspects, not for their trial. In this aspect, the order implied an understanding that when ordeal was the appropriate historical proof, there was no substitute for it. Fourth, the order spoke of persons accused and about whom there was or was not suspicion. In

19. More correctly, it had forbidden clerical participation in the ordeal: "Nobody [i.e., no cleric] shall perform any rite of blessing on the occasion of compurgation by hot or cold water or hot iron. . . ." R. C. van Caenegem, "The Law of Evidence in the Twelfth Century. European Perspective and Intellectual Background," in *Proceedings of the Second International Congress of Medieval Canon Law*, ed. S. Kuttner and J. Ryan (1965), 1·310.

20. Chapter 36, which made the writ of inquisition of life and limb obtainable without payment, was the clause most likely to affect jury development. The writ mentioned has been identified with the writ de odio et atia, but payments for the latter continued immediately and long after Magna Carta.

21. D. M. Stenton, ed., *Rolls of the Justices in Eyre for Yorkshire, 1218–19* (1937), xl.

this aspect, the order was monumentally important. It assumed that there were accused persons who were not suspected; it thus recognized and assumed the continuation of the older medial jury verdict, which had been the mechanism that distinguished the merely accused from the truly suspected.

The only extant Crown pleas roll of the 1218–19 phase is from York. Because the York session had commenced before the 1219 order was issued, it is difficult to know which cases preceded its receipt at York and which cases followed.[22] There are tantalizing hints in the earlier cases that the justices were willing to try final jury verdicts.[23] Perhaps that was one of the solutions that had been discussed but not decided before the justices went out from Westminster. Finally, however, the only case on the earlier part of the roll containing an award of proof was an appeal of wounding in which combat was adjudged.[24] Several other cases, both presentments and appeals, were set over to February 1219, as if the justices were anticipating the arrival of instructions.[25]

Presentments that went to judgment do not permit the conclusion that a new system was operating. In one case it was reported that a wife who had been beaten by her husband had said that the husband had killed a priest. The husband was not suspected by the jurors and so was put on pledges to answer any appeal that might be made.[26] This case is identical to the many pre-1215 cases in which a person was accused but not suspected.[27] The release under pledges was either an ap-

22. The York session was held in two parts. The first ran from 25 November to Christmas 1218 and the second from 21 January to April 1219. Ibid., xx–xxi. The reference in ibid., pl. 727, to 15 December places it in the first part. Pickering hundred was ordered to make presentments on 3 February (ibid., pl. 41), and those presentments begin at ibid., pl. 953. I cannot determine where the break between the first and second parts occurs. Neither does the roll indicate when, in relation to itself, the order from Westminster was received.

23. Two appellees put themselves on the countryside *de bono et malo*. Ibid., pl. 727. This formula became, a little later, the symbol for a final jury verdict. Its first appearance came to naught, as the whole case involving these apparently guilty persons was concorded. In another case, four arson suspects were ordered taken and four vills were told to stay behind. Ibid., pl. 494. An opinion was wanted from the vills about these suspects, but it is not obvious why that opinion was necessary. An appellor offered to prove by verdict of the vills and visne, but the verdict declared the appellee to be not guilty. It is not clear whether an unfavorable verdict would have been medial or final. Ibid., pl. 692. Twice appellees put themselves upon verdicts *si culpabilis sit*. Ibid., pl. 707, 1022. In the first, the appellor then retracted. The second appears to be a plea for a medial verdict.

24. Ibid., pl. 579.

25. Ibid., pl. 505 (Alan of Follifoot), 592 (John of Heck), 707 (the accessories).

26. Ibid., pl. 855.

27. See above, text at n. 10.

plication of the third clause of the 1219 order—light suspicion—or a continuation of a pre-1215 practice. In another case, an accused uxoricide was suspected by the jury because he admitted finding the body but did not raise the hue and cry; instead, he fled toward a church and was captured in flight. This accused was declared guilty by the jury and four vills and was hanged.[28] This is a case of manifest guilt, but an obvious, if slippery, point must be made. The facts, the evidence, making out manifest guilt had to come to the justices from some local source. One local source that could report those facts was the presenting jury.[29] So it was perfectly possible to have a conviction based on a jury statement which is not a substitution of a jury verdict for other proof. Perhaps the justices were too eager to find manifest guilt in the case of the uxoricide.[30] Perhaps the joinder of the vills to the hundredors has some significance. But there is little in these presentment cases that predicts the jury as proof. Among the appeals, however, real change can be seen.

Of greatest importance are those appeals in which the appellee appeared but did not seek an inquest. Before 1215 it was unusual for such appellees to be subjected to inquests. At York in 1218–19 an unsought jury verdict was taken in almost every appeal. For example, in an appeal of rape, the appellor appeared and offered to prove; the appellee appeared and denied. But the jurors and vills attested that suit was reasonably made; the defendant was incarcerated until he paid a fine.[31] The defendant was not fully convicted, but the verdict was used as a sufficient base for a punitive sanction.

These unsought inquests were had whether the appellor had died,[32] failed to appear,[33] retracted the appeal,[34] or appeared to prosecute and the appeal was nullified.[35] In many instances the verdict was "not suspected" or "not guilty" and the appellees were acquitted. But in others

28. *Rolls for Yorkshire, 1218–19*, ed. Stenton, pl. 842.

29. E.g., *Pleas of Gloucester, 1221*, ed. Maitland, pl. 174.

30. But see D. M. Stenton, ed., *Pleas before the King or His Justices, 1198–1202* (1952), pl. 618 (slayer attested by hundredors to have been taken in flight; manifestly guilty and hanged).

31. *Rolls for Yorkshire, 1218–19*, ed. Stenton, pl. 1029. This may be Bracton's pecuniary penalty upon the king's suit after a failed appeal. S. E. Thorne, ed., *Bracton on the Laws and Customs of England* (Cambridge, Mass., 1968), 2.403.

32. E.g., *Rolls for Yorkshire, 1218–19*, ed. Stenton, pl. 444. There are nine such cases.

33. E.g., ibid., pl. 541. There are thirty-seven such cases.

34. E.g., ibid., pl. 473. There are six such cases.

35. Ibid., pl. 553, 585, 941.

the appellee was said to be either suspected or guilty. In such cases, which previously would have gone to the ordeal for proof, the appellees were gaoled until they paid a fine.[36] Although these appellees, even if called "guilty," were not treated as if they had been fully convicted of a felony, it is nonetheless apparent that the jury verdict was the basis for a milder punitive action.

It is important that the justices took a verdict by unsought inquest in the very first case that presented the opportunity.[37] The timing means that these verdicts were not the product of the 1219 order; the immediacy indicates that a decision to take such verdicts had been made before the eyre. Here is another piece of evidence that the handling of criminal cases had been discussed in some detail before the eyre and that broader use of the jury had been part of those discussions.[38]

Two questions present themselves: Why did the justices decide to use these jury verdicts, and in what cases did they do so? The second is easier to answer than the first. The jury verdict was taken when the appeal was one that, for any reason, could not be proved by combat. Concerning the first question, the decision to take verdicts in these appeals was not a direct outcome of the loss of the ordeals. Before 1215 there were two instances in which ordeal-proof was adjudged in appeals: first, when the appeal was in all respects appropriate for combat-proof, but one of the parties was unable to fight; second, in those rare instances when a defaulted, retracted, or nullified appeal was referred to a jury for an unsought verdict and that verdict was unfavorable to the appellee.[39] But before 1215 the overwhelming majority of defaulted, retracted, or nullified appeals were not referred. Rather, the appellees were simply adjudged *quietus* or *sine die*. It is this group of cases, to which the ordeals had no pre-1215 application, that were uniformly referred for verdict in 1218–19.

The power to refer, as it existed before 1215, was sparingly exercised because its use conflicted with the appellor's expectation of reparations.[40] The judicial attitude about reparations and concords seems to have changed. When the parties had actually concorded an appeal of rape or wounds before the eyre, the appellee was fined. In some of the

36. Ibid., pl. 449, 473, 522, 583, 585, 594, 603, 671, 698, 839, 850, 941, 955, 957. All are rape or wounds except plea 449, involving an accessory to homicide.

37. Ibid., pl. 444 (Swan of West Bretton).

38. See above, n. 21.

39. Groot, "Jury in Private Criminal Prosecutions," 130–31.

40. Ibid., 132–36.

cases there was also an inquiry into guilt, but the fine appears to have been imposed for making the unlicensed concord rather than for the offense.[41]

During John's reign the underlying assumption, at least when direct personal injury was at issue, was that the primary harm was to the appellor. It followed that the Crown should not pursue its interest in the secondary harm, breach of the peace, by interfering with the availability of reparations to the appellor. In 1218–19 there is a subtle change. The assumption seems to have been that inflicting injury was equally an offense against the victim and the Crown;[42] the Crown was willing to give precedence to the victim, by way of reparations and concord, but only until the eyre. If no concord had been made by then, the Crown's interest in its own peace took precedence. This change in assumption was probably pragmatic. There must have been judicial dissatisfaction with the litany in the earlier eyres of "non est prosecutus . . . sine die" and "retraxit se . . . quietus." In fact, that dissatisfaction is evidenced by the occasional taking of unsought inquest verdicts at the pre-1215 eyres. Moreover, the nation had recently suffered years of turmoil and war. It must have been important to re-establish royal control over a countryside that had been fragmented into factions, and it must have been equally important to re-establish order by wiping clean all prior disorder. Of course, history could not be ignored. To have disallowed all pre-existing concords might have been too big a step. It might also have been counter-productive. Concords did, after all, create peace; they were a way of terminating discord. Crediting pre-eyre concords in 1218–19 should have encouraged concords, and therefore stability, between this eyre and the next.[43] Taking verdicts yielding quasi convictions in unconcorded cases should also have encouraged concords.[44] The taking of unsought verdicts, then, represents a significant, considered change. It demonstrates some growth in the perception that individualized harm offends the peace

41. *Rolls for Yorkshire, 1218–19*, ed. Stenton, pl. 649, 695, 866, 923, 944, 1044. One who had concorded a homicide was nonetheless outlawed. Ibid., pl. 766.

42. Bracton's statement about this is even stronger. *Bracton on the Laws of England*, ed. Thorne, 2:402.

43. The counter is obvious: that crediting concords encouraged violence by providing the offender with an easy way out This assumes that an offense and its consequences were thought through before its commission.

44. The counter is that the fine for the unlicensed concord approximated the fine following a quasi conviction, and in any event, a quasi conviction was not a certainty. This assumes that peace between the time of the event and the next eyre had no value to the offender.

of the state. It also broadened the jury's role in criminal cases. But it did not abolish concords, at least in cases of direct personal injury.

Unlike these cases of unsought inquests, almost no change can be seen when inquests were sought.[45] There are nine cases in which appellees specifically pleaded de odio et atia. In six of them the verdict is recorded. Five verdicts were favorable to the appellee and nullified the appeals.[46] The sixth case involved two appellees. One specifically pleaded de odio et atia, but no verdict was recorded. The second, who apparently only denied, was suspected by the jurors and combat was adjudged.[47] It is not clear whether the verdict was elicited by the first appellee's plea or was given gratuitously when the jurors were asked about the sufficiency of the pre-proof.[48] In either event, the verdict was medial only—it only sent the appellee to proof by combat.

The only real change apparent in the 1218–19 phase is the pervasive use of the unsought jury verdict in appeals deprived of combat as proof. This is a significant change because it manifested a change of perception about the role of the state in maintaining order and, by accepting jury verdicts as a foundation for imposing penalties, was one more step toward final, convicting jury verdicts. But such verdicts did not appear in 1218–19.

The 1219–21 Interim

The 1218–19 phase wound down during the spring and summer of 1219.[49] Between that time and the 1221–22 phase, recorded judicial activity was at Westminster. A roll of every term from Michaelmas 1219 through Easter 1221, when the justices next went out, is extant, and there is nothing on the roll of Michaelmas 1219 to indicate that a significant change was in the making. A few confessed and manifestly guilty criminals were hanged.[50] Appeals other than by approvers were left unresolved.

There were a number of appeals by approvers. William de Stancs ap-

45. See above, n. 23, for cases hinting at the possibility of final verdicts upon sought inquests.

46. *Rolls for Yorkshire, 1218–19*, ed. Stenton, pl. 570, 581, 669, 734, 939.

47. Ibid., pl. 579.

48. Ibid., pl. 911, in which the coroners attested pre-proof and suspicion. Combat could be adjudged upon pre-proof alone. Ibid., pl. 823, 843.

49. Ibid., xx–xxi; D. M. Stenton, ed., *Rolls of the Justices in Eyre for Lincolnshire, 1218–9, and Worcestershire, 1221* (1934), xlvii.

50. *Curia Regis Rolls*, 8:112 (Simon de Edesburg), 142 (Richard of Leicester).

pealed five others but was defeated in his first combat and hanged. That precluded proof against the remaining appellees. Two of them abjured and three were committed to pledges; apparently the former were more heavily suspected than the latter.[51] William Smalwude, another approver, appealed many men. One of them, Hugh de Solers, put himself upon his neighborhood, but twelve jurors summoned ad hoc supported the appellor's allegations. Hugh was committed to his lord and tithing to await summons.[52] William Smalwude's appeals reappear in important ways in the roll of the next term. For the moment it is enough to note that the inquest sought by Hugh de Solers was an inquest de fidelitate. Such inquests had existed in approvers' appeals before 1215. Verdicts from them were medial only; an unfavorable one only sent the appellee to combat against the appellor.[53] Thus the inquest upon Hugh de Solers is not evidence for the existence of a convicting jury during Michaelmas 1219, and there is, in fact, strong evidence that it did not exist. The heirs of two men hanged in Devon during the 1218–19 phase complained at Westminster that the convictions were improper and that they should be permitted to inherit. The convicts had been accused of receiving a robber; they had admitted receiving him but only as a relative and had neither admitted nor denied receipt of the booty. Because the hundred jury said they were of ill fame and were reputed to have divided the booty in the barn of one of them, they were hanged. The council and bench justices held the convictions improper because the two were not seized of the booty, had not confessed, and *could not be condemned by the speech of the jurors*.[54] This action by the council and bench justices, the very highest juristic authorities, approved conviction on proof of manifest guilt and so in concept approved the conviction of the Yorkshire uxoricide.[55] Possession of stolen goods made out manifest guilt in a case of larceny or robbery, just as flight made out manifest guilt in a homicide case. The reference to the speech of the jurors must be understood in this context. The council and bench justices would permit conviction upon a jury report of evidence constituting manifest guilt; the speech of the jurors that could not convict was a simple assertion by the ju-

51. Ibid., 141, 207, 270.

52. Ibid., 134, 143.

53. D. M Stenton, ed., *Earliest Northamptonshire Assize Rolls, AD 1202–1203* (Lincoln and London, 1930), pl. 723–30.

54 *Curia Regis Rolls*, 8 80 [F. W. Maitland, ed., *Bracton's Note Book* (reprint, Littleton, Colo., 1983), vol. 2, pl 67].

55. See above, text at n. 28

rors, even if based upon reputation and rumor, that the accused was guilty.

Although a simple assertion of bad reputation by a jury sent the accused to the ordeal while the Assize of Clarendon was in force, that possibility had disappeared by the 1190s. At the beginning of the thirteenth century, an accused was adjudged the ordeal if the hundred jury supported its suspicion with inculpatory evidence or if the hundred jury *and the vills* joined in an assertion of suspicion, which could be based upon reputation. In effect, the assertion of suspicion by the augmented jury was substituted for inculpatory evidence. In the case of the Devon receivers, where the ultimate issue was condemnation rather than proof by ordeal, the council and justices refused to make a new but similar substitution. They refused to allow an assertion of guilt, at least by the hundred jury alone, to be substituted for a report of inculpatory evidence sufficient to make out manifest guilt.[56]

This whole situation changed radically during Hilary term 1220. At the end of the roll for that term there is a subroll entitled *Rotulus latronum*. The early part of it is unremarkable, but the appeals of William Smalwude, the approver, reappear and need mention. Several of his appellees sought inquests de fidelitate. One of these, Adam son of the priest, was said by his inquest to be of ill fame; combat was therefore adjudged between them. Adam defeated William, who was hanged.[57] Once William had been hanged, the cases against his remaining appellees were left without proof. These are clustered with another set of cases in which Alice, a confessed and condemned homicide, had accused several others.[58] Like William's cases, these latter ones were without proof because the female accuser could not offer combat.[59] But a solution suddenly appeared. Two men accused by the

56. Vills did not participate in the case of the Devon receivers, nor did the receivers request a jury verdict, but I do not think these factors controlled the eventual result. The timing of the original judgment and of its review at Westminster are important to this conclusion. Joscelin, bishop of Bath, was the senior justice on the southwestern circuit in 1218–19. E. Foss, *The Judges of England* (1848), 2.515. He was called from the eyre to a royal council by a letter issued 12 February 1219. *Rolls for Worcestershire, 1221*, ed. Stenton, xliv. He was absent from the bench and from Devon when the receivers were condemned. *Curia Regis Rolls*, 8:80 [*Bracton's Note Book*, ed. Maitland, vol. 2, pl. 67]. Since the 12 February letter had reached the bishop before the receivers were tried, the 1219 order, issued 26 January, must also have been received. The order did not anticipate assertive convicting verdicts by any kind of jury. It prescribed, at most, that the Devon receivers should have been imprisoned for safekeeping.

57. *Curia Regis Rolls*, 8:270. Earlier portions of the same case are in ibid., 143, 269.

58. Ibid., 273 [*Select Pleas*, ed. Maitland, pl. 191], 274–76.

59 Maitland gives the appeals of William Smalwude until he was hanged,

woman were hanged "because they put themselves for good and ill (*de bono et malo*) upon a verdict and the vills say that they are thieves."[60] In the next case three of her suspects "put themselves for good and ill (de bono et malo) upon a verdict of the countryside." The vills said that two were thieves, and they were hanged; the other was said to be lawful (*fidelis*), and he was put on pledges.[61] Immediately there appeared Roger Wauding, an appellee of William Smalwude who had apparently failed an inquest de fidelitate. He should have been awarded combat as proof, but William had already been hanged. Roger "puts himself upon his neighborhood for good and ill (de bono et malo) so that if the neighborhood acquits him he is to be quit, if otherwise, he is to be convicted."[62] Here is the first active appearance of the formula de bono et malo.[63] The four men accused by Alice were the first persons properly convicted by an English jury.

Roger Wauding's case clearly expresses the meaning of the de bono et malo formula. It also helps to explain its creation. Roger Wauding was suspected by many of receiving and other evils. The 1219 order required his imprisonment, and that imprisonment, because no proof was available, would be perpetual. Long-term imprisonment in a medieval English prison was insupportable to the prisoner.[64] The government necessarily recognized that it could not continue indefinitely to send suspects to prison. The decision must have been taken that these heavily suspected defendants would be offered an alternative—a jury verdict of guilty or innocent.

This new convicting jury verdict combined features found in extant jury forms. First, the new jury verdict is assertive rather than evidentiary. Similar verdicts, sufficient only to elicit proof, were the pre-1215 "suspected" verdict of the hundred jury and four vills, the "ill fame" verdict of the de fidelitate jury, and the "guilty" verdict of the de odio jury.

The notion that an assertive, nonevidentiary verdict was sufficient for the imposition of *some sanction* was contributed by the quasi-convicting verdicts first found in 1218–19. The same idea can be found in

---

and Alice's condemnation. *Select Pleas*, ed. Maitland, pl. 190, 191. He does not follow the cases into the sequence I describe below.

60. *Curia Regis Rolls*, 8:274.

61. Ibid.

62. Ibid., 275.

63. The phrase first appeared at York in 1218. *Rolls for Yorkshire, 1218–19*, ed. Stenton, pl. 727. See above, n. 23.

64. See, generally, R. B. Pugh, *Imprisonment in Medieval England* (Cambridge, 1968), chap. 15.

the pre-1215 requirement that a suspect who purged himself by ordeal must nonetheless abjure. What was first needed to create the de bono et malo jury from the earlier forms was a decision that an assertive, nonevidentiary verdict could condemn. In modern terms, the decision in the case of the Devon receivers—that an assertive verdict could not condemn—had to be overruled.[65] An analogous step had already been taken when the assertive verdict of the four vills had been added to the unsupported suspicion of a hundred jury. Of course, the older assertive verdict of the hundredors and vills had not condemned. On the other hand, it was forced upon the accused. But sought verdicts, medial only, were well known in the de odio et atia and de fidelitate forms.

These first convicting juries arose in appeals by approvers.[66] The issue de fidelitate was the classic medial jury issue in such cases. Its very name, and certainly its application, asked about the accused rather than the crime.[67] It was therefore an issue closely associated with the vills. In the first two convicting jury cases, vills only decided the de bono et malo issue. In the first, the accusation was homicide, but these vills were asked about repute, and they said the defendants were thieves. In the second, one defendant was returned fidelis and the other two were said to be thieves. Even allowing for some clerical confusion in describing a novel event,[68] it is clear that these first inquests de bono et malo flowed most directly from the inquest de fidelitate, that they were largely character inquests, and that they were closely associated with the vills.[69] They were also, in theory, sought inquests.

65. Making that decision still left questions about the conditions for such a verdict. Eventually the answers were that the accused had to seek the verdict and that it required the hundredors and vills. Thus the judgment on the Devon receivers, who did not seek a verdict, would have still been improper in 1220 or 1221. Some sought verdicts in 1220 and 1221, however, were apparently rendered by hundredors alone; e.g., *Rolls for Worcestershire, 1221*, ed. Stenton, pl. 1218 [*Select Pleas*, ed. Maitland, pl. 144].

66. The female accuser was not, strictly speaking, an approver but was the equivalent.

67. This was true of all pre-proof issues in approvers' appeals. Was the appellee in frankpledge? Would his lord claim him? See, for example, *Curia Regis Rolls*, 9:186 (appeal of Robert Medicus); see also *Bracton on the Laws of England*, ed. Thorne, 2:433.

68. There was some obvious confusion; e.g., *Curia Regis Rolls*, 8:278 [*Select Pleas*, ed. Maitland, pl. 193] (appellee reported to have put himself on jury "de fidelitate sua ita quod eum aquietent quietus sit, sin autem convincatur").

69. I claim only a close association, not a dependency. Even in these first de bono et malo cases, acquitting verdicts by vills are set over to be tried by knights (ibid.,

A suspect who had to decide upon accepting a de bono et malo verdict was on the horns of a dilemma. One horn was a possible final conviction by a jury, while the other was his immediate disposition under the 1219 order. Those who were the objects of significant suspicion faced imprisonment or abjuration. A suspect who faced only abjuration under the 1219 order could choose it rather than a de bono et malo verdict.[70] It was only the most heavily suspected person, the person most likely to be convicted by a jury, who had to make the choice between imprisonment and a jury verdict. That was doubtless a most unpleasant choice; it is doubtless, also, that choosing the jury was motivated by a fear of imprisonment. Still, it is important to avoid anachronism. In 1220 the suspect was being told in effect: The law ordains that you should be imprisoned, but you can avoid imprisonment by your plea de bono et malo. By the last quarter of the century the statement was reversed: You must be tried by a jury; should you refuse, you will be punished by *prisone (peine) forte et dure*.[71]

For all of this, the 1220–21 interim is a time of uncertainty. Roger Wauding, the very suspect whose case most clearly expresses the meaning of the plea de bono et malo, was freed pending his trial at an eyre. This somewhat surprising result can be explained. Roger's immediate interest was to avoid imprisonment; he had been promised that he would be spared imprisonment if he pleaded de bono et malo. The state's primary interests were to empty the prison and to obtain the power to try the suspect, and both of these primary goals had been accomplished by the plea.[72] When there was no immediately available jury to try Roger, he obtained the temporary benefit of the state's inability to complete his trial.[73]

276 [Richard Roper], 277 [Jordan Oggesfot]), appellees bargain for special juries (e.g., ibid., 278 [*Select Pleas*, ed. Maitland, pl. 193] [William Barreville]), and juries of twelve were ordered (e.g., ibid., 276 [Hugh de Solers])

70. Ibid., 279 [*Select Pleas*, ed. Maitland, pl. 196] (Gilbert of Tolesthorpe); see also *Rolls for Worcestershire, 1221*, ed. Stenton, pl. 1208 [*Select Pleas*, ed. Maitland, pl. 143].

71. 3 Edw I, c. 12 (1275); F. M. Nichols, ed., *Britton* (reprint, Holmes Beach, Fla., 1983), 1:26–27; H. G. Richardson and G. O. Sayles, eds., *Fleta* (1955), 2:85. I believe the *prisone*, and probably the *peine*, began in the 1220s. See below, n. 157

72. It is clear that Roger, if he appeared before the next itinerant justices, would not be permitted to refuse a jury. The idea that the plea de bono et malo vested in the state the power to try the accused at its next opportunity seems to have been revived in the later writ de bono et malo. See R. B. Pugh, "The Writ de Bono et Malo," *Law Quarterly Review* 92 (1976): 264–66.

73 This deferral is similar to that enjoyed by appellees who pleaded de odio et atia at Westminster and was not uncommon in these early de bono et malo cases. See, for example, *Curia Regis Rolls*, 9:286, 309 (appeal of Nicholas fitz Robert).

The rolls of Trinity 1220 through Easter 1221 contain only one conviction after a plea de bono et malo, but this defendant's guilt was probably manifest in any event.[74] Several persons appealed by approvers had inquests de fidelitate. Those who were judged to be fidelis were permitted pledges; those who were not were awarded combat against their appellors.[75] These cases make clear that the de fidelitate verdict still existed in its medial form; it had spawned, but had not become, a final verdict. Thus, as the 1221–22 phase of the eyre approached, the plea de bono et malo and its assertive, final jury verdict had come into existence, but its exact application across the generality of criminal prosecution was unsettled.

The 1221–22 Phase

The shift from Westminster to the eyre was a shift from an essentially non-jury system to one in which juries were omnipresent. This immediately meant that trial upon a plea de bono et malo never needed to be deferred; some jury was available or could be formed to try it. The indirect effects are less clear. Because suspects could not expect deferral, they might be more likely to refuse a jury at eyre than at Westminster. Suspects at eyre were also likely to know before plea the composition of the jury that would try them. A suspect anticipating a favorable jury was likely to accept it.[76] The converse was also true.[77] The availability of the jury also caused it to be offered more freely to suspects at eyre than at Westminster.[78]

These readily available juries also allowed the justices to continue throughout this phase the practice, begun in 1218, of taking unsought inquests in appeals not provable by combat. For those appellees returned as suspected or guilty, they again applied the system of coer-

74. Ibid., 198 (Hugh of Upton).

75. Ibid., 186 (appeal of Robert Medicus), 199–200 (appeals of Roger fitz Geoffrey), 285 (appeal of John fitz Nicholas).

76. E.g., *Rolls for Worcestershire, 1221*, ed. Stenton, pl. 1132 [*Select Pleas*, ed. Maitland, pl. 134], 1208 [*Select Pleas*, ed. Maitland, pl. 143] (suspects not in custody came forward to plead de bono et malo).

77. E.g., *Pleas of Gloucester, 1221*, ed. Maitland, pl. 111 (refused jury because hated by many).

78. E.g., D. M. Stenton, ed., *Rolls of the Justices in Eyre for Gloucestershire, Warwickshire and Staffordshire, 1221–1222* (1940), pl. 1239 (lightly suspected person); *Rolls for Worcestershire, 1221*, ed. Stenton, pl. 1218 [*Select Pleas*, ed. Maitland, pl. 144] (confessed suspect); ibid., pl. 1100 (manifestly guilty suspect); see also *Curia Regis Rolls*, 9:198 (manifestly guilty suspect at gaol delivery where a jury was available).

cive confinement and fines. In general, the cases involving an unsought inquest and coercive confinement were for rape and wounding. In homicide cases, the justices seemed to have pressed harder for full jury resolution.[79]

But it is important to remember that the juries of the eyre were present in the first instance to report and, in particular, to report persons about whom there were suspicions—to make presentments. Glanvill says that the justices made many and varied inquiries into the foundation of a presentment.[80] This apparently occurred after the hundredors had presented *and* asserted suspicion. Its function was to determine if inculpatory evidence existed or if there was need to consult the vills. Bracton also describes a judicial inquiry into presentments.[81] Bracton's inquiry apparently occurred after presentment but before the hundredors gave their opinion. Its function was to determine if the presentment had any worth at all. Stated simply, Glanvill's inquiry asked if there was reason to go forward, while Bracton's asked if there was any reason *not* to go forward. Between Glanvill and Bracton, of course, the whole system had shifted from one based primarily on private prosecution to one largely dependent on public prosecution. This change in judicial inquiry into presentments is a manifestation of that shift. So when a hundred jury presented someone, its presentment was scrutinized. While making their inquiry the justices sometimes seem to have elicited a preliminary opinion from the hundredors. If the presentment failed at this stage, there was no trial. For example:

> Anketil the miller and Unfridus of Shipton were accused of receiving [an arsonist]; Anketil died and Unfridus comes and is not suspected and is therefore quit. . . .[82]

More frequently, the unverified suspicion cases are in this form:

> Stephen the baker and Adam Kang, attached for ill repute, are not suspected, and therefore let them be under pledges.[83]

79. *Pleas of Gloucester, 1221*, ed. Maitland, pl. 261–62, 320; *Rolls for Warwickshire, 1221–1222*, ed. Stenton, pl. 910. Pre-eyre concords of rape and wounding were honored. *Pleas of Gloucester, 1221*, ed. Maitland, pl. 320; *Rolls for Warwickshire, 1221–1222*, ed. Stenton, pl. 910. But a concord of a homicide most emphatically was not. *Pleas of Gloucester, 1221*, ed. Maitland, pl. 101, discussed below in text at n. 116.

80. *Treatise Called Glanvill*, ed. Hall, 171.

81. *Bracton on the Laws of England*, ed. Thorne, 2:404.

82. *Pleas of Gloucester, 1221*, ed. Maitland, pl. 216. See also *Rolls for Warwickshire, 1221–1222*, ed. Stenton, pl. 1263 [*Select Pleas*, ed. Maitland, pl. 170].

83. *Rolls for Worcestershire, 1221*, ed. Stenton, pl. 1266.

There are many such cases. Certainly Stephen the baker would have been put under pledges before 1215 after a finding of nonsuspicion, but the same disposition was directed in 1219 for lightly suspected defendants. I am unable to distinguish those cases in which the suspicion is in fact nonexistent from those in which light suspicion invoked the third clause of the 1219 order.

Despite the difficulty in classification, two things are clear: first, these placed-under-pledges cases are not full jury trials to determine guilt or innocence; second, the 1219 order is still in effect. At the Shropshire session of this phase, a defendant taken for ill repute refused a jury and, after paying twenty shillings, was put under pledges.[84] Clearly, no jury trial was had, yet suspicion reported by some agency, presumably a jury, was sufficient for a full jury trial to be offered. That suspicion, perhaps lightened by the oblation, invoked the third clause of the 1219 order. At Gloucester a family group accused of homicide refused a jury; the jury nonetheless reported that the mother and son had killed the victim and that the father had assented; the mother and son were gaoled, while the father was gaoled only until he found pledges.[85] Again, it is clear that there was no trial, and it is equally clear that the dispositions are appropriate to the 1219 order.

Martin of Pattishall was the leading professional among the justices sent on the eyre in 1221–22.[86] He had been at York in 1218–19 and was one of the bench justices who decided, during Michaelmas term 1219, that an assertive verdict should not have convicted the Devon receivers. He was on the bench during Hilary term 1220, when the convicting jury was first approved, and he had hanged a man upon a de bono et malo verdict when he headed a gaol delivery in Hereford during Trinity term 1220.[87] As the convicting jury continued to develop in the course of this phase of the eyre, it did so under the watchful eye of this important and knowledgeable justice.

It is also significant that the four surviving rolls of this phase are sequential. As the justices moved from place to place with their entourage, they must have created a stir. As the judicial train arrived for a session, so too did all of the county and local officials, the jurors and vills, litigants, and all others attached for appearance. There must

84. *Rolls for Warwickshire, 1221–1222*, ed. Stenton, pl. 1239.

85. *Pleas of Gloucester, 1221*, ed. Maitland, pl. 213.

86. *Rolls for Worcestershire, 1221*, ed. Stenton, xlix–l.

87. *Rolls for Yorkshire, 1218–19*, ed. Stenton, xxi-xxxiii; *Curia Regis Rolls*, 8:1, 247; 9:198.

have been a keen interest in what had happened at earlier sessions. Questions were asked and answered. Gloucester defendants acted in response to information from the Worcester sessions. The justices, administering a new system, had in their turn to react. This means that a search for consistency across the rolls, a synchronic treatment of them, is futile. Their relationship is temporal, and there is a general flow from one to the next. Certainly there are individual entries that, even when viewed temporally, appear erratic. Perhaps they are just that; perhaps they are clerical mistakes, for the clerks were also attempting to describe new events. Perhaps they are special exercises of discretion. But most of the apparent eccentricity is resolved when the rolls are examined in sequence.

The Worcester roll has seven public prosecutions that resulted in true jury trials. Those seven cases involved twelve defendants who accepted trial and one who refused. Only two of these defendants were incarcerated before trial. The first, who was almost manifestly guilty, accepted jury trial, was convicted, and was hanged.[88] He would certainly have remained in gaol had he refused the jury and might have been hanged in any event.[89] The other imprisoned defendant had been taken for ill fame; he refused a jury and abjured.[90] Obviously the possibility of acquittal was not enough to entice a plea de bono et malo when the alternative was only abjuration. It is more difficult to decide if the other ten defendants accepted jury trial because they expected acquittal or because they feared imprisonment. I believe it was the former. Seven of the ten did not appear at the proper time;[91] they waited, it seems, until the judicial waters had been tested. The clearest case involves two foresters accused of a homicide in Worcestershire. Three other men came forward and promised to have them before the justices when the eyre reached Staffordshire. They did appear there and put themselves upon a Staffordshire hundred jury. They were acquitted.[92] These foresters did not pay for their inquest, but

88. *Rolls for Worcestershire, 1221*, ed. Stenton, pl. 1099

89. See, for example, *Curia Regis Rolls*, 8:396 (confessed thief refused jury; hanged).

90. *Rolls for Worcestershire, 1221*, ed. Stenton, pl. 1208 [*Select Pleas*, ed. Maitland, pl. 143]. This defendant followed his brother into the dock; the brother had accepted a jury and had been hanged.

91. Ibid., pl. 1098 [*Select Pleas*, ed. Maitland, pl. 130], 1130 [*Select Pleas*, ed. Maitland, pl. 133], 1132 [*Select Pleas*, ed. Maitland, pl. 134], 1208 [*Select Pleas*, ed. Maitland, pl. 143].

92. Ibid., pl. 1130 [*Select Pleas*, ed. Maitland, pl. 133].

most publicly prosecuted defendants did so.[93] They must have thought that the oblation provided some advantage, but the nature of that advantage is not apparent.[94] And neither late appearance nor oblation guaranteed an acquittal. Osbert Alfolc was reported by the jurors to be a slayer; the jurors were quite clear about the fact and the context. Osbert came late and paid one mark for an inquest "si culpabilis sit . . . necne." Osbert was convicted and hanged.[95]

Finally there is Franke of Knighton, accused of harboring an outlaw robber. In such cases the accused frequently admitted the person's presence but denied knowledge of his status.[96] Franke first admitted the man's presence and then, in an interlineation, is said to have confessed to knowing that the man was an outlaw. He then "willingly" put himself upon twelve jurors de bono et malo, was convicted, and was hanged.[97] Franke's admissions were sufficient to condemn him; he willingly accepted a jury because it was his only hope of avoiding hanging.[98]

The final, convicting jury had now been extended from approvers' appeals to regular public prosecutions. The next step would be application of that jury to appeals. On this point the Worcester roll is equivocal. The phrasing of pleas for a jury verdict at Worcester was richly diverse. There were two introductory phrases: *ponit se super* and *pro habenda*. The latter tended to be used when there was an oblation, and the former when there was not. There were also two substantive phrases: *de bono et malo* and *si culpabilis sit necne*. Either introductory phrase was joined with either substantive phrase, though sometimes there is no substantive phrase.

Until this time, presented persons had never, at eyre, put themselves upon juries.[99] When a presented person did so at Worcester, whatever the description of his action, he surely was putting himself

93. Ibid., pl. 1098 [*Select Pleas*, ed. Maitland, pl. 130], 1100, 1132 [*Select Pleas*, ed. Maitland, pl. 134], 1208 [*Select Pleas*, ed. Maitland, pl. 143].

94. There is no evidence on this roll that the oblation was related to the composition of the trial jury.

95. Ibid., pl. 1208 [*Select Pleas*, ed. Maitland, pl. 143]. This accused homicide had been bailed. This should have required a favorable inquest. Perhaps the earlier favorable outcome created a false hope of acquittal.

96. *Bracton on the Laws of England*, ed. Thorne, 2:361–62.

97. *Rolls for Worcestershire, 1221*, ed. Stenton, pl. 1218 [*Select Pleas*, ed. Maitland, pl. 144].

98. Franke's interlined confession of knowledge and consequent willingness to accept a jury may be an early example of judicial trickery. See J. M. Kaye, ed., *Placita Corone*, Selden Society Supplementary Series (1966), 4:xxxvi–xxxvii.

99. A presented person who was incarcerated could have had a bail inquest.

upon that jury for conviction or acquittal. But appellees had long since put themselves upon juries at eyre. In the past, whatever the description of the plea, it was clearly a plea for a medial verdict. This was so even when the plea was "utrum culpabilis sit . . . necne."[100] When appellees appeared at Worcester and put themselves upon a jury, even when they did so "si ipsi culpabiles sint . . . necne," it is impossible to know from the plea whether they were seeking a medial or a final verdict.[101] If there were a conviction, the appellee obviously had sought a final verdict, but no Worcester appellee who put himself upon a jury was convicted.

The Gloucester session immediately followed that at Worcester.[102] There was a lower rate of jury acceptances, a lower rate of jury convictions, and a higher rate of jury refusals at Gloucester than at Worcester.[103] Sixteen defendants in ten publicly prosecuted cases accepted jury trials.[104] The language of the Gloucester roll is more formulaic than that of the Worcester roll. Two defendants made oblations for their juries; in each case this is expressed by: "pro habenda inquisicione . . . si sit culpabilis necne."[105] The other eight cases, in which there are no oblations, are in the form "ponit se . . . de bono et malo."[106] When no oblation is mentioned, the acquitting jury seems to have been the presenting hundred jury.[107] In the only jury conviction among the presentments, the defendants put themselves upon twelve jurors and the countryside de bono et malo. They were said by the jurors to be guilty, and the jurors were supported by four named

100. E.g., *Staffordshire Suits*, ed. Wrottesley, 92–93.

101 There are four instances. Twice the plea was for a verdict only (*Rolls for Worcestershire, 1221*, ed. Stenton, pl. 1124, 1142 [*Select Pleas*, ed. Maitland, pl. 136]), and twice for a verdict re guilt (ibid., pl. 1145, 1210).

102. Ibid., xlviii.

103. The Worcester roll contains 203 pleas of the Crown; these produced eleven jury acceptances, one jury refusal, and three jury convictions. The Gloucester roll contains 507 pleas of the Crown; these yielded twenty-one jury acceptances, eight jury refusals, and two jury convictions.

104. I do not include an inquest, directed to the county, asking whether the accused had a royal pardon. *Pleas of Gloucester, 1221*, ed. Maitland, pl. 362.

105. Ibid., pl. 52, 436. The cases were referred to multiple hundred juries. Maitland thought the oblation produced the special jury. Ibid., xli. Bracton, however, says that an accused could not choose a special jury. *Bracton on the Laws of England*, ed. Thorne, 2:390.

106. *Pleas of Gloucester, 1221*, ed. Maitland, pl. 228, 257, 289, 326, 364, 378, 384, 414.

107. One defendant was not suspected by the hundred or the vills. Ibid., pl. 326.

vills.[108] These cases, taken together, imply that the hundred jurors alone could acquit but that conviction required joinder of the hundred jurors and the vills.

A final, assertive verdict of the hundredors plus the four vills would be a direct descendant of the earlier assertive, medial verdict of the same augmented jury. Participation by the vills should also be suggested by the derivation of the original de bono et malo plea from the plea de fidelitate. Unfortunately, each of the three convictions at Worcester was reported to have been pronounced simply by "juratores."[109] The difference between the Worcester and Gloucester cases may be only clerical, but it may also be more than that. The Worcester cases were unusually strong: a homicide taken after flight, a confessed harborer of an outlaw, and a slayer whose act was known in detail to the jurors. The justices may have thought, extrapolating from earlier manifest guilt cases, that the hundredors alone were sufficient to convict in these instances.

Among the Gloucester appeals are three clear instances of medial verdicts. Two were rendered upon pleas de odio et atia; one appellee was acquitted,[110] but the other was adjudged combat.[111] The third appellee simply put himself upon his visne, was returned guilty, and went to combat.[112] Excluding an approver's appeals,[113] four appellees apparently put themselves upon final verdicts. A brief description of the cases, all of them appeals of homicide, is necessary:

1. The appellor had died and the jurors were amerced for concealing the appeal; the appellee paid one-half mark for an inquest; he was acquitted.
2. The appellor did not appear; the appellee put himself on the verdict of twelve; he was acquitted.
3. The appellor retracted and the jurors were amerced for concealing the appeal; the appellee paid ten marks for a verdict of twelve; he was acquitted.

108. Ibid., pl. 228.

109. *Rolls for Worcestershire, 1221*, ed. Stenton, pl. 1099, 1208 [*Select Pleas*, ed. Maitland, pl. 143], 1218 [*Select Pleas*, ed. Maitland, pl. 144] (defendant put himself upon twelve jurors).

110. *Pleas of Gloucester, 1221*, ed. Maitland, pl. 76.

111. Ibid., pl. 434.

112. Ibid., pl. 87.

113. Ibid., pl. 73–75. Two appellees, after the approver was hanged, pleaded de bono et malo. There are no verdicts.

4. The appellor did not come, the appeal had been privately concorded, and the jurors were amerced for concealment; the appellee put himself upon the jurors de bono et malo; he was convicted and hanged.[114]

I believe a simple unsought inquest followed by coercive confinement upon an adverse verdict was not appropriate for these appellees. Such inquests were frequent in rape and wounding cases, but in homicides the justices seem to have pushed appellees to put themselves upon juries. Of course, these appellees could have refused a jury entirely and taken a chance upon what disposition would be made of them.[115] It is also possible, since the phrase de bono et malo does not appear in the first three cases, that these appellees were seeking a medial verdict, which, if adverse, would have required a new choice. The fourth appellee did fully expose himself to conviction and was in fact convicted. I believe these appellees all put themselves upon final verdicts. The jurors, who would also ultimately decide the cases, had concealed—failed to report—three of them. These appellees thought the jurors were favorably disposed toward them and would acquit.

Of course, one of them was wrong, and his case deserves special attention. After the widow of the victim had appealed the defendant, she made an elaborate concord with him. She did not appear at eyre, and the hundred jury did not report the appeal. In fact, a son of the victim and the appellor was a member of this jury and apparently aided the concealment. However the fact of the crime came to the justices, the appellee apparently thought that he would not be convicted. But upon his plea de bono et malo he was convicted by the jurors and four vills and was hanged.

This is an important case. It is the first clear example of one whose prosecution began privately, other than in approvers' appeals, and who was convicted by a jury. This could almost be the case Bracton had in mind when he described the necessity of proof by the country after an appeal was not prosecuted by the appellor or was made by a female (this case was both). In such cases there could not be combat, but the appellee was "bound to answer not only the appellor but the lord king."[116] And clearly the concord did not, in this homicide case, stand in the way of full prosecution. It may have satisfied the appellor,

114. Ibid., pl. 12, 343, 396, 101. See also ibid., pl. 426 (one report says the appellee put himself on a jury, but the other does not).

115. See below, text at nn. 121–29.

116 *Bracton on the Laws of England*, ed. Thorne, 2·402.

but the appellee was bound to answer the king as well, and the king had made no concord.[117]

This conviction was obtained upon verdict of the hundredors and the vills. It is, in this way, the exact cognate of the only conviction among the presentments, which also depended upon a verdict of the twelve and the vills. I suggested in discussing that case that the augmented convicting jury was a descendant of the older augmented medial jury. The closeness of the connection can now be seen even more clearly. Before 1215, when the justices subjected an appellee to an involuntary inquest he was awarded an ordeal only after adverse verdict by an augmented jury.[118] That is, when appeals were converted into public prosecutions only an augmented jury could issue an adverse verdict. That notion was carried forward so that in 1221 when an appeal was converted, when the appellee answered the king, only an augmented jury could convict.[119]

Finally, it is now clear that medial and final verdicts coexisted. An appellee who put himself on a jury de odio et atia obtained a medial verdict, while one who put himself on a jury de bono et malo obtained a final verdict. An analog has already been noticed: A medial verdict upon a plea de fidelitate continued to be available after it generated the final verdict upon the plea de bono et malo.[120] Presumably, one whose medial verdict de odio et atia was adverse would, if proof by combat was not available, be made to choose between a new plea de bono et malo and imprisonment, and this is the same choice as that made by approvers' appellees who failed their de fidelitate inquests.

The difficulty with this new system was its dependence upon the willingness of defendants to submit to final verdicts. Gloucester defendants were notably stubborn; eleven of them in eight cases refused.[121] Perhaps they had heard about defendants at Westminster and Worcester who had refused to plead and who had been permitted to

117. Concords, sanctioned by custom, were still permitted in homicide cases. See *Curia Regis Rolls*, 9:201 [*Bracton's Note Book*, ed. Maitland, pl. 1474] (John Sanctus)

118. Groot, "Jury in Private Criminal Prosecutions," 139.

119. This corresponds to Bracton's description. His discussion of defaulted appeals flows directly into his discussion of public prosecutions. He says suspicion may arise from rumor among responsible men on the presumption created by an appeal. He then describes trial by the hundredors and four vills. *Bracton on the Laws of England*, ed. Thorne, 2:402–5.

120. See above, text at n. 75.

121. *Pleas of Gloucester, 1221*, ed. Maitland, pl. 111, 161, 213, 229, 316, 330, 414, 435. Maitland listed only seven cases in his introduction. Ibid., xxxix He missed plea 229.

abjure.[122] Perhaps they thought conviction was certain: one refused because many people hated her;[123] another because he had done evil during the civil war;[124] and one came on for trial immediately after two others had pleaded de bono et malo and been hanged.[125] At least six individuals were said by augmented juries to be guilty.[126]

If conviction was certain, so was imprisonment. The 1219 order was still in effect. It is doubtful that these people were tougher than the approvers' appellees who accepted jury trial at Westminster. Of course, those appellees were transported from their home counties to the central gaols. Perhaps the likelihood of outside sustenance made gaol less fearsome to these Gloucester defendants. In any event, all of those who refused juries were initially incarcerated. Two were properly permitted pledges.[127] Eventually the justices released two more to pledges[128] and permitted another to abjure.[129] All three were fairly clearly guilty of homicide. If these releases began while the pleas of the Crown were still being heard, that undoubtedly strengthened the resolve of later defendants.

There is no doubt that the justices considered these refusals a problem. Toward the end of the session they seem to have offered a thief several different forms of jury in an effort to obtain a plea; he refused them all.[130] This is a critical point for jury trial. Release under pledges and abjuration could empty the gaols but could not convict. If the jury was to replace the ordeal, it would need to be effective, and it was not effective at Gloucester.

After the Gloucester sessions, the eyre moved to Hereford and Leicester, for which no rolls survive. It came to Warwick in late September 1221.[131] Somewhere between Gloucester and Warwick the justices had made a decision. The first two cases on the roll are simple

122. *Curia Regis Rolls,* 8:279 (Gilbert of Toleshorpe); *Rolls for Worcestershire, 1221,* ed. Stenton, pl. 1208 [*Select Pleas,* ed. Maitland, pl. 143].

123. *Pleas of Gloucester, 1221,* ed. Maitland, pl. 111.

124. Ibid., pl. 161.

125. Ibid., pl. 229. The same thing happened at Worcester. *Rolls for Worcestershire, 1221,* ed. Stenton, pl. 1208 [*Select Pleas,* ed. Maitland, pl. 143].

126. *Pleas of Gloucester, 1221,* ed. Maitland, pl. 111, 213, 229, 330, 414. One, a homicide, was hanged for breaking gaol. Ibid., pl. 316.

127. Ibid., pl. 111, 213. The text refers to the disposition of the daughter in plea 111 and of the father in plea 213.

128. Ibid., pl. 161, 414.

129. Ibid., pl. 330. This defendant stood upon his right to defend by combat; the case is strikingly similar to the hypothetical one in *Placita Corone,* ed. Kaye, 18.

130. *Pleas of Gloucester, 1221,* ed. Maitland, pl. 435.

131. *Rolls for Warwickshire, 1221–1222,* ed. Stenton, xii.

unsolved homicides that elicited the rules of *murdrum* applied in Warwick. These are immediately followed by a widow's appeal of her husband's homicide. Since she had a new husband, who did not join the appeal, it was null. The justices ordered an inquiry by the countryside into the truth of the matter; the appellee was apparently heavily suspected but refused a jury. The justices had seen enough of recalcitrant defendants. They added twenty-four knights to the twelve hundredors. This jury of thirty-six declared the appellee guilty, and he was hanged.[132] Some forty cases later, the very next case in which an accused refused a jury verdict, a presented thief was suspected by the hundredors. As in the prior case, he was put upon an additional jury of twenty-four knights, which condemned him, and he was hanged.[133]

These cases, early in the Warwick session, stopped jury refusals.[134] How they did so tells us much about this early jury system. Defendants who came on to plead had already been presented by the hundred jury, and each presentment had survived initial scrutiny. If it had not, they would have been acquitted or released to pledges and would not have needed to plead.[135] What the defendant faced was a choice of an augmented jury. He could plead de bono et malo and be tried by the hundredors and four vills, or he could refuse to plead and be tried by the hundredors and twenty-four knights. Since the hundredors were fixed, his real choice was between twenty villagers[136] and twenty-four knights. This was a real choice only if two conditions were met: first, that the vills and knights might decide the same case differently; second, that if the vills or knights disagreed with the hundredors, the former would control. The first seems clear. Even a guilty defendant with a bad reputation could at least hope for mercy from his peers, but he was less likely to get it from the knightly jury chosen from the county at large. The second is borne out by the cases.[137]

132. Ibid., pl. 728 [*Select Pleas*, ed. Maitland, pl. 153].

133. Ibid., pl. 767 [*Select Pleas*, ed. Maitland, pl. 157].

134. But see ibid., pl. 877. This very cryptic entry states that a captured homicide abjured because he refused a jury. Presumably he was not heavily suspected of the actual slaying.

135. This does not mean that the hundredors were prepared to convict; it means that judicial inquiry had not found a reason why the prosecution should not proceed, and the hundredors had not given one. See text at nn. 80–81 above and at n. 149 below.

136. Four vills, each represented by four men and the reeve. *Bracton on the Laws of England*, ed. Thorne, 2:310 (writ of 1226, the sheriff was ordered to summon to eyre "from each vill four lawful men and the reeve"); W. Stubbs, *Select Charters*, 9th ed. (Oxford, 1921), 358 (writ of 1231; identical).

137. The Warwick appeals add nothing. I list them with their salient features: *Rolls for Warwickshire, 1221–1222*, ed. Stenton, pl. 738 (de bono et malo), 751

Thirteen publicly prosecuted defendants in seven cases put themselves upon verdicts.[138] Two cases began by indictment. In this context, indictment means that the hundred jurors had named these men in their *rotulus de privatis* as suspects and that they had been arrested.[139] In one of these cases, the suspects put themselves upon the countryside, the hundred jurors did not suspect them, and they were acquitted.[140] There are two important features to this case: first, the hundred jurors, by simple, *self-contradictory* statement, could forestall further prosecution; second, because the hundred jury did not suspect, participation by the vills was unnecessary. In the other case, the hundred jurors did not retract their indictment, the suspect put himself upon the countryside, but he was not suspected by the vills and was placed under pledges.[141] The lessons of this case are similar to the first: If the hundredors suspected, the vills were consulted, because they were necessary to conviction, but even a simple statement of the vills that the defendant was not suspected terminated his prosecution. The other public prosecutions lead to the same conclusions. When the hundred jurors did not suspect a defendant who had sought a verdict, he was either acquitted or put under pledges without participation by the vills.[142] Only if the hundredors did suspect was the case referred to the vills, and absence of suspicion by the vills terminated the prosecution.[143]

This is, of course, precisely the way in which pre-1215 assertive, medial verdicts screened suspects.[144] These vills apparently remembered that before 1215 they had the power, by refusing to join hundredors in suspicion, to spare a defendant the ordeal. When they exercised a similar power in 1221, they may have done so because they thought the defendant was innocent, or from mercy, or in reaction to perceived judicial high-handedness in condemning men through

(de odio et atia), 832 [*Select Pleas*, ed. Maitland, pl. 161] (oblation; special jury), 875 (oblation), 886, 899 (oblation; de bono et malo), 906 [*Select Pleas*, ed. Maitland, pl. 163], 945 [*Select Pleas*, ed. Maitland, pl. 165], 966 [*Select Pleas*, ed. Maitland, pl. 166] (oblation; de bono et malo), 976. There were no convictions.

138. Ibid., pl. 839, 885, 891, 901, 925, 949, 958 All used the ponit se formula, and there were no oblations.

139. *Bracton on the Laws of England*, ed. Thorne, 2:329.

140. *Rolls for Warwickshire, 1221–1222*, ed. Stenton, pl. 958.

141. Ibid., pl. 839

142. Ibid., pl. 885, 891 [*Select Pleas*, ed Maitland, pl. 162] (William Goman), 925 (Gilbert le Eskermissur), 949 (Henry Cut).

143. Ibid., pl. 891 [*Select Pleas*, ed. Maitland, pl. 162] (John Kynebaut)

144. See above, text at nn. 10–13.

"blue-ribbon," knightly juries. Whatever the motivation, the justices' solution to the problem of recalcitrant defendants could be thwarted by recalcitrant villagers. The justices must have recognized that possibility, but they took these verdicts calmly. Neither the hundred juries that did not suspect after first presenting nor vills that disagreed with hundred juries were amerced. Again, this is precisely the pre-1215 pattern.[145] Not even the jurors who disavowed their own indictment and who were placed in mercy at the time finally had to pay an amercement.[146] Here is the power of the English jury to acquit.

After Warwick the eyre visited Staffordshire and then Shropshire.[147] The Stafford roll is lost, and the Shropshire roll is fairly small and has only two cases of interest. No appellee put himself upon either a medial or a final jury verdict. One person, taken for ill fame, was offered but refused a jury; he paid twenty shillings to be under pledges.[148] Presumably he was not heavily suspected of a specific serious crime and therefore saw no reason to chance a verdict. Two men were taken by the sergeant upon an indictment after stolen meat was found in their barn. The hundred jury *sua sponte* reported that the principal defendant was a lawful man and not guilty, and that he had been framed. The defendants were acquitted.[149] This case again makes the point that the hundred jury, as it had been since the beginning of the century, was pressed to report completely but could immediately thereafter terminate the proceedings.

In early 1222 a final session of this eyre was held at Warwick. There is a little cluster of Crown pleas,[150] apparently a proceeding in the nature of a gaol delivery with the suspects transported to Warwick for this final session. A suspect who pleaded de bono et malo was said by the "juratores" to be more thief than lawful, but he was permitted abjuration.[151] Probably no vills were present at this little session. Does this case predict the gaol delivery jury of twelve with which some identify the modern petty jury?[152]

145. Groot, "The Jury of Presentment," 22.

146. *Rolls for Warwickshire, 1221–1222*, ed. Stenton, pl. 958 and p. 426.

147. Ibid., xii.

148. Ibid., pl. 1239.

149. Ibid., pl. 1263 [*Select Pleas*, ed. Maitland, pl. 170]. This case fits precisely into the judicial inquiry asking if there was any reason the case should not go forward *Bracton on the Laws of England*, ed. Thorne, 2:404. It even matches one of Bracton's reasons: a lord trying to obtain his tenant's land.

150. *Rolls for Warwickshire, 1221–1222*, ed. Stenton, pl. 1473–76.

151. Ibid., pl. 1474.

152. See *Crown Pleas of the Wiltshire Eyre*, ed. Meekings, 52–53.

Conclusion

In the short period from 1216 to 1222, the true trial jury was born and matured into the form it would have for many decades. The immediately precipitating event was the abolition of the ordeal by the Roman church in 1215. But the development of the jury in its medial form before 1215 made it a ready substitute for that form of physical proof.

The first major step in the transition of the jury from medial to final was the taking of quasi-convicting, sanctioning verdicts in nonprovable appeals during the eyre proceedings of 1218–19. The first true jury trials appeared during Hilary term 1220. These were trials in a specialized form of prosecution—approvers' appeals. These trial juries were most directly descended from an older medial form that was unique to approver cases, the inquest de fidelitate.

The true jury trial in criminal cases generally appeared during the second phase of the 1218–22 eyre, first in the trial of presented defendants at Worcester and then in the trial of an appellee at Gloucester. But extending the new convicting jury to appeals did not erase the older de odio et atia inquest; that medial form continued to exist alongside the new, final form. At Gloucester the structure of the convicting jury, at least at eyre, was fixed as the twelve hundredors and four vills. But the new system, as applied through the Gloucester sessions, depended upon defendants' willingness to put themselves upon jury verdicts. The stubbornness of Gloucester defendants in this regard caused a judicial reaction at Warwick.

The first two Warwick defendants who refused trial—that is, trial by the hundredors and the vills—were involuntarily placed upon a jury of the hundredors and twenty-four knights and were convicted. This judicial action produced the desired response from defendants—pleas de bono et malo. But the juries upon which these defendants put themselves were less tractable. Either the hundredors refused to suspect, or if they did suspect, the vills refused to join them in convicting defendants. There was no obvious judicial reaction to these not-guilty verdicts, probably because juries in their medial form had long since developed the power to terminate prosecutions.

The Warwick experiment with involuntary trial by twenty-four knights is important. The new jury trial system had not worked well at Gloucester; some change was necessary. The jury as judge of guilt or innocence might even have been abandoned. That the justices decided only to change the form of the jury is evidence of a commitment to the concept of lay judging. That the experiment ended as soon as defendants began to accept trial by hundredors and vills indicates that community lay judging was preferred. That the experiment was not repeated after vills regularly began to acquit is more evidence of a strong commitment to community lay judging.[153]

This commitment was so strong that verdict by the community was entrenched as *the only way* in which an accused could be condemned.[154] This, of course, required a mechanism for insuring that a defendant would accept trial by his community. I have found few cases in the printed post–1221 rolls in which defendants steadfastly refused jury trial. Some mechanism, perhaps simple incarceration as in 1220,[155] continually generated pleas de bono et malo. Bracton speaks frequently, but not very clearly, of suspects compelled to put themselves upon juries.[156] Whatever this mechanism was, and it may have been more than simple imprisonment,[157] its effect was trial by the hundreds and vills, by the visne. Thus jury trial, as developed between 1216 and 1222, continued as judgment by the locality, by common folk who could say no to the king.

Acknowledgments

Research for this essay was supported, in part, by the Frances Lewis Law Center, Washington and Lee University. I must also thank two Washington and Lee students: Martha Petrey (law '86) was my able research assistant, and Thomas W. Thagard III (arts '87), whose research overlapped mine, was a valuable sounding board.

153. The two Warwick cases are well known, probably because they were much later cited for the proposition that persons were regularly tried involuntarily in the 1220s. Matthew Hale, *The History of Pleas of the Crown* (1800), 2:321 note n. The cases deserve fame, but for the reason stated in the text. I have found only one similar case, but it may be a medial verdict: *Curia Regis Rolls*, 13:297.

154. Condemnation after failure of proof by combat remained a possibility in appeals, but realistically, that occurred only in some approvers' appeals.

155. E.g., *Curia Regis Rolls*, vol. 11, pl 2309; ibid., vol. 13, pl. 2781.

156. *Bracton on the Laws of England*, ed. Thorne, 2:402–5.

157. *Curia Regis Rolls*, vol. 11, pl. 1903. Two approvers' appellees, brought to a gaol delivery, could not be tried by combat. They refused a jury. Later they reappeared before the court and "of their own spontaneous volition" put themselves upon a jury.

Two

Juror Attitudes toward Local Disorder: The Evidence of the 1328 Lincolnshire Trailbaston Proceedings

Bernard William McLane

Thomas Brinton, the late-fourteenth-century bishop of Rochester, believed that criminals were not punished as they should have been. In one of his surviving sermons he complained that:

> If a voluntary murderer or most notorious thief who according to every law ought to pay the just penalty of his wickedness, is captured in order that justice may be done upon his person, as though in compassion, they strive to keep him from danger, some saying, "He is young: if a youth has gone wrong, the old man will be able to amend." Others declare, "He is of our blood: if the Law proceeds against him, the whole of our clan will be shamefully disgraced."[1]

A century earlier the Crown had made a similar complaint in the Statute of Westminster (1275): "the peace is less kept, and the laws less used, and offenders less punished than they ought to be."[2] The reason for this laxity, according to the Crown, was that local inhabitants preferred that strangers be robbed rather than offenders punished because oftentimes either the offenders or their protectors were local men.

Scholars have long noted the apparent contradiction between numerous charges of criminal behavior and low conviction rates for those who stood trial.[3] It is difficult, however, to test the assertion that local communities were unwilling to deal forthrightly with criminal offenders, especially during the years between 1290 and 1350, de-

1. Quoted in G. R. Owst, *Literature and Pulpit in Medieval England* (Oxford, 1966), 340.

2. *Statutes of the Realm* (1810), 1:26.

3. See the comments in J. G. Bellamy, *Crime and Public Order in England in the Later Middle Ages* (1973), 124.

spite abundant evidence that disorder was endemic. The statutes promulgated and the judicial commissions issued during the late thirteenth and early fourteenth centuries testify to an apparent epidemic of crime throughout England. The Statute of Winchester (1285) echoed the Statute of Westminster: "from day to day, robberies, murders, burnings and thefts be more often used than they have been heretofore."[4] In 1304 justices were assigned to investigate the activities of "malefactors and peacebreakers who are moving about the woods and parks and committing murders, depredations, burnings and other misdeeds to the peril of travellers and dwellers" in Lincolnshire and the rest of England.[5] Special commissions, which led to inquests popularly known as trailbastons, were issued in the following year and periodically throughout this period to deal with these "malefactors and peacebreakers."[6]

Justices were similarly appointed in 1317 to investigate and deal with "diverse homicides, felonies, conspiracies, and other crimes committed in the county of Lincoln which go unpunished."[7] In 1325 specially appointed officials were to "pursue and arrest disturbers of the peace who join together and make raids by day and night, commit robberies, imprison people until they make ransom, go to fairs and markets and take goods without paying for them, beat those who will not be of their party and waylay merchants."[8] Three years later it was ordained in the Statute of Northampton (1328) that:

> No man great or small, of what condition soever he be . . . be so hardy [as] to come before the King's justices or other of the King's ministers during their office, with force and arms, nor having no force in affray of the peace, nor to go nor ride armed by night and day, in fairs, markets, nor in the presence of the justices or other ministers, nor in no part elsewhere.[9]

Conditions apparently remained unchanged in 1338, when keepers of the peace were appointed in Lincolnshire, Northamptonshire, and Rutland because "it is reported that there are many disturbers thereof

4 *Statutes of the Realm*, 1:96

5. *CPR, 1301–1307*, p. 343 (23 Nov.).

6. Ibid., 354, 542 (6 Apr. 1305 and 21 Feb. 1307, respectively). See Alan Harding, "Early Trailbaston Proceedings from the Lincoln Roll of 1305," in *Medieval Legal Records: Edited in Memory of C.A.F. Meekings*, ed. R. F. Hunnisett and J. B. Post (1978), 143–68.

7. *CPR, 1317–1321*, p. 91 (3 Nov.).

8. *CPR, 1324–1327*, p. 228 (27 July).

9. *Statutes of the Realm*, 1:258.

and suspected persons who run from county to county and cannot be apprehended and brought to justice," while in 1340 trusted royal justices and local men were commissioned throughout England to investigate and deal with allegations of widespread official misconduct and numerous complaints that "malefactors and peacebreakers in gangs were wandering about day and night in various counties beating and wounding people in cities, towns and other places, committing robberies and imprisoning people until they paid fines and redemptions."[10]

It is difficult to use the evidence contained in the surviving inquest records because of the restructuring undertaken by the Crown during this period of those parts of the legal system that dealt with criminal matters. This process began with the introduction of new gaol delivery and assize circuits in the early 1290s and ended in the 1340s with the emergence of the justices of the peace and their associates, the justices of assize and gaol delivery, as the chief judicial agents of the Crown in the English countryside.[11] This reorganization, which was rather more haphazard than planned, and the subsequent lack of continuity in the operation of the royal criminal courts make it impossible to determine whether there was an actual increase in the number of crimes committed or either a new or an increased unwillingness to tolerate what may have been a constant problem of disorder.[12] Despite this uncertainty, there seems no reason to doubt that a crisis of law and order existed during this period or to believe that the preambles to the statutes and the wording of the judicial commissions quoted above were simply rhetorical flourishes advanced by members of the royal bureaucracy to justify the expansion of its influence and an increase in its sources of revenue.

A further word of caution is necessary. The enrolled complaints and charges are extremely terse. Entries in the surviving court records of

10. The commissions are in *CPR, 1334–1338*, p. 141 (1 Aug. 1338); and *CPR, 1340–1343*, pp. 106–7 (10 and 16 Dec. 1340), respectively. The Lincolnshire inquest that resulted from the latter commissions is calendared in *The 1341 Royal Inquest in Lincolnshire*, ed. B. W. McLane, Lincoln Record Society, 78 (forthcoming).

11. The changes are discussed in McLane, "The Royal Courts," chap. 1; and Alan Harding, *The Law Courts of Medieval England* (New York, 1973), 86–92. See also David Crook, "The Later Eyres," *EHR* 97 (1982): 241–68.

12. G. O. Sayles declares that "it is impossible to know whether the increase was more apparent than real, reflecting the attempt to apply the rule of law more widely and more meticulously." *Select Cases in the Court of King's Bench*, Selden Society, 7 vols. (1936–71), 7:xxxvi, n. 7. See also K. B. McFarlane, *The Nobility of Later Medieval England* (Oxford, 1973), 114–15, and R. B. Pugh, "Some Reflections of a Medieval Criminologist," *Proceedings of the British Academy* 59 (1973) 84.

this period typically are limited to those details that the enrolling court clerks considered absolutely essential: the names of the accused and victim, the crime, and the date when and the place where the crime allegedly took place. Background evidence, such as the circumstances of the offenses and the motives involved, were rarely noted, except in a few homicide cases in which jurors stated that the deaths had been in self-defense.[13]

Finally, it is impossible to conduct a study of law and order during the late thirteenth and early fourteenth centuries based on the evidence of a series of records from a single royal court. There was no comprehensive criminal court that operated continuously during this period, as had, for example, the eyre *ad omnia placita* for much of the thirteenth century or the peace and assize sessions from the late fourteenth century onward, whose surviving records have provided scholars with evidence with which to examine purported fluctuations in criminal behavior.[14] Nevertheless, to admit that the nature of the evidence of widespread disorder in the late thirteenth and early fourteenth centuries makes analysis difficult and generalizations hazardous does not mean that this evidence cannot be profitably studied and valuable lessons learned concerning the interrelationship between the royal administration of justice and local attitudes toward disorder, only that any findings must be tentative and subject to further testing and revision. The purpose of this study is to conduct a preliminary examination of the extent to which the complaints registered by Thomas Brinton and the Crown in the Statute of Westminster reflected popular attitudes toward local disorder and the role played by the royal courts in dealing with it. Given the general lack of continuity in the royal administration of criminal justice, the approach adopted has been to examine a large number of charges made during a single important judicial inquest: the 1,915 presentments brought

13. Thomas Green has made extensive use of jurors' declarations of self-defense to examine popular attitudes. See, for example, his early article, "Societal Concepts of Criminal Liability for Homicide in Medieval England," *Speculum* 47 (1972) 669–94, and his recent book, *Verdict According to Conscience: Perspectives on the English Criminal Trial Jury, 1200–1800* (Chicago, 1985). James Cockburn produced the classic study of the limits and inaccuracies of law-court evidence for the early modern period in his "Early Modern Assize Records as Historical Evidence," *Journal of the Society of Archivists* 5 (1974): 215–31. See also J. B. Post, "Some Limitations of the Medieval Peace Rolls," *Journal of the Society of Archivists* 4 (1973): 633–39

14. One example is J. B. Given, *Society and Homicide in Thirteenth-Century England* (Stanford, 1977), which made extensive use of eyre roll material. An important contribution for the early-fourteenth-century scene, based on a good set of gaol delivery rolls, is B. A Hanawalt, "Economic Influences on the Pattern of Crime in England, 1300–1348," *AJLH* 18 (1974): 281–97.

against 1,513 individuals during trailbaston proceedings conducted in Lincolnshire in 1328.[15] Although this approach does not allow for the study of changes in patterns of criminal behavior—or, more accurately, patterns of criminal prosecutions—it does make possible the examination of the prosecution of a wide range of felonies and misdemeanors.

A commission, dated 15 May 1328, authorized John Stonore, justice of Common Pleas, John Cambridge, a sergeant at law, and William Ross and Richard Grey, local magnates, to hold inquests in the counties of Lincoln, Nottingham, Derby, Leicester, and Warwick. These inquests were part of an extensive campaign against disorder that the Crown conducted throughout England between 1328 and 1332.[16] The terms of the commission were in standard trailbaston terminology: homicides, robberies, and other serious crimes were being committed day and night, and criminals were wandering throughout the countryside "to the great peril of inhabitants and travellers and in contempt of the king and to the manifest terror of his people." Accordingly, the justices were to investigate and deal with "common malefactors and breakers of the king's peace"; their procurers and receivers; those who paid these offenders to assault and kill their enemies "in fairs, markets and other places, both public and private"; those who threatened jurors so that they would not tell the truth; those who "by reason of their power and state" protected criminals in return for fees; conspirators; and those who were "malefactors in fish ponds and parks." In addition, the justices were to deal with the misdeeds of local officials: "sheriffs, coroners and their clerks, bailiffs and ministers, constables and gaol keepers, and bailiffs of liberties and their assistants."

The Lincolnshire inquest began at Lincoln on 6 June, when juries representing the major county divisions of Holland, Kesteven, and each of the three ridings of Lindsey, the towns of Stamford and Grimsby, and the city of Lincoln began to make their presentments to

15. PRO, JUST 1/516. Unless otherwise stated, all records cited are from the Public Record Office

16 *CPR, 1327–1330*, p. 297. The full commission is on C 66/169, m 7d, and also on JUST 1/516, m. 1 The Crown's campaign in Lincolnshire is examined in detail in McLane, "The Royal Courts," 62–79, and more generally in E.L.G. Stones's doctoral dissertation, "Sir Geoffrey Le Scrope (*c*. 1285–1340)" (University of Edinburgh, 1950), 142–77. See also Helen Cam, "The General Eyres of 1329–30," *EHR* 39 (1924): 241–52, and *The Eyre of Northamptonshire, 3–4 Edward III, A.D. 1329–1330*, ed. D. Sutherland, Selden Society, 97 (1983), 1.xxii-xxvii.

the justices.[17] On the same day the justices also began to hear private complaints (*querelae*) prosecuted by alleged victims.[18] Trials of those arrested were conducted, and additional presentment sessions were held on 20 June and between 18 and 28 July.[19] On 18 July the sheriff was ordered to begin outlawry proceedings against accused felons who had not appeared before the justices, and further sessions were planned for 22 August and 13 October.[20] Apparently those sessions were never held, and the inquest lapsed until Trinity term 1331, when the justices of King's Bench began a thorough review of the proceedings.[21] Ross was ordered to send the names of all those who had been outlawed for nonappearance or had had outlawry proceedings begun against them, and the sheriff was ordered to arrest those he could and bring them before the court.[22] On 7 June and 19 July the justices presided over the trials of those arrested.[23] In addition, a list of those who had been indicted for felonies in 1328 and subsequently outlawed for nonappearance was transcribed onto the term roll.[24] The comprehensiveness of this review is testimony to the seriousness with which the Crown and the local communities took the problem of disorder in Lincolnshire.

A total of 248 men were identified as jurors during the sessions of June and July 1328: 18 served on both presentment and trial juries, another 148 only on presentment juries and 82 others only on trial juries.[25] The small number of men who sat on both presentment and trial juries is perhaps surprising and is discussed below. There was also a strong correlation between the social status and administrative experience of certain jurors and the type of jury service they performed (see

17 JUST 1/516, mm. 1, 7, 8, 10, 21.

18. Ibid., m. 35.

19. The gaol deliveries are recorded on mm. 15–18, and the second series of presentments is on mm. 21d, 23, 24, 24d, 26, 26d, 31, 32d.

20. JUST 1/516, mm. 3, 3d, 5, 6d–7d, 8, 8d, 9d–10d, 11d, 13, 13d, 23, 24, 24d.

21 KB 27/285, Rex m. 1.

22. The writs to Ross and the sheriff, dated 8 May 1331, are on ibid., m. 17.

23. KB 27/285, Gaol Delivery mm. 1–10d.

24. The list is on KB 27/285, Rex mm. 17–21. The review of the trailbaston proceedings continued through Michaelmas term 1333. KB 27/294, Rex mm. 1, 5, 28.

25. Although the list of jurors on the fifteen presentment juries seems to be a complete listing of those who performed such service, the names of the members of the twelve recorded trial juries may be only a partial listing. In contrast to the lists of presentment juries that were enrolled at the beginning of each new section, the names of trial juries were recorded at the end of only certain otherwise routine trial entries. For citations to the presentment juries, see nn. 18, 20. The trial juries were identified on JUST 1/516, mm. 15–17d

Table 2.1).[26] Fully 81 percent (34 of 42) of the county gentry and prominent residents of the city of Lincoln who performed jury service sat as presentment jurors, and only the remaining 19 percent (8 of 42) served exclusively as trial jurors. Similarly, 78 percent (42 of 54) of those who held appointments as local or royal officials and served as jurors sat on presentment juries, while only the remaining 22 percent (12 of 54) sat exclusively on trial juries.

Local notables, when called upon to perform jury service during the 1328 Lincoln trailbaston proceedings, were thus far more likely to serve as presentment jurors than just as trial jurors. Whether this pattern of jury service was typical for the period is unknown, and further study is required. But although it is hazardous to generalize on the basis of a single inquest, the Lincoln evidence suggests that the local elites and perhaps the Crown considered presentment jury service to be more prestigious and important than service on trial juries. Local notables (and the Crown or its justices?) may have believed that during special royal inquests it was more important to identify offenders considered to be beyond the control of local authorities than to spend time on the more mundane task of determining the guilt or innocence

Table 2.1. Composition of the Trailbaston Juries

Type of Service	No. of Jurors	Gentry or Equivalent Status	Experience as a Local or Royal Official
Presentments and trials	18	11	10
Presentments only	148	23	32
Trials only	82	8	12
Total	248	42	54

SOURCE: JUST 1/516.

26. Gentry status has been accorded to individuals described as knights on the inquest roll or identified as such by the sheriff during the 1324 levy of the county gentry (*Parliamentary Writs and Writs of Military Summons*, 2:644–45), and those identified by the sheriff in 1316 as having lands worth £50 in the county (C 47/1/8, mm. 14, 15). An equivalent rank was given to residents of Lincoln who, according to the 1327 subsidy (E 179/135/12), were among the four wealthiest members of individual city parishes. Experience as a royal or local official included serving as a sheriff, a member of Parliament, a justice of special oyer and terminer, the mayor of Lincoln, and a member of the Lincoln Council of Twenty-four. The evidence of this service is based on information in the printed calendars and J.W.F. Hill, *Medieval Lincoln* (Cambridge, 1948).

of those few who were actually brought before the justices to answer the charges against them.

The offenses publicly prosecuted by presentment during the 1328 proceedings fall into three basic categories: 53 percent (1,019 of 1,915) dealt with felonies, 27 percent (507 of 1,915) dealt with trespasses committed by nonofficials, and 20 percent (389 of 1,915) with trespasses committed by local and royal officials (see Table 2.2).[27] The large number of felony presentments is not surprising. There had not been a major royal inquest into crime in the county since 1318, and these offenses, especially homicide, had long been regarded as pleas of

Table 2.2. Types of Offenses Presented during the 1328 Proceedings

Types of Offenses	Number of Presentments
Felonies	
Homicides	506
Thefts[a]	401
Fel. accomplices	104
Arsons	8
	1,019
Trespasses by nonofficials	
Assaults	257
Thefts[b]	96
Conspiracies	46
Trespass accomplices	27
Other trespasses	81
	507
Trespasses by officials	389
Total presentments[c]	1,915

SOURCE JUST 1/516.
[a] Includes 141 burglaries and 40 robberies.
[b] Includes 86 charges of extortion.
[c] Many presentments mentioned more than one type of offense or more than one instance of the same offense. In order to gauge the relative frequency of the different offenses prosecuted, each offense and each instance of the same offense has been counted separately.

27. B. H. Putnam, who examined the Lincolnshire roll, stated that "it is a roll that gives a particularly complete picture of criminal proceedings [and] bears a close resemblance to the rolls of the criminal side of an eyre." "Shire Officials. Keepers of the Peace and Justices of the Peace," in *The English Government at Work, 1327–1336*, ed. J. F. Willard et al., 3 vols. (Cambridge, Mass., 1940–50), 3:298.

the Crown. As such, they were generally reserved for prosecution in the royal courts unless the Crown had granted specific jurisdictional privileges to local magnates (lay or ecclesiastical) or urban communities.[28]

The large number of homicides publicly prosecuted by jury presentment and the absence of private appeals brought by the alleged victims' next of kin during the 1328 proceedings very probably reflect the decline of the appeal as a useful judicial mechanism for most people. Appeals were still lodged during this period, but they had become increasingly difficult to prosecute and, indeed, had always been primarily intended to secure out-of-court settlements satisfactory to the appellors.[29] It is also relevant to point out that prosecuting one's grievances in the royal courts was only one way, and perhaps not always the most effective way, of obtaining justice or, more accurately, restitution.[30] Perhaps the local communities and the Crown had decided that in an era of widespread disorder, it was of the utmost importance for the maintenance of some semblance of good order that serious crimes be prosecuted publicly in the royal courts (which, in theory at least, were beyond the control of local influences) even when the victims or the next of kin had reached settlements with the offenders.[31]

28. J. B. Post, "Local Jurisdictions and Judgment of Death in Later Medieval England," *Criminal Justice History* 4 (1983):1–21.

29. The appeal has been the subject of two important recent studies. C. H Whittick, "The Role of the Criminal Appeal in the Fifteenth Century," in *Law and Social Change in British History*, ed. J. A. Guy and H G. Beale (1984), 55–72; and Daniel Ernst, "The Moribund Appeal of Death: Compensating Survivors and Controlling Jurors in Early Modern England," *AJLH* 28 (1984): 164–88. Whittick and Ernst argue that one of the primary goals of prosecuting appeals was to force the accused to provide compensation acceptable to the appellor. See also C.A F. Meekings's comments in *Crown Pleas of the Wiltshire Eyre, 1249*, Wiltshire Archaeological and Natural History Society, 17 (1961), 70–76, 83, 87–88.

30. J. R. Kent, for example, states that "it was only after local attempts to settle a dispute had failed that inhabitants brought suit at law, that they appealed to authorities outside the village for assistance in resolving a dispute." " 'Folk Justice' and Royal Justice in Early Seventeenth-Century England: A Charivari in the Midlands," *Midland History* 8 (1983): 70. See also the comments of J. A. Sharpe in " 'Such Disagreement betwyx Neighbors': Litigation and Human Relations in Early Modern England," in *Disputes and Settlements: Human Relations in the West*, ed. John Bossy (Cambridge, 1983), 167–87; and Given, *Society and Homicide*, 201. These citations and others that follow that reference sixteenth- and seventeenth-century studies suggest that certain attitudes toward dealing with local disorder at the community level were similar whether one is dealing with the late medieval or the early modern period.

31. The private settlement of disputes has attracted recent attention. J. B. Post, "Equitable Resorts Before 1450," in *Law, Litigants and the Legal Profession*, ed. E W. Ives and A H. Manchester (1983), 68–79; Edward Powell, "Arbitration and the

Equally as unsurprising as the numerous felony charges were the presentments made concerning official misconduct. Although abuses of authority by local and royal officials have been examined in connection with the assessment and collection of wartime levies, misconduct resulting from the ordinary administration of government has been largely neglected.[32] Based on the evidence of the 1328 proceedings, local inhabitants had legitimate grounds to complain about such officials as those of Somerton Castle in Kesteven, who often did not pay for supplies taken from neighboring villages, or Ralph Cressy, coroner of Kesteven, who, if over a hundred presentments are accurate, routinely demanded and collected fees before providing services that were supposed to be free. To many inhabitants of the local communities, the trailbaston sessions at Lincoln must have been an all-too-infrequent occasion on which to register complaints about the malpractices of local and royal officials.

The trespasses presented during the 1328 proceedings provide some limited evidence of what may have been a significant change relative to the prosecution of trespasses in the royal courts in the early fourteenth century. During this period, inhabitants of Lincolnshire increased their use of judicial mechanisms available in the royal courts. The number of trespass lawsuits prosecuted in the court of King's Bench by county residents steadily increased between 1301 and 1322 and rose dramatically in 1323, while the more elevated segments of county society obtained ever larger numbers of special commissions of oyer and terminer after 1300 to adjudicate their disputes.[33] An ap-

Law in the Late Middle Ages," *TRHS*, 5th ser., 33 (1983) 49–67, and Michael Clanchy, "Law and Love in the Middle Ages," in *Disputes and Settlements*, 47–67. See also J. W. Bennett, "The Mediaeval Loveday," *Speculum* 33 (1958). 351–70; and J. M. Kaye, "The Making of the English Criminal Law," *Criminal Law Review* 23 (1977): 4–13.

32. The connection between official corruption and war finance is examined in J. R. Maddicott, *The English Peasantry and the Demands of the Crown, 1294–1341*, Past and Present Supplement no. 1 (Oxford, 1975); Dorothy Hughes, *A Study of Social and Constitutional Tendencies in the Early Years of Edward III* (1915), chap. 10; and McLane, "The Royal Courts," chap. 3. The only extended discussions of "ordinary" official misconduct are Helen Cam's *Studies in the Hundred Rolls: Some Aspects of Thirteenth-Century Administration*, Oxford Studies in Social and Legal History, 6 (Oxford, 1921), and *The Hundred and the Hundred Rolls: An Outline of Local Government in Medieval England* (New York, 1960).

33. The increase in trespass litigation is examined in McLane, "The Royal Courts," 15–22, and McLane, "Changes in the Court of King's Bench, 1291–1340: The Preliminary View from Lincolnshire," in *England in the Fourteenth Century: Proceedings of the 1985 Harlaxton Symposium*, ed. W. M. Ormrod (Woodbridge, Suff., 1986), 152–60. The increased use of special commissions of oyer and terminer is discussed in Kaeuper, "Law and Order in Fourteenth-Century England: The Evidence of Special Commissions of Oyer and Terminer," *Speculum* 54 (1979) 734–84, and McLane, "The Royal Courts," 23–30.

parent result of this increase in private litigation in the royal courts was the relative decline in the importance allotted to prosecuting trespasses publicly by presentment during royal inquests. The evidence of the Lincolnshire presentments is inconclusive, but it does suggest a shift in attitude: While 60 percent (639 of 1,071) of the presentments made during the 1305 trailbaston proceedings involved trespasses, they comprised only 26 percent (507 of 1,915) of those made during the 1328 sessions.[34] Obviously this topic needs additional study; however, because of the evidence of the statutes and commissions quoted at the beginning of this study and the charges in surviving legal records, it is unlikely that there had been a decrease in the number of assaults, extortions, and similar petty offenses committed in Lincolnshire between 1305 and 1328. A more probable explanation is that there was a change in the attitude of the local communities toward dealing with these offenses. By 1328, local inhabitants may have been unwilling to rely exclusively or even primarily on public prosecution by presentment to deal with ordinary petty disorderly behavior, especially when alleged victims apparently had ample opportunity to prosecute their own grievances and, if successful, to receive court-sanctioned damages. In this vein it is worth pointing out that 315 private informal complaints were brought before the justices during the 1328 proceedings and that there is no evidence connecting any of these querelae with the presentments.

The anonymous author of the "Trailbaston Song" warned that if certain royal justices did not mend their ways, he would "teach them the game of Trailbaston": "I will break their back and rump, their arms and legs. . . . I will cut out their tongue and their mouth in the bargain."[35] As already noted, inquests like the one held at Lincoln in 1328 were described as trailbastons because they were intended to deal with offenders who traveled about the countryside, killing, robbing, assaulting, and threatening local inhabitants. Studies of two early-fourteenth-century gangs, the Folvilles and the Coterels, who operated in the east Midlands, including Kesteven, suggest what can only be described as professional gangsters. The gang members killed their enemies, robbed with impunity, hired themselves out to local gentry and ecclesiastical houses, and did not hesitate to kidnap and hold for

34 For the 1305 figures, see McLane, "The Royal Courts," 12, Table 1.1

35. Printed and translated in *Anglo-Norman Political Songs*, ed. I.S.T Aspin, Anglo-Norman Text Society (Oxford, 1953), 67–78.

ransom Richard Willoughby, a justice of King's Bench. In fact, several members continued their active careers by putting their talents and experience to good use in the king's service.[36]

A survey of those accused during the Lincoln proceedings, however, suggests that even in an era of widespread disorder the activities of the Folvilles and Coterels were atypical. Very few of the Lincoln accused, for example, were alleged to have committed the wide variety of offenses perpetrated by the Folvilles and Coterels. Indeed, only 7 percent (108 of 1,513) of the Lincoln accused were charged with both felonies and trespasses. Moreover, although 71 percent (1,078 of 1,513) of the Lincoln accused were charged with felonies, only 29 percent (313 of 1,078) of these alleged felons were accused of more than one offense. Based on the Lincoln evidence, the image of thugs engaged in repeated serious criminal activity on the scale of the Folville and Coterel gangs is difficult to maintain. This does not mean that the apparent crisis of law and order during this period was illusory, only that according to the presentment jurors the most troublesome sorts of disorder did not consist exclusively, or perhaps even primarily, of legally defined serious offenses, such as arson, rape, or homicide.

In addition to making mandatory presentments about felonious criminal activity, notably homicide, the presentment jurors focused much of their attention on habitual petty offenders. Prominent among the accused were 276 individuals identified as "common malefactors and peacebreakers in fairs and markets." These petty offenders had been the subjects of inquiry as early as 1194, but they seem to have been particularly troublesome at the end of the thirteenth century and throughout the first half of the fourteenth century.[37] "Malefactors" accounted for 74 percent (189 of 255) of all those charged with assault and 53 percent (75 of 142) of all those accused of petty theft and extortion. In addition, while 75 percent (207 of 276) of the malefactors were alleged to have committed their offenses with others, 55 percent (680 of 1,237) of the remaining accused were so charged. Finally, 81 percent (223 of 276) of the malefactors were ac-

36. E.L.G. Stones, "The Folvilles of Ashby-Folville, Leicestershire, and Their Associates in Crime, 1326–1347," *TRHS*, 5th ser., 7 (1957): 117–36, and J. G. Bellamy, "The Coterel Gang: An Anatomy of a Band of Fourteenth-Century Criminals," *EHR* 89 (1967): 698–717. See also Bellamy, *Crime and Public Order*, chap. 3; B. A. Hanawalt, *Crime and Conflict in English Communities, 1300–1348* (Cambridge, Mass., 1979), chap. 6; and Given, *Society and Homicide*, chap. 6.

37. See the comments of Meekings in *Crown Pleas*, 29; Harding, "Early Trailbaston Proceedings," 144–48; and especially F. M. Nichols, "Original Documents illustrative of the Administration of the Criminal Law in the time of Edward I; with Observations," *Archaeologia* 40 (1866): 89–105, esp. 93–94.

cused of multiple offenses, in sharp contrast to only 36 percent (445 of 1,237) of the others. The Lincoln evidence therefore suggests that the widespread problem of disorder during this period resulted only partly from a ready willingness to resort to deadly violence. Perhaps equally important in the eyes of the respectable members of the local communities, who were the dominant members of the presentment juries, was the disorder caused by habitual petty offenders, who only rarely committed homicides and robberies but who engaged in repeated disorderly behavior such as assault and extortion, usually in groups of kindred spirits and often during local markets, thereby disrupting the good order of village life.[38]

Several presentments are worth examining to illustrate the types of disorderly behavior the presentment jurors associated with these habitual offenders. West Riding jurors charged Robert Lake, John son of Robert, Simon Polayn, William Stiry, Robert son of Richard, and William Hichon, inhabitants of Alkborough; John Lamb of Walcot, Henry Chaloun, John Andrew, and Nicholas Lake, residents of Doldingthorp; and Roger Bigot of Witton and his brothers John and Thomas with being "malefactors, fighters and peacebreakers in fairs and markets" and accused them of taking "fines and redemptions from various people on the way to the market of Burton and other places and forcing them to pay 40*d.* or 2*s.* by threatening to beat them."[39] Two specific beatings were mentioned, presumably to substantiate the general allegations. Likewise, North Riding jurors presented William Quarrington of Barrow upon Humber and his brothers Peter, John, and Thomas; William Melton of North Ferriby; and William Martin and his brother Robert, Richard Boller, Robert Haston, William Spitelhog, and John Shelton, inhabitants of Barton upon Humber, with having beaten and wounded three men on 10 August 1327 at the fair of Thornton and with having assaulted a chaplain the next day and imprisoned him in the church at Thornton until he paid forty shillings.[40] The jurors ended the charges against these offenders by describing them as "common malefactors in fairs and markets."

38. Keith Wrightson in "Two Concepts of Order: Justices, Constables and Jurymen in Seventeenth-Century England," in *An Ungovernable People: The English and Their Law in the Seventeenth and Eighteenth Centuries*, ed. J. Brewer and J. Styles (1980), 21–46, draws attention to the gradual differentiation within local society during the early modern period between "the better sort" and "the others." Such a distinction may partly explain the concern Lincolnshire presentment jurors had about "common malefactors" and, more specifically, about safeguarding the orderly business of local markets. See also Post's comments in "Some Limitations," 636–38.

39. JUST 1/516, m. 31.

40. Ibid., m. 32.

John Paris of Humby was similarly prosecuted by presentment jurors, and not just for having accepted half a mark to beat William Athelard, which he was alleged to have done on 4 October 1322. Significantly, the jurors declared that he had made a living by hiring himself out to perform similar services on a contractual basis for sixpence a year for periods of up to ten years.[41] The presentment jurors in most such cases were probably much more concerned with establishing the notoriety of these habitual petty offenders than with prosecuting specific offenses they had committed. An established reputation for disorderly behavior seems to have been the key element in being identified as a "common malefactor" during the 1328 proceedings.[42] Thomas son of William Hood and Hugh Hood, residents of Gedney, for example, were first labeled "common malefactors and breakers of the king's peace" and then charged with assaulting Richard Chapel, William Gedney, Geoffrey Carter, "and many others in Fleet and other places." For good measure, the jurors ended their presentment by adding that the Hoods were also "common wanderers at night against the peace."[43] Similarly, William Ingelby was first accused of being a "common beater and breaker of the king's peace in fairs and markets" and then charged with beating Robert West "and others at Glentham and other places."[44] This particular presentment graphically illustrates the jurors' apparent primary concern, that of identifying the most troublesome offenders in their neighborhoods, since the "common beater" label was transcribed on the inquest roll by one clerk, and the specific assault charge was added later by another clerk.

Most thefts prosecuted by presentment were treated by the jurors as felonies; only 19 percent (96 of 497) were prosecuted as trespasses (petty theft and extortion; see Table 2.3). How common this pattern

41. Ibid., m. 26d.

42. Wrightson, in "Two Concepts of Order," 29, states that for the seventeenth-century scene "one finds a reluctance of village officers to present to the justices offenders other than those who had scandalized, threatened or alienated the greater part of the community; who had stepped outside the moral economy as it were." See also the comments in P. Hyams, "Trial by Ordeal: The Key to Proof in the Early Common Law," in *On the Laws and Customs of England: Essays in Honor of Samuel E. Thorne*, ed. M. S. Arnold et al. (Chapel Hill, 1981), 107–18. F. B. Sayre, "*Mens Rea*," *Harvard Law Review* 45 (1932): 976; T.F.T. Plucknett, "The Origins of Impeachment," *TRHS*, 4th ser., 24 (1942): 60–61; and T. Curtis, "Explaining Crime in Early Modern England," *Criminal Justice History* 1 (1980): 120.

43. JUST 1/516, m. 19.

44. Ibid., m. 30.

was is difficult to gauge, because historians of crime have generally ignored trespasses and focused their attention on felonies. R. B. Pugh, for instance, in a study of late-thirteenth-century gaol delivery hearings, concluded that "much evidence could be found to show that in the Middle Ages men customarily equated felony with theft."[45] Yet the evidence of any court, including the trailbaston proceedings of 1328, does not include the prosecution of all offenses committed in a particular area during a certain period, but only a selected number of offenses that, for one reason or another, had been chosen by the victims or the local communities to be prosecuted in a particular court.[46] Most thefts, for example, must have been dealt with through the various informal and formal mechanisms within the local communities.[47] Only when an agreeable settlement could not be reached

Table 2.3. Theft Presentments during the 1328 Proceedings

Type of Theft	Number of Presentments
Larceny	220
Burglary	141
Robbery	40
Petty theft	10
Extortion	86
Total	497

SOURCE: JUST 1/516.

45. Pugh, "Some Reflections," 87 n. 4.

46. L. A. Knafla, in " 'Sin of All Sorts Swarmeth': Criminal Litigation in an English County in the Early Seventeenth Century," in *Law, Litigants and the Legal Profession*, 53–54, points out that "the type and extent of recorded crime changes significantly when one moves from a court concerned solely with indictable criminal offenses to courts . . . which heard a wide range of indictable and non-indictable criminal and semi-criminal offenses." J. A. Sharpe, in "Enforcing the Law in the Seventeenth-Century English Village," in *The Social History of Crime in Western Europe since 1500*, ed. V.A.C. Gatrell et al. (1980), 99, similarly states that "the archives of no single court in seventeenth-century England (or, one suspects, in any other past society) gives a complete picture of the quality or quantity of crime in that society."

47. Prosecutions for theft can be found in village court records. See, for example, *Court Rolls of the Manor of Ingoldmells in the County of Lincoln*, ed. W. O. Massingberd (1902), 13, 14, 33, 38, 52–53, 55, 58, 62, 91; and also Britton, *The Community of the Vill: A Study of the Family and Village Life in Fourteenth-Century England* (To-

through informal means or when the circumstances of a particular theft were heinous was recourse made to formal mechanisms, first within the local communities and then through other increasingly impersonal and formal institutions. The predominance, therefore, of presentments of felonious theft over trespass theft during the 1328 proceedings probably reveals more about local attitudes toward dealing with thieves in a special royal inquest than the actual number of thefts committed in Lincolnshire during the 1320s.

Members of the local communities apparently believed that ordinary petty theft should be prosecuted by the victims. The private prosecution of theft as a trespass was a common phenomenon in the royal courts. For example, 37 percent (39 of 106) of the querelae prosecuted during the 1328 proceedings that have a recorded verdict involve theft. Similarly, Lincolnshire trespass lawsuits involving theft prosecuted in King's Bench steadily increased from 50 percent (133 of 264) of all such lawsuits in the 1290s to 68 percent (1,013 of 1,487) in the 1330s.[48] With the opportunities available to victims of theft to adjudicate their complaints, the local communities may have held that only the most serious thefts or the most dangerous and troublesome thieves should be prosecuted publicly by presentment in royal inquests, such as the 1328 proceedings.[49]

In determining the gravity of a theft, the value of the allegedly stolen goods was relatively unimportant. Not surprisingly, all thefts prosecuted as felonies involved goods worth more than 12*d.* (the theoretical dividing point between felony and trespass), yet virtually every theft prosecuted as a trespass, whether by jury presentment or private querela, also involved goods valued at more than 12*d.* Typical examples of stolen goods prosecuted as trespasses would include grain worth £20, 200 sheep, livestock worth £40, one horse worth 1 mark and clothes and dishes worth 40*s.* Of course, the circumstances surrounding the thefts must have been crucial in determining whether

ronto, 1977), 116, Table 36. Prosecutions for theft are also recorded in the Burwarmotebook, which contains entries of court sessions held in the city of Lincoln (Diocese of Lincoln, Dean and Chapter MS. 169, mm. 83, 84, 91)

48. The King's Bench figures are based on the number of new lawsuits recorded on the term rolls.

49. J. A. Sharpe, in "Enforcing the Law," 110, has argued that for the early modern period "an indictment for theft might only be made after a lengthy period in which the person accused had established a local reputation for stealing." See also the comments concerning the various possibilities of prosecuting theft in the royal courts in T.F.T. Plucknett, "A Commentary on the Indictments," in *Proceedings before the Justices of the Peace in the Fourteenth and Fifteenth Centuries, Edward III to Richard III*, ed. B. H. Putnam (1938), clix.

the theft would be prosecuted at all, and, if prosecuted, whether it would be prosecuted as a felony or a trespass. Unfortunately, the lack of detail in the enrolled entries precludes an examination of these circumstances.

An equally important factor in determining the action taken by the local communities must have been the reputations of those involved. In this connection, two apparently similar presentments are worth examining. William Bradley, John Baker, Thomas Baker, Geoffrey Tailor, Henry Burgess, Thomas Gernoun, John Salisbury, and Roger son of John allegedly broke into the grange of Riby with force and arms during the night of Good Friday 1326 and stole goods worth £10.[50] Similarly, Peter Swine, Walter son of Philip, Peter son of Thomas Manning, William Godfrey, William Westmells, John son of William Lawrence, and Alan Dale allegedly broke into the buildings of William Master in the village of Wrangle with force and arms during the night of 5 April 1321 and stole goods worth £10.[51] According to the recorded presentments, both thefts involved goods worth £10, violence, breaking and entering at night, and roughly the same number of accused. If the circumstances of these thefts had been recorded, they might have revealed the reasons why the jurors prosecuted those in the first presentment as felons and those in the second as trespass offenders. The jurors presumably had taken into account the reputations of Peter Swine and his accomplices, who were charged with only this offense, and those of William Bradley and his accomplices, who faced thirty-three additional felony and trespass charges. Prior to the beginning of the trailbaston proceedings, the presentment jurors apparently had decided that Peter Swine and the others accused of the Wrangle theft did not merit felony prosecution, even though they could have been charged with burglary, and that William Bradley and those accused of the Riby grange theft should be prosecuted as felons because of their apparent penchant for serious criminal behavior, which must have been seen as a dangerous threat to the well-being of the entire community.

Additional evidence from the 1328 proceedings supports this concept of a pre-inquest sorting process. Only 52 women (3 percent of the 1,513 accused during the inquest) were presented, yet 45 (87 percent of the women) were charged with felonies. Women were thus much more likely to be prosecuted as felons than as petty offenders during the 1328 proceedings, whereas "only" 70 percent (1,024 of 1,461) of

50. JUST 1/516, m. 10d.

51. Ibid., m. 19.

the men were prosecuted as felons. As with the thefts, this pattern of female prosecution seems to reflect a selective pattern of prosecution rather than the criminality of female offenders in general, and a working hypothesis that needs to be tested by other scholars is that disorderly women were usually dealt with by their neighbors through local institutions. The Lincolnshire evidence is slight but worth mentioning. During Stamford town court sessions in October, November, and December 1319, 18 of the 57 people (32 percent) fined for various offenses, including assault, were women.[52] It may be that only when a woman committed a homicide (which ten were alleged to have done during the 1328 proceedings) or alienated her neighbors (by acting as accomplices in homicides or felonious thefts, which twenty-eight were alleged during the 1328 proceedings to have done) was she brought before the more formal and impersonal institutions of royal justice. The presentment jurors during the 1328 proceedings seem to have had considerable latitude in determining the severity with which particular offenders would be prosecuted and took into consideration factors, such as the reputation of the accused or the appropriateness of dealing with certain offenders in a special royal inquest, that were extralegal from a strictly judicial perspective.[53]

The inability of the Crown and the local communities to apprehend alleged offenders was chronic throughout the thirteenth and fourteenth centuries. J. G. Bellamy remarked that "in the more lawless decades of the later middle ages, a felon could consider himself distinctly unlucky if he were captured by the authorities."[54] This was clearly the situation in Lincolnshire, since only one-third (514 of 1,513) of those accused during the 1328 proceedings were brought before royal justices to answer the charges against them, despite the rigorous review conducted by King's Bench in 1331 (see Table 2.4).

52 The record of the fines levied is on SC (Special Collections) 2/188/1, m. 1.

53 M. S. Arnold, in "Law and Fact in the Medieval Trial. Out of Sight, Out of Mind," *AJLH* 18 (1974): 278, declares that "custom, derived from shared societal assumptions, was the legal norm, not what some sovereign or his agent decreed." See also the comments of C. B. Herrup in "Law and Morality in Seventeenth-Century England," *Past and Present* 106 (1985): 106.

54 *Crime and Public Order*, 201. Similarly, Maitland, in F. Pollock and F. W. Maitland, *The History of English Law*, 2d ed. (Cambridge, 1968), 2:557, stated, "whatever the law might wish, the malefactor's fate was likely to be outlawry rather than any more modern punishment." See also *Some Sessions of the Peace in Lincolnshire, 1381–1396*, ed. E. Kimball, Lincoln Record Society, 49 (1955), lvii.

Moreover, although many of the accused apparently had been "hand-picked" by the presentment jurors for prosecution, when in most cases, excluding homicide, they might have been dealt with elsewhere in some less formal and public manner, those who stood trial actually had little reason to fear.

Convicted trespassers were usually imprisoned for a brief period and then released after being fined. In fact, most individuals accused of trespasses acknowledged their guilt and asked to be allowed to pay a fine. These petty offenders, especially those designated as "common malefactors," must have been aware that they had been singled out for public prosecution by presentment and therefore had little chance of acquittal, since public opinion was against them. In addition, these fines were levied according to the ability of the accused to pay rather than according to the number and type of charges a person faced.[55] There are numerous cases in which different individuals were fined different amounts even though they had been charged with the same offense, or in which those charged with a few offenses were fined more than those who faced many charges. Ralph Payknave, for example, was accused in six presentments of assault, false imprisonment, and extortion, as well as being a "common malefactor," while Hugh Tyler was presented only once on a charge of conspiracy. Yet Tyler was fined £10 and Payknave only 40*d*. The reason, no doubt, was that Payknave was of moderate means in the city of Lincoln and Tyler was one of the city's wealthiest citizens. Indeed, Ralph Cressy, coroner of Kesteven—who, according to more than one hundred presentments, had illegally taken £30 11*s*. 4*d*.—was fined only £20, which apparently left him with an illegal profit of more than £10.

Felony conviction, on the other hand, was punishable by execution, but very few alleged felons were convicted, and even fewer were hanged. As shown in Table 2.4 only 18 percent (34 of 193) of the alleged felons who were tried were found guilty, and only 18 of those tried (53 percent of those convicted and 10 percent of those tried for felonies) were sentenced to be hanged. Sixteen others who were convicted were granted benefit of clergy and turned over to the ordinary of the bishop of Lincoln. Another forty men produced royal pardons, usually for service in Scotland, and the trial jurors declared that three who were tried had acted in self-defense and were therefore eligible for royal pardons "of course." The remaining 81 percent (156 of 193) of the alleged felons who were tried were acquitted and released.

55. See C.A.F. Meekings's comments in "The Veredictum of Chippenham Hundred," *Collectanea*, ed. N J. Williams (Devizes, 1956), 72.

Table 2.4. Disposition of the Accused during the 1328 Proceedings

	No. of Accused	Felonies	Felonies and Trespasses	Ordinary Trespasses	Trespasses by Officials
Total Disposition					
Outlawed for nonappearance	780	723	39	6	12
Appeared during 1328 Proceedings	253	58	34	137	24
Appeared during King's Bench review	261	118	28	103	12
Charges sent to Chancery	12	9	3	—	—
No recorded action	207	62	4	126	15
Total	1,513	970	108	372	63
Disposition of Those Who Appeared before Royal Justices					
Acquitted	143	114	3	22	4
Acquitted of felony, fined for trespass	39	—	39	—	—
Guilty, hanged	18	11	7	—	—
Guilty, fined	235	—	—	208	27
Guilty, benefit of clergy	17	13	3	1	—
Self-defense verdict	3	3	—	—	—
Presented pardon	42	30	10	1	1
No information	17	5	—	8	4
Total	514	176	62	240	36

SOURCE. JUST 1/516 and various King's Bench court rolls (KB 27 series) for the period Trinity term 1331 through Michaelmas term 1333.

The reasons for this high acquittal rate are not difficult to discern, but they are very difficult to document, because of the lack of detailed information in the legal records of this period, including the 1328 inquest roll and the related King's Bench rolls.[56] The first and most obvious reason for the low conviction rate must have been that those who stood trial were actually innocent of the crimes with which they were charged. A self-selecting process must have taken place to some extent, since so many accused felons (72 percent or 780 of 1,078) did not appear before the trailbaston justices or the justices of King's Bench and were outlawed. Aside from those who had been captured and others who had obtained royal pardons for their offenses, probably the only individuals who willingly stood trial were those who were sure of their innocence, or at least confident of the treatment they would receive from the trial jurors. In addition, many of those tried must have been acquitted not because they were actually innocent but because the trial jurors did not know whether they were guilty. R. B. Pugh, after conducting a study of gaol delivery sessions in the 1290s and in 1302, concluded that trial jurors "must often have acquitted because they were convinced of their own ignorance rather than the suspects' innocence."[57]

Such a conclusion goes against accepted scholarship that medieval trial jurors, in Pugh's words, "were supposed to know [the truth] before the trials began."[58] In theory, trial jurors were selected from local inhabitants who would be familiar with "the facts" of the offenses being deliberated, including the involvement of the accused. The evidence of the 1328 proceedings is admittedly limited, but it does suggest that practice did not necessarily follow theory.[59] As is evident from Table 2.5, Holland trial jurors were rarely drawn from those who lived at the scene of the crime and only infrequently came from villages within five miles of the scene.[60] Indeed, many of these jurors came from between six and nine miles from the scene, and a surprising number came from ten or more miles away. An apparently similar

56. See the comment in Arnold, "Law and Fact," 267–68, 274–77.

57. "The Duration of Criminal Trials in Medieval England," in *Law, Litigants and the Legal Profession*, 110.

58. Ibid

59. See the comments in Pugh, "Reflections," 93–95, and especially Edward Powell, below, chap 4, text at n. 68.

60. A number of the jurors were local gentry whose residence was not listed. They have been counted as of unknown residence. Because of their status, however, even if they had lands in the immediate area where a crime had been committed, they may not have known very much about the details.

Table 2.5. Residence of Holland Trial Jurors Relative to the Scene of the Crime

Jury No.	Scene of Crime	Distance of Jurors' Residence from Scene of Crime (mi.) Scene	1–3	3–5	5–9	10+	Unknown*
1	Holbeach	4	2	1	—	—	5
2	Holland marsh near						
	Wigtoft	—	2	—	6	1	3
	Boston	3	1	3	1	1	3
	Surfleet	—	1	1	4	3	3
3	Spalding	1	—	1	1	5	4
4	Wyberton	—	2	1	5	—	4
	Spalding and Pinchbeck	—	—	3	2	3	4
	Swineshead	—	2	1	2	3	4
	Wigtoft	—	2	—	4	2	4
	Fleet	1	2	—	2	3	4
5	Spalding	—	1	4	6	—	1
Total		9	15	15	33	21	39

SOURCE: JUST 1/516, mm 15, 17d.
*Jurors whose residence was not recorded

situation was faced by a panel of Lindsey jurors responsible for adjudicating three homicides, three burglaries, and two felonious thefts allegedly committed as early as 1309 in nine different villages and granges located in six different hundreds in the three ridings of Lindsey.[61] Obviously, in such circumstances neither the Holland nor the Lindsey jurors could have had much firsthand knowledge of the crimes they were dealing with. In the absence of any evidence of witnesses testifying during the presentment sessions, the jurors may have relied primarily on those among them who did come from near the scene of the crime or who knew something of the accused, and also on the manner in which the accused handled themselves in court.[62]

A second reason for the trial jurors' leniency toward accused felons,

61. JUST 1/516, m. 16.

62. See the comments in Pugh, "Duration of Criminal Trials," 109–10; Green, *Verdict According to Conscience*, 18, 26, 58, 98; and J. M. Beattie, "Crime and the Courts in Surrey, 1736–1753," in *Crime in England, 1550–1800*, ed J. S. Cockburn (1977), 173. J. M. Kaye states that "juries decided cases as much on the basis of the prisoner's general reputation as on that of the specific charge against him": J. M. Kaye, ed., *Placita Corone*, Selden Society, Supplementary Series, 4 (1966), xxxvi.

especially alleged killers, was the inflexibility of the common law regarding felonies.[63] Except for cases in which the trial jurors declared the accused to have killed in self-defense or when he was found to be mentally incompetent or had been granted benefit of clergy or had obtained a royal pardon, felony conviction carried the death sentence. In many cases, trial jurors may have acquitted the defendants because they believed that they did not deserve to be hanged, even though they may actually have committed the crime for which they were being tried. Such leniency, however, varied according to the type of crime. Alleged felonious thieves were convicted twice as often during the 1328 proceedings as accused killers (22 percent, or 15 of 67, compared to 11 percent, or 15 of 139). R. B. Pugh found a similar trend in a study of late-thirteenth-century Newgate gaol delivery records: 31 percent of the alleged felonious thieves were convicted, compared to 21 percent of the accused killers. Also, Barbara Hanawalt found conviction rates for felonious theft and homicide to be 31 and 12 percent respectively during early-fourteenth-century gaol delivery sessions.[64] The higher conviction rate for felonious theft, however, does not mean that "property took precedence over life" but rather that the attitudes of the local inhabitants toward these two types of crime were crucial in determining the actions taken against those who stood trial.[65]

Trial jurors either simply acquitted most alleged killers or, in a few cases (three during the 1328 proceedings), declared that they had killed in self-defense, thereby making them eligible for royal pardons "of course."[66] William son of William White of Holbeach, for example, stood trial for having feloniously killed Richard Fowler, also of Holbeach, on 14 January 1328 at Holbeach.[67] According to the jurors' statement, Fowler had maliciously attacked White with a knife in order to kill him. White was wounded in the head and fell to the ground. He got up and fled but was cornered. White "could not escape unless he killed Richard in self-defense." The justices apparently questioned

63. The best discussion of this topic is Green, *Verdict According to Conscience*, 28–64. See also Beattie's comments in "Crime and the Courts," 170–71.

64. Pugh, "Some Reflections," 86–87, and Hanawalt, *Crime and Conflict*, 59, Table 2. Given, in *Society and Homicide*, 133, states that during selected thirteenth-century eyre sessions, the conviction rate of homicide was 17 percent but that the rate rose dramatically to 43 percent when felonious theft was involved with homicide See also Green's figures in *Verdict According to Conscience*, 32 n. 10.

65. The quote is from B. A. Hanawalt, "Violent Death in Fourteenth- and Early Fifteenth-Century England," *Journal of Comparative Studies in Society and History* 18 (1976): 317.

66. They are enrolled on JUST 1/516, mm. ld, 15, 17.

67. Ibid., m. 15.

the jurors about their verdict, since the court clerk noted at the end of the entry that the jurors had said "that he could not have escaped and the deed was not done with malice aforethought."[68] Why the jurors did not simply acquit White instead of resorting to such a hackneyed verdict is unknown. Perhaps the jurors felt that the circumstances of Fowler's death, which were not fully recorded, rendered outright acquittal inappropriate.

Trial jurors generally may have had a "live and let live" policy toward accused killers, especially in cases where the homicides were alleged to have been the unexpected outcome of an argument or a fight that had begun in a tavern or some other public place.[69] An unwritten assumption may have been that if a person were killed in the course of a fight in which the deceased had not been put at an unreasonable disadvantage, the survivor was not held culpable. West Riding jurors, for example, charged that William Paris, a knight, had feloniously killed John Kirkbride, another minor local knight, in the village of Torksey in May 1327.[70] According to the enrolled presentment, which is unusual in its detail, an argument had broken out between Kirkbride and Paris, an elector of infantry for Scottish war service. Kirkbride "maimed" Paris's hand with a sword blow and was then set upon and mortally wounded by Paris and several others. When brought to trial in 1331, Paris was acquitted, and no mention was made of self-defense.[71] Perhaps in certain instances, as Professor Green has suggested, "from the community's point of view, a violent attack could be met with a violent response. A man whose life was threatened did not have to seek some means of escape; indeed, he need not do so though he was not in danger of losing his life."[72]

The element of fairness must have been important in determining the attitude of the trial jurors toward the accused, and it apparently rendered alleged thieves more at jeopardy than accused killers. Robbery, by definition, involved at least the threat of violence and was often perpetrated by several offenders, while burglary, especially when committed at night, often must have caught the victim off-guard and therefore unable to prevent the crime. To many inhabitants

68. For discussion of the jurors' behavior in this regard, see Green, *Verdict According to Conscience*, 77, 96.

69. See, for example, the following Lincolnshire cases: C 260/24/40, mm. 1, 2, 38/20, mm. 1, 2; 23/16, mm. 1, 2, 19/7, mm. 1, 2; 54/21, mm. 1, 2.

70. JUST 1/516, m. 10.

71. KB 27/285, Gaol Delivery m.17.

72. *Verdict According to Conscience*, 38, with examples on pp. 38–40.

of the local communities, this type of crime may have seemed more unfair than assault or even homicide, which was favorably contrasted with murder, or homicide by stealth, in the popular mind long before the distinction received official sanction at the end of the fourteenth century.[73] That contrast was pointed out by Maitland, who declared that the participant in a fight "was expected to kill his enemy in a fair, open honest manner, not to take mean advantage, not to fall upon him like a thief in the dark."[74] From this perspective it is worth asking why most cases involving extortion were not treated as robberies. Extortion, especially when committed by "common malefactors," usually involved the seizure of more than twelve pence in cash, implied or actual violence, and several perpetrators. Most extortions thus combined all the elements usually associated with robbery. Perhaps extortionists were prosecuted as trespassers rather than as felons because they were considered less dangerous than robbers in the sense of being either younger or less hardened and therefore not yet considered to be beyond redemption.[75] Perhaps extortionists were treated more leniently because they were usually more open in carrying out their nefarious activities. In any event, the lack of fairness in certain circumstances, especially when stealth was suspected, seems to have aggravated a particular offense and led to felonious thieves being more harshly judged than alleged killers.

A third factor in the low conviction rate may have been the belief

73. See ibid., 30–35, and Green's earlier article, "The Jury and the English Law of Homicide, 1200–1600," *Michigan Law Review* 74 (1976): 415–99. T.F.T. Plucknett, in "A Commentary on the Indictments," cxlvii, declared that "slaying in ambush is prominent no doubt because of the clear proof of premeditation. Here, too, we find the justices and the jurors in the county making distinctions that the common law as yet did not recognize."

74. Quoted in Charles Radding, "Evolution of Medieval Mentalities A Cognitive-Structural Approach," *American Historical Review* 83 (1978): 586. See also J. M. Kaye's comments in "The Early History of Murder and Manslaughter, Part 1," *Law Quarterly Review* 87 (1967) 387; and Bellamy, *Crime and Public Order*, 54

75. Thomas Brinton's allusion to the popular inclination to be merciful to youthful offenders in the sermon quoted at the beginning of this study is fascinating Unfortunately, as was usually the case, the ages of the accused and their victims were not recorded on the trailbaston roll. Perhaps many of the "common malefactors and wanderers in fairs and markets" were the humble equivalents of Duby's *juvenes*, twelfth-century French aristocratic youths who had no fixed place in society and who accordingly "formed the cutting edge of feudal aggressiveness, . . fanned the fires of trouble in areas of instability and provided the best contingents for distant expeditions." Georges Duby, "In Northwestern France: The 'Youth' in Twelfth-Century Aristocratic Society," translated in *Lordship and Community in Medieval Europe*, ed. F. L Cheyette (New York, 1968), 199–200. See also Cockburn's comment in "Trial by the Book? Fact and Theory in the Criminal Process, 1558–1625," in *Legal Records and the Historian*, ed. J. H. Baker (1976), 75.

that in some instances the accused had been sufficiently punished by being presented and forced to come before specially appointed royal justices. Local opinion may have held that the process of being publicly prosecuted was an unambiguous means of putting certain individuals on notice that they had seriously, but not fatally, violated accepted standards of conduct and should mend their ways. That may have been the feeling with regard to many thieves, especially habitual offenders. Fulk Julian of Whaplode was thus presented for being a "common beater and peace breaker" and for beating Nicholas Finn of Sutton St. Mary, Geoffrey Caddock, and "many others."[76] When brought before the justices of King's Bench, Julian admitted his guilt and was fined half a mark. In addition, he had to produce two men to act as pledges for the fine and to ensure "his future good behavior toward the king and others."[77] Similarly, Alexander son of Robert Holbeach admitted having broken into William Farford's close at Holbeach during a night in January 1313 and having beaten Farford's daughter. Holbeach was fined ten shillings and forced to produce six pledges for the fine and to ensure that he would "henceforth behave well and peacefully toward the king and everyone else."[78] Trespassers could safely admit their guilt; alleged felons could not, but guarantees could still be demanded. William Paris, the knight who was acquitted of having killed John Kirkbride in the case mentioned above, was forced to find six of his local peers to act as guarantors for his "future good behavior toward the king and everyone else."[79] This process of binding over has been well documented for the early modern period, but, based on the evidence of the 1328 proceedings, it was also a mechanism whose value in promoting good order was appreciated in early-fourteenth-century Lincolnshire.[80]

A fourth reason for the low conviction rate had to do with problems inherent in the legal system. During a period when the royal system

76. JUST 1/516, m. 19

77. KB 27/285, Gaol Delivery m. 8

78. The original presentment is on JUST 1/516, m. 19d. The trial is on KB 27/285, Gaol Delivery m. 8.

79. KB 27/285, Gaol Delivery m. 17. Other examples of acquitted offenders who had to find pledges for their good behavior are on KB 27/285, Gaol Delivery mm. 17, 18.

80. For the early modern period, see Sharpe, "Enforcing the Law," 116–17; Wrightson, "Two Concepts of Order," 40; and Knafla, " 'Sin of All Sorts Swarmeth,' " 55–56. The use of pledges to ensure future good behavior is referred to on JUST 1/516, m. 19d, and KB 27/285, Gaol Delivery mm 8d–9d, 10d, 11d, 12; and KB 27/294, Rex m. 32d. Other less specific pledges are noted on JUST 1/516, mm. 17, 19, 19d, 21, 23, 26d, 28d, 31, 32d, 34d, 35d, 36, 38d–40d.

of criminal justice was being transformed and the opportunities to use mechanisms available in the royal courts greatly expanded, complaints about corruption and coercion increased.[81] The May 1328 commission to the justices, which authorized them to hold the trailbaston session, ordered them to investigate and deal with those who "by means of their power and state" protected criminals in return for fees, and those who threatened jurors so that they would not tell the truth.[82] The last part of this order was a summary of the second article of the original 1304 trailbaston commission: "Of those who have disturbed jurors on assizes, that they dare not speak the truth, for if they do so they cause them to be so beaten and ill-treated that many lose their lives, or are maimed for ever more, so that for fear of them the truth cannot be known before the king's justices."[83]

The prevalence of corrupt practices and coercion cannot be measured, but presentments made during the 1328 proceedings indicate that both were utilized when needed. Richard Thurger, coroner of Holland, for example, was accused of receiving five marks from William Ironside of Holbeach so that he would not be charged with the death of William Virly, while William Manby was prosecuted not only for having taken twenty shillings from William Cotelyn to ensure that he would not be accused of the death of Robert Smith of Little Carlton but also for having arranged to have an innocent man charged with Smith's death.[84] Likewise, Henry, parson of Barkston, was presented for paying five pounds to William Paris, the local knight, to disrupt an inquest that had been convened at the suit of the prioress of Stixwould against Henry. Paris threatened the appointed jurors and assaulted several of them, with the result that they did not appear at the inquest.[85] Sometimes direct coercion of jurors was unnecessary. John son of Ranulph Rye of Gosberton prosecuted a querela against William son of Roger Cressy, knight, and three others for having assaulted him at an inquest he had obtained by special commission of oyer and terminer "so that the jurors fled."[86]

In circumstances such as these, it would hardly be surprising if cer-

81. See *Select Cases in the Court of King's Bench under Edward I*, ed. G. O. Sayles, Selden Society, 58 (1939), liv. See also Harding, "The Origins of Conspiracy," *TRHS*, 5th ser., 33 (1983): 89–108.

82. See above, n. 16

83. Quoted in Nichols, "Original Documents," 96.

84. JUST 1/516, mm. 3 and 29 respectively.

85. Ibid., m. 28.

86. Ibid., m. 41.

tain offenders who should have been found guilty were acquitted. Perhaps the possible hazards of jury service partly explain why six individuals who served as jurors during the 1328 proceedings subsequently received from the Crown "exemption for life from being put on assizes, juries or recognizances and from appointment as mayor, sheriff, escheator, coroner or other bailiff or minister of the king."[87] Indeed, it is also not surprising that on certain occasions members of the local communities were unwilling to rely on due process in the royal courts. Presentment jurors charged that servants of David Strathbogie, earl of Angus, released Richard Boarhead, who had allegedly stolen grain from the earl's grange at Temple Bruer, in exchange for livestock and cash.[88] Similarly, Robert Langton, parson of Doddington, was accused of taking fourteen shillings from William Hoodman, who had allegedly stolen the parson's cow, "to forget the theft."[89] Finally, according to Holland presentment jurors, Jordan Wing of Spalding had got into a fight with John Hanwell, also of Spalding, in 1327. Hanwell was killed, and Jordan was immediately seized and imprisoned in the local gaol. Unfortunately for Wing, the next day a group of villagers broke into the gaol, "rescued" him, took him outside the village, and then beheaded him.[90] The reasons for Wing's "execution" were not recorded, but the unwillingness of certain villagers to await formal proceedings before royal justices is clear.

S.F.C. Milsom has stated that "the legal historian . . . has a mass of original documents produced for business purposes; but they do not explain the ideas and assumptions underlying the business. . . . [Y]ou have to reconstruct those for yourself, to find a pattern which fits the detail."[91] The intention of this study of the 1,915 presentments made during the 1328 Lincolnshire trailbaston proceedings and the actions taken against 1,513 individuals who were accused of various offenses

87. E.g., *CPR, 1330–1334*, pp 9 (16 Oct. 1330), 173 (22 July 1331), 190 (16 Oct 1331)

88. JUST 1/516, m. 5.

89. Ibid., m 5d.

90. Ibid., mm. 2d, 8.

91. "F W. Maitland," *Proceedings of the British Academy* 66 (1980): 275. Green, in *Verdict According to Conscience*, 29, similarly states: "The early history of English criminal law lies hidden within the laconic formulas of the rolls and law books. The rules of the law, as expounded by the judges, have been the subject of many studies; but their practical application in the courts, where the jury of the community was the final and unbridled arbiter, largely remains a mystery."

has been to examine the attitudes of local jurors toward using a specially convened royal inquest to deal with local disorder. Many homicides were presented, and many habitual petty offenders were prosecuted. Thefts were usually treated as felonies, and the few women who were charged with offenses before the justices were usually prosecuted as felons. When brought before the justices, most alleged trespassers admitted their guilt and were fined. Very few alleged felons appeared before the justices, and the small number who appeared were usually acquitted. These patterns are clear, but it is also clear that they are patterns of prosecution and treatment rather than patterns of criminal behavior.

T.F.T. Plucknett once characterized the indictment as a "conspicuously unprofessional" instrument in which "the layman [tells] in his own words what he thinks of the local criminals, simply and directly."[92] The evidence of the 1328 proceedings is admittedly limited, but it suggests that the local communities exercised considerable latitude in dealing with local disorder. This evidence also suggests that a pre-inquest sorting process had taken place and that, with the exception of alleged killers, only those who had been determined by the members of the communities to be beyond local control or who had outraged local opinion in some manner were prosecuted publicly by the presentment jurors. From that perspective, the 1328 proceedings were something of a last resort.

Acknowledgments

This study is based on research that began as part of my unpublished doctoral dissertation, "The Royal Courts and the Problem of Disorder in Lincolnshire, 1290–1341" (University of Rochester, 1979). A draft of this study was read at the Eighteenth International Congress on Medieval Studies in Kalamazoo, Michigan, on 7 May 1983. Support from the Harry Frank Guggenheim Foundation, the American Philosophical Society and the American Bar Foundation allowed me to conduct research on this and other aspects of early-fourteenth-century social and legal history. I would like to thank Professors Thomas Green and James Cockburn for their comments on a draft of this study, as well as Dr. Edward Powell for his valuable remarks and for allowing me to see a draft of his contribution to this volume.

92 "A Commentary on the Indictments," cxxxv–cxxxvi.

Three

Jury Lists and Juries in the Late Fourteenth Century

J. B. Post

It is a commonplace among lawyers that the behavior of juries is unpredictable and their motives unfathomable. In the retrospect of centuries, the problems of perception are greatly magnified, since the mechanisms of trial procedure are shadowy, and the interplay of personalities and private interests can be discerned only rarely. The formal enrollments are sparing in their clues to the functions of the jury. What follows is a preliminary attempt to evaluate the evidence of jury lists—which survive in large numbers, although they are small and uneven by comparison with the plea rolls—and to draw tentative inferences about the administration of criminal trials in the last quarter of the fourteenth century.

The ideal jury list, for the historian at least, is filed with, and probably attached to, a parent writ or precept.[1] The writ is addressed to the sheriff, bailiff, or other appropriate officer, and it orders the summons of a jury at a specific date. It bears an endorsement of execution by the recipient. The list itself is headed with the name of the visne, or neighborhood (hundred, wapentake, or liberty). It lists twenty-four men, each with his place of residence and the names of two persons who pledge his appearance to the summons. It is annotated with the name of the defendant. The names of those on the panel who are present at the session are pricked with a heavy dot in the margin; twelve of these are marked as sworn (*Jur'*). The names of the nonattenders are annotated with a sum of money for amercement or distraint. If necessary, the names of talesmen (*tales de circumstantibus*, added to remedy absences from the panel) are noted at the foot of the list.

1. Strictly speaking, *panel* is the proper term both for the list of persons summoned and for the body of persons summoned. For the sake of clarity, here *list* refers to the list itself and *panel* to the potential jurors.

Few jury lists conform to this ideal, and many fall almost unrecognizably short of it. The reasons for the vagaries vary both in character and in significance. First, much can be attributed to lazy or slipshod clerical work. This is a treacherously easy refuge for the documentary critic, but it is safe to suppose, for example, that the omission of a visne or a defendant at the head of a list, annoying though it may be now, was inconsequential to the clerk at the time. Similarly, the treatment of jury pledges followed a very common practice. Occasionally the pledges named may have been genuine pledges; sometimes the jurors are cited as pledges for each other; but the vast majority, with monosyllabic and often rhymed surnames (John Lone, John Stone, John Gore, Richard Dore, Richard Cake, Henry Blake),[2] were close relatives of John Doe and Richard Roe, and they served bureaucratic convenience in the same manner.

Even when clerical standards cannot be impugned, differences in the presentation of jury lists do not necessarily betoken differences in procedure. A writ or precept may show that the sheriff instructed the hundred-bailiff, and the hundred-bailiff summoned the jurors, but the absence of a writ or precept does not mean that this procedure was not followed; a jury list without a writ (and without the sewing-holes where one had been) may represent an oral, less fully recorded process rather than a less complex one. Variations in procedure cannot be deduced quite as simply as that.

On the other hand, variations in procedure cannot be discounted as explanations of divergences in the form of the lists, and they may be variations of great significance. If the jury lists from a session are all without precepts, all without pledges, all drafted with an air of haste, and perhaps all apparently in the same hand, there must be a possibility—to put it no more strongly—that the panels were prepared centrally, during or just before the session. Such an inference implies, in turn, that the selection of the panel was from persons available (for whatever reason) at the time and place of the session and may not, therefore, represent recruitment from properly qualified residents of the visne. For the records of many sessions, moreover, the balance of probabilities is uncertain, giving no strong warrant for inferring one mode of impaneling rather than another.

In these circumstances, deductions about the motives or behavior of the juries are even more hazardous than might have been supposed. Procedural divergences deduced from jury lists may reflect local, prag-

2. Selected at random, in this instance from PRO, JUST 3/216/5, m. 5. All unpublished documents cited are in the Public Record Office.

matic attitudes toward administration, but they may also, or alternatively, reflect deliberate or conscious acceptance of principles at variance with those of the jurists. If it had become common for the courts to accept jurors who were interested parties, or unchallengeable, or not of the visne, then the purpose of jury trial and the function of the jurors in the courts must have been somewhat different from the models of textbook theory.

The commonest observable fault of medieval juries is their persistent failure to appear. Every roll of every court has its quota of cases respited until the next session or term "for default of jurors," and every file of judicial writs has its quota of jury distraints. The jury lists confirm and illustrate the problem. The typical list has the slightly scruffy appearance of a document drafted at leisure and then much amended in practice. Deletions, interlineations, and other rough emendations give the overwhelming impression that securing a jury of twelve was a haphazard and, when the day came, rushed procedure. An arbitrary sample from a typical gaol delivery file exemplifies these difficulties: with an average panel of twenty-one and an average attendance of ten, it is scarcely surprising to find that only half the juries could be sworn exclusively from among those originally summoned.[3] It is perhaps suggestive, too, that the figures are enhanced by some of the smaller panels with less formal lists (including two cases of twelve present out of twelve summoned), which, in the light of the average attendances, look suspiciously like juries of talesmen—panels "summoned" from those already known to be available at the session. The efficacy of the routine summons in advance is exposed further by a *nomina ministrorum* list from the same file, showing that none of the four coroners from Surrey and Sussex, and only six of the twelve liberty and hundred-bailiffs, appeared when required to do so.[4]

If a panel produced an insufficient number of jurors, it was open to the court to adjourn the case, pending fresh summons and jury distrainder, until a full jury could be sworn, and that is what commonly happened in litigation between parties. Pressures and priorities in routine criminal trials (mostly at gaol delivery) were clearly different, for the standard practice seems to have been to ensure the trial, without

3. The sample consists of the first twenty-one annotated (and hence evidently used) lists from JUST 3/216/5. Overzealous statisticians will want to know that the average panel was 20.76, that the average attendance was 10.33, and that 47.62 percent of the juries were insufficient without talesmen. The serious historian, realizing that 0.33 of a juror is as insignificant now as he was in court, will prefer the approximations in the text.

4. JUST 3/216/5, m. 40.

respite or adjournment, by recruiting talesmen. In the arbitrary sample, half the juries were supplemented in this way. This proportion may or may not be higher than was generally the case, but it fairly represents the very frequent resort to an expeditious administrative convenience.

Everything about the jury lists therefore suggests that the main difficulty—assembling the requisite jury of twelve—was met summarily in ordinary cases by making up the numbers at the last minute. This procedure does not necessarily imply a dilution or denial of the policies and purposes of impaneling, since these remain to be established with any certitude, but the composition of a jury inevitably has some bearing upon the exercise of its functions. The main criteria for judging the panel as summoned and the jury as sworn must be their social and administrative status, their relationship to the visne, and their possible involvement in the sessions or cases on which they were expected to serve.

The status of the jurors, where it can be established, is entirely consistent with the fifteenth-century evidence assembled by Dr. Powell.[5] They came from a broad band in the middle classes of society: tax collectors, bailiffs, the occasional coroner, and other officials, together with men whose standing in the county was unrecorded and probably unremarkable but who were nevertheless among the most prosperous persons in their own communities. One example will serve to illustrate: a panel from East and West Goscote hundreds in Leicestershire, at gaol delivery in 1380.[6] Sixteen were summoned, of whom the identifiable members were two subsidy collectors, one of whom had been a commissioner on a criminal inquisition,[7] a probable churchwarden,[8] and a free tenant assessed at the highest rate in a busy market town.[9] When too few appeared, talesmen were added, including one of the county coroners.[10] Others, notably for want of a stated residence, are not positively identifiable. In this respect it is a typical list, as it is also in the similarity in the mix of original panel and talesmen.

Some relationship between the jurors and the visne of the offense is a matter of general assumption, and the working details are poten-

5. See below, chap. 4.

6. JUST 3/31/2, m. 7.

7. Roger Somervile and William Chamberlain. See *Calendar of Fine Rolls, 1377–1383*, p. 53, *CPR, 1377–1381*, p. 130.

8. William Lane of Arnesby. See JUST 3/31/2, m. 8.

9. Richard Leicester of Market Harborough. See E 179/33/35.

10 John Charnels of Snarestone. See JUST 3/31/2, m. 3.

tially significant. A jury summons for a case might be specific; two writs in the prosecution of Sir Thomas Ardern for procurement of felony specified, respectively, jurors from Pipe Ridware, Lichfield, and Elford, and jurors from the visne of Cannock Wood "not of the affinity."[11] More commonly and observably, the visne was defined in conventional administrative units. The county was a universal requirement; it was the widest catchment for gaol delivery juries, and sheriffs were the returning officers for summonses emanating from King's Bench. When a Gloucestershire man was appealed, at Winchester gaol delivery, of a larceny at Winchcombe, the case was adjourned pending the summons of a Gloucestershire jury. It may have been the protocol for securing an out-county jury that caused the case to be called into King's Bench.[12]

Usually the visne was the hundred, as the headings of the jury lists indicate, and the intention to observe this is reflected, albeit imperfectly, in the panels. The sheriff of Surrey was amerced for producing a panel from Godley hundred for a case from Woking.[13] More nearly typical panels show strong representation from the hundred stated—all ten identifiable places of residence in an Edwinstree list of twenty-four names,[14] for example, and fourteen from a Guthlaxton panel of nineteen.[15] In some cases, one or more of the panel came not merely from the hundred but from the very place of the alleged offense: John Smith of Chedzoy sworn to try the parson of Chedzoy for murder,[16] John Hunt and John Butcher of Buckland to try a case of larceny at Buckland, and John Baker of Barkway to try another at Barkway,[17] and John Webb of Watton impaneled for a case of reset by a Watton man.[18] In other cases, some jurors were out-hundredal, especially talesmen, but in general, panels seem to have been predominantly from the hundred, and juries substantially so.

To what extent this represented adherence to a principle and to what extent it was merely the symptom of an administrative tradition is inevitably obscure, and cases can be found that fall definitively into

11. KB 37/2/3/3. The same panel is listed each time, quite reasonably, since the greatest distances are about nine miles

12. JUST 3/179, mm. 7d, 9d, 10, 10d.

13. JUST 3/216/5, mm. 41, 50.

14. Ibid., m. 159.

15. JUST 3/31/2, m. 6.

16. JUST 3/60/4, mm. 16, 21.

17. JUST 3/216/5, m. 159.

18. Ibid., m. 157.

one category or the other. At one extreme, perhaps, is the anomalous jury in the curious case of John Shropshire—a case that is enrolled in King's Bench as a memorandum, clearly defying any attempt to couch it in terms of routine procedure.[19] Shropshire was caught in Westminster Hall by Roger Welby, "apprentice of the court," and others, trying to steal Welby's dagger by cutting the belt it was on. Because Welby had hold of the dagger at the time, only the belt was actually removed. Whether as a handhaving thief (a thief caught with the stolen property) or as an appellee, Shropshire was accused and committed to the marshal. He was immediately produced in court and was asked why he had done it (apparently without an opportunity to plead), to which he replied that he wanted to reimburse his unmet expenses in London. Then, "because the court wishes to be certified to the full about the whole matter," the marshal was ordered to summon a jury "of officials within the hall and traders then present." These jurors, when sworn, returned a verdict that substantially followed the preliminary accusation, adding "words of felony" to the simple description of the stealing of the belt but accepting the theft of the dagger as an unfulfilled intention. They also appraised the dagger at half a mark and the belt at fourpence. Shropshire was committed to the marshal, and Welby got his dagger back. The whole episode has an air of spontaneity—more than just presentment, but less than a trial at bar—but a jury was making a formal finding upon accusation and examination of the prisoner in court, and the restitution of the alleged mainour (the stolen property) smacks of a conclusion. Furthermore, that jury was explicitly impaneled from persons who could not help but be informed of the circumstances already.

At the other extreme—again, perhaps—is the case of Richard Chike. This time the jury was an irrelevant formality. Chike's homicide was sixteen years past; the coroner's jury had brought in a verdict of self-defense; he had a pardon in his pocket; and in any case, as bailiff of Ringwood hundred he was himself a returning officer and a member of the administrative establishment. Nevertheless, a jury was impaneled. When no members of the panel appeared, it was replaced by a panel of talesmen from different parts of the county.[20] In the wholesale absence of jurors from the visne, therefore, the verdict was potentially committed to men who were unlikely to have had prior knowledge and who can have had scant time to gather hearsay.

It is likely, indeed, that the known difficulties of successfully sum-

19. KB 27/475, Rex m. 29d.

20. KB 37/2/16/2; JUST 2/155, m. 1; KB 27/527, Rex m. 1.

moning an adequate panel conditioned the initial composition. Criminal trial jurors usually had little incentive to turn up; the amounts of distraints upon defaulters were often small by the socio-economic standards of the panel, and the prospect of successful distraint was anyway less than perfect. If impaneled jurors were to appear, they needed compelling reasons for attending the sessions, and this, rather than any more sinister motive, may account for the high incidence on original panels of court officers, local officials, and others who had other business at the sessions—prosecution pledges, for example, who may have been witnesses or supporters of the victim,[21] or appellors in one case impaneled as jurors in another.[22] If defaulting jurors eventually had to be replaced by talesmen from among those present, it made sense to impanel probable attenders in the first place.

The obtrusive dominance of pragmatism over any jurisprudential nicety is emphasized by the absence of jury challenges. The received opinion of the lawyers allowed a defendant to challenge jurors, peremptorily or for cause, and a maximum of thirty-five is the number usually cited.[23] It was also accepted in principle that a defendant could object to the impaneling of his personal enemies or of jurors who had been on the grand jury that brought the indictment.[24] Of this procedure the records of routine jury trials show not a trace. In the great majority of jury lists, the twelve men sworn are the first twelve to have been pricked as present, and there is usually no marking that could represent the process of trying the jurors between selection and swearing, as the theory (and the formulas of enrollment) required. If jury challenge were common in criminal trials, some trace would have been left in the documents.

There is no overt explanation for this apparent lack of challenges, but the counterfactual inference is simple and powerful. If jury challenge were available in practice, it would have been used. The successful challenge of one or two jurors would have been sufficient to exhaust the attendance on many panels; the challenge of any more than that would have embarrassed almost every summoning officer at almost every session. If it had been possible to challenge thirty-five jurors on panels of twenty-four or eighteen, many men and women in

21. E.g., John Hale of Barnet. JUST 3/216/5, mm. 221, 225.

22. E.g., William Odam, John Gantroun, and William Lane, of Arnesby, apparently churchwardens there. JUST 3/31/2, mm. 6–8.

23. A. Fitzherbert, *La Graunde Abridgement* (1577), Corone 56.

24. Cf. W. Holdsworth, *History of English Law*, 7th ed. (1956), 1:324–25; 25 Edw. III, c. 3. In 1393 Cassy and Gascoigne respited a death sentence as "erroneous and revocable" on such grounds. *CPR, 1391–1396*, p. 338

the shadow of the gallows would have claimed their right. Since a panel of thirty-five, let alone a margin of thirty-five, was beyond the requirements, or indeed the reasonable powers, of any sheriff attempting to observe the doctrine of the visne, the system of jury trial could not realistically sustain a procedure that allowed the arbitrary or preferential rejection of its sketchily assembled dozens. It seems very likely that the typical defendant was not allowed to challenge his jury and thus delay his trial.

The obvious way in which a defendant (or plaintiff or appellor) could expect to affect the composition or character of a jury was the simple expedient of bribery.[25] Jurors paid for favorable verdicts were very far from unknown, and the "assizers" and "inquest-mongers" were common subjects of complaint in this period. Complacent or biased officials could also ensure that only sympathetic or malleable jurors were impaneled, as when an undersheriff turned up at dawn to recruit jurors from a single manor belonging to an interested party.[26] Such practices flourished predominantly in the lucrative field of private litigation, but there are strong inferential grounds for supposing that criminal trials could be affected similarly. It is not easy, in the almost invariable absence of circumstantial information, to distinguish between a jury that was assembled impartially by the machinery of justice to swear to the innocence or guilt of the accused and did so, and a jury that was impaneled by favor, fear, or fraud from the local allies of one party or the other or, however impaneled, returned a verdict as bribed. What is possible is a deduction from acquittal and conviction rates in King's Bench. Cases brought into King's Bench at the instance of one party were normally determined in favor of that party; jury verdicts on appeals were usually convictions (at a far higher rate than convictions at gaol delivery upon indictment), whereas jury verdicts on indictments brought into King's Bench upon certiorari (normally regarded as the defendant's writ) were, in this period at least, invariably acquittals. No individual case can be exposed as corrupt, but it would be naive to suppose that these jury verdicts in King's Bench reflected either community opinion or the burden of the evidence, and other criminal courts can hardly be immune from suspicion.

The available evidence for the assembling of criminal trial juries thus suggests that legal principle, if considered at all, was heavily sub-

25. This paragraph is based on the slightly fuller treatment in J B. Post, "The Justice of Criminal Justice in Later Medieval England," *Criminal Justice History* 7 (1986): 33–49.

26. *Medieval Legal Records· Edited in Memory of C A.F. Meekings*, ed R. F. Hunnisett and J. B. Post (1978), 320, no 101.

ordinated to administrative reality, and the aggregated evidence of jury behavior suggests no greater respect for legal principle once the jurors were sworn. The wide variety of juries, moreover—varying from panels of the visne duly summoned to probably uninformed talesmen—does not allow simple assumptions about the duties of the jurors. What can be said with considerable confidence is that no theoretical model or practical generalization can comprehend the assorted practices of different courts, different officials, and different circumstances. Some juries were, or were in a position to be, self-informing as to the evidence or opinion for or against the defendant; others were not. By the middle of the fifteenth century, Fortescue could apparently regard the jury as "a body of impartial men who came into court with an open mind,"[27] and the lawyers who accepted the idea of thirty-five jury challenges evidently envisaged the exhaustion (if indeed they ever envisaged the presence) of self-informed jurors. But there is no clear evidence of the basis (bribery and favor apart) on which a jury in the late fourteenth century was expected to decide.

Even if the jurors were not returning verdicts on the basis of their personal knowledge, the evidence on which they based their opinions was obviously of miscellaneous derivation. The admission of a fact, like a confession, was irrebuttable, and if the jury exculpated a defendant by denying a fact to which he had pleaded, their verdict was ignored.[28] The defendant was thus in a position to testify against himself. There are also some indications that his testimony could be accepted in his favor. These are curious, for they fly in the face of the very ancient and persistent principle of the common law that the handhaving thief was liable to the most summary and merciless of procedures.[29] While the formalities of public prosecution were gradually superseding the brisk justice of earlier times, the effect was commonly much the same. In a typical case, Thomas Puttock was taken with the mainour, which corresponded closely to a list of stolen goods attributed to him by a peace sessions jury. On examination, he admitted that the goods did not belong to him, and appropriate judgment

27. T.F.T. Plucknett, *A Concise History of the Common Law*, 5th ed. (1956), 129; J. Fortescue, *De Laudibus Legum Angliae*, ed. S. B. Chrimes (Cambridge, 1949), chap. 25

28. *Select Cases in the Court of King's Bench*, ed. G. O. Sayles, Selden Society, 7 vols. (1936–71), vol. 6, no. 95.

29. F. Pollock and F. W. Maitland, *The History of English Law*, 2d ed. (Cambridge, 1968), 2:495–97; J. B. Thayer, *A Preliminary Treatise on Evidence at the Common Law* (Boston, 1896), 71–72 n. 3; J. B. Post, "Local Jurisdictions and Judgment of Death in Later Medieval England," *Criminal Justice History* 4 (1983): 1–21.

followed.[30] Nevertheless, the courts often took a different attitude; in a number of cases the defendants disavowed the mainour and were promptly acquitted.[31] It had always been allowed in defense that the alleged mainour rightfully belonged to the defendant,[32] but disavowal was a different sort of claim. Nicholas Cory, for example, claimed a ham and a tunic as his own but disavowed two brass bowls.[33] The point of objection does not seem to have been the proof of unlawful possession, because it was possible to disavow successfully mainour whose rightful owner had been identified,[34] and a deliberate plant by an ill-wisher or an official seems unlikely, since stolen goods were forfeit to the Crown unless an appeal had been brought by the victim. Pending firmer evidence, it seems probable that disavowal meant denying all knowledge of mainour, which by the time of the trial may no longer have been available to be exhibited as evidence anyway and which had been part of a generalized accusation of suspicious behavior. A disavowal could be sufficiently hard as evidence to preclude reference to the jury at all, giving the defendant's word a remarkably high standing.

The defendant's word was not the only evidence available to the jury. In private actions for debt and the like, documentary evidence was frequently admitted,[35] and witnesses to a charter might be produced (although no procedure existed for their compulsion) to confirm or deny its provenance and content.[36] This use of a document as a record of a transaction was a natural extension of the use of witnesses and participants; the kinds of lawful dealings that might provide a defense to an accusation of theft were seldom likely to have been recorded, and it was therefore reasonable for the courts to admit oral evidence, as they seem to have done.[37] Other kinds of documents could also be admitted; the trial on a peace sessions indictment for false im-

30. JUST 3/179, m. 5d.

31. *E.g., ibid.*, m. 13 (Richard Huggin).

32. J. M. Kaye, ed., *Placita Corone*, Selden Society Supplementary Series, 4 (1966), 24. The testimony of this treatise is deeply suspect and is cited here only when it is likely to be reasonably representative.

33. JUST 3/179, m. 7.

34. JUST 3/174, m. 1 (Thomas Pinchbeck).

35. Thayer, *Evidence*, 104ff.

36. *King's Bench*, ed. Sayles, vol. 4, no. 32. In vol. 5, no. 9, the distinction of function between jurors and witnesses is blurred by the statement that the defendants "put themselves on a jury of the country and on the witnesses named in the said writing."

37. The example given in *Placita Corone*, ed. Kaye, 25, shows the acceptance of such testimony from an abjured felon, but he was only produced because he was spotted by the defendant while passing the window of the courthouse.

prisonment was adjourned to allow the defendant to produce the *venire facias* upon which he claimed to have acted.[38]

Of a different order was the examination of witnesses to events. This was, again, a feature of many private actions,[39] but in criminal prosecutions there is no evidence of a regular procedure. It seems likely that justices felt at liberty to interrogate defendants and their accusers to elicit claims and statements well outside the formal needs of appeal and exception,[40] and the justices of gaol delivery might allow a peace sessions indictment to be supported by the sworn testimony of the alleged victim.[41] On the other hand, there may have been some expectation that the jurors, guided perhaps by the bench, would use their discretion and initiative. Fortescue subsequently emphasized that since jurors (however impartial) were from the neighborhood of the facts at issue, they were peculiarly able to assess the credibility of the allegations on either side,[42] and in a suit between parties he further declared, from the bench, that legitimate attempts by jurors to seek out witnesses and their evidence should be clearly distinguished from approaches made by witnesses to jurors, which he regarded as maintenance.[43] Whatever the preliminaries may have been, Fortescue treated witness evidence in court as a commonplace,[44] and Chancery was then already developing the modern use of the subpoena.[45] It is probable, despite the relatively slow development of procedural modifications in the criminal sphere, that by the end of the fourteenth century witnesses were an acceptable feature of criminal trials, while having no formal or essential part in the process.

A further use of witness testimony is implicit in the obscure manner of acquittal without jury inquest. This occurred quite frequently at gaol delivery, most commonly in cases of persons arrested on suspicion. After mention of the cause of imprisonment (there is rarely, in these cases, any sign of a specific accusation in indictment form),[46]

38. JUST 3/170, m. 2.

39. *King's Bench*, ed. Sayles, vol. 1, no. 114; vol. 5, p. xcv.

40. *Placita Corone*, ed. Kaye, 8–9, 15–22.

41. JUST 3/179, m. 2 (Philip Bullingdon). The defendants were nevertheless acquitted; their accuser, by acting as witness and not as appellor, seems to have avoided the amercement consequent upon a failed appeal.

42. Fortescue, *De Laudibus*, chap. 28.

43. P. 28 Hen. VI, fol. 6, pl. 1, quoted in Thayer, *Evidence*, 128–29.

44. Fortescue, *De Laudibus*, chap. 26.

45. Thayer, *Evidence*, 129.

46. Entries usually take the form "taken at A. on suspicion" (e.g., JUST 3/179, m. 5d), but occasionally the suggestion is amplified to "suspicion of larceny" (e.g.,

the record states that "because it is testified in this court by many trustworthy persons (*fidedignes*) that N. is of good repute (*de bona fame*)," he is acquitted and released. Sometimes this discharge is preceded by a judgment of "not guilty."[47] In the early fifteenth century the procedure is clearer. Many suspects are "delivered after proclamation," provided that no accuser comes forward.[48] Some of them are said to have taken oaths of good behavior, occasionally in respect of specified persons, and to have found sufficient security. The cases are noted on the sheriff's calendar of prisoners but do not always find their way to the enrollment.[49] The additional note "40d." over several names suggests either security or an amercement.

This form of acquittal without reference to a jury presumably had its origins as a procedural corollary of the terms upon which persons were arrested as being of ill repute; this would certainly explain the use of such forms with persons arrested by justices of the peace,[50] pursuant to the statute of 1361.[51] The bulk of arrests on suspicion, however, were not attributed to justices or to any specific officers; the invariable mention of the place of arrest suggests that arrests without indictment were part of the routine duties of local officials, under the broad terms issued in 1331.[52] This strengthens the supposition that "good repute" was established by witnesses; an arresting official could hardly have been expected to provide a favorable testimonial from the local community. No responsibility attached to anyone speaking for the defendant, and mainpernors (persons offering security for the defendant's bail or good behavior) were often not required. The regular use of this procedure implies very strongly that direct testimony was normally required for a successful prosecution.

The procedure of acquittal in this fashion was nevertheless far from automatic, as its converse shows. Two men charged separately with homicides, and a third with larceny, were acquitted by jury, notwith-

John Jardevyle, m. 12), and the arresting officer may be mentioned (e.g., the case of Giles Zelond, m. 13d).

47. E.g., John Boys. JUST 3/179, m. 5d.

48. E.g., JUST 3/218/1, mm. 198, 206, 231–32, 242.

49. Cf. the file (n. 48 above) with the roll at JUST 3/194, JUST 3/205, m 6d.

50. E.g., Robert Webbe (JUST 13/174, m 1d) and Giles Zelond (JUST 3/179, m. 13d).

51. 34 Edw. III, c. 1 gave the justices generalized authority over "evil-doers, rioters, and all other barretors," wandering "pilferers and robbers," and "all those who are not of good repute (*bone fame*)." For the possible interpretations of this statute to cover, for example, nightwalkers, whoremasters, drunkards, and eavesdroppers, see W. Blackstone, *Commentaries on the Laws of England*, 8th ed. (Oxford, 1778), 4:256.

52 5 Edw. III, c. 14.

standing which they were remanded in custody because they were not of good repute. Whether objections to the verdict were raised by the indicting officials, or discretion was exercised by the justices, or further charges were pending is not clear.[53] If the first, the objections lapsed with time, since one of the men was found to be of good repute at the next gaol delivery.[54] In this type of case, as in other less seriously regarded cases, the justices may have felt entitled to use or count remand in custody as a punitive sentence.[55] If concrete suspicions were entertained, the remand could be genuine; two men disavowed the mainour with which they were said to have been taken, and when proclamation failed to produce an accuser, they were mainprised (conditionally released to mainpernors) pending the next delivery; the next defendant, also disavowing the mainour, was remanded in custody so that further inquiries could be made.[56] The discharge on "good repute" of three men supposedly taken with the mainour emphasizes the flexibility that procedures upon vaguely specified or unsupported allegations had attained.[57]

The omission of a jury inquest in cases such as these underlines the obscurity of the jury's function in ordinary criminal trials. Cases were being tried summarily which might otherwise have gone to a jury, and were, as far as can be discerned, decided upon evidence, or lack of evidence, which an uninformed jury might reasonably have been asked to assess. There may have been evidential or procedural defects that left no case to answer, the justices feeling that a jury was unnecessary. If so, the very fact of summary procedure usually prevents us from knowing the details. Equally, the varied composition and variable motives of juries prevent us from deducing the features that consigned a defendant to the verdict of his country. We can only be sure that the court records of the time support no single or simple hypothesis about the functions of a criminal trial jury.

53. JUST 3/179, mm. 8 (John Skit), 9d (Richard Reynes), 10 (John Sibley).

54. JUST 3/179, m. 10d

55. At the Winchester delivery in February 1409, three defendants complained that they had already been in custody, two of them for six years and one for one year. JUST 3/218/1, m. 218.

56. JUST 3/174, mm. 1 (Thomas Pinchbeck), 1d (Walter Tyler).

57. JUST 3/179, m. 13.

Four

Jury Trial at Gaol Delivery in the Late Middle Ages: The Midland Circuit, 1400–1429

Edward Powell

It is a maxim of English legal history that the medieval jury was self-informing. That orthodoxy was established at the turn of the century through the immensely durable work of F. W. Maitland and J. B. Thayer, and it has recently been restated by Professors J. H. Langbein and T. A. Green.[1] Trial jurors were, in Thayer's words, "men chosen as being likely to be already informed."[2] They were drawn from the visne, the neighborhood of the offense, and were thus supposed to be witnesses rather than triers of fact. Presentation of evidence to the jury therefore played no part in courtroom procedure. Langbein summarizes these points succinctly:

> The Angevin system of self-informing juries had required no outside officer to investigate crime and to inform the jurors of the evidence. . . . Denunciation (to the jury of accusation) and proof of guilt (to the jury of trial) operated informally, that is, out of court and in advance of the court's sitting. . . . Medieval jurors came to court more to speak than to listen.[3]

One fundamental problem arises from this interpretation: that of transformation. How and when did the self-informing jury evolve into the modern trial jury, which is informed entirely in court through the presentation of evidence? As Langbein admits, "this transformation of the active medieval juries into passive triers is among the great

1 F. Pollock and F. W. Maitland, *The History of English Law*, 2d ed. (Cambridge, 1968), 2:624–25, J. B. Thayer, *A Preliminary Treatise on Evidence at the Common Law* (1898), 90–129, J. H. Langbein, *Prosecuting Crime in the Renaissance* (Cambridge, Mass., 1974); idem, "The Origins of Public Prosecution at Common Law," *AJLH* 17 (1973). 313–35, Green, *Verdict According to Conscience*, chaps 1–4.

2. Thayer, *Evidence*, 90.

3. Langbein, "Public Prosecution," 314

mysteries of English legal history, still no better understood than when Thayer wrote."[4] Langbein himself has argued persuasively, however, that the effects of this change were being felt by 1550, and that they were greatly accelerated by the bail and committal statutes of 1554–55.[5] The assumption has therefore been made that during the late Middle Ages the jury underwent major change whereby it ceased to be a self-informing institution, thus necessitating the overhaul of prosecutorial and trial procedure in the second half of the sixteenth century.[6]

Any attempt to investigate the history of the jury in the late Middle Ages must address this central question. The aim of this essay is therefore to explore the extent to which the trial jury had already ceased to be self-informing by the early fifteenth century. Was the jury still "medieval" in character, gathering its information outside the courtroom and coming into court to speak rather than to listen? Or was it becoming "modern," coming into court largely ignorant of the offenses to be tried and reliant on the presentation of evidence in court by the prosecution? There is, of course, a third possibility: that the contrast between "medieval" and "modern" criminal trial procedure has been overemphasized and that supposedly modern features such as the presentation of evidence in court and the use of witnesses were as much a part of medieval trials as of trials after 1550. This essay will also seek to test the adequacy of the hypothesis regarding the workings of the medieval jury and its transformation outlined above.

Sir John Fortescue's description of the trial jury, written in the mid fifteenth century, endorses the theory of the jury as witnesses:

> The "witnesses" are neighbours, able to live of their own, sound in repute and fair-minded, not brought into court by either party, but chosen by a respectable and impartial officer, and compelled to come before the judge.[7]

Fortescue was referring to juries in civil cases, but his terse treatment of criminal procedure echoes these sentiments, and there can be little

4. Ibid.

5. Langbein, *Prosecuting Crime*, passim. Langbein's purpose in this book was, of course, to investigate the character and consequences of the Marian statutes rather than their long-term causes.

6. Green, *Verdict According to Conscience*, 105–6; Langbein, "Public Prosecution," 314.

7. J. Fortescue, *De Laudibus Legum Anglie*, ed. S. B. Chrimes (Cambridge, 1949), 63.

doubt that he viewed the criminal trial jury in a similar light.[8] Cases from the central courts in the late Middle Ages can be adduced in support of Fortescue's assertions. Thayer provided several examples,[9] and there are good illustrations from the court of King's Bench in the early fifteenth century. In 1403, following the theft of bundles of feet of fines from the Treasury of Receipt at Westminster, a jury of clerks and officials of that department was summoned to try the accused man, John Freeman.[10] Again, in Trinity term 1413, John Shaw was tried in King's Bench on a charge of attempting to rescue a prisoner from custody in open court, by a jury of King's Bench filazers and officials.[11] Clearly, such jurors were summoned because of their firsthand knowledge and professional expertise. By definition, however, such cases were exceptional, and while they provide useful impressionistic evidence, they can hardly be regarded as typical. The vast majority of criminal trials took place not at Westminster but in the provinces, before justices of gaol delivery and justices of the peace, and it is upon the evidence of trials at that level that our general conclusions must be based.

After the demise of the general eyre in the early fourteenth century, there were three regular kinds of royal commission which conferred the power to determine cases of felony: gaol delivery commissions issued to assize justices for each county of their circuit and valid until superseded by fresh circuit commissions; gaol delivery commissions *pro hac vice*, valid for one delivery only and most commonly issued to justices of the peace of the relevant county; and the peace commissions, which empowered such justices to determine all indictments for felony taken before them.[12] Very few records exist of felony trials be-

8 "Who, then, in England can die unjustly for a crime when . . . none save his neighbors, good and faithful men, against whom he has no manner of exception, can condemn him?" Ibid., 65.

9. Thayer, *Evidence*, 90–92

10. PRO, KB 27 (Court of King's Bench, Plea Rolls)/567, Rex m. 18d Unless otherwise stated, all records cited are from the Public Record Office.

11. *Select Cases in the Court of King's Bench*, ed. G. O. Sayles, Selden Society, 7 vols. (1936–71), 7:215–17. The first jury panel returned for Shaw's trial was found to have been nominated by his accuser, John Swan, who was the deputy marshal, and a second panel had to be drawn up by Thomas Cowley, the king's attorney. Both panels are on file at KB 9 (Court of King's Bench, Ancient Indictments)/993, mm. 10–14.

12. M. Gollancz, "The System of Gaol Delivery as Illustrated in the Extant Gaol Delivery Rolls of the Fifteenth Century" (M.A. thesis, London Univ., 1936), 48, 128, *Calendar of General and Special Assize and General Gaol Delivery Commissions on the Dorses of the Patent Rolls: Richard II, 1377–99* (PRO Search Room), introduction, R. B. Pugh, *Imprisonment in Medieval England* (Cambridge, 1968); B. H. Putnam, ed , *Early Treatises on the Practice of the Justices of the Peace in the Fifteenth and Six-*

fore the justices of the peace, and with a few exceptions, surviving peace rolls consist of undetermined indictments enrolled for submission to the court of King's Bench.[13] Records of deliveries pro hac vice are similarly fragmentary, but there remains a substantial archive of circuit gaol delivery records stretching from the late thirteenth to the mid fifteenth century. In many instances the county files also survive, including gaol calendars, jury lists, and other material, all of which complement the enrolled record of trial proceedings.[14] For most circuits, these records are comprehensive and continuous enough to permit systematic analysis. The present study is based upon an examination of the circuit gaol delivery records of three counties in the Midland circuit—Derbyshire, Leicestershire, and Warwickshire—between 1400 and 1429.[15]

Medieval legal records are notoriously uninformative about trial procedure. The only matters routinely recorded in criminal trials were the indictment or appeal, the defendant's appearance and plea, the selection and swearing in of the trial jurors, their verdict, and the sentence. The gaol delivery records do allow us, however, to approach the problem of trial procedure and jury behavior indirectly through an analysis of the composition of trial juries—the frequency of service of jurors, their administrative experience, geographical distribution, and social status—and of the speed and outcome of trials. The first half of this essay presents the results of such an analysis for the three counties examined, and the second half considers the implications of those findings for our understanding of the nature of criminal jury trial in the late Middle Ages.

The circuits of assize and gaol delivery took shape in the course of the fourteenth century, and by 1400 the circuit groupings of counties and the timing of sessions familiar from the early modern period were all but established.[16] Assizes were usually, but not invariably, held twice

teenth Centuries (Oxford, 1924), 88–89; *Proceedings before the Justices of the Peace in the Fourteenth and Fifteenth Centuries: Edward III to Richard III*, ed. B. H. Putnam, Ames Foundation (1938), civ–cv.

13. *Proceedings*, ed. Putnam, lvii–lxxvi.

14. Gollancz, "Gaol delivery," 16–47.

15. The Midland circuit was comprised of Northamptonshire, Warwickshire, Leicestershire, Derbyshire, Nottinghamshire, Lincolnshire, and Rutland. These are the latest medieval Midland circuit records to survive. After 1429 there are no gaol delivery records from the circuit until 1818. Cockburn, *Assizes*, xii.

16. Ibid., 15–48

a year, during the Lent and Trinity vacations.[17] The judges had a wide variety of business to transact. As well as being commissioned to hear possessory assizes and deliver gaols throughout their circuits, they heard cases delegated *nisi prius* from the courts of King's Bench and Common Pleas. These might include criminal as well as civil trials.[18] Assize judges were also appointed as justices of the peace in each county of their circuit and frequently took indictments in that capacity.[19] Finally, the judges received all manner of ad hoc judicial or administrative commissions to discharge while on circuit. In 1419, for example, a nationwide inquiry into treasons, escapes of felons, and concealments of the forfeited chattels of convicted felons was carried out largely through commissions to the assize judges.[20]

Business was conducted at breakneck speed. In the early fifteenth century the Midland circuit lasted from thirteen to fifteen days from the date of the sitting at the first county town, Northampton, to that in the last, Lincoln.[21] In between, the judges visited Warwick, Leicester, Derby, Nottingham (where Derbyshire as well as Nottinghamshire prisoners were delivered), and Lincoln. Sometimes the judges included Coventry and Oakham in Rutland in their itinerary.[22] Allowing five days' travel between venues, this left at most two days, and sometimes only one, for sittings in each county. The judges and their staff obviously worked under immense pressure, which must have severely restricted the time available for criminal trials.[23]

Before each visitation the senior assize judge, through his clerk, sent precepts to all the sheriffs of the circuit instructing them to pre-

17. Early in Henry IV's reign the winter assizes on the Midland circuit were held several times during the Michaelmas rather than the Lent vacation, while in Henry V's reign the suspension of possessory assize business disrupted the routine of circuit visitation. See Gollancz, "Gaol delivery," appendix B.

18. For examples of criminal nisi prius cases, see KB 27/631, Rex m. 5 (1419); 634, Rex m. 33 (1419); 635, Rex m. 2d (1420).

19. E. Powell, "Public Order and Law Enforcement in Shropshire and Staffordshire in the Early Fifteenth Century" (Ph.D. thesis, Oxford Univ., 1979), 123–29. On the Midland circuit the assize judges sat as justices of the peace in Leicestershire in February 1422 and February 1426, and in Warwickshire in July 1414 and February 1420. JUST 3 (Gaol Delivery Rolls)/31/9, m. 7; 31/10, m. 9; 67/8, m. 15; 67/11, m. 3.

20. *CPR, 1416–22*, pp. 205–6; KB 9/1056, mm. 23–32, 39–51; 214, mm. 1–4; 213, mm. 39–42, 49–51; *Calendar of Inquisitions Miscellaneous, 1399–1422*, nos. 563–79.

21. Gollancz, "Gaol delivery," 138. By the 1580s it had lengthened to twenty-one days. Cockburn, *Assizes*, 25.

22. The Midland circuit rolls for 1400 to 1429 are JUST 3/188, 195, and 203.

23. See below, text at n. 70

pare for the business of the forthcoming sessions.[24] The gaol delivery precept included *inter alia* an order to summon panels of twenty-four knights and other free and lawful men, each of whom had one hundred shillings' worth of land or rents per annum, from the visne of each township where an offense had been committed.[25] This was clearly an impracticable order. To take an extreme example, there were ninety-one prisoners from Nottinghamshire and Derbyshire to be delivered at Nottingham in July 1412. A panel for each would have involved over two thousand men from the two counties, each with a landed income of £5 a year.[26] More realistically, a statute of 1414 stipulated an income of forty shillings for jurors in cases of homicide, implying that a smaller income was acceptable for jurors trying lesser felonies.[27] In practice, the sheriff would have observed the spirit of the precept if he had summoned a panel of jurors from each hundred within the shire, who might reasonably be expected to have acquired some knowledge of the offenses they were to try.[28] The files show, however, that this was never achieved for the three counties under study. There were four hundreds in Warwickshire, five in Leicestershire, and six hundreds and wapentakes in Derbyshire, but in none of them were there more than three trial juries at any delivery between 1413 and 1429, the period for which files, and thus jury lists, survive. Even the summons of three juries to a session was exceptional, occurring only twice in sixteen files from Leicestershire and three times in sixteen files from Warwickshire. In Derbyshire there was without exception only a single trial jury for the whole county, probably because the delivery of Derbyshire prisoners took place outside the county at Nottingham, thereby increasing the problem of securing the attendance of jurors.[29] This pattern does not appear to be anomalous. Similar practice is ob-

24. Separate writs were sent out for assize and gaol delivery business; compare Justice John Cockayne's precepts to the sheriff of Leicestershire and Warwickshire for the Lent assizes 1423 (JUST 4 [Eyre, Assize, etc., Writ Files]/8/2, mm. 107, 190) with those for gaol delivery (JUST 3/31/11, m. 10 and JUST 3/68/1, m. 6), all dated 9 November 1422.

25. Fortescue, *De Laudibus*, 64–65, is thus formally correct in spite of Professor Chrimes's strictures. Ibid., 176–77.

26. See below, Fig. 4.1.

27. 2 Hen. V, st. 2, c. 3

28. Cf. Putnam, *Early Treatises*, 271–72.

29. Derbyshire is the only county of the three to show a marked geographical clustering of jurors. Over half the jurors who served more than once at gaol delivery lived in the southern half of the county, within ten miles of Derby and twenty of Nottingham.

servable in Northamptonshire within the Midland circuit, and outside it in Buckinghamshire.[30] In Nottinghamshire, another Midland circuit county, the practice early in Henry V's reign was to summon panels from groups of wapentakes, but by the late 1420s that had been abandoned in favor of a single county panel.[31]

At first sight, therefore, there seems to be no obvious geographical basis for jury summons. Furthermore, it was unusual for accused felons to be arraigned individually before separate juries. As was the practice in later centuries, juries generally tried several cases at a time.[32] Table 4.1 analyzes the number of accused tried by each jury between 1413 and 1429.[33] There were wide fluctuations between individual juries, but on the average, Derbyshire juries tried between eight and nine prisoners at a sitting, Leicestershire juries between four and five, and Warwickshire juries between three and four. The largest number of prisoners arraigned before a single jury during the period

Table 4.1. Number of Prisoners Tried by Midland Circuit Juries, 1413–1429

	Derbyshire		Leicestershire		Warwickshire	
No. of Prisoners Tried by Jury	No. of Juries	No. of Prisoners	No. of Juries	No. of Prisoners	No. of Juries	No. of Prisoners
11 or more	5	104	1	12	0	0
10	3	30	2	20	2	20
9	1	9	1	9	0	0
8	3	24	1	8	1	8
7	3	21	1	7	0	0
6	4	24	1	6	3	18
5	0	0	1	5	3	15
4	1	4	4	16	3	12
3	1	3	2	6	9	27
2	3	6	2	4	5	10
1	3	3	7	7	6	6
Total	27	228	23	100	32	116

SOURCES: JUST 3/13/1; 31/6–21; 56/8–27; 67/7–13, 68/1–11; 188, 195; 203, 218/4, 5, 7; 219/4.

30. JUST 3/52/15–31 (Northants., 1413–29); JUST 3/220/1 (Bucks, 1430–36).

31. JUST 3/56/8–10, 21–27.

32. Cockburn, *Assizes*, 117–18; Thomas Smith, *De Republica Anglorum*, ed. M. Dewar (Cambridge, 1972), 114.

33. This table does not represent a complete record of deliveries between 1413 and 1429, but only of those prisoners tried by jury at sessions for which jury lists survive.

was thirty-nine, tried by a Derbyshire jury at Nottingham in July 1420.[34] Throughout the three counties, only sixteen persons were tried individually out of nearly 450 who were tried by jury. Normally, gaol delivery juries were expected to render verdicts on a batch of cases placed before them.

How far was this pattern of jury trial compatible with the principle that jurors should be drawn from the neighborhood of the offenses? Did the sheriff attempt to group cases from a single hundred together for determination by a jury from that hundred? Table 4.2 explores

Tables 4.2. Residence of Trial Jurors and Scene of Offenses, by Hundred or Wapentake

Jury Ref. (JUST 3)		Hundred or Wapentake							
Derbyshire		High Peak	Scarsdale	Wirksworth	Appletree	Morleyston	Repton	Derby Town	Total
56/8 m. 14	Jurors	3	2	2	2	1	1	0	11
July 1413	Offenses	0	4	2	2	0	0	0	8
56/12 m. 21	Jurors	0	0	1	5	2	4	0	12
Feb. 1416	Offenses	1	2	0	1	0	2	0	6
56/12 m. 22	Jurors	2	2	0	0	1	7	0	12
Feb. 1416	Offenses	0	0	0	0	0	1	0	1
56/13 m. 14	Jurors	0	2	2	1	3	4	0	12
Oct. 1416	Offenses	0	0	0	1	1	3	0	5
56/14 m. 17	Jurors	0	4	1	0	3	4	0	12
Mar. 1417	Offenses	0	5	0	0	0	1	0	6
56/19 m. 19	Jurors	1	2	2	2	2	2	0	11
Mar. 1422	Offenses	1	1	0	1	2	2	0	7
56/21 m. 26	Jurors	1	2	4	2	2	0	0	11
July 1423	Offenses	2	1	1	0	2	2	1	9
13/1 m. 2	Jurors	0	0	0	3	8	0	0	11
Mar. 1425	Offenses	0	0	0	0	1	0	0	1
219/4 m. 13	Jurors	5	2	0	0	3	0	2	12
July 1426	Offenses	2	0	0	0	0	1	1	4
56/25 m. 10	Jurors	1	0	0	1	3	0	6	11
Aug. 1427	Offenses	0	0	0	0	2	0	0	2

34. Thirty of these were tried on a single indictment for robbery.

these questions by correlating the geographical location of offenses with the principal residence of jurors for ten juries from each county.[35] In Derbyshire, where a single trial jury was the rule, offenders from all parts of the county had to be tried together, and there is little correlation except in the unusual circumstances of February 1416 and March 1425, when individual prisoners (both gentlemen) were acquitted at special deliveries at Derby. In July 1413 three jurors were drawn from High Peak wapentake, where no offenses had occurred. In February 1416 there were no jurors from Scarsdale on the jury that tried the two

Table 4.2. (*cont.*)

Leicestershire		Framland	Gartree	Goscote	Guthlaxton	Sparkenhoe	Leicester Town	Total
31/6 m. 8	Jurors	2	1	7	2	0	0	12
Feb. 1414	Offenses	1	0	1	3	1	0	6
31/7 m. 2	Jurors	2	2	4	2	2	0	12
Feb. 1420	Offenses	0	0	1	1	0	1	3
31/9 m. 8	Jurors	4	2	2	1	2	0	11
Feb. 1422	Offenses	0	3	2	1	3	1	10
31/14 m. 9	Jurors	0	3	6	3	0	0	12
Feb. 1425	Offenses	0	0	1	1	0	0	2
31/14 m. 10	Jurors	0	12	0	0	0	0	12
Feb. 1425	Offenses	0	1	0	0	0	0	1
31/14 m. 11	Jurors	1	0	9	0	1	0	11
Feb. 1425	Offenses	0	0	1	0	0	0	1
31/15 m. 3	Jurors	0	1	6	1	4	0	12
July 1425	Offenses	0	0	3	1	1	0	5
31/19 m. 5	Jurors	1	11	0	0	0	0	12
Feb. 1428	Offenses	1	1	2	0	1	0	5
31/20 m. 3	Jurors	0	12	0	0	0	0	12
July 1428	Offenses	0	1	0	0	0	0	1
31/20 m. 4	Jurors	0	0	0	2	10	0	12
July 1428	Offenses	0	0	0	0	3	0	3

35. Correlation has been attempted only where the residence of at least ten jurors on a panel is known.

offenses committed there.[36] At the sessions of July 1423, two prisoners accused of crimes in Repton were convicted, although there were no jurors from that hundred.[37] In Leicestershire the results are mixed. Where juries tried several prisoners at once, as in February 1414, February 1422, and February 1428, there was little geographical link between jurors and places of offense. In the last example, eleven of the jurors came from Gartree hundred, where only one of the five offenses had taken place. On the other hand, where prisoners were

Table 4.2. (*cont.*)

Warwickshire		Hemlingford	Knightlow	Barlichway	Kineton	Warwick Town	Coventry Town	Total
67/10 m. 8	Jurors	2	5	2	0	2	0	11
Feb. 1417	Offenses	2	1	4	0	2	0	9
67/11 m. 2	Jurors	2	5	0	3	1	0	11
Feb. 1420	Offenses	1	0	0	0	0	0	1
67/11 m. 4	Jurors	1	5	3	0	2	0	11
Feb. 1420	Offenses	0	1	0	0	0	0	1
67/12 m. 9	Jurors	4	4	0	0	2	0	10
July 1420	Offenses	1	0	0	1	0	0	2
68/1 m. 3	Jurors	1	1	0	0	10	0	12
Feb. 1423	Offenses	1	0	0	1	0	0	2
68/2 m. 3	Jurors	0	5	0	2	2	3	12
Feb. 1424	Offenses	1	1	1	1	0	0	4
68/4 m. 4	Jurors	9	3	0	0	0	0	12
July 1424	Offenses	3	5	0	0	0	0	8
68/4 m. 5	Jurors	3	4	1	2	1	0	11
July 1424	Offenses	2	2	0	1	0	0	5
68/5 m. 11	Jurors	3	4	2	0	1	0	10
Feb. 1425	Offenses	1	1	0	1	0	0	3
68/5 m. 12	Jurors	0	1	1	7	1	1	11
Feb. 1425	Offenses	1	1	0	0	0	0	2

36. JUST 3/56/12, m. 22.

37. The men convicted were John Rawlyn and William Pulton. JUST 3/203, mm. 38–38d.

tried in ones and twos the correlation is quite strong. The three juries at the February 1425 sessions and the two at the July 1428 session all include large numbers of jurors from the hundreds in which the alleged crimes took place. Both sessions reveal the sheriff successfully matching juries against the offenses to be tried. Warwickshire, with the lowest ratio of prisoners to jurors, might be expected to show the strongest correlation, but again the pattern is contradictory. On occasion, as with the two juries of July 1424, a clear geographical link was preserved even while several prisoners were tried together. Yet in February 1420 and February 1425 one and two prisoners respectively were tried by juries whose members were mostly not drawn from the neighborhood.

In all three counties the vast majority of trial juries included at least one or two jurors from each hundred where the offenses had been committed. Within the hundreds, however, there is no consistent geographical correlation between the location of offenses and the domicile of jurors. It is visible from time to time but not often enough to allow the conclusion that the principle of neighborhood juries was observed in a modified form through the inclusion on panels of a few men drawn from the visne of each offense to be tried.[38]

This sample of thirty juries is, of course, a comparatively small one, and it is important not to place too much reliance upon the findings it yields. The overall pattern, nevertheless, allows the tentative conclusion that while sporadic efforts were still being made to ensure that juries in criminal trials were drawn from the neighborhood where the offense had occurred, those efforts were more successful in the small minority of cases where prisoners were tried on their own or in pairs. Where three or more prisoners were tried at one time, the geographical correlation between jurors and offenses tended to break down.

If, as the preceding section suggests, jurors were not always selected on a geographical basis, the question arises as to what other criteria were used in their selection. Perhaps the most likely alternatives are legal and administrative experience and social standing within the shire. Did the sheriff and his staff rely upon experienced and respected jurors who were *liberi et legales homines*, as the judge's precept required, even if they were not always from the visne? Tables 4.3 and 4.4 analyze the frequency with which men served on juries during the pe-

38. At the Derbyshire assizes in Nottingham at Michaelmas 1416, cases were heard involving offenses at Brampton and Milton, and jurors from these two villages appeared on the panel. JUST 3/56/13, mm. 13–14. At the Derbyshire assizes of Lent 1417, two jurors were summoned from Ashover, where one of the accused, John Stubbing, lived. JUST 3/56/14, mm 16–17.

Table 4.3. Frequency of Jury Service, 1413–1429

No. of Times Served	Number of Jurors		
	Derbyshire	Leicestershire	Warwickshire
10	1	0	0
9	0	0	0
8	1	0	0
7	1	0	4
6	1	2	1
5	1	0	2
4	2	4	10
3	15	18	13
2	26	31	42
1	162	132	186
Total	210	187	258

SOURCES JUST 3/13/1; 31/6–21; 56/8–27; 67/7–13; 68/1–11; 218/4, 5, 7; 219/4.

riod.[39] No jury lists survive for roughly one-third of all deliveries, so that the figures probably underestimate the frequency with which some jurors served. Despite this, a clear pattern of repeated service does emerge, with over 50 percent of jury seats in Leicestershire and Warwickshire, and 45 percent in Derbyshire, occupied by jurors serving more than once (Table 4.4). In all counties, a small number of jurors served with some regularity.

Service on trial juries at gaol delivery was only one of the many minor legal and administrative burdens imposed on the king's subjects by the routine of royal government. Comparable duties included sitting on presenting juries at peace sessions, before the sheriff's tourn, or on special inquiries such as the Lollard commissions of 1414; acting as recognitors (jurors) in possessory assizes heard before the assize judges; and serving as coroners, subsidy collectors, hundredal and seigneurial bailiffs, and village constables. Royal legal and administrative records for the period were searched in order to assess the extent to which gaol delivery jurors, particularly those who served more than

39. Because of documentary loss, the tables should be regarded as of relative, rather than absolute, significance. For the period covered, no jury lists survive for 8 out of 29 Derbyshire deliveries, 9 out of 25 Leicestershire deliveries, and 9 out of 25 Warwickshire deliveries. In addition, no account can be taken of trial jury service before justices of the peace and gaol delivery commissioners pro hac vice, for which no records survive.

Table 4.4. Representation of Jurors Serving Twice or More, 1413–1429

	Derbyshire		Leicestershire		Warwickshire	
	No.	%	No.	%	No.	%
Total no. of juries	26		23		33	
Total no. of jury seats	312		276		396	
Seats occupied by jurors serving once only	162	52	132	48	186	47
Seats occupied by jurors serving twice or more	142	46	144	52	207	52
Names lost or illegible	8	3	0	0	3	1

SOURCES: JUST 3/13/1; 31/6–21; 56/8–27; 67/7–13; 68/1–11; 218/4, 5, 7; 219/4.

once, were active in these other capacities. The results are presented in Table 4.5.

The fragmentary and uneven nature of the evidence helps to explain the disparities between the counties and suggests that these figures offer a highly conservative estimate of the involvement of trial jurors in other duties. Thus the number of jurors who were also assize recognitors is based on a single surviving Midland circuit assize file, for 1423–29, which contains fifteen Derbyshire panels, eight Warwickshire panels, and only four for Leicestershire. By contrast, only ten peace sessions juries for Derbyshire have been found, as against twenty-eight for Leicestershire and thirty-three for Warwickshire.

There is a striking incidence of coroners and bailiffs among trial jurors in Derbyshire and Warwickshire. Coroners provided some of the most regular jurors: Thomas Bradshaw of Chellaston served ten times during his career as a Derbyshire coroner; and his colleague William Woodroffe of Hope, four times.[40] In Warwickshire the coroners John Brome of Warwick, Roger Bulston, and William Dassett of Thurlaston all served seven times, although Bulston's recorded service took place after he had ceased to be coroner in about 1415.[41] The presence of cor-

40. The other Derbyshire coroners were Roger Wormhill, Henry Wychard, and William Ulgerthorpe.

41 No inquests by Bulston are found after this date. This does not mean, of course, that he did not serve as a trial juror while he was a coroner, since no jury lists survive for Warwickshire before 1414. Other Warwickshire coroners who served as jurors were William Reynold of Attleborough (who served on four juries), Richard Hall of Stratford (five), Richard Stafford of Wappenbury (one), John Tolas of Warwick (one), and William Hopkins of Warwick (one). I am very grateful to Dr. M. C. Carpenter of New

Table 4.5. Participation of Gaol Delivery Jurors in Other Official Duties

	Derbyshire Jurors serving		Leicestershire Jurors serving		Warwickshire Jurors serving	
	Twice or More	Once Only	Twice or More	Once Only	Twice or More	Once Only
Total no. in sample	48	162	55	132	72	186
Coroners	4	1	1	0	4	3
Hundred-bailiffs	7	3	2	0	5	1
Tax collectors	8	15	6	4	13	18
Assize recognitors	26	23	13	5	25	18
Jurors on special comm.	27	30	18	25	20	18
Jurors at peace sessions and tourn	7	9	26	19	45	50
Constables	0	6	11	8	—	—
No other duties found	9	93	14	91	13	117

SOURCES: KB 9/200–225; JUST 4/8/2 (Midland circuit assize file, 1423–1429); *Cal. Close Rolls, 1405–29; Cal. Fine Rolls, 1405–30;* KB 37 (court of King's Bench, Brevia Regis Files)/4/2/1, unnumbered membranes (Leicestershire constables lists, 1414).

oners on juries raises the intriguing possibility that in some homicide cases they participated in the trial of prisoners who had been indicted before them as coroners, and that in fact occurred at least twice in Derbyshire during the period. In the first instance, at the Lent assizes in 1414, there were no less than four past and present coroners, including Henry Wychard, who presided over the inquest, on a jury that tried three persons for murder.[42] In the second, Thomas Bradshaw sat on a jury that acquitted Richard Shavington on an indictment of homicide in self-defense which had been taken before him at the inquest.[43] No such cases have been detected for the other two counties. In Warwickshire, when coroners performed jury service at the delivery at which an indictment taken before them was determined, they sat on juries hearing other cases.[44]

Hall, Cambridge, for providing me with much valuable information on these and other Warwickshire jurors.

42. JUST 3/56/11, m. 13, and JUST 3/195, m. 60d.

43. JUST 3/56/21, mm. 25–26, and JUST 3/203, m. 38d.

44. As did Richard Hall in February 1417 and Richard Stafford in July 1424.

Bailiffs were as prominent as coroners on Derbyshire and Warwickshire juries, although again they were less in evidence in Leicestershire.[45] Bailiffs from every hundred and wapentake saw service in Derbyshire, led by Henry Rolleston of Etwall, the bailiff of Appletree hundred in Henry V's reign, who sat on eight juries.[46] In Warwickshire only two hundredal bailiffs appeared on jury lists,[47] but seigneurial bailiffs were better represented. Richard Hall and William Reynold, as well as being coroners,[48] were, respectively, bailiff of the bishop of Worcester's liberty of Pathlow and bailiff of the duchy of Lancaster in Leicestershire, while John Warin, who served seven times, was bailiff of Nuneaton, presumably in the service of the duchy of Lancaster.[49]

The number of trial jurors who served as recognitors in assizes and as jurors at peace sessions, on the sheriff's tourn, and before special commissions suggests that many of them possessed broad experience in both the civil and criminal aspects of the legal system. In particular, service on juries of presentment gave trial jurors firsthand knowledge of the procedures that led to the arraignment of accused felons before them at gaol delivery. In Leicestershire 24 percent of all trial jurors had also served on juries of presentment; in Warwickshire, 37 percent.[50] For trial jurors who served twice or more, the figures rise to 47 percent and 62 percent respectively.[51] Since assizes were held at the

JUST 3/67/10, m. 7, and JUST 3/195, m. 83 (Hall); JUST 3/68/4, m. 5, and JUST 3/203, m. 51 (Stafford). These cases suggest that even if coroners did not attend every delivery, as the judge's precept ordered, they were present when indictments taken before them were determined.

45. Names of hundred-bailiffs appear in some gaol delivery calendars; e.g., JUST 3/56/12, m. 7d (Derbs.), 31/7, m. 3 (Leics.), 67/11, m. 5 (Warwicks.).

46. The others were Simon Allerton, bailiff of Gresley (who served on two juries), William Bagshaw of High Peak (two), Gilbert Ince of Repton (two), Roger Sergeant of Scarsdale (three), John Buxton of Wirksworth (three), Richard Congleton of Appletree and Wirksworth (one), and Robert Winter of Morleyston (one). William Bate, bailiff of the seigneurial liberty of Sawley, served seven times.

47. Robert Hatch, who served on two juries, and Thomas Craklawe, on one, both of Knightlow.

48. See above, n. 41.

49. JUST 3/67/11, m. 5 (Hall); 31/7, m. 3 (Reynold); 188, m. 23 (Warin). William Rokesley, bailiff of Stratford-upon-Avon (JUST 3/188, m. 20), served twice as a trial juror.

50. Insufficient peace sessions juries survive from Derbyshire to produce a meaningful statistic.

51. There are not enough data to test the hypothesis that a *cursus honorum* existed whereby men were selected as trial jurors only after acquiring experience of criminal procedure on juries of presentment. It is not common, however, to find men recorded as gaol delivery trial jurors before they have appeared on presenting juries. The opportunities for service on presenting juries were much greater, since peace sessions,

same time as gaol delivery, and before the same judges, the number of jurors who served in both capacities should occasion no surprise. A comparison between jury lists from the same session does not suggest, however, that gaol delivery jurors were systematically "poached" from assize panels.[52] Nevertheless, overlaps did occur. Peace sessions, assize, and gaol delivery juries all survive from the summer assizes at Northampton in 1428, and they reveal that seven trial jurors sat on the peace sessions jury and three on all three bodies.[53]

The fortuitous survival of lists of village constables from Derbyshire and Leicestershire in 1414 makes possible some tentative suggestions as to their role as trial jurors. Given their local police duties, constables would seem to be obvious candidates for such a role. They were responsible for leading the hue and cry, making arrests on suspicion or at the order of superior officials, and ensuring the safe-conduct of those arrested to gaol or before royal judges, where they were also answerable for the chattels of fugitive felons. In these capacities their presence might frequently be required at gaol delivery. In the mid fourteenth century they had also acquired important responsibilities for the enforcement of the Statutes of Labourers.[54] In addition they frequently acted as presenting jurors before justices of the peace and special commissions.[55] During the period of exceptional judicial activity at the beginning of Henry V's reign, juries of constables are recorded in several counties, and it is from that period that the Derbyshire and Leicestershire lists survive.[56]

---

to which juries from each hundred were summoned, were held four times a year, in contrast to the semiannual gaol deliveries, where no more than three juries were summoned at one time. See above text at n. 29.

52. At Leicester in February 1427 ten men were impaneled as recognitors and trial jurors, but none actually served in both capacities. JUST 3/13/21, mm. 5–6; JUST 4/8/2, m. 633.

53. The three were Thomas Burdon, John Dawes, and Richard England. JUST 3/52/30, m. 2; JUST 4/8/2, m 554; KB 9/224, m. 164. This is the only instance I have so far discovered where juries from all three agencies survive for a single session.

54. H. M. Cam, "Shire Officials," in *The English Government at Work, 1327–1336*, ed. J. F. Willard et al., 3 vols. (Cambridge, Mass., 1940–50), 3.169–71; L. R. Poos, "The Social Context of the Statute of Labourers Enforcement," *Law and History Review* 1 (1983). 31–37, Smith, *De Republica*, 107–10. They also retained local military duties. See Putnam, *Early Treatises*, 271.

55. *Proceedings*, ed. Putnam, xcix.

56. G. L Harriss, ed., *Henry V. The Practice of Kingship* (Oxford, 1985), 60–72. Derbyshire and Leicestershire lists are to be found in the returns to the Lollard inquiries of 1414. KB 9/204/1, mm. 57–83, 128–45. A fuller list survives for Leicestershire from the superior eyre of the same year: KB 37/4/2/1. There are also jury lists of Derbyshire constables from 1419 and 1423 at KB 9/1056, m. 34; and 218/2, m. 43.

The names of 158 constables have been recovered for Derbyshire,[57] and 157 for Leicestershire. No data survive for Warwickshire. Such a sample, drawn mainly from a single year, probably represents a very small proportion of those who served as constables throughout the period, and we may therefore be grossly underestimating the number of those who were, or had been, constables and who served on trial juries. In Derbyshire very few constables appeared on jury lists; of 210 jurors, only six can be shown to have been constables, and none served more than once.[58] That is consistent with the comparatively restricted nature of jury service in Derbyshire, with a single county jury at gaol delivery and a strong representation of higher officials. In Leicestershire, by contrast, where two or three juries were regularly summoned to gaol delivery and where higher officials rarely appeared on juries, 10 percent of jurors (19 out of 187) can be identified as having served as constables. Seven of these appeared on two juries, and four on three.[59] Within this small sample there is a slight tendency for constables to appear on juries drawn from the near vicinity of an offense. At the Lent assizes in 1425, for example, Robert Swyndriver was acquitted for clipping coin at several places in Gartree hundred by a jury that was drawn entirely from Gartree and that included four men who had been constables in 1414.[60] Similarly, at the summer assizes in 1428, William Hill was acquitted of homicide at Horninghold, also in Gartree hundred, by a Gartree jury that included two constables.[61]

As we have seen, theoretically trial jurors were selected from knights and other men possessing at least £5 a year of landed income, although in practice 40*s*. was prescribed as a more realistic expecta-

57. The figure includes those named in the 1419 and 1423 lists.

58. John Ball (constable of Duffield), Robert Clerk (Melbourne), John Cook (Morley), John Jowdrell (Hartshorne), William Normanton (Horsley), and John Sherwynd (Hathersage). Four served as jurors in the year they were recorded as constables.

59. Those who served on three juries were John Janyn (Welham), John Russell (Kibworth Harcourt), John Symmes (Galby), and John Thorpe (Cranoe). Those who served twice were John Boudon (Great Stretton), John Brown (Ibstock), Thomas Collinson (Gumley), John Jeffs (Foston), William Goodfellow (Hallaton), William Harcourt (Bruntingthorpe), and John Hardwin (Whitwick).

60. JUST 3/31/14, m. 10, JUST 3/203, m. 43. See above, Table 4.2. The four constables were Thomas Collinson (Gumley), Robert Polle (Kibworth Harcourt), John Russell (Kibworth Harcourt), and John Merchant (Kibworth Beauchamp). The offenses took place at Harborough, Gumley, Foxton, and Kibworth.

61. JUST 3/31/20, m. 3; JUST 3/203, m. 40. The constables were William Goodfellow (Hallaton) and John Thorpe (Cranoe).

tion.[62] The results from the shires studied reveal that the "county gentry"—the leading knightly and armigerous families, who filled the offices of sheriff, justice of the peace, and shire-knight—rarely staffed trial juries unless the defendant was himself a gentleman.[63] Any attempt to enforce the £5 qualification might nonetheless involve those on the lower fringes of the gentry,[64] and the appearance on juries of several coroners and tax collectors certainly suggests the active participation of some lesser gentlemen.[65]

The data from Leicestershire and Warwickshire are insufficient to attempt an estimate of the levels of gentry representation on juries in those counties, but for Derbyshire such an attempt is worthwhile owing to the coincidence of full returns from the 1431 tax subsidy and the 1434 oath against lawbreakers, and the recent appearance of a detailed study of Derbyshire gentry in the fifteenth century.[66] Jurors are assumed to have been gentry if they were styled esquire, armiger, or gentleman; if they served as coroners or tax collectors; if they took the 1434 oath; if they are included in Dr. Wright's list of Derbyshire gentry;[67] or any combination of these. The results of this admittedly rough-and-ready assessment are summarized in Table 4.6. They suggest that nearly 60 percent of jurors who served twice or more, and nearly 30 percent of those who served once only, were of gentle status, or 35 percent of jurors overall.

Such figures should be treated with great caution. Derbyshire jurors may in any case have been of a higher-than-average social status because of the restricted nature of jury service in the county. What can perhaps be said with safety is that an appreciable number of trial jurors were drawn from the lower ranks of the gentry. The remainder were presumably yeomen and prosperous husbandmen.[68]

62. See above, text at n. 27.

63. The jury that acquitted William Rolleston, gentleman, of asportation of goods at Derby in 1414 included Avery Longford, Ralph Francis, Thomas Okeover, Henry Bradshaw, and Robert Sacheverell. JUST 3/56/9, mm. 6–7; JUST 3/195, m. 61d.

64. M. J. Bennett, *Community, Class and Careerism* (Cambridge, 1983), 83; S. M. Wright, *The Derbyshire Gentry in the Fifteenth Century* (Chesterfield, 1983), 4–6.

65. See Table 4.5. Wright, *Derbyshire Gentry*, 4; N. Saul, *Knights and Esquires. The Gloucestershire Gentry in the Fourteenth Century* (Oxford, 1981), 141–45. The minimum property qualification for a coroner was probably £5 a year. R. F. Hunnisett, *The Medieval Coroner* (Cambridge, 1961), 176.

66. *Feudal Aids, 1284–1431* (1899–1921) 1: 272–310 (1431 tax returns); *CPR, 1429–36*, pp. 410–13 (1434 oath); Wright, *Derbyshire Gentry*, appendix I.

67. Wright, *Derbyshire Gentry*, appendix I.

68. The status of seventeen Derbyshire jurors who were not gentlemen has been established, of whom twelve were yeomen and five were husbandmen.

Table 4.6. Derbyshire Jurors of Gentle Status

	Jurors Serving Twice or More	Jurors Serving Once Only	Total
Styled esquire or armiger	5	10	15
Styled gentleman	9	5	14
Took 1434 oath	10	17	27
Officeholders (coroners and tax collectors)	13	18	31
Appear in Wright, *Derbs. Gentry*, App. I	15	26	41
Total no. of gentry	28	45	73
Total no. of jurors	48	162	210
Percent gentry is of total no. of jurors	58%	28%	35%

SOURCES. See n. 66.

The general picture that emerges from this detailed study of Midland circuit trial jurors in the early fifteenth century may be summarized as follows. Except in the minority of cases where prisoners were tried individually or in pairs, the theory that defendants should be tried by jurors from the vicinity of the offense was rarely observed. Most juries were expected to try several cases at once, and their members were drawn indiscriminately from all parts of the shire. On the other hand, a significant minority of jurors in all counties served twice or more, and many had experience of other aspects of judicial administration, whether as officials—coroners, bailiffs, or constables—or as jurors at assizes, peace sessions, the sheriff's tourn, or special commissions of inquiry and oyer and terminer. Experience of this kind was most common among those who served more than once as trial jurors. Finally, the evidence from Derbyshire suggests that some jurors, perhaps a majority of those who served more than once, enjoyed gentry status.

The most significant conclusion to emerge is that by 1400 the selection of trial jurors at gaol delivery was determined at least as much by status and administrative experience as by geographical proximity to the offense. The Midland evidence reveals a group of men in every county, at the fringes of the gentry and just below, who were regularly called upon to fulfill a variety of minor judicial duties and without whose cooperation the machinery of royal justice in the shires would have ceased to function. By no means all jurors fell into this group,[69] but the numbers and experience of those who did must have exercised a decisive influence in most jury deliberations.

What implications, then, do these findings carry for the character and development of the criminal trial jury in the fifteenth century? How far did these Midland circuit juries conform to the medieval "self-informing" archetype? Clearly the efficacy of the self-informing jury, whose members came to court as witnesses, depended upon observance of the instruction contained in the judge's precept that jurors be drawn from the neighborhood of each offense. Once they ceased to be truly local, juries must have found insuperable difficulties in acquiring knowledge of crimes before they came to court. It strains credulity to suggest that jurors from every hundred in the county, faced with four or five equally widespread cases, would have been sufficiently well apprised of the circumstances of each before coming to court to render verdicts upon them without seeking further information. Our hypothesis must be that by the early fifteenth century the criminal trial jury was no longer self-informing in the accepted sense—if indeed it ever had been. The corollary is that evidence in some form must have been presented at the trial itself. The second part of this essay explores these points more fully in the context of a general consideration of criminal trial procedure in the late Middle Ages.

Before proceeding to such a consideration, however, it is necessary first to analyze the Midland circuit evidence for three further aspects of jury trial that are relevant to our discussion. These are the number, duration, and outcome of trials at gaol delivery.

Table 4.7 and Figures 4.1 through 4.3 indicate the total and average numbers of prisoners tried at gaol delivery at Nottingham (where Nottinghamshire as well as Derbyshire prisoners were tried on circuit), Leicester, and Warwick between 1400 and 1429. The numbers fluctuated widely between sessions. For example, whereas ninety-one prisoners were tried at Nottingham in July 1412 (thirty-five of them on a single indictment), only four were tried there in February 1429. A decline in the numbers delivered is evident in all counties during the 1420s; in Leicestershire and Warwickshire it is perceptible from 1415 onward. It is unlikely that this was the result of a falling crime rate; more likely an increasing proportion of felony trials was being determined before justices of the peace or under gaol delivery commissions

69. See Table 4.5.

Table 4.7. Numbers of Prisoners Delivered and Deliveries, 1400–1429

	Total No. of Prisoners Delivered	Total No. of Deliveries	Average No. Delivered per Session
Nottingham	1,493*	50	30
Leicester	503	46	11
Warwick	587	46	13

SOURCES: JUST 3/188, 195, 203.
* Includes both Nottinghamshire and Derbyshire prisoners

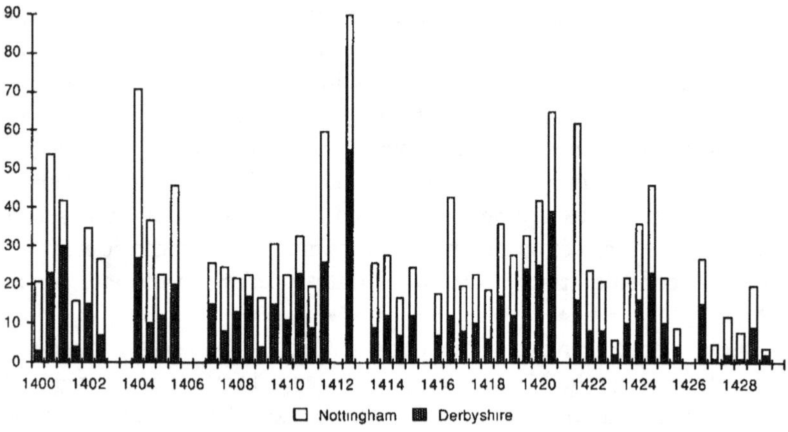

Figure 4.1. Number of Prisoners Delivered per Session at Nottingham Gaol, 1400–1429.

pro hac vice, perhaps to relieve the pressure of business on assize judges.

There is general agreement that before the beginning of the nineteenth century, criminal trials were extremely short and perfunctory,[70] and the Midland evidence offers little to contradict that view. At Leicester and Warwick it was common for ten or more prisoners to be arraigned at a time, and at Nottingham twenty or more. It is im-

70. Cockburn, *Assizes*, 109–11; J. H. Baker, "Criminal Courts and Procedure at Common Law, 1550–1800," in *Crime in England, 1550–1800*, ed. J. S. Cockburn (1977), 37–38; R. B. Pugh, "The Duration of Criminal Trials in Medieval England," in *Law, Litigants and the Legal Profession*, ed. E. W. Ives and A. H. Manchester (1983), 104–15.

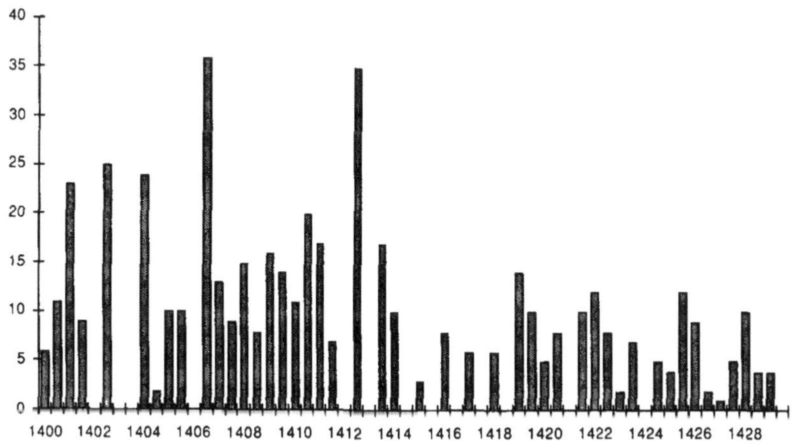

Figure 4.2. Number of Prisoners Delivered per Session at Leicester Gaol, 1400–1429.

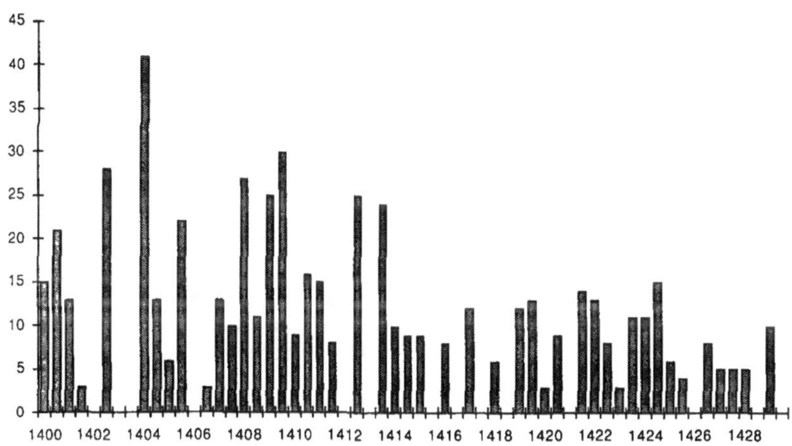

Figure 4.3. Number of Prisoners Delivered per Session at Warwick Gaol, 1400–1429.

possible to say with any precision how long trials lasted on average, since we do not know the length of the judges' working day, the exact duration of their stay in each county town on the circuit, or the amount of time taken up by assize, nisi prius, and other business. We do know that all business in each county was completed before the circuit judges in two days at most, and if half that time was devoted to gaol delivery, trials can rarely have taken as much as an hour, and they frequently must have taken much less time than this.

Tables 4.8 through 4.16 summarize the results of trials at gaol delivery in the three counties between 1400 and 1429. In many respects the figures tell a familiar story. Larceny was, as ever, the staple of gaol delivery business. The consistently high overall rates of acquittal—70 percent in Derbyshire, 71 percent in Leicestershire, and 74 percent in Warwickshire—are in line with existing studies.[71] As Green's work leads us to expect, indictments for murder produced the highest rates

Table 4.8. Outcome of Trials of Derbyshire Prisoners, 1400–1429

	Confessed	Convicted	Acquitted	Pardoned	Pardoned & Acquitted	Indictment Insufficient	Approver	Stood Mute	Sine Die	Other	Total
Murder	0	8	4	1	3	0	0	0	0	0	16
Homicide	0	0	13	15	0	3	0	0	0	0	31
Robbery	0	16	72	3	0	4	4	1	0	0	100
Larceny	1	66	234	11	2	6	3	1	0	0	324
Rape	0	0	48	1	0	0	0	0	0	0	49
Accessory	0	1	62	2	0	17	0	0	18	0	100
Miscellaneous	0	2	16	1	0	1	0	0	0	2	22
Total	1	93	449	34	5	31	7	2	18	2	642

SOURCES: JUST 3/188, 195, 203.

Table 4.9. Outcome of Derbyshire Trials, by Percentage, 1400–1429

	Convicted (%)	Acquitted (%)	Pardoned (%)	Other (%)	Total No. in Sample
Murder	50	25	6	19	16
Homicide	0	42	48	10	31
Robbery	16	72	3	9	100
Larceny	20	72	3	4	324
Rape	0	98	2	0	49
Accessory	1	62	2	35	100
Miscellaneous	9	73	5	14	22
All crimes above	15	70	5	10	642

SOURCES: JUST 3/188, 195, 203.

71 J. B. Given, *Society and Homicide in Thirteenth-Century England* (Stanford, 1977), 91–105; Green, *Verdict According to Conscience*, 32, 59–60.

of conviction, the contrast with homicide being particularly marked in Derbyshire and Leicestershire.[72] There are two areas, however, in which the figures provide unexpected results, and both are worthy of consideration for the light they may throw on the nature of jury trial at gaol delivery. These are the outcome of trials on indictments for rape and the contrasting pattern of verdicts on charges brought by appeal as against indictment.

Not a single person was convicted of rape out of nearly 280 indicted for the offense in the three counties between 1400 and 1429. This is a remarkable statistic even by medieval standards, and it raises the question of whether we should take the accusations at face value. Were all of them genuinely brought for violent sexual assault or ab-

Table 4.10. Outcome of Derbyshire Trials on Appeal and Indictment, 1400–1429

		Convicted	Acquitted	Pardoned	Default	Other	Total
Appeals	No.	49	6	0	4	0	59
	%	83	10	0	7	0	100
Indictments	No.	44	439	34	0	66	583
	%	8	75	6	0	11	100

SOURCES: JUST 3/188, 195, 203

Table 4.11. Outcome of Trials of Leicestershire Prisoners, 1400–1429

	Confessed	Convicted	Acquitted	Pardoned	Pardoned & Acquitted	Indictment Insufficient	Approver	Stood Mute	Sine Die	Other	Total
Murder	1	6	12	2	1	0	0	1	0	0	23
Homicide	0	0	24	23	0	1	0	0	0	0	48
Robbery	0	8	20	3	0	0	1	0	0	0	32
Larceny	0	46	139	9	0	1	2	0	0	2	199
Rape	0	0	113	1	0	1	0	0	0	0	115
Accessory	0	1	28	3	0	1	0	0	29	0	62
Miscellaneous	0	2	21	2	0	0	0	0	0	1	26
Total	1	63	357	43	1	4	3	1	29	3	505

SOURCES: JUST 3/188, 195, 203.

72. Green, *Verdict According to Conscience*, 33–34.

Table 4.12. Outcome of Leicestershire Trials, by Percentage, 1400–1429

	Convicted (%)	Acquitted (%)	Pardoned (%)	Other (%)	Total No. in Sample
Murder	26	52	9	13	23
Homicide	0	50	48	2	48
Robbery	25	63	9	3	32
Larceny	23	70	5	3	199
Rape	0	98	1	1	115
Accessory	2	45	5	48	62
Miscellaneous	8	80	8	4	26
All crimes above	13	71	9	8	505

Sources: JUST 3/188, 195, 203.

Table 4.13. Outcome of Leicestershire Trials on Appeal and Indictment, 1400–1429

		Convicted	Acquitted	Pardoned	Default	Other	Total
Appeals	No.	31	0	0	0	0	31
	%	100	0	0	0	0	100
Indictments	No.	32	357	43	0	42	474
	%	7	75	9	0	9	100

Sources: JUST 3/188, 195, 203.

duction? Our suspicions are further raised by the large number of clergy indicted for rape—14 out of 49 accused in Derbyshire, 50 out of 115 in Leicestershire, and 80 out of 114 in Warwickshire—which suggests that in many cases the true offense was clerical fornication or adultery in breach of the vow of celibacy. This is confirmed by the case of Ralph Taillour, chaplain of Moreton in Warwickshire, who was indicted for rape at the sheriff's tourn and tried at gaol delivery in 1427 because he kept a concubine, Alice Begger, in defiance of an order from the bishop of Worcester to remove her from his house.[73] This cannot have been an isolated instance. Among the *gravamina* of the clergy of the province of Canterbury presented to Archbishop Arundel in the convocation of 1411, there was a demand that clergy accused of adultery or fornication should not be indicted for rape before the king's judges like common thieves, without the consent of the ordi-

73. JUST 3/203, m. 49.

Table 4.14. Outcome of Trials of Warwickshire Prisoners, 1400–1429

	Confessed	Convicted	Acquitted	Pardoned	Indictment Insufficient	Approver	Sine Die	Other	Total
Murder	1	12	20	0	0	0	0	0	33
Homicide	0	4	13	7	0	0	0	0	24
Robbery	0	9	25	0	0	1	0	1	36
Larceny	1	51	192	2	3	1	0	0	250
Rape	0	0	111	1	2	0	0	0	114
Accessory	0	0	28	3	3	0	26	0	60
Miscellaneous	0	0	20	6	5	2	0	1	34
Total	2	76	409	19	13	4	26	2	551

SOURCES JUST 3/188, 195, 203.

Table 4.15. Outcome of Warwickshire Trials, by Percentage, 1400–1429

	Convicted	Acquitted	Pardoned	Other	Total No. in Sample
Murder	36	61	0	3	33
Homicide	17	54	29	0	24
Robbery	25	69	0	6	36
Larceny	20	77	1	2	250
Rape	0	97	1	2	114
Accessory	0	47	5	48	60
Miscellaneous	0	59	18	23	34
All crimes above	14	74	3	9	551

SOURCES. JUST 3/188, 195, 203.

naries.[74] There can be little doubt that indictment for rape at peace sessions or the sheriff's tourn was being used as a popular expression of disapproval of clergy who broke their vows of celibacy. By implication, of course, the practice also reflected dissatisfaction with the failure of the ecclesiastical courts to take action in the matter. It is possible that rape indictments were used in a similar way against laymen who had committed adultery.

74. Lambeth Palace Lib., Register of Archbishop Thomas Arundel, vol. 2, fol. 23v.

Table 4.16. Outcome of Warwickshire Trials on Appeal and Indictment, 1400–1429

		Convicted	Acquitted	Pardoned	Default	Other	Total
Appeals	No.	23	3	0	1	0	27
	%	85	11	0	4	0	100
Indictments	No.	53	405	19	0	47	524
	%	10	77	4	0	9	100

SOURCES: JUST 3/188, 195, 203.

In such circumstances, which must have produced many but, of course, not all of the indictments for rape, there can have been no question of conviction. The punishment lay in the inconvenience and humiliation of indictment and arraignment. The trial itself was a formality and a foregone conclusion. Criminal trial procedure was thus being used by local society in a sophisticated manner as a formal sanction against sexual impropriety. The point is an important one because it establishes that a sizable proportion of defendants at gaol delivery were, strictly speaking, not accused felons at all.[75]

The second distinctive feature of the figures on trial verdicts is the marked contrast in results between cases brought by appeal and those brought by indictment.[76] Whereas cases brought on indictment show the usual high levels of acquittal, those brought on appeal show very high levels of conviction. In Derbyshire 83 percent of those arraigned on appeal were convicted and only 10 percent were acquitted, as against 8 percent convicted and 75 percent acquitted on indictment. In Leicestershire there was a remarkable 100 percent conviction rate on appeal as against the 7 percent convicted and 75 percent acquitted on indictment. In Warwickshire 85 percent were convicted and 11 percent acquitted on appeal, 10 percent convicted and 77 percent acquitted on indictment. The numbers of those appealed were certainly small—59 in Derbyshire, 31 in Leicestershire, and 27 in Warwickshire—but because of the sharp distinctions between the proportions of those convicted and those acquitted, the results cannot be dismissed as statistically insignificant. In Derbyshire those arraigned on appeal accounted for only 9 percent of those accused but 53 percent of those convicted; in Leicestershire the figures are 6 percent and 49 percent, and in Warwickshire, 5 percent and 30 percent, respectively.[77]

75. See below, text at n 111.

76. See Tables 4.10, 4.13, and 4.16.

77. Most of those appealed were charged with larceny. In Derbyshire, 44

Why should the difference of procedure have had such an effect upon the outcome of trials, especially given the notorious reluctance of medieval juries to convict? One answer may be that appeals were brought only in cases where the defendant's guilt was so manifest as to guarantee conviction, thereby minimizing the financial risk to the appellor of a false appeal. On the other hand, the correlation between procedure and outcome is so strong as to suggest that part of the explanation lies in the nature of the appeal itself—the presence of the victim or his kin in court as the accuser, in direct confrontation with the accused. Once more this raises the central question of criminal trial procedure and the means whereby evidence was presented to the jury.

The continued use of the private criminal appeal in the fifteenth century provides a valuable reminder of the double-sided character of medieval criminal law. The perpetrator of a felony had committed a twofold offense—against his victim and against the king, for breach of his peace—and might be prosecuted in two distinct and independent ways: at the suit of the party by appeal, and at the suit of the Crown by indictment. Royal pardons explicitly safeguarded the rights of the appellor,[78] and in cases of homicide the appeal continued to take precedence in procedural terms over indictment.[79]

Procedure by appeal provides unequivocal evidence of the active role played by the private accuser in bringing felons to justice. As we have seen, however, appeals provided the mode of prosecution in only a small minority of cases. Indictment was the norm, where the role played in the prosecution by the victim and his or her kin is almost entirely concealed from view. Later evidence suggests that in the sixteenth century it was very important, and in the exploration of trial procedure that follows I argue that the role of the private accuser, long neglected by historians, provides a key to an understanding of the workings of the criminal jury in the late Middle Ages.

---

were appealed of larceny, 12 of robbery, and 3 of murder. In Leicestershire, 21 were appealed of larceny, 6 of robbery, 3 of murder or homicide, and 1 of accessory to murder. In Warwickshire, 14 were appealed of larceny, 6 of murder or homicide, 5 of robbery, 1 of rape, and 1 of accessory to murder.

78. E.g., C 67 (Patent Rolls, Supplementary)/37, m. 60 (general pardon of 1414), Smith, *De Republica*, 125.

79. Trial proceedings upon homicide indictments were deferred for a year after the offense in order to allow the victim's kin to sue by appeal if they chose. A. Fitzherbert, *La Graunde Abridgement* (1577), Corone, pl. 4, citing a Year Book of 1482. The rule was observed on the Midland circuit in the early fifteenth century. See JUST 3/56/13, mm. 13, 17, 31/6, m. 1; 52/22, mm. 2–3.

On the basis of the Midland circuit evidence analyzed above, I suggested that in the early fifteenth century, trial juries could not have been truly self-informing in the sense that they came to court already apprised of the facts of the cases they were to try.[80] That is not to say that no juror had any knowledge of the facts and personalities involved, but rather that it was not sufficient for them to arrive at a verdict without further evidence. Information must therefore have been presented to them in some form during the course of the trial.

A prime source was, of course, the defendants themselves. They replied to the charges against them and the judge's examination unaided by defense counsel, and the plausibility of their denials, as well as their general demeanor, must have weighed heavily with the jury.[81] For obvious reasons, many defendants probably contributed little to the jurors' knowledge except to deny any involvement in the offense. Occasionally, though, sensational disclosures might be made. At the Leicester Lent assizes in 1419, Margery, widow of John Chaloner, appealed two men of the murder of her husband. They were both convicted, but Margery herself was immediately appealed of the same murder by Chaloner's brother, John Smith, and she was convicted. Margery's part in her husband's death must have been revealed by her former accomplices.[82]

Defendants aside, there were two other possible sources of evidence for the jury in court: (1) the victim or the victim's kin and other witnesses for the Crown; and (2) royal officials such as justices of the peace, coroners, and constables. Sir Thomas Smith's description of criminal trial procedure at gaol delivery, written in 1565, leaves no doubt as to the victim's importance to the prosecution:

> The Judge first after they [the jurors] be sworne, asketh first the partie robbed, if he knowe the prisoner, and biddeth him looke upon him: he saith yea, the prisoner sometime saith nay. The party pursuivant giveth good ensignes *verbi gratia*, I knowe the well ynough, thou robbest me in such a place, thou beatest mee, thou tookest my horse from mee, and my purse, thou hadst then such a coate and such a man in thy companie: the theefe will say no, and so they stand a while in altercation.[83]

80. See above, text at nn. 68–69.

81. Baker, "Criminal Courts," 36–38; Green, *Verdict According to Conscience*, 134–38.

82. JUST 3/195, m. 72d.

83. *De Republica*, 114.

The expectation in the mid sixteenth century, therefore, was that the injured party would act as accuser and leading witness for the prosecution, and the "altercation" between accuser and accused must have been of crucial importance in shaping the jury's verdict. Is there reason to believe that this was already the expectation a century and a half before Smith wrote?

Perhaps the most telling evidence is that the sixteenth-century reform of criminal procedure took for granted the existence of the private prosecutor. The Marian committal statute was predicated upon the assumption that too often private parties who made accusations failed to discharge their duty to follow them up in court. In Langbein's words, "[I]t transformed the role of the private accuser from option to obligation" by instructing the justice of the peace to bind him over by recognizance to give evidence at the trial.[84] This legislation is a classic example of the phenomenon elucidated by Professor Milsom whereby limited and conservative measures have unforeseen and far-reaching consequences.[85] The purpose of the Marian statutes was thus to make the traditional system of criminal prosecution operate according to its own assumptions by attempting to ensure that private accusers did not default on their obligation to appear in court to substantiate charges previously made before the justices of the peace.[86] In other words, late-medieval prosecutorial procedure relied upon the testimony in court of the accuser, who was usually the victim or the victim's kin.

What evidence is there specifically from the late Middle Ages to confirm this line of argument? There is explicit reference to the private accuser in the judge's precept to the sheriff ordering preparations for gaol delivery.[87] The sheriff was instructed to make proclamation throughout the county summoning all those who wished to prosecute prisoners about to be delivered.[88] A similar procedure was followed when criminal cases from the court of King's Bench were referred nisi

84. Langbein, "Public Prosecution," 322.

85. S.F.C. Milsom, *The Legal Framework of English Feudalism* (Cambridge, 1976).

86. My views on the causes of the Marian statutes therefore differ from Langbein's. Where he sees them as the product of "the growing inability of the jury to inform itself" (*Prosecuting Crime*, 22), my hypothesis is that they resulted from the frequent failure of the private accuser to appear in court to inform the jury.

87. See above, n. 24.

88. Ibid. The sheriff was ordered to proclaim that "omnes illi qui versus huiusmodi prisones prosequi voluerint, quod tunc sint ibidem versus eos prout justum fuerit prosecuturi si sibi viderunt expediri."

prius to the assizes. In 1419, for example, when the trial of Richard Hillay on an indictment for murder was passed to the Derby assizes, public proclamation was made, as was customary, that if anyone wished to prosecute, accuse, or give information on the matter on the king's behalf to the jurors, then he should come forward.[89] On that occasion no one came forward, but the proclamation did occasionally meet a response, as happened twice within a year at the Lincoln assizes on the Midland circuit. At the summer assizes in 1419, a group of merchants led by Nicholas Blackburn of York was tried at nisi prius for price fixing. In answer to the call for information on the king's behalf, William Babington, a king's sergeant, came forward to allege that the jury had been impaneled in Blackburn's favor by the undersheriff.[90] In the following February at the Lent assizes in Lincoln a certain John Fleet offered to give evidence for the king at the trial at nisi prius of Simon Manfeld of Navenby, gentleman, for receiving robbers.[91] The proclamation for evidence on the king's behalf appears to have been customary, too, in non-criminal cases to which the Crown was party. In 1406 it was made *prout moris est* at an inquest into the grant of lands in Gloucestershire made by John Holland, late earl of Huntingdon, to John Boteler and others. John Deerhurst appeared and gave evidence for the king.[92]

There can be no doubt, then, that witnesses and informants were sought in Crown proceedings. The customary proclamation may provide the basis for the single rule of evidence cited in Staunford's *Les Plees del Coron*: "anyone may be admitted to give evidence for the king."[93] It is harder to find incontrovertible proof from the fifteenth century that those who appeared for the Crown in proceedings upon indictment included the victim of the offense concerned, who was thus effectively acting in the manner Smith described, as both accuser and witness.[94] There is, however, an extraordinarily interesting case

89. KB 27/631, Rex m. 5. ". . . facta publica proclamacione prout moris est si quis pro domino Rege prosequi, calumpniare aut informare sciret vel vellet dictos juratos super infracontentis, quod tunc veniret ibidem eosdem juratos pro dicto domino Rege inde plenius informand'."

90. KB 27/634, Rex m. 33. The jury acknowledged the truth of the accusation and was dismissed.

91. KB 27/635, Rex m. 2d: " . . . quidam Johannes de Flete asserit se pro domino Rege in premissis informare. Super quo in presencia eiusdem Johannis processum est ad capcionem inquisicionis predicte." Manfeld was acquitted.

92. *Calendar of Inquisitions Miscellaneous, 1399–1422,* no. 325.

93. Baker, "Criminal Courts," 39; also, see Langbein, *Prosecuting Crime,* 122.

94. See above, text at n. 83.

from 1461 that shows the victim of a crime acting in exactly that capacity. Richard Hayward was on his way to King's Bench in Trinity term of that year to prosecute on the king's behalf John Young of London, who had been indicted for a robbery (or theft) committed against Hayward.[95] He was accosted in Westminster Hall by John Davy, who assaulted him there while the courts of Chancery and Common Pleas were in session and threatened him with death if he gave evidence to secure Young's conviction.[96] Davy confessed to this offense and was condemned to perpetual imprisonment and to amputation of his right hand for violent contempt in the face of the court. It is only in unusual circumstances of this kind, where the record reveals procedural details that are normally omitted, that we see the victim-prosecutor at work in Crown criminal proceedings in the fifteenth century. There is nothing about the case, however, to suggest that Hayward's role was in any way exceptional.

The second possible source of evidence to inform the jury in court lay with officials involved in the processes of arrest and indictment—justices of the peace, coroners, bailiffs, and constables. The judge's precept ordered the sheriff to summon all justices of the peace, coroners, and hundred-bailiffs to be present at gaol delivery with their rolls and memoranda, and to submit a list of those summoned to him at the sessions.[97] Many such lists of officials survive in the gaol delivery files, and they record the attendance or non-attendance of bailiffs (though unfortunately not of justices of the peace and coroners) with pricks and crosses respectively.[98] It is likely that the most conscientious, "working" justices of the peace attended gaol delivery sessions, since peace sessions were often held at the same time as assizes.[99] We

95. KB 27/801, Rex m. 3. ". . . ad prosequend' pro ipso Rege versus Johannem Yonge nuper de London, dyker, de feloniis indictatum pro roberia ipsius Ricardi Hayward per prefatum Johannem eidem Ricardo facta." See J. H. Baker, "Le Brickbat Que Narrowly Mist," *Law Quarterly Review* 100 (1984) 545

96. Davy said he would kill Hayward, " . . si idem Ricardus . . . aliquam evidenciam aut materiam versus prefatum Johannem Yong ad barram in curiam predictam coram prefato Rege presentem pro convictione sue feloniarum predictarum . . dederit sive declareret." KB 27/801, Rex m. 3.

97. See above, n 24

98. E.g., JUST 3/56/12, mm. 1d, 3d, 7d; 56/13, m. 1; 31/7, m. 3; 67/11, m. 5. Bailiffs were fined for non-attendance. See E 101 (Exchequer, Accounts Various)/667/15.

99. *Proceedings*, ed. Putnam, lxxxvii, Powell, "Public Order and Law Enforcement," 123–28. At the Lent assizes at Northampton in 1419, for example, the senior assize judge, John Cockayne, delivered the gaol with Thomas Waldeby on 3 March and held peace sessions with the local working justice of the peace, Thomas Billing, on 4 March. JUST 3/52/20; JUST 3/195, m. 92; KB 9/83, m 11

have also seen that some coroners frequently appeared at gaol delivery as trial jurors, and those who did not were probably present when prisoners were being tried on homicide indictments taken before them.[100] All four Warwickshire coroners were present at the Lent assizes in 1415, when they were examined by the judges to verify a claim made by the Warwick gaoler that a prisoner had died in custody.[101] It is likely that in the course of taking indictments and making arrests, these officials became well acquainted with the facts of most cases and with the parties involved. Justices of the peace in particular might have examined the defendant and his accuser before committal, as was the practice in the sixteenth century, although as yet they had, of course, no statutory obligation to record the examination in writing.

Sir Thomas Smith emphasized the role of the village constables in making arrests and giving evidence at gaol delivery, and this accords with what we know of their medieval functions.[102] Some coroners' rolls record the committal of accused slayers to the custody of the constable until the next gaol delivery, usually in cases of self-defense.[103] The judge's precept ordered the sheriff to summon four men and the reeve of each township where an offender had been arrested.[104] We have no means of knowing whether this was still observed in the fifteenth century, but what we know of jury composition makes it seem unlikely. It is clear, however, that in cases of arrest on suspicion, representatives of the township concerned, presumably the constables, were expected to appear and the townships were amerced if they did not.[105] Constables must therefore have appeared often at gaol delivery, providing an important source of evidence concerning the offense and the arrest which was more disinterested than that of the victim or the accused. A coroner's indictment from Leicestershire in 1379 illustrates the point. Thomas Randolf of Braunstone was indicted for slaying John Sherman in self-defense. Randolf found Sher-

100. See above, n. 44. Two Nottinghamshire coroners, Peter Strelley and Ralph Bingham, appeared as trial jurors at the summer assizes in 1423, when both had indictments on the calendar. JUST 3/56/21, mm. 17–19.

101. JUST 3/195, m 84d.

102. *De Republica*, 107, 109–10, 113. See above, text at n. 54.

103. E.g., JUST 2 (Coroners' Rolls)/52, mm. 2, 3d (1366); 58, mm. 1, 9 (1377, 1379).

104. See above, n. 24.

105. E.g., JUST 3/56/10, m. 6, where the township of Norwell, Nottinghamshire, was amerced for nonappearance. The estreats roll for the Western circuit for 1459–60 records the amercement of several townships for nonappearance. E 101/667/15.

man lurking outside his house at night and challenged him; Sherman assaulted Randolf, who struck him with a stick in self-defense, overpowered him, and took him to the house of the constable of Braunstone for custody until daylight. Later Sherman died of his wounds, and Randolf gave himself up to the constable's custody until the next gaol delivery.[106] What would have been more obvious than for the judge to examine the constable of Braunstone on the case when he brought Randolf to court, just as Sir Thomas Smith describes for the sixteenth century?[107]

In summary, my hypothesis is that in the fifteenth century, trial juries were not usually self-informing but relied upon the presentation of evidence in court, most probably by the private accuser and by the officers of the law. Apart from the requirement of written examinations by justices of the peace laid down in the Marian statutes, procedure was very similar to that described by Smith in the mid sixteenth century.

If this hypothesis is accepted, it still remains to account for the very high levels of acquittal on prosecution by indictment, which averaged 70 percent or more in the counties examined.[108] Green explained similar levels of acquittal during the thirteenth and fourteenth centuries through the workings of the self-informing jury.[109] He argued that because the trial juries were the source of practically all evidence, they were able systematically to nullify the law of felony, that is, to acquit those who were technically guilty of felony but whom the community did not regard as deserving of the death penalty. But if evidence was presented openly in court by the early fifteenth century, such manipulation would have been far more difficult, if not impossible. Why then were acquittal rates so high?

There are probably several related reasons, turning on the nature of the offenses involved, the character of the prisoners who appeared, and the effectiveness, or otherwise, of criminal procedure. As to the first, the pattern of rape indictments is indicative. A substantial proportion of rape defendants were clergy, many of whom were probably guilty only of breach of celibacy, and rape indictments may have been used more widely as a sanction against sexual impropriety.[110] There

106. JUST 2/58, m. 1. Cf. Green, *Verdict According to Conscience*, 41–42. I have not been able to trace a trial enrollment for this offense.

107. *De Republica*, 113.

108. See Tables 4.10, 4.13, and 4.16.

109. *Verdict According to Conscience*, chaps. 1–3, esp. pp. 25–27.

110 See above, text at n. 75.

was thus an identifiable category of offender at gaol delivery who was not in fact being accused of felony and for whom conviction would have been entirely inappropriate.[111] This was an essentially tactical use of the machinery of criminal justice for secondary purposes.

It is highly likely that tactical indictments were commonly used in another way as well: to harass one's opponent as part of an overall strategy for the waging of disputes in and out of court. In such circumstances, indictments became an extension of civil litigation. A good example was the indictment of Ralph Huse, esquire, in Derbyshire for feloniously breaking into the close of Thomas Dethick at Dethick. Huse was acquitted at gaol delivery in 1420 and subsequently secured compensation by arbitration against Dethick for false indictment.[112] This was merely one incident in a long-running dispute between Huse and the Dethick family over the dower of Huse's wife, Margery, widow of Thomas's brother Robert.[113] Huse and Dethick were both substantial gentry, but their behavior was probably imitated lower down on the social scale. The huge number of larceny indictments, for example, may conceal cases arising from village disputes over the sale or ownership of goods and livestock. If that were so, it would partially explain the interesting phenomenon found by Professor Hanawalt that defendants at gaol delivery tended to come from the higher levels of village society.[114] Second, and related to the first point, I suggest that there was a category of defendants who came to court voluntarily because they were virtually certain of an exculpatory verdict or acquittal, although they had committed a felonious offense. This category is very much the same as that which Green saw as benefiting from jury nullification at an earlier period and may be typified as being comprised of people who slew feloniously but without true premeditation.[115] For such prisoners, the keys to escaping conviction were their refusal to flee after the offense, their standing in local society and the good opinion of their neighbors, and their readiness to make com-

111. Rape defendants totaled some 20 percent of all those tried in Leicestershire and Warwickshire and about 8 percent in Derbyshire.

112. JUST 3/195, m. 43d; KB 7/640, m. 12.

113. *Collections for a History of Staffordshire*, William Salt Archaeological Society, 17 (1896), 115, CP 40 (Court of Common Pleas, Plea Rolls)/616, m. 7d; 619, m. 122, 621, m. 136; JUST 4/8/2, m. 240. For another case of false indictment, see E. Powell, "Proceedings before the Justices of the Peace at Shrewsbury in 1414," *EHR* 99 (1984): 535–50

114. B. A Hanawalt, *Crime and Conflict in English Communities, 1300–1348* (Cambridge, Mass., 1979), 173–76.

115. Green, *Verdict According to Conscience*, 32–46.

pensation to the victim's kin.[116] All this could have been confirmed in court by witnesses and officials. In addition, there were probably many incidents in which the circumstances were by no means clear and where there was legitimate room for doubt as to the culpability of the accused, especially in cases of homicide, where the victims were not available to give their version of the events.[117]

The question of evidence must indeed have been of critical importance in determining trial jury verdicts. If the self-informing jury no longer explains the problem of high acquittal rates, the obvious answer is that juries acquitted not in the teeth of the evidence but for lack of it. When the presentation of evidence in court was inadequate, the prisoner enjoyed the benefit of the doubt. As Smith asserted in 1565: "If none come in to give evidence, although the malefactor hath confessed the crime to the Justice of the peace . . . the twelve men will acquite the prisoner. . . ."[118] The central figure here was the victim or private accuser, and the pivot of the trial was the "altercation" between accuser and accused. If the former failed to appear and prosecute, the case against the latter fell by default. This state of affairs no doubt occurred all too often, and it ultimately led to the Marian committal statute of 1555.[119]

No mention has yet been made of the role of one major protagonist in trial procedure—the judge himself. Once again the records offer very little direct evidence, but some assessment must be attempted if only because of the markedly contrasting images of the medieval and early-modern judge presented by Green and Cockburn respectively. Green sees the fourteenth-century judge as powerless against and frustrated by the wall of silence maintained against him by the defendant and the trial jury, a situation made possible by the total control over evidence enjoyed by the self-informing jury.[120] For Cockburn, working

116. According to R. B. Pugh, "When acquitting, [jurors] often said no more than that a suspect's character was good. He who had the reputation of *Fidelitas* must have had a flying start toward liberation." "Some Reflections of a Medieval Criminologist," *Proceedings of the British Academy* 59 (1973): 98, cited in Green, *Verdict According to Conscience*, 26. For a case of men acquitted on an appeal of homicide in King's Bench after providing compensation, see E. Powell, "The Settlement of Disputes by Arbitration in Fifteenth-Century England," *Law and History Review* 2 (1984): 27–28.

117. Green, *Verdict According to Conscience*, 25–26.

118. *De Republica*, 113.

119. See above, text at n. 86.

120. *Verdict According to Conscience*, 28–33, 66–69.

from sixteenth- and seventeenth-century evidence, the judge dominated all proceedings, constantly intervening and browbeating defendant and jurors alike.[121]

There can be no certainty as to which image corresponds more closely with the fifteenth-century reality, but if the hypothesis advanced in this essay is correct, it is probably the latter. Green's view of the judge depends upon the existence of the self-informing jury and assumes that trial juries regularly nullified the law of felony by concealing the true facts of cases from the judge.[122] If, as I have argued, evidence was heard in court in the fifteenth century, such a situation could not have arisen except where the private accuser failed to appear. Otherwise it is more likely that the judge came to know as much of the facts as the jury did and that verdicts of self-defense were returned on the basis of the evidence supplied in court. For example, self-defense may have been considered appropriate in cases where the accused was known to have committed the offense but where there had been no witnesses and it was thought that the slayer should be given the benefit of the doubt because of his or her general reputation and demeanor after the incident.[123] The relative social standing of slayer and victim may also have been an important consideration. The slayer who killed a social inferior was probably more likely to be allowed self-defense by the judge and jury than one who slew his social superior.[124] In such circumstances there is no reason why the judge should not have concurred wholeheartedly with the jury's verdict, or even have directed them to return it.

In practice, the attempts of trial juries to nullify the law of felony must have been of lesser concern to medieval assize judges than the corruption and inefficiency that pervaded the legal system.[125] Gaolers were repeatedly fined for allowing prisoners to escape. The Warwickshire coroner Richard Hall was fined in 1416 for failing to draft indictments correctly.[126] Hundred-bailiffs Thomas Craklawe of Warwickshire and John Buckby of Northamptonshire were fined for

121. *Assizes*, 109–10, 114, 122–23.

122. *Verdict According to Conscience*, chap. 2.

123. Homicide cases, of course, presented peculiar procedural difficulties related to the fact that the victim did not live to tell the tale.

124. The special category of petty treason existed, with particularly severe penalties, for servants who killed their masters, and wives their husbands.

125. Cockburn, *Assizes*, 104–9; Green, *Verdict According to Conscience*, 66–69.

126. JUST 3/67/10, m. 3.

concealment of the mainour taken from arrested thieves.[127] In February 1422 two trial jurors at the Worcester assizes were gaoled and fined for receiving food and drink after they had been sworn.[128] Non-attendance at sessions was also a serious problem. A complete roll of estreats from the Western circuit at the end of Henry VI's reign consists almost entirely of fines for non-attendance of jurors, bailiffs, and townships.[129] The main concerns of the judges at gaol delivery were probably to get through the calendar of prisoners as quickly and uneventfully as possible and to ensure the enforcement of the financial exactions accruing to the Crown from its jurisdiction over felony. Both financially and intellectually, criminal business was far less rewarding to men of law than the civil side of assize work.

The argument of this essay has been that in the early fifteenth century the criminal jury trial already bore a close resemblance in important respects to that of the late sixteenth century.[130] The trial jury was not usually self-informing but relied for its information upon the hearing of evidence in court. By 1400 the active "medieval" jury had begun to give way to the passive triers of the modern courtroom, and the fundamental changes in trial procedure that Green and Langbein saw as taking place in the two centuries before 1550 were well advanced.[131] To pursue the origins of these changes back into the fourteenth century and their consequences forward into the sixteenth is a task beyond the scope of this inquiry, but its wider implications warrant some concluding speculation.

In view of the findings presented here, it seems unlikely that the transition from the medieval to the modern jury was the product of a short period of rapid, revolutionary change. My suspicion is that crim-

127. JUST 3/67/12, m. 13 (1420); 52/21, m. 5 (1421). In 1424 Craklawe was indicted and acquitted for homicide "contra coronam et dignitatem domini Regis." JUST 3/68/4, m. 2; JUST 3/203, m. 50.

128. JUST 3/218/3, m. 36d.

129. E 101/667/15.

130. There can be no doubt that there were significant developments during the sixteenth century that must have influenced the conduct of criminal trials—for instance, the refinement of the criminal law, especially regarding homicide; the use of Star Chamber to investigate corrupt or recalcitrant juries; and the Marian statutes See Green, *Verdict According to Conscience*, 105–52. My contention is that the "altercation" between accuser and accused described by Sir Thomas Smith was as much the essence of the trial in the early fifteenth century as it was a century and a half later.

131. Green, *Verdict According to Conscience*, 112; Langbein, "Public Prosecution," 314.

inal trial juries were never entirely self-informing in the strict sense in which the term has been interpreted, and that even in the earliest days of jury trial, accusers and witnesses had the chance to inform the jury in court. Witnesses to felonies are known to have been summoned before the general eyre, and already by the end of the thirteenth century some juries lacked the local knowledge necessary to be truly self-informing.[132] For much of the medieval period, general acceptance of the self-informing character of the trial jury was probably accompanied by a recognition of the duty of accusers and witnesses to present their case in court on the king's behalf. The later history of criminal trial procedure reveals equally well the vigor with which the traditional prerogatives of the jury were defended long after it had ceased, in procedural terms, to be self-informing.[133] The development of the modern criminal trial was a centuries-long process marked more by gradual evolution than by sudden transformation.

Acknowledgments

I am grateful to Professor J. S. Cockburn, Professor T. A. Green, and Dr. J. B. Post for their constructive help and criticism in the writing of this essay.

132. C.A.F. Meekings, ed., *Crown Pleas of the Wiltshire Eyre, 1249*, Wiltshire Record Society, 16 (1961), 46, 103, 173, 217, 231; R.B. Pugh, ed., *Wiltshire Gaol Delivery and Trailbaston Trials, 1275–1306*, Wiltshire Record Society, 33 (1978), 17–20.

133. Green, *Verdict According to Conscience*, chaps. 5–8.

Five

Lawless Juries? The Composition and Behavior of Hertfordshire Juries, 1573–1624

P. G. Lawson

Historians of English criminal justice have long puzzled over the behavior of juries. In particular they have puzzled over the apparent willingness of juries to reach verdicts contrary to the law—what Roscoe Pound called "jury lawlessness."[1] Legal historians have seen this trait as one of the virtues of the common-law system. S.F.C. Milsom's view is typical: "So far as justice was done throughout the centuries, it was done by jurors and in spite of savage laws."[2] According to this view, juries were a force for moderation in the application of the criminal law, regularly overriding harsh legal codes to protect defendants from punishments that were seen as excessively severe.

The view expressed by Pound and Milsom is undoubtedly an attractive one, and it has recently surfaced in a particularly sophisticated form in the work of several historians who are primarily concerned to probe the social context of Tudor and Stuart criminal justice. Thus Cynthia Herrup suggests that in addition to the formal legal definitions of culpability, there existed in the seventeenth century an informal, religiously inspired, community-based set of definitions.[3] Joel Samaha argues in similar fashion, noting that the rule of law was "tempered to accommodate strong feelings in the community with respect to felony and its punishment."[4] These alternative definitions and community feelings shaped the activities of all who enforced the criminal law, from the victim to the judge. By implication, juries

1. "Law in Books and Law in Action," *American Law Review* 44 (1910): 18.

2. *Historical Foundations of the Common Law*, rev ed. (1981), 403.

3. "Law and Morality in Seventeenth-Century England," *Past and Present* 106 (1985). 102–23.

4. "Hanging for Felony: The Rule of Law in Elizabethan Colchester," *Historical Journal* 21 (1978): 763–82; also, see Green, *Verdict According to Conscience*, 125ff, 375ff

emerge as articulators of a widely shared body of norms that might limit, even contradict, the formal criminal law. Once again jury lawlessness appears as a force for moderation. But if one strand of recent research stresses the social context of criminal justice, a second stresses its procedural context, and the result is a rather different view of the behavior of Elizabethan and Jacobean juries. In his recent study of the court of assizes, J. S. Cockburn suggests that by its very nature trial procedure undercut the independence of juries and strengthened the position of the judge, thereby ensuring that the behavior of juries was in large part determined by the bench. He concludes that the prevailing form of criminal trial was one "in which the role of the jury was subordinate to and conditioned by the will of the assize bench."[5] By implication, jury lawlessness becomes at best a limited and superficial phenomenon, and at worst an illusion.

Although recent research on Elizabethan and Jacobean criminal justice yields differing, even contradictory, views of the forces that shaped jury behavior, the original observation seems valid: Whatever their origin and true significance, the symptoms of jury lawlessness are clearly apparent. Contemporary commentators insisted that the principal function of both grand and trial juries was the evaluation of evidence. The grand jury was required to evaluate prosecution evidence in support of each bill of indictment and to decide whether there was a case to answer; it was not necessary that the grand jurors be convinced of the truth of the case, but only that it was "meet" or "fit" to be brought to trial.[6] If a prisoner was indicted, the trial jury was required to hear the evidence presented by both the prosecutor and the prisoner, deciding, ultimately, if the latter was guilty as charged. The aim of the trial jury was thus slightly different from that of the grand jury, but the essence of its function was still the evaluation of evidence. John Lilburne might make wider claims on its behalf, arguing that trial jurors were not only judges of fact but judges of law, but most commentators disagreed.[7] Fitzherbert stated the ac-

5 *Assize Introduction*, 131–33.

6. Sir Matthew Hale, *Historia Placitorum Coronae: The History of the Pleas of the Crown*, ed. S. Emlyn, 2 vols. (1736), 2:157. See also Z. Babington, *Advice to Grand Jurors in Cases of Blood* (1677), 124–25; J. Cowell, *The Interpreter* (Cambridge, 1607), under "Jurie." Cf. John Hawles, *The Englishman's Right* (1680), 125.

7. On the attitudes of Lilburne and the Levellers to the trial jury, see T. B. Howell and T. J. Howell, eds., *Complete Collection of State Trials*, 24 vols. (1809–28), 5:444; Christopher Hill, "The Norman Yoke," in idem, *Puritanism and Revolution. Studies in Interpretation of the English Revolution of the Seventeenth Century* (New York, 1964), 76–77; Donald Veall, *The Popular Movement for Law Reform, 1640–1660* (Oxford, 1970), 100, 156–59.

cepted wisdom: "Our Jurers are not to Judge de Jure, but de facto, not of matter of Lawes, or right itself, but of matter of fact only." Trial jurors were reminded of this as they recited their oaths: "a true Verdict shall [you] give according to your Evidence."[8] But against contemporary prescriptions for proper jury behavior we must set the various indications that juries were not adhering to their assigned role. In the case of the grand jury we may note not only those indictments for property crime in which the charge was reduced but also contemporary complaints that they were doing much the same thing in homicide cases.[9] In the case of the trial jury, we may note, most obviously, the so-called "partial verdicts," for here was a widely recognized means by which jurors could ignore the evidence by simply reconstructing the facts of a case. But partial verdicts are not the only manifestation of the apparent refusal of trial juries to be bound by the evidence. Instances of judicial dissatisfaction with decisions other than partial verdicts and complaints that juries were willing to acquit against the evidence also point in this direction.[10]

But if jurors might adopt a flexible attitude toward the evidence, it is not necessarily true that they did so in response to a community-based set of norms somehow distinct from the criminal law. Such an argument is at risk of foundering on the very real difficulties involved in extracting from a society as highly stratified as Tudor and Stuart society a coherent "community" that is at once "popular" in nature but which can also accommodate the jurors. It will be part of the argument of this paper that far from being representative members of their communities, jurors occupied a position of importance within the early-modern structures of wealth and power—a position much closer

8. Thomas Fitzherbert, *A Defence of the Catholyke Cause* (1602), pt. 2, 12. T. W., *The Office of the Clerk of Assize . . .* (1682), 45; Bodleian Lib., Rawlinson MS. C 271, fol. 8.

9. For examples of altered indictments, see Hertfordshire Record Office (hereafter HRO), HAT SR5/27, 7/70, 8/21, 13/24, 16/38, 23/92, 28/152, 32/77; PRO, ASSI 35/39/3/12, 35/55/3/9. See also Cockburn, *Assize Introduction*, 52–53. On the powers of grand juries to alter indictments, see Michael Dalton, *The Countrey Justice* (1618), 229. For contemporary complaints, see C. Read, ed., *William Lambarde and Local Government: His "Ephemeris" and Twenty-nine Charges to Juries and Commissions* (Ithaca, 1962), 119–20; Hale, *Pleas*, 2:157–59, 162, Babington, *Advice*, "To the Reader," also pp. 67, 79–82, 94–95.

10. Judicial dissatisfaction with a jury verdict might be registered overtly through a decision to punish the jurors (see below, text at n. 95), or implicitly through a judgment that undercut, or at least modified, the effect of the verdict (see Cockburn, *Assize Introduction*, 115). See also Green, *Verdict According to Conscience*, 139–40. For contemporary complaints concerning the behavior of trial juries, see *Lambarde and Local Government*, ed. Read, 119–20, 171–72, 175–76; W. C. Abbott, ed., *The Writings and Speeches of Oliver Cromwell*, 4 vols. (Cambridge, Mass., 1937–47), 4:274.

to those who made the laws than to those who bore the brunt of their enforcement. This was the crucial feature of the social context of the jury system. As to its institutional context, there undoubtedly were aspects of the trial process that constrained the conduct of the jurors. Nonetheless, any attempt to make this the key to their behavior runs the risk of underestimating both their social position and the very real skills they brought to their task. In what follows it will be argued that these skills were sufficiently developed for jurors to be able to preserve a degree of practical independence, even in the face of an overbearing bench. Ultimately, the behavior of juries was shaped neither by procedural constraints nor by community-based definitions of right and wrong but by the logic of exemplary punishment. It was the need to make the message of the gallows as effective as possible which not only gave early-modern criminal justice its particular character but also shaped the behavior of its principal decision makers, including the jurors. Seen in this light, the signs and symptoms of jury lawlessness become symptoms of a deeper obedience, an obedience to the fundamental logic of the system itself.

In developing these arguments I have relied primarily on the quarter sessions rolls and assize indictment files belonging to the county of Hertfordshire.[11] These have been supplemented by formal accounts of trial procedure and descriptions of actual trials. The first group of accounts, although fairly full, is of limited value because the discussions are usually quite formal. The second, although potentially more useful, is especially sparse.[12] Possessing few direct descriptions of ju-

11. Hertfordshire's quarter sessions rolls commence in 1589 and survive almost unbroken until 1618. HRO, HAT SR1–32. The assize files begin in 1573, and although their survival is irregular for the first two decades of the series, thereafter they are fairly complete. PRO, ASSI 35/15/4–35/66/2.

12. Of the first group of accounts, I have relied primarily on the following: Bodleian Lib., Rawlinson MS. B. 257, fols. 77–78 ("The Style of the Sessions"); ibid., fols. 85–87v ("The holding of a Sessions in Sandwich"); Bodleian Lib., Rawlinson MS. C. 271, fols. 5–15 ("The Manner and forme of proceedings at the Assizes . . ."); BL, Lansdowne MS. 569, fols. 2–4v ("Instructions for Proceedings at the Sessions of the peace"); ibid., fols. 5–19 ("Manner and forme of proceedings"); B. C. Redwood, ed., *Quarter Sessions Order Book, 1642–49*, Sussex Record Society, 54 (1954), 210–14 ("Regule per Clericum ad Generalem Sessionem Pacis Observande"), M. Reed, ed., "The Keeping of Sessions of the Peace in the Borough of Hastings," *Sussex Archaeological Collections* 91 (1962): 55–59 ("Direccons to hold a Sessions for a Port"); Thomas Smith, *De Republica Anglorum* (1583), 75–84, *Clerk of Assize*, passim. As to the second group of accounts, it should be noted that while historians of criminal justice in the eighteenth century are able to draw on newspaper and pamphlet accounts of trials, these are quite rare before the 1670s. Most of the surviving pamphlets have little to say about trial procedure, being more concerned with the lurid details of the crime. As for the accounts contained in the various series of law reports, and among the "State Trials" (T. B. Howell and T. J. Howell, eds., *Complete Collection of State Trials*, 30

ries, the historian is forced to draw inferences about their character and behavior from the records they have left among the sessions rolls and assize files.

The qualities required for jury service were several. Legal commentators, of course, called for a degree of impartiality. But beyond this they noted several specific requirements. Of these the most important were the age qualification, the legal or moral qualification, the residential qualification, and the property qualification. According to the first of these, the juror was to be an adult but not in his dotage. Unfortunately, jury lists do not give the ages of the jurors. Although it may be assumed that most satisfied the basic requirement, it is difficult to answer the more interesting question of precisely at what stage in their lives most men served as jurors. The second requirement raises equally insoluble questions. Sheriffs were warned against nominating individuals who had a criminal record or who were suspected of any sort of wrongdoing; jurors were to be "legales homines."[13] It seems probable that most sheriffs approached this requirement with a degree of flexibility. None of Hertfordshire's jurors had been convicted of a felony, but several had been indicted for lesser offenses, such as riot and assault, and one grand juror, Thomas Kent, had been the subject of several complaints by women who had claimed he had molested them.[14] But in addition to formal legal wrongs, the moral qualification seems to raise the issue of general reputation. It may be assumed that jurors were supposed to be men of high repute within their own communities, but whether that was so is difficult to say.

During the medieval period the crucial qualification for jury service, and in particular for service on the trial jury, was the residential qualification. When jurors were assumed to have prior knowledge of an offense it was essential that they be drawn from the same neighborhood as the accused; only in this way could they furnish the evidence on which the verdict would be based.[15] In the late sixteenth cen-

vols. [1809–26]), these deal with cases that by their very nature were exceptional. They are therefore of only limited use. See also J. H. Langbein, "The Criminal Trial before the Lawyers," *University of Chicago Law Review* 45 (1978). 264–72; Green, *Verdict According to Conscience*, 106.

13. William Lambard, *Eirenarcha; or, Of the Office of the Justices of the Peace* (1581), 304–6; Michael Dalton, *Officium Vicecomitum: The Office and Authority of Sheriffs* (1662), 394ff; Hale, *Pleas*, 2:264.

14. HRO, HAT SR2/129.

15. J. G. Bellamy, *Crime and Public Order in England in the Later Middle Ages* (1973), 145–46.

tury the notion of "neighborhood" still figured in the formal residential qualification for service on both grand and trial juries. In the case of the grand jury, the sheriff was instructed to nominate only residents of the county. Beyond this it was emphasized that the grand jury ought to represent all parts of the county, with several members being selected from each hundred.[16] The few surviving sheriff's panels suggest that the recommended geographic balance was established at the start, among those nominated for service at both quarter sessions and assizes.[17] To some extent this balance was maintained among those finally chosen to serve, and again, each of the hundreds is usually represented. Nonetheless, a more detailed examination of the records suggests that the jurors from Hertford hundred worked harder than their colleagues. Residential information survives for 147 of the assize grand jurors who served between 1589 and 1618. Those of the jurors who resided outside Hertford hundred each attended an average of 4.7 times; in the case of the jurors who resided within Hertford hundred the average was 8.1.[18] Although it is less pronounced, a similar pattern can be detected among the members of the quarter sessions grand jury. In this case, residential information survives for 549 of the jurors who served between 1589 and 1618. Those who resided outside Hertford hundred each attended an average of 1.9 times, but for those who resided within Hertford hundred the average was 2.8.[19] The reasons for this bias are fairly clear. The town of Hertford was the usual venue for both assizes and quarter sessions, and it was therefore convenient to draw especially heavily on the local population.

Despite this bias toward Hertford, the composition of the two grand juries does reflect at least a degree of the prescribed residential characteristics. Much the same is true of the trial jury, although, again, only if the residential requirement is interpreted quite widely. Commentators continued to suggest that trial jurors should be chosen from the neighborhood in which the offense had occurred, from "the place where the question is moved."[20] Indeed, until the late seven-

16. *Clerk of Assize*, 15, 17.

17. See, for example, HRO, HAT SR27/27, 63, 105, 140; SR28/41, 105, 211; SR29/80, 195, 219; SR30/30, SR31/46; SR32/84. PRO, ASSI 35/37/3/2; 35/42/4/26; 35/44/3/31; 35/46/1/74; 35/47/1/70; 35/47/2/28; 35/48/1/28; 35/48/2/25, 35/49/4/1; 35/52/4/37; 35/54/3/90. See also Cockburn, *Assize Introduction*, 45.

18. This analysis is based on PRO, ASSI 35/32/3–35/60/3; HRO, HAT SR1/65, 98; SR2/36; SR6/171, SR7/115; SR9/92; SR10/139 (grand jury lists).

19. This analysis is based on HRO, HAT SR1–32 (grand jury lists).

20. Hale, *Pleas*, 2.262–64; Lambard, *Eirenarcha*, 305; Dalton, *Office and*

teenth century some commentators assumed that jurors retained at least a portion of their medieval role as witnesses.[21] Nonetheless, by the late sixteenth century, residence in the county was the only absolute requirement.[22] Moreover, the limited evidence provided by the jury lists suggests that there was little correspondence between the parish in which an offense occurred and the parishes in which the jurors resided. Three of the surviving lists of assize trial jurors contain residential information, and the last of these is both typical and fairly complete. It describes a trial jury that sat at Hertford assizes in March 1615 and that heard five different cases.[23] These cases had diverse beginnings; they originated in four different parishes that were located in three different hundreds. The origins of the jurors were equally diverse. Of the ten whose residences are given, all came from different parishes, and those parishes were divided among five different hundreds. But more important, not a single juror came from a parish in which one of the offenses had occurred, nor even from an adjacent parish. Indeed, six of the ten jurors did not even come from one of the three relevant hundreds. Whatever legal commentators thought about the role of the jury in the early-modern criminal trial, the simple facts of geography would seem to contradict the suggestion that its members might still be, in any meaningful sense, self-informing.

Despite the past importance of the residential qualification, by the late sixteenth century the qualification that most concerned contemporaries was the property qualification. They assumed, with some justification, that there was an intimate link between the economic status of jurors and the sort of decisions they rendered. A moderate degree of wealth was seen as the necessary prerequisite of impartiality and independence, and as the best guarantee of socially acceptable verdicts.[24] Ideal grand jurors were described as "grave and substantial gentlemen," and as "the most sufficient freeholders in the county." Ideal trial jurors were described as men "most sufficient, both for un-

Authority, 398; PRO, SP 14/190/44 ("Concerning Jurors," ca. James I).

21. See also Barbara J. Shapiro, *Probability and Certainty in Seventeenth-Century England* (Princeton, 1983), 176. The notion that jurors continued to be self-informing survived into the seventeenth century. Sir Matthew Hale, *The History of the Common Law of England*, ed. Charles Gray (Chicago, 1971), 165; 1 Vaughan 135–149, 124 *Eng Rep.* 1006–1013.

22. Cockburn, *Assize Introduction*, 57.

23. PRO, ASSI 35/57/3/28. See also ASSI 35/34/3/11, 35/55/3/12.

24. *Commons Journals*, 1:582; Wallace Notestein et al., eds., *Commons Debates, 1621*, 7 vols. (New Haven, 1935), 3:19–21.

derstanding, and competency of estate."[25] The statutory underpinnings of these prescriptions were, however, anything but straightforward. The basic property qualification for trial jurors was the possession of freehold land to the annual value of forty shillings. But the passage of time had seen the piecemeal alteration of that qualification, and the result was a somewhat confusing body of legislation.[26] In the case of grand jurors, the law was even more obscure. Having searched the statutes, Sir Matthew Hale found himself somewhat perplexed: "I do not find anything determined but freeholders they ought to be."[27] For his part, Michael Dalton believed that the property qualification for grand jurors amounted to only twenty shillings freehold. As his authority he cited simply "the old statutes."[28] As late as 1769, Blackstone could still complain that the qualification for grand jurors lacked clarity: "They ought," he concluded, "to be freeholders, but to what amount is uncertain."[29]

Whatever the precise statutory requirements, neither Parliament nor the government were convinced that most jurors could be described as "sufficient freeholders." During the seventeenth century the government repeatedly criticized bailiffs and sheriffs for nominating individuals it believed were unqualified to serve. The problem was compounded by the poor attendance of those who were nominated and by the consequent heavy reliance on talesmen—individuals who were chosen from among the bystanders in court and who might be of questionable character and social status.[30] The supposed inevitable result was a dilution of the social composition of juries. Thus the preamble to a draft bill of 1571 complained that those responsible for selecting trial jurors persistently omitted the better sort, returning in-

25. Cowell, *Interpreter*, under "Jurie"; *Clerk of Assize*, 102; Dalton, *Office and Authority*, 398. See also PRO, SP 14/190/44.

26. Hale, *Pleas*, 2:272; Dalton, *Office and Authority*, 398, 402ff., *Clerk of Assize*, 43–44; 2 Hen. V, st 2, c. 3; 8 Hen. VI, c. 29; 19 Hen. VII, c. 13; 22 Hen. VIII, c. 10; 23 Hen. VIII, c. 13, 27 Eliz. I, c. 6. See also Cockburn, *Assize Introduction*, 57; Green, *Verdict According to Conscience*, 114, 132, J. C. Oldham, "The Origins of the Special Jury," *University of Chicago Law Review* 50 (1983): 214–21.

27. Hale, *Pleas*, 2:155.

28. Dalton, *Office and Authority*, 402.

29. William Blackstone, *Commentaries on the Laws of England*, 4 vols. (Oxford, 1765–69), 4:299. See also Cockburn, *Assize Introduction*, 46–47.

30. On the use of talesmen, see 4 & 5 P. & M., c. 7; 14 Eliz. I, c 9. Lambard, *Eirenarcha*, 307. See also Cockburn, *Assizes*, 118; idem, *Assize Introduction*, 60; Green, *Verdict According to Conscience*, 114, 132; Oldham, "Origins of the Special Jury," 146–47.

stead "men of weake Judgement and verie meane estate whose educacon and capacitie have not . . . made them fitt for this service."[31] In a similar vein, a statute of 1584 complained that trial jurors were recruited from the "poor and simpler sort"; that sheriffs refused to nominate "the ablest and fittest persons"; and that because of "vaine and untrue conceit" individuals of "the best qualitie refuse to serve."[32] Likewise, a proclamation of 1607 noted that local officials "do not onely spare Gentlemen of qualitie, in a kind of awe . . . but do likewise for lucre, gaine and reward, forebeare to returne many of the ablest and fittest persons." As a result, juries were often recruited from the "simple and ignorant," or from "those that are so accustomed and inured to passe and serve upon Juries, as they have almost lost that tendernesse of Conscience which in such cases is to bee wished."[33] Similar complaints were voiced in the House of Commons in 1621 during debate on a bill "for the avoideing of insufficient jurors."[34] Nor were these complaints restricted to official circles. Sir Thomas Smith and Thomas Fuller might imply that trial jurors were substantial yeomen,[35] but according to William Harrison they were often drawn from "the fourth and last sort of people": day-laborers, poor husbandmen, and small craftsmen.[36] As the movement for law reform gathered momentum during the seventeenth century, moderate reformers emphasized the need to improve the social and economic status of jurors.[37] Those criticisms persisted, even after the issue of law reform had subsided.[38]

31 PRO, SP 12/77/48 ("Byll for Juryes"); *Commons Journals*, 1:84.

32. 27 Eliz. I, c. 6.

33. J. Larkin and P. Hughes, eds., *Stuart Royal Proclamations*, 2 vols. (Oxford, 1973–83), vol. 1, no. 77. See also Sir Henry Nevill's proposal entitled "A Project to raise a present somme of money for his Ma[jesty's] use" (PRO, SP 14/31/55) and a discussion of abuses committed by sheriffs and their subordinates (SP 14/31/57), both of which seem to date from the same year as the proclamation. In addition, see the Commons debate of the previous year on a bill "to reform Abuses in impanelling of Juries at Westminster and at the Assizes " *Commons Journals*, 1:261.

34. Notestein et al., eds., *Commons Debates*, 3:19–21; *Commons Journals*, 1:582.

35. Smith, *De Republica*, 79; Thomas Fuller, *The Holy State and the Profane State*, ed. M. Walten, 2 vols. (New York, 1938), 2:106.

36. William Harrison, *The Description of England*, ed. G. Edlen (New York, 1968), 118.

37. Veall, *Popular Movement*, 114, 117–18; S. Prall, *The Agitation for Law Reform during the Puritan Revolution* (The Hague, 1966), 54–60.

38. Richard Bernard, *A Guide to Grand Jury Men* (1627), 12–13. See also Cockburn, *Assize Introduction*, 58–63.

No doubt the abuses described by contemporaries did occur. Hertford's quarter sessions records suggest that bailiffs were often negligent and sometimes corrupt. In 1597 the quarter sessions grand jurors complained that the bailiff of Hertford hundred not only gave insufficient warning to jurors but also overcharged those who failed to appear. In the following year they made a similar complaint, in this case that the deputy bailiff for Braughing hundred was warning inhabitants for service without showing proper warrant. On several occasions justices of the peace were even forced to excuse individuals who had not been properly notified.[39] The quarter sessions records also suggest that absenteeism was common. During the period 1590–1614 the average number of absentees recorded on the final lists of quarter sessions grand jurors was nine; during the same period the average size of the jury itself was fifteen.[40]

Yet, while abuses did occur, their impact on the composition of the juries may not have been as severe as contemporaries implied. Although Somerset jurors were probably as reluctant as many others to attend, Edward Hext was still able to inform the Council that not one of them was willing to pay a sum of money in lieu of service, for fear that jury duties might, as a result, be "layde upon the meanest sorte."[41] In Hertfordshire, despite absenteeism and shrieval negligence, there are few signs that judges and justices of the peace had any difficulty filling juries. Not only were grand juries at both quarter sessions and assizes generally larger than the required minimum of thirteen, but an examination of the surviving sheriff's panels indicates that the court was usually able to swear enough jurors from among those originally summoned.[42] There is little indication that it was

39. HRO, HAT SR9/31; SR10/179; SR29/76. See also Cockburn, *Assize Introduction*, 58–59. For more general discussions of corruption and negligence among bailiffs, see Anthony Fletcher, *A County Community in Peace and War: Sussex, 1600–1660* (1975), 223; A. H. Smith, *County and Court: Government and Politics in Norfolk, 1558–1603* (Oxford, 1974), 145; Peter Clark, *English Provincial Society from the Reformation to the Revolution: Religion, Politics and Society in Kent, 1500–1640* (Hassocks, 1977), 114; M. J. Ingram, "Communities and Courts: Law and Disorder in Early-Seventeenth-Century Wiltshire," in J. S. Cockburn, ed., *Crime in England, 1550–1800* (1977), 123–25.

40. This analysis is based on HRO, HAT SR2–26 (grand jury lists). Unfortunately, the lists of assize grand and trial jurors do not name absentees, and therefore systematic analysis of absenteeism on these juries is impossible. But see Cockburn's discussion in *Assize Introduction*, 58–59.

41. PRO, SP 14/32/80 (Edward Hext to Salisbury, 1608).

42. See the sheriff's panels listed above, n. 17. For discussions of the proper

necessary to recruit from bystanders.[43] Much the same was true in the case of the trial jury. Between 1573 and 1624 an average of 2.5 trial juries sat at each session of the assizes. Candidates were not in short supply. Only rarely did jurors serve on more than one jury at a single session, and in only one instance—the especially busy session of March 1598—was a jury required to hear a second group of cases.[44] The court records are less clear on the role of talesmen. The sheriff's panels do not survive, and talesmen are not identified as such in the final lists of jurors. It is therefore difficult to know how widely they were used. Nonetheless, the tell-tale signs are lacking. Any widespread use of talesmen should be reflected in the appearance in the jury lists of the names of individuals who had been summoned to court for some other purpose—perhaps as witnesses or prosecutors. In Hertfordshire's assize records such a correspondence is rare. A survey of the records relating to four different sessions (those for 1614 and 1615) reveals no overlap between the lists of trial jurors and the remaining records of court appearances.[45] It would seem that contemporaries exaggerated the effects of absenteeism and official negligence.

It would also seem that they underestimated the social status of the jurors. An examination of court records and related probate records suggests that far from being men of "meane estate," Hertfordshire jurors were men of at least moderate wealth and social status. The court records are most informative in the case of the assize grand jury, and they suggest that here the gentry predominated. As can be seen from Figure 5.1, gentlemen were in a minority during the 1570s and 1580s. From the early 1590s an increase in their numbers is unmistakable, and by 1609 gentry domination was virtually complete.[46] Admittedly, the court records may exaggerate the extent of the change. Indeed, it has been suggested that the designation "gent" was applied indiscriminately by the clerk and therefore has little value as an indicator of so-

size of the grand jury, see PRO, SP 14/190/44; Babington, *Advice*, 4–5, *Clerk of Assize*, 30. See also Cockburn, *Assize Introduction*, 44–45. During the period 1573–1624 the average size of the assize grand jury was seventeen. PRO, ASSI 35/15/4–35/66/2; HRO, HAT SR1/65, 98; SR2/36; SR6/171; SR7/115; SR9/92; SR10/139 (grand jury lists).

43. Cf. *Clerk of Assize*, 29–30; Cockburn, *Assize Introduction*, 49.

44. An examination of the records of five different assize sessions reveals only two individuals who served on more than one jury at the same session. PRO, ASSI 35/50/4, 51/3, 51/4, 52/3, 53/3. For the 1598 panel that served twice, see ASSI 35/40/2/44, 58. Also, see Beattie, *Crime and the Courts*, 380.

45. PRO, ASSI 35/56/1–35/57/4. Cf. Cockburn, below, chap. 6, text at n. 18.

46. Analyses of the social status of the assize grand jurors are based on PRO, ASSI 35/15/4–35/66/2; HRO, HAT SR1/65, 98; SR2/36; SR6/171; SR7/115; SR9/92; SR10/139 (grand jury lists).

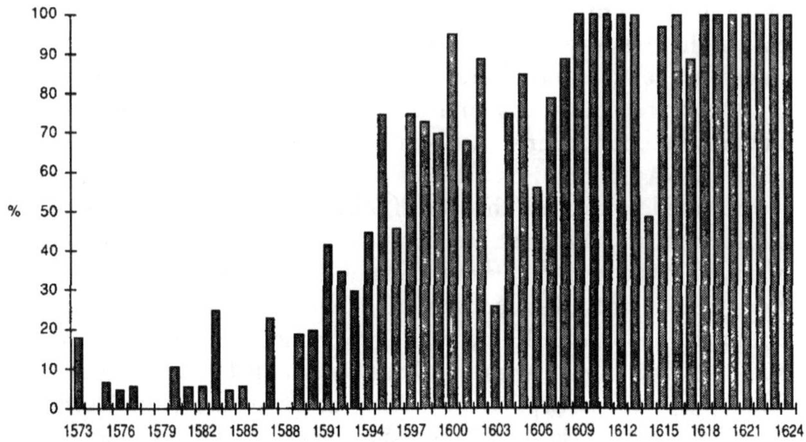

Figure 5.1. Gentry Representation on the Hertfordshire Assize Grand Jury, 1573–1624.
SOURCES: See n. 46.

cial status.[47] Some support for this claim can be found in a comparison of the lists of grand jurors with the records of the heralds' visitations.[48] During the period 1589–1618, 246 individuals served as grand jurors, and 166 (67 percent) of these are described as gentlemen in the jury lists. Despite this description, only 13 percent belonged to families that are recorded in the heralds' returns as being armigerous.[49] However, like most sets of returns, Hertfordshire's are clearly incomplete; the families of a number of individuals who belonged to the magisterial class, and whose gentility is not in doubt, are not included. These deficiencies are further highlighted by probate records. Grand jurors who are described as gentlemen in the jury lists but who are not mentioned in the heralds' returns are nonetheless described as gentlemen in their wills and inventories. Thomas Pigott of Tewin served on the grand jury nineteen times between 1591 and 1606. When he died in 1611 his goods were valued at £338, and his inventory describes a well-furnished fifteen-room house with several outbuildings. Although he is not mentioned in the heralds' returns, Pigott is usually described as a gentleman in the grand jury lists, and he is described in

47. Cockburn, *Assize Introduction*, 49.

48. Morrill notes the importance of inclusion in the heralds' visitations as a test of gentility. J. S. Morrill, *The Cheshire Grand Jury, 1625–1629* (Leicester, 1976), 18.

49. C. Metcalfe, ed., *Visitations of Hertfordshire, 1572 and 1634*, Harleian Society, 22 (1886), passim.

similar fashion in his inventory.[50] Like Thomas Pigott, Samuel Mitchell of Welwyn is not mentioned in the heralds' returns. Nonetheless, he is described as a gentleman in the jury lists, and that description is confirmed in his will. The same is true of Robert Eames of Little Gaddesden and Edward North of Tewin.[51] Although the evidence is fragmentary, it does suggest that it would be wrong to dismiss the status descriptions included in the jury lists.

Thomas Pigott and his colleagues were, of course, not members of what we may call the magisterial gentry.[52] Only five justices of the peace served as grand jurors, and four of these served only once, in July 1607.[53] Moreover, contemporaries drew a clear distinction between the status of justices of the peace and that of grand jurors. In the course of a series of arguments against the notion that such justices might serve on the grand jury, one contemporary noted that because of his elevated social status a justice of the peace would exercise too much influence.[54] Rather than the magisterial gentry, those grand jurors who are described as gentlemen in the jury lists were probably recruited from the "lesser" or "parish" gentry—individuals of moderate prosperity who occupied positions of importance within their own parishes and who stood on the bottom rung of the ladder of gentility.[55] The remainder of the grand jurors were probably substantial yeomen—men such as George Neale of Harpenden. Neale served on the assize grand jury once, in 1605. When he died, in 1611, he left an inventory valued at £664.[56] Other examples may be cited. Thomas Ewer of Watford, Thomas Yonge of Bendish, and Robert Kympton of Walkern were all called to serve on the assize grand jury with some regularity. None is given a style in the grand jury lists, but all are described

50. PRO, ASSI 35/33/3–35/48/1; HRO, H22/849.

51. For Samuel Mitchell, see PRO, ASSI 35/46/1–35/47/1; HRO, 89 HW 27. For Robert Eames, see PRO, ASSI 35/52/4–35/60/2; HRO, 37 HW 39. For Edward North, see ASSI 35/54/4–35/60/3; HRO, 96 HW 11

52. See also Morrill, *Cheshire Grand Jury*, 17–18.

53. PRO, ASSI 35/49/5/25 Service by justices of the peace on the assize grand jury was equally rare in other counties. See Cockburn, *Assizes*, 112–13, 115, 251; *Order Book*, ed. Redwood, xxiii.

54. PRO, SP 14/190/44.

55. On the parish gentry, see L. Stone, *The Crisis of the Aristocracy, 1558–1641* (Oxford, 1965), 51–52; G. E. Mingay, *The Gentry. The Rise and Fall of a Ruling Class* (1976), 13; K. Wrightson, *English Society, 1580–1680* (1982), 25.

56. PRO, ASSI 35/47/2/28; *Victoria County History of Hertfordshire* (1908), 2.307; Lionel Munby, ed., *Wheathampstead and Harpenden*, 3 vols. (Harpenden, 1973–75), 2:76.

as yeomen in their wills or inventories.[57] It is unclear whether this mix of lesser gentry and wealthy yeomen formed the social foundation of the assize grand jury in other counties, but there is at least some evidence that it did. A detailed list of Herefordshire's grand jurors compiled in 1610 describes eight as gentlemen and the remaining eight as substantial farmers.[58]

Although the lesser gentry dominated the assize grand jury, their presence on the county's second grand jury—the grand jury sitting at quarter sessions—was negligible. The surviving jury lists for the period 1589–1618 describe only 1.5 percent of the jurors as gentlemen.[59] But more than this, the lists suggest that the two grand juries differed not only in their social composition but also in their actual personnel, something that may have been unique to Hertfordshire. In both Essex and Cheshire those who served on one grand jury usually also served on the other.[60] By contrast, in Hertfordshire only fifty-three quarter sessions grand jurors served on the assize grand jury, and this figure represents less than 6 percent of all quarter sessions grand jurors. Moreover, most of the overlap occurred during the early part of our period. Thirty-four of the fifty-three individuals who served on both juries had completed their assize careers before Elizabeth's death in 1603. There may once have been a greater overlap in membership, but by the late sixteenth century, as the lesser gentry strengthened their hold, the assize grand jury seems to have begun to drift away from its quarter sessions counterpart.

With gentry representation so limited, the class that apparently dominated Hertfordshire's quarter sessons grand jury was the county's yeomanry. Because the lists of jurors do not contain status designations other than that of gentleman, the route to this conclusion is a circuitous one. Despite their deficiencies, the jury lists do contain residential information, and it is therefore possible to isolate a group of jurors from a particular locale and to construct a picture of social status through an examination of collateral sources. All the sessions and assize records have been searched for references to the forty-four men

57. For Thomas Ewer, see PRO, ASSI 35/47/2/28; HRO, HAT SR9/92; A25/2720 For Thomas Yonge, see PRO, ASSI 35/33/2/32–35/46/1/74, HRO, HAT SR1/65; 53 AW 22; A25/2303. For Robert Kympton, see PRO, ASSI 35/32/3/3–35/46/1/74; HRO, 74 HW 21.

58. PRO, SP 14/58/561.

59. HRO, HAT SR1–32.

60. Morrill, *Cheshire Grand Jury*, 11; Joel Samaha, *Law and Order in Historical Perspective* (New York, 1974), 49.

who were called to serve from the four parishes of Wheathampstead, Harpenden, Flamstead, and Great Gaddesden. The references gleaned from the court records have been supplemented with social and economic data gathered from probate records.[61] Taken together, these records yield information on twenty jurors. Two are described as gentlemen (and are so described in the jury lists), and one is described as a husbandman. However, the remaining seventeen (85 percent) are all described as yeomen.[62] Inventories survive for only seven of these yeomen, too few to allow a proper analysis of personal wealth. But those that do survive indicate that at least a few of these men were quite prosperous. By far the wealthiest was George Neale of Harpenden—the same George Neale who served on the assize grand jury. A second juror who was probably wealthier than most was William Halsey of Great Gaddesden. Halsey's inventory lists property valued at £454 and describes a six-room house with several outbuildings. Probably more representative were William Cooke of Flamstead and Thomas Wells of Great Gaddesden. Cooke's house included four rooms, and his property was valued at £153; Wells's house included eight rooms, and his possessions were valued at £130.[63] Although the wealthiest yeomen may have served, the typical quarter sessions grand juror was probably a yeoman of more modest means.

The task of establishing the social status of the typical trial juror is more difficult. Only a handful of assize trial jury lists contain residential information, and it is to these that we must confine our analysis. When taken together, two of the most complete lists give the residences of twenty-two jurors, and of these, probate records survive for thirteen.[64] Two are described as husbandmen, one as a craftsman (a carpenter), and the remaining ten as yeomen.[65] Like the quarter sessions grand juries, the assize trial juries appear to have been composed mainly of yeomen. None were as wealthy as George Neale, but some

61. HRO, 22 HW 24; 118 HW 9, 4 HW 2, 10 HW 90; 22 HW 62; 55 HW 21; 100 HW 85; 116 HW 69; 54 HW 58; 74 HW 48; 139 HW 19; 9 HW 108; 55 HW 89; 74 HW 53; 3 HW 60; *Wheathampstead and Harpenden*, ed. Munby, vol. 2, appendix 3.

62. For the two jurors who are described as gentlemen, see HRO, HAT SR1/123, 29/80, 113.

63. HRO, 55 HW 9; 4 HW 32; 139 HW 19.

64. PRO, ASSI 35/55/3/12; 35/57/3/28.

65. HRO, 139 HW 3; H22/896; 79 HW 28; 74 HW 25; 56 AW 3; A25/2395; H22/1110; 131 HW 50; H22/820; 74 HW 25; 139 HW 180; H23/948; 116 HW 70; 79 HW 46. A third trial jury list, dating from 1592 (PRO, ASSI 35/34/3/11), yields residential information on eight jurors. Of these, probate records survive for only one, William Chaundler of Bennington (HRO, 2 AR 160r). He too is described as a yeoman.

were moderately prosperous; the surviving inventories include one valued at £255 and a second at £285. But if the yeomanry dominated, the assize trial jury, like the quarter sessions grand jury, was leavened with a sprinkling of gentlemen. For the period 1573–1624, eleven trial jurors are described as gentlemen.[66] Once again these were undoubtedly members of the lesser gentry. The John Christian who served as an assize trial juror in 1616 may have been the same John Christian who was called to quarter sessions to serve on the grand jury in 1617 and who died in 1638, leaving a substantial estate to his children. In both jury lists and in his will Christian is described as a gentleman.[67] Moreover, the similarity between these two juries goes even further. Not only were they recruited from the same class, but as the example of John Christian indicates, there was also some overlap in their actual membership. Of the individuals listed in the two relatively complete lists of assize trial jurors, fourteen also served on the grand jury at quarter sessions.

Very few trial jury lists survive among the quarter sessions records, and it is therefore difficult to establish social status. Of the few lists that do survive, none contain any information other than the names of the jurors. Yet, while the evidence is fragmentary, it does suggest that quarter sessions trial juries were recruited from essentially the same social class as the quarter sessions grand jury and the assize trial jury. Indeed, once again there appears to have been some overlap in membership. Six lists of trial jurors survive in the quarter sessions records, and they contain a total of seventy-two names.[68] Forty of those names (56 percent) correspond with the names of quarter sessions grand jurors, and thirty-six (50 percent) with the names of assize trial jurors. Like these other juries, the quarter sessions trial jury was probably composed mainly of yeomen. The same can be said of the more specialized trial juries summoned to quarter sessions to hear traverses.[69] Once again the jury lists only rarely survive, but those that do contain residential information, and it is therefore possible to establish links with collateral sources. The probate records of the members of two juries called to quarter sessions to try traverses in

66. This count is based on PRO, ASSI 35/15/4–35/66/2 (trial jury lists).

67. PRO, ASSI 35/58/4/12; HRO, HAT SR29/113. In his will Christian left £200 and the bulk of his estate to his eldest son, £100 each to his remaining six children, and smaller bequests to his grandchildren. HRO, 22 HW 74.

68. HRO, HAT SR6/71, 82, 209, 211; SR12/44; SR32/63.

69. On traverse procedure, see Lambard, *Eirenarcha*, 438–40, 445.

1617 have been examined. Taken together, these records yield information on twenty-one of the total of forty-five jurors. Of the former group, eighteen are described as yeomen and three as craftsmen.[70]

It was thus Hertfordshire's yeomanry that formed the social backbone of the county's jury system, supported on the one hand by the lesser gentry and on the other by wealthier husbandmen and craftsmen. Those contemporaries who implied that the jurors were primarily men of the "middling sort" were therefore closer to the mark than those who complained of men of "meane estate." But even the former description is somewhat misleading. It is correct insofar as it implies that most jurors stood between the gentry on the one hand and the laborers and smallest property owners on the other, but it is incorrect insofar as it implies that the jurors were, in economic terms, equally distant from the two. The jurors were men of property; they were above that fundamental barrier that separated those who owned property from those who did not.[71] The pattern of social alignment implicit in this economic distinction is underlined by a consideration of Gregory King's analysis of the social distribution of wealth.[72] Cressey suggests that the yeomen correspond with King's "freeholders of the better sort," and possibly with his lesser freeholders.[73] Taken together, these two categories composed 12 percent of England's families in 1688. Most of Hertfordshire's jurors were thus recruited from a relatively small section of the population.[74] But what is more important for our purposes, only 5 percent of all families had annual incomes higher than those of the freeholders' families. By contrast, 83 percent had lower incomes.[75]

70. HRO, HAT SR29/46, 51; 47 HW 103; 103 HW 21; 79 HW 58; 48 HW 40; H22/595; H23/2106; 77 AW 34; A25/3225; 65 AW 10; 111 HW 14; H23/1843; 81 AW 17; 55 HW 95, H22/595; H22/239.

71. Wrightson, *English Society*, 37.

72. Joan Thirsk and J. P. Cooper, eds., *Seventeenth-Century Economic Documents* (Oxford, 1972), 780–81.

73. David Cressy, "Describing the Social Order of Elizabethan and Stuart England," *Literature and History* 3 (1976): 40.

74. The proportion may have been even smaller than King's data suggest. According to the Tawneys, of the 19,402 men mustered in Gloucestershire in 1608, less than 5 percent were yeomen. If the analysis is restricted to heads of households, the proportion was still only 8 percent. A. J. Tawney and R. H. Tawney, "An Occupational Census of the Seventeenth Century," *Economic History Review* 5 (1934–35): 25–64.

75. In addition to King's data, we might also consider data gathered from pro-

Hertfordshire's jurors were thus recruited from a comparatively wealthy section of English society. However, even this sort of calculation tends to undervalue their economic importance, for it treats the whole of the country's population as part of a single social structure. But as Christianson notes, England's social hierarchy was not a unitary structure; rather it was a composite of many local structures.[76] When the jurors are considered within the context of the village community, their economic importance is magnified. We may recall here the example of George Neale. Since the late fifteenth century the Neale family had been building up their farm, known as Hammondsend. By 1599 George Neale was able to purchase the manor of Ing's (named for its thirteenth-century owner, William Inge, chief justice of King's Bench). When he died, in 1611, Neale was not only one of the wealthiest inhabitants of Harpenden but also one of its largest landowners.[77] Admittedly, this is an extreme example, for Neale was wealthier than most yeomen. However, the Neales counted among their neighbors other yeoman families that also sent jurors to quarter sessions—families such as the Carpenters, the Catlyns, and the Grunwins.[78] Although not as wealthy as the Neales, all three families had deep roots in Harpenden and neighboring Wheathampstead, and all three were important landholding families. In addition, all three were connected to the Neales through kinship ties.[79]

As members of the yeomanry, the jurors thus occupied positions of importance within England's economic structure, particularly within the economic structure of their village communities. Moreover, recent local studies indicate that this importance was growing more pronounced during the Elizabethan and Jacobean periods. The peculiar pattern of sixteenth-century economic growth ensured a redistri-

bate records. On the basis of a survey of 2,256 inventories relating to the period 1580–1700, Cressey has calculated an average inventory value for each of the basic social classes. These values make it possible to quantify the economic distance between classes. The average value of the inventories of the yeomen was 595 percent greater than that of the laborers. By contrast, the average value of the inventories of the gentry was only 66 percent greater than that of the yeomen. These calculations are my own and are based on data in David Cressy, *Literacy and the Social Order: Reading and Writing in Tudor and Stuart England* (Cambridge, 1980), 139.

76. Paul Christianson, "The Causes of the English Revolution: A Reappraisal," *Journal of British Studies* 15 (1976): 58–59. See also Alan Everitt, *Change in the Provinces: The Seventeenth Century* (Leicester, 1969), 6.

77. *Wheathampstead and Harpenden*, ed Munby, 2:76, *VCH Hertfordshire*, 2:307.

78. See, for example, HRO, HAT SR2/59; SR5/20, SR9/28; SR10/171; SR14/63.

79. *Wheathampstead and Harpenden*, ed. Munby, 2:64ff.

bution of wealth in favor of the propertied classes, and the yeomanry were among the principal beneficiaries.[80] But just as important as this process of economic polarization was the corresponding process of political polarization. In their study of the Essex village of Terling, Wrightson and Levine note that the local yeomanry were exercising an increasing domination over the public life of the village through their hold on the most important local offices. Not only did Terling's yeomen and wealthier craftsmen account for most of the jurors at quarter sessions, they also accounted for most of the churchwardens, overseers, and manorial jurors.[81] In Terling, jury service was simply one aspect of a more wide-ranging power. Much the same was true across the border in Hertfordshire. An examination of the forty-four individuals who were called from the parishes of Great Gaddesden, Wheathampstead, Harpenden, and Flamstead to serve as quarter sessions grand jurors reveals a wide range of public activities. For example, many of these individuals were also members of the presentment jury that represented their region at quarter sessions. The "hundred jury," as it was called, was an institution of importance in the maintenance of law and order at the local level, for it was charged with identifying ("presenting") minor offenses and administrative inconveniences.[82] Altogether twenty-one of the forty-four grand jurors served on the hundred jury. Besides these additional duties at quarter sessions, the jurors were also active in parochial affairs. The Harpenden parish register lists fourteen churchwardens between 1606 and 1626. Eight of these served on the quarter sessions grand jury. The Flamstead register is slightly less complete, listing eleven churchwar-

80. On the process of social and economic polarization, see Lawrence Stone, "Social Mobility in England, 1500–1700," in *Seventeenth-Century England: Society in an Age of Revolution*, ed. Paul Seaver (New York, 1976), 33–36, 38; J. D. Chambers, *Population, Economy and Society in Pre-Industrial England* (1972), 27, 134, 139; D. Felix, "Profit Inflation and Industrial Growth: The Historic Record and Contemporary Analogies," in *Essays in Quantitative Economic History*, ed. R. Floud (Oxford, 1974), 134–39; Peter Bowden, "Agricultural Prices, Farm Profits, and Rents," in *The Agrarian History of England and Wales, vol. 4, 1500–1640*, ed. Joan Thirsk (Cambridge, 1967), 598–601, 608–9, 695; Alan Macfarlane, *Reconstructing Historical Communities* (Cambridge, 1977), 162–63; Victor Skipp, *Crisis and Development. An Ecological Case Study of the Forest of Arden, 1570–1674* (Cambridge, 1978), 65, 68, 78–79, 103; Keith Wrightson and David Levine, *Poverty and Piety in an English Village: Terling, 1525–1700* (New York, 1979), 34–36, 108–9.

81. *Poverty and Piety*, 103–6.

82. Lambard, *Eirenarcha*, 300; *Clerk of Assize*, 110–11. Although Hertfordshire had three hundred-juries, some counties had no equivalent bodies. S.A.H. Burne, ed., *The Staffordshire Quarter Sessions Rolls*, William Salt Archaeological Society and Staffordshire Record Society, 5 vols. (1931–40), 4.xxiv; Morrill, *Cheshire Grand Jury*, 42.

dens between 1605 and 1620. Of these, five served on the grand jury. Of the fifteen grand jurors from Great Gaddesden, at least nine served as churchwardens between 1591 and 1625, and at least four served as stonewardens between 1615 and 1625.[83] Manorial affairs provided a further sphere of activity. Of the eleven inhabitants of Wheathampstead and Harpenden summoned to quarter sessions to serve as grand jurors, nine sat at least once on the homage of the court baron of the manor of Rothampstead.[84] The specialized juries summoned to inquire into local incidents offered yet another area of activity. In May 1597 a special sessions was held at Great Gaddesden to inquire into a riot, and eight residents of Flamstead and Great Gaddesden were required to serve on the jury. Of these, five had served as grand jurors.[85] In a very practical sense, those who served as jurors were the rulers of their parishes.

Just as significant as the possession of power was the use to which it was put. Wrightson and Levine note that from the early years of the seventeenth century the farmers and wealthier craftsmen who dominated Terling were beginning to use their powers to impose a new standard of order and discipline on their fellow villagers, particularly on the village poor.[86] The same pattern can be detected in Hertfordshire. From the 1590s the presentment juries show an increased inclination to present church non-attendance, alehouse offenses, drunkenness, and squatting—offenses primarily associated with the poor.[87] Undoubtedly, Parliament and the government paved the way with new legislation and with exhortations to greater diligence relayed through the assize and county benches.[88] But as Wrightson and Levine

83. HRO, D/P 122A 1/1 (Harpenden parish register); D/P 38 1/1 (Flamstead parish register), D/P 39 1/1 (Great Gaddesden parish register). Although the references to churchwardens are fragmentary, it is clear that many of the grand jurors who served in this office did so more than once.

84. HRO, D/ELW M35.

85 HRO, HAT SR9/97–98

86. *Poverty and Piety*, 110–41, 178–79 See also William Hunt, *The Puritan Moment: The Coming of Revolution in an English County* (Cambridge, Mass , 1983), 140ff; Keith Wrightson, "Two Concepts of Order: Justices, Constables and Jurymen in Seventeenth-Century England," in *An Ungovernable People· The English and Their Law in the Seventeenth and Eighteenth Centuries*, ed. J. Brewer and J. Styles (1980), 32–46; Peter Clark, "The Alehouse and the Alternative Society," in *Puritans and Revolutionaries· Essays in Seventeenth-Century History Presented to Christopher Hill*, ed. D. Pennington and K. Thomas (Oxford, 1978), 69–71; J. A. Sharpe, *Crime in Seventeenth-Century England: A County Study* (Cambridge, 1982), 173ff.

87. P. G. Lawson, "Crime and the Administration of Criminal Justice in Hertfordshire, 1580–1625" (D. Phil. thesis, Oxford Univ., 1982), 180ff.

88. For the relevant legislation, see J. R. Kent, "Attitudes of Members of the

note, the turning point came when village notables abandoned their traditional preoccupation with community harmony in favor of the preoccupations with order, discipline, and the poor that were current among county and national rulers.[89] Thus, if the process of economic polarization had a political dimension, it also had a cultural dimension; the interests and preoccupations of those who served as jurors were increasingly at variance with the interests and preoccupations of many of their fellow villagers.

The social context of the jury system seems clear. In a very precise sense, it was a class institution. It was dominated by a small but distinct stratum of Tudor and Stuart society. The members of this stratum were propertied, they ranked well up in the national scale of wealth, and they exercised a tangible power over the lives of their own communities. Moreover, the manner in which they used this power reinforced the widening economic division between themselves and the poorer residents of their villages. Indeed, seen from the perspective of the village community—and that must have been the perspective of most men and women—juries comprised not simply a class institution but a ruling-class institution.

A question remains about the extent to which this social context shaped the decisions of the jurors themselves. Gerrard Winstanley thought that it did. In a well-known passage he complained that the jury that convicted the Diggers for their activities on St. George's Hill was composed of "rich freeholders and such as stood strongly for the Norman power."[90] But, of course, the case of the Diggers was not an ordinary case; it is not necessarily true that the logic implicit in Winstanley's complaint can be applied to the grand and trial juries hearing routine felonies. To fully understand the behavior of the jurors, we must consider all possible influences, including not only those drawn from the social context of the jury but also those drawn from its procedural context—the context of the courtroom itself.

Within the courtroom the most obvious influence was the judicial bench. In his study of assize procedure, Cockburn notes that the judge exercised considerable power over the prosecution process as a whole

House of Commons to the Regulation of 'Personal Conduct' in Late Elizabethan and Early Stuart England," *BIHR* 46 (1973): 41–71. For examples of exhortations from the county bench, see *Lambarde and Local Government*, ed. Read, passim.

89. Wrightson, "Two Concepts of Order," 33–46; Wrightson and Levine, *Poverty and Piety*, 115–16

90. *The Works of Gerrard Winstanley*, ed. G. H. Sabine (1941), 327.

and over juries in particular.[91] Before the start of proceedings the judge could shape and even reshape the composition of a jury.[92] During the course of the indictment process he could influence the deliberations of the grand jury through specific directions and through his control over the flow of evidence.[93] Once the trial was under way he could influence the presentation of the evidence—and therefore its effect on the trial jury—through interjected comments and questions, and these interjections might be reinforced at the end of the trial by his final summation and direction. According to Hale, the judge was

> able in Matters of Law emerging upon the Evidence to direct them [the jury]; and also, in Matters of Fact, to give them a great Light and Assistance by his weighing the Evidence before them, and observing where the Question and Knot of the Business lies, and by shewing them his Opinion even in Matter of Fact, which is a great Advantage and Light to Lay-men.[94]

Even after the verdict had been returned, the judge could force a jury to reconsider its verdict, and if the members proved obstinate, they might be fined or brought before Star Chamber or King's Bench.[95]

If the independence of the jury was threatened by the powers of the bench, it was also threatened by the practical inconveniences under which jurors, particularly trial jurors, labored. Most trials were brief; the average length of fourteenth-century gaol delivery trials was only about fifteen minutes, and the situation was probably little improved by the sixteenth century.[96] Jurors therefore had little time to absorb

91. *Assize Introduction*, 70–71, 111–12, 132–33.

92. Hale, *Pleas*, 2:155, 296, 309–10. See also Dalton, *Office and Authority*, 394; *Clerk of Assize*, 40–41.

93. Cockburn, *Assize Introduction*, 104.

94. *History of the Common Law*, 164–65. See also Cockburn, *Assize Introduction*, 70, 109; Langbein, "Criminal Trial before the Lawyers," 285–87; Shapiro, *Probability and Certainty*, 191.

95. Smith, *De Republica*, 88; *Lambarde and Local Government*, ed. Read, 59, 121; Hale, *Pleas*, 2:158–60, 310–12; Babington, *Advice*, "To the Reader;" J. H. Baker, "Criminal Justice at Newgate, 1616–1627: Some Manuscript Reports in the Harvard Law School," *Irish Jurist*, new ser., 8 (1973), 313. The judge could also minimize the effects of a verdict with which he disagreed. In the case of a guilty verdict he could grant a reprieve, and in the case of an acquittal he could sentence the prisoner to the house of correction. For examples of the former, see PRO, ASSI 35/22/2/25v; 35/44/4/6, 7; HRO, HAT SR1/65. For examples of the latter, see PRO, ASSI 35/57/3/32, 33, 108v; 35/58/4/19, 28, 88v; 35/59/3/22, 33–35, 124v; 35/60/2/14, 30, 101v. See also Cockburn, *Assize Introduction*, 71, 131–33.

96. B. A. Hanawalt, *Crime and Conflict in English Communities, 1300–1348* (Cambridge, Mass., 1979), 41; R. B. Pugh, "The Duration of Criminal Trials in Medie-

the details of individual cases. Moreover, the constraints imposed by the brevity of the trial were compounded by the practice of multiple arraignment. At both quarter sessions and assizes, groups of prisoners were arraigned together, and a single jury would hear the cases in rapid succession. According to Sir Thomas Smith, juries dealt with no more than three prisoners at a time, and "many times they are charged but with one or two."[97] But Smith's reckoning may have been too optimistic. As Figure 5.2 indicates, Hertfordshire's trial juries usually dealt with more than three prisoners; the typical number was, in fact, seven.[98]

Given both the power of the bench and the practical difficulties under which juries labored, it is tempting to view the latter as necessarily passive bodies and to treat their decisions as articulations of the wishes of the judge. But as tempting as it is, such a view seems too extreme. For its part, the grand jury enjoyed a degree of practical immunity from judicial pressure simply because it heard its evidence and considered its verdict in isolation, away from the watchful eye of the judge. Although trial juries were more vulnerable, it seems unlikely that the powers of the bench were used to anything like their

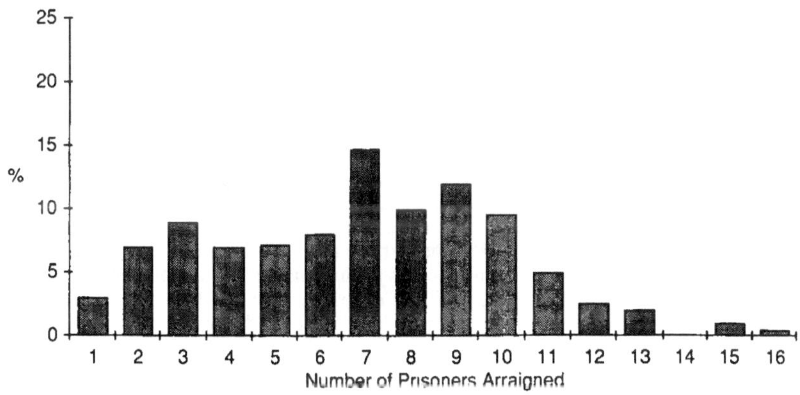

Figure 5.2. Arraignments before Hertfordshire Trial Juries, 1573–1624.
SOURCES: See n. 98.

val England," in *Law, Litigants and the Legal Profession*, ed. E. W. Ives and A. H. Manchester (1983), 108. The assize judges had only seventeen days in which to complete the whole of the Home circuit. It is therefore not surprising that trials were speedy. BL, Lansdowne MS. 53, fol. 198. See also Green, *Verdict According to Conscience*, 134; Cockburn, *Assize Introduction*, 110, 131

97. *De Republica*, 81.

98. PRO, ASSI 35/15/4–35/66/2 (trial jury lists and indictments). See also *Clerk of Assize*, 41; Cockburn, *Assize Introduction*, 63–65.

full extent, at least in routine cases. Scattered instances of decisive judicial intervention during trials, and aggressive directions at their conclusion, can certainly be cited,[99] but many of them occurred in the course of trials involving religious and political issues.[100] Where such issues were not at stake, it seems unlikely that judges would have been so aggressive; the use of their powers took time, and time was at a premium.[101] It is therefore not surprising that Thomas Smith's description of criminal trials in the mid sixteenth century indicates that directions from the bench were usually brief in duration and neutral in content.[102] Descriptions of Old Bailey trials dating from both the early and later seventeenth century suggest that judges might direct juries to reach a specific verdict.[103] However, the more usual approach seems to have been a cursory, fairly neutral direction of the sort described by Smith.[104] Moreover, these same accounts suggest that if judicial pressure was applied, juries might show some resistance.[105] Only rarely did judges invoke their disciplinary powers.[106] Nonetheless, there are enough examples to make it clear that juries were not

99. Examples of aggressive judicial intervention and direction can be found in the *State Trials*. For other examples, see J. H. Pollen, ed., *Unpublished Documents Relating to the English Martyrs*, Catholic Record Society, 5 (1908), 28–32; W. Urwick, *Nonconformity in Hertfordshire* (1884), 533, Cockburn, *Assizes*, 122, idem, *Assize Introduction*, 70.

100. In trials such as these, juries were especially likely to be disobedient See John Bellamy, *The Tudor Law of Treason: An Introduction* (1979), 171–73; Hunt, *Puritan Moment*, 205–6; Veall, *Popular Movement*, 79, 153, 158 n. 1, 162–66; J. R. Jones, *Country and Court: England, 1658–1714* (Cambridge, Mass., 1979), 221.

101. One other area, however, where aggressive jury directions may have been a common feature was in witchcraft trials in the latter part of the century According to both Thomas and Shapiro, leading members of the Restoration bench used their powers to undercut witchcraft prosecutions and so, as Shapiro notes, "make the witchcraft statute inoperative many decades before final repeal." Shapiro, *Probability and Certainty*, 206; Keith Thomas, *Religion and the Decline of Magic: Studies in Popular Beliefs in Sixteenth- and Seventeenth-Century England* (Harmondsworth, 1973), 547.

102. *De Republica*, 80–81.

103. Baker, "Criminal Justice," 313; *An Exact Account of the Trials of the Several Persons Arraigned at the Sessions-house in the Old Bailey for London and Middlesex* (1678), 11, 15, 23; Langbein, "Criminal Trial before the Lawyers," 285–87. See also Shapiro, *Probability and Certainty*, 205.

104. Baker, "Criminal Justice," 316–17; *An Exact Account*, 6, 9, 10, 11, 18. See also Beattie, *Crime and the Courts*, 376; Green, *Verdict According to Conscience*, 139.

105. *An Exact Account*, 15–16.

106. Smith, *De Republica*, 80–81; Hale, *Pleas*, 2:310–12, Bellamy, *Tudor Law of Treason*, 173.

invariably passive instruments at the disposal of the bench.[107] This is not surprising. Tudor and early-Stuart society was, of course, highly deferential, and jurors were the social inferiors of judges. Nevertheless, as we have seen, they were men of some importance within their own communities. A degree of independence would have been only natural. Thus, while judicial power might limit the independence of juries, it did not necessarily extinguish it.[108]

Much the same can be said of the constraints imposed by trial procedure. The speed of the proceedings need not have prevented jurors from reaching an independent verdict. Research on modern trial juries suggests, in fact, that most jurors reach a decision early in the trial, usually long before they begin to deliberate.[109] It may be assumed that in routine cases Elizabethan and Jacobean jurors did not require a lengthy presentation in order to formulate an opinion. When the case was more difficult, it seems likely that the court would have proceeded at a more leisurely pace, a possibility suggested by the long lists of witnesses that often accompany indictments for homicide and witchcraft.[110] If the duration of the trial was not an insurmountable difficulty, neither was the practice of multiple arraignment.[111] Jurors were usually supplied with a list of prisoners in their charge (the *aide mémoire*), and although they may not always have done so, they were at least able to retire to consider their verdict.[112] Moreover, pamphlet

107. PRO, ASSI 35/38/2/20; Cockburn, *Assize Introduction*, 71, Green, *Verdict According to Conscience*, 140–42, 147. See also T. G. Barnes, ed., *List and Index to the Proceedings in Star Chamber for the Reign of James I (1603–1625) in the Public Record Office, London*, 3 vols. (Chicago, 1975), vol. 3, passim

108 See Green, *Verdict According to Conscience*, 150 n. 179.

109. J. Kessler, "The Social Psychology of Jury Deliberations," in *The Jury System in America*, ed. R. Simon (Beverly Hills, 1975), 70 See also Green, *Verdict According to Conscience*, 150 n 179.

110. See, for example, the indictments of Eleanor Swyft for murder (PRO, ASSI 35/42/3/10v, 11v) and the indictment of George and Sarah Adownes for witchcraft (ASSI 35/55/2/85v). Shapiro cites witchcraft trials in which as many as nineteen witnesses were called. She also notes that some witchcraft trials were long enough to include the performing of "experiments." *Probability and Certainty*, 205, 207, 211.

111. Green, *Verdict According to Conscience*, 150 n. 179. Cf. Cockburn, below, chap 6, text at n. 101.

112 *Clerk of Assize*, 48, 157; Bodleian Lib., Rawlinson MS. C 271, fol. 10. Noting that some jurors may have been illiterate, Cockburn questions the significance of the *aide mémoire*. He also questions whether trial juries routinely retired to consider their verdicts *Assize Introduction*, 65, 110. The second query is especially tantalizing. However, as Cockburn himself notes, most commentators implied that juries did indeed retire. See, for example, Smith, *De Republica*, 81; *Clerk of Assize*, 48–49; Hale, *History of the Common Law*, 165. See also Green, *Verdict According to Conscience*,

descriptions of witchcraft trials indicate that deliberations might be lengthy.[113] Although we know little of the substance of those deliberations, recent examinations of sixteenth-century Star Chamber records suggest that they could be both detailed and searching.[114] In the seventeenth century, Hale would advocate precisely this sort of deliberation, noting that jurors ought to weigh individual testimonies before accepting them as fact:

> It is one of the Excellencies of this Trial . . . that altho' the Jury ought to give a great Regard to Witnesses and their Testimony, yet they are not always bound by it, but may either upon reasonable Circumstances, inducing a Blemish upon their Credibility . . . pronounce a Verdict contrary to such Testimonies, the Truth whereof they have just Cause to suspect. . . .[115]

All this is not to deny the limiting effects of trial procedure. Had the jurors been as simple and ignorant as the government claimed, they probably could not have coped.[116] But they were not. Cressey's examination of illiteracy in the diocese of London (including part of Hertfordshire) during the years 1580–1640 indicates that only 3 percent of gentry deponents before the ecclesiastical courts were unable to sign their names. In the case of yeoman deponents, the proportion was 33 percent.[117] It seems probable that many, possibly most, of Hertfordshire's grand and trial jurors were literate. In this connection it may be noted that most of the presentment jurors who were required to sign presentments between 1589 and 1618 were able to do so with a signature rather than a mark.[118] Of course, the ability to read need not

---

139 n. 142. Beattie notes that by the late seventeenth century jurors were no longer retiring. *Crime and the Courts*, 395ff

113. An account of a series of witchcraft trials at York assizes in 1612 implies that the deliberations of the trial jury were indeed quite lengthy: "Heere the Iurie of Life and Death, hauing spent the most part of the day, in due consideration of their offences; Returned into the court to deliuer up their Verdict." G.B Harrison, ed , *The Trial of the Lancaster Witches A.D. MDCXII* (1929), 128, 146, 159, 185; quotation is from p. 128.

114. G. R. Elton, *Policy and Police· The Enforcement of the Reformation in the Age of Thomas Cromwell* (Cambridge, 1985), 312, Green, *Verdict According to Conscience*, 142. Cf. Cockburn, *Assize Introduction*, 110–12.

115. Hale, *History of the Common Law*, 164.

116. *Stuart Proclamations*, ed. Larkin and Hughes, vol. 1, no. 77.

117. Cressy, *Literacy and the Social Order*, 121.

118. See, for example, HRO, HAT SR27/49. See also Wrightson, "Two Concepts of Order," 28; and Cockburn, below, chap. 6, text at n. 35.

always have led to a greater knowledge of the law, but in at least some cases it did. The Yorkshire yeoman Adam Eyre included among his books a copy of Dalton's *The Countrey Justice*, and in his diary he indicates that it was an especially popular book with his neighbors.[119] But even though literacy may have encouraged a knowledge of the law, it must not be assumed that illiterate jurors were inevitably ignorant of the law. Recent studies of popular protest indicate that members of the laboring classes, most of whom were illiterate, shared a rudimentary knowledge of the law.[120] Nor is this surprising. As Macfarlane's study of Earls Colne makes clear, law had a pervasive presence in Tudor and early Stuart society, touching most aspects of life, and most sections of the community.[121] Among the property-owning classes, knowledge of the law must have been heightened by the growing taste for litigation. The latter part of the sixteenth century saw a dramatic increase in civil litigation, and as contemporaries complained, the "middling sort" were active participants.[122] While John Norden reproached greedy lawyers for creating animosity among the yeomen, merchants, and husbandmen of Cornwall, he noted that those men were themselves "verie litigious" and "muche inclined to lawe quarrels for small causes."[123]

As important as it may have been to any juror, a general knowledge of the law was not quite the same thing as experience. Many could, of course, draw on their background as local officials. Although not im-

119. H. J. Morehouse, ed., "A Dyurnall . . . ," in *Yorkshire Diaries and Autobiographies*, Surtees Society, 65 (1875), 43, 92–93.

120. John Walter, "Grain Riots and Popular Attitudes to the Law: Maldon and the Crisis of 1629," in *Ungovernable People*, ed. Brewer and Styles, 51–52, 62–64.

121. In the course of his intensive examination of the records of the village of Earls Colne, Macfarlane notes that during the five-year period from 1589 to 1593 more than 200 legal actions "left their mark . . on this village of roughly 1,000 inhabitants." *Reconstructing Historical Communities*, 183. In a similar vein, Ives reminds us that "Land was bought and sold through the court of Common Pleas. Estates were still largely managed through manorial courts. Family life was dominated by legal considerations of inheritance, marriage and death." E. W. Ives, "Social Change and the Law," in *The English Revolution, 1600–1660*, ed. E. W. Ives (New York, 1968), 119. See also Brewer and Styles, Introduction, in *Ungovernable People*, 17.

122. On the increase in civil litigation, see Mildred Campbell, *The English Yeoman under Elizabeth and the Early Stuarts* (reprint, 1967), 108, 366–68; Stone, *Crisis of the Aristocracy*, 240–42; Ingram, "Communities and Courts," 113ff., Penry Williams, *The Tudor Regime* (Oxford, 1979), 248–51; J. A. Sharpe, " 'Such Disagreement betwyx Neighbours': Litigation and Human Relations in Early Modern England," in *Disputes and Settlements. Law and Human Relations in the West*, ed. J. Bossy (Cambridge, 1983), 168.

123. Quoted in Campbell, *English Yeoman*, 366.

mediately relevant, this sort of experience must have offered a general introduction to decision making within an institutional context.[124] But the sort of experience most likely to ensure the independence of the juries was jury service itself. That too was available. Among the whole body of Hertfordshire jurors there was, in fact, a fair degree of practical experience.

Previous experience was most pronounced among the members of the assize grand jury. Between 1589 and 1618, 246 individuals served as grand jurors at the assizes.[125] Taken together, these jurors each served an average of 3.9 times. However, as Figure 5.3 indicates, this average conceals considerable variation. At one extreme are the eighty-five jurors (34 percent of the total) who attended only once; at the other extreme is the much smaller group of thirty-two jurors (13 percent) who served on more than twice the average number of occasions. Among this last group were individuals who served with remarkable regularity. Henry Bull, an esquire from Hertford, served

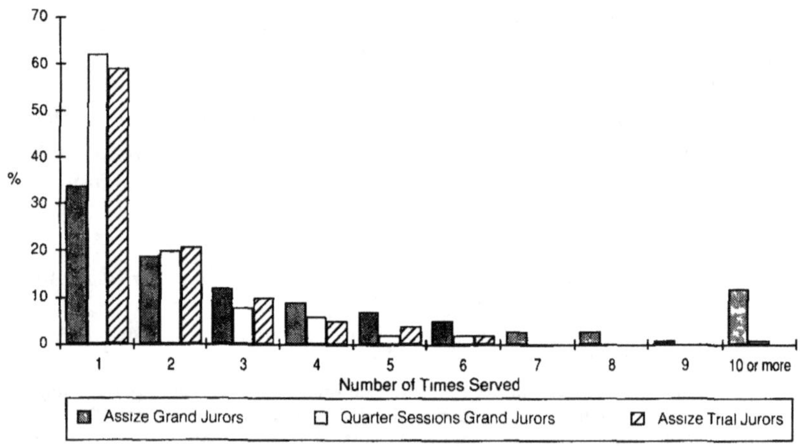

Figure 5.3. Service on Hertfordshire Juries, 1589–1618.
SOURCES: See nn. 125, 128, 130.

124. Cf. Cockburn, below, chap. 6, n. 40.

125. The analysis of assize grand jurors is based on PRO, ASSI 35/32/3–35/60/3; HRO, HAT SR1/65, 98; SR2/36; SR6/171, SR7/115; SR9/92, SR10/139 (grand jury lists). The terminal dates 1589 and 1618 have been chosen so as to ensure comparability with the analysis of the quarter sessions grand jury lists; the latter do not begin until 1589. In addition, it was necessary to exclude the early lists of assize grand jurors because only a small proportion survives. If these lists were included, the service records of many of the early jurors would be diluted, and the results of the analysis would inevitably suggest a lower level of experience than was actually the case. Cf. Cockburn, *Assize Introduction*, 50–51, 54

thirty-one times; Walter Graye, a gentleman from Codicote, served twenty-two times; and William Preston, a gentleman from St. Michaels, served twenty times.[126] While this group was small, its members could not help but form a permanent presence on the grand jury. At least two attended every sitting of the assizes, giving each jury a considerable depth of experience. Moreover, the contribution of these especially active jurors was buttressed by the contribution of less experienced jurors. An examination of the last five panels in our series indicates that of the eighty-seven jurors listed, seventy-eight (90 percent) had served on at least one previous occasion.[127]

The total number of individuals who served as assize grand jurors was comparatively small, but each of the remaining juries drew on a much larger group of potential members. In consequence, the general level of experience was lower. Altogether, 906 quarter sessions grand jurors have been identified, and between 1589 and 1618 they served a total of 1,636 times. Each juror therefore served an average of 1.8 times.[128] Those who attended only once included 62 percent of the total; those who attended more than twice the overall average (five or more times) included 5 percent of the total. These especially active quarter sessions grand jurors thus formed a relatively smaller group than their counterparts at the assizes. Nonetheless, their level of experience was still substantial, and their numbers were sufficiently large that most quarter sessions grand juries could rely on their presence. An average of almost three members of this group attended each sitting of the court. Moreover, their fellow jurors usually included men with at least some experience. The last five panels in our series contain a total of seventy jurors; of these, thirty-eight (54 percent) had served at least once before.[129]

A similar pattern of service can be found among the assize trial jurors. In this case 832 individuals have been identified, and between 1589 and 1618 they served a total of 1,539 times.[130] Trial jurors there-

126. For Henry Bull, see PRO, ASSI 35/37/3–35/66/2; for Walter Graye, see ASSI 35/42/4–35/58/4; for William Preston, see ASSI 35/42/3–35/60/2.

127. PRO, ASSI 35/58/4/86; 35/59/3/122; 35/59/4/63; 35/60/2/100, 35/60/3/68.

128. The analysis of quarter sessions grand jurors is based on HRO, HAT SR1–32 (grand jury lists).

129. HRO, HAT SR29/113, 195, 219; SR30/30; SR31/46

130. The analysis of assize trial jurors is based on PRO, ASSI 35/32/3–35/60/3 (trial jury lists). Once again the above terminal dates have been chosen to ensure comparability with the analyses of the other juries, and because inclusion of the few surviving jury lists from the 1570s and 1580s would inevitably dilute the results of the analysis. Cf. Cockburn, *Assize Introduction*, 61–62.

fore served an average of 1.8 times each—a level of attendance similar to that calculated for the quarter sessions grand jurors. Once again, the majority of jurors (59 percent) attended only once. At the other extreme, those who attended on more than twice the average number of occasions (five or more times) comprised 6 percent of the total. Although this second group was small, its members can be found serving on most trial juries. An examination of the last five panels in the series indicates that each one included at least two of these jurors, and in each case they were supported by a minimum of four others who had served at least once before. Of the sixty jurors who are listed, thirty-nine (65 percent) had some previous experience.[131]

In coping with the difficulties imposed by early-modern trial procedure, Hertfordshire's juries were therefore able to draw on fairly substantial reservoirs of practical experience. Although this experience was most extensive in the case of the assize grand jury, the other juries typically included several individuals who had served once before and several more who had served on a number of occasions. Moreover, because this fairly specific sort of experience was buttressed on the one hand by moderately high levels of literacy and a rudimentary knowledge of the law, and on the other hand by a more wide-ranging experience in village government, it must have ensured at least a modicum of practical independence.[132]

Assuming that Hertfordshire's juries did enjoy a degree of independence, we may conclude that their decisions were in large part their own. Although features of the procedural context did impose constraints, the jurors remained the principal architects of their own verdicts. As Fuller noted, although the trial juror might be guided by the judge in matters of law, "he needs not to be led by the nose in matters of fact. . . . [H]e cares not whom he displeaseth so he pleaseth his own conscience."[133] But to insist that there was a degree of independence is not to imply that juries were therefore pitted against the bench in a state of continuous conflict. Too often historians confine their attention to the evidence of conflict between judge and jury.[134] Of course,

131. PRO, ASSI 35/60/2/12, 21, 31; 35/60/3/8, 17. See also Beattie, *Crime and the Courts*, 385ff.

132. See also Green, *Verdict According to Conscience*, 150 n. 179. Cf. Cockburn, below, chap. 6, text at n. 100.

133. *Holy State*, 2:117.

134. But see Green, *Verdict According to Conscience*, 129; Beattie, *Crime and the Courts*, 408–10, 421.

this evidence exists. Legal commentators such as Babington dwell at length on the negative aspects of courtroom relations.[135] And as we have seen, the court records themselves suggest that in the face of judicial bullying, jurors might become obstinate. But it is not at all clear that this evidence reflects the true state of relations between judge and jury. After all, Babington was primarily concerned with a quite specific situation—the behavior of grand juries in cases of homicide. Moreover, the records of Star Chamber indicate that judges were rarely forced to use their coercive powers.[136] One suspects that the normal state of courtroom relations was one of cooperation. Rather than stressing the drama of the conflict between judge and jury, we should note that together they participated in a larger drama, the drama of the criminal trial. It was the logic of that drama, particularly its symbolic function, which probably determined the behavior of both participants.

Symbol and ritual were crucial ingredients in the exercise of authority and the maintenance of order in Tudor and early-Stuart England. In the 1530s, while advocating the use of plays in the struggle against the pope, Richard Morison noted that "into the common people things sooner enter by the eyes than by the ears; remembering more better that they see than that they hear."[137] As Penry Williams notes, this sort of argument continued to inform discussions of authority through the sixteenth century.[138] One need only point to the large body of secular and religious symbolism that was constructed around the monarchy.[139] This approach to the maintenance of authority is hardly surprising. As Mervyn James notes, in a society in which the instruments of physical coercion were either nonexistent or difficult to wield, the state was forced to place a special reliance on ideological instruments.[140]

135. Babington, *Advice*, passim.

136. See in particular *List and Index*, ed. Barnes, vol. 3, passim. See also Smith, *De Republica*, 80–81; Hale, *Pleas*, 2:310–12; Cockburn, *Assize Introduction*, 71.

137. Quoted in Williams, *Tudor Regime*, 359.

138. Ibid., 359–60.

139. In addition to Williams see David Bergeron, *English Civic Pageantry* (1971); Roy Strong, *The Cult of Elizabeth: Elizabethan Portraiture and Pageantry* (1977); Paul S. Fritz, "From 'Public' to 'Private': The Royal Funerals in England, 1500–1830," in *Mirrors of Mortality: Studies in the Social History of Death*, ed. Joachim Whaley (1981), 61–79.

140. *English Politics and the Concept of Honour, 1485–1642*, Past and Present Supplement, no 3 (1978), 44. For a particular example of the way in which order was maintained through ideology rather than physical coercion, see John Walter and

This ideological aspect of authority must be kept in mind as we turn to the criminal trial, for here, too, authority was presented in symbolic and ritual form. Each stage of a sitting of the assizes had about it a theatrical quality, from the ceremonial arrival of the judges at the borders of the county, to their procession into court, and finally to that solemn moment when the presiding judge pronounced the death sentence.[141] But if the assizes was a particular instance of social theater, it was also a theater of blood. For the crucial ceremony, the one that gave all the earlier ones their meaning, was the ceremony of the gallows. The public execution underlined the power of the state and conveyed, in the most graphic terms possible, the twin messages of deterrence and obedience.[142] These messages were repeated several times each year, not only in London but throughout the country, before large and attentive audiences. Time and again these audiences watched the unfolding of essentially the same melodrama: the march to the gallows, the sermon, the dying speech full of remorse and warnings against the consequences of crime, and finally the execution itself.[143] Nor can we doubt that these ceremonies made an impression. In his account of the execution of a convicted murderer in 1582, Holinshed noted that the prisoner's clear repentance and "patheticall speeches" had a great effect on the crowd: "all (where of some were such as a man would have thought had never a teare to shed at such a sight, having viewed diverse the like and more lamentable spectacles) with wet eies beheld him."[144] Those who made the laws and guided their enforcement no doubt counted on this effect; it was crucial to

Keith Wrightson, "Dearth and the Social Order in Early Modern England," in *Rebellion, Popular Protest and the Social Order in Early Modern England*, ed. Paul Slack (Cambridge, 1984), 108–28.

141. *Clerk of Assize*, 23–29; *Calendar of State Papers, Domestic, 1667*, 337, Smith, *De Republica*, 83; Cockburn, *Assizes*, 65, 297–302, T.S.P Woods, *Prelude to Civil War, 1642: Mr. Justice Malet and the Kentish Petitions* (Wilton, 1980), 20–21; T. G. Barnes, ed., *Somerset Assize Orders, 1629–1640*, Somerset Record Society, 65 (1959), xviii.

142. Preface, in *Albion's Fatal Tree: Crime and Society in Eighteenth-Century England*, ed. Douglas Hay et al. (Harmondsworth, 1975), 13; Douglas Hay, "Property, Authority and the Criminal Law," in ibid., 56–57. Peter Burke, *Popular Culture in Early Modern Europe* (New York, 1978), 196–98; J. A. Sharpe, " 'Last Dying Speeches': Religion, Ideology and Public Execution in Seventeenth-Century England," *Past and Present* 107 (1985): 144–67; Beattie, *Crime and the Courts*, 423.

143. Sharpe, *Crime in Seventeenth-Century England*, 142; idem, " 'Last Dying Speeches,' " 148ff.

144. Raphael Holinshed, *Chronicles of England, Scotland, and Ireland*, ed. Henry Ellis, 6 vols. (1807–8), 4:495. See also Bellamy, *Tudor Law of Treason*, 209. Cf. Sharpe, " 'Last Dying Speeches,' " 167; Peter Linebaugh, "The Tyburn Riot against the Surgeons," in *Albion's Fatal Tree*, ed. Hay et al., 66.

the maintenance of order. As Robert Greene argued, "he that fears the gallows shall never be [a] good thief."[145]

Exemplary punishment was thus central to early-modern criminal justice, and the logic of exemplary punishment exercised great influence over the whole process of law enforcement. Inevitably, law enforcement was selective; the whole process of prosecution and trial was, in fact, a process of selection.[146] Given the extent of the existing body of capital legislation, there could be no thought of applying the law according to its letter.[147] Such an approach would only prove counter-productive. As Coke noted, "it is not frequent and often punishment that doth prevent . . . offences . . . for the frequency of the punishment makes it so familiar as it is not feared." Moreover, he implies that the terror induced by a single hanging might turn to compassion if too many offenders were sent to the gallows.[148] In the end, only certain individuals would be selected to face the full rigor of the law, and those prisoners would, by the nature of their character or deed, reinforce the message of exemplary punishment—they would be suitable participants in the ceremony of punishment. Nor should they include individuals whose execution might weaken the legitimacy of the sanction. Thus Bacon advised judges to moderate their sentences according to "person, place, time and occasion or other circumstances."[149]

Just as the logic of exemplary punishment shaped the administration of criminal justice in general, so it shaped in particular the behavior of juries. They, too, participated in the process of selection. Through their verdicts they recommended some prisoners for release and others for punishment. In making their selection they no doubt

145. Robert Greene, *A Disputation . . .*, in *Cony-Catchers and Bawdy Baskets: An Anthology of Elizabethan Low Life*, ed. Gamini Salgado (Harmondsworth, 1972), 272.

146. In his discussion of law enforcement in eighteenth-century England, Beattie notes that "[t]he law was applied, and was meant to be applied, selectively." "Crime and the Courts in Surrey, 1736–1753," in *Crime in England*, ed. Cockburn, 171. See also Beattie, *Crime and the Courts*, 421.

147. Although the number of capital statutes was not as large as it would be by the end of the eighteenth century, the sixteenth century did see a widening of the scope of capital punishment. Parliament introduced capital statutes in connection with buggery, witchcraft, horse theft, theft by servants, theft from the person, and theft with breaking. 25 Hen. VIII, c. 6; 5 Eliz. I, c. 17; 33 Hen. VIII, c. 8; 2 & 3 Edw. VI, cc. 29, 33; 21 Hen. VIII, c. 7; 5 Eliz. I, c. 10; 8 Eliz. I, c. 4; 39 Eliz. I, c. 15.

148. Sir Edward Coke, in Epilogue, *The Third Part of the Institutes of the Laws of England* (1797). See also Babington, *Advice*, 52–53. In addition, see the views of Edmund Burke noted in Hay, "Property, Authority and the Criminal Law," 50.

149. Quoted in Samaha, "Hanging for Felony," 775.

began with the evidence. But consideration of the evidence proceeded against a backdrop imposed by the necessity of selection. Indeed, to some extent it was overshadowed by this necessity. It was the process of selection that gave rise to the apparent signs of jury lawlessness—the altered indictments, the partial verdicts, and the verdicts that contradicted the facts of the case. All these suggest that jurors adopted an essentially strategic approach to their task. Evidence might be adapted or even ignored so as to achieve the desired end. At a general level, that end was the designation of appropriate candidates for the ceremony of the gallows. But at a more basic level the decisions of the juries were shaped by specific selection criteria. In principle it should be possible to clarify these criteria through aggregate analyses of the decisions of each of the juries. Unfortunately, this sort of approach is not always possible. Many of the *ignoramus* bills do not survive, and it is therefore difficult to analyze the decisions of the grand juries.[150] For Hertfordshire the most complete body of documentation relates to the verdicts of the assize trial jury. Of the known verdicts returned by the assize trial jury between 1573 and 1624, 41.3 percent were acquittals, 48.3 percent were absolute convictions, and 10.4 percent were partial verdicts.[151]

More important for present purposes, however, is the fact that these general proportions conceal a good number of variations, and many of these variations reflect distinct criteria of selection. The most obvious variation emerges when we compare the treatment of men and women. As Table 5.1 indicates, conviction levels for women were much lower.[152] This is not surprising. Women, like children, were viewed as dependent and inferior. The sight of too many suffering the ultimate sanction would have brought the whole ceremony into disrepute. In addition to the prisoner's sex, it seems clear that juries were also influenced by the prisoner's character. Eighteenth-century juries

150. According to several commentators, *ignoramus* bills were destroyed. Smith, *De Republica*, 69; Cowell, *Interpreter*, under "Jurie."

151. Unless otherwise stated, analyses of the assize trial jury verdicts are based on PRO, ASSI 35/15/4–35/66/2; HRO, HAT SR1/65, 98; SR2/36; SR6/171; SR7/115; SR9/92; SR10/139 (indictments and gaol delivery calendars, 1573–1624). Cf Cockburn, *Assize Introduction*, 177.

152. Of course, women were associated with certain types of crime, and this may have affected the distribution of verdicts. However, the differences persist even when an effort is made to exclude these effects. Thus a comparison of the verdicts for a single offense—grand larceny—only confirms the general picture. In the case of men, 48 percent of the verdicts were convictions and 37 percent were acquittals. For women the comparable proportions were 25 percent and 55 percent. For similar findings, see Hanawalt, *Crime and Conflict*, 54, and Beattie, "Crime and the Courts," 182.

Table 5.1. Assize Trial Jury Verdicts for Male and Female Prisoners, 1573–1624

	Male (%)	Female (%)
Convictions	52	30
Acquittals	38	59
Partial verdicts	10	11
Total	100	100

SOURCES: See n. 151. $N = 1{,}282$

were more inclined to convict prisoners with dubious pasts, particularly prisoners with criminal records.[153] Late-seventeenth-century trials at the Old Bailey suggest that the identification of a prisoner as an "old offender" was itself often enough to ensure conviction.[154] Rare surviving accounts of early-seventeenth-century trials convey the same impression.[155]

The inadequacies of the assize records make it difficult to identify prisoners with criminal records, but it is possible to distinguish between those who, when indicted, were charged with one offense and those who were charged with a series of offenses. It seems probable that multiple offenders were viewed in a particularly negative light and would therefore have made especially appropriate candidates for public execution. As can be seen from Table 5.2, prisoners accused of one offense had a lower proportion of convictions and a higher proportion of acquittals than those accused of multiple offenses. Table 5.2 also suggests that there may have been a countervailing tendency, because the level of partial verdicts was higher for the latter group of prisoners. But this assumes that a partial verdict was invariably a form of discretionary lenience. That may have been true in the case of non-

153. Beattie, "Crime and the Courts," 171–73; Langbein, "Criminal Trial before the Lawyers," 303–5. Cf. Herrup, "Law and Morality," 112ff. Herrup argues that recidivism might be tolerated so long as the offence did not violate certain moral criteria and the offender seemed open to rehabilitation.

154. See, for example, *The Proceedings on the King's Commissions of the Peace, and Oyer and Terminer, and Gaol Delivery of Newgate, Held for the City of London, and the County of Middlesex, at Justice Hall, in the Old-Bayly* (August 1685), 2, 3; *The Proceedings on the King's Commissions of the Peace, and Oyer and Terminer, and Gaol Delivery of Newgate, Held for the City of London and County of Middlesex at Justice-Hall in the Old-Bayly . .* (February 1686), passim.

155. See, for example, Richard Gough, *The History of Myddle*, ed. Peter Razzell (Firle, Sussex, 1979), 82.

Table 5.2. Assize Trial Jury Verdicts for Prisoners Accused of Single and Multiple Offenses, 1573–1624

	Number of Offenses	
	One (%)	Two or More (%)
Convictions	46	62
Acquittals	44	19
Partial verdicts	9	19
Total	99	100

SOURCES: See n. 151. $N = 1{,}282$

clergyable felonies such as burglary. However, a large proportion of the partial verdicts were returned in cases of simple grand larceny; here, a partial verdict amounted to a conviction for petty larceny, and the prisoner would almost certainly be whipped. By contrast, because grand larceny was clergyable, those convicted absolutely stood a good chance of being released unpunished. In these circumstances, as Beattie notes, a partial verdict might be less a form of lenience than an attempt to ensure that a prisoner received at least some form of punishment.[156] The fact that prisoners accused of several offenses received a higher proportion of partial verdicts may simply reflect an attempt by juries to ensure that those among them whose offenses included only grand larcenies would not escape punishment through the protection granted by benefit of clergy.

The jurors thus tailored their verdicts to fit the attributes of the prisoner. Male prisoners with doubtful characters and criminal records were best suited to the needs of exemplary punishment, and they were therefore the most likely to be convicted; the execution of an "old offender" gave the terror of the gallows an undeniable legitimacy. But if the attributes of the prisoner were the crucial criteria, they were not the only ones.

To some extent, trial jurors were also influenced by the character of the prisoner's crime. An examination of verdicts in cases of robbery, burglary, and larceny with breaking indicates that the seriousness of the offense—as measured both by the amount stolen and by the number of participants—exercised some effect.[157] As Table 5.3 indicates,

156. Beattie, *Crime and the Courts*, 486–87.

157. Cf. Sharpe, *Crime in Seventeenth-Century England*, 107–10.

the level of convictions rose with the value of the goods stolen. A similar pattern emerges when prisoners who were indicted alone are compared with those who allegedly acted in the company of accomplices (Table 5.4). Juries were more likely to convict prisoners who fell into the latter category. It would seem that thieves who committed major crimes, or who committed crimes that displayed the attributes of gang activity, were judged as particularly appropriate candidates for the ceremony of the gallows.

It may be that the character of the crime did not provide an independent set of criteria. In apparently responding to the nature of the crime, juries may in fact have been responding to the character of the prisoner. It seems likely that those who committed serious crimes, and who did so with the help of accomplices, were also those who had

Table 5.3. Assize Trial Jury Verdicts for Robbery, Burglary, and Breaking, Compared According to the Value of the Stolen Property, 1573–1624

	Value of the Stolen Property		
	Less than £1 (%)	£1–£10 (%)	More than £10 (%)
Convictions	30	62	70
Acquittals	53	27	23
Partial verdicts	17	10	7
Total	100	99	100

Sources: See n. 151. $N = 281$

Table 5.4. Assize Trial Jury Verdicts for Robbery, Burglary, and Breaking, by Lone and Group Offenders, 1573–1624

	Prisoners Indicted	
	Alone (%)	As Part of Group (%)
Convictions	47	59
Acquittals	39	31
Partial verdicts	14	10
Total	100	100

Sources: See n. 151. $N = 284$

some criminal experience. Although the nature of the crime was not unimportant, the character of the prisoner probably remained the crucial criterion of selection.

A final, though less pronounced, set of criteria emerges when we consider more general social and economic conditions. As Table 5.5 indicates, high crime levels were associated with moderately high levels of convictions and moderately low levels of acquittals.[158] When crime levels were low, the level of convictions fell and the level of acquittals rose.[159] Of course, jurors had no independent source of information about prosecution levels, but they could see the number of prisoners waiting to be tried. It would seem that when this number was large, and when crime levels could be presumed to be high, juries were inclined to strengthen the message of deterrence by sending a larger group to the gallows.[160]

But if juries were influenced by crime levels, they appear to have been largely unaffected by price levels. As Tables 5.6 and 5.7 indicate, prices seem to have had little influence on their verdicts, either in

Table 5.5. Mean Annual Proportions of Assize Trial Jury Verdicts Compared According to Prosecution Levels, 1576–1624

	Prosecution Levels	
	Low (%)	High (%)
Convictions	45	50
Acquittals	45	38
Partial verdicts	10	13
Total	100	101

SOURCES: See n. 158.

158. This and the following analyses are based on PRO, ASSI 35/18/5–35/66/2, HRO, HAT SR1/65, 98; SR2/36; SR6/171; SR7/115; SR9/92; SR10/139 (indictments and gaol calendars, 1576–1624). These analyses have been restricted to those years for which the information on verdicts appears to be complete.

159. Here and elsewhere in the discussion, "high" and "low" are categories defined by the trend. Thus years of "high" crime are years in which the number of persons indicted at the assizes rose above the trend. All trends have been calculated using the regression routines in SPSS-6000.

160. See Samaha, "Hanging for Felony," 777; idem, *Law and Order*, 57; Beattie, "Crime and the Courts," 183–84; Douglas Hay, "War, Dearth and Theft in the Eighteenth Century: The Record of the English Courts," *Past and Present*, 95 (1982): 155.

general or in the more specific case of property crime.[161] Of course, the effect of prices may be masked here by the effect of crime levels. During the late sixteenth and early seventeenth centuries, high prosecution levels usually coincided with high prices. It is therefore difficult to isolate the effect that each might have exerted on juries. Nonetheless, it is noteworthy that some contemporaries implied that economic need was grounds for lenience. Thus, according to Baker, necessity was considered a good defense in cases of larceny.[162] Likewise,

Table 5.6. Mean Annual Proportions of Assize Trial Jury Verdicts for All Offenses Compared According to Price Levels, 1576–1624

	Price Levels	
	Low (%)	High (%)
Convictions	47	48
Acquittals	42	40
Partial verdicts	11	12
Total	100	100

SOURCES: See n. 158.

Table 5.7. Mean Annual Proportions of Assize Trial Jury Verdicts for Property Offenses Compared According to Price Levels, 1576–1624

	Price Levels	
	Low (%)	High (%)
Convictions	49	48
Acquittals	41	39
Partial verdicts	10	12
Total	100	99

SOURCES: See n. 158.

161. The price series used to determine years of high and low prices is Bowden's "average of all grain prices" index. Peter Bowden, Statistical Appendix, in *Agrarian History*, ed. Thirsk, 4:815–21.

162. *The Reports of Sir John Spelman*, vol. 2, ed. J. H. Baker, Selden Society, 94 (1977), 300, 323. See also Green, *Verdict According to Conscience*, 128 and n. 87. Cf. Samaha, *Law and Order*, 57.

William Perkins suggested that crimes that resulted from poverty should be dealt with less severely than other offenses.[163] Moreover, it was in 1596, a year of severe harvest failure, that Edward Hext complained of the reluctance of victims to prosecute: "most comonly the simple Cuntryman and woman, lokynge no farther then ynto the losse of ther owne goods, are of opynyon that they wold not procure a mans death for all the goods yn the world."[164] Jurors may have shared these attitudes. The most suggestive example is the year 1623. Here the effect of prices appears in undiluted form, for although prices were high, prosecution levels were low. Taken together, the court records indicate that convictions accounted for only 25 percent of the verdicts in cases of property crime, while acquittals accounted for 57 percent and partial verdicts for 28 percent.

But rather than any inclination toward mercy, this shift in the balance of verdicts may simply reflect a change in the character of the prisoners brought to trial. It seems probable that during periods of high prices a larger-than-normal proportion of the prisoners would have been members of the "respectable poor"—individuals driven to crime through economic necessity.[165] As a result, a smaller proportion of the prisoners would have satisfied the criteria for inclusion among those selected for execution. During years of economic crisis, jurors may therefore have found themselves caught between conflicting imperatives. On the one hand, rising levels of prosecutions may have encouraged them to increase the number of prisoners sent for punishment; on the other, this inclination was probably muted by the somewhat different character of the prisoners arraigned before them.

The behavior of juries was thus determined first and foremost by the requirements of exemplary punishment and the consequent need to enforce the law selectively. In playing their part in this process of selection, juries were influenced by the character of the accused, the nature of the crime, and certain features of the social and economic environment. Of these criteria, the most important was the character of the accused. The influence exercised by the other criteria was more limited, and to some extent it was simply an extension of the first. The principal task of the jurors continued to be the selection of pris-

163. Christopher Hill, "William Perkins and the Poor," in *Puritanism and Revolution*, ed. idem, 227 n. 4.

164. R. H. Tawney and Eileen Power, eds., *Tudor Economic Documents*, 3 vols. (1924) 2:341.

165. See Hay, "War, Dearth and Theft," 155–56.

oners whose execution would provide an appropriate, and therefore deterrent, example.

To the extent that they adopted a flexible, strategic approach to their task, Elizabethan and Jacobean jurors can be described as lawless. But at a deeper level the description seems inappropriate. While they did violate the letter of the law, jurors did not violate its spirit. Early-modern criminal justice was founded on the logic of exemplary punishment, and this logic demanded that the law be enforced selectively rather than absolutely. It was this demand that shaped the deliberations of the jurors; it was this demand that ensured that the jurors were likely to convict men more than women, "old offenders" more than inexperienced offenders, and serious offenders more than those who committed less serious crimes. This same demand ensured that jurors would adopt a more intolerant stand toward those charged when crime levels were high, and possibly a more tolerant stand toward those charged when prices were high. Far from attempting to moderate the law, the jurors emerge as willing and largely obedient participants in the early-modern system of law enforcement. To some extent, this obedience was ensured by the judge, particularly by his considerable power to guide and control. But this was not the most important factor, for the jurors enjoyed a good deal of practical independence. More important was the fact that the jurors were themselves men of property; they occupied positions of importance within the prevailing structure of wealth and power. Moreover, the patterns of sixteenth- and seventeenth-century economic and cultural polarization ensured that their natural social alignment was with the larger landowners immediately above them in the social structure rather than with the landless and near-landless mass that stretched out below them—and that supplied the bulk of the prisoners who stood before them in court.

Six

Twelve Silly Men? The Trial Jury at Assizes, 1560–1670

J. S. Cockburn

It is often said that familiarity breeds contempt. That maxim finds no place in the literature of the law, but it may help to explain why by the middle of the sixteenth century praise for the criminal trial jury, a familiar institution for three centuries, was limited to the formal panegyrics of legal writers.[1] Criticism of the jury in action was, on the other hand, almost universal. Even Sir Thomas Smith—never slow to extol English institutions—could find few wholly praiseworthy features in the mid-sixteenth-century jury trial. Rather, he was concerned to play down the worrying anomalies that by the 1560s had undermined the ancient safeguard of trial by peers. Although seldom from the same social stratum as the accused, jurors were still, Smith claimed, drawn from the general locality of the crime.[2] If they—like the suspects arraigned before them—were kept uncomfortable prisoners until they reached a verdict, that at least accelerated their decision.[3] To be sure, they were liable to be fined or bound over to Star Chamber by trial judges dissatisfied with their verdicts, but such proceedings were, Smith assured his readers, more sound than substance and, in the rare instances where they were pursued to a conclusion, were thought "very violent, tyrannical and contrary to the liberty and custom of the realm of England."[4]

1. For some seventeenth-century examples, see J. C. Oldham, "The Origins of the Special Jury," *University of Chicago Law Review* 50 (1983): 141 n. 17.

2. They were, Smith thought, "substantial yeomen, that dwell about the place, or at least in the hundred, or near where the felony is supposed to be committed, men acquainted with daily labour and travail, and not with such idle persons as be ready to do such mischiefs." *De Republica Anglorum* (1583), 79. Smith's work was written in about 1565.

3. Ibid., 82: "Considering that [the jurors] be themselves all this while as prisoners . . . it is no marvel . . . they make expedition."

4. Ibid., 88–89.

Most of the jury's critics were less disingenuous. Jurors, they asserted, were usually unwilling, often illiterate, and frequently overburdened.[5] They were routinely intimidated by overmighty judges[6] or stampeded by a dominating foreman into unjust verdicts.[7] A former lord mayor of London openly ridiculed the possibility of twelve jurors, "eleven of which it's possible can neither write nor read," actually presuming to judge law.[8] Zachary Babington, for twenty years of the seventeenth century an assize clerk on the Oxford circuit, characterized the composition of juries there as a "scandal."[9] Robert Parsons simply dismissed the trial jury as "twelve silly men" compelled by an uncaring oligarchy to decide matters of life and death in an atmosphere of partiality, haste, and confusion.[10]

Parsons was, of course, a Jesuit, viewing with dismay the increasingly hostile proceedings against adherents of the old faith. Similarly, the most strident of the jury's seventeenth-century critics were dissenters, like John Lilburne, whose reservations about jury trial reflected both their reversals at law and their deep commitment to the ideal of a godly magistracy.[11] To that extent, their strictures should perhaps be discounted. But Zachary Babington; the Essex clergyman William Harrison; those who promoted the attempted reforms of

5. For full citations, see Cockburn, *Assize Introduction*, 58–61.

6. Smith (*De Republica*, 88) alluded to the practice by which judges conveyed their wishes to the trial jury by means of "some watchword."

7. At Northampton in 1665 the foreman of a jury that convicted Quakers for offenses against the Conventicle Act was said to have bullied into silence or agreement the ten jurors who originally favored an acquittal. C. W. Horle, "Partridges upon the Mountains: The Quakers and the English Legal System, 1660–1688" (Ph.D. diss., Univ. of Maryland, 1985), 153–54.

8. [Samuel Starling], *An Answer to the Seditious and Scandalous Pamphlet* (1671), 2, quoted in Horle, "Partridges upon the Mountains," 288.

9. Zachary Babington, *Advice to Grand Jurors in Cases of Blood* (1677), 12–13. For Babington's circuit service, see Cockburn, *Assizes*, 81, 127, 132, 317, 324–25.

10. Robert Parsons, *The Jesuit's Memorial for the Intended Reformation of England under their First Popish Prince*, ed. E. Gee (1690), 248–51. Parsons's tract was written in 1597. Dr. Stephen Roberts has pointed out to me, quite rightly, that in the early modern period *silly* was probably understood to mean unsophisticated or simple rather than foolish.

To an Italian commentator, writing about twenty-five years earlier, even torture seemed a less arbitrary way of deciding life and death: "The lives of many wretches [are] taken away by the judgment of men who understand little, being people of low class . . . who through not understanding or wanting to hurry too much, resolve it perhaps to the contrary of the way they should. In other states people are rarely put to death before being made to confess the truth either by torture or by other means." PRO, SP 12/78/34 ("Considerationi sopra la justitia criminale") [translated].

11. Green, *Verdict According to Conscience*, 153–207.

1571, 1607, 1621, and 1665; the judges and local magistrates who periodically lamented the dearth of jurors at assizes and quarter sessions; and the grand jurors who complained in 1629 and 1648 about the indiscriminate use of talesmen were not disappointed litigants and had no political ax to grind.[12] Rather, like Christopher St. German and Thomas More earlier in the sixteenth century, they were persuaded by practical experience that the trial jury had become the weak link in the chain of judicial process.[13]

Any assessment of the nature of jury trial in early modern England must take into account that possibility and the vein of adverse criticism that supports it. A failure to do so is one of several flaws in the most recent attempt to represent the early-seventeenth-century jury as a largely autonomous vehicle of community discretion.[14] Much of the argument against that view has been set out elsewhere, and the detailed evidence will not be repeated here.[15] The main purposes of this essay are, rather, to augment that evidence by extending the statistical analysis of jury service down to 1670; to investigate two further issues raised by contemporary critics of the jury system (juror literacy and the role of the foreman in jury deliberations); and finally, in the light of the additional evidence, to reconsider the case for and against jury initiative in the century after 1560.

That service on a trial jury in the sixteenth and seventeenth centuries was unpopular and that jurors at both assizes and quarter sessions were often in short supply seems now beyond doubt.[16] Contemporaries assumed that efforts to combat a chronic shortage of jurors resulted automatically in the impaneling of unqualified men "of all

12. William Harrison, *The Description of England*, ed. A. Edelen (Ithaca, 1968), 91; PRO, SP 12/77/48 ("Byll for Juryes," 10 Apr. 1571); *Stuart Royal Proclamations . . . 1603–1625*, ed. J. F. Larkin and P. Hughes (Oxford, 1973), 167–71; 16 & 17 Chas. II, c. 3; Cockburn, *Assizes*, 313; "The Note Book of a Surrey Justice," ed. G. Leveson-Gower, *Surrey Archaeological Collections* 9 (1888): 180, PRO, ASSI 35/70/1; *Western Circuit Assize Orders, 1629–1648*, ed. J. S Cockburn, Royal Historical Society, Camden, 4th ser., 17 (1976), 1190.

13. *St German's Doctor & Student*, ed. T.F.T. Plucknett and J. L. Barton, Selden Society, 91 (1974), 299; *The Reports of Sir John Spelman*, vol. 2, ed. J. H. Baker, Selden Society, 94 (1978), Introduction, 106.

14. C. B. Herrup, "Law and Morality in Seventeenth-Century England," *Past and Present* 106 (1985): 102–23.

15. Cockburn, *Assize Introduction*, 56–71, 131–33.

16. Ibid., 59. The shortage continued into the early eighteenth century. Beattie, *Crime and the Courts*, 378–79.

sorts,"[17] and it is easy to overlook the fact that most talesmen were, by definition, those with either the leisure or a reason to attend court. Mere spectators impaneled *de circumstantibus* are hardly likely to have included many of the laboring poor, whose ignorance so appalled critics of the jury system. Men with business at court typically included victims, witnesses, and those who had entered bonds for the appearance or good behavior of others. Such men were certainly coopted onto deficient trial juries.[18] But whether or not their inclusion offended the letter as well as the spirit of the law was purely a matter of chance. Doubtless some witnesses were, as the abortive bill of 1571 alleged, "men of very mean estate."[19] But most victims of property crime and those standing surety were, by definition, men of modest means,[20] and it is reasonable to assume that at least some of them satisfied the statutory property qualifications for jury service.[21] The same may also have been true of constables, who were intermittently impaneled, and it was certainly true of grand jurors sworn for petty jury service.[22] Although the potential for dilution is obvious, it seems likely that contemporaries routinely overstated the impact on the social composition of petty juries of men impaneled de circumstantibus. But whether the bulk of trial jurors were, as Smith asserted, "substantial yeomen" is very difficult to ascertain.[23] The limited investigations so far completed suggest only that a majority of trial jurors at assizes and quarter sessions during this period were probably yeomen or craftsmen.[24] How "substantial" they were remains unclear.

17. PRO, SP 12/77/48; ASSI 35/70/1. There was apparently no property qualification for talesmen until 1692, when it was established by statute at one-half of that for regularly impaneled jurors. 4 W. & M., c. 24, repeated by 3 Geo. II, c. 25 (1730).

18. Cockburn, *Assize Introduction*, 60–61.

19 PRO, SP 12/77/48.

20 The amount of bonds entered at assizes in this period ranged between £5 and £20. Most of those standing surety are described as yeomen or tradesmen. Cockburn, *Assize Introduction*, 274–75; *Cal. Assize Records. Hertfordshire Jas. I*, passim.

21. For the qualifications, see Cockburn, *Assize Introduction*, 57; Oldham, "Origins of the Special Jury," 214–21.

22. Cockburn, *Assize Introduction*, 51, 59; Joan Kent, "The English Village Constable, 1580–1642: The Nature and Dilemmas of the Office," *Journal of British Studies* 20 (1981): 26–49. However, the data for the Essex village of Terling tabulated in K. Wrightson and D. Levine, *Poverty and Piety in an English Village: Terling, 1525–1700* (New York, 1979), 105, suggest that constables were of lower social status than sessions jurors and, by implication, than assize jurors as well.

23. *De Republica*, 79.

24. See above, chap. 5, text at n. 65; C. B. Herrup, "The Common Peace: Legal Structure and Legal Substance in East Sussex, 1594–1640" (Ph.D. diss., Northwestern Univ., 1982), 201–6, 463–65.

Since contemporaries equated wealth and social status with intelligence and good judgment, the failure to establish the economic status of individual jurors is particularly tantalizing.[25] It means that for the time being we cannot use even that dubious measure of intelligence to test contemporary assertions of widespread juror ignorance. We know that in Mary's reign eleven members of a trial jury could claim that only their foreman was able to read the evidence submitted to them,[26] and in 1565 Smith implied that, although trial jurors were given the indictments before they retired to consider their verdicts, it was assumed that they could not read them.[27] A century later, however, the authoritative *Clerk of Assize* spoke of a written note stating the prisoners' names and offenses that was given to the jurors "for their better direction and help of their memory to know who they have in charge."[28] Hawles, writing in 1680, assumed, perhaps a trifle idealistically, that jurors had the leisure and ability to read such works as Horne's *Mirror*, Coke's *Institutes*, and Vaughan's *Reports*.[29] This could be taken to indicate that by the late seventeenth century most trial jurors could read and that the century after 1560 had seen significant advances in juror literacy.

Direct evidence of this development—if, indeed, it took place—is lacking. But if we accept the ability to write one's name as an index of literacy, then some tentative inferences can be drawn from an analysis of the juror signatures that infrequently appear on assize indictments.[30] The evidence is, admittedly, very limited. Trial jurors signed only "special" verdicts—the effect of which was to reserve the issue for discussion by the judges assembled in Serjeants' Inn—and such cases were rare. Only four special verdicts were returned on the Home circuit between 1560 and 1625 and, unfortunately, none of them are

25. Cockburn, *Assize Introduction*, 61.

26. PRO, STAC 4/3/43.

27. *De Republica*, 81. The indictment was, of course, in Latin.

28. T. W., *The Office of the Clerk of Assize* . . . (1682), 48.

29. J. Hawles, *The Englishman's Right* (1844 ed.), 76–77.

30. See Cressy, *Literacy and the Social Order: Reading and Writing in Tudor and Stuart England* (Cambridge, 1980), 53–61, for a discussion of signatures as a measure of literacy. Dr. Cressy's assessment of the course of yeoman literacy in southeastern England (which includes no data from Kent) is broadly compatible with the pattern suggested here. Ibid., 100, 107, 121, 125–27, 154–56. For a stimulating discussion, in a medieval context, of the significance of literacy, see B. Stock, *The Implications of Literacy: Written Language and Models of Interpretation in the Eleventh and Twelfth Centuries* (Princeton, 1983), esp. pp. 88–240. I am grateful to Dr. G. M. Spiegel for bringing this work to my attention.

signed.[31] Between 1650 and 1685, however, Home circuit juries returned at least eight special verdicts, all of which bear the signatures or marks of the jurors concerned.[32] In addition, a jury at Chelmsford assizes in March 1651 submitted and signed a unique memorandum of its verdicts on the ten suspects arraigned before it.[33] The sample is completed by two coroners' juries which, although suggestive rather than strictly comparable, have the advantage of being dated 1625 and 1639, respectively.[34]

Analysis of these data strongly suggests that most late-seventeenth-century jurors—at least on the Home circuit—were literate. Of the 108 jurors signing documents in the thirty-five years after 1650, only 11 (10.2 percent) did so by mark,[35] and all 36 who witnessed special verdicts after 1673 signed their own names.[36] On the other hand, only 10 (35.7 percent) of the 28 jurors who endorsed coroners' inquests in the first half of the century were able to sign their own names.[37] It is doubtful that these figures indicate an increase in the percentage of literate jurors on the Home circuit from approximately 36 percent in the first half of the seventeenth century to almost 90 percent in the second. But they do raise the possibility of a steady improvement in literacy during the century and the probability that seventeenth-century reports of juror ignorance were, at least in the narrow sense, much exaggerated.

The broader question of juror experience is equally debatable. A case has been made for local administrative office as an important component in the experience of assize and quarter sessions jurors,[38] and it is certainly true that some jurors had served as constables or in other local offices.[39] But the value of such service to those sworn to

31. For the references, see Cockburn, *Assize Introduction*, 112 n. 192.

32. PRO, ASSI 35/91/1, m. 44; 92/6, m. 35; 95/7, m. 37, 103/5, m. 35; 114/4, m. 61, 115/5, m. 48; 120/6 (unnumbered membrane); 126/5 (unnumbered membrane). For some later examples not considered here, see Beattie, *Crime and the Courts*, 81 n. 18

33. PRO ASSI 35/92/1, m. 47.

34. Ibid., 35/67/5, m. 40v, 81/4, m. 71.

35. Ibid., 35/92/6, m. 35 (Kent, July 1651): 3 marks; 103/5, m. 35 (Kent, July 1662): 4 marks, 114/4, m. 61 (Kent, Mar. 1673): 4 marks.

36. Ibid., 35/115/5, m. 48 (Kent, Apr. 1674); 120/6 (Kent, July 1679); 126/5 (Kent, Sept. 1685).

37. Ibid., 35/67/5, m. 40v (Kent, July 1625): 5 signatures; 81/4, m. 71 (Kent, July 1639) 5 signatures.

38. See above, chap. 5, text at n. 124.

39. For a spectacular example, see below, text at n. 68.

jury service is uncertain. Local office probably served as an introduction to the vagaries of those in authority and to the inadequacy of local law enforcement agencies. But the extent to which it prepared jurors for the acute and particular pressures of the assize courtroom or for the fundamental moral dilemma of deciding life and death remains questionable.[40]

Attempts to equate "experience" with repeated jury service are more persuasive. Repeated exposure to the relatively narrow range of legal issues raised by the bulk of assize business probably meant that some jurors accumulated a superficial familiarity with the substantive criminal law, at least insofar as it protected property. Such familiarity led to an overall acceleration in the pace of criminal proceedings in the eighteenth century as judges were able to cut short their instructions and juries were able to minimize their deliberations.[41]

Much of the data on trial jury service at assizes between 1559 and 1603 has already been published.[42] In general the data suggest that most trial jurors served only once or twice in a lifetime: of 6,408 men sworn to service on the Home circuit between 1559 and 1603, only 1,417 (22 percent) served more than twice.[43] Moreover, each juror normally served on only one panel at a given assizes before being discharged, perhaps to serve at a subsequent sitting or, more likely, never again. On the face of it, these patterns suggest that the vast majority of late-sixteenth-century trial jurors were unfamiliar with legal and procedural issues, and they may have required careful tutoring from the bench. A small number, it is true, were exceptionally active, serving as many as thirty or forty times. But even if men from this pool were systematically included in trial juries,[44] perhaps at several consecutive sittings, their impact remains unclear. One possibility, of course, was a jury dominated by one or two "experienced" members—something that seventeenth-century critics found even less palatable than uniform ignorance.[45] Be that as it may, occasional and unsystem-

40. That dilemma, of course, lies at the root of the "jury lawlessness" discussed above in chapter 5. Jurors who had served in other local government capacities may have developed a certain shrewdness, and it is also true that the Puritan view of the world did involve an awareness of fairly sophisticated moral choices. I am grateful to Dr. Stephen Roberts for pointing this out. For further discussion of the general issue, see Beattie, *Crime and the Courts*, 387–89.

41. Beattie, *Crime and the Courts*, 165, Langbein, "The Criminal Trial before the Lawyers," *University of Chicago Law Review* 45 (1978): 277, 284.

42. Cockburn, *Assize Introduction*, 61, 62.

43. Calculations based on ibid., 62.

44. For this suggestion, see above, chap. 5, n. 131.

45. See above, n. 7.

atic service on a single jury at each assizes continued to dominate the pattern throughout the early seventeenth century. Approximately 80 percent of those impaneled for trial jury service at Kent assizes between 1603 and 1649 served only once or twice, and 64 percent only once.[46]

At the summer assizes of 1650, however, the traditional pattern changed abruptly. In Kent and Surrey—two of the three largest counties on the Home circuit—the established custom of swearing jurors for service on only a single panel was suddenly replaced by a more coherent system in which men were instead impaneled on up to five juries at the same assizes.[47] Thus at Croydon assizes in July of that year, the six juries impaneled were filled by only twenty-four men: twelve served on two separate juries, and the remaining twelve on four.[48] At Maidstone assizes on 5 August, thirty-six men made up six juries, and seven months later, in March 1651, the three juries impaneled there required only fourteen men.[49] This pattern was maintained until at least as late as 1675,[50] and since it is very similar to that already identified in eighteenth-century Surrey,[51] it seems likely that repeated, or serial, service at one assizes remained the norm, there and in Kent, for more than a century after 1650.

Some of the advantages of serial service are fairly clear. Table 6.1 indicates that the average number of jurors sworn at each assizes in Kent between 1650 and 1669 was almost exactly half what it had been in the twenty-five years before 1650. Indeed, by the 1660s the average number of men needed to fill each panel was down from almost twelve to less than five, and at several winter sessions in that decade it dropped to as low as three. Such a radical reduction in the number of men sworn at each assizes must have brought several benefits. It greatly reduced—perhaps even eliminated—the possibility that unqualified men or talesmen might have to be sworn, and thus it removed a routinely criticized feature of jury composition; it reduced

46. These statistics were drawn from *Cal. Assize Records: Kent Jas. I* and Kent jury panels in PRO, ASSI 35/67–90. For similar conclusions based on the Hertfordshire data to 1624, see above, chap. 5, text at n. 130.

47. The following section is based on an examination of trial jury panels in PRO, ASSI 35/91–111 (1650–1670).

48. PRO, ASSI 35/91/5.

49. Ibid., 91/7; 92/5.

50. Based on trial jury panels in ibid., 112–16 (1671–1675). The rolls from the period after 1675 are currently being repaired. For similar changes in Essex in the 1780s, see below, chap. 9, text at n. 114.

51. Beattie, *Crime and the Courts*, 380–82.

Table 6.1. Number of Jurors Sworn at Kent Assizes, 1625–1669

	Assizes	Juries	Jurors	Average No. per Panel
1625–29	9	30	343	11.4
1630–34	9	31	356	11.5
1635–39	10	33	388	11.8
1640–44	6	16	168	10.5
1645–49	8	27	285	10.6
1650–54	10	36	266	7.4
1655–59	8	27	171	6.3
1660–64	9	48	233	4.9
1665–69	4	12	59	4.9
Total	73	260	2,269	8.7

SOURCE: ASSI 35/67–111.

the time required to call and swear new jurors; and, presumably, it allowed judges to accelerate the proceedings by paring or eliminating altogether the charge traditionally given to each jury before it considered its verdicts.[52]

We know very little about the effect of serial service on jury deliberations. It seems reasonable to assume, however, that twelve men who remained together while deliberating on forty or more suspects, arraigned in four batches, did so with increasing familiarity, confidence, and expedition. Although we can only guess at the total time saved in this way,[53] the overall gains in both time and efficiency were surely considerable. It is probably no accident that the evidence of serial service is strongest in the circuit's largest and most populous counties, where gaol calendars were consistently heavy and the demand for jurors was particularly acute. In Essex, where in the 1650s between two and four juries were normally required at each assizes, the introduction of serial service was delayed until 1653 and was only a sporadic feature thereafter.[54] Hertfordshire and Sussex, whose tra-

52. Even before 1650 the charge was probably cursory. Cockburn, *Assize Introduction*, 109.

53. Assuming that before 1650 it might take as long as twenty minutes to make up and swear a jury, that each jury was given some sort of charge before retiring, and that jury deliberations accelerated after that date, total savings of more than two hours seem possible.

54. In consequence, the average number of men needed to fill each Essex panel between 1650 and 1654 was almost ten.

ditionally light calendars could usually be dealt with by one or two juries, yield few instances of serial service.

We can be reasonably certain, then, that the change introduced in 1650 was designed to turn weakness into strength by formalizing the fact of endemic juror shortages in the interest of improved efficiency.[55] Whether or not the modification was a direct response to criticisms of the existing system is, however, unclear. Since the change occurred at the same time in two of the circuit's five counties, it seems likely that it originated in some central directive, perhaps a decision taken by the assembled judges or, more probably, a directive of the Rump, emanating from one of its committees. In the 1640s and 1650s, as Dr. Roberts has pointed out, "the jury was the target of Leveller pamphleteering and a talking-point for radical lawyers in the Rump and the nominated assembly."[56] Against that background, a central directive introducing serial jury service seems entirely consistent. Since there is some evidence that in the mid 1650s attempts were made in at least one county to purge political undesirables from the lists of those eligible for jury service, a political motivation for changes in Home circuit practice cannot be entirely ruled out.[57] However, serial jury service there not only antedated the reforming activity concentrated in 1655–56 but also survived the Restoration of the Stuart monarchy in 1660. This suggests that the reasoning behind the rationalization of 1650 transcended political considerations.

In at least one county the rationalization of jury recruitment took a further, related form. From about 1640 there are signs, in Kent if not elsewhere, that attention was focusing on the qualifications and role of the jury foreman. To that point, the foreman appears to have been merely the first among equals; he spoke for his fellow jurors, was listed first on the panel,[58] and presumably was selected from its literate members.[59] But there is no indication, either in contemporary sources or Home circuit practice, that jury experience was considered a necessary prerequisite for service as a foreman, or that holders of the

55. For a discussion of earlier efforts to increase efficiency, see Cockburn, *Assize Introduction*, 59–60.

56. S. K. Roberts, "Initiative and Control. The Devon Quarter Sessions Grand Jury, 1649–1670," *BIHR* 57 (1984), 168 The proximity of the Home circuit changes to the trial of John Lilburne in September 1649 should not, perhaps, be overlooked. See Green, *Verdict According to Conscience*, 160, 170–77.

57. Roberts, "Initiative and Control," 168–71; see also N. L. Matthews, *William Sheppard, Cromwell's Law Reformer* (Cambridge, 1984), 156–59, 163–64.

58. Smith, *De Republica*, 82.

59. See above, text at n. 8.

office exercised exceptional influence. For eighty years after 1558 most Home circuit foremen, like rank-and-file jurors, served only once or twice, not always in that capacity, and rarely more than once at a single assizes. In 1638, however, that pattern began to change. At the Kent winter assizes of that year, Robert Day was returned as the foreman of one of the four juries impaneled.[60] He had last served as a juryman in February 1635[61]—his only appearance to that point—and the traditional pattern of service suggested that he would not be called again for several years. In fact, over the next ten years Day was sworn to a further ten juries—one-quarter of the total extant—and on each occasion he was designated the foreman.[62] On two occasions, in 1641 and 1642, he served as the foreman of two different juries at the same assizes,[63] thereby anticipating the pattern of serial service introduced in 1650. In the course of a thirteen-year career as an assize juror, Day participated in at least 118 trials, 111 of them as foreman.

Robert Day's experience of assize trial, considerable though it must have been, pales into insignificance, however, beside that of Bernard Ellis. Between February 1640 and March 1663 Ellis attended twenty-one of the thirty-eight assizes for which records survive.[64] During that time he was sworn to at least fifty juries, on forty-one of which he was the foreman. From 1650 onward he invariably served as the foreman, usually of several juries at the same assizes and frequently of all those impaneled at that session. During a career that spanned twenty-four years and three regimes, Ellis was directly involved in the trial of almost 400 prisoners.

Beyond the bare facts of his extraordinary career as an assize juror, we know tantalizingly little about Bernard Ellis. He appears to have been born in 1605, which would mean that he was thirty-five years old when first sworn to jury service in Kent.[65] That may indicate that he had recently moved to the county and was, in fact, a younger son of the Cumberland gentleman of the same name who was admitted to Gray's Inn in 1587.[66] In any event, by 1640 he had settled at Darenth,

60. PRO, ASSI 35/80/2.

61. Ibid., 35/77/4.

62. Ibid., 35/80–88.

63. PRO, 30/26/104; ASSI 35/84/11.

64. This discussion is based on an analysis of ASSI 35/82–104.

65. Kent Archives Office (hereafter KAO), P109/25/3 (Darenth parish records), note on a copy of the will of Bernard Ellis (d. 1713) referring to an epitaph in the chancel of Darenth church. I am grateful to Katherine Topping of the Kent Archives Office for a copy of this document and for other references to Ellis.

66. *Register of Admissions to Gray's Inn, 1521–1889*, ed. J. Foster (1889), 71.

where he lived until his death in July 1667. Under the terms of his will, Ellis left twelve shillings a year to the poor of Darenth, and it is clear that, although consistently styled a "yeoman," he had accumulated a modest estate.[67] In 1651, and possibly 1652, he served as constable of Axton hundred.[68] Later generations of the family attended Gray's Inn and held property in both Darenth and Dartford.[69]

Although he is easily the most spectacular example of an institutionalized foreman, Ellis's career is in fact only one illustration of a pattern of service that in Kent continued to the end of our period.[70] Between 1651 and 1663 the foreman of several juries upon which Ellis did not serve was Thomas Brewer of Bearsted. During a career that began in 1646 and ended twenty-one years later, Brewer was sworn to at least forty juries, on thirty-one of which he served as the foreman. Either Ellis or Brewer presided over fifty-nine of the one hundred juries known to have been impaneled in Kent between 1650 and 1663. After Ellis's retirement in 1663, Brewer joined forces with Henry Toller of Westerham, who between 1660 and 1670 served on twenty-four juries, eleven times as the foreman.

The introduction of a virtually institutionalized foreman and serial service for rank-and-file jurymen brought an unprecedented degree of stability to the Kent trial jury in the second half of the seventeenth century. Broadly speaking, the mid-century innovations meant that after 1650 virtually all Kent panels contained experienced jurors, one of whom almost always served as the foreman. Indeed, in the sense that after 1650 most jurors were sworn to several panels at one assizes, almost all, in the short term at least, were "experienced." The sharp contrast between this state of affairs and the pre-1650 pattern of random and occasional service is to some extent revealed by Table 6.1. It is even more clearly illuminated, however, by the statistics of individual service after mid century. At the five assizes held between March 1653 and March 1655, for example, fifty-three men were sworn to fill fourteen juries.[71] Bernard Ellis presided over twelve of the fourteen; the foreman of the remaining two was William Hayes of Cobham,

67. KAO, P109/25/3; E. Hasted, *History of Kent*, 2d ed. (1797), 2:376. At the winter assizes 1657 an information was entered against Ellis alleging that he had failed to enclose fifteen acres of coppice in Darenth. PRO, ASSI 35/98/11, m. 114.

68. PRO, ASSI 35/92/6, mm. 1–2v This probably explains why Ellis was not sworn as an assize juror during those two years, which was unusual for him.

69. *Register of Admissions to Gray's Inn*, ed. Foster, 297, 335; KAO, P109/25/3; Hasted, *History of Kent*, 376.

70. This section is based on an analysis of ASSI 35/91–111.

71. This section is based on an analysis of ASSI 35/94–101.

who also served with Ellis on the other twelve. Of the forty juries impaneled between 1653 and 1660, twenty-six were presided over by Ellis, four by Hayes, and four by Thomas Brewer. In addition, Hayes served as a juror on a further sixteen occasions, and Brewer on ten. As a result, only six of the forty juries sworn during these seven years were not presided over by one of the three men, and on twenty occasions two or all three of them were sworn to the same jury. During the same period, fourteen different judges rode the Home circuit, only four of them on more than three occasions, and the circuit clerkship changed hands once.[72] Looked at from this point of view, the most stable element in criminal justice administration in Kent during these years was the trial jury.

Although both serial and repeated service played a part in establishing the extraordinary continuity of the Kent jury, surely the key role was that taken by the five men who in the twenty years after 1650 virtually monopolized the office of foreman.[73] The experience of men like Bernard Ellis and Thomas Brewer obviously transcended a familiarity with the superficial forms of assize trial. Their combined jury service spanned twenty-seven years, during which they tried almost seven hundred prisoners accused of a relatively narrow range of offenses. In that time twenty-five judges traveled the Home circuit, seldom for more than two consecutive years, and three different men held the circuit clerkship.[74] These statistics, taken together, indicate that although Ellis and Brewer had, as far as we know, no formal legal training, their experience of the criminal law in action compared favorably with that of any member of the Home circuit establishment.

Long familiarity with the limited range of legal issues involved in most assize cases and with the variety of verdicts available to the trial jury suggests that members of this foreman elite also exercised an extraordinary degree of control over the jury's deliberations and verdict. Hawles thought that rank-and-file jurors in the late seventeenth century normally deferred to the foreman and other experienced members of the panel.[75] Quakers, too, believed that seventeenth-century

72. Cockburn, *Assizes*, 273–74, 314.

73. Bernard Ellis of Darenth (foreman 1649–1663), William Godfrey of Boxley (foreman 1651–1662); Thomas Brewer of Bearsted (foreman 1651–1666); Henry Toller of Westerham (foreman 1661–1670); William Hayes of Cobham (foreman 1646–1660).

74. Cockburn, *Assizes*, 272–75, 314.

75. Hawles, *Englishman's Right*, 69–70.

foremen exercised a decisive, and often malign, influence on jury verdicts.[76]

Statistical analysis lends some support to the notion of a connection between juror experience and the pattern of verdicts at assizes. Table 6.2, which tabulates jury verdicts between 1560 and 1670, indicates that the acquittal and conviction rates for crimes against property in Kent averaged approximately 37 and 63 percent respectively (counting partial verdicts as convictions). Although there were significant short-term fluctuations—notably between 1560 and 1569 and in the war period 1640–1649, when acquittals rose to over 47 percent—these rates remained fairly stable until 1650. Thereafter, acquittals rose to 39 percent of those indicted between 1650 and 1659 and to 41 percent in the following decade. This trend alone may point to a modest, though apparently sustained, change in juror attitudes after 1650.

A general verdict of guilty or not guilty did not, however, exhaust the possibilities open to trial jurors in the early modern period. They could, alternatively, find the accused guilty of a lesser offense than that formally charged in the indictment. In the context of property crime, such "partial verdicts," as contemporaries often called them, typically reduced a capital charge of burglary to clergyable larceny or

Table 6.2. Kent Jury Verdicts in Property Crimes, 1560–1670

		Acquitted		Convicted as Charged		Partial Verdict	
Decade	Tried	No.	%	No.	%	No.	%
1560–69	237	113	47.7	124	52.3	none	
1570–79	257	89	34.6	166	64.6	2	0.8
1580–89	445	149	33.5	291	65.4	5	1.1
1590–99	569	184	32.3	367	64.5	18	3.2
1600–09	376	132	35 1	219	58.2	25	6.6
1610–19	159	50	31.4	89	56.0	20	12.6
1620–29	216	64	29.6	123	56.9	29	13.4
1630–39	474	172	36.3	250	52.7	52	11.0
1640–49	276	130	47.1	119	43.1	27	9.8
1650–59	303	118	38.9	134	44.2	51	16.8
1660–69	298	122	40.9	121	40.6	55	18.5
Total	3,610	1,323	36.6	2,003	55.5	284	7.9

SOURCE: ASSI 35/2–111.

76. See above, n. 7.

one of grand larceny to petty larceny, a misdemeanor punishable by whipping. They could also, of course, be used to reduce charges of murder to clergyable manslaughter. Influenced, no doubt, by their potential in capital cases, contemporaries interpreted partial verdicts as expressions of jury clemency,[77] and that line has been followed by most modern commentators. Recently, however, Professor Beattie has pointed out that in many instances the jury's intention may well have been to strengthen judicial sanctions by substituting a more painful, and public, whipping for the formal branding that followed a successful plea of benefit of clergy.[78] Beattie's suggestion seems entirely reasonable and serves to alert us once again to the danger of accepting contemporary criticisms of jury behavior at face value. Nevertheless, it does not threaten the general assumption that partial verdicts are a reliable, if somewhat opaque, guide to jury attitudes.

Table 6.2 and Figure 6.1 demonstrate that at Kent assizes partial verdicts were unknown in the 1560s and very uncommon before 1590.[79] Thereafter, their use steadily increased until by the 1660s more than 31 percent of all convictions were the product of partial verdicts. This overall pattern was punctuated by two dramatic surges. The first, in the twenty years after 1600, took the incidence of partial

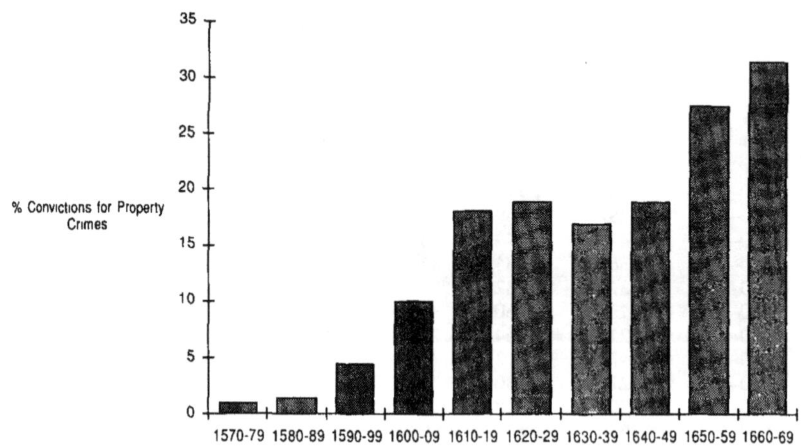

Figure 6.1. Partial Verdicts at Kent Assizes in Convictions for Property Crimes, 1560–1669.

77. See below, text at n. 83.

78. Beattie, *Crime and the Courts*, 486–87.

79. They were somewhat more frequent in Essex and Hertfordshire and common at the Old Bailey during this period. Cockburn, *Assize Introduction*, 115, 175–81.

verdicts from less than 5 to over 18 percent of all convictions for property crimes. The second saw the incidence of partial verdicts increase even more abruptly, from just over 18 percent in the decade ending in 1649 to more than 27 percent ten years later and to over 31 percent by 1669.

To some extent, this pattern defies explanation. We cannot, of course, know whether the dearth of partial verdicts throughout the circuit in the 1560s, and in some counties well beyond, indicates that jurors were unaware of their discretionary powers, were unwilling to use them, or were prevented from doing so by the assize bench. Legal writers before 1560 were certainly familiar with the possibility of charge reduction by the trial jury. Indeed, the Marian assize judge William Staunford, writing in 1557, listed the types of charges in which partial verdicts, which he called "special verdicts," were possible.[80] However, Sir Thomas Smith, describing trial procedure less than a decade later, spoke as if a general verdict of guilty or not guilty was the only possibility open to trial juries.[81] On balance, it seems more likely that Elizabethan jurors were unwilling to exercise, rather than unaware of, their discretionary powers.

We cannot, however, discount the possibility that charge reduction was in fact regulated by the assize bench and that some, if not all, partial verdicts in the early part of our period are a measure of judicial rather than juror discretion. A theory of judicial control is consistent with Smith's allusion to the "watchword" by which early Elizabethan judges communicated their wishes to the trial jury.[82] It may also help to explain the hostility with which late-sixteenth-century assize judges viewed the increasing tendency of both trial and grand jurors to "usurp" the discretionary powers of judge and sovereign.[83] Indeed, William Lambard's account of this, and the fact that many of the earliest examples of partial verdicts reduce a charge of murder to one of clergyable homicide, may point to the gradual extension in the late sixteenth century of a discretion that at first had been sanctioned and regulated by the bench and, perhaps, limited in practice to cases of homicide.

It seems clear that by the 1590s assize judges on the Home circuit

80. W. Staunford, *Les Plees del Coron* (1557), 165.

81. *De Republica*, 82, 87–88

82. Ibid., 88.

83. *William Lambarde and Local Government: His "Ephemeris" and Twenty-nine Charges to Juries and Commissions*, ed. C. Read (Ithaca, 1962), 119–20, cf pp. 172, 175–76

were attempting in vain to discourage the unauthorized exercise of discretionary powers by both trial and grand jurors. Judicial attempts to limit grand jury discretion continued into the seventeenth century, during which there were, according to Babington, "great contests and differences" between the judge and the grand jurors over charge reduction in "cases of blood."[84] Direct opposition to the exercise of discretionary authority by trial jurors, however, appears to have been replaced in part by an informal system of judicially controlled plea bargaining in which charge reductions were exchanged for guilty pleas. In this way, Home circuit judges were able to exclude the jury from between 10 and 30 percent of the criminal cases heard on each circuit in the thirty years after 1590.[85] But despite a significant reduction in the opportunities for jury discretion, the number of partial verdicts continued to rise.

The explanation for this paradox remains unclear. Professor Hay has suggested that in the eighteenth century, jurors' attitudes were influenced by economic conditions,[86] and we might therefore expect to find some correlation between the exercise of "pious perjury" and periods of economic hardship, particularly during the severe crises of the late sixteenth century.[87] But in our period jury verdicts in general appear to have been largely unaffected by short-term economic fluctuations.[88] In fact, the dramatic surge in partial verdicts which followed changes in the recruitment of Kent jurors made in 1650 suggests that the explanation for earlier fluctuations in the pattern of discretionary verdicts may lie not in external variables but in changes in the internal dynamics of the trial jury itself. The precise nature of those changes in the years before about 1640 is, however, unclear. There is, as we have seen, little evidence in the early seventeenth century of systematic service by "experienced" jurors, although it is possible that a more sophisticated analysis might reveal patterns of experience less obvious than those demonstrated here. On the other hand, there are indications in the seventeenth century of a significant advance in juror literacy, which may well reflect a more general improvement in

84 Babington, *Advice to Grand Jurors*, passim.

85. These figures are from Cockburn, *Assize Introduction*, 67.

86. D. Hay, "War, Dearth and Theft in the Eighteenth Century: The Record of the English Courts," *Past and Present* 95 (1982): 154–55.

87. For a recent reexamination of the impact of economic changes on the pattern of property crime during this period, see P. Lawson, "Property Crime and Hard Times in England, 1559–1624," *Law and History Review* 4 (1986): 95–127.

88. For confirmation of this conclusion, see ibid., 126.

the quality of trial jurors—at least in some areas.[89] The caveat is important because the evidence of juror literacy is not only inconclusive, but it also contradicts contemporary assertions of widespread ignorance and illiteracy among trial jurors.[90] Moreover, the pattern of discretionary verdicts on the Home circuit reveals appreciable local variations: In the period before 1625 the incidence of partial verdicts ranged from 3 percent of all verdicts returned in Kent to 9 percent in Hertfordshire.[91] Such discrepancies imply that, in the early seventeenth century at least, verdicts were the product of variables that did not operate uniformly even within the counties of a single circuit. Thus, although it seems reasonable to suppose that increasing literacy resulted in improved confidence and efficiency, any theory that seeks to explain discretionary verdicts solely in terms of juror education must be advanced with considerable caution.

After 1650 the evidence for linking fluctuations in the exercise of discretionary power to changes in the internal dynamics of the trial jury is much stronger. The nature of the changes themselves and their uniformity in at least two of the circuit's counties is clear. Nor can there be much doubt about the increased stability and self-confidence that they brought to trial juries in Kent and Surrey after mid century. The appearance in Kent of an institutionalized foreman is particularly significant, both to theories of the foreman's role in later periods[92] and to any explanation of the sustained increase in discretionary verdicts after 1650. Although at this stage we can only speculate about the precise impact of the foreman on the complex dynamics of the assize courtroom, it seems reasonable to assume that the long-term presence on the trial jury of men as experienced as Bernard Ellis not only boosted the knowledge and self-confidence of rank-and-file jurors but also significantly increased judicial confidence in their ability to reach speedy, principled, and consistent decisions. Whether the result was a relaxation in judicial control, an increasingly confident assumption of discretionary authority by knowledgeable and well-organized jurors, or a combination of both need not, for the moment, concern us. The important point is that if, as seems likely, partial verdicts are a reliable guide to juror discretion in the seventeenth century, then in at least one county on the Home circuit the years after 1650 brought

89 See above, text at n. 36.

90. See above, text at n 8

91. These figures are from Cockburn, *Assize Introduction*, 114.

92. Beattie, *Crime and the Courts*, 397–98.

a significant, and apparently sustained, increase in the autonomy of the trial jury.

I have argued elsewhere that in the sixteenth and seventeenth centuries the trial jury was dominated by the assize bench and imprisoned in recruitment patterns and trial procedures that severely inhibited its capacity for independent action.[93] To the extent that such judicial domination implies jury passivity, that view has been challenged, notably by Professor Green, who believes that "amid all the abuses, shortcuts, and cynicism, from the perspectives both of jurors and of the observing community, the exercise of jury-based discretion remained a part of the doing of justice, even at Home circuit assizes."[94] Up to a point, this analysis is unexceptional. Professor Green and I agree that the trial judge dominated a courtroom in which procedural abuses and shortcuts abounded; the discretionary authority of trial jurors was certainly enshrined in contemporary lawbooks, and, as we have seen, from about 1580 examples of what is undeniably jury-*based* discretion was a fairly regular feature of criminal trial on the Home circuit. But there is still considerable doubt about the way in which a tradition of juror discretion was translated into fact. Are we to believe that for thirty years after 1558 Home circuit jurors found almost no cases in which they thought mercy appropriate? Or could it be that they did not know, and were not told, of the existence of their mitigatory power? And how can we be sure that when jurors eventually began to return discretionary partial verdicts they did not do so on instructions from the bench? These are troublesome questions that Professor Green parries by arguing that there were enough instances in which the inclinations of judge and jury coincided to maintain, in the eyes of an "observing community," the illusion of juror discretion. That line of reasoning, however, serves only to carry us into deeper water.

We know that throughout the early modern period assize courtrooms were crowded,[95] but how representative the onlookers were of the local community and what they made of what they saw—or thought they saw—at assizes is difficult to discover. If popular attitudes to public execution are any guide, community perspectives were rooted in a pervasive cynicism that threatened the carefully

93. Cockburn, *Assize Introduction*, 56–71, 130–34.

94. Green, *Verdict According to Conscience*, 152.

95. Cockburn, *Assizes*, 53, 110.

staged rituals of criminal justice. Hanging was "nothing . . . but a wry neck, and a wet pair of breeches," said one commentator.[96] "He will read as well as my horse," called out a Kent justice of the peace as a felon who claimed benefit of clergy was offered the book.[97]

Against this background, we might doubt whether bystanders even detected the hints by which, according to Smith, judges communicated their wishes to the jury. If they did detect them, they may well have interpreted them as simply confirmations of the widespread impression of judicial domination. The few observers who did comment on the relationship between judge and jury apparently received mixed signals. Smith seems to have thought that in the 1560s the jurors' choice was limited to conviction or acquittal. They sometimes exercised it contrary to the judge's wishes, he notes, and were then threatened with punishment, although after a show of contrition the possibility of further proceedings usually "passed away."[98] Thirty years later, Lambard wrote as if judges and local magistrates were struggling helplessly to stem a rising tide of discretionary verdicts.[99] But in 1680 Hawles could claim that jurors were fearful slaves to judicial whim, men who routinely disregarded the evidence and merely echoed back "what the bench would have done."[100] These examples suggest that community perspectives are not, perhaps, the best vantage point from which to view shifts in the balance of power in the assize courtroom. Since we have almost no direct indication of juror perceptions, this realization forces us to look again at the evidence of juror conduct at assizes—at the pattern of verdicts and at the procedural framework within which jurors reached their decisions.

The procedural argument for jury passivity seems to me very strong. Most assize cases were discharged very rapidly, with little or no time for meaningful deliberation by the jury, which normally did not leave the courtroom. Judicially controlled plea bargaining deprived the jury of many opportunities to exercise discretion in the late sixteenth and early seventeenth centuries. Most important, the practice of multiple arraignment persisted throughout our period. In view of the interest in juror perspectives, it might be well to remind our-

96. J. A. Sharpe, " 'Last Dying Speeches': Religion, Ideology and Public Execution in Seventeenth-Century England," *Past and Present* 107 (1985): 167.

97. *The Diary of John Manningham of the Middle Temple, 1602–1603*, ed. R. P. Sorlien (Hanover, N. H., 1976), 54.

98. *De Republica*, 88–89.

99. *Lambarde and Local Government*, ed. Read, 119–20.

100. *Englishman's Right*, 36.

selves of the implications of multiple arraignment. According to Smith, trial jurors in the 1560s, if they were charged with more than two or three prisoners, protested to the bench: "My Lord, we pray you charge us with no more, it is enough for our memory."[101] Smith thought, or pretended, that because of this, judges normally limited the number of suspects arraigned before a single jury to one or two. But, at least on the Home circuit, this was never the case. Judges there apparently ignored juror reservations and arraigned as many as eighteen prisoners before a single panel. Between 1559 and 1625 the average number of suspects with which each jury was charged was 6.7, and between 1625 and 1670 it rose, in Kent, to almost 8.[102]

The implications of these statistics cannot be ignored. Twentieth-century jurors, despite the benefits of professional assistance and unlimited time, find considerable difficulty in distinguishing between several defendants grouped together in one indictment.[103] How, then, did Elizabethan jurors—illiterate, impressionable, and inexperienced as most of them appear to have been—make sense of their task of returning verdicts almost instantaneously on a dozen indictments after hearing, seriatim, the evidence on all twelve? Professor Beattie is surely correct in suggesting that one way was to sacrifice discussion altogether and instead simply to endorse a decision reached by the foreman or one or two experienced members of the panel.[104] Such a theory fits perfectly within the picture of juror selection that emerged in Kent after 1640. But it is not so easily accommodated within the pattern of random and occasional service that appears to have dominated throughout the circuit before that date. In these circumstances is it not likely that overburdened jurors commonly acquiesced in a decision reached not by their equally inexperienced foreman but by the trial judge? I am not saying that judges deliberately set out to stifle juror initiative by overloading each panel with more suspects than it could handle, although they can hardly have been unaware of that possibility. My contention is simply that, in practice, assize procedure operated in ways that heavily qualified the theoretical autonomy of the trial jury.

An obvious casualty in all this is, of course, the theory of jury delib-

101. *De Republica*, 81.

102. Cockburn, *Assize Introduction*, 64. The figure for 1625–1670 is based on an examination of trial jury panels in PRO, ASSI 35/67–111.

103. I am grateful to Dr. J. B. Post for corroborating this point from his own experience of jury service.

104. Beattie, *Crime and the Courts*, 397–98.

erations. There is really no way in which meaningful jury discussion could have taken place within the context of what we know about the actual conduct of assize trials. In that sense the early-modern trial jury was essentially passive. It was passive, too, in the sense that dependence on either the foreman or the judge, or even on an experienced few, automatically relegated the bulk of those impaneled to a subordinate and virtually silent role. Undoubtedly there were many instances in which the inclinations of rank-and-file jurymen coincided with the wishes of the foreman or the bench. Almost certainly, too, there were cases that, by virtue of their extraordinary interest to the community, generated discussion within the jury and even disagreements with the bench. It can surely be no coincidence that most of the late-sixteenth-century cases in which assize juries were punished in Star Chamber involved acquittals "against the evidence" of suspects charged with homicide,[105] and that Babington's account of courtroom tension after the Restoration concentrates exclusively on "cases of blood."[106] Professor Green, too, relies heavily upon the evidence of homicide cases,[107] and that documentary bias probably helps to explain some of the discrepancies between his view of judge-jury relations and one that rests almost exclusively upon evidence drawn from offenses against property—which, after all, comprised some 75 percent of criminal business at assizes throughout this period.

I have argued hitherto that almost all we know of routine assize cases in the early modern period points toward a form of trial in which the balance was heavily weighted against jury initiative. Much of the material considered in this essay supports that view. It suggests that for the bulk of Elizabeth's reign the trial jury at assizes remained an essentially passive body, its independence stifled by judicial and procedural pressures, ignorance, and a general unwillingness to serve. In this context it seems likely that the few discretionary verdicts returned before the 1580s—and possibly some after that date—reflect judicial rather than jury initiatives.

From about 1590, however, there are signs of a change in the court room balance of power. Discretionary verdicts not only become more

105. Huntington Lib., MS. 2657. I am grateful to Mr. A. J. Fellows of Trinity College, Oxford, for confirming this point from his study of Star Chamber cases in the 1570s.

106. Babington, *Advice to Grand Jurors*, sigs. A3v–4. Cf. Cockburn, *Assize Introduction*, 52–53.

107. T. A. Green, "The Jury and the English Law of Homicide, 1200–1600," *Michigan Law Review* 74 (1976): 413–99; Green, *Verdict According to Conscience*, 119–29.

common, but if we are to believe Lambarde, they must be seen, at least in part, as the expression of a novel, and unwelcome, assertiveness on the part of both grand and trial jurors.[108] Neither the chronology of, nor the reasons behind, this development is very clear. It is possible that the increase in unauthorized partial verdicts represents a tentative, and perhaps delayed, response to the economic downturn of 1585–87, which hardened into a policy of juror mitigation in the deepening crisis and the rapid rise in property offenses that marked the 1590s.[109] The pattern of acquittals, however, appears to provide little support for such a thesis, and it is clear that, for the moment at least, an economic rationale for jury mitigation can be advanced only with the greatest caution. Nevertheless, the possible correlation of jury verdicts and economic trends deserves further exploration, as do changes in both juror literacy and patterns of service at assizes and elsewhere. The work will be slow and demanding, but we cannot hope to resolve satisfactorily the ambiguities and uncertainties surrounding criminal trial in the sixteenth century until it has been attempted.[110]

Although significant reservations remain—notably about the impact of multiple arraignment and unsystematic service—it is now clear that the picture of judge-jury relations in the seventeenth century requires some modification. Again, the reasons for the further expansion of jury mitigation in the early years of the century are unclear, but it seems unlikely that the continued increase in partial verdicts, which by the 1620s accounted for almost 20 percent of all convictions for property offenses, can be wholly explained by a theory of judicial control. Whether the apparent growth in juror independence stemmed directly from improvements in the quality of trial jurors—a development of which increased literacy was one manifestation—or from a more subtle shift in courtroom dynamics cannot at present be ascertained. If the Kent evidence is typical, part of the answer may well lie hidden in the details of juror selection and service. From about 1640 there are clear signs in the Kent data of a rationalization that linked the short-term benefits of serial service by rank-and-file jurors

108. See above, text at n. 83.

109. See Cockburn, "Nature and Incidence of Crime, 1559–1625: A Preliminary Survey," in *Crime in England, 1550–1800*, ed. J. S. Cockburn (1977), 67–70.

110. For an indication of the techniques and limitations, see chap. 5 and, in the context of quarter sessions, Herrup, "East Sussex," 201–6, 463–65.

to the long-term stabilizing effect of repeated service by an increasingly experienced foreman. That the regularization of that pattern after 1650 was accompanied by a further surge in discretionary verdicts tends to confirm the importance of juror "experience" in the emergence of a coherent philosophy of jury discretion.

It is possibly premature—as well as uncomfortably precise—to characterize the rationalization of 1650 as a watershed in the uneasy relationship between judge and jury. We do not know, and will probably be unable to discover, if those changes extended beyond the Home circuit. In the meantime, the experience of Western circuit jurors at the hands of Chief Justice Kelyng in the 1660s serves as sufficient warning against easy generalizations.[111] Even after the decision in Bushel's case, judicial coercion—albeit of an informal variety—remained a feature of assize trial: As late as 1687 Justice Holloway could speak quite naturally of "menacing and threatening" a trial jury on the Oxford circuit.[112] Nevertheless, the emergence in at least some counties after 1650 of a literate, experienced, and well-organized jury surely made judicial bullying more difficult. Indeed, in routine property cases, which were never as prone to generate judge-jury tensions as political and homicide trials, intimidation by the bench probably became unnecessary.

We have no way of knowing what John Lilburne would have made of the Kent trial jury after 1650—whether he would have thought it superior to the bench or would have derided its foreman for his undoubted knowledge of the law. But perhaps we should not too easily assume that Interregnum law reformers, of whom Lilburne was only the most vocal, were all sound and fury and that all the major events in the later evolution of the trial jury occurred after the Restoration. In two counties at least, the mid-century changes in jury composition represented a decisive break with the stultifying patterns of the preceding century. If, as seems likely, they also brought to jury practice a new coherence and self-confidence that was never thereafter entirely lost, then the innovations of 1650 stand as one of the earliest mile stones on the road to jury independence.

111. Green, *Verdict According to Conscience*, 208–21. It is perhaps significant that most of the episodes complained of involved homicide cases.

112. Cockburn, *Assizes*, 115 n. 2.

Seven

Juries and the Middling Sort: Recruitment and Performance at Devon Quarter Sessions, 1649–1670

Stephen K. Roberts

In the seventeenth century the jury was the most representative institution available to the English people. More than any other organ of local government, it attracted the attention of princes and parliaments and was the focus of much rhetoric and polemical debate. For the Levellers the jury could become a powerful measure of liberty and a concrete prototype for a new political order. For others it was a symbol of decay in the body politic.[1] Yet despite its potency as a symbol, no other institution of government depended so much on the good will of obscure officials and on a system of enforcement so fumbling and haphazard. The most recent treatments of the jury have been in the context of the criminal trial process and have concerned the rhetoric of charges to juries as examples of thinking on central and local government relations.[2] On the performance of the jury there is a division between those who see it as capable of independent action and those who see it as confined and dependent on the initiative of others.[3] Keith Wrightson has portrayed jurymen as brokers mediating between the governors and the governed.[4] Elsewhere I have tried to emphasize the importance of geography and administrative weakness in the summoning and performance of quarter sessions grand juries.[5]

1. For a survey of the local context, see S. K. Roberts, "Jury-Vetting in the Seventeenth Century," *History Today*, Feb. 1982, 25–29.

2. Green, *Verdict According to Conscience*, chaps. 4, 5; R. Cust and P. G. Lake, "Sir Richard Grosvenor and the Rhetoric of Magistracy," *BIHR* 54 (1981): 44–49.

3. J. S. Morrill, *The Cheshire Grand Jury, 1625–59* (Leicester, 1976), Cockburn, *Assize Introduction*, 56–71.

4. "Two Concepts of Order: Justices, Constables and Jurymen in Seventeenth-Century England," in *An Ungovernable People: The English and Their Law in the Seventeenth and Eighteenth Centuries*, ed. J. Brewer and J. Styles (1980), 21–46.

5. "Initiative and Control: The Devon Quarter Sessions Grand Jury, 1649–1670," *BIHR* 57 (1984): 165–77.

Here I hope to argue that, at least in one southwestern English county, recruitment to both grand and trial juries at quarter sessions was more attuned to the social and economic order of the region than some of the evidence has hitherto suggested, even if the capacity of juries for initiative was severely circumscribed. I hope to show that the jury class was not in itself quiescent or docile, but that the task of the gentry, as represented on the bench of magistrates, was to shape, channel, and subdue the capacity for action of the "middling sort." A docile jury became the proof of an effective magistracy.

Political behavior is necessarily influenced by geography. The most striking feature of the topography of Devon is that the so-called Tees-Exe line, dividing the highland zone of Britain from the lowland, runs through it. The western side, west of the River Exe, is a landscape that recalls parts of Wales. It is hilly, and travel across it on horseback, as Thomas Risdon remarked, was not always easy: "Be they never so well mounted upon horses out of other countries, when they have travelled one journey in these parts they can, in respect of ease of travel, forbear a second."[6] In the heart of the county is the imposing massif of Dartmoor, and on its perimeter were the proto-industrial villages and townships in valleys where wood and water were plentiful and which harbored the clothing (serge cloth) trades and what remained of the tin industry. Devon has two coastlines that supported fishing communities and made the county a natural point of embarkation for Ireland and the New World.[7] It was the mercantile clothing interests and the contact with Ireland that gave Devon Puritanism its characteristics of social conservatism and a propensity to believe in an imminent popish invasion.[8] Devon was a fertile breeding ground for the "natural backbenchers" who filled early-Stuart and Cromwellian parliaments.[9]

Devon was a county of many gentry families. Estimates of the total number of families that could be accurately described as "gentry" vary between three and five hundred, and these were spread evenly

6. T. Risdon, *The Chorographical Description or Survey of the County of Devon* (1811), 4.

7. H.E.S. Fisher, "The South-west and the Atlantic Trades, 1660–1770," in *The South-West and the Sea*, ed. idem (Exeter, 1968), 7–14.

8. A. Fletcher, *The Outbreak of the English Civil War* (1981), 212, 250; S. K. Roberts, *Recovery and Restoration in an English County: Devon Local Administration, 1646–1670* (Exeter, 1985), introduction and chap. 1.

9. Roberts, *Recovery and Restoration*, 53–60. The phrase is, of course, Hugh Trevor-Roper's.

across the county.[10] They crowded the bench of magistrates, and after the quarterly sessions meetings at Exeter Castle, went home to govern their parishes and hundreds like demigods from their rural seats, secure in their right to rule. For purposes of tax collection, Devon was divided into three "grand divisions," but for the day-to-day administration of criminal justice and local government in its wider sense, the pivotal unit of local administration above the parish was the hundred. Devon contained thirty-three hundreds and an anomalous "artificial" hundred comprising the manors of the Duchy of Lancaster. It was from the hundreds of Devon that the sheriff and his bailiffs summoned the juries to the jury chamber at Exeter Castle four times a year for quarter sessions.[11]

The evidence for the behavior of the quarter sessions juries of Devon comes from the sessions bundles, a rich miscellany of the court's working papers.[12] The principal source for attendances on the grand jury are the grand jury panels, lists of those summoned to serve and shorter lists of those finally sworn from the reservoir of available men. Some men were repeatedly named on sheriff's lists but were never sworn to a jury in the twenty-year period under consideration here. There were 281 such "ghosts," some of whom were considered unsuitable on grounds of age or occupation, and some were chronically sick. Others were perhaps considered not wealthy enough to deserve a place, and still others had simply not been crossed off the sheriff's lists. There may have been political and religious objections to some, as we shall see. The list of active jurors comprised the names of 391 individuals, almost two-thirds of whom served on more than one occasion; the remaining 149 served once only. So the Devon grand jury involved a large number of individuals, drawn from an even larger pool of available manpower. There can be no doubt that of all the institutions of local representation, the sessions grand jury was the closest thing to a mouthpiece for the yeomanry of the county. It was nearly a parliament of the middling sort, but it lacked a vital ingredi-

10. The varying estimates may be found in T. Westcote, *A View of Devonshire in 1630*, ed. G. Oliver and P. Jones (Exeter, 1845); F. T. Colby, ed., *The Visitation of Devon in the Year 1620*, Harleian Society (1872); W. G. Hoskins, "The Estates of the Caroline Gentry," in *Devonshire Studies*, ed. H.P.R. Finberg and W. G. Hoskins (1952); Roberts, *Recovery and Restoration*, xvii, xviii.

11. Fuller details of the workings of Devon local administration may be found in Roberts, *Recovery and Restoration*, passim.

12. Devon Record Office (hereafter DRO), Quarter Sessions (hereafter QS) in boxes.

ent, that of self-regulation. Quarter sessions juries were at the beck and call of the class that summoned and dismissed them: the gentry.

The quarter sessions grand jury usually consisted of seventeen men who represented the villages and small towns of rural Devon. The larger towns were practically unrepresented on the county sessions juries; most had their own courts. The cloth towns of the Exe, Culme, and Creedy valleys above Exeter were better placed geographically to send jurors to Exeter than, for example, far-flung Bideford, Barnstaple, and Okehampton, so it is not surprising that the cloth towns did have some representatives on the grand jury from time to time. But even where the grand jury represented the needs and preoccupations of industry, it was "industry in the countryside,"[13] cloth weaving, in a close relationship with the overwhelmingly agrarian local economy, which ensured that urban-rural tensions were not a feature of grand jury consciousness.

Evidence for the quarter sessions trial or petty juries is less plentiful. Lists of impaneled jurors, without any complementary listings of the pool from which they were drawn, are to be found among the sessions bundles, with bills of indictment attached. Trial jurors were a separate and lower caste. The grand jurors occupied houses with an average of just over five hearths, while a sample of fifty-two trial jurors' homes contained a more modest three hearths each.[14] Grand jurors were community leaders, "parish elites"; petty jurymen were yeomen of some standing but with a markedly lower status. Few petty jurors (about 10 percent) were promoted to the grand jury. Three-fourths of the trial jurors served on only one occasion, in contrast to the grand jury, on which most men served more than once. But the justices and sheriffs strongly offset this spreading of the burden of attendances by the raising up of a cadre of trial jurors of great experience who could be relied upon to act as bellwethers. The significance of multiple attendance in the trial jury is considered below, but here it should be noted that the jury leaders (it seems likely that this is how those who attended many times were regarded) came from villages within an easy ride of Exeter.

It is now necessary to look at the work of the grand jury in the two areas of local government and criminal justice. The principal task of the grand jury, in its role in county administration rather than in the criminal-law process, was to deliver presentments to the court. The

13. The phrase is from the title of Joan Thirsk's essay in *Essays in Social and Economic History Presented to R. H. Tawney*, ed. F. J. Fisher (Cambridge, 1961), 70–88.

14. DRO, QS Hearth Tax Returns; PRO, E 179/245/17, 375/13, 102/530.

surviving presentments blend together moral censure, a listing of lapses in community life, and a tendency toward attacks on specific individuals, including other jurors. An interest in roads and bridges was natural in those who had to foot the bill for their repair and supervise their upkeep, and who needed them for trade. Such presentments were usually of specific neglect. At Easter sessions 1667, roads at Halberton, Tiverton, Poltimore, and between Pinhoe and Huxham parishes were presented; at Michaelmas sessions 1664, Wonford bridge at Heavitree was said to be in disrepair. Such presentments were likely to be repeated, a pattern also discernible in the orders of magistrates.[15] The Easter 1667 road presentment had first been made, in its essential details, at Michaelmas 1661.

Presentments also reflected moral concern, as in the "grievance of unlicensed alehouses," or merely the jurors' anxiety to be seen to be diligent. At Epiphany sessions 1649 it was ordered that "upon petition of the grand jury in respect of this week's service, no amerciament should be extracted against them for not appearing at the precedent sessions." There could be a virtual cash reward for dutiful conduct, and hard work could redeem an earlier dereliction of duty.[16]

The deliberations of the grand jury did not, however, ignore matters of state concern completely. In 1659, after a decade of centralized probate administration, the jury requested a local court of probate.[17] In so doing it seemed to advocate a measure of devolved government, and it voiced concern over the reestablishment of the Church of England in 1660.[18] Although the jury singled out thirty-five individuals as absentees from church and condemned those ministers who neglected to administer the Anglican rite, there is little evidence that in doing so the jury was voicing an independent judgment of the small freeholders. The parishes that the jury singled out for complaint were those in which the gentry's rights of patronage had been overidden during the Interregnum, and presentments followed at a respectful distance the decisions on religious policy taken at the national level.

Jostling with appeals for ecclesiastical revival and secular reform were less lofty concerns. Minor infringements of respectable behavior

15. DRO, QS Box 70, bundle for Epiphany 1665 (misplaced presentment of October 1661); Box 72, loose presentments of October 1664 and April 1667.

16. QS Box 68, loose presentment of January 1663; Box 67, bundle for Easter 1662; Box 72, loose presentment of April 1667; Box 73, loose presentment of July 1668; Box 64, bundle for Easter 1660; Devon QS Order Book (hereafter DQSOB), Epiphany 1649.

17. Presentment of April 1660.

18. For details, see Roberts, "Initiative and Control," 166–67.

and actions detrimental to public welfare were frequently presented. The tithingmen of Farringdon, Aylesbeare, and Poltimore had failed to keep nets to catch rooks; Hugh Smeardon of Ilsington had diverted a watercourse; John Penny of Halwell had laid "dung and soil in the king's highway leading from Dartmouth and Totnes." Thomas Venning of Abbotskerswell was presented for the "keeping of geese in our potwater and other annoyances to the sum of the parishioners." Jurors presented their colleagues, and there was no "professional" unity or defense against outsiders. Hugh Smeardon of Ilsington was sworn to five grand juries between 1665 and 1670, but he was presented for diverting water. An erstwhile mayor of Bradninch, Robert Jerman, was presented by his fellow townsman John Venman as "a common drunkard and an encourager and procurer of others as commit the same sin."[19] Commonly the grand jury had no presentments of its own to make or simply endorsed those of other officers—constables and surveyors of highways, for example—without comment.

The contribution of the jury system to trials at law at quarter sessions may be assessed by examining indictments, true bills, gaol calendars, and endorsements by court officials on jury lists.[20] Indictments of suspected criminals were framed by the clerks of the peace, considered by the grand jury, and if delivered as true bills were passed to the court for hearing before a trial jury. Great caution is required in interpreting this evidence, however. The least ambiguous sources for the volume of business before the court are the indictments before the grand jury, which endorsed them as true bills or *ignoramus* bills. The Devon archive is defective, however, in that there are some sessions for which there are no surviving indictments and many sessions for which the record is incomplete. Judging by the number surviving, the Devon quarter sessions would seem to have been quieter than their counterpart in Wiltshire.[21] There was an average of a hundred true bills a year there, compared to about seventy-five in Devon. There were no significant differences between the two decades in this; continuity seems to have been the hallmark of the work of quarter sessions despite radical political change at the Restoration.

Another source to be used with care is a good series of gaol calendars

19. QS Box 68, loose presentment of Epiphany 1663; Box 67, bundle for Easter 1662 (misplaced presentment of April 1659); Box 70, loose presentments and bundle for Epiphany 1665 (misplaced, of Michaelmas 1661).

20. All in QS bundles.

21. M.J. Ingram, "Communities and Courts. Law and Disorder in Early Seventeenth-Century Wiltshire," in *Crime in England, 1550–1800*, ed. J. S. Cockburn (1977), 111.

in the sessions order books and among the papers of the court.[22] Gaol calendars are simply lists of prisoners delivered from gaol by the sheriff, and they usually consist merely of the numbers released, branded, hanged, and so on. Occasionally names are given. The problems are, first, that the calendars of assizes and quarter sessions seem to be conflated and confused, especially in the late 1640s and early 1650s. They were kept as a running total, not as a formal and final record. Second, there is a constant risk of double-counting if this source is used to calculate gross annual totals of offenders. For example, those who were fined but were unable to meet the penalty languished in gaol until they could, or until the court had mercy on them, and their names appear in successive gaol calendars. Others appear as "discharged from gaol," but it is often far from clear when they were first imprisoned, why they were gaoled, or why they were released. The calendars sometimes include the names of those who were acquitted by proclamation and released with those who had served sentences after conviction. Gaol calendars are particularly suspect in an appraisal of the jury system because there is much evidence, paralleled elsewhere, that prisoners found not guilty by a jury could nevertheless be punished—like the three acquitted by the trial jury in January 1654 who were then gaoled while their friends or relatives found sureties for their good behavior.[23]

These defects counsel caution. Just as indictments are likely to underestimate the volume of business, so calendars tend to inflate the court's workload. Careful and detailed research could reconstruct at least some of the sessions and would minimize the dangers of using evidence impressionistically, but that is beyond the scope of this study. Here it may simply be observed that a sample of the gaol calendars suggests that the county was in line with the kind of caseload described by Dr. Ingram for Wiltshire.

Indictments were framed in response to presentments by jurors, constables, surveyors of highways, and other minor officials. By the mid seventeenth century, however, most were the result of a pre-trial examination of suspects by justices of the peace in response to information lodged by wronged parties.[24] As the century progressed, the

22. The calendars of gaol delivery are at the end of the order book entry for each quarter sessions.

23. Gaol calendars, DQSOB, Epiphany 1654. J. A. Sharpe, *Crime in Seventeenth-Century England: A County Study* (Cambridge, 1983), 152.

24. Examinations are to be found in the sessions bundles. Cf. J. H. Langbein, *Prosecuting Crime in the Renaissance* (Cambridge, Mass., 1974), 118–21; J. H. Baker,

grand jury became more and more marginal to the judicial process. Presentments did include the names of individual offenders but, as I have tried to show, that cannot be taken to indicate political initiative by the jury. Offenders indicted thus were those who had fallen foul of political campaigns by the gentry—absentees from church, uncooperative clergy, engrossers of grain—or those who had broken social or economic regulations—diverters of watercourses or spoilers of roads. Grand jury presentments tended on the whole to avoid naming individuals and instead spoke to the general issue.

Constables' presentments—made both by constables of the hundreds and by the much less exalted petty constables of the parishes—were given a temporary new lease of life by the development, or revival, of petty sessions in the countryside after 1660. These, too, were firmly under the control of the gentry, but the gentry worked in a close and mutually beneficial relationship with the yeoman parish elites, ably supported by a cadre of increasing importance: the justices' clerks. Constables' presentments covered the same issues as those of the grand jury but were more expansive on local problems, since they were made on a hundred-by-hundred, not a county-wide, basis. In Devon by the 1680s even the presentments of constables showed the symptoms of arid formalism and subservience displayed by the grand jury twenty years earlier, as the grip of the county gentry grew ever tighter.[25]

The number of indictments framed by genuine presentment of the jury was very small. By far the largest source of grist to the judicial mill was the procedure by which an offender would be apprehended by the parish constable or other community servant or ruler—minister, select vestryman, or perhaps even a powerful yeoman farmer—and taken to a justice or his clerk for examination before commitment for trial. Care must be taken here to distinguish legal theory from practice. J. H. Baker reminds us that an indictment by at least twelve men was a precondition of a trial for felony,[26] but the evidence from Devon suggests that the grand jury, if not yet a rubber stamp, had become the second stage in the prosecuting process, a point on the quasi-bureaucratic road to criminal conviction.[27] The most important sin-

"Criminal Courts and Procedure at Common Law, 1550–1800," in *Crime in England*, ed. Cockburn, 20.

25. Roberts, *Recovery and Restoration*, 114ff.

26. Baker, "Criminal Courts," 18.

27. C. B. Herrup, "Law and Morality in Seventeenth-Century England," *Past and Present* 106 (1985): 102–23, summarizes the prevailing view that the business in the courtroom was "the end of an elaborate selection process." This view, however, is

gle source of prosecuting energy was the bench of magistrates acting extramurally, examining suspects in the halls of their county seats, confident in their authority and in their power.

The grand jury was not, therefore, a notable initiator of prosecutions, but it was not a meaningless cypher, either. It judged whether an indictment was worthy of trial, that is, whether the prosecution had made a case to be answered. And it was here, rather than in the more overtly political and open-ended procedure of presentments, that the jury was at its most unpredictable. Unfortunately, it is here, too, that the judicial record for mid-seventeenth-century Devon is at its most incomplete. The examination of bills of indictment took most of the grand jurors' time at sessions. It is difficult to estimate whether there were certain offenses that grand jurors were more likely to prosecute in true bills or whether juries were likely to reject a determinable number of indictments. A random sample of the surviving indictments shows that there were occasions when the grand jury rejected up to two-thirds of the indictments before it. This was particularly so in the case of the Cromwellian "Reformation of Manners," when a determined drive by magistrates met with a cool response not only in the jury chamber but in the parishes too, where petty officialdom showed no enthusiasm for a judicial violation of community harmony.[28]

More readily analyzed is the last chronological contribution of the jury system to due process. True bills became the legal basis of trial before petty juries, details of whose verdicts may be found in the quarter sessions rolls.[29] Two-thirds of the defendants appearing before the trial jury were found guilty in the 1650s and a slightly lower proportion in the following decade. Such were the cold statistics over the long term, but in individual sessions a defendant's chances of acquittal might be higher. At the Michaelmas sessions of 1656, for example, a trial jury found seven defendants guilty and fourteen not guilty.[30] At the Midsummer sessions of 1659—a politically chaotic year, it must be admitted—two prisoners were found guilty and five not guilty.[31] Even in more settled times, when the rights of the propertied were so

not incompatible with an emphasis on the inadequacy of the bureaucratic structure available to magistrates.

28. S. K. Roberts, "Fornication and Bastardy in Mid-Seventeenth-Century Devon: How the Act of 1650 Was Enforced," in *Outside the Law. Studies in Crime and Order, 1650–1850*, ed. J. G. Rule (Exeter, 1982), 1–20.

29. Indictments attached to lists of petty juries.

30. QS Box 61, bundle for Michaelmas 1656, petty jury list.

31. QS Box 63, bundle for Midsummer 1659, petty jury list.

firmly secured, the trial jury could convict seven prisoners and acquit ten, as it did at Easter sessions 1667.[32]

Caution is required here, too, however. The record of acquitted and traversed cases seems confused, and there is another danger of double-counting cases in sessional totals, especially in cases traversed to the next sessions or removed to assizes because of the seriousness of the offense. All misdemeanors were prosecuted at sessions, but if the grand jury decided that an alleged offense was sufficiently grave to be classed as a felony, it was likely to be reserved for the next assizes. It can nevertheless be judged that the greatest single category of cases coming before the trial jury was theft. Nearly 70 percent of the defendants were suspected thieves. Other frequent offenses were forcible entry, assault, and vagrancy. A small but significant group of of fenders in the 1650s had denounced Parliament or drunk healths to King Charles, or in the 1660s (one assumes they were different persons) had spoken against the Prayer Book or refused the Oath of Allegiance. The volume of cases was sometimes swollen by groups of offenders: fifteen rioters at Easter sessions 1658,[33] seven attenders at a nonconformist conventicle at the Epiphany sessions 1671.[34] If the two decades each have a peculiar flavor, it is in that the Interregnum decade saw a busy trade in fornication cases at sessions, brought under the 1650 Act for Suppressing the Detestable Sins of Incest, Adultery and Fornication,[35] while the 1660s were marked by a revival of prosecutions under the game laws. Among those found guilty under the latter were a man who had killed a pigeon and two who had taken salmon.[36] Such offenses had, of course, been prosecuted in the 1650s but, as with moral regulation in the Interregnum, there was now a scrupulous, vindictive zeal in response to new legislation.

A study of punishments meted out to convicts is beyond the scope of this study, but it is worth noting that there was a degree of plea bargaining in certain cases at sessions. Two Quakers who pleaded guilty in the sessions of Michaelmas 1662 to membership in the sect were fined five shillings each; one who put himself "on his country" was

32. QS Box 72, bundle for Easter 1667, petty jury list.

33. QS Box 63, bundle for Easter 1658, petty jury list.

34. QS Box 75, bundle for Epiphany 1671, petty jury list.

35. QS Box 63 contains a bundle of indictments for fornication from 1655 to 1660. Also, see Roberts, "Fornication and Bastardy," passim.

36. QS Box 72, bundle for Easter 1667; Box 73, bundle for Midsummer 1668, petty jury list.

subsequently fined twenty shillings.[37] But plea bargaining was beyond the power of the jury and depended wholly on the fiat of the magistrates. To ascertain the views of the trial jury on crime is a hazardous task. C. B. Herrup has argued that both individuals and the courts distinguished redeemable recidivists from those who deserved capital punishment by invoking a system of moral values based on the universality of sin.[38] "Sinners" needed rehabilitation; hardened, willful "criminals" did not. Plausible though this suggestion is as a description of the *mentalité* of lawgivers, it may not do justice to the separate class interests of judges and juries; one can never be sure that juries were untrammeled by magisterial pressure, and in the presentment system at least, the jury was consistently pliant. We simply do not know what the expressed views of jurors were. On the other hand, there is some evidence that juries were reluctant to follow government policy slavishly and that they were constrained by local precedent, hallowed procedure, and a concept of community at odds with that of their superiors. In the cases of fornication, for example, magistrates relied on confessions by suspects as a means of evading trial by jury and the risk of acquittal.

Only half of a bundle of ninety-six true bills returned between 1655 and 1660 went to trial, and on those, three people were found guilty and twenty-seven were acquitted.[39] Two adulterers were acquitted and two were sent to assizes. Except for those who could successfully claim benefit of clergy, conviction for felony meant, in theory, punishment by hanging. Quarter sessions dealt with clergyable felonies, assizes with both clergyable and nonclergyable ones. There were no executions at quarter sessions between 1649 and 1670, although there may have been six at sessions in January 1648 and another one or two later that year.[40] We have evidence for Exeter assizes only for the late 1640s,[41] but executions there were running at about twenty each year. At the end of most sessions meetings, however, between two and four prisoners were burnt in the hand after having successfully claimed benefit of clergy. The largest number punished in that way was seven in the Epiphany sessions in 1653 and six at Michaelmas 1660.

Petty juries showed a readiness to convict for theft but some cau-

37. QS Box 67, bundle for Michaelmas 1662, petty jury list.

38. Herrup, "Law and Morality."

39. See the sources cited in n. 35 above

40. Evidence of DQSOB gaol calendars.

41. Assize gaol calendars appear in DQSOB for Midsummer 1646, Midsummer 1647, Epiphany 1648, Midsummer 1648, Epiphany 1649, and Midsummer 1651.

tion when dealing with other offenses. Thefts of sheep and lambs seem to have been among the most common of grand larcenies. Juries, perhaps justices too, were willing to undervalue the animals stolen in order to reduce the gravity of the offense.[42] For example, even though in the mid seventeenth century a sheep could be valued at anything from nearly ten to sixteen shillings, at the Midsummer sessions in 1652 the court did not value the stolen animals at more than eight shillings in any of the eight thefts under consideration.[43] Clothes, food, and saddlery were among the other items most frequently stolen, as one would expect in any pre-industrial society. The court was cautious in dealing with other offenses. The sessions of Easter 1657 was typical. Five defendants accused of theft were found guilty, while two accused of assault, one of barratry (disturbing the peace persistently by quarreling or verbal provocation), two of fornication, and one of diverting a watercourse were found not guilty.[44] But here the ready refusal of the trial jury to convict in difficult cases would suggest prudence and referral to further process rather than fearless repudiation of those who had framed the indictment. Those acquitted included extortioners, barrators, those accused of taking excessive tolls, perjurers, and a man tried in 1658 for "giving of love powder unto one Joan Westlake."[45] These acquittals may have led to the transfer of the cases to assizes or to a newly framed indictment.

The trial jury may have taken on some of the work of the semidormant grand jury. Its composition was certainly more reliable, as we shall see. But more research needs to be done on the pattern of crime in Devon before conclusive answers can be offered to questions about the criminal side of the jury's work. Suffice it to say that the trial and grand juries were subordinated in the legal framework of seventeenth-century England to the justices and sheriffs who summoned and directed them. A single legalistic and moral framework supporting the dominant legal philosophy can be conceived of only if the interests of jurors and justices are regarded as identical, as they seem to be by Herrup. Unfortunately, however, a deferential jury cannot be taken a priori to be a jury and a class genuinely in accord with the gentry's views of godliness and good order.

42. Cf. Sharpe, *Crime in Seventeenth-Century England*, 142–46, and Herrup, "Law and Morality," 106–7.

43. QS indictments, Midsummer 1652. Prices of sheep and lambs are from the appendixes in *The Agrarian History of England and Wales*, vol. 4, ed. J. Thirsk (Cambridge, 1967).

44. QS Box 61, bundle for Easter 1657.

45. QS Box 62, bundle for Easter 1658.

Devon juries seem to have been tame, but magistrates showed no complacent satisfaction at their workings. Throughout the 1650s and 1660s they consistently behaved as if the jury were a wayward, unpredictable force. Interest in jury reform had a respectable pedigree and appeared in the parliaments of the 1620s, reaching a climax in the 1640s and 1650s. Recent work by Professor Green has shown how the idea of the jury as an expression of the local community was central to the theory and the history developed by the radicals of the mid seventeenth century,[46] and I have outlined elsewhere the contrast between Leveller theory and local practice.[47] The Levellers insisted that juries should be recruited from the neighborhood of the offender, and they developed a view of the law that Green has described as "community self-identification."[48] Practically speaking, in Devon, as in any other county, judgment by one's neighbor meant simply judgment by a Devonian, and the ideas of community expression advocated by John Lilburne and John Jones were never even on the agenda of the "natural rulers" of Devonshire, even when the bench of magistrates was filled with gentry, merchants, and lawyers of a lower standing than their predecessors of the pre-war period.[49]

Juries could be "tuned" on a piecemeal basis by reviewing the lists of freeholders, a task undertaken jointly by the sheriff and the justices. The Commonwealth bench was enthusiastic in its scrutiny. Between Epiphany 1650 and Michaelmas 1652 the magistrates discharged ten men from future jury service, in most cases because of old age. Roger Fowler of East Budleigh was allowed to go because he was a professional man, "both a physician and a chirugeon."[50] In these cases the decision to discharge was taken by the justices alone; the sheriff was simply to take note of the exemptions. The deliberations took place in court after the jury had been summoned, however, and were necessarily a rather cosmetic exercise. The basic weakness in the system itself called for more drastic action, as the magistrates themselves had come to realize by the time Oliver Cromwell was sworn in as Protector.

At the Epiphany quarter sessions in 1655, the Devon bench made

46. Green, *Verdict According to Conscience*, esp. chap. 5.

47. Roberts "Jury-Vetting in the Seventeenth Century."

48. Green, *Verdict According to Conscience*, 186.

49. Roberts, *Recovery and Restoration*, 24–28.

50. DQSOB Epiphany 1650, Epiphany 1651, Easter 1651, Michaelmas 1651, Epiphany 1652, Michaelmas 1652.

plain its intention to alter the procedure by which juries were summoned, and it instituted a system of closer scrutiny by justices of the peace over the details of procedure, supplanting the sheriff as the principal controller of all juries, grand and petty, at assizes and quarter sessions. A group of justices who were committed to the Protectorate met to draft a number of resolutions to improve the quality of juries in order to prevent any resurgence of royalism. They resolved to be "very wary of returning any to serve in juries who have aided the late king etc. and continue their affections unto that interest."[51] This determined expression of local concern in Devon at the openness of the jury was almost certainly a prefiguring of, and the prompting for, Oliver Cromwell's letter to Major General John Desborough on the subject, and for the element of jury-vetting in the campaign of 1655–56 as a whole.[52]

The experiment of the major generals was begun during the summer of 1655, with Desborough visiting the west country to settle the local militias.[53] Jury administration proceeded normally for a while, with no perceptible alteration in the pattern of summoning, but the subject was important enough to the Protector for him to write personally to Desborough on 29 January 1656 solely on the issue of controlling juries. The letter was to be forwarded to the sheriff of Devon. Cromwell wrote that he was responding to having been "much pressed" to instigate reform. The letter came at the end of a period of magisterial anxiety in Devon about the strength of godly rule, and it suggests that Cromwell was responding to pressure specifically from within the county. His opening sentence made it clear where he believed the problem lay: "The law and justice hath been much liable to be perverted by the way that is generally held by deputy sheriffs in the choice of juries." This criticism was leveled at those charged with the permanent administration of the system; it was an attack on the professionals. Cromwell endorsed the proposals of the magistrates:

> If . . . the justices of the peace, especially such of them as are best spirited for work, name some of the freeholders of clearest integrity and prudence, of honest and blameless conversation, which for their number may be proportioned to the business of the county to which they relate, to serve upon juries for the year next ensuing, both between party and party and in

51. DQSOB Epiphany 1655; BL, Add. MS. 44058, fols 42–44.

52. The details are in Roberts, *Recovery and Restoration*, 49–53, 81–87.

53. *Calendar of State Papers, Domestic, 1655*, 77–78, 92–93, A. H. Woolrych, *Penruddock's Rising, 1655* (1955).

> cases criminal, and offer the names so agreed upon to the sheriff and undersheriff of the county; I doubt not but that they would be found willing to receive kindly such an assistance.[54]

Cromwell was here endorsing the Devon recommendations of the previous year and was commending them to the country as a whole. He argued that under the old way, the names of the jurors who were going to serve were known before the trial, since the undersheriff delivered the names to the clerk of the court. The result, Cromwell said, was "the ensnaring of the weaker and the tempting the avarice of the more subtle, wholly in wait for their own advantage." Typically, the Protector saw the issue as a moral crusade and equated royalism with corruption.

Justice Christopher Savery was one of the most concerned about jury regulation, and in his home district near Dartmouth he listed "the names of such persons as were presented by the gentlemen and the chief inhabitants of the several parishes within the hundreds of Coleridge and Stanborough."[55] The help of parish leaders was enlisted to compile lists of suitable jurors. No other lists have come to light. The compiling of lists, so typical of seventeenth-century reform drives, was no guarantee that changes in the jury system would actually occur. In Plymouth on 4 February 1656 at the end of a trying tour of duty, Desborough wrote pessimistically to Secretary Thurloe of the likely outcome of the campaign.[56] Nevertheless, Cromwell's initiative did mark a move away from simple censorship by sheriffs and justices of the peace. The government provided the stimulus and the policy, and the parish elites, the ministers, and the gentry provided the manpower. It was an attempt to enlist the support of the godly.

The success of the venture may be judged on the evidence of the sessions files. Until Midsummer quarter sessions 1656, there is nothing to suggest that the jury system had been moved from its wonted course. But in that summer, at a time when the vigorous campaign by the "men on horseback" to secure reliable returns to the forthcoming second Protectorate Parliament was under way, the trial jury displayed some unusual features. Its twelve members apparently had never served before and were not to do so again before 1670. They came from a wider geographical area than usual, and the customary

54. *The Writings and Speeches of Oliver Cromwell*, ed. W. C. Abbott, 4 vols. (Cambridge, Mass., 1937–47), 4:87–88.

55. BL, Add. MS. 44058, fols. 44v–52v.

56. *A Collection of the State Papers of John Thurloe, Esq.*, ed. T. Birch, 7 vols. (1742), 6:501.

freeholders lists were replaced by a shorter list of seventeen names from which the twelve were sworn. They tried twenty-one cases, seventeen of which resulted in convictions. The grand jury proved less easy to purge, but seventeen out of the twenty-five were new men. Ten of the seventeen jurors sworn were new.[57] By mid-seventeenth-century standards this had been a notable success.

Jury control was a realistic aim when the central government, the shrievalty, and the bench of magistrates were agreed on common ends. The following sessions of Michaelmas 1656 showed, however, how difficult it was to sustain reform. To a grand jury list of twenty-six names the sheriff or his deputy added: "Those above named were returned the last sessions by the justices but no others except three by the justices being returned the sheriff also returned these following so as the service may not be neglected,"[58] and inserted a further twenty-one names. The sheriff had doubtless employed his bailiffs to produce them. Ironically, Cromwell had feared the consequences of over-reliance upon subordinate local officials, a fear inculcated in him by these magistrates, who were keen to detect a threat to their own position but who were less capable of sustaining executive action. But 1656 was a year of common agreement on the aims of government, which assured reformers of at least some success.

The Restoration brought with it no moderation in the justices' pretensions to complete administrative control; in the unique Cavalier euphoria of the early 1660s, they were as committed to the policies of central government as those in power in the mid 1650s had been. Attacks were made on the sheriffs' bailiffs, and instead of the panacea of listing, the justices resorted to a system of direct accountability to themselves by all minor officials charged with summoning juries. This was a modified version of what had been tried in 1656; not the comprehensive listing of jurors, but only magisterial approval was now the self-assigned task of the bench. On this occasion, the good will of the parish gentry was not sought; here was a centralizing move to reinforce quarter sessions power. It was the secular local equivalent of the exclusivist policies pursued by the Church of England after 1660: orthodoxy was now defined very narrowly. For a few sessions around 1661, freeholders lists were endorsed with justices' signatures as an indication of approval, but again the magistrates failed to sustain their scrutiny.[59]

Not even the act "for the returning of able and sufficient jurors,"

57. QS Box 61, bundle for Midsummer 1656, jury lists and indictments.

58. QS Box 61, bundle for Michaelmas 1656.

59. DQSOB Michaelmas 1661; freeholders lists, QS boxes 67, 68.

which passed the Lords on 2 March 1665, achieved much success. The preamble spoke of "the reformation of abuses in sheriffs and other ministers who for reward do oftentimes spare the ablest and sufficientest and return the poor and simpler freeholders less able to discern the causes in question and to bear the charges of appearance and attendance thereon."[60] Penalties were to be imposed on negligent sheriffs and corrupt bailiffs, and again the justices were empowered to review the books of freeholders. The only evidence that the act was observed in Devon is the greater-than-average number of new men sworn to the quarter sessions grand jury during 1665 and 1666. There were no purges or general orders arising from the statute, however, and from 1667 the pattern of recruitment resumed its usual course. The act produced the merest hiccup in the procedure of jury summoning. The intentions of the statute and the aspirations of Devon justices of the peace were not in harmony. Despite its directions for registration, the act regarded the justices as the temporary agents of reform, an inspectorate whose task was to be completed within the space of one session, whereas since the mid 1650s at least, the magistrates had seen themselves as the principal and regular directors of local administration and local justice. During the Interregnum, reformers had eventually appealed to public opinion and the self-interest of community leaders, above the heads of the jury, whose proponents' own claim for it as the representative of the people was treated with scant respect. During the 1660s, by contrast, there was no appeal to the community at all. The gentry were in full control and would brook no interference from anyone. The jury was a nuisance and would be reformed by direct intervention. But what and whom did the jury represent, and what was this really a struggle to control? To answer these questions it is necessary to examine the relationship between participation in sessions juries and agrarian wealth.

Elsewhere I have drawn attention to the principal features of recruitment to the Devon grand jury.[61] Settlements in the south and east of the county returned the largest numbers, and these were the nucleated villages of arable farming. The larger industrial communities were under-represented. There was a connection between manorial representation and service on the sessions jury: healthy representation of a community on the sessions jury often corresponded to an active manorial elective system at home. Manors like Alphington (three grand jurors, ten petty jurors), Kenton (two grand jurors, five

60. *Statutes of the Realm*, 5:553–54 (16 & 17 Chas II, c. 3).

61. "Initiative and Control," 173–76.

petty jurors), Morchard Bishop (five grand jurors, one petty juror) and Newton St. Cyres (one grand juror, five petty jurors) maintained a vital tradition of manorial jury meetings and presentments. There is also an administrative momentum to consider; parishes sending the most grand jurors to Exeter were those that were on main roads to the city or were otherwise well situated for travel to it. On the whole, the parishes that sent the most men to Exeter were not those dominated by magisterial families, but some—like Alphington, Aylesbeare, Chudleigh, Newton St. Cyres, Rockbeare, and Sowton—were near Exeter or were on main roads. Others—Bishopsteignton and Halberton are good examples—were farther away but were still on principal highways. Others were simply large settlements. Administrative effectiveness diminished as the distance from Exeter increased, and the north of the county was ill-served by this pattern of participation.

The sessions trial jury displayed in a more pronounced form the tendency for jury recruitment to be concentrated in the Exeter area. We know the residence of the members of sixty juries sworn between 1649 and 1670. Of the hundreds of the county producing more than a dozen attendances each, only one, Lifton in west Devon, lay outside a sixteen-mile radius of the city of Exeter. This does not take account of jurors sitting on more than one occasion, and the figures for the hundreds nearest Exeter are swollen by those who came many times. Thomas Eliot of Upton Pyne in the hundred of Wonford sat on fifty-two juries, Thomas Harris of Kenton in the hundred of Exminster on forty-eight, John Turner of Alphington on forty-six, and his fellow parishioner John Pawling on forty-two. They may also have served on juries before 1649 and after 1670. Yet a good three-fourths of the jurors came only once or twice, so that the prominence of the "suburban" hundreds cannot be gainsaid. Within these hundreds, the numbers of sworn petty jurors bore no relation to the population of the parishes. Doddiscombsleigh, nestled in the Haldon Hills to the southwest of Exeter, had an adult male population of 102 in 1642 and sent one man as a trial juror; neighboring Dunchideock, even more remote and with an adult male population of only 50, sent seven. Alphington had 196 adult males and sent eight.[62] There was a trend toward multiple attendances, which the case of Dunchideock illustrates. Taking the period 1649 to 1659 as a whole, four Dunchideock men sat on the jury sixteen times. For the decade 1660 to 1670, four men (one served on either side of the Restoration) sat a combined total of thirty-seven

62. Population estimates are from A. J. Howard, ed., *The Devon Protestation Returns, 1641*, 2 vols. (1973).

times. This is the pattern in the whole county. Between 1649 and 1659, 111 different men sat on twenty-one juries; between 1660 and 1670, 76 were sworn to a total of thirty-eight. The trial jury was developing into a reliable cadre that was within easy reach of the magistrates and their clerks and that was not subject to the vagaries of the hundred-bailiffs, who undermined reform campaigns.

The notion of the petty jurors as semi-professional trusties is supported by the seasonal pattern of attendances by the leading jurors. Although normally there was a nucleus of seasoned jurymen at hand at all sessions, men like Thomas Eliot and Thomas Harris proved particularly useful for the Epiphany sessions, held in January. The southwest is always prone to heavy falls of snow in winter, and the short journeys that could be made by those from nearby parishes were not only convenient to the court but also probably necessary to sustain the judicial process at the worst time of year. All who sat on more than a dozen juries each in their careers sat more often at Epiphany sessions than at any of the other three. As a quid pro quo, many "regulars" were excused attendance during the Summer and Michaelmas sessions, when the demands of the farming year were at their heaviest. Thomas Harris of Kenton, for example, sat on twice as many Epiphany sessions as Midsummer ones; Richard Lowe of Bishopsteignton on four times as many. Service during the summer months could be spread more evenly among the larger pool of jurors.

There would thus appear to be an association between jury service and the imperatives of the agrarian society of rural Devon, and this relationship went further: most petty jurors came from farming areas long enclosed, suggesting a link between a developed agrarian community, where room for economic expansion was limited, and service in local administration. In the southern and eastern part of the county, the enclosed landscape was at its most mature, although as H.S.A. Fox points out, there were important differences between the two districts: "Pre-enclosure farm and field structure in South Devon was characterised by compact holdings and large square closes; in East Devon most holdings were fragmented and their scattered closes smaller in size and more elongated in shape, fossilizing as it were pre-enclosure patterns of strips."[63] David Levine has developed Fox's argument to show how east Devon in the late sixteenth century was ripe for proto-industrial development.[64] There was considerable pressure on

63. "The Chronology of Enclosure and Economic Development in Medieval Devon," *Economic History Review*, 2d ser., 27 (1975): 188.

64. *Family Formation in an Age of Nascent Capitalism* (New York, 1977), 105–7.

land in the eastern part of the county, and the maturity of the enclosed landscape offered little room for expansion or development to the prosperous yeomen and tenant farmers. The farther west one went in Devon, the less intense were the pressures on land: the ultimate in land availability was Dartmoor, which was used freely by those requiring summer grazing.[65] Petty jurors were likely to come from parishes where land was not freely available and from districts where fields were small.

Evidence of field size can also be found in manorial surveys and rentals, but a general source for the whole of the county is the series of glebe terriers in the Devon Record Office.[66] Glebe terriers are surveys of lands attached to parochial benefices, and they were compiled by churchwardens for the benefit of the diocesan authorities. They describe the condition and the acreage of church-owned lands farmed by the incumbent or for his profit. If one is prepared to assume that glebe lands would be representative of land-use patterns in the parish as a whole, they are a helpful guide. The Devon glebe terriers give the size of each enclosure in acres and note any glebe in open fields. It is therefore possible to reach an average field size for every parish surveyed.

This crude method confirms that parishes in the south and east of the county had smaller fields than those in the north and west. Thus East Budleigh, Alphington, Aylesbeare, Newton St. Cyres, Sidbury, and Tiverton had glebe holdings of an average of three acres per enclosure or less, sometimes much less, as in the case of Alphington, which in 1601 had fields averaging only 1.9 acres, although by 1680 this figure had risen to 2.3 acres. Some other average close sizes in the southwest were higher, and as Fox suggested, field sizes in the South Hams around Dartmouth were larger: Halwell's average in 1680 was 7.9 acres, swollen by several large fields of 16 and 22 acres.

On the whole, however, the western part of the county had the largest glebe enclosures. Bere Ferrers, in the southwest, had an average of 8.4 acres but contained three fields of over 15 acres; Black Torrington (averaging 13.4 acres) included an 80-acre "close" in 1602, although later terriers suggest that this was a large tract of moorland. The returns to the Milles inquiries of about 1750 and John Grant's survey of East Devon of 1844 confirm the prevalence of a pasture economy in the highland zone of the county and of arable farming in the south and

65. *Agrarian History*, ed. Thirsk, 4:76–77.

66. What follows is based on an examination of ninety-six glebe terriers (DRO GT) of fifty-two Devon parishes. For glebe terriers as a source, see the introduction by Molly Barratt to *Ecclesiastical Terriers of Warwickshire Parishes*, vol. 1, Dugdale Society (1955).

east, and confirm that even in the mid nineteenth century, fields around Exeter were especially small.[67] Not only was this a long-enclosed landscape in the seventeenth century, it was also a remarkably persistent landscape pattern.

This digression into economic history has been necessary to emphasize the fact that quarter sessions jurors came from areas of the county that were most developed economically. At the risk of laboring the point, one further piece of evidence must be discussed. Outfield cultivation, the sporadic or seasonal use of common land or wasteland to augment the usable land in a parish, has long been noted as a practice in the highland zone of Britain, especially in the southwest of England.[68] Outfield cultivation was a useful means of containing pressures on land, and it was practiced in the north and west of Devon, whence comparatively few jurors came, and less in the south and east, the natural recruiting ground for jurymen.

Devonshire thus seems capable of being divided into two sectors according to land use. In the south and east the landscape was frozen into a pattern of small fields and scattered holdings, although this was a wealthier area than the west, where fields were larger and where there was a surplus of land that could be exploited when pressures dictated. The jury system in Devon, and in an acute form the petty jury, was serviced by men from the area that was economically advanced but that seemed incapable of further expansion.

David Levine has shown how east Devon conforms to Joan Thirsk's model for the development of industries in the early-modern countryside.[69] The cloth trades, including the specialist crafts like lace making, were concentrated in the heartland of the jury-forming parishes. It is my suggestion that the petty jurors, coming from the industrial and agrarian economy of south and east Devon, represent a swollen yeoman/husbandman class in those areas. Part of Dr. Thirsk's thesis was that pastoral farming was more manageable and limited than ar-

67. Bodleian Lib., MS Top Devon b. 1 (for an extended analysis, see R. Stanes, "Devon Agriculture in the Mid-Eighteenth Century: The Evidence of the Milles Enquiries," in *The South-West and the Land*, ed. M. A. Havinden and C. M King [Exeter, 1969], 43–65); J. Grant, "A Few Remarks on the Large Hedges and Small Enclosures in Devonshire and the Adjoining Counties," *Journal of the Royal Agricultural Society* 5 (1844): 420–29.

68. H.S.A. Fox, "Outfield Cultivation in Devon and Cornwall: A Re-interpretation," in *Husbandry and Marketing in the South-West, 1500–1800*, ed. M. A. Havinden (Exeter, 1973), 35. Cf. G. E. Fusell, "Four Centuries of Farming Systems in Devon, 1500–1900," *Trans. Devonshire Assoc.* 83 (1951): 179–82.

69. Levine, *Family Formation*, 105–6; Thirsk, "Industries in the Countryside," in *Essays in Social and Economic History*, ed. F. J. Fisher, 70–88.

able agriculture and that subsidiary economic activity was a natural response to under-employment. Levine has shown this to have been the case in east Devon. Petty jurors seem to have had plenty of time—time available in a static, if prosperous, pastoral economy that could only be expanded by economic diversification. The cloth trade was scattered extensively throughout south and east Devon, and participation in local government may itself have been a response to the history of enclosure, an inflexible pattern of farming and a political counterpart to "industry in the countryside." Political consciousness could be defined as simply a willingness to serve in the process of government, and perhaps historians have for too long considered the rhetoric of overt political action to be the only criterion of political activity.

Magistrates kept a watchful eye on the jury, as the history of intervention and "tuning" shows, so we should not be surprised that its public façade was one of compliance with the policies of the bench. Nevertheless, it would be unwise to conclude that there was no connection between religious radicalism and jury participation. The public record of the jury alone is not sufficient evidence on which to judge the tone and political disposition of the "middling sort" of Devon.

Puritanism in Devon was of a cautious and conservative kind. Opposition to bishops and a fear of popery were among its principal characteristics, and in the early 1640s its leading exponents were leaders among the squirearchy.[70] Typical Devon lay Puritans were Sir John Northcote (1599–1676), active in the House of Commons during 1640–42, Sir William Morrice, later Charles II's secretary of state, and Thomas Bampfield (1620–93), barrister, recorder of Exeter, MP for the city, and Speaker of the lower house in the second Protectorate Parliament.[71] A tendency toward moral censoriousness, underpinned by a rigid concept of social hierarchy, emerged among the more austere Puritans; Bampfield and Edward Raddon, clerk of the peace during the Commonwealth, inherited the Sabbatarian and authoritarian mantle of Ignatius Jourdain, the scourge of Exeter's drinking fraternity.[72] During the 1650s these men were a powerful voice among the ruling re-

70. E. A. Andriette, *Devon and Exeter in the Civil War* (Newton Abbot, 1972) offers the best narrative.

71. Extensive references to all three men may be found in Roberts, *Recovery and Restoration*.

72. Ibid., 48, 59. F. Nicholls, *The Life and Death of Ignatius Jourdain* (1654), Keith Thomas, "The Puritans and Adultery: The Act of 1650 Reconsidered," in *Puritans and Revolutionaries: Essays in Seventeenth-Century History Presented to Christopher Hill*, ed. D. Pennington and K. Thomas (Oxford, 1978), 267, 274, for Jourdain.

gime, and it was during their ascendancy that a new religious radicalism, having its seat among the middle and lower classes, came to the fore.

Quakers were active in Devon from the mid 1650s, but their number bore no relation to the violence of the response against them from the Devon bench. Quarter sessions ordered Quaker books to be burned and lumped Quakers with vagrants as threats to the social order.[73] Much has been written about the political significance of Quakerism; it had at its heart a reaction against authority, discipline, and the hierarchical social code.[74] It was, in local terms, a reaction against the local ruling elite, and it was treated accordingly by it. Devon MPs were among the most vehement and intemperate denouncers of the west country Quaker James Nayler during his "trial" before the second Protectorate Parliament in 1656.[75]

At the Restoration the political initiative swung nationally toward Anglicanism, but because of the unique influence on the king of Devonian Presbyterians—William Morrice and George Monck, duke of Albemarle, being among the most eminent—a measure of continuity with the Interregnum bench was assured. The prosecution of sexual offenders at quarter sessions was abruptly dropped, but Quakers continued to be persecuted, and new magistrates appeared whose Anglicanism was not of a liberal kind and who cooperated with successive bishops of Exeter to hound "dissenters," now more widely defined to include Independents and Baptists, who had enjoyed the personal protection of Oliver Cromwell during the Protectorate.[76] In a sense, the Restoration encouraged the authoritarian instincts of the Devon gentry to develop still further.

Post-1660 dissent and the official response to it sharpened the class divisions in Devon society. Nonconformists were more numerous among the middling sort; there had been few religious radicals among the magistrates of the 1650s. Those who now became "known to the government" as men to be monitored were former soldiers and central government officeholders pushed into a demimonde of plotting and, in the case of Samson Larke, who was executed after Monmouth's

73. DQSOB Midsummer 1656, Midsummer 1658; A.H.A Hamilton, *Quarter Sessions from Queen Elizabeth to Queen Anne* (1878), 164–65.

74. The best recent treatment is B. Reay, *The Quakers and the English Revolution* (1985).

75. Roberts, *Recovery and Restoration*, 56–59.

76. J. Simmons, "Some Letters from Bishop Ward of Exeter, 1663–1667," *Devon and Cornwall Notes and Queries* 21 (1940–41): 222–27, 282–88, 329–36, 359–68; *Calendar of State Papers, Domestic, 1655–56*, 224.

Rising of 1685, into open revolt after maltreatment at the hands of the Cavalier regime.[77] It was therefore natural that there should be some people of nonconformist sympathies among the Devon jurymen, particularly as recruitment to the jury was centered on areas in which dissent flourished. The government and the bench were shrewd enough to be able to exploit this in the interest of good order.

The Indulgence of 1672 was granted as a response to high politics, which must have seemed peculiarly remote to Devon people. The penal laws against Protestant nonconformists and Roman Catholics alike were suspended, and nonconformity in general came under the auspices of the local state. In these circumstances, the two qualifications in jurors and constables of a dissenting background and experience in local administration proved irresistible to the bench. At least ten men whose houses were licensed to hold religious conventicles in 1672 were grand jurors and high constables.[78] Andrew Holwell of Woodbury was sworn to the grand jury in 1664 and 1665 and was then dropped before being licensed in 1672; Richard Burthogg and William Venner were both prosecuted for sectarian activities after receiving licences in 1672, although in most cases a license seems to have bestowed a degree of immunity from later prosecution. This episode is one of the very few in which the bench recognized independent thinking by jurors for what it was and rewarded them with heavier public responsibilities.

But the jury was not the totally dependable body that this delegation of authority would suggest. We already know that jurors strayed into crime of a conventional kind. Several petty jurors came from families not above theft or delinquency. If the jury was a bulwark in the defense of property, its members individually were not necessarily exemplars of the sanctity of the rights surrounding it. Juror Peter Bartoe's son, John, was accused of stealing a saddle; juror Hugh Bidwell of Newton St. Cyres had a brother tried at quarter sessions for adultery.[79] These were petty jurors, but even the grand jury was scandalized from time to time by offenses perpetrated by its own members against the norms of good moral or neighborly conduct. The treatment accorded those who drank or swore or who diverted water-

77. Roberts, *Recovery and Restoration*, 154–55.

78. Their names are in the *Calendar of State Papers, Domestic, 1672*, and the lists of constables and jurors are in QS.

79. QS Box 72, bundle for Michaelmas 1667, examinations; Box 68, bundle for Midsummer 1663, examinations. For more on Bartoe, see S. K. Roberts, "Participation and Performance in Devon Local Administration 1649–1670" (Ph.D. diss., Univ. of Exeter, 1980), 125.

courses, blocked drains, or simply habitually failed to turn up for jury service sent a frisson of righteous indignation around the jury chamber and reminded its occupants that their status granted them no immunity.

Apart from infringements of the criminal law and the "annoyances" that disturbed social and economic life in seventeenth-century Devon, jurors and constables could fall foul of "political" laws, those laws against religious dissent promulgated so vigorously in the 1660s, 1670s and 1680s. Work in progress by Peter Jackson on nonconformity in the diocese of Exeter has produced a comprehensive listing of those convicted at quarter sessions of attending conventicles, and in the church courts of not taking the sacrament of Holy Communion. By this time the church courts had been rehabilitated as an agency to deal with moral and religious offenses. A considerable number of these offenders were involved in the middle ranks of local administration as head constables and grand or petty jurors. Jackson's own work will offer a definitive view of the prosopography of dissenters in Devon and Cornwall, but here some characteristics of the patterns of service in county government by some sixty nonconformists may be outlined.[80]

A number of men serving as jurors in the 1650s were later prosecuted for dissenting activities. Abraham Pounsford, a petty juror in 1656, the year of the Protectorate's sharpest impact on the localities, was prosecuted three times after 1660 in the bishop's consistory court for not receiving the sacrament of the Lord's Supper. John Lidstone, a cooper by trade and a grand juror sworn regularly from 1651 to 1653, was another persistent nonconformist, staying away from church and not receiving the sacrament. George Young of Crediton was a Commonwealth juror prosecuted for absence from church in 1662. Altogether, some twenty men who served on grand juries in the 1650s found themselves in trouble for these "political" offenses a decade later, suggesting that although there was no immediate or spectacular purge of juries at the Restoration itself, there was a significant degree of difference in composition between juries of the 1650s and those of the succeeding regime. This is despite the overwhelming evidence that Commonwealth and Protectorate juries were pliable and not active politically. It suggests that the Restoration may have seen a hardening of attitudes among the Devon middling sort to create a climate of "conscientious objection" among a group that had gained its polit-

80. What follows is based on a list of dissenters' names culled by Peter Jackson from QS and consistory court records and checked against names of jurors in QS. I am very grateful to Peter Jackson for allowing me to see this list.

ical experience, or at least its tutelage, under a more sympathetic regime.

It is notable that the offenders of the 1660s were much more likely to have served the county on juries under the Commonwealth rather than after 1653 and that the only other dissenting jurors to be prosecuted who had served during the Interregnum were those who had been drafted in during Major General Desborough's visitation in 1656. Abraham Pounsford, John Viccary, William Sumpter, and John Fry all appeared on juries in 1656 and then disappeared to emerge again later as defendants in the church courts. It is equally interesting, however, that many nonconformists seem to have been removed from the jury in the period after 1656 but before the Restoration. John Viccary of Farway served in 1656, but his name was subsequently erased from jury lists and he was excused from service from 1660 to 1662 before being prosecuted in 1665. Augustine Skinner was excused on several occasions between 1658 and 1670. William Starr of Seaton was spared jury service in 1658, and in 1665 his widow, Grace, a Quaker, was haled before the church courts and accused of absence from church. Nowhere was the gentry more alive to the dangers of the sects in the later 1650s than in Devon, and after the traumas of the major general's visitation and the case of James Nayler, there seems to have been a weeding-out of anyone with sectarian views.

But there was no simple division between jurors of the 1650s who became nonconformists and those serving in the following decade who did not. Some of the prosecuted jurors served in the 1660s, some up to the time of prosecution. John Yeo, alias Bawden, of Whitestone, for example, was last sworn in 1663 and was prosecuted in the consistory court in May of that year for not attending church. Silvanus Evans was sworn in 1660 and prosecuted in 1662; Henry Stoy was summoned, but not sworn, six times in the 1660s and was later convicted for not receiving the sacrament of the Lord's Supper. Altogether nine sessions grand jurors appeared on juries after 1660 before being prosecuted in the church courts or at quarter sessions for not complying with the rites and ceremonies of the Church of England. As in the previous decade, however, the bench of magistrates and the sheriff frequently had time to remove likely dissidents from the jury panels before any damage ensued. Men like Henry Stoy and William Venner, both of Chittlehampton, were summoned to quarter sessions but were never sworn by the sheriff in the 1660s, and both were prosecuted for offenses against the church. William Choldich of Aveton Gifford was summoned five times between 1665 and 1668 but was never sworn and in 1670 was prosecuted at quarter sessions for attending a conventicle. By 1678 he felt alienated enough to withhold payment of the rate for the upkeep of the church and was prosecuted in the consistory court.

What is clear is that although the dissenting jurors were a small minority, they were significant enough as a group to merit the attention of those who manipulated the jury and who ruled Devon. There were no pronouncements at sessions about the problem, and there was no need for any public discussion; behind-the-scenes consultations between sheriffs and bailiffs would ensure that unsuitable freeholders were simply overlooked. Although it has been argued here and elsewhere that the jury was no wayward force in local politics, the same cannot necessarily be said for the whole class from which juries were recruited. East Devon Puritanism and jury quiescence were both cultural manifestations of the same socio-economic class, but a measure of how hard the justices had to work to nurture quiescence may be the frequency with which dissenters appeared in the jury chamber before anyone noticed. Magistrates continued to work in a semi-bureaucratic administrative system that could not guarantee that "troublemakers" would be eliminated.

To control the grand and petty juries at quarter sessions was to control the middling sort of men, as the gentry realized. They were prepared to invest time and energy in the task because the rewards, in terms of an ordered county, were considerable. But what of juries in other geographical contexts? What happened when recruitment and performance sprang from the narrow confines of the borough? A brief study of two of the large towns of Devon may throw the class basis of the tensions at county quarter sessions into relief.

During the seventeenth century, Barnstaple in north Devon had been eclipsed as an economic center by the rise of new kinds of cloth, the "new draperies," and by the development of the east Devon cloth trade. Even its role as a point of embarkation and as a landing place for imports of Irish wool was undermined by the silting up of the River Taw. It proved impossible to dredge, and the port of Bideford grew at Barnstaple's expense.[81] In its politics Barnstaple was suspicious both of county government and of the central authority. Its own economic welfare came before wider issues. In 1647 the military governor of the town was a local man, Richard Harris, who supported municipal interests against the county committee. During the 1650s the principal government agent in the town was a merchant, Lionel Beecher, who by 1657 was sorely repenting his commitment to the Protectorate and

81. W. G. Hoskins, *Devon* (1954), 327–30.

the consequent decline of his business.[82] Religion divided the town from the county: the moderate Puritan minister Martin Blake, who was supported by townsmen, was hounded by county committeemen and the local military establishment throughout the 1650s.[83]

Barnstaple could not be relied upon by Interregnum governments, but the restored monarchy was no more popular there. From the first moves to re-establish the local militia, the town opposed what it took to be the attempt by George Monck, duke of Albemarle, to overturn local customs by Privy Council diktat. By February 1662 the government was facing a strike by Barnstaple ratepayers, who resented the introduction of military rates without reference to the aldermanic body.[84] As in the 1650s, local privileges and interests were defended fiercely against encroachment or intrusion. How far did the jury structure of the town contribute to this spirit of truculent independence?

At Barnstaple, the court leet and the local sessions or aldermanic court had been amalgamated into one court dealing principally with minor civil cases and criminal matters involving property rights, including trespass. Jury lists have survived from the 1670s, and they show that presentments were regular and lengthy. At a meeting of the "general sessions of the peace and court leet held before the mayor, deputy recorder, alderman and steward" on 12 October 1674, no fewer than forty-five separate presentments were offered by the grand jury.[85] An alehousekeeper, "although bound yet very unfit," six unlicensed alehousekeepers, an idle beadle, and a man whose swine "run the street" were reported, but most cases were of broken pavements, noisome dunghills, and weaknesses in the masonry and equipment of the quay. Dilapidated "penthouses" (outhouses) were a matter of great concern to the Barnstaple jurors, and their prominence indicates the operation of elementary planning laws or the internal regulation of business premises. Merchants and tradesmen who developed their property were carefully scrutinized. The quay was naturally an area of interest and was keenly watched. In August 1674 three "penthouses," two access roads, and a pavement there were presented, and the quay itself needed attention.[86] From the late 1670s, presentments for absenteeism from church began to appear, possibly to reflect concern about

82. PRO, SP 18/153/48.

83. Bodleian Lib., MS. J. Walker, c. 4, fols. 176–90, 350, 356, 369, J. F. Chanter, *The Life and Times of Martin Blake, BD* (1910), esp. chap. 4.

84. North Devon Athenaeum, Barnstaple, Barnstaple Borough MSS. 576–90.

85. Barnstaple Borough MS. 1856.

86. Ibid., MS. 1858.

the popish plot and the exclusion crisis, but otherwise presentments related to internal regulatory matters only.

Those presented for their neglect or deliberate infringement of local standards were punished by an established scale of fines. In the county, by contrast, penalties were determined by the discretion of the magistrates. A broken pavement attracted a fine of three shillings, a "broken penthouse" five shillings, and all other misdemeanors six shillings and eightpence, except the offense of allowing a house to fall into dangerous disrepair, which carried a penalty of ten shillings.[87] Compare these with three shillings and fourpence for illegal drinking, five shillings for drunkenness, and twenty shillings for running an unlawful alehouse—penalties determined in early-Stuart statutes—and it becomes apparent that the Barnstaple court took regulative presentments seriously. Their effect was to reinforce the introspective tendencies in Barnstaple's government: to focus popular participation on issues crucial to the economic life of the town, which in the mid seventeenth century must have caused concern in most propertied residents. Here was the middling sort in control.[88]

At first glance, Dartmouth had much in common with Barnstaple. Both were seaports, both were parliamentary boroughs with a freeman franchise, and both had flourishing local courts. But apparent similarities concealed many differences. In Dartmouth, quarter sessions and the court leet remained separate, even if their civil and criminal functions overlapped. Dartmouth was a primary port for the "new draperies" cloth exports and had adapted to economic necessity. Dartmouth, unlike Barnstaple, had seen much military action during the civil war, and it was dominated in the 1650s by Puritans like Thomas Boone, one of the few Devon survivors of Pride's Purge of Parliament in December 1648. Although Major John Blackmore advised the demolition of Dartmouth Castle in May 1650, his fears sprang from the possibility of a sea invasion by Irish rebels or exiled royalists, not from any imagined designs by the local populace.[89] Barnstaple and Dartmouth were "Puritan" in their government, but Dartmouth was not introspective. Merchants and mayors there, like John Budley and William Barnes, became county tax assessment commissioners, and Barnes presided at the town customs office.[90] The town was open to

87. Dorse of ibid., MS. 1856.

88. Ibid., MSS. 1857, 1859, 1860, 1861, 1862, 1865.

89. *Calendar of State Papers, Domestic, 1650,* 137.

90. *Acts and Ordinances of the Interregnum,* ed. C. H. Firth and R. S. Rait, 3

benign intervention, and good will was offered by outside authorities. When Christopher Savery and Edmund Fowell, two Devonshire justices of the peace, arbitrated in a tithes dispute there, they made it clear that they had acceded to "all your demands, which we seldom or never do to any."[91] Major General Desborough settled amicably a dispute there over a church living in 1656.[92] After 1660, however, good will faded. Dartmouth considered itself betrayed by the Privy Council, which was alleged to have favored Merchant Adventurers' trade monopolies. In the 1667 by-election at Dartmouth the government's candidate was defeated in a contest in which complex sectional interests, blurring national and local perspectives, were marshaled vigorously.[93]

Jury presentments at sessions and leets contain many of the same items as those made in Barnstaple. Neglected roads, pigs in the streets, dunghills in public places, walls in imminent danger of collapse—these are plentiful. But a striking difference was the readiness of jurors to attack prominent individuals and the chamber itself for their shortcomings not only with regard to local matters of concern to tradesmen and property holders but also in their enforcement of statutes and proclamations. In July 1660 the Presbyterian minister James Burdwood, who enjoyed the support of Thomas Boone, was presented "for riding on Whitsunday last." The churchwardens were criticized for not erecting the king's arms in the church, the receiver was censured for not repairing the north conduit, and the chamber was accused of granting "foreign" shopkeepers the same privileges as freemen.[94] No one was exempt from criticism, however eminent; leading townsmen Thomas Boone, Captain John Pley, and Mr. William Spurway were censured for minor neglects of pavements and property.[95] But this was October 1660, and the temerity of the court leet in pursuing these affairs may have owed not a little to Restoration politics; all three had been notable Commonwealthsmen. The presentments may simply reflect the royalist euphoria so prevalent in 1660. Also to the fore of the 1660 presentment is concern for the observance of the Sabbath, church attendance, and the maintenance of the church fab-

vols. (1911), 2:660–61; *Calendar of State Papers, Domestic, 1652–53*, 584, PRO, E 122/222/66.

91. DRO, Dartmouth Corporation MS. DD 62722.

92. Ibid., MS. DD 62817B; Edmund Calamy, *The Nonconformists' Memorial*, ed. Samuel Palmer (1802–3), 1:14.

93. See Roberts, "Participation and Performance," 143–44, for details.

94. Dartmouth Corporation MS. DD 63018.

95. Ibid., MS. DD 63020.

ric. Even as late as July 1662 the neglects of the town scavengers were presented with the civic leaders "for not having the commandments in the church of St. Saviours."[96] Unfortunately, the series of Dartmouth presentments is brief and fragmentary, and perhaps the years 1660 to 1662 were not typical ones in the consciousness of the jury. But if the series is compared with that for the county in the same period, the Dartmouth jury seems much more abrasive.

In both Barnstaple and Dartmouth the jurors were minor freeholders, but they were prepared to speak their mind, in Barnstaple against those who failed in their obligations to the community and in Dartmouth against those who transgressed against government edict and the prevailing religious code. In both cases the jury harmonized with the impression offered by the townsmen to the world outside, and in neither instance was the jury in any way moribund. In both cases the tyranny of geography held no sway, and the freeholder class was vigorous and assertive, a force to be reckoned with.

Historians of the jury divide quite neatly into those who see it as enjoying wide initiative in government and in fact finding and those who see little evidence of jury independence. Professor Green is the latest historian to argue that the form of control that emerged at the assizes in the later sixteenth century was one that allowed juries a measure of independent judgment in questions of life and death.[97]

It has been my argument here that the trial jury in the chamber at quarter sessions in the 1650s and 1660s was the product of such a degree of intervention and manipulation by the gentry that to describe the choices before it (in misdemeanors) as "independent" ones would be to misuse the word. The view of the selected quarter sessions trial jurors as the stooges of the gentry is reinforced by the evidence I have tried to present on the liveliness of the jury class. Jurors were small businessmen and industrialists as well as farmers, and many were the products of an economy in which surplus energies sought an outlet. Many were religious dissenters. When national politics and local gentry preoccupations coincided, then the experience and priorities of the jury class could be utilized, as in the Cromwellian reformation of manners in 1656 and in the licensing of houses during the Indulgence. On other occasions, however, which means for most of the period un-

96. Ibid., MS. DD 63114. The other presentments examined were DD 63017, 63019, 63112, 63113.

97. Green, *Verdict According to Conscience*, 369.

der review here, the jury was patrolled and policed by the class immediately above it and was forced into the Procrustean mold of deference and passivity cast for it by the gentry. When John Willoughby, esquire, was approached by the sheriff in 1659 to serve on the assize grand jury, he was told his presence would "put a lustre on the representative body of the county." In the recruitment of quarter sessions grand and petty jurors, however, it was a matter of ensuring that their light remained firmly under a bushel.

Eight

London Juries in the 1690s

J. M. Beattie

The late seventeenth century was the heroic age of the English jury, for in the political and constitutional struggles of the reigns of Charles II and James II, trial by jury emerged as the principal defense of English liberties. The grand jury that refused to indict the earl of Shaftesbury and the trial jury of twelve citizens who acquitted the Seven Bishops were to be celebrated as saviors who had prevented the establishment of tyrannical government and had confirmed the jury, as Blackstone was to say, as the "sacred bulwark of the nation."[1] But the constitutional significance of the right to trial by jury went much deeper than that. The jury was also seen as protecting ordinary individuals from arbitrary power and from malicious and unfounded charges, and as supporting a form of trial that gave English subjects a much fairer hearing when they were brought before a criminal court than the subjects of less happy regimes across the Channel. Trial by jury was thus widely thought to be crucial to the defense of the most basic and fundamental of English liberties, a view that was to be asserted frequently in the eighteenth century, particularly when the role of the jury was seen as being unfairly limited and restricted, as in trials for seditious libel.[2]

The study of the composition and character of an institution as important in national life as the jury thus hardly requires justification—particularly, perhaps, for juries in London, where the political trials of

1. William Blackstone, *Commentaries on the Laws of England* (1769), 4:344. On the political trials of the 1670s and 1680s, see G. W. Keeton, *Lord Chancellor Jeffreys and the Stuart Cause* (1965), passim; and Green, *Verdict According to Conscience*, chap. 6.

2. Green, *Verdict According to Conscience*, chap. 8.

the 1670s and 1680s were centered and where the busiest of the criminal courts were to be found. But there are other good reasons for examining juries in the capital in the late seventeenth century and the early decades of the eighteenth, for this was a period of particular significance in the history of the criminal law and the administration of justice. In the decades following the Restoration, many of the assumptions upon which the judicial system had rested were beginning to erode, and new solutions were being sought to the problems posed by crime and social disorder. Dissatisfaction in the courts and in Parliament with the ineffectiveness of the law gave rise to a variety of efforts to enlarge its powers of deterrence, efforts that can be seen to include (although they were by no means limited to) attempts to develop transportation as an effective sanction in the hands of the courts and to enlarge the scope of capital punishment.

In the search for more effective punishments and in the administration of the changing criminal law, the jury played an important role, for jurors were allowed a great deal of discretion in the way they rendered their verdicts and applied the law. Discretionary powers were not exercised for the first time by juries in the late seventeenth century,[3] but the importance of the jury and its independent role in the courtroom were significantly extended and secured in this period by the decision in the case of Edward Bushel in 1670 and particularly by the subsequent elaboration of Chief Justice Vaughan's decision in that case by the proponents of jury rights.[4] Of course, it was not only juries in London that were enabled after 1670 to reach verdicts free of the judge's coercion and free of the fear that they might be fined or imprisoned by a trial judge who disagreed with them. And it was not only London juries that could shape the way the criminal law was administered by their choices among the variety of verdicts open to them. But it is possible that juries in the capital were particularly influential in enlarging the habits of discretionary justice that were to characterize the administration of the law in the eighteenth century. The London courts dealt with a much larger number of criminal cases than courts elsewhere in the country, and the way they dealt with the capital statutes and with the capital provisions of the law generally was widely reported in this period through the pamphlet accounts of trials

3. For juries in the late sixteenth and early seventeenth centuries, see in particular Cockburn, *Assize Introduction*, 56–71; and C. B. Herrup, "The Common Peace. Legal Structure and Legal Substance in East Sussex, 1594–1640" (Ph.D. diss., Northwestern Univ. 1982), chap. 5. Also, see above, chap. 6.

4. Green, *Verdict According to Conscience*, chap. 6.

at the Old Bailey (the main criminal court in London) that were published regularly—eight times a year—from the late 1670s.[5]

The late seventeenth century is thus a useful period in which to investigate juries at the Old Bailey and at the other criminal courts of the capital. That is the aim of this essay. I will concentrate on the last decade of the century and on juries in the City of London—in the City, that is, as against the county of Middlesex, the point of which distinction will be clarified when we come to deal with the structure of the criminal courts in the metropolis. I have chosen to study the 1690s because it was in the reign of William III that the efforts to increase the effectiveness of the courts resulted in several statutes that began the process of extending the range of capital punishment and in other changes in the administrative system, and this essay forms part of a larger study of the way the courts received and adapted those alterations. My object here, however, is not to analyze what the London juries did—the verdicts they reached and the way they put the criminal laws into effect. That will have to be left to subsequent work. My concern is, rather, to investigate the membership of London juries in this period and the way they were constituted, as a necessary preliminary to that larger study of the role of juries in the metropolis in the administration of the criminal law.

The business of dealing with crime in the metropolis was divided among several jurisdictions. In the City of London, the mayor and a number of aldermen were magistrates ex officio,[6] and by the end of the seventeenth century they and the recorder of the City were holding sessions of the peace in the Guildhall eight times a year. Their jurisdiction at these sessions extended over the ancient City within the walls and the several extramural wards under their purview (including Farringdon Ward Without, Bishopsgate Without, and Cripplegate

5. For the character of these Old Bailey Sessions Papers (hereafter OBSP) see J. H. Langbein, "The Criminal Trial before the Lawyers," *University of Chicago Law Review* 45 (1978): 267–72; and idem, "Shaping the Eighteenth-Century Criminal Trial: A View from the Ryder Sources," *University of Chicago Law Review* 50 (1983): 3–5; M. Harris, "Trials and Criminal Biographies: A Case Study in Distribution," in *The Sale and Distribution of Books from 1700*, ed. R. Myers and M. Harris (1982), 1–15.

6. By the 1638 Charter, the mayor, the recorder, the aldermen who had served as mayor, and the next three most senior aldermen were to be included in the City commission of the peace. The 1692 charter added six more aldermen—the next six by seniority who had served as sheriff. Finally, by the Charter issued in 1741 all the aldermen were to be named as justices of the peace. [P. E. Jones], *The Corporation of London: Its Origins, Constitution, Powers and Duties* (1950), 59–60.

Without), an area that included a population in the 1690s of perhaps close to 125,000 and about a quarter of the total population of the larger metropolis. Outside the City itself, that population lived largely in Middlesex and came under the jurisdiction of the magistrates of that county. By the second half of the seventeenth century, the Middlesex sessions also met at Hicks' Hall in Clerkenwell eight times a year at the same time as the City sessions in the Guildhall, for reasons we will come to. Two other jurisdictions may be noted briefly. The City of Westminster, although it was in Middlesex, had its own commission of the peace and its own quarter sessions. Cases arising in Westminster could also be dealt with at the county sessions, however, and the most important matters tended to be taken there. The Borough of Southwark, south of the Thames, was in some respects and for some purposes within the City of London, and the mayor and aldermen of London had the right to hold their sessions of the peace there once a year. But, in fact, this court handled few cases, and none of any seriousness. Criminal matters arising in Southwark and in the other populous parishes along the south bank of the river were dealt with by the courts of Surrey—the county quarter sessions and the assizes.

The main criminal courts of London were those of Middlesex and the City. At the sessions of the peace in both jurisdictions the magistrates dealt with the range of business common to county and borough sessions elsewhere: administrative matters arising from the poor laws and vagrancy, the organization of the watch, licensing, and so on (though in the City such matters were also dealt with by the Common Council and the Court of Aldermen); and minor criminal offenses like assault, disturbances of the peace, fraud, and cheating. As in other counties by the end of the seventeenth century, the Middlesex and London magistrates left the more serious criminal cases—not just capital cases, but felonies in general—to courts presided over by the judges of the high courts. In the counties this meant the assizes, the twice-yearly sessions held by the two judges of the king's courts at Westminster who went on circuit out of term.[7] In London and Middlesex this arrangement did not obtain. There were no assizes there on the pattern familiar in the rest of the country. Since the courts of King's Bench and Common Pleas sat in the county of Middlesex, there was no need to arm the judges appointed to hear criminal cases with additional powers to take civil pleas by means of the commissions of assize and *nisi prius*, as was required elsewhere. In London and Mid-

7. Cockburn, *Assizes*, 87–93.

dlesex, serious criminal cases were dealt with by a body of commissioners merely empowered to hold sessions of oyer and terminer and of gaol delivery.

The crucial point about these sessions in the metropolis is that although two jurisdictions were involved, there was only one gaol to be delivered, for Newgate (in the City of London) was the common gaol not only of the City but also of Middlesex. Defendants from the county's prisons were transferred to Newgate to take their trials at the sessions held in the justice hall known as the Old Bailey, which was attached to the prison. These cases were heard under commissions of oyer and terminer and gaol delivery addressed to the lord mayor of London, who presided, to the aldermen of the City, the recorder and Common Sergeant, and to the judges of the high courts. In practice, the Old Bailey sessions were very largely in the hands of the professional judges, several of whom took turns hearing the cases. But the mayor and aldermen were by no means excluded from the bench, and the recorder of the City played an important role at the Old Bailey, for it was his duty to pronounce the sentences at the conclusion of the session and to report in person to the sovereign the cases of those prisoners condemned to death.[8]

The trials at the Old Bailey were heard before a single group of judges, but the prisoners were brought before them from both London and Middlesex, and this meant that these were in effect double sessions, for each prisoner had to be tried by a jury from the appropriate jurisdiction. Juries were thus called to the Old Bailey from London and from Middlesex, and the prisoners were tried before them in interspersed batches. Several prisoners from London would be arraigned together, for example, and their trials would go forward immediately, one after the other, to the London jury. When that group of as many as eight or ten trials was completed, the jury would retire to deliberate on all of them. While they were out, a batch of Middlesex prisoners would be arraigned and tried in a similar way before the Middlesex jury. It seems clear from some of the printed Old Bailey Sessions Papers of the late seventeenth century that as soon as the London jurors had reached their verdicts they would return to the court and report them, even if this meant interrupting the Middlesex cases then in progress.[9] When the Middlesex cases were completed, that jury would

8. Langbein, "Eighteenth-Century Criminal Trial," 31–36.

9. For jury practices at the Old Bailey in the late seventeenth and early eighteenth centuries, see Langbein, "Criminal Trial before the Lawyers," 272–77. For the London jury returning to court to report their verdicts and interrupting the Middlesex

retire, another group of London prisoners would be arraigned, and thus the trials would proceed.

It might be noted parenthetically that the practice at the Old Bailey was for the same twelve men to serve through the entire session on the London jury and the same twelve Middlesex men to serve for the county. This was quite unlike the pattern of service at the county assizes, where several dozen jurors were often required for each session. That situation was changing at the provincial assizes in the second half of the seventeenth century, but the assize courts never came to expect that the twelve men who formed the trial jury on the first day would hear every case on the calendar. That was clearly the expectation and the practice at the Old Bailey. Presumably, it depended in large part on the willingness of these London and Middlesex jurors to devote the better part of a week to this duty. But it was also made possible by the double nature of the Old Bailey session and by the way the juries deliberated there and found their verdicts. That is suggested by the changes that can be seen in jury practice at the county assizes in the second half of the seventeenth century.

In the late sixteenth and early seventeenth centuries, on the Home circuit at least, assize trial juries heard cases in batches and then left the court to find verdicts on them all at once in the way we have described the Old Bailey juries working in the 1690s. At the county assizes, however, when one jury retired, a second group of twelve men had to be sworn in if the court's business was not to be brought to a standstill while the first jury deliberated. In fact, at the county assizes the practice was to constitute a succession of juries, and, depending on the length of the calendar, a second jury might be followed by a third, a fourth, or even a fifth. Some of the men from one jury might subsequently serve on a later panel. But more often than not, each panel consisted largely of fresh jurors, and the result was that a large number of men served at each session of the provincial assize courts, indeed as many as fifty or sixty.[10] There is no doubt that sheriffs had frequently found it difficult to assemble a sufficient number of qualified men to meet the demands of this system and that the courts often had to scramble to find suitable jurors.[11] It is hardly surprising, then, that this method of creating juries—a series of essentially separate panels following each other—gave way in the middle of the seven-

trials to do so, see OBSP, Dec. 1678, which, as Langbein has said, provides an unusually full and detailed account of the procedure and practice of the court (ibid., 274–75).

10. Cockburn, *Assize Introduction*, 61–62.

11. Ibid., 58–61; see above, chap. 6, text at n. 16.

teenth century to a system in which these successive panels were largely made up of jurors who had served earlier in the session. This allowed for a significant reduction in the number of individuals required for jury service at the assizes. Cockburn has found the precise moment at which this new system began: the summer assizes of 1650. It seems reasonable to think that this striking change came after a decade of particular difficulty—through civil war and revolution—in getting a sufficient number of qualified jurors to attend the assizes. But the fundamental problem had clearly troubled the courts for a long time by then, and the introduction of a system that required fewer jurors must have been a welcome development to judges, sheriffs, and court officials alike. And the number of men serving at each assize session certainly did go down after 1650 and continued to shrink further through the second half of the seventeenth century.[12]

One consequence of this reduction in the number of jurors required at the assizes may well have been some raising of the social status of those who sat on provincial trial juries. The new system also seems to have had a profound effect on the way juries deliberated and reached their verdicts. At some point in the decades that followed the mid-century change in the way juries were constituted on the Home circuit the assize courts found that the repeated service of individual jurors on successive panels—serial service, as Cockburn has called it[13]—was not compatible with the form of deliberation that had clearly been the general pattern before mid century, a system in which a jury heard a batch of cases one after the other without pause and then left the court to deliberate on them all. That had required a series of separate juries, or at least two separate juries, and when the courts adopted a system in which some men were placed on successive panels and might serve through the entire session, juries could no longer leave the court to deliberate if the court's business was not to come to a halt from time to time. This is probably why at some point in the late seventeenth century—whether immediately in 1650 or sometime thereafter remains unclear—assize juries on the Home circuit began to deliberate in open court on each case as it was concluded. In particularly contentious cases, juries continued to find it necessary to leave the court to deliberate in private. But by the late seventeenth century the common practice on the Home circuit was

12. See above, chap. 6, text at n. 52; also, Beattie, *Crime and the Courts*, 380–82.

13. See above, chap. 6, text at n. 51.

for the jurors simply to huddle around their foreman when each case ended and to announce their verdict immediately.

It seems reasonable to assume that there was a connection between the changes in the way the jury was created and the changes in the mode of deliberation. The jury could no longer leave the court to find verdicts on a group of cases when several of its members were to be included on the next jury to be charged with a batch of prisoners—unless, of course, the court went into recess while the first jury deliberated or perhaps occupied itself with other business, and there is no evidence that the provincial assize courts did either of these things. The system of deliberation was tied to the membership of the jury panels and the way they were constituted, and the change to deliberation in public at the end of each case was much more a matter of necessity than of ideology. This is clearly the implication of the striking fact that for half a century or more after the new mode of deliberation had been introduced at the assizes on the Home circuit the Old Bailey continued with the former practice. It was not until 1738 that trial juries at the Old Bailey began to deliberate in open court at the conclusion of each trial.[14] The change had been resisted, it was said then, because it was thought that juries would take too long with each case if they had to find their verdict in public, and the session would thus be extended by several days. That fear proved groundless. But it is also clear that the change had not been necessary at the Old Bailey in the second half of the seventeenth century, when it had occurred at the provincial assizes. For one thing, the Old Bailey did not require such large numbers of jurors, because one jury of twelve heard all the cases from London and another all the cases from Middlesex. But the main reason that the old system continued to function reasonably well at the Old Bailey into the eighteenth century was perhaps because two separate juries were essential to its institutional structure, essential to the way it worked. There was always a second jury ready to hear cases from its own jurisdiction when the first left the court to deliberate on a group of trials it had just heard. What was required at the Old Bailey, perhaps, was a rough equality in the number of prisoners from Middlesex and from London to allow a reasonable alternation between the juries. The inexorable growth of Middlesex cases in the early eighteenth century to the point that they increasingly and significantly outnumbered those from the City may have encouraged the abandonment of the old system in 1738. Public deliberation may have been adopted to enable twelve jurors to continue to hear all the cases

14. Beattie, *Crime and the Courts*, 396.

from Middlesex—which they could do if they did not leave the court to deliberate—rather than calling in further panels from the county.

The judicial system of the metropolis was thus in the hands of courts of quarter and general sessions of the peace meeting eight times a year in the City and in Middlesex (the latter supplemented by the quarter sessions held in Westminster) and the sessions of oyer and terminer and gaol delivery at the Old Bailey, at which prisoners from both London and Middlesex were tried. The Old Bailey sessions had been held a varying number of times each year in the sixteenth century and the first half of the seventeenth. But in 1669 they settled into the pattern of meeting eight times a year that was to be observed through the eighteenth century.[15] The court met in the periods between the four law terms and the times of the two assize circuits, generally in January, February, April, May, June, August, October, and December.[16] It met at the same time that the sessions of the peace were held in the City and in Middlesex. This was no accident, for the two levels of courts were intimately related in ways that were fundamentally different from the relationship of the quarter sessions and assize courts in the rest of the country and in ways that determined the nature of the jury service that men in the metropolis were called upon to give.

In the provinces the county courts of quarter sessions and the assizes were independent of one another and were held at different times. Each had its own sphere of jurisdiction well marked out. Cases might occasionally be sent from one to the other. In particular, the magistrates in quarter sessions might leave a difficult matter to be dealt with by the professional judges at their next assizes. But in the main, cases were committed by examining magistrates either to the assizes or quarter sessions, and each court proceeded independently of the other. Each also had its own clerical staff and its own records. In the metropolis there was no such clear separation between the sessions of peace, of oyer and terminer, and of gaol delivery. The relationship between the sessions at the Guildhall in London and those at the Old Bailey illustrates this point.

The Guildhall sessions of the peace began with the swearing of a grand jury and a trial jury and with the trial before the mayor and al-

15. *London Sessions Records, 1605–1685*, ed. H. Bowler, Publications of the Catholic Record Society, 34 (1934), vii.

16. See Langbein, "Eighteenth-Century Criminal Trial," 12 n. 29, for a useful explanation of the timing of these sessions.

dermen of some of those accused of minor offenses. After two days, however, these sessions were invariably adjourned, whether the business had been completed or not, because the sessions at the Old Bailey always began then, and the mayor and aldermen and the recorder were named in the commissions under which they were held. The Guildhall sitting remained in adjournment so long as the Old Bailey sessions continued and then resumed, if there was business still outstanding, when that session had concluded. In the 1690s more than half the sessions of the peace were interrupted in this way and then resumed "by adjournment." In January 1698, to take one example, the sessions opened at the Guildhall on the twelfth, and on that and the next day the trial jury returned verdicts in twelve cases. The list of minor offenders to be tried had not been completed, however, when the Old Bailey sessions began on the fourteenth, and the Guildhall sessions were adjourned until the Old Bailey trials were concluded. On 20 January the Guildhall sessions were resumed, and the trial jury completed its work by hearing four outstanding cases. That was a common pattern. In the summer months an adjourned session might not be required, but as often as not the sessions of the peace had to be continued in the Guildhall when the trials were concluded at the Old Bailey. The trial jury that had assembled at the Guildhall on the first morning of the sessions generally returned unchanged to the adjourned meeting a week or two later to complete the work that had been interrupted by the beginning of the gaol delivery session.

Those called to serve on the grand jury on the first morning at the Guildhall did not adjourn when the court opened at the Old Bailey, for they were the only grand jury that would be called to scrutinize the bills laid before both the sessions of the peace and the gaol delivery. They had begun their work at the Guildhall, and when the sessions began at the Old Bailey, they appear to have moved there to continue their work. The same grand jury that had been sworn at the Guildhall was sworn again before the court authorized to deliver Newgate and stayed to hear the cases against the London prisoners in that gaol, sending them for trial, as we have seen, before a jury summoned especially to the Old Bailey for that purpose.[17]

17. Bowler (above, n. 15) assumed that the London grand jury stayed at the Guildhall when the Old Bailey sessions began and sent the true bills to that court for trial as they found them (p. xxxii). I do not have a great deal of evidence on this as yet, but the OBSP for December 1678, p. 5, suggests the account I have given in the text—that is, that the London grand jury actually came to the Old Bailey to continue its work when the Guildhall session was adjourned. The account of that December 1678 session reports, for example, that on the first morning six London prisoners and ten Middlesex prisoners were arraigned, and then, the report continues, "the Grand Jury for London,

There was thus a close relationship between the sessions that began at the Guildhall and the sittings of the commissioners to deliver the gaol of Newgate. The sessions of the peace were adjourned; the lord mayor, the recorder, and the aldermen were named in the commission of gaol delivery; and the recorder, if not always the others, played an important role at the Old Bailey. The grand jury that had begun its work at the Guildhall also dealt with the cases of those to be tried at the Old Bailey and moved there when that session began. In addition, the clerical staffs of the two courts appear to have been identical, or at least very similar. Certainly the clerk of the peace in London, who was appointed by the Court of Aldermen, was also the clerk of the arraigns at the Old Bailey.[18] Also, the London clerical staff conceived the proceedings of the two courts to be different aspects of one session, for they kept the records of the Guildhall sittings and of the Old Bailey together. The indictments, recognizances, and other essential evidence from the two courts were put together in one composite roll, and the record of their proceedings was kept in a single minute book.

The relationship between the Middlesex sessions of the peace and the Old Bailey was fundamentally the same as that between the Guildhall sessions and the Old Bailey. Middlesex prisoners were dealt with in the way that London prisoners were dealt with at the Old Bailey; their bills were examined by a Middlesex grand jury and those indicted were tried by a Middlesex trial jury. As in the case of London, a grand jury had been summoned to the Middlesex sessions, also held in the same week as the Old Bailey sitting, and this grand jury had also dealt with the misdemeanors that would be tried before the magistrates and the more serious cases that would be reserved for the judges at the Old Bailey. But perhaps because the Old Bailey was in the City and because the Middlesex magistrates were not essential to the functioning of the gaol delivery sessions, the Middlesex sessions were not quite as closely bound up with the Old Bailey as were the proceedings of the London magistrates. The Middlesex sessions do not appear to have adjourned, for example, when the Old Bailey began. Sir John

coming in to bring in their bills, were sworn anew, to enquire upon the New Commissions, which being done the Clerk for London arraigned another Prisoner . . . " I take this to mean that the grand jury brought the bills they had already scrutinized at the Guildhall, that they were sworn again under the commissions of oyer and terminer and gaol delivery, and that they remained at the Old Bailey to deal with the outstanding bills. Apparently they were not charged again, however. There seem to have been no charges at the Old Bailey—certainly there are none in print. J. N. Adams and G. Averley, comps., *A Bibliography of Eighteenth-Century Legal Literature* (1982), 403–6.

18. *London Sessions Records*, ed. Bowler, xvii–xviii.

Reresby, who was a Middlesex magistrate in the 1680s, noted in his memoirs for 18 May 1686 some details about a case of personal interest to him because it involved a man who had stolen from him. He recorded that "the Sessions began at Hicks Hall, wher [*sic*] the bill was found against one Spencer that robb'd me of my plate, and the 19 [i.e., the next day] he was found guilty at the Old Bailiff [*sic*] and burnt in the hand." Earlier, under the date 15 January 1684, Reresby described "The sessions for Middlesex at Hicks his Hall and the ould Bailiff" in such a way as to make it clear that they were going on concurrently.[19] Nor does it appear that the Middlesex grand jury actually went to the Old Bailey to deliberate on bills brought against Middlesex prisoners who would be tried in that court. Rather, they seem to have stayed at Hicks' Hall and sent on the true bills as they found them to the Old Bailey. Apparently this was their practice in the seventeenth century and into the nineteenth.[20]

The pattern of court sessions in the City of London required that several juries be called. The sessions of the peace at the Guildhall required a grand jury and a trial jury on opening day, and further trial juries were needed at the Old Bailey and at the resumed sessions of the peace if they met by adjournment. Since the combined sessions normally lasted well over a week, it would not have been surprising if a large number of individual jurors had been pressed into service at the meetings of these courts. In fact, generally speaking only about forty

19. *Memoirs of Sir John Reresby*, ed. Andrew Browning (Glasgow, 1936), 426, 328.

20. J. C. Jeaffreson quotes an early-nineteenth-century edition of *The Crown Circuit Companion* on the practice at the Westminster and the Middlesex sessions as follows: "At both the last-mentioned sessions, indictments are preferred for felony, which, when returned to the grand jury into Court, are, by the respective Clerks of the peace, transmitted to the Sessions House at the Old Bailey." *Middlesex County Records*, ed. J. C. Jeaffreson, Middlesex County Record Society, 4 vols. (1886–92), 1:xxvi n, and see p. xxii. As to the involvement of Middlesex magistrates at the Old Bailey, Bowler believed that they were excluded from the commission of gaol delivery in the seventeenth century, except for some years in the 1680s. I am as yet unclear whether Middlesex magistrates sat on the bench at the Old Bailey with any regularity after the Revolution of 1689. Some appear to have been present at the April 1716 session (OBSP, April 1716, 1), but for the most part Middlesex magistrates must have been excluded, for they petitioned the lord chancellor in 1717 to be included in the commission of gaol delivery, a petition strongly opposed by the Court of Aldermen of London. Corporation of London Record Office (henceforth CLRO), Repertories of the Court of Aldermen (henceforth Rep.), 122, fols. 3, 263; London Sessions Papers, Dec. 1718 ("Answer to the Justices of Middlesex Representation to the Lord Chancellor about the Commission of Gaol Delivery").

men were required altogether: seventeen on the grand jury and twelve each on the trial juries at the sessions of the peace and the Old Bailey. These men normally served through the whole session. Occasionally one or two of the men who had been on the original sessions jury at the Guildhall were replaced when that court met again after its adjournment, and occasionally more than twelve trial jurors were required for the London cases at the Old Bailey. But for the most part the jurors sworn on the first day at the Guildhall and the Old Bailey served through the entire session at each of these courts.

This was strenuous and time-consuming duty for the individuals concerned. They would be expected to give as much as a week to jury service, and since these courts met eight times a year (and they were by no means the only courts in the City that required juries, for the mayor's and the sheriffs' courts that dealt with civil pleas also did so) jury duty in London had clearly to be shared in some settled way. This had early been recognized. In 1520 by order of the Common Council the twenty-five wards into which the City was then divided agreed on a plan by which they shared the duty of providing grand and trial jurors throughout the year, one or more wards being designated as responsible for each month. The principle that jury duty would be distributed among the wards was retained in the late seventeenth century, although, as we shall see, they no longer shared it equally—if they ever had—because some of the wards provided jurors on several occasions during the year for both grand and trial juries, while others contributed only once and then to only one jury. By the 1690s a pattern of service was well established. At the January session, two or three wards (generally the same wards every year) were called upon to provide men for jury service at the sessions of the peace and the gaol delivery. In February men from other wards were summoned, and so on. We shall explore that pattern of service and the results it produced in some detail in a moment, but several other features of the system of jury selection in the City of London are worth pointing out first.

The jurors were summoned by sheriffs' officers known as sergeants of the mace, sixteen of whom were attached to the two sheriffs' prisons, the comptors. The sergeants of the mace served notice of jury duty to men included on lists provided to them by the sheriffs or more likely by their assistants, the secondaries.[21] It is not entirely clear where these names of potential jurors came from. Some may have been taken from lists of inhabitants provided by the wardmote, the

21. Betty R. Masters, "City Officers. II: The Secondary," *The Guildhall Miscellany* 2 (1968): 425–33.

annual meetings of the inhabitants of the wards that were convened by the aldermen every St. Thomas's Day (21 December) and which remained the most significant institution of local government in the city other than the Court of Aldermen and the Common Council.[22] At the wardmote a group of men were named as grand and petty jurors for the coming year, but they may have been intended principally as the men who would be asked to serve on the juries at the mayor's and the sheriffs' courts. At least it is clear from some of the wardmote inquest books that survive for this period that those who chose the jurors for the Guildhall sessions and for the jury at the Old Bailey did not confine themselves to the list of jurors for the year chosen at the annual meeting. Other lists of likely jurors were provided by the aldermen, who must have known a large number of the eligible men in their wards and who on occasion were encouraged by a mayor to nominate jurors as a way of preventing richer men from escaping service altogether. The wardmote inquest nominations and the aldermen's lists may thus have been the main sources of jurors' names.[23]

Eligibility for jury service in London had been established by an act of Henry VIII's reign that set the qualification as the possession of lands, tenements, or goods of a hundred marks in value, a requirement that recognized that many men of substance in London might not hold freehold land.[24] This established a standard that by the end of the seventeenth century must have made a large number of men eligible for jury service. It is likely that the assumption in the sixteenth century was that such men would also be householders in the City, but that requirement was not actually spelled out until 1730, when many of those who owned property and goods in the City no longer lived there.[25]

22. Valerie Pearl, "Change and Stability in Seventeenth-Century London," *London Journal* 1 (1979): 15–27.

23. For a mayor's request to the aldermen to prepare lists of jurors, see CLRO, Rep. 114, p. 8; and see S. Webb and B. Webb, *English Local Government from the Revolution to the Municipal Corporations Act: The Manor and the Borough* (1908), pt. 2, p 606. For the contribution of both the wardmote inquests and the aldermen to the lists of eligible jurymen, see Joseph Newell, *Inquest Jurymen: An Enquiry into the Nature and Duties of Inquest Jurymen of the city of London . . .* (1825), 88.

24. 4 Hen. VIII, c. 3 (1512).

25. The requirement that jurors be inhabitants of the city was included in the jury act of 1730, which also slightly increased the value of the property requirement to a hundred pounds (3 Geo. II, c. 25). For juror qualification acts over the early modern period see J. C. Oldham, "The Origins of the Special Jury," *University of Chicago Law Review* 50 (1983): 137–221, which, although it is particularly concerned with special juries, includes a great deal of evidence and discussion about juries in general. See pp. 212–13 for London juries; and in particular the extremely valuable list in the Appendix,

The sheriffs and their officials thus marked out a number of men for jury service from the wards whose turn it was to provide jurors. Generally about seventy men were summoned for the opening day of the sessions at the Guildhall. Two lists of names on long strips of parchment—each list summoned by a different sergeant of the mace—were submitted to the court on the first morning, and those present were marked as having appeared. The absence of the others was noted or accounted for. Some were marked as being ill, and others were said to be out of town. Occasionally a man was noted as being "very aged," and a significant number were marked as "excused" or "spared" by a sheriff or the mayor. There were assertions in this period that such favors were corruptly available, and there is perhaps some support for this in the fact that some men were excused frequently.[26] The vast majority of those summoned, however, presented themselves in court.

Generally about fifty men stood in the court on the first morning and from them twenty-five were invariably chosen and their names recorded. The first seventeen on this list would form the grand jury, and soon after being chosen they must have been sent off to consider the bills that awaited their scrutiny. The other eight men were perhaps thought to be in reserve for grand jury service should the need arise. But, perhaps by custom and long usage, they had also come to serve another function: they formed the nucleus of the trial jury that dealt with cases of assault and the other minor offenses sent to trial at the sessions by the grand jury. The other four jurors were generally chosen from those who had been summoned to court but who had not been among the twenty-five first picked. Thus were two juries formed, a grand jury and a trial jury. They began their work, and the rest of the men called to the first day of the sessions were dismissed.

Two days later the court was adjourned when the sessions of gaol delivery began. At the Old Bailey another trial jury of twelve men was required and was assembled by the same process by which the juries had been called to the Guildhall. Two sergeants of the mace summoned a group of about sixty men from the wards usually called upon for that particular session. Those who appeared in court were marked as present, and the absence of the others was noted or explained as before. From this group the twelve jurors who would try the London

pp. 214–21, of acts of Parliament affecting jury qualification before 1730. A committee of the Common Council studied the question of juror eligibility in London, in 1817, and its report is also informative. See CLRO, Misc. MSS. 174.3.

26. CLRO, Rep. 81, fol. 135; Rep. 97, p. 264. And see below, text at n. 41, where the numbers summoned and excused and the number of men who appeared in court are investigated more fully.

prisoners were chosen, and the rest were allowed to leave, without any apparently being retained as alternates.

In examining the jurymen who served for the City of London in the 1690s, we will thus be studying three juries assembled at each session of the courts, eight times a year, amounting to more than three hundred men each year. I propose to look at three broad questions concerning them: first, the differing contributions that the wards made to these juries; second, the pattern of service of individual jurors—how often they were called, how often they were sworn, and whether they served on one or more of the three juries summoned from the city; and finally, the identity of those who served in the 1690s, their experience of decision making in other areas of local administration, and what this suggests about the role of the jury in the administration of the law and in the wider governance of the City at the end of the seventeenth century.

The number of men involved in the process of jury selection in the 1690s is quite striking. Something on the order of 1,000 men were summoned every year to the eight sessions of the London courts, and of those, close to 800 actually appeared, and about 320 were sworn. For the most part, the wards of the City contributed regularly to only one of the eight sessions, generally the same one each year. The ward of Aldgate provided jurors at each of the February meetings of the courts between 1692 and 1699, for example; men from Bridge ward were on the juries at every May session; and men from Billingsgate every October. Half the wards contributed in this way. The numbers of jurors who actually served on these occasions varied considerably from ward to ward, in part because some wards provided men for all three juries when their turn came, others for only one. But at least it was clearly established in the case of such wards that they would be called upon only once during the year. Others were asked to send jurors much more often, and others less frequently. Farringdon Without regularly provided jurors at four of the eight annual sessions and occasionally at two others, and jurors from the ward of Cheap normally served at three sessions each year. There were some distinctions among the five wards that were called upon more often than once a year, because three, including Cheap, not only provided jurors frequently but provided them for all three juries, while two, Farringdon Without and Cordwainer, sent men for one of the three juries only. On the other side, a few wards—Dowgate and Aldersgate, for example—were drawn on less frequently than once a year. On only one occasion in the eight years I have examined in the 1690s were men summoned from Bassishaw, and then none was actually selected to sit on a jury. No one from Queenhithe or Portsoken was even summoned.

This pattern of service, the number of times that wards contributed to the juries that tried London prisoners at the eight sessions held each year between 1692 and 1699, is shown in Table 8.1, along with the number of men who actually served on the three juries.[27] There was an obvious correspondence, as one would expect, between the frequency with which a ward was called upon to contribute to the panel and the number of men from that ward actually sworn, although it was not an exact correspondence. Some wards contributed a disproportionately large or small number of candidates when they were called upon. Coleman Street ward, for example, ranked fourteenth in frequency of contribution to jury panels but fifth in the number of jurors sworn. On the other hand, Bread Street ward was called upon to send jurors very often—indeed, it was second in frequency only to Cheap in this period—and yet it ranked only sixth in the number of jurors who actually served. Still, with these few exceptions, there was a broad relationship between the number of times the wards were called upon and the number of jurors they provided, and this confirms a pattern of service under which some wards contributed heavily to juries, and others more lightly.

Why these differences existed is unclear. It is possible that they simply reflected the habits of the summoning officers as they had developed over time and as they had been confirmed by the repetition of a practice that seemed to work. But they also clearly derived from real differences among the wards in terms of the number of their inhabitants or in the distribution of wealth and thus in the size of the population eligible for jury service. Some evidence about this is included in Table 8.2, in which the wards for which tax records provide some indication of the numbers and relative wealth of the inhabitants are ranked in the order in which they contributed to the three juries in the

27. These figures are shaped—one might say slightly distorted—by the way juries were assembled. As we have seen, there was a close link between the grand jury and the sessions trial jury, since both were drawn from the same list of jurors summoned on the first day of the sessions. Wards that contributed regularly to the grand jury were thus likely to contribute to the sessions trial jury too, while those that were not called upon for grand jury service did not—could not—provide men to the sessions trial jury. Only a few wards were in this latter category, however—most notably Castle Baynard, Aldersgate, and Lime Street. For some reason, a few wards contributed only rarely to the trial jury at the Old Bailey while sending men regularly to serve on the grand jury and sessions jury: Coleman Street, Cornhill, and Cordwainer were all in this category.

Table 8.1. Jury Service by Wards, 1692–1699

Ward	Number of Times Contributed to Jury				Number of Jurors Sworn			
	Old Bailey Trial Jury	Grand Jury	Sessions of the Peace	Total	Old Bailey Trial Jury	Grand Jury	Sessions of the Peace	Total
Aldersgate	3	—	—	3	6	—	—	6
Aldgate	4	3	2	9	39	35	2	76
Bassishaw	1	—	—	1	—	—	—	—
Billingsgate	8	8	7	23	37	34	60	131
Bishopsgate Within	1	7	8	16	1	30	55	86
Bishopsgate Without	5	4	3	12	18	17	5	40
Bread Street	12	15	10	37	50	65	32	147
Bridge	8	8	9	25	44	47	44	135
Broad Street	8	7	6	21	49	33	22	104
Candlewick	4	7	7	18	14	36	16	66
Castle Baynard	8	—	—	8	52	—	—	52
Cheap	15	19	16	50	36	121	63	220
Coleman Street	1	7	8	16	8	82	67	157
Cordwainer	—	15	14	29	—	148	108	256
Cornhill	1	8	7	16	3	72	22	97
Cripplegate Within	16	11	9	36	44	71	82	197
Cripplegate Without	8	6	7	21	34	21	33	88
Dowgate	4	1	—	5	20	7	—	27
Farringdon Within	11	9	9	29	52	82	43	177
Farringdon Without	21	3	2	26	110	6	10	126
Langbourn	7	1	1	9	56	10	5	71
Lime Street	8	—	—	8	51	—	—	51
Portsoken	—	—	—	—	—	—	—	—
Queenhithe	—	—	—	—	—	—	—	—
Tower	3	5	4	12	10	54	11	75
Vintry	5	7	8	20	7	41	31	79
Walbrook	4	6	3	13	27	34	5	66
Total					768	1,046	716	2,530

SOURCES: CLRO, Sessions Rolls and Minute Books

Table 8.2. The Contribution of Wards to the London Juries, 1692–1699, and Their Wealth as Reflected in the Poll Tax of 1692

Rank Order of Wards as Contributors	Number of "Substantial Ratepayers" in Ward*	Rank Order	Percentage of "Substantial Ratepayers"*	Rank Order
Top eight wards.				
Cordwainer	208	12	52	11
Cheap	341	6	74	1
Cripplegate Within	270	8	35	16
Farringdon Within	391	3	30	20
Coleman Street	184	16	34	17
Bridge	209	11	58	5
Billingsgate	254	9	57	6
Bottom eight wards:				
Castle Baynard	205	14	29	21
Lime Street	87	25	41	14
Bishopsgate Without	161	18	16	24
Dowgate	105	23	32	18
Aldersgate	51	27	12	26
Bassishaw	118	22	70	2
Portsoken	126	20	14	25
Queenhithe	125	21	32	18

SOURCES: CLRO, Sessions Rolls, Minute Books, and 1692 tax returns.
* "Substantial ratepayers" are those assessed in the middle and upper categories in the 1692 poll tax. Data on the number and percentage of such ratepayers are derived from De Krey, "Trade, Religion, and Politics in London in the Reign of William III," 335–37.

1690s, taking all three juries together. The measures of wealth are derived from the returns of the poll tax collected in 1692. For the purposes of this tax, the ratepayers of the City were divided into three categories. In the first, every person except for the very poor—those in receipt of alms, householders exempted from paying the poor rates, children of day laborers, and servants in husbandry—was to pay a basic tax of a shilling per head four times a year. In the second category, shopkeepers, tradesmen, and artisans whose worth was assessed at more than £300 were to pay an extra ten shillings beyond the shilling per head for everyone in their household. A third group composed of merchants, lawyers, physicians, gentlemen, and a few others were to pay a surtax of a pound, and another pound if they kept a coach.[28] I

28 On this tax, see G. S. De Krey, *A Fractured Society: The Politics of London in the First Age of Party, 1688–1715* (1985), 172.

have derived my information about the returns on this tax from the work of Gary De Krey, in particular from his calculation of the heads of households who paid at the three rates in each ward.[29] In using De Krey's figures in Table 8.2, I have combined the householders in the two surtax groups (since the distinction between them was not wealth but status) and characterized them as "substantial ratepayers." The number of such ratepayers ranged from close to a thousand in Farringdon Without to fifty-one in Aldersgate. Table 8.2 shows the top eight and bottom eight wards in rank order with respect to that figure, and also the percentages of such ratepayers in those wards and their rank order in that respect too. Thus in Cordwainer, which contributed more jurors in total than any other ward, 208 heads of households paid a surtax of ten shillings or a pound in 1692, and that accounted for 52 percent of the ward's ratepayers. In these respects Cordwainer ranked twelfth and eleventh respectively among the City's wards.

The evidence in Table 8.2 confirms what one would expect, given the property qualification for jury service. There was a broad connection in the City between the number and proportion of "substantial" householders in a ward and the contribution made by the men of that ward to the juries at the Guildhall sessions and the Old Bailey. There was no direct and simple relationship; indeed, there could hardly have been such a relationship, since the system by which juries were assembled distributed the burden so unevenly. Langbourn, for example, which included a large number and a high proportion of ratepayers in the surtax brackets, ranked only seventeenth in the list of wards providing jurors, presumably because men from Langbourn were called upon for jury service only once a year, and then mainly at the Old Bailey, which required twelve jurors for each session, rather than at the Guildhall, where a grand jury of seventeen and a trial jury of twelve had to be assembled. Nonetheless, despite the disparities of service that this made for, one can still see in Table 8.2 a general relationship between the number and concentration of wealthier inhabitants in a ward and that ward's contribution to jury service. The connection is perhaps clearest at the bottom of the table, because the wards that ranked in the lowest third of contributors to the juries were with few exceptions also the wards with the fewest inhabitants paying the surtax and with the smallest concentration of such inhabitants. There was no simple relationship between wealth and jury service, but at

29. For these figures, see De Krey, "Trade, Religion, and Politics in London in the Reign of William III" (Ph.D. diss., Princeton Univ., 1978), 335–37, Table V.

the least one can say on the basis of the evidence in Table 8.2 that the richer wards do not seem to have opted out and left service on the grand and trial juries to their poorer neighbors.

Of course, such an analysis can take us only so far. It is useful to know how jurors were summoned and the wards from which they came in the largest numbers. But this does not tell us what kinds of men actually served. There were rich and poor inhabitants in all wards of the city. To take this aspect of the subject further, we must examine the membership of the juries and the patterns of service of individual jurors. We may begin by asking how often men served in the 1690s and on which juries, and then go on to examine a sample of jurors in more detail.

Throughout the early modern period in England, juries in criminal cases normally included a number of men with considerable experience of jury service behind them. A man serving for the first time on either a grand or trial jury would have found himself in the company of men who had served before and who could thus anticipate the hectic pace at which trials would move and the range of verdicts that would be open to them. At the Surrey assizes in the late seventeenth century, more than half the members of a typical grand jury and almost a third of the twelve trial jurors would have seen previous service.[30] Such repeated service was even more common among London jurors in the 1690s. The frequency with which men did jury service in the capital is explained partly by the fact that the courts met eight times a year—as against the two sessions of the assizes and four of the quarter sessions in most counties. But it was also encouraged by another characteristic of jury duty in London that was not to be found in Surrey or perhaps elsewhere in the country by this period: In London the membership of the juries was not determined by social considerations and requirements to anything like the extent it was at the county quarter sessions and assizes.

By the last decade of the seventeenth century a sharp division had arisen in Surrey and Sussex (and, it seems clear, elsewhere) among the men called to serve on the various juries in the county courts. Certainly the grand jury at the assizes was by then the preserve of the gentry and even included a significant number of justices of the peace. The men who served on the grand jury at the assizes never served on the trial jury in that court or on the juries at the quarter sessions. Sim-

30. Beattie, *Crime and the Courts*, 327–29, 385–87.

ilarly, the men called to serve on the assizes trial jury were not likely to be asked to sit in judgment on the prisoners tried at the sessions. A marked sense of exclusivity had developed in the provincial courts by this period.

There is some evidence of this in London. The members of the grand jury were likely to be slightly more wealthy and more prominently engaged in other aspects of the government of the city than those who served on the trial juries. But no social gulf separated such men. There remained a more open approach to jury service in London, a greater willingness of men to serve on both grand and trial juries and in both courts, and a tolerance of men on one jury who had served on another. This emerges from the figures presented in Table 8.3, which reveal in a broad way the pattern of jury service in the 1690s. These figures show that the incidence of repeated service was very high indeed. Almost half the men sworn to jury service in these years were called to two or more court sessions. Also, the largest proportion of such men returned to the same jury each time. But a significant number of the repeaters—indeed, four out of ten—served on two juries, and a few served on all three. Such overlapping of personnel would certainly not have happened in Surrey or Sussex in this period, and on the face of it, it seems that the sharp social distinctions that defined several layers of jurymen in the provincial courts did not operate in London in quite the same way. The London grand jury remained open to those who served on the trial juries at the sessions of the peace and the Old Bailey. Nor was it the case that the grand jury represented the pinnacle of achievement for men who had worked their passage on the other juries. Men who served on more than one jury were as likely as

Table 8.3. Patterns of Jury Service in London, 1692–1699

Jury Service	No. of Jurors	Percentage
Single jury service	744	55.1
Repeated Service		
On same jury	340	25.2
On sessions and grand jury	150	11.1
On sessions and Old Bailey jury	24	1.8
On grand and Old Bailey jury	67	5.0
On all three juries	25	1.9
Total	1,350	100.1

SOURCES: CLRO Sessions Rolls and Minute Books.

not to have served on the grand jury first; at least membership on the grand jury did not mean that a man would not subsequently take a turn on one of the trial juries. This may, incidentally, help to explain why the London grand jury remained invariably at seventeen members in the 1690s. In Surrey, and presumably in other counties, the grand jury at the assizes tended to increase in size over the late seventeenth century and into the eighteenth, and certainly to vary considerably from one session to the next.[31] It seems reasonable to think that this was one consequence of the enlarging social distinction of its membership in this period, since one might presume that the clerk of the court would not have wanted to insult the men summoned by failing to swear them for service if they actually made their appearance. If no particular distinction was accorded service on the grand jury in London, there would be little pressure to enlarge its numbers.

The relative openness of London juries may also help to explain the frequency with which some men served. Table 8.4 sets out the incidence of repeated service in the years 1692 to 1699, counting, it should be made clear, service on all juries together (the grand jury and the trial juries at the sessions and the Old Bailey) on the grounds that each would have extended a man's experience of jury duty and equally equipped him for the tasks jurymen had to perform. What seems par-

Table 8.4. Patterns of Repeated Service on London Juries, 1692–1699

No. of Sessions Sworn as Juror	No. of Men	No. of "Appearances"
1	744	744
2	265	530
3	168	504
4	87	348
5	48	240
6	26	156
7	10	70
8	2	16
Total	1,350	2,608
First-time attenders		1,350
Jurors with previous experience		1,258
Proportion of experienced jurors:		$\frac{1,258}{2,608} = .48$

SOURCES: CLRO Sessions Rolls and Minute Books.

31. Ibid., 324–27.

ticularly striking about these figures is the number of men sworn to serve four, five, and six times in the eight years examined. For some men this must have meant that they were chosen virtually each time their turn came around, for we must remember that while the court met eight times a year, men were at risk only when their ward was called upon to provide jurors for service on one of the juries. For most, that would have been only once a year. The high incidence of repeated service seems particularly striking in view of that pattern of jury selection.

It is clear, nonetheless, that London juries were dominated by men who had had some experience of the work they would be called upon to perform. A typical grand jury of seventeen men would have included eight who had seen service on that jury or on one of the trial juries at least once before; and even more significantly, in view of the seriousness of the decisions they had to make and the pressures under which they had to work, almost half the men who sat on the London trial juries at the Old Bailey in the 1690s had had previous jury experience and to that extent knew something about court procedure, the nature of criminal law, and the way juries typically deliberated and reached their verdicts.

The experience that so many London jurors had acquired no doubt had a direct bearing on the way they dealt with the accused whose cases they tried. Their familiarity with the procedures of the courtroom and the range of verdicts they were able to arrive at, particularly in capital cases, must also have shaped the relationship between the jury and the judges, who—in the absence of lawyers from the criminal courts in this period—played such a prominent role in the conduct of trials.[32] As important in these matters, however, was the question of who the jurors were—their place in the community, their wealth and social status, and their more general experience of office-holding and decision making. What can be learned about these matters in the 1690s?

The returns from two taxes collected in London in this period provide some evidence about jurors' wealth and occupations. The first, the poll tax of 1692, mentioned earlier, established three rates of payment for all the inhabitants of the City: a basic tax of a shilling a head four times a year to be paid by everyone except the very poor; a surtax on top of that of ten shillings to be paid by shopkeepers, tradesmen, and artisans whose worth was assessed at more than £300; and a sur-

32. Langbein, "Criminal Trial before the Lawyers."

tax of one pound assessed against merchants, lawyers, physicians, gentlemen, and a few other such people. Gary De Krey has used these returns to calculate a "socio-economic profile" of each of the wards of the city, which reveals that, broadly speaking, about 65 percent of the city's ratepaying households fell into the first category; that is to say, they were estimated to be worth less than £300; about 21 percent fell into the second category, that of shopkeepers and the like assessed at more than that sum; and about 14 percent were merchants and others who paid the additional surtax beyond that second level.[33] These categories are, of course, very broad indeed, but they do help us to place jurors in a general way in relation to the London ratepaying population at large. I have taken the jurors sworn in 1692 as a sample. Table 8.5 includes the numbers of such men in the three categories of the poll tax, so far as the records make it possible to determine them. This reveals that jurors were drawn very largely from the upper end of the ratepaying hierarchy. Despite a rule that exempted a number of men from jury service who would have appeared in the third category—lawyers and surgeons most prominently[34]—fully 82 percent of the jurors sworn in 1692 paid the surtax above the basic level and thus were among the shopkeepers, tradesmen, and artisans assessed at more than £300, or the merchants, gentlemen, and professionals. Together, these groups included just over a third of the heads of ratepaying households.

The poll tax returns of 1692 are particularly useful in that they not only place the householder in one of these three categories of wealth and status and (because it was a per capita levy) give the structure of his household, they also reveal his occupation. This provides further evidence of the relatively high standing of London jurors. In Table 8.6

Table 8.5. Tax Categories of Jurors Sworn in London in 1692[a]

	Tax Categories			
	Basic tax	Surtax 10/-	Surtax £1	*N*
Jurors	17.7%	64.2%	18.1%	271
All ratepayers[b]	65.4	20 8	13.8	18,580

[a] SOURCE CLRO, 1692 tax returns; for tax categories, see text

[b] SOURCE: De Krey, "Trade, Religion, and Politics in London," 335–37.

33. De Krey, "Trade, Religion, and Politics," 335–37.

34. See below, chap. 9, text at n. 24.

I have divided the occupations given for the jurors who served in 1692 into four categories. Some of these divisions are arbitrary, and the division cannot be entirely relied on, since one cannot always be certain that a man belongs in one category rather than another. I have placed shoemakers and watchmakers among the skilled trades, for example, although these men may belong among the retail trades. Some others were perhaps not as skilled as I have assumed. But the divisions are likely to be broadly coherent, and they do serve to confirm the picture that emerges from the tax categories that these jurors fell into. The vast majority of those whose occupations are identified were in wholesale and retail trades; fully 70 percent could be so classified. Of these men, only fifteen were in the basic tax category; only fifteen, that is, were thought by the assessors to own goods of less than £300 in value. Seventeen of the jurors in skilled trades and manufacturing were in this group, too, but the men I have placed in this category

Table 8.6. Jurors' Occupations and Tax Categories in the Poll Tax of 1692

	Tax Category[a]			
Occupation Group	1	2	3	*N*
Wholesale trades[b]	9.5%	55.6%	34.9%	63
Retail trades[c]	11.9	81.0	7.1	84
Manufacturing and skilled trades[d]	35.3	60.8	3.9	51
Professions and others[e]	9.1	54.5	36.4	11
N	35	140	34	209

SOURCES: CLRO 1692 tax returns.

[a] For the categories of the 1692 poll tax, see text. The jurors are those jurors sworn in 1692. The occupations are those occupations identified in the 1692 poll tax returns. The occupations of 85 jurors were not given.

[b] Cloth-worker (2); corn chandler (1); factor (2); mercer (6); merchant (22); oilman (3); packer (3); piece broker (1); salesman ("sailsman") (6); salter (7); skinner (3); tobacconist (2); warehouseman (5).

[c] Bookseller (6); baker (1); button seller (2); cheesemonger (4); cottoner (1); fustian seller (1), grocer (7); haberdasher (13); hosier (5); hemp seller (1); innholder (2); linen draper (9); leather seller (3); milliner (2); silkman (7); shopkeeper (2); seedsman (1); stationer (1); stocking seller (1); tradesman (8); tallow chandler (1); woollen draper (1); druggist (4); coffeeman (1).

[d] Boxmaker (1); brewer (1); cabinetmaker (1); carpenter (1); cooper (1); cutler (1); colorman (1); chairman (1); distiller (2); dyer (5); flatter (1); joiner (4); plumber (2); sawyer (1); shoemaker (2); silversmith (2); potter (1); printer (2); tailor (1); tinman (1); upholsterer (upholder) (9); watchmaker (3); wiredrawer (wiredresser) (6); soapmaker (1).

[e] Apothecary (2); "captain" (1); coachman (1); exchangeman (1); gentleman (1); goldsmith (4); scrivener (1).

made up only a quarter of the jurors who served in 1692. The stated occupations and the tax categories together suggest that jurors were very largely men in trade, particularly retail trades in the city, although a significant number were merchants, warehousemen, and others in wholesale businesses, and one might say about them at a minimum that they were at least relatively prosperous in that they were drawn overwhelmingly from the upper third of the ratepaying population.

Rather more specific evidence than this can be derived from another set of tax returns, in which the sums paid were based on an assessment of the annual value of real estate owned and the value of personal goods and trade stock. This was the aid authorized by Parliament in 1694.[35] The tax, charged at the rate of four shillings on the pound, was collected by wards in London. The returns make it possible to establish a little more precisely the wealth of the jurors sworn in 1692, at least as it was estimated by the assessors for this tax. I have followed Gary De Krey, who used these returns to estimate the wealth of members of the Common Council in this period, in confining my analysis to the assessed value of the jurors' real property in order to make comparison possible.[36] I have, in fact, used the same categories of wealth in Table 8.7 as he employed in that analysis, and I have also reproduced his figures, slightly reworked, in order to get some sense of how jurors compare to this group of important London citizens.

The Common Council of London included 234 councilmen elected by the wards at the annual wardmote inquest. It was the legislative body of the City, and although its business was to a considerable extent controlled by the aldermen (themselves members of the council) and the lord mayor, who summoned it into session and presided over its deliberations (a control that was the subject of considerable dis-

35. 6 & 7 W. & M. c. 3. For the various taxes of William's reign, see W. Kennedy, *English Taxation, 1640–1799 An Essay on Policy and Opinion* (1913; reprint, 1964), 44–50.

36. De Krey, "Trade, Religion, and Politics," 326–28, Table I. As De Krey has pointed out, these estimates undoubtedly exaggerate the wealth of some men whose trades required large property holdings—warehousemen, for example—and undervalue the income of men whose wealth was more heavily invested in stock in trade. And it is also possible that since the tax paid was based on assessed values, the wealth of some men was deliberately understated (ibid., 326–28). For a valuable discussion of the problems surrounding the use of tax records as a means of estimating the wealth of individuals, see N. Rogers, "London Politics from Walpole to Pitt: Patriotism and Independency in an Era of Commercial Imperialism, 1739–1763" (Ph.D. diss., Univ. of Toronto, 1974), 347. Rogers provides a great deal of evidence about the wealth of several groups within the London elite at a slightly later period than the one I am concerned with.

Table 8.7. Wealth of Jurors and Common Councilmen in 1694

Assessed Value of Property, per Annum (in pounds)	Jurors[a]	Common Councilmen[b]
20 or less	19.4%	11.3%
21–40	44.0	35.1
41–60	23.8	29.1
61–80	7.3	11.1
81–120	2.8	7.5
Over 120	.8	3.1
Lodgers in 1694	2.0	2.9

[a] SOURCE: CLRO. For the 1694 tax, see text. Tax assessments are available for 248 jurors, but missing for 45

[b] SOURCE: De Krey, "Trade, Religion and Politics in London," 327.

pute in this period and into the eighteenth century), the Common Council played an important role in the political and administrative life of the city.[37] The social character of common councilmen was frequently the subject of sneering condescension in the eighteenth century, particularly because the greatest overseas merchants, the bankers, and the financiers avoided service on this as on other bodies—a circumstance that was made the more likely by the resolutions of the Court of Aldermen in 1710 and the Common Council in 1716 that common councilmen had to be residents of the wards they represented.[38] De Krey's analysis of their assessed wealth suggests that the social status of common councilmen varied widely. But his figures also make it clear—in conjunction with the occupational evidence from the 1692 poll tax—that the Common Council included prosperous and eminently respectable men. A fifth of the members in the 1690s were overseas merchants, for example.

As one might anticipate, jurors were rather less wealthy as a group than the men who served on the Common Council. But they were men of the same broad type. Indeed, as we shall see, a significant number of jurors of the 1690s were, had been, or would become common

37. Webb and Webb, *Manor and Borough*, pt. 2, pp. 626–56, Rogers, "London Politics from Walpole to Pitt," 19–27; A. Henderson, *London and the National Government, 1721–42* (Durham, N.C., 1945); G. Rudé, *Hanoverian London, 1714–1808* (1971). For the "rise" of the Common Council in the early eighteenth century, see De Krey, *A Fractured Society*, 209–12, 233–38.

38. Webb and Webb, *Manor and Borough*, pt. 2, pp. 626–27.

councilmen. About half the members of the council owned property with an annual value estimated by the assessors in 1694 at more than forty pounds, while just over a third of jurors were in that category. Rather more of the jurors were in the lowest of De Krey's assessment levels, and it is possible that on some juries there were men of very modest wealth. There were, indeed, occasional complaints in London about jurors who were thought to be too poor to be able to render an independent verdict. But, apart from the relativity and distortion and foreshortening of the social world involved in such judgments, it seems clear that complaints about "poore, ignorant, and mercenary jurymen" (to quote a mayor's precept, several times reissued) were principally directed at the juries that tried civil cases in the mayor's and sheriffs' courts rather than at the criminal juries at the Guildhall and Old Bailey.[39] The evidence of the tax returns suggests, in any case, that such criticism would have been misplaced. As a group, the jurors who served in the criminal courts came largely from the ranks of the merchants and retail tradesmen of the City and were securely within the prosperous and respectable communities in their wards. If, like the Common Council, the London juries did not include the merchant princes and the governors of the bank and of the large trading and financial companies, they did include some men of considerable wealth, men such as Richard Chancey, a linen draper of Cornhill whose property was assessed at £150 annual value and who served on both the sessions jury and the grand jury, and Thomas Phipps, another Cornhill linen draper, who had property estimated to be worth £100 a year.

The indications of the wealth of jurors that can be derived from the tax returns of the 1690s also help to clarify the question of whether London juries were as socially homogeneous and exclusive as those at the county assizes. In Table 8.8 I have divided the jurors sworn in 1692 according to their tax and occupational groups and according to the juries on which they served, both in 1692 and later if they returned to sit on another jury between 1692 and 1699. The picture that emerges confirms what one would expect from the experience of the provincial assizes in this period: that there was a tendency for wealthier men to serve on the grand jury (or, to a lesser extent, on the sessions of the peace trial jury to which the grand jury was tied by the way they were summoned) rather than on the trial jury at the Old Bailey. More than 90 percent of grand jurors paid the surtax in the assessment of 1692;

39. CLRO, Small MS Box 38, no. 25. For a helpful discussion of these social judgments, see below, chap. 9, text at nn. 179–93.

Table 8.8. Wealth and Occupation of Jurors Who Served between 1692 and 1699[a]

	Jury		
	Sessions of the Peace Trial Jury	Grand Jury	Old Bailey Trial Jury
Tax category in 1692 poll tax[b]			
Assessed 1s.	21.7%	9.4%	20.8%
Assessed 11s.	62.5	63.8	70.8
Assessed 21s.	15.9	26.8	8.3
N	120	149	96
Wealth, based on 1694 asessment[c] (annual value of property, in pounds)			
20 or less	22.5	11.0	23.0
21–40	45.0	47.1	46.0
41–60	24.2	26.5	25.3
61–80	4.5	8.8	3.4
81–120	1.8	5.1	2.3
Over 120	1.8	1.5	0.0
N	111	136	87
Occupational group[d]			
Wholesale trades	26.3	37.6	21.3
Retail trades	47.4	41.0	42.7
Manufacturing and skilled	23.2	17.1	29.3
Professions and others	3.2	4.3	6.7
N	95	117	75

SOURCES: CLRO, 1692 and 1694 tax returns.
[a] Based on service on the three juries in the period 1692–99 of the jurors sworn in 1692, counting each juror's appearance on a jury once only.
[b] For the tax categories in the 1692 poll tax, see text.
[c] For the calculation of annual property values from the returns of the 1694 assessment, see text and Table 8.7.
[d] For these occupation categories, see text and Table 8.6.

42 percent were thought to own property of more than £40 annual value; and nearly 80 percent were in wholesale or retail trades. In each case, these indicators of their wealth and social standing suggest that they were wealthier and higher up the social scale than the men who sat on the trial jury at the Old Bailey, who were more likely to be manufacturers or skilled tradesmen and more likely to have lesser amounts of assessed wealth. Another way to look at this is to examine the juries on which the twenty men assessed at the highest rates in 1694 served. Besides Chancey and Phipps, this would include another linen draper from Cornhill and a haberdasher and a bookseller from

the same ward; an apothecary from Cordwainer; an oilman, a druggist, and a haberdasher from Cheap; several other tradesmen; and three merchants. These men together served on juries on forty-eight occasions in the 1690s. On thirty-one of those occasions they sat on the grand jury and on twelve occasions on the sessions jury at the Guildhall; only five times, and these accounted for by two men, did they serve on the trial jury at the Old Bailey.

There seems to have been a clear preference among these wealthier men for the comparative dignity of the grand jury room, or at least of the jury at the sessions, over the bustle and anxiety and stench of the Old Bailey courtroom, in which they would have to deal with the accused felons from Newgate and decide how many of them would be condemned to die at Tyburn. Service on the grand jury presumably accorded them more honor. They may also have been anxious to sit on that jury because it had the right to issue presentments and to speak for the community on important subjects.[40] In this respect, jury service in London may have mirrored the pattern of the Surrey and Sussex assizes, where the grand jury was taken over by the gentry in the last two decades of the century, in part at least to gain command of an institution that could be of immense political importance. But the data in Table 8.8 also confirm what seemed clear from the way the juries were recruited: that however much the London grand jury might be dominated by the more prosperous men, the jury was not closed to those of more modest means. A number of artisans whose wealth was assessed at a very low level sat on the grand jury along with merchants and the prosperous linen drapers from Cornhill. By the same token, the men in the higher categories of assessed wealth did not entirely disdain service on the trial jury, even the trial jury at the Old Bailey. There were tendencies toward social divisions on the juries, but there was no social gulf. It seems reasonable to think that by the end of the seventeenth century there was more of a homogeneous jury class in London than was the case in the courts of quarter sessions and the assizes in the counties.

Why were particular men chosen for jury service? What determined who would be summoned and who would be chosen actually to serve

40. This prompts the question of whether service on the grand jury or any other jury was determined by political considerations. Party loyalties were well defined in London in this period—as De Krey has revealed—and party conflicts were fierce. I have not yet investigated the possibility that politics helped to determine the shape of the grand jury and the two trial juries in London, but this seems a question worth pursuing.

on a jury? Answers to these questions would tell us a good deal about the way the jury and jury service were regarded in this period. Unfortunately, there is little evidence to go by, and it is likely to remain difficult, perhaps impossible, to discover how decisions were made at the two stages of juror selection—the summoning of several dozen men and the choice in court of the seventeen grand jurors and twelve trial jurors who would hear the cases. But we can discover who was summoned, who among them responded by coming to court, and who was selected, and I have done this for two wards—Cheap and Bridge—in the years 1692 to 1699. In particular, I have tabulated the number of times individuals were summoned for jury service, how often they actually appeared in court or were excused in some way, and the number of times they were then included in a jury. And to see what broad socio-economic distinctions there might have been between men summoned often and those called upon only once or twice in these eight years, and between those sworn often and those rarely chosen actually to sit on a jury, I have located as many as possible in the returns of a tax collected in 1695 on marriages, births, and burials and on bachelors and childless widowers—a tax I have chosen to use for this purpose because the returns are said to be relatively complete and because there is an index in print to the returns for London parishes within the walls.[41] The act authorizing the tax established a system of payments graduated according to social status and wealth. The status categories are too elevated to be of relevance to my investigation, running as they do from duke to gentleman. But the broad distinctions in wealth are more useful, for the act established a basic tax for everyone not in those named status groups and added a surtax for householders who owned land with an annual value of at least £50 or personal estate with a value of £600. We can thus discover how many of the men summoned from Cheap and Bridge wards paid the surtax and were what Glass reasonably calls "substantial householders."[42] And we can discover if these richer men were summoned more often and sworn to sit on juries more often than those paying the basic tax, or whether richer men succeeded more readily in removing themselves from the jury pool assembled in court.

The results of this investigation are presented in Table 8.9. Over the years 1692 to 1699, 135 men were summoned for jury service on at least one of the eight occasions on which grand and trial jurors were drawn from Bridge ward, in Cheap, 193 men were named at least once

41. *London Inhabitants within the Walls, 1695*, Introduction by D. V. Glass, London Record Society (1966).

42. Ibid., xx.

Table 8.9. Men Summoned for Jury Service in Bridge and Cheap Wards, 1692–1699[a]

		Those Identified in Returns of 1695 Tax[b]		
	Total	Number	Paid Surtax (%)	Paid Base Tax (%)
Bridge Ward[c]				
Summoned (individuals)	135	91	62.6	37.4
Summoned more than twice	86	72	65.3	34.7
Summoned more than four times	46	41	78.0	22.0
Sworn (individuals)	61	45	66.7	33.3
Sworn more than twice	18	16	68.7	31.3
Sworn more than four times	2	2	50.0	50.0
Cheap Ward[d]				
Summoned (individuals)	193	115	53.9	46.1
Summoned more than four times	58	41	65.9	34.1
Summoned more than eight times	11	10	70.0	30.0
Sworn (individuals)	92	58	53.4	46.6
Sworn more than four times	13	12	58.3	41.7
Sworn more than eight times	4	4	50.0	50.0

[a] SOURCE: CLRO, Sessions Rolls, Minute Books, and 1695 tax returns.
[b] SOURCE: *London Inhabitants within the Walls, 1695,* Introduction by D V. Glass (London Record Society, 1966). In a number of cases the identity of a juror could not be established with certainty, usually because there were two men in the ward with the same or similar names. In many more cases, a summoned juror could not be found in the 1695 tax returns. They were missing for several reasons. The wardmote inquest book for Bridge (see n. 45), which includes lists of inhabitants in the ward drawn up for the annual meeting, makes it clear that the tax returns for at least one of the ward's fourteen precincts are entirely missing. But the largest number of those whose 1695 tax category is unknown were simply not living in the ward in that year. The jurors we are concerned with were summoned between 1692 and 1699. Many of those called before 1695 had died or left the ward before the tax assessment was made, and some of those summoned after 1695 must have come of age or moved to the ward after the assessment was completed.
[c] Grand juries and Old Bailey trial juries were summoned in Bridge ward on eight occasions each between 1692 and 1699.
[d] Grand jurors were summoned on twenty occasions, and trial jurors for the Old Bailey on seventeen occasions, in Cheap between 1692 and 1699. Men from the ward were included in the juries actually chosen on nineteen and fifteen occasions respectively.

on the twenty occasions on which grand jurors were called or the seventeen on which men were summoned for service on the trial jury at the Old Bailey. Bridge and Cheap were both relatively wealthy wards. The heads of roughly 41 percent and 44 percent respectively of ratepaying households within the wards paid the surtax, compared to approximately 27 percent in the City within the walls as a whole.[43] Unfortunately, not every juror summoned from Bridge and Cheap between 1692 and 1699 is included in the returns of the tax collected in 1695.[44] But of those who can be identified, approximately 63 percent in Bridge and 54 percent in Cheap were heads of "substantial households" and paid the surtax. Wealthy men were thus summoned in larger numbers than their proportion in the ratepaying population of these wards would have warranted. Even more striking perhaps, wealthy men were also, as individuals, summoned for jury service more often than their poorer neighbors. In both Bridge and Cheap, men paying the surtax formed an even larger proportion of those summoned "often" (by which I mean more than twice in Bridge out of the eight times juries were called from that ward, and more than four times in Cheap, whence juries were summoned more frequently) and "very often" (more than four and eight times respectively) than of those called for jury service only once.

It is also true that men in the highest tax group were excused more often than other men; that is, they were allowed more readily than others to ignore the summons and not to appear in court. This may reflect the reluctance of some richer men to serve and also their ability to earn the favor of the mayor or the sheriff, who could excuse men from having to respond to the summons. But, more simply, it also reflects the fact that richer men were summoned more often. Their willingness to serve is indicated by the fact that men who paid the surtax in 1695 were not only summoned more often than those who paid the basic rate, but they also responded more often and were actually sworn to sit on a jury more often. Some richer men were clearly anxious to avoid jury service, but many more seem to have been happy to serve or even sought to do so. Men in the higher tax brackets were prominent among those called upon again and again for jury service, and it seems reasonable to think that they welcomed this as an honor and a reflection of their standing in the community. But it is also pos-

43. Ward percentages have been calculated from the 1695 tax data presented in P. E. Jones and A. V. Judges, "London Population in the Late Seventeenth Century," *Economic History Review* 6 (1935): 59–62. Ward calculations remain approximate because the tax was collected and the assessments were made on a parish basis, and the ward and parish boundaries did not coincide. In addition, some of the parish returns are missing. The 27 percent figure for the City as a whole is Glass's calculation (*London Inhabitants within the Walls*, xx–xxi) based on the figures in Jones and Judges's study.

44. About 31 percent of the men summoned from Bridge ward between 1692 and 1699 and 40 percent summoned from Cheap could not be found or identified in the index to the returns of the 1695 tax provided by *London Inhabitants within the Walls*. For an explanation of this, see Table 8.9 n. b.

sible that they regarded jury service as an aspect of local governance and as one means of participating in the maintenance of order in their neighborhoods. And indeed, that jury service was regarded in this way is strongly suggested by another characteristic of the men who served as jurors in London in the 1690s: their experience in other aspects of the government of the City.

The men who served on the London juries in the 1690s were typically very experienced; many of them sat on several juries in the course of that decade. But many had also had other kinds of experience that must have helped to shape their views of the cases they dealt with. For a significant number of jurors, their service at the Guildhall and the Old Bailey was only one aspect of their wider engagement in the governance of the city, for many were also involved in public affairs in their parishes, in their wards, and in the wider arena of the City itself.

The central focus of local service and local government in London was in the twenty-six wards into which the City was divided. The wards were headed by an alderman, who was responsible for calling and presiding over the annual wardmote inquest at which, in the manner of a court leet, matters of local concern could be presented and sent for adjudication before the Court of Aldermen. The ward remained the principal provider of a number of municipal services—including watching and lighting—and the constables, the beadle, and the scavengers were also appointed for their year of service by the wardmote inquest. Many of the offices filled at the annual meeting were largely ceremonial, and indeed, by the end of the seventeenth century the inquest was itself becoming an occasion merely for feasting and drinking. But it did appoint some important local officials, and it also elected the men who would represent the ward on the Common Council.[45]

Many of the jurymen who served at the Guildhall and the Old Bailey in the 1690s were also active in their wards. In Cornhill, for example, the wardmote inquest book reveals that fully 80 percent of the men who served on juries also held a ward office at one time or another in this decade. Many of these offices were obviously entirely ceremonial. The annual meeting in Cornhill elected a foreman of the

45. For the wardmote inquest, see Webb and Webb, *Manor and Borough*, pt 2, pp. 594–606; and Pearl, "Change and Stability." Wardmote inquest books for the 1690s are available in the Guildhall Library for the following wards: Aldersgate (MS. 2050), Bridge Within (MS. 3461/3), Candlewick (MS. 473), Cornhill (MS. 4069/2), Portsoken (MS. 2648), Vintry (MS. 68).

inquest, four speakers, a pricker, a treasurer, a controller, and two each of scribes, stewards, butlers, and porters—as well as nine common councilmen, four constables, four scavengers, and a beadle.[46] It does not, perhaps, signify a great deal that a large number of jurors held one of the ceremonial positions in the Cornhill wardmote in the course of the decade, although it does suggest something about their local standing. It is even more revealing of that local standing that as many as eleven of the fifty-seven men who sat on London juries from Cornhill ward between 1692 and 1699 also sat, at one time or another, on the Common Council of the City. (They included, incidentally, Richard Chancey, the wealthy linen draper we met earlier, who sat on the sessions trial jury once and the grand jury twice in these years and who was to be on the Common Council for a long period after 1700. He also served in the ward in the 1690s as foreman of the inquest, twice as speaker, and as pricker.) Cornhill was not unusual in this regard, for just about two hundred of the jurors we have been concerned with had been, were, or were to become members of the Common Council. Seventy of the jurors in the years 1692 to 1699 were on the Common Council when they served as jurors, so there was obviously no thought that service on the jury at the Guildhall or the Old Bailey was in any sense demeaning for a member of the Common Council of the City.

At another level of local life, a significant number of jurors were also experienced in the affairs of their parishes. The City contained 111 parishes, several of which were included in each ward (although the boundaries were rarely contiguous). As in the rest of the country, the parishes in London collected and administered the poor rate, and for this purpose collectors and overseers were appointed each year. Men also served in London in the other usual parish offices, as churchwardens, sidesmen, and members of the vestry. I have not yet searched extensively for jurors among the officials appointed in the London parishes every year. Indeed, the erratic survival of the appropriate parish records may make a full and systematic search impossible. In Bridge ward, for example, there are good runs of records in this period for only two of the four parishes within or partially within the ward, and this may turn out to be a common pattern. But even this fragmentary evidence makes it clear that jurors were often experienced at this very important level of administration. In the two parishes in Bridge ward, twenty men who served as jurors between 1692

46. Guildhall Lib., MS. 4069/2. The wards each had different structures of officials (Webb and Webb, *Manor and Borough*, pt. 2, pp. 599–600).

and 1699 held one or more of the parish offices in the 1690s. They had served as churchwardens, overseers, or collectors of the poor, as well as sidesmen and vestrymen. Sixty men from Bridge sat on the London juries in these years, and presumably others among them held similar positions in the two parishes whose records are incomplete.[47]

It seems clear that the men who served as jurors at the Guildhall and the Old Bailey were also engaged in the government of the City in a variety of other ways. They can also be found on other juries. A survey of the fragmentary evidence that survives of the juries called to the mayor's court in the early 1690s—one of the City courts that dealt with civil cases—discloses some seventy-six men serving in that court who also sat on the juries we are concerned with at some point between 1692 and 1699.[48] We can be reasonably certain that if the evidence could be recovered, they would also be found to have served on the coroners' juries and the juries in the sheriffs' courts, and to have been involved in the meetings in their precincts that resulted in nominations of men for wardmote office and for the Common Council.

The implications of the social character of the jurors who dealt with criminal cases at the Guildhall and the Old Bailey and of their broad experience of the working of the courts and other institutions of government in the City seem to me to be important in two areas in particular. In the first place, these matters have some bearing on the process of deliberation undertaken by criminal trial juries in this period and the verdicts they arrived at. Jurors brought to their work in the courts the views and prejudices shaped by their interests as men of particular kinds of property, as merchants and tradesmen, as artisans and small masters. London juries included some men of modest means, but they were drawn preponderantly from among the City's more substantial and prosperous citizens. In addition, most of them had clearly not been selected at random or chosen as representative citizens simply to make impartial determinations of the guilt or innocence of those charged with offenses in the criminal courts. Many had frequently served on juries before and with men well known to them and with whom they had worked in other aspects of local

47. Vestry Minutes of St. Magnus and St. Margaret's Fish Street, Guildhall Lib., MSS. 2791/1 and 1175/1.

48. CLRO, MC2C/3: Mayor's Court Books. This is a volume kept by one of the four attorneys who practiced in the mayor's court. I have surveyed only the juries called in 1691 and 1692—a total of twenty-two grand and trial juries, which required the services of about 265 men.

administration. The reappearance on the ward lists of the same men over and over again, and particularly of men with long experience of jury service and of local office, suggests that juries were to some extent self-selected and that those who served on them regarded the work of the jury in broad terms as an aspect of local governance.

Whether these characteristics of London jurors in the 1690s—their respectability, experience, and engagement in local affairs—were reflected in their verdicts is a difficult question that remains to be investigated. But it is worth noting that there was a good deal of scope for jurors in the criminal courts to apply to the prisoners at the bar the kinds of judgments that poor-law officials, constables, or other local officers would have thought appropriate in dealing with the poor of a parish or with vagrants—that is, judgments based on an assessment of character and disposition. The scope for the application of such judgments by jurors was, if anything, enlarged in this period with the extension of capital punishment to a larger number of relatively minor offenses. It was obvious even as these statutes were passed in the reigns of William and Anne (and after) that the courts would put them into force selectively and with discretion—that while some of those accused under them might be hanged, large numbers would not be, and that juries and judges together would in effect choose some of the accused to be executed and others to be punished in some other way.

Criminal trial juries were centrally involved in these judgments because of their capacity, not merely to find the accused guilty or not guilty of the charge in the indictment, but to find a so-called partial verdict by which a capital charge could be reduced to a noncapital sentence. In the period we are concerned with and through the eighteenth century, such mitigating verdicts were very common indeed, and they were crucial to the way the criminal law was administered and interpreted.[49] It is usually impossible to discover why such verdicts were arrived at in particular cases, but it is clear that in deciding whether to convict a prisoner capitally or to spare his life, jurors commonly put a great deal of weight on the prisoner's character, disposition, and previous conduct as these matters had been revealed in the trial. Such personal judgments of the prisoner's worthiness were central to a large number of the decisions made by criminal trial juries in a period in which many defendants faced capital charges, particularly in London, where the courts dealt with more serious offenders than normally came before the provincial assizes. It is clear that in administering a criminal law dominated by the threat of capital punishment,

49. Beattie, *Crime and the Courts*, 419–30.

jurors at the Old Bailey had a great deal of opportunity to express in their verdicts the concerns and standards they brought with them to the courtroom as men of property and as men engaged in the management of local affairs.

A second implication of the character of juries in this period will also be worth following up and is perhaps more susceptible of investigation. This concerns the possible role played by the City of London in shaping the development of the criminal law. As is well known, both the law and its administration were altered strikingly in the generation following the Revolution of 1689. Not only was the scope of capital punishment broadened by several statutes of William's reign and of Anne's, but attempts were also made then to encourage prosecutions and to increase the effectiveness of the punishments the courts could impose upon convicted felons. Much remains to be discovered about the forces and influences at work behind these significant changes in policy. But one possible source of concern and pressure for change seems to me to be London, where much of the crime problem that these changes in the law were designed to combat was to be found and where reformers could bring to bear a large and influential body of opinion. There is some evidence that at least one of the major statutes of this period resulted from a petition to the House of Commons from the government of London,[50] and it seems likely that the influence of the authorities in the metropolis could be found behind other of the initiatives being taken. If that turns out to be the case, it seems to me a reasonable speculation that will repay detailed investigation that the authorities of the City were themselves being pushed and encouraged by the kinds of men who sat on juries, men with experience of crime in their daily lives and with experience of the way the criminal courts worked, and men who also had frequent contact with the institutions and the men who governed and spoke for the City. It seems reasonable to think that these men with broad experience of the criminal courts and of all levels of government in the City may well have played an important part in the encouragement of changes that were beginning to transform the criminal law and criminal administration in this period.

Acknowledgments

I am grateful to the Social Sciences and Humanities Research Council of Canada and to the Ministry of the Solicitor General of Canada,

50. Ibid., 491–92.

through its contributions grant to the Centre of Criminology, University of Toronto, for financial assistance. I wish to thank Tony Doob, the Director of the Centre, for his help with the analysis of the data, and Tammy Landau and Elizabeth Elbourne for research assistance. I am grateful to James Cockburn, Douglas Hay, Peter King, and Peter Lawson for allowing me to see early versions of their essays and for offering advice on my own. I would also like to thank Donna Andrew, Joanna Innes, Nicholas Rogers, and James Sewell for their helpful comments on an earlier version of this essay. I am particularly grateful to Gary De Krey for generously sharing with me the results of his own work and for giving me a great deal of help with the tax records of London in the 1690s.

Nine

"Illiterate Plebeians, Easily Misled": Jury Composition, Experience, and Behavior in Essex, 1735–1815

P.J.R. King

When Smollett's Lismahago described the juries of the later eighteenth century as "generally composed of illiterate plebeians, apt to be mistaken, easily misled,"[1] he was attacking one of the central components of the criminal justice system. The eighteenth-century criminal trial jury operated at a vital crossroads in the judicial process. The jurors' decisions both affected and were affected by the attitudes and behavior of prosecutors, witnesses, and committing magistrates. Although their verdicts were to all intents and purposes sentencing decisions in some types of cases,[2] jurors' findings might also be deeply influenced by the sentencing options open to the court and by the pardoning policies of those involved at later stages in the penal process. The trial before the petty jury was the principal public moment in the long chain of individual and collective choices and interactions that determined the fate of the accused. Trial outcomes were also the most systematically recorded point in that chain, and jury verdicts have therefore become an important focus of attention for historians of the criminal law.

As county studies have accumulated, a common pattern of verdicts has emerged. Inevitably there were local variations, and the overall picture disguised significant differences between types of offense, but the Essex and Home circuit patterns do not appear to have been untypical. Around one-seventh of those indicted for property crimes in

1. T. Smollett, *The expedition of Humphry Clinker*, ed. A. Ross (1771, reprint 1967), 241.

2. In burglary and aggravated larceny cases, a partial verdict effectively limited the range of sanctions available by preventing the judge from passing a capital sentence.

the major courts of Essex between 1740 and 1805 had their indictments dismissed as "not found" by the grand jury. The petty jury acquitted almost a third of the remainder and brought in partial verdicts, reducing the charge and effectively lessening the sentence, in a further 10 percent.[3] On the Home circuit between 1782 and 1787, acquittal levels at the assizes varied little between the five counties of Surrey, Essex, Hertfordshire, Kent, and Sussex, averaging 34 percent of true bills. Partial verdicts affected a further 12 percent of indictments.[4] Clearly the juries' decisions had a vital impact on the judicial process. Less than half of those indicted for major property crimes in southeastern England were found to be guilty as charged.

Although it is difficult to uncover the underlying criteria that influenced these highly selective processes, it is evident that these were principled decisions.[5] In particular, the use of partial verdicts was related to various aspects of the character of the offender and the nature of the offense. Quantitative evidence indicates, for example, that females, the young, and those with families to support were much more likely to be given partial verdicts, while in some periods of high food prices those verdicts also showed a general tendency to increase.[6] Age-related verdict patterns on the Home circuit in the 1780s suggest that, despite the hurried nature of the decision-making process, verdicts reflected subtly different levels of evaluation. While the accused's chances of obtaining a partial verdict varied dramatically with his or her age, the chance of gaining an outright acquittal did not. In most types of cases the mitigating circumstances that enabled certain offenders to obtain a lighter sentence appear to have had much less influence on initial judgments about guilt or innocence.[7]

3 P. King, "Crime, Law and Society in Essex, 1740–1820" (Ph.D. diss., Cambridge Univ., 1984), 301–2. Surrey and Staffordshire acquittal and partial verdict rates were slightly higher. J.M. Beattie, "Crime and the Courts in Surrey, 1736–1753," in *Crime in England, 1550–1800*, ed. J.S. Cockburn (1977), 175–76; D. Hay, "Crime, Authority and the Criminal Law: Staffordshire, 1750–1800" (Ph.D. diss., Warwick Univ., 1975), 476. Surrey figures for a much more extended period are available in Beattie, *Crime and the Courts*, 411, 425, 437.

4. King, "Crime, Law and Society," 302.

5. J. H. Langbein, "Albion's Fatal Flaws," *Past and Present* 98 (1983): 106.

6. P. King, "Decision-Makers and Decision-Making in the English Criminal Law, 1750–1800," *Historical Journal* 27 (1984): 34–44; Beattie, *Crime and the Courts*, 429–49; D. Hay, "War, Dearth and Theft in the Eighteenth Century: The Record of the English Courts," *Past and Present* 95 (1982): 155; King, "Crime, Law and Society," 308–9.

7. King, "Crime, Law and Society," 310. This evidence that acquittal rates were the same for every age group over fourteen needs to be confirmed by research in other courts and periods. However, apart from highway robbery cases, where high hang-

When allied with recent work on trial procedures,[8] these verdict patterns have enabled historians to gain substantial insights into the role that juries played in the increasingly elaborate system of mitigation that developed during this period.[9] However, several important and related clusters of questions about judge-jury relations and the degree of independence enjoyed by the jurors, about the deeper assumptions on which selection processes were based, and about the degree to which the interests and attitudes of jurors overlapped with or opposed those of the gentry elite remain intractable. These questions, in turn, cannot be adequately answered without a detailed understanding of who the jurors were and of the relationship between contemporary perceptions of the capacities and social status of jurors and their actual wealth, status, and abilities. It is this final set of issues, raised both implicitly and explicitly by Lismahago's critique, that forms the main focus of this essay. From what social and economic backgrounds did the jurors come? How did their patterns of wealth, occupation, age, and household structure vary both between different courts and over time? Were a significant proportion of jurors illiterate? Could they be easily misled, or had they already gained considerable experience of individual and joint decision-making processes both inside and outside the courtroom? Using the Essex freeholders books, which offer a depth of information not available in any other county so far studied, and a variety of court records and parish-based sources, the central sections of this paper analyze these aspects of jury composition and experience and re-examine the comments of contemporaries in light of that information. The final section explores the complex links between the behavior and decision-making processes of jurors and their experience levels and background.

Contemporaries were not slow to voice their opinions of the quality and social background of those who sat on juries. Eulogistic generali-

ing rates and the lack of a partial-verdict tradition may have produced a small minority of acquittal decisions based on character-related criteria, initial acquittal decisions were not as closely related to character as partial verdicts or punishment policies were. Jurors did not make a strict division between the two issues—the character of the prosecutor vis-à-vis the accused was clearly important in evaluating guilt—but the age-related evidence is difficult to explain unless jurors were making a two-level evaluation.

8. J. H. Langbein, "The Criminal Trial before the Lawyers," *University of Chicago Law Review* 45 (1978): 263–316; idem, "Shaping the Eighteenth-Century Criminal Trial: A View from the Ryder Sources," *University of Chicago Law Review* 50 (1983): 1–136, Beattie, *Crime and the Courts*, 340–99.

9. Green, *Verdict According to Conscience*, 267–317, provides a detailed discussion of the mitigation system and of the contradictory reactions of contemporary writers to it.

zations about jury trial such as that published by the *Chelmsford Chronicle* in 1784, which stressed that trial by jury "is the union of wisdom with integrity, impartiality with humanity," were by no means always accompanied by complimentary remarks about the jurors themselves.[10] To Madan they were usually "low and ignorant country people" while Adam Smith described them as "the meaner sort."[11] Less frequently quoted but equally vehement critics offered more detailed comments. To William Hutton the jury was a grand and well-founded building, but its superstructure was rotten and in urgent need of repair."The better informed and more opulent persons to whom this duty of attendance belongs, escape through private avenues such as pride, business interest, pretended sickness, secret fees, etc.," he suggested in 1789. "The weight, therefore, of this important concern falls upon the lower class, who are utterly unable to sustain it. The bailiff . . . has been so distressed for a jury that I have seen him pick up idle people in rags, while loitering in the open hall at Warwick."[12] A year earlier *The Times* had touched on similar themes when it complained that "persons of education and property are too often ready to evade serving" as jurymen, the net result being that "juries frequently consist of ignorant and illiterate persons."[13] Dagge was milder if rather less consistent, writing at one point of juries "being generally composed of persons whose knowledge is confined to moderate bounds" but later characterizing jury trial as involving "twelve illiterate and the greatest part of them perhaps ignorant men."[14]

Bamford, in discussing the jurors of the early nineteenth century from an overtly democratic standpoint, "thought the English jury one of the most bungling pieces of judicial machinery which could have been put together" and linked his analysis to "the manner in which jurymen were selected," noting that "In the county I come from they were generally men who had just the brute instinct of beavers to scrape a little subsistence together, and to keep it; but who for all other purposes were far behind their neighbours, and infinitely so in

10. *Chelmsford Chronicle*, 24 Dec. 1784.

11. M. Madan, *Thoughts on Executive Justice, with Respect to the Criminal Laws, Particularly on the Circuits*, 2d ed. (1785), 142, A. Smith, *Lectures on justice, police, revenue and arms*, ed. E. Cannon (1763), 52.

12. *A dissertation on juries; with a description of the hundred court: as an appendix to the Court of Requests* (Birmingham, 1789), 22–23. For the full context of this quotation, see Hay's essay, text at nn. 1–12.

13. *The Times*, 13 Oct. 1788.

14. H. Dagge, *Considerations on criminal law* (1772), 154–61.

qualifications necessary for deciding betwixt right and wrong, guilt and innocence."[15]

Some of these writers were presenting specific and sometimes highly polemic arguments, however, within which their analysis of the quality of serving jurors played only a minor part. Madan was attacking the whole panoply of institutions and practices that had led to the mitigation of the capital sanction. Hutton was angrily defending part of his life's work, the local court of requests, against Blackstone's pejorative remarks.[16] Bamford, the only one of these writers to have suffered at the hands of a jury, had bitter memories of the experience and attacked the jury from a different direction, demanding that the rhetoric of "trial by his peers" be made a reality for the workingman.[17] Since none of these writers appears to have engaged in, or had access to, any systematic research on the wealth, literacy, or social experience of jurors, their views need to be tested against other forms of evidence. It is here that the detailed information available in the Essex freeholders books is particularly useful.

Eighteenth-century parish constables were bound by law to return yearly lists to the quarter sessions of the names, places of abode and titles or additions of all the inhabitants of their parish qualified to serve on juries.[18] In the great majority of counties this was all that was recorded, but in Essex a tradition had been established by the 1730s whereby three other pieces of information were also returned: the age of the juror, the value of his estate, and the parish in which the largest proportion of his holdings lay (usually, but not always, the same place as his parish of abode).[19] Most of the freeholders books compiled each year from these returns have not survived, but they are available for twelve individual years in the period 1734 to 1815, the only sizeable

15. S. Bamford, *Passages in the Life of a Radical* (1984), 295. Although writing in the 1840s, Bamford was recalling a conversation held twenty-five years earlier. Complaints of the ignorance of jurors were not new. See Cockburn, *Assize Introduction*, 61, for some similar early-seventeenth-century remarks.

16. Hutton, *Dissertation on juries*, 8–12.

17. Bamford, *Passages*, 295; *The Autobiography of Samuel Bamford*, vol. 1, *Early Days*, ed W. H. Chaloner (1848–49, reprint 1967), 49–50.

18. R. Burn, *The justice of the peace and parish officer*, 10th ed. (1766), 2:467. They were to "be careful to insert the Christian names, occupations and places of abode of such persons to enable the sheriff to summon them." J. Paul, *The parish officer's complete guide*, 6th ed. (1793), 187.

19 The Kent freeholders books, for example, give only name, parish, and status. F. Hull, ed., *Guide to the Kent County Archives Office* (Maidstone, 1958), 25.

gaps in the series being between 1734 and 1759 and between 1783 and 1815.[20] These books can be combined with the assize and quarter sessions jury lists to develop detailed profiles of the age, wealth, and occupational structures not only of the eligible freeholders as a whole but also of the main types of criminal trial jury: the petty and grand juries of the quarter sessions and assizes. Within the assize petty jury it is also possible to develop a separate analysis of jury foremen.[21]

Although the Essex quarter sessions authorities were almost completely successful in obtaining returns of this level of detail from every parish within the court's jurisdiction,[22] the consistency of the information they received is sometimes open to question. Parish vestries and their officers were highly individual in their approach to local matters such as rating assessments,[23] and the criteria on which the value of a man's estate was estimated may have varied considerably between parishes. Policies about who should be excluded from the freeholders books were also inconsistent. A minority of constables included groups—such as surgeons, apothecaries, attorneys, Quakers, and clergy—who were specifically exempted by statute,[24] and it seems likely that some parish officers were either wrongly or incompletely informed about exemptions. Even those who were conscientious enough to consult one of the relevant printed handbooks were not necessarily well advised. Joshua Shaw's *Parish Law*, for example, suggested, with no apparent basis in law, that butchers were not eligible for jury service.[25] Some exemption categories were difficult to define and were therefore negotiable. In 1786 a Loughton horse and cow farrier claimed exemption because his profession was closely allied to that of a surgeon and having "care of more than 2,000 cattle . . . many

20. Essex Record Office (hereafter ERO), Q/RJ 1/1–12. The years covered are 1734, 1759, 1768–72, 1779–81, 1783, and 1815.

21. Assize jury lists survive in a complete series: PRO, ASSI 35. The quarter sessions lists, which were written on the large sheet usually placed on the outside of the rolls, have often been destroyed Grand jury lists from before the 1780s are rarely available. Petty jury lists were sometimes duplicated in the inner documents, but their survival is also patchy. The quarter sessions lists do not usually note who was the foreman. (ERO, Q/SR 800 to 900 form the main subnumbers used here)

22. Just over 1 percent of entries by the 1780s do not include age and estate.

23. Paul, *The parish officer's complete guide*, 63–69, indicates the legal complexities. Certain categories of wealth were only assessable "in those places in which a usage to assess such stock has been proved." For a discussion of practice rather than legal theory, see *Gentleman's Magazine* 14 (1744), 654–57. (I am grateful to John Styles for this reference.)

24. Burn, *Justice of the Peace*, 2:466–67.

25. J. Shaw, *Parish Law* (1743), 354.

beasts may be lost by my being absent two or three days."[26] The constables' attitudes toward the disabled, the deaf, and the infirm are also problematic. If an individual had a sufficient estate and was within the age limits for jury service (over twenty-one and not more than seventy) some constables included him in their returns even though they knew that he was handicapped. Others, lacking any clear guidelines, excluded the long-term disabled from their lists.[27] Occasionally, those who had served on a jury within the last two years, and who therefore could not legally be recalled,[28] were also omitted from the freeholders books, but in Essex this seems to have been rare.[29]

A few potential jurors may have avoided being included in the freeholders books by offering monetary or non-monetary inducements to their local constables, but the latter were obliged to post a copy of their list on the door of the parish church as well as having it ratified by a local magistrate, and any officer found guilty of malpractice might be heavily fined.[30] More names were probably lost through the laziness or inattention to detail of some constables. Where the books of consecutive years are available, however, it is clear that only a small minority of constables failed to revise their parish list each year. Although estate and age valuations occasionally oscillated in rather idiosyncratic ways,[31] names were regularly added or removed in al-

26. ERO, Q/SBb 322/55.

27. The situation allowed for three possible responses Some constables included the disabled and then added a note describing their infirmity. Others included them but, either from ignorance of their condition or negligence, gave no indication that they were disabled. This may help to explain why a considerable number of impaneled jurors claimed various long-term disabilities as grounds for exemption after being called to attend the court. Finally, many constables may well have automatically excluded the long-term disabled from their returns.

28. Burn, *Justice of the Peace*, 2.472–73.

29. For example, thirty-five of the thirty-seven petty jurors who served at the Summer assizes in 1778 and the Lent assizes in 1779 can be found in the freeholders book compiled in the summer of 1779.

30. Burn, *Justice of the Peace*, 2:467–68. Positive evidence of corruption is difficult to find. Prosecutions were very rare. Relatively few of the largest owner-occupiers in the parishes whose land tax returns I have analyzed seem to have escaped being listed in the freeholders books, suggesting that the wealthy rarely attempted to avoid inclusion or that the safeguards created by the lists being publicly displayed usually prevented any of the more obvious candidates from being accidentally or deliberately omitted. Alternatively, some parishioners may have positively courted inclusion in the jury lists because this was a public indication that they were men of wealth and credit.

31. The age of a specific juror did not always rise by one unit each year; in these cases successive constables probably guessed the man's age. However, differences are relatively small. Estate valuations also showed very few wide oscillations, although long-term changes are sometimes observable, and, indeed, were inevitable, given the active state of the land market and the changing levels of rents and land values.

most every parish and the lists were clearly not frozen by inertia or uninformed repetition.

Despite the considerable number of potentially eligible jurors that were excluded from the freeholders books by these processes, the first surviving list in 1734 contains over 2,300 names, while later lists fluctuated between just under 2,000 and 2,900.[32] After allowance is made for the 11 percent of the Essex population excluded because they lived in boroughs or liberties with their own jurisdictions[33] and for exempt occupations, female household heads and underage or overage male householders, these figures suggest that just under 10 percent of nonexempt household heads in Essex were listed as having a sufficient estate to serve on a jury in 1734, the equivalent figure after mid century being about 8 percent.[34]

What were the principal characteristics of those who found themselves included in the Essex freeholders books? Throughout the period 1734–1815, between half and two-thirds of the eligible jurors were in their forties or fifties (Table 9.1). Only just over a quarter were under forty despite the fact that those aged between twenty and thirty-nine constituted more than 55 percent of all the people between twenty and seventy in the population.[35] Inheritance practices, partic-

32. Both the 1759 and 1783 lists contained about 1,950 names. By 1815 this had risen to just over 2,900. It is not clear why the numbers fell between 1734 and 1759 and then remained static for twenty-five years at a time when the Essex population was rising. Double-counting was rare in the late eighteenth century, but it may have been more common in 1734. *Essex Free-holders Book*, 1734, ed. F.G. Emmison (Chelmsford, 1982), vii-ix.

33 The boroughs of Colchester, Harwich, Maldon, and Saffron Walden and the Liberty of Havering had courts exercising quarter sessions jurisdiction. They therefore needed local freeholders to man their own juries. The Cinque port of Brightlingsea had no such courts but enjoyed the privilege of exemption throughout this period. E. P. Dickin, *A History of Brightlingsea* (Brightlingsea, 1939), 115. In 1801 the population of these exempt areas was 25,128.

34. Based on Brown's estimate of 31,000 household heads in 1723 (the Essex population grew very little between 1723 and 1734), the county total outside exempt jurisdictions was apparently 27,590. After excluding an estimated 12 percent as female householders or male householders aged over seventy or under twenty-one and another 500 for those who were in exempt occupations (allowing for the small number still included in freeholders books), the best guess appears to be 2,328 eligible jurors out of a potential nonexempt male householder population of 23,780, i.e., 9.8 percent. Similar exercises for 1779 and 1815 produce estimated figures of between 7.9 and 8.0 percent. A. Brown, *Essex at Work, 1700–1815* (Chelmsford, 1969), 108. These are, of course, very approximate figures.

35. This is based on the age structure of the population of England and Wales in 1786. The figures are from E. A. Wrigley and R. S. Schofield, *The Population History of England, 1541–1871* (1981). My thanks to Roger Schofield for making this information available under more convenient age groupings. The age structure of eligible jurors changed little over time, apart from a slight tendency for the average age to rise.

Table 9.1. Age Distribution of Eligible and Serving Jurors in Late-Eighteenth-Century Essex

Age	QS Petty Jury (%)	QS Grand Jury (%)	Assizes Petty Jury (%)	Assizes Petty Jury Foreman (%)	Assizes Grand Jury (%)	Freeholders Books General (%)
20–29	10.1	9.7	9.9	1.6	9.8	7.5
30–39	28.2	16.0	27.3	12.9	18.2	19.0
40–49	32.0	28.6	30.1	41.9	31.2	28.8
50–59	22.6	32.0	26.1	33.9	28.1	29.0
60–69	6.4	12.0	6.4	9.7	12.3	15.7
70+	0.7	1.7	0.3	0.0	0.4	0.1
Total	100.0	100.0	100.1	100.0	100.0	100.1
N	425	175	785	62	285	1,579

NOTES: Serving jurors rather than impaneled ones form the basis of the first five columns (PRO, ASSI 35). Assize petty jurors sample years are 1766–1803, grand jurors, 1766–1774 and 1790–1800 (ERO, Q/SR). Quarter sessions petty juries, 1775–1796; grand jurors, 1781–1796 (for earlier years, quarter sessions rolls are damaged). ERO, Q/RJ 1/4, 11 and 12 (1769, 1783, 1815) were sampled for "freeholders books general." ERO, Q/RJ 1/1–12 were used to trace the ages of serving jurors.

ularly the age at which sons came into possession of their fathers' lands, undoubtedly had an important influence on this pattern, but whatever its underlying causes, the age structure of jurors ran parallel to those of other officials serving in the judicial process, including judges, justices of the peace, borough aldermen, and sheriffs. This offers further support to Keith Thomas's suggestion that in early modern England "it was men in their forties and fifties who ruled."[36] Since the vast majority of males had married and begun to bring up a family by that time in their lives, it is not surprising to find that the mean size of jurors' households tended to be larger than average. In the Terling census of 1809, for example, listed jurors averaged 7.4 persons per household, compared to 4.9 in the parish as a whole, and in the Bocking census taken two years earlier the equivalent figures were 7.2 and 4.3. In the Harlow census of 1797, 43 percent of jurors had households of 7 or more persons, while only 29 percent of all Harlow households were in the same category.[37] This difference is less, however, if jurors'

36. *Age and Authority in Early Modern England*, 1976 Raleigh Lecture (1976), 9.

37. Sample sizes for jury households are small. The largest were Bocking

households are compared only with those of tradesmen, artisans, and farmers.[38] Moreover, in Ardleigh, where the number of servants per household can also be analyzed, the difference disappears completely once servants are allowed for. Although the vast majority of jurors would have had the experience of bringing up a family by the time they sat on a jury, they would not necessarily have had a greater-than-average number of children still at home. They were, however, much more likely to be concerned with the management of apprentices or living-in servants. In Ardleigh, jurors had five times as many servants as the parish average.[39]

Despite some obvious cases of rounding, when the ages given in the freeholders books are cross-checked with parish registers or informal censuses, significant discrepancies are rare. The freeholders' occupations also match up well with evidence about the same individuals in other sources, such as wills.[40] Unfortunately, information about jurors' occupations was not as systematically collected as age or estate, which may have produced some distortions in Table 9.2.[41] Since occupational labels often disguised wide discrepancies of wealth, differences between employees and employers, and dual or multi-occupational practices, this evidence must be treated with caution, but a comparison of 1734, 1783, and 1815 does suggest both specific economic changes and an enduring structure.

The proportion of eligible jurors labeled as artisans or tradesmen increased after the middle of the eighteenth century (Table 9.2), reflecting, it would seem, the growing prosperity of Essex commerce, although this rise may have been due mainly to changes in administrative practice. In 1734 constables often used the label

(with 550 households and 18 jurors' households) and Harlow (with 282 households and 23 jurors' households). The Terling census is the least reliable, with only 7 jurors' households to compare with 142 others. ERO, D/P 32/28/2; W. F. Quin, *A History of Bocking and Braintree* (Brentwood, 1981), 215.

38. In Harlow, 33 percent of the households of tradesmen or farmers who were not traceable to jury lists contained seven or more persons. The equivalent figure for laborers' households was 18 percent.

39. F. Erith, *Ardleigh, 1796* (East Bergholt, 1978) reprints the census in full, from which a mean household size for jurors can be calculated as 6.5. For the population as a whole, the figure was 5.5. Ibid., 107. Jurors averaged 2.5 servants per household, while the general figure was 0.5.

40. *Essex Free-holders Book*, ed. Emmison, ix.

41. Only 37 entries out of over 1,900 had no age information attached in 1779, but in some hundreds less than half the parish constables listed occupations. Some of the constables living in parishes where all jurors were farmers may have been more inclined to take the view that occupational information was unnecessary. The sample may therefore be biased in favor of tradesmen and artisans.

Table 9.2. Occupation of Eligible and Serving Jurors in Essex, 1734–1815

	All Essex Household Heads	Freeholders Books 1734	Freeholders Books 1783	Freeholders Books 1815	QS Petty Jury	Assizes Petty Jury	QS Grand Jury	Assizes Petty Jury Foremen
Gentry	3.0	24.4	10.9	11.8	0.3	2.7	6.0	11.1
Professionals	2.0	2.1	2.1	1.5	0.3	0.6	0.0	2.2
Farmers and yeomen	11.5	42.5	45.1	46.8	50.0	37.9	44.0	26.6
Artisans and tradesmen	31.5	30.2	39.1	36.3	47.0	58.0	46.0	60.0
Maritime occupations	6.5	0.2	1.0	1.6	1.0	0.2	4.0	0.0
Husbandmen	45.5	0.5	1.4	0.8	0.3	0.4	0.0	0.0
Laborers and paupers		0.1	0.4	1.3	1.0	0.2	0.0	0.0
N		866	768	2,594	302	483	50	45
Specific Trades within Artisans and Tradesmen Category (Percent of Total Sample)								
Clothier		2.7	1.6	0.1	0	1.9		
Miller		1.5	3.9	3.5	1.5	3.9		
Maltster		1.7	1.6	1.2	0.6	3.2		
Victualer		1.7	5.1	2.7	7.9	9.9		
Tailor		0.5	1.3	0.8	2.0	1.1		
Blacksmith or Wheelwright		1.0	2.1	2.5	4.0	1.1		

NOTE: All figures are percentages except sample sizes.
SOURCES: Freeholders books ERO, Q/RJ 1/11 and 12. For sources and sample periods for jurors, see Table 9.1 For Essex household heads, see King, "Decision-makers," 28

"gent" in a blanket fashion. By 1783 they were much more selective and the proportion of jurors labeled in this way had fallen drastically.[42] More obviously, the collapse of the Essex cloth industry, which was effectively dead by 1815, can be seen in the disappearance of clothiers from the freeholders books. In the mid eighteenth century, cloth manufacturing occupations also provide evidence of the basic division brought about by the property-based qualifications for jury service. In 1734 and 1783 there were thirty-five clothiers or baymakers listed but only three weavers and five wool combers, despite the fact that in the population as a whole the latter groups greatly outnumbered their putting-out masters. Unlike the maritime occupations and certain less profitable or less highly capitalized trades, clothmakers were relatively well represented in the jury books, partly because Essex clothiers had a habit of buying their way into land. Shopkeepers, merchants, and trades such as innkeeper, which often

42. This was partly allowed for by excluding from the occupational count all parishes in which every juror was labeled as "gent," but in 1734 its use was so widespread that this can only have eliminated a minority of false labels.

necessitated some landholding, were also fairly well represented, but only two categories, farmers and gentry, made a much larger impact on the jury books than they did on the general occupational structure of the county. Despite the widespread use of the problematic label "yeoman,"[43] it is clear that nearly half the eligible jurors were farmers.

Since a few men described as laborers did serve as petty jurors in late-eighteenth-century Essex, and a total of thirty-three laborers were listed in the 1815 freeholders book, it appears that in a minority of parishes those who owned very small pieces of land and earned most of their living by working for other, more substantial landholders were still deemed to be liable for jury service. However, the existence of these men cannot disguise the essential division about which Bamford complained so bitterly—a division that can be most clearly seen by linking the jury lists to the four detailed parish censuses available.[44] Thirteen of the forty-two farmers listed in the Harlow census of 1797 and eleven of the eighty-five tradesmen can be definitely identified in the freeholders lists of 1783 and 1815. One gentleman and none of the town's professionals, all of whom were exempt, appear on these lists. None of the 49 percent of Harlow household heads labeled as laborers were eligible for jury service.[45]

Bocking, like Harlow, was a market town. It was also an important cloth-manufacturing center until that industry's decline in the later eighteenth century. Of the twenty-three Bocking men listed in the 1815 freeholders book, eighteen can be found in the detailed occupational census of 1807.[46] Three were clothmakers or retired clothiers now labeled as gentlemen, four were farmers, and the remainder, apart from one schoolmaster, were members of the more highly capitalized trades. Laborers, weavers, and wool combers—the latter groups being by that time very much part of the town's poor—were once again unrepresented in the jury books, although just over 50 percent of household heads followed these occupations. There were many similarities with Harlow. Overall, less than one in twelve of the town's tradesmen

43. The label "yeoman" may have been applied to some tradesmen, which probably canceled out some of the bias toward the latter in Table 9.2. Occasionally it was used as indiscriminately as "gent," but in general, after 1750 at least, it was largely confined to farmers who were owner-occupiers.

44. Unfortunately, three of the four Essex censuses, which go beyond the simple categories of "trade," "agriculture," and "other" used in the early enumerator's returns, were taken in the 1790s or 1800s, when linking with the jury books is more difficult.

45. ERO, D/P 32/28/2.

46. ERO, Q/RJ 1/12; Brown, *Essex at Work*, esp. chap. 1.

and artisans but about a quarter of its small collection of farmers can be found in the jury books.[47]

The Ardleigh census of 1796 and Erith's detailed reconstruction of the parish at that date provide comparable rural material.[48] Here 51 percent of household heads were laborers or husbandmen. None appear in the jury books. Tradesmen and artisans were about equally represented in these two sets of documents, but jury service was concentrated in only three of the twenty trades found in the census: millers, blacksmiths, and wheelwrights.[49] Yeomen and farmers represented 21 percent of household heads and 72 percent of listed jurors. The occupational structure of jury lists varied widely between parishes, depending on local patterns of landholding, trade-based wealth, and gentry residence. Ardleigh was a large parish situated near the biggest town in Essex. It had no resident gentry.

Great Braxted, a medium-sized agricultural parish in central Essex, presents a rather different picture. As expected, the majority of the population, those listed as agricultural laborers, left no trace in the jury books. However, the presence of two resident gentlemen with large local landholdings meant that two of the four eligible jurors in 1783 were gentry, the others being farmers.[50]

Since eligibility for jury service was based on a substantial property qualification, it is hardly surprising that the occupational data suggest that jurors were drawn exclusively from the top half of the spectrum of wealth and social status. However, the fact that only between 8 and 10 percent of nonexempt household heads found their way onto the Essex lists does not mean that jurors were drawn exclusively from the richest tenth of the population. The statutory qualifications for jury service did not attempt to measure total income or wealth. They were

47. The picture in 1779 was rather less stark. The rapid decline of Bocking's cloth-manufacturing enterprises in the late eighteenth century was accompanied by a considerable decline in the size of its jury lists, from fifty-two in 1779 to twenty-three in 1815. The 1779 list includes two wool combers and a weaver, who may well have been employers on a small scale themselves, as well as several clothiers and a dyer.

48. Erith, *Ardleigh*.

49. These three trades represented 7.5 percent of household heads and 18.7 percent of jury-list entries. ERO, Q/RJ 1/8–12. The remaining artisan occupations in 1796, which included some trades such as shoemakers and tailors that were less frequently associated with wealth or heavy capital requirements, made no impact on the jury books, although by 1815 two trades not found in the census—baker and jobber—were to be found on the freeholders list.

50. This is based on the listings for the 1780s printed in W. A. Gimson, *Great Braxted, 1086–1957* (Chelmsford, 1958), 34–36. By 1815 Braxted had only one resident gentleman, but the jury list, like that of many other agricultural parishes in this period, had expanded to include five tradesmen as well as three farmers.

based on one indicator of wealth—the possession of certain categories of landed property—and they therefore excluded various relatively well-off non-landowning groups while including many small freeholders with rather limited resources.

The most important qualification for jury service in the English counties had been established in 1692, when it was laid down that "every juror shall have in his own name or in trust for him within the county, £10 a year of freehold or copyhold lands or tenements."[51] Certain very limited categories of leaseholders—those holding land by lease of the yearly value of at least £20 for one or more lives or for at least ninety-nine years— were also made eligible in 1730, but by that date the vast majority of Essex tenancies were based either on yearly agreements or on leases of twenty-one years or less, and this new category therefore seems to have had little impact on the freeholders books.[52]

Any attempt to locate the jurors more precisely within the top half of the scale of individual wealth is severely hampered by the absence of suitable tax records. Apart from poor-rate assessments, which are available for only a small proportion of Essex parishes and which list occupiers rather than owners, the only tax returns that can provide anything approaching a systematic picture of wealth and income structures are those of the land tax, the drawbacks of which are well known to historians.[53] Although the land tax schedules do include payments for some minor forms of wealth apart from landholding,[54]

51. Burn, *Justice of the Peace*, 2:464. For a concise summary of changing legal qualifications, see J. C. Oldham, "The Origins of the Special Jury," *University of Chicago Law Review* 50 (1983): 216–21.

52. Burn, *Justice of the Peace*, 2:464. The £20 a year had to be "above the reserved rent" which would have involved some constables in more complex forms of evaluation; ibid. None seem to have given separate treatment to this type of holding. For leasehold patterns, see A. Young, *General view of the agriculture of the county of Essex* (1807), 1:41–42, 97–102; J. D. Chambers and G. E. Mingay, *The Agricultural Revolution* (1966), 46; C. Shrimpton, "The Landed Society and the Farming Community of Essex in the Late Eighteenth and Early Nineteenth Centuries" (Ph.D. diss., Cambridge Univ., 1965), 265. In any case, leases for lives were sometimes seen as a form of freehold. J. Paul, *Laws relative to landlords, tenants and lodgers* (1806), 22.

53. For this debate, see G. E. Mingay, "The Land Tax Assessments and the Small Landowner," *Economic History Review*, 2d ser., 17 (1964): 381–88; D. B. Grigg, "The Land Tax Returns," *Agricultural History Review* 11 (1963): 82–94; J. M. Martin, "Landownership and the Land Tax Returns," *Agricultural History Review* 14 (1966): 96–103.

54. Some payments were made in respect of houses alone or of the property of canal companies and mill owners. Mingay, "The Land Tax," 383. The proportion of houses on which payments were made, however, was usually small. H. G. Hunt,

by the mid eighteenth century the tax had come to fall almost entirely on land.[55] The returns therefore fail to deal systematically with such forms of wealth as trade stocks, raw materials, capital equipment, bonds, and business credits—that is, those forms in which many commercial and industrial men held the vast bulk of their wealth. In the small minority of parishes where a systematic attempt was made to rate capital stock as well as physical buildings or land, they might be traceable in parish rate assessments, but in general these records also appear to have systematically under-represented commercial wealth. Even where they do appear as landowners, tenants, or ratepayers, the tax paid by tradesmen or artisans offers no real comparative guide to their wealth vis-à-vis the local farmers and landowners.[56]

Even the comparatively simple task of placing those jurors involved in agriculture or landowning within the wealth and income structures of their communities is fraught with difficulties. Neither the extent of landownership nor the size of tenancies alone provides a sufficient guide in late-eighteenth-century Essex. Many large tenant farmers possessed considerable stock, working capital, and personal wealth but were not landowners. Many small owner-occupiers had extremely limited resources, were loaded with debts (which were sometimes a greater burden than rents),[57] and were reduced to a very frugal and arduous lifestyle. Shrimpton, the leading authority on Essex landholding in this period, concluded that, "compared with the average size of tenanted holdings, owner-occupied properties were much smaller,"[58]

"Landownership and Enclosure, 1750–1830," *Economic History Review*, 2d ser., 11 (1959): 498.

55. S. Dowell, *A History of Taxation and Taxes in England* (1965), 2 50–51; W. R. Ward, *The English Land Tax in the Eighteenth Century* (1953), 87. As Adam Smith noted, "It is easy to lay a tax upon land . . . but it is very difficult to lay a tax upon stock or money without very arbitrary proceedings." W. Kennedy, *English Taxation, 1640–1799* (1964), 125. Although the business and merchant sectors did not contribute in due proportion to the land tax, the problems were so great and the alternatives so lucrative that governments gave up trying to tax income realistically. J. V. Beckett, "Land Tax or Excise: The Levying of Taxation in Seventeenth- and Eighteenth-Century England," *EHR* 100 (1985). 296–97.

56. For a discussion of the way "houses are not rated one fourth so much as lands" and the problems posed by the fact that "as it is impossible to know every man's circumstances, stock is generally unrated," a discussion which finally concluded that although they had the same income "where the shopkeeper pays one shilling, the farmer pays forty," see *Gentleman's Magazine* 14 (1744)· 654.

57. B. H. Slicher Van Bath, *The Agrarian History of Western Europe, A.D. 500–1850* (1963), 311, astutely points out that "Landownership and wealth were far from always going hand-in-hand. And where do we place the owner-occupier so burdened by debt that the annual interest he has to pay is higher than the tenant farmer's rent?"

58. "The Landed Society," 373. Colquhoun estimated the farmers' incomes

while at the same time showing that neither form of landholding can be treated in isolation, since about a quarter of Essex was farmed by men who owned and leased land simultaneously.[59]

Without a full survey of the county's land tax assessments, any attempt to compare the size of jurors' and non-jurors' landholdings also encounters difficulties, because those holdings were sometimes situated in more than one parish or locality.[60] However, despite these problems and those associated with attempts to use the land tax as a direct guide to acreage or relative landholding size, some limited parameters can be established by using these returns in conjunction with the information given in the freeholders books about where each juror's landholdings were situated.

From an analysis of eight predominantly rural parishes in central and northern Essex, four of which were clustered together near the Suffolk border, it soon becomes clear that the choice of potential jurors open to the constables of any given parish was often very limited.[61] The majority of the landowners listed in the returns did not occupy land in the parish concerned, and many of them were almost certainly town-dwelling professional or commercial men.[62] Although the number of parish residents eligible for jury service was increased to a certain extent through the inclusion of those who were tenants in their parish of abode but who owned some freehold land in other par-

at a third above those of the lesser freeholders, although the distinction was rarely this clear-cut. G. E. Mingay, *English Landed Society in the Eighteenth Century* (1963), 24.

59. Shrimpton, "The Landed Society," 383.

60. Many larger gentry landowners, for example, not only possessed consolidated holdings in one cluster of parishes but also had many smaller holdings in outlying areas. Nor was it that uncommon for even the smaller owners to have land in more than one parish. Mingay, "The Land Tax," 387.

61. The cluster of northern parishes were Langham, Dedham, Lawford, and Ardleigh. The other four were St. Osyth on the eastern coast, Layer Bretton to the south of Colchester, and Great Braxted and Messing nearer the center of the county. The land tax references are ERO, Q/RPL 1057, 582, 793. All were in 1783. For the use of land tax returns to calculate acreage equivalents and the attendant problems, especially where the rent per acre was not reasonably uniform throughout the parish, see Grigg, "The Land Tax Returns," 85–86; and Martin, "Landownership and the Land Tax," 99–103. The very smallest categories of landholder may have been excluded from the land tax returns altogether.

62 This is one of the reasons occupiers rather than owners have been the main focus here. Slicher Van Bath, *Agrarian History*, 311, has suggested that "a knowledge of the distribution of landownership adds little to our understanding of rural society, since the owners, in many cases living in towns, were no part of that society." In the eight parishes studied here, just over 40 percent of the landowners were owner-occupiers, a figure that appears to have been fairly typical of Essex (Shrimpton, "The Landed Society," 371) and of Leicestershire (Hunt, "Landownership," 502–3).

ishes, the freeholders lists were usually based on a fairly small subgroup. Of the seventy-six landowners listed in the Ardleigh land tax of 1783, only sixteen were also occupiers, half of them renting land as well as farming their own. Eight of the fifteen male owner-occupiers were listed as jurors, a further three potential jurors being included in the freeholders books because they owned land in neighboring parishes while living in Ardleigh. With one exception, those eight were the largest landowners among this subgroup of fifteen. However, they held only about a quarter of the land of the parish. Tenant farmers, many of them with more substantial holdings than some of the owner-occupier jurors, were extremely influential in the parish, although entirely absent from the freeholders books. Phillips Bromley, for example, whom Erith describes as having "dominated" the Ardleigh vestry from the early 1780s until the census year of 1796, cannot be found in the jury books.[63] In the neighboring parish of Lawford the two largest farmers, who between them leased over a quarter of the land in the parish, if the proportion of the land tax they paid is any guide, were not eligible for jury service because they owned no part of their holdings. Thus, while Edmund Cook, who farmed only about 1.5 percent of the parish, was eligible, Thomas Jarmains, who cultivated nearly 14 percent, was not.[64] If the amount of land held and farmed, rather than the amount owned, is used as a measure, it becomes evident that many non-jurors had a much greater income than those whose names were recorded in the freeholders books.

The other two parishes in this northern grouping of four, Dedham and Langham, suggest a similar pattern. Of the six Langham farmers who cultivated enough land to generate a land tax assessment of £60 or more, only two were jurors. Four of the seven Langham jurors on the 1783 list farmed land assessed at less than £30. Nearly a dozen tenant farmers who were not jurors had larger holdings than this, and several had holdings two or three times as large. Since none of the jurors listed in either Langham or Lawford in 1783 were described in the jury books as having major holdings outside their parish and since cross-checking with the land tax returns of neighboring parishes broadly supports the jury book evidence,[65] these distributions were not usu-

63. Erith, *Ardleigh*, 6.

64. Thomas Jarmains's land tax suggests that he farmed just under 400 acres. Cook probably held about one tenth of that amount.

65. The freeholders books name only one parish as the place where the juror's qualifying estate lies. Presumably, if it was spread across more than one parish, the place where the most valuable part lay would be named. The books therefore only tell us that no Lawford or Langham juror in 1783 held the largest part of his freehold

ally the result of extra-parochial holdings among jurors being left out of the calculations. Many of the wealthiest farmers and most prominent members of the local community were excluded from jury service, while some men of lesser status were not.

The evidence gathered from all but one of the four central and eastern Essex parishes sampled broadly supports this conclusion. In St. Osyth more than twenty tenant farmers had larger holdings than the majority of eligible jurors, and once again the parish's largest resident farmer was not in the freeholders book. At Messing, farther south, only half of the handful of large farmers who dominated the parish were among those listed as potential jurors. At Great Braxted the two resident gentry and the largest farmer were all jurors, but the fourth juror paid less land tax than more than half of the parish's thirty or so tenants. The tiny parish of Layer Bretton was the only area in this random sample to suggest a different pattern. Here all four of the owner-occupiers were jurors, and these four were by far the largest cultivators in the parish.

Without a vast amount of detailed research, it is not possible to establish how typical the pattern found in the great majority of these parishes is of Essex as a whole.[66] Since no attempt has been made to reconstruct ownership patterns—which would require the analysis of much broader areas—or to overcome completely the problems implicit in any study of tenancy structures based on single parishes, no final conclusions can be advanced. However, the main purpose here has been to show that it was not just the wealthy commercial, trading, and manufacturing groups who were under-represented in jury books. Essex contained a large number of wealthy tenant farmers whose prosperity grew in the later eighteenth century and continued to grow until the end of the Napoleonic wars.[67] Some used their increasing wealth to buy freehold property, but many remained large tenant farmers only, and were therefore excluded from the jury books. The numerical growth of the small owner-occupier in the same period and the decline in the average size of owner-occupied farms which accom-

land outside the parish. This is confirmed by the land tax evidence, which shows that only one juror from these parishes had any holdings in the other three neighboring parishes analyzed and that this holding was extremely small. The total holdings of the thirty-seven jurors from these four parishes are only increased by 2.3 percent by adding the lands listed as theirs in all the parishes surveyed. In this area at least, jurors' holdings appear to have been fairly concentrated.

66. Griggs, "The Land Tax Returns," 86–90, indicates the wide differences that can occur within a county.

67. Shrimpton, "The Landed Society," 336.

panied it[68] led to an increase in the number of small freeholders listed in the jury books but did nothing to counteract the fact that large numbers of prosperous tenant farmers, who played such an important part in many farming communities, continued to be excluded from jury service. In parishes such as Lawford or St. Osyth, which also had a considerable number of inhabitants with commercial, trading, or maritime interests, the top quarter or third of village society in terms of income may well have excluded a significant proportion of the small owner-occupiers listed as potential jurors.[69]

Since very few listed jurors in the parishes investigated were not either entered as landowners in their parish land tax returns or described in the jury books as owning land elsewhere, it appears that the constables stuck fairly closely to the basic criteria of landownership laid down in the jury acts. However, their interpretation of the amount of income required from these lands was often more flexible than the acts implied. Thomas Sach of Layer Bretton, for example, owned only a tiny piece of freehold land, which almost certainly was not worth £10 a year,[70] but he was included on the jury lists, perhaps because he was also a tenant farmer on a rather larger scale.

On what basis did the constables make their estimates of the value of jurors' estates? The prevalence of rounding in many parishes suggests that a precise calculation was rarely regarded as necessary. Although in law every constable had "free liberty to inspect" both the land tax and the parish rate books,[71] valuations only very occasionally corresponded exactly with, or were in a regular proportionate relationship to, either the jurors' land tax levels or their rate assessments.[72] In collecting the parish rates and in normal everyday contact with their fellow parishioners, constables would have had ample opportunity to ask the potential jurors themselves both the yearly rental value and

68. Ibid., 371–73.

69. This tentative conclusion indicates a slightly broader range than that suggested by Hay's findings (see chap. 10, text at n. 103), but it is not entirely clear whether this is due to real differences in landownership and administrative practices between the counties involved or to the different ways in which the evidence has been analyzed

70. Sach's land tax rental quota was £3. Land tax assessments in Essex were usually around three-fourths of gross rent. Shrimpton, "The Landed Society," 351.

71. Burn, *Justice of the Peace*, 2.467. The majority of estate valuations were rounded to £10, £20, £30, etc.

72. On one occasion in 1780 three Ardleigh jurors' valuations of £11, £23 and £20 were exactly the same as their land tax rentals, but this was exceptional, and by 1783 the relevant entries had been rounded slightly upward and there was no longer an exact correlation.

the location of their freehold property. If their answers were not glaringly at odds with the other information available, the constables may well have taken this as their basis. When jurors' estate valuations are plotted against their land tax assessments, a clear overall correlation emerges in most parishes. Individuals making above-average land tax payments were, in the vast majority of cases, also among the top half of estate valuations in the jury books. In Lawford the eligible jurors end up in almost exactly the same rank order whichever set of documents is used and, although the correspondence is not always as close, when allowance is made for the possible existence of lesser holdings in other parishes, it appears that most constables made reasonably effective efforts to ascertain the relative size of jurors' landholdings. Provided fairly large samples are involved, the valuations in the freeholders books can be used as a broad indicator of the relative size of landholdings among those freeholders deemed eligible for jury service, despite the lack of uniformity in the constables' approaches to evaluation.

More than a third of those listed in the Essex freeholders books of the later eighteenth and early nineteenth centuries were described as having an estate of the yearly value of between £10 and £19 (Table 9.3). The vast majority of these were given the lowest eligible income, which may indicate that unless they also farmed leasehold land or followed a non-agricultural occupation, many eligible jurors were by no means wealthy men.[73] More than two-thirds received a valuation of less than £50, but the remainder were spread across a much broader range, just over 2 percent being valued at £500 or more. While the overall distribution of estate valuations remained much the same throughout the period 1734–1815, between 1779 and 1815 they moved slightly toward the higher income groups, reflecting, it seems, the rapid rise of rents and land values that took place during the Napoleonic Wars.[74]

Given the small samples available, it is difficult to monitor changes in jurors' literacy levels over time. However, by laboriously tracing the marks or signatures of individual listed jurors in documents such

73. Not all the £10 valuations can be read in this way, however. Some constables were highly idiosyncratic, while others used a fairly limited scale of valuations even when there appear to have been large differences in wealth within the parish. One or two parishes, such as Bocking, refused to make estate valuations and gave every inhabitant a nominal £10 figure. These have been excluded from Table 9.3.

74. The proportion of eligible jurors with estates valued at £200 or more doubled between 1779 and 1815, while the proportion with £10–£29 estates fell by nearly a quarter. A sample of ten trades whose estate valuations were compared over this period revealed no overall changes.

Table 9.3. Estate Valuations of Eligible and Serving Jurors in Late-Eighteenth-Century Essex

Estate (in pounds)	QS Petty Jury (%)	QS Grand Jury (%)	Assizes 1766–1800 Petty Jury (%)	Assizes Petty Jury Foremen (%)	Assizes Grand Jury (%)	Freeholders Books General, 1779 and 1815 (%)
10–19	66.1	15.0	38.4	26.3	0.8	35.9
20–29	24.5	26.8	21.3	10 5	0.0	18.7
30–39	5.8	14.0	13.2	12.3	3.1	9.1
40–49	1.0	14.0	5.3	8.8	0.8	6.2
50–59	1.2	8.4	6.2	10.5	0.0	7.2
60–69	0.2	7.8	1.8	0.0	0.0	2 8
70–79	0.5	1.7	2.3	1.8	0.0	1.4
80–89	0.0	1.1	1.5	3.5	0.0	1.3
90–99	0.5	2.2	0.5	0.0	0.8	0.4
100–199	0.2	6.1	8.1	15.8	33.3	10.9
200–299	0.0	2.2	1.2	10.5	7.8	2.3
300–399	0.0	0.0	0.0	0.0	5.8	1.4
400–499	0.0	0.0	0.1	0.0	1.9	0.2
500–999	0.0	0.6	0.0	0.0	29.1	1.1
1,000–1,499	0.0	0.0	0.0	0.0	8.1	0.7
1,500+	0.0	0.0	0.0	0.0	8.5	0.3
Total	100.0	99.9	99.9	100.0	100.0	99 9
N	416	179	778	57	258	2,040

NOTE: Sources and sample years as for Table 9.1 except for freeholders books, which are based on 1779 and 1815.

as parish agreements or depositions, it has been possible to refute, for Essex at least, contemporaries' often-repeated accusations of juror illiteracy. In the resulting sample, which includes members of every major occupational group found in jury lists and covers a fairly balanced sample of levels of estate valuation, 98 percent of jurors signed their names rather than using a mark.[75] This is not necessarily so surprising. About 85 percent of all the farmers making depositions, and 75 percent of all tradesmen and artisans, had similar skills in late-eighteenth-century Essex,[76] and some of the less wealthy and presum-

75. This is based on a sample of all surviving depositions from 1748–49, 1754–65, 1771–74, 1783–86, 1792–94, and 1800 (ERO, Q/SBb 180–380) and parish agreements (D/P 263/8/1; D/P 21/8/1; Q/RJ 11/1–12). The total sample size of 63 is, unfortunately, still rather small. For comparable late-seventeenth-century literacy levels among jurors, see chap. 6, text at n. 36.

76. King, "Crime, Law and Society," 189. These levels are each about 10 percent higher than those of similar groups in the diocese of Norwich at the beginning of

ably less literate members of these occupations would have been excluded from the jurors' ranks by the vagaries of the property qualifications. However, even if the ability to sign was not necessarily an indicator of complete literacy in some cases, it seems certain that the majority of jurors, including those on the least prestigious quarter sessions petty jury, would have been able not only to read but also to take basic notes if they so desired.[77]

A large number of jurors used their skills of literacy and numeracy extensively as parish officers drawing up churchwardens', overseers', surveyors', or constables' accounts during their terms of office. How extensive was the average juror's experience of parish office? Levels of office-holding could differ considerably between parishes, depending on the size of the group available to serve and on local traditions about office-holding and about the employment of paid substitutes. In two Essex parishes situated near the outskirts of London, Barking and Woodford, between 85 and 90 percent of the listed jurors (excluding those who were either esquires or London residents with a second home in southwestern Essex) had served in an office at least once.[78] The majority served several times. In Woodford between 1759 and 1783 the average number of service years was four; in Barking the average figure in 1779 was well over six. About 80 percent of these Barking jurors had served as churchwardens while 75 percent had been overseers, and these figures only began to decline at the end of the century, when professional overseers were introduced and the office of churchwarden ceased to be rotated.[79] Rural jurors had equally impres-

the eighteenth century D. Cressy, *Literacy and the Social Order: Reading and Writing in Tudor and Stuart England* (Cambridge, 1980), 160–63.

77. Cressy, *Literacy*, 54–55.

78. In Barking, where both esquires and landowners with a second house in the parish were largely exempt from parish office, 90 percent of the remaining twenty jurors listed in 1734 had served at least once. The average number of years served was 4.8. The equivalent figures for 1779 were 85 percent and 6.2. These are minimum figures. They relate to only three of the major offices, since constables' names are not available. In Woodford, where information is available for all four parish offices, 87 percent of listed jurors between 1759 and 1783 served in an office at least once. These figures were calculated by comparing the freeholders books with officeholders listed in J. E. Oxley, *Barking Vestry Minutes* (1955), 317–27; and E. J. Erith, *Woodford, Essex, 1600–1850: A Study of Local Government in a Residential Parish*, Woodford and District Historical Society Proceedings and Transactions, 10 (1950), 110–30. The Barking list covers four wards, each of which had its own officers, which may partly explain the frequency of office-holding.

79. Although the jurors labeled as esquires were rarely asked to be parish constables, until the last quarter of the eighteenth century non-esquire jurors seem to have served in all four main offices in roughly equal proportions in Woodford—57 percent as churchwardens, 67 percent as overseers, 57 percent as surveyors, and 63 percent

sive office-holding records. In Ardleigh the slightly incomplete information provided by Erith suggests that at least three-fourths of the jurors traceable in the 1796 census served in at least one parish office in their lifetime, and the average number of years served was a minimum of 3.8.[80] Since more than 80 percent of the non-gentry jurors listed for the less populated rural parish of Messing also filled a parish office at least once in the later eighteenth century, with one of these serving thirteen periods of office in fourteen years, this pattern was almost certainly a general one.[81] The vast majority of jurors had some experience of local office, and a considerable number would have had behind them many years of service in administrative posts requiring continued use of the holder's judgment and discretion.

The jurors' experience of group decision making would partly depend both on the customs and power structure of the local vestry and on their own willingness to be present. Their record of attendance was often extensive. The four non-gentry jurors listed for the Surrey parish of Wimbledon in 1762 attended an average of 132 vestry meetings each during the middle decades of the eighteenth century. The eleven listed in 1788 had already clocked up more than 800 vestry meetings and thirty-seven office-holding years between them by that date.[82] While the diaries of vestry members such as Thomas Turner sometimes cast doubt on the sobriety and honesty of the men who attended the meetings, discussions were often prolonged, and the decisions the members reached suggest that they were quite capable of making astute and penetrating assessments of the character and prospects of members of the laboring poor.[83] If jurors were "easily misled" it was not for lack of experience in dealing with, and making group decisions about, the poorer sections of the local community.[84]

as constables. For similar patterns of high parish officeholding experience in London, see chap. 8, text at n. 47.

80. Erith, *Ardleigh*, 36–106, does not appear to record office holding completely. Here, as in Messing, there was a tendency for a few large farmers to dominate the more prestigious post of churchwarden (p. 6).

81. ERO, D/P 188/12/1. Only the years between 1776 and 1792 have been surveyed and linked to jury lists for the years between 1772 and 1783. All six of the non-gentry jurors were nominated for a parish office in these years, but one avoided actually serving.

82. F. M. Cowe, ed., *Wimbledon Vestry Minutes 1736, 1743–88*, Surrey Record Society, 25 (1964), 95–102, 144. One 1762 juror, the shopkeeper Charles Piggott, attended 341 vestries in these years.

83. G. H. Jennings, ed., *Thomas Turner: The Diary of a Shopkeeper* (1979), 17, 37, 45, 57. For the large quantities of liquor consumed, see A Stokes, *East Ham: From Village to County Borough* (Stratford, 1933), 41–57.

84. Not every Essex parish had open vestry debates of the sort recorded by

Many jurors would also have belonged to a variety of other bodies with joint decision-making processes. The membership lists and standing committees of the numerous prosecution associations that grew up in the later eighteenth century usually included several eligible jurors. In 1781 seven of the Ardleigh Prosecution Association's eighteen members were listed in the freeholders books, and the majority of these had also been members of the larger Colchester Association against Horse-stealers since its inception in the mid 1770s.[85] It is hardly necessary to list the many types of social, political, and charity-related associational forms that jurors might have belonged to. As these voluntary associations mushroomed in the later eighteenth century, so, no doubt, did many jurors' experience of committee meetings and joint decision making.[86]

The judgments of the contemporary commentators who labeled serving jurors as ignorant or illiterate are clearly challenged by this analysis of those listed in the freeholders books as eligible for jury service. However, these critics remain unanswerable unless an assessment is made of the relationship between those who actually served on a jury and those who were merely eligible to do so. If, as was sometimes the case in the early seventeenth century, extensive use had been made of talesmen, that relationship might have been highly tenuous.[87] In fact, by the mid eighteenth century, talesmen were rarely used in Essex. On a handful of occasions one or two extra names were added to the assize petty jury panel during the court's proceedings because no more impaneled jurors were available, but that remained an exceptional practice.[88] The right of jury challenge was rarely used, and the need for

Turner. Little is known about the way vestry meetings were run, but it seems unlikely that many were controlled strictly by one or two individuals. For a corrective against an overcomplimentary view of the wisdom of farmers and its application to vestry meetings, see John Clare's portrayals of "rich plain and superstitious" farmer Wormstall or young farmer Bigg, "wise among fools and with the wise an ass." *Selected poems and prose of John Clare*, ed. E. Robinson and G. Summerfield (Oxford, 1978), 19–25.

85. See King, "Crime, Law and Society," 193–236, for an analysis of the growth of prosecution associations in Essex. ERO, D/P 263/8/1; *Chelmsford Chronicle*, 23 June 1775.

86. R. J. Morris, "Voluntary Societies and British Urban Elites, 1780–1850: An Analysis," *Historical Journal* 26 (1983), 95–118

87. The Home circuit assizes were sometimes chronically short of jurors, and widespread recourse to talesmen was one response. Cockburn, *Assize Introduction*, 59–61.

88. Talesmen were also rarely used in other counties. See chap. 10, text at n. 86 In PRO, ASSI 35/206/1, at the end of the petty jury panel for Lent 1766, Samuel

talesmen, whose property qualifications were much lower, was kept to a minimum because jury panels were usually large enough to allow considerable leeway even in the later eighteenth century, when rising caseloads increased the average number of jurors sworn.[89] The sheriff's officials stuck strictly to the book. The assize jurors of 1780, for example, can all be found in the freeholders book they would have used that year.[90] Jury panels appear to have been exclusively drawn from the official lists. "Idle people in rags" almost certainly did loiter around the courts of mid-eighteenth-century Chelmsford, but there is no evidence that they were coopted in any numbers onto the county's juries.

Each type of criminal trial jury had its own particular character in terms of the subgroup of eligible jurors most likely to be found serving on it. Despite the problems caused by the very patchy survival of the quarter sessions jury lists, the Essex jury profiles (Tables 9.1–9.3) show both the well-known division between the grand jury at the assizes and all the other juries, and several more subtle differences. From the estate valuations alone it is clear that by the second half of the eighteenth century the assize grand jury in Essex, as elsewhere, was confined to the county elite (Table 9.3).[91] Nearly half of those who served had estates valued at five times the legal minimum for service as a justice of the peace. Among their foremen were men of the first consequence in the county; Sir William Smyth, Sir John Griffin, and Sir William Maynard all filled the office at some time in the 1760s and 1770s. Many assize grand jurors were on the commission of the peace, a considerable number were active justices of the peace in their divi-

Manning's name has been added in a later hand. Every juror on the panel seems to have been used. Cottu also found that talesmen were rarely used. M. Cottu, "On the administration of the criminal code in England," *The Pamphleteer* 16 (1820): 46–47.

89. The numbers impaneled, that is, those whose initial attendance at the court was demanded—fluctuated but rose only marginally in the long term. (The average panel size of the assize petty jury was 45.25 in 1766–69 and 35.9 in 1770–74; it was always 48 in the 1790s. The grand jury was also standardized at 49 in the 1790s.) However, the number of jurors actually sworn rose between 1760 and 1790 as caseloads swelled and it became increasingly difficult to use just one jury to hear all the cases. (The average number of assize petty jurors serving was 12.95 in the 1760s, 16.18 in the 1770s, 19.7 in the 1780s, and 16.1 in the 1790s. The grand jury averaged only 18 or 19 in the 1760s and 1770s, but by the 1790s this had been standardized at 23.)

90. That is, the 1779 freeholders book: ERO, Q/RJ 1/8. Hay finds a similarly tight use of the books. See below, chap. 10, text at n. 90.

91. This had not been the case in the seventeenth century. Cockburn, *Assize Introduction*, 49–51; Beattie, *Crime and the Courts*, 320–23. In Surrey by the mid eighteenth century, grand juries had been taken over by "gentlemen of the best figure in the county." Beattie, *Crime and the Courts*, 322, quoting William Blackstone, *Commentaries on the Laws of England* (1769), 4:299.

sions, and the majority sat at least occasionally on the quarter sessions bench.

By contrast, the quarter sessions grand jurors, when their occupations can be traced, appear to have been composed almost entirely of farmers, artisans, and tradesmen with an occasional smattering of individuals of rather higher status, who were styled "gentlemen" (Table 9.2). Despite their broad similarity, jurors' occupations also provide some indications of differences between the two types of petty jury. The poorer trades, such as mariners and tailors, were better represented at the quarter sessions, as, of course, were laborers. Those labeled as "gentlemen" were almost nonexistent. The more prosperous trades such as millers, maltsters, and clothiers were more frequently found on the assizes petty jury.[92]

More fundamental differences emerge from the age and estate data (Tables 9.1 and 9.3). On average, grand jurors, whether serving at the quarter sessions or the assizes, were older than petty jurors and were closer in age structure to the eligible jurors as a whole. Petty juries were particularly poorly endowed with men in their sixties, reflecting, perhaps, either the higher estate valuations of older freeholders or their more energetic attempts to avoid serving on the much more arduous lower jury.[93] The estate valuations reveal a distinct hierarchy of wealth among the three non-elite juries. The quarter sessions grand jury contained many more substantial farmers and tradesmen and drew a larger-than-average proportion of its members from estate values between £30 and £100. The assize petty jurors were less wealthy; 60 percent had estates valued at less than £30. Apart from a gap in the highest categories, they represented a fairly typical sample of the freeholders books. Quarter sessions petty jurors were overwhelmingly drawn from the lowest end of the scale, nearly two-thirds having only the minimum estate level necessary to qualify. Thus, in contrast to the interchangeability that often characterized early-seventeenth-century trial juries,[94] each of the four main juries of late-eighteenth-century Essex was distinct in character. A small minority of individ-

92. The use of the courtesy title "gent" remains problematic. Although 2.7 percent of assize petty jurors and 6 percent of quarter sessions grand jurors were so described, the individuals involved would not necessarily have been recognized as members of the gentry by contemporaries. The average estate valuations of the tailors listed in the 1779 freeholders book was £16.0. Maltsters averaged £25.9 and clothiers £50.0.

93. Estate valuations may have shown a tendency to rise with age. Grand jurors not only enjoyed higher status, they also met in private and were able to complete their business in a much shorter time.

94. Cockburn, *Assize Introduction*, 50–51.

uals did serve on more than one jury during their lifetime, and there was no strict division by level of wealth, but each jury covered a particular spectrum, and the wealth structures of the four juries followed a definite order.

The quarter sessions records do not identify jury foremen, but on the assizes petty jury the foreman was much less likely to be from the younger age ranges (Table 9.1). Although the majority of foremen had only small estates, a significantly larger proportion were drawn from the wealthier end of the assize petty jury scale (Table 9.3). Older and better-off jurors apparently stood a rather greater chance of being appointed foremen even though the majority of foremen were neither especially wealthy nor over fifty.

One specific Essex jury list offers insights into a more obscure area of jury practice. The jury that tried Henry Simons for assault and false accusation in 1752 appears to have been a special jury.[95] More than half of its members were drawn from the grand jury panel at the same assizes. Three of them were on the commission of peace, and the remainder had estate valuations that were also in the higher ranges usually associated with assize grand jurors.[96] Their levels of status and wealth therefore tended to be rather higher than the typical pattern for early-eighteenth-century special jurors suggested by Oldham.[97]

Returning to the four main juries, it seems clear that those responsible for impaneling jurors followed specific and fairly consistent policies at both the quarter sessions and the assizes. Although they did not reserve certain particular levels of estate for each type of jury, their selection mechanisms did result in a different spectrum of valuations for each jury. While no direct record of them appears to have survived, some rough policy guidelines were clearly being laid down.

The impaneling policies of the sheriff's officials were not the only factors that influenced the makeup of Essex juries. Many of those called for jury service avoided fulfilling this often-onerous duty either by paying a fine or by successfully pleading special circumstances. Illnesses, especially the diseases and infirmities of old age, were frequently used as excuses. The cryptic comments entered on the petty

95. Sir Gurney Benham's essay, "Strange Story of a Polish Jew," *Essex Review* 69 (1940): 65–70, briefly describes the case and lists the jurors.

96. Four of the seven actually served on the grand jury at that assizes. Apart from those on the commission of the peace, the special jurors estate valuations varied between £90 and £500. Special jurors in Bedfordshire were also drawn from among the grand jurors. J. Godber, ed., "John Salisbury of Leighton Buzzard," in *Some Bedfordshire Diaries*, Publications of the Bedfordshire Historical Records Society, 40 (1959), 50.

97. Oldham, "Origins of the Special Jury," 164.

jury lists included "deaf," "diseased eyes," "wife sick," "infirm," "fits," and simply "not able," as well as some other types of criteria, such as "no freehold," "gone away," "Quaker," or "dead."[98] In most cases, however, the assize and quarter sessions clerks merely wrote "excused" on the jury list. The process by which exemption was obtained can therefore be better approached through jurors' letters, which can sometimes be found in the quarter sessions bundles. By the late eighteenth century, local surgeons often wrote on a juror's behalf. The excuses varied from major illnesses to "painful plax of the leg" and even "lameness of the arm,"[99] but often a rather vague reference to the fact that the patient was undergoing treatment seems to have sufficed.[100] Some jurors wrote directly, claiming urgent business priorities. The timber dealer William Newman claimed that the Michaelmas quarter sessions were "a very ill convenient time for me to leave my home" because he would miss the Braintree fair, at which many "tradesmen round my neighbourhood 20 miles . . . settle with me and give fresh orders."[101] The elderly and wealthy farmer William Haylock, having already used his connections to obtain a previous exemption, wrote again in 1811, advancing the thinnest of health grounds and requesting that "as you have been my friend to get me off before . . . I hope you will be my friend again this time."[102] It is more than possible, as Hutton implied in the 1780s, that the wealthier potential jurors, who could more easily afford the services of a surgeon and who had better opportunities, perhaps, to cultivate the right connections, would in general have found it somewhat easier to avoid jury service. Although it was rare for more than 10 or 15 percent of jurors to be excused from any single panel, and although the majority of exemptions may well have been obtained on genuine health grounds, this would have resulted in a significant reduction in the average wealth of serving jurors.

Some movement in this direction is definitely indicated by an anal-

98. The "no freehold" entries are relatively rare, however, suggesting that few constables made the mistake of listing men who owned no land.

99. ERO, Q/SBb 325/32, 422/51. Broken legs and infectious diseases such as fever and dropsy were also popular.

100. At times it appears that a note from a surgeon was sufficient, no further detail being required. See, for example, ERO, Q/SBb 329/47.

101. ERO, Q/SBb 421/63. Newman achieved his aim. His triennial service was moved to another quarter.

102. ERO, Q/SBb 422/52. Haylock lived in the farthest corner of northwest Essex and at the age of sixty he had every reason to try to avoid this arduous journey. His excuse "that he was likely to catch cold" was hardly persuasive in itself.

ysis of those who did not seek exemption but merely paid the fine exacted for non-attendance. Only 9 percent of quarter sessions grand jurors had estates of £100 or more, while 30 percent of those fined for non-attendance on that jury had a similar estate valuation. Since the fines ranged from £2 to £5 men of considerable estate would not have found them a major inconvenience but some small owner-occupiers stood to lose a significant portion of their annual income.[103] A considerable number only became willing to risk a fine as old age approached. The jurors who were fined at the quarter sessions between 1767 and 1785 included a much larger than average number of men in their sixties.[104] Thus, those who were called to jury service might respond in a number of ways according to their age, material resources, and connections. Overall, their decisions almost certainly reduced the average age and wealth levels of the jurors who eventually served on the three non-elite juries, although the constables who drew up the freeholders lists and the impanelment policies of the sheriff's officers remained the central determining factors.

Since the four main Essex juries each had their own distinctive character by the mid eighteenth century, it is difficult to use them to evaluate the very generalized comments of contemporaries, whose remarks often failed to distinguish between civil and criminal juries, let alone between the four variations of the latter. Nor have I yet been able to uncover any substantial debate within the county about the quality of its jurors. Even though the least prestigious jury in Essex, the quarter sessions petty jury, was drawn from the lowest echelons of the county's eligible freeholders, it does not appear to have suffered from the problems and criticism experienced by its counterpart in Surrey, where until 1770, hundredal presentment juries were used as a basis for petty jury recruitment, and many complaints about unqualified jurors resulted.[105] At a general level, however, the detailed evidence available in Essex does raise many questions about the crit-

103. Seventeen of the fifty-six potential grand jurors fined between 1767 and 1785 had estates of £100 or more. Considerable numbers of freeholders with lower valuations were also willing to pay, however. A total of 48 percent of the fined jurors had estates of less than £40. ERO, Q/SPe 2/3. The estreat books recording these fines have not survived for the assizes in this period. Petty jurors were less frequently fined. The sample is therefore too small. Quarter sessions fines ranged from £1 to £3 but three-fourths were for £2. The assize fines occasionally recorded on the rolls ranged from £2 to £5. Fines of over £4 were not infrequent.

104. ERO, Q/SPe 2/3, when linked to age information in the freeholders books, indicates that 20 percent of fined grand jurors were under forty, 27 percent were in their forties, 25 percent were in their fifties, and 27 percent were in their sixties.

105. Beattie, *Crime and the Courts*, 390–93.

icisms leveled at jurors by their contemporaries. Although they may not have been widely read, jurors were not illiterate. Nor can it be assumed, in view of their wide experience of local office-holding, that they were easily misled. It is difficult to interpret most of the derogatory remarks made by contemporary writers as balanced and well-informed judgments, and a minority, in their less polemic moments, sometimes admitted that lower-status jurors were not without some abilities. The correspondent of the *Gentleman's Magazine* who lambasted both quarter sessions and assize jurors as being so inadequate "that often their slender capacities scarcely enable them to discriminate plaintiff from defendant," had to concede that "there are many husbandmen and farmers very useful and intelligent men."[106] An earlier pamphleteer, while criticizing the ways that jurors were subject to outside influence, stressed the quality of shopkeepers and merchants as jurors.[107]

The pejorative labels bandied about by many elite commentators may well have been based more on their reactions to jurors' decisions than on their knowledge of the actual status and attributes of serving jurors, a theme that is developed further at the end of this essay. They also showed little knowledge of the amount of experience jurors had already gained in the courtroom itself. While Madan admitted that jurors' knowledge of "their duty" would be enhanced by "repeated services" in the court, he seems to have assumed that petty jurors did not usually have any previous experience.[108] Recent research on patterns of jury service in both London and Surrey has suggested that this was a rash assumption.[109] In Essex in the middle of the eighteenth century it was not necessarily an invalid one, but at almost exactly the time when Madan was writing his famous critique, those responsible for the administration of the jury system in Essex decided to alter their impaneling and selection policies in a fundamental way in order to ensure that inexperienced jurors would no longer predominate. This decision may well have had far-reaching effects on the balance of courtroom relations in the county.

106. *Gentleman's Magazine* 62 (1792): 1194.

107. *A dissertation on the constitution and effects of a petty jury* (1737), 18.

108. *Thoughts on executive justice*, 142. Madan contrasted the ability of grand jurors "to know their duty" with the incapacity of petty jurors. He acknowledges that grand jurors "from their repeated services" and because of their higher status might be more capable, but he seems to assume implicitly that petty jurors did not have the advantage of previous experience to draw on.

109. Beattie, *Crime and the Courts*, 385–86; Langbein, "Criminal Trial before the Lawyers," 276. For the later-seventeenth- century pattern, see above, chap. 8, Tables 8.3 and 8.4.

Before the early 1780s, Essex impaneling and jury selection policies did not follow the pattern used in Surrey, where the freeholders of a few towns in close proximity to the court's meeting place were very heavily utilized.[110] In Essex this system would have been completely unworkable because, unlike Surrey, all the major court hearings were held in one town, Chelmsford, which contained relatively few eligible jurors.[111] Instead, the burden of jury service was more evenly spread across Essex. For each specific assizes, jurors were usually drawn from only a few hundreds, but the area from which they were chosen was changed each session so that between 1760 and 1770, for example, every hundred except one supplied men to an assize petty jury panel. Since the system was not based on a strict rotation, it was not entirely equitable, and the burden fell rather more heavily on some areas than on others. However, service was never mainly confined to one section of the county; jurors from distant hundreds were just as likely to serve as those who lived near Chelmsford.[112] This policy, combined with the large pool of men available, meant that few of those listed in the freeholders books served more than once on an assize petty jury in any given decade. Between 1759 and 1774 about 4 percent served twice, and only one served three times. The lack of systematic quarter sessions records makes it difficult to evaluate either the extent to which quarter sessions practice differed from that of the assizes or the frequency with which individual freeholders were impaneled on both quarter sessions and assize juries during this period, but service on both juries was almost certainly confined to a small minority.[113] The overall impression is one of relatively inexperienced jurors. In the late

110. Beattie, *Crime and the Courts*, 382–84.

111. Chelmsford's population in 1801 was 3,755. In 1815 it had just enough eligible jurors for one complete petty jury panel.

112. Staffordshire also had a roughly proportionate system. See below, chap. 10, text at n. 118. In Essex the three most populated hundreds—Becontree, Lexden, and Hinckford—were by far the most frequently called upon. Becontree, situated in the southwestern corner of Essex, contributed 146 men to the 1779 freeholders books and filled 179 seats on assize petty juries between 1775 and 1786. Tendring, in the far northeast of the county, contributed above-average numbers (189 and 119) The Chelmsford hundred had very similar figures (179 and 118), but some fairly central hundreds, such as Waltham (61 and 12) and Dunmow (104 and 20), got off lightly on this jury. However, they may have supplied more jurors for the quarter sessions juries or for the civil side at the assizes.

113. Out of a sample of 141 quarter sessions grand and petty jurors drawn from the period 1775–89, only 12 (8 5 percent) served on an assize petty jury between 1759 and 1800.

1770s and early 1780s the proportion of jurors coming to the assize petty jury with some previous experience rose slightly to an average of between one in six and one in eight, but only a handful had served on more than one previous occasion (Table 9.4).

This pattern changed fundamentally from the summer assizes of 1784 onward. At that point, a new policy based on recalling almost all those who had been impaneled exactly three years earlier was instituted. Some new jurors were introduced into every panel, mainly to replace the minority who had moved, died, or reached the age of seventy in the intervening three years, but the great majority of the previous panel was recalled en bloc. For example, thirty-seven of the forty-eight names on the assize petty jury panel of Lent 1794 can also be found in almost exactly the same order on the equivalent panel of Lent 1791. On some panels the change was as little as 10 percent.[114] The process by which men were selected from these panels for actual jury service was also reformed. Usually at least six and sometimes as many as nine of the twelve selected for the initial trial jury had served

Table 9.4. Experience Levels of Assize Petty Jurors and Foremen in Essex, 1770–1809

	Assize Jurors with Experience					Foremen		
	No. of Jurors Serving	No. with Previous Experience	Level of Previous Experience	Percent Experienced	Average Experience Level	Percent with Previous Experience as Jurors	Level of Previous Experience	Percent with Previous Experience as Foreman
1770–74	157	5	6	3	1.2	14	1.5	0
1775–79	165	27	29	16	1.1	31	1.0	0
1780–84	175	21	24	12	1.1	33	1.0	15
1785–89	219	115	149	53	1 3	67	1.5	27
1790–94	148	81	139	55	1.7	86	1.7	21
1795–99	174	110	243	63	2.2	92	2.6	33
1800–09	108	69	184	64	2.7	100	3.6	82

NOTES: The level of previous experience consists of the total number of previous sittings as jurors among those who came to sit on a jury in the period specified. Average experience levels are calculated only for the subgroup of jurors with at least one previous experience. The jurors at the summer assizes 1784 were placed in the 1785–89 period to highlight the change that occurred in that session. The 1800–09 period is based on the sample years 1800, 1803, 1806, 1809. Experience levels are based on a survey of ASSI 35 from 1758 onward.

114. Only five out of forty-eight names were different between the Summer assize panels of 1796 and 1799. A few may have managed to get themselves removed even though they remained resident and eligible.

three years earlier.[115] Presented with the opportunity of selecting any twelve jurors from a panel of forty-eight, all but a handful of whom had usually turned up at the court, the assize officials did not use procedures based on random selection but deliberately chose to ensure that at least half of those sworn had already done jury service.[116] This change was not confined to the assize petty jury. Both the quarter sessions jury panels began to be selected on the same three-year repeating pattern from about this time. Only the assize grand jury, many members of which were already serving year after year, was not affected.[117]

For many separate blocks of individuals, the mid 1780s therefore marked the beginning of a triennial pattern of jury service that continued well into the nineteenth century. Both Samuel Cole of Finchingfield and Samuel Hudson of Dedham, for example, became locked into the pattern when they served on the petty jury at the summer assizes in 1782 at the ages of thirty-nine and forty-four respectively. Thereafter they found themselves making the journey to Chelmsford every three years until the early 1800s, when, by reaching the age of seventy, they both obtained exemption. Neither of them served every time he was impaneled, but after most of these journeys they sat together on the same jury. Given the long distances involved, they must have spent well over a month of their lives in getting to, serving at, and returning from the assizes during these two decades.[118] Extended service of this kind became the typical pattern at the assizes, and to a lesser extent at the quarter sessions, in the late eighteenth and early nineteenth centuries.[119] For example, thirty of the forty-eight jurors

115. The policy seems to have been that by only swearing about half of the previous jury, some experienced jurors would remain available to form the core of a second jury should one be necessary.

116. In civil cases statute law required that the names be drawn from the panel by ballot, but the legal framework in criminal cases seems to have been more flexible. Dogherty, *The Crown circuit companion* (1799), 12. The practice on the Northern circuit when Cottu traveled it was similar to that of Essex. Cottu, "Administration of the criminal code," 41.

117. Many assize grand jurors served very regularly. Samuel Bosanquet, John Strutt, and Joseph Strutt, for example, sat on every jury between 1796 and 1800. At least seven men sat on more than half the assize grand juries sworn between 1766 and 1774.

118. Assize juries spent an average of between two and three days actually hearing cases in the 1790s, but when the court's preliminary procedures and at least a day each way for traveling are included, the better part of a week was probably consumed on most occasions (Hudson lived thirty miles from Chelmsford).

119. This pattern continued well into the nineteenth century. For example, James Winterbourne of Southminster made eight trips to serve on assize juries between his first appearance at the age of twenty-seven in 1788 and his fiftieth birthday in 1811.

impaneled at the Lent assizes 1791 can be found on all four panels between 1791 and 1800, while at least a third of both the grand and petty jurors impaneled at the October quarter sessions in 1796 can also be found on all four juries between 1787 and 1796.

Why was such a decisive change in policy made at this point? Since Essex was the only Home-circuit county to introduce a strict triennial system, the initiative clearly came from within the county rather than from the assize officials, but there is no record of any discussion of jury selection policies at the quarter sessions.[120] The timing of the change, which coincided with a large post-war boom in recorded crimes, is highly suggestive.[121] At a time when court schedules were in danger of becoming unduly clogged or extended by rapidly expanding gaol calendars, more experienced jurors may well have been favored on the grounds that they might require less time to instruct and less time to decide their verdicts. More experienced jurors may also have been viewed as a possible means of changing the quality or nature of verdicts during this period of acute anxiety about law-and-order issues, but lacking any more substantial evidence, it seems likely that the convenience of the court was the most pressing reason for the reform.

The inequity of the new system is easily demonstrated. It confined jury service to three relatively small groups and froze the geographical distribution of jury impanelment so that the areas unfortunate enough to be picked between late 1781 and the summer of 1784 bore the main burden from that point onward.[122] However, I have found no real signs of overt opposition to the new policy. Freeholders were certainly well aware of the inevitability of the three-year cycle, but in their letters to the quarter sessions at least, they appear to have accepted its legitimacy. "I do not . . . spurn my regular turn which I understand to be once in three years," wrote one juror in 1811 in an attempt, not to avoid jury service, but simply to change the quarter of the year on which it fell.[123]

It is difficult to assess how far the disadvantages of jury service—the time and money lost, the waiting around, and the possibility of incur-

120. ERO, Q/Smg 24. The sessions books make no reference to any decision or discussion. Unfortunately, the sheriff's records are not available, nor are those of the assize clerks.

121. King, "Crime, Law and Society," 35, 64–73; Hay, "War, Dearth and Theft," 121–23.

122. After 1784, when a name was dropped from the panel a substitute was usually chosen from the same parish.

123. ERO, Q/SBb 421/63.

ring the displeasure of customers, creditors or neighbors through an unpopular verdict[124]—may have outweighed the advantages. Regular jury service could perhaps have enhanced the status of the individual juror within his own community. To some it was probably a welcome break from work routines and domestic duties, a chance to visit the county town and mingle with those who gathered there for one of the most important social events of the year. The triennial system does not seem to have produced a significant increase in the number of jurors seeking exemption or wishing to pay a fine, but these are not adequate indicators of attitudes, particularly in view of the fact that the payment of a fine on one occasion did not enable an individual to break out of the three-year cycle.[125]

Whatever the responses it evoked in the jurors themselves, the new triennial system immediately produced a much more experienced group of jurors, quadrupling at one stroke the percentage of serving jurors with previous experience of service (Table 9.4). In the long term it also produced an accumulating level of experience. In the mid 1780s the great majority of experienced jurors had served at only one previous assizes, but by the opening years of the nineteenth century most were sitting at their third or fourth assizes, and a significant subgroup had already served on half a dozen occasions. Not only were two-thirds of assize petty jurors and nearly all their foremen (Table 9.4) able to draw on the lessons of previous jury service, but their level of experience was also deepening to the point where some would already have heard not dozens but hundreds of cases. By the late eighteenth century, despite the fairly frequent use of two juries to cover the caseload of a specific assizes,[126] each petty juror was involved in verdicts on an average of about twenty indictments. For those jurors who were usually selected for the initial petty jury, which did the bulk of the work at most assizes, an average year would have involved making evaluations on about thirty defendants.[127] Thus, when the victualer John Webb, who served at the Lent assizes every third year after 1783,

124. This last disadvantage is stressed in the anonymous pamphlet, *A dissertation on the constitution and effects of a petty jury*, 17–18.

125. Those who had been fined the last time they were on the panel almost always found themselves on the panel again three years later. Jurors may also have gained some intrinsic satisfaction from being involved in an institution so widely lauded as the great defender of the Englishman's liberty.

126. Toward the end of a significant proportion of assize hearings a second jury would be sworn in to speed things up by dealing with cases under the *nisi prius* judge.

127. Many indictments involved several defendants.

was sworn onto the petty jury in 1801, he had already heard nearly two hundred cases.

The new system had important effects not only on individual jurors but also on their collective consciousness. Every assize and quarter sessions jury after 1784 contained a core of men who had already sat together at a previous session of the court. Usually these men formed a majority, and as the eighteenth century drew to a close they got to know each other very well. Eight of those who sat on the initial petty jury at the summer assizes in 1791 sat together on every subsequent triennial occasion until the early nineteenth century.[128] Men of the same town often found themselves serving together. Four Bocking men—a victualer, a cardmaker, a grocer, and a blacksmith—traveled up to the same Lent assizes every third year between 1783 and 1801. The logical thing to do in this situation was to hire a horse and cart and travel up together, as William Newman and Charles Peers of neighboring Braintree did in 1811.[129] Jurors not only entered the courtrooms of late-eighteenth-century Essex with extensive experience of trying various types of cases, they also knew many of their fellow jurors well from past interactions both inside and outside the courts.

Although the verdicts and decision-making processes of juries were almost certainly linked in a variety of ways to the backgrounds and experience levels of the jurors themselves and to the degree of cohesion they achieved as a group, the precise relationship between jury behavior and jury composition is extremely difficult to assess. Eighteenth-century jurors have left virtually no record of their opinions. On the rare occasions when a diarist records his jury service, a cryptic note, such as James Oakes's entry "I was upon the jury," usually sufficed.[130] Can the main evidence available, the verdict patterns themselves, suggest any fruitful hypotheses about the relationship between rising experience levels and jury behavior?

One theory sometimes advanced by modern commentators—that

128. The eight included the long-serving Samuel Cole of Finchingfield and Samuel Hudson of Dedham, as well as Edward Betts of Dedham, John Burrell of Thorndon, Edward Graygoose of Royden, William Seabrook of Boreham, William Hooper of Kelvedon, and Isaac Watson of Braintree. Three of these men were foremen at some time between 1790 and 1802.

129. ERO, Q/SBb 422/53.

130. Suffolk Record Office, Bury, 1461 Diary of James Oakes, 24 Mar. 1784. Henry Purefoy confined himself to describing his fellow grand jurors as "gentlemen of figure." L. G. Mitchell, ed., *The Purefoy Letters, 1735–53* (1973), 49–50.

older and more experienced jurors are much less likely to acquit than young and inexperienced ones[131]—receives no support from the Essex verdict patterns of the late eighteenth century. During the first fifteen years of the new triennial system, acquittal rates increased steadily from 27 percent in 1780–84 to nearly 37 percent by 1795–99. In Essex as a whole, the advent of older and more experienced petty jurors coincided with a movement toward greater leniency. Was this a causal relationship? As jurors became more experienced they may either have become inherently more lenient or have felt able to follow their own inclinations toward mercy more often as they gained in confidence and independence in their relationship with the bench. However, the use of rising acquittal rates as supporting evidence for this alternative hypothesis is fraught with difficulties. Although the triennial system continued to produce highly experienced jurors and foremen well into the early nineteenth century (Table 9.4), after 1800 the rising trend of acquittal rates was reversed and a continuous decline set in, a decline that was paralleled in the national statistics.[132] By 1815–19, less than a quarter of those indicted before Essex petty juries were found not guilty.

More important, perhaps, a wide variety of changes, whose precise effects are often impossible to estimate, could have produced the rising Essex acquittal rates between 1785 and 1799. Jurors' decisions, taken at the crossroads of the judicial system, were sensitive not only to changes in trial procedure, such as the introduction of stricter rules of evidence or the introduction of lawyers into criminal trials,[133] but also to pre- and post-trial actions. The decisions of committing magistrates, prosecutors and witnesses might alter the proportion of less clear-cut cases passed on to the major courts.[134] Jurors may also have

131. On the effects of jury inexperience, see W. R. Cornish, *The Jury* (1968), 173–77. S. S. Diamond and H. Ziesel, "Jury Behavior," in *Encyclopedia of Crime and Justice*, ed. S. H. Kadish (New York, 1983), 931, link younger jurors with acquittals. J. Baldwin and M. McConville, *Jury Trials* (1979), 101-5, note the prevalence in current work of two assumptions—that acquittals are more frequent when jurors are inexperienced and that young jurors are much more systematically inclined toward the defense, being better able to identify with the accused—but use their Birmingham-based research from the 1970s to cast doubt on these assumptions.

132. King, "Crime, Law and Society," 306.

133. Both of these processes were clearly occurring during this period, although they had begun well before the 1780s. Beattie, *Crime and the Courts*, 352–75; Langbein, "Criminal Trial before the Lawyers," 307–11; Langbein, "Eighteenth-Century Criminal Trial," 84–134.

134. A period of acute anxiety about crime such as the 1780s might, for example, persuade prosecutors or magistrates to push a higher proportion of cases through the pre-trial filters and into the major courts even when the evidence was not

reacted to changing post-verdict judicial strategies, counteracting the stricter pardoning policies and rising hanging rates of the mid 1780s with a more lenient attitude.[135] The wide range of alternative and sometimes contradictory explanations tends to obscure the relationship between jury experience levels and changing acquittal rates. Some answers may emerge as parallel work is done on other counties. A comparison of acquittal levels in 1782–87 and 1799–1800 indicates that Essex assize verdict patterns did not deviate substantially from those of the Home circuit as a whole during the first fifteen years of the triennial system, despite the fact that most of the other counties on the circuit do not appear to have introduced any equivalent method of ensuring that a high proportion of their jurors were experienced.[136] In Kent, for example, where only a handful of assize jurors in 1801 had served on a jury in the previous five years, acquittal rates were almost identical to those of Essex in both 1782–87 and 1799–1801.[137] At this early stage of research the quantitative evidence therefore suggests that the triennial system may have had relatively little impact on aggregate acquittal levels. However, this does not mean that it had no influence on the balance between the judge and the jury or on the internal dynamics of the jury itself.

Despite the central role played by the assize judge in trial proceedings and the many areas of basic agreement between the jurors and the bench, judge-jury relations in the later eighteenth century were balanced in such a way that jurors might also have an important influence.[138] Jurors were most heavily reliant on the judge's legal knowl-

particularly conclusive. Acquittal rates might then rise in response to a decline in the quality of the evidence being presented by prosecutors. Alternatively, of course, jurors might wish to come down harder on offenders, which could produce a countervailing movement.

135. Romilly certainly believed they might well do this. However, acquittal rates in Essex continued to rise after hanging rates returned to normal at the end of the 1780s. S. Romilly, *Observations on a late publication entitled Thoughts on executive justice* (1786), 88–89.

136. Home circuit acquittal rates were untypically low in the period 1799–1800, but the parallel trend is clear. Essex acquittal rates were 32.7 percent of found bills in 1782–87, and the figure for the rest of the circuit was 34.4 percent. In 1799–1800 the acquittal rates were 30.1 percent in Essex and 30.2 percent elsewhere.

137. Essex acquittal rates were 32.7 percent in 1782–1787 and 28.9 percent in 1799–1801. In Kent the figures were 32.5 percent and 29.2 percent. Other Home-circuit counties may have had rather larger numbers of experienced jurors but not, it seems, a rotating system.

138. For a more extended discussion of the factors affecting judge-jury relations in this period, see King, "Crime, Law and Society," 321–33. This theme will be further developed in P.J.R. King, *Crime, Justice and Discretion: Law and Society in Es-*

edge, and therefore most susceptible to his influence, where none of them had previous experience of hearing a particular kind of case. Faced by a highly exceptional plea of insanity in 1754, for example, the Chelmsford assize petty jury capitulated to Judge Ryder's forceful arguments for a guilty verdict.[139] However, the presence of highly experienced jurors such as Samuel Hudson or John Webb, a few of whom could be found on most Essex petty juries by the 1790s, meant that fewer types of cases would put the jurors at this kind of disadvantage in relation to the judge. As their practical knowledge of trial procedures, of verdict options, and of what was possible or permissible in judge-jury relations grew, the jurors' capacity for independent action and their tactical sense of how best to put their wishes into effect must have also increased considerably. Although the judge remained the formal legal expert, the jurors had their own expertise, which probably increased both the speed at which cases were dealt with and the jurors' own confidence in their decision-making capacities. Most assize judges did not serve regularly enough, or over sufficiently extended periods on this circuit, to develop a personal knowledge of specific triennially appearing sets of jurors.[140] Although this may have been less true at the quarter sessions, few trial judges would have gained a more intimate relationship with the jurors through the triennial system. It was the relationship between the jurors that was reshaped.

What specific effects did the new system have on the internal dynamics of jury decision making? The content and nature of jury interaction is extremely difficult to assess. Contemporaries generally noted the exceptional rather than the typical. Grand jury decisions were shrouded in secrecy,[141] while those of the petty jurors were only reported in detail when they had had protracted difficulty in reaching a unanimous verdict and had therefore resorted to illegal or highly questionable solutions. In the sessions book of the Havering liberty, which exercised quarter sessions jurisdiction over a small area of

sex and South-eastern England, 1740–1820, forthcoming. It can only be touched on here in relation to the specific issues raised by changes in jury composition.

139. King, "Crime, Law and Society," 321.

140. Of the forty-five judges who presided at the Essex assizes between 1750 and 1800, only six came to Chelmsford more than ten times. The majority came only once or twice. One or two developed a regular pattern of coming, but they might sit on either the Crown or the civil side, and it is unlikely that continuity was sufficient to enable them to develop a personal knowledge of the jurors. PRO, ASSI 31/3–18.

141. The oath taken by the grand jurors contained a secrecy clause, but the petty jurors' oath did not. P. Devlin, *Trial by Jury* (1956), 46–47; Dogherty, *Crown circuit companion,* 18–20.

south Essex, a memorandum of 1730 records that "the jury could not for several hours agree on their verdict, seven being inclinable to find the defendant guilty and the others not guilty. It was proposed by the foreman to put twelve shillings in a hat and hussell most heads or tails whether guilty or not guilty. The defendants therefore were acquitted the chance happening in favour of not guilty."[142] A better-publicized case in the 1780s, that, like the Havering one, did not involve an indictment for felony, revealed a similar incident in which a jury that was divided six to six had tossed to decide the verdict. This case also prompted Lord Mansfield to discuss a previous occasion when a verdict had been set aside because the bailiff had observed the jury determining their verdict by ballot.[143]

At the Sudbury borough court, a few miles north of Essex, the jurors of the October sessions in 1791, having kept the court waiting through numerous adjournments from noon until 10 P.M., could still only agree that they had "a wish to be released" and that "unanimity of verdict . . . would never be obtained if they were closeted forever." However, "oppressed as they were by hunger and thirst," at midnight they came to a second decision "to burst open the door of the room in which they were confined and to betake themselves everyone to his own house." For this exodus they were in danger of being prosecuted themselves, and the first response by the mayor of Sudbury was to consult the attorney general about the correct legal action to be taken.[144] However, there were constraints on the authorities in such a situation. An extended debate had arisen during the eighteenth century over the unanimity rule and its tendency to force dissenting jurors through physical duress "to break their oath and commit a kind of necessary perjury."[145] The *Gentleman's Magazine*, in commenting on the case, recommended compromise rather than coercion:

> The institution of juries . . . has its defects. That of a compulsive union of sentiment and opinion is one of them; this effect of it seldom happens; and happening so seldom is better passed over than, by criminal process against jurors, incurring

142. ERO, Q/HM.1. 16.7 1730. The case was one of assault, and the clerk seems to have recorded this procedure without any sense that it might be illegal, but illegal it undoubtedly was. Burn, *Justice of the Peace*, 2:486.

143. The practice was revealed by two of the jurors. *The Times*, 9 Nov. 1785.

144. *The Times*, 17 Oct. 1791.

145. The pamphlet *A dissertation on the constitution and effects of a petty jury* recommended a secret ballot. Another pamphlet, *On Unanimous verdicts by jurymen* (1798), took a very critical view, a line of which is quoted here. This piece was reprinted and then attacked in the *Gentleman's Magazine* 81 (1811): 319–20, 407.

> the risk of weakening in the public mind the reverance due to the great palladium of our freedom.[146]

Such cases suggest that the court's control over jury behavior in these specific circumstances was extremely limited. A lack of information would usually have prevented any action being taken against jurors who chose illegal methods of decision making such as a show of hands or a coin toss. More important, if the jurors refused to accept the physical coercion implicit in the ruling that until they had agreed on a verdict, they were "to be kept together . . . without meat or drink, fire or candle," the full force of the law could not be brought to bear upon them without calling into question the legitimacy of the jury system itself.[147] However, these forms of jury interaction, which all occurred after a petty jury had retired from the court, were highly exceptional. The vast majority of petty juries made their decisions in a few minutes in a huddle in open court.[148] On the relatively rare occasions when petty jurors did retire, less extreme forms of dispute resolution were usually sufficient. Forceful argument, teasing, accusations of bias, and finally threats of personal or commercial ostracism were, according to at least one contemporary observer, the primary ways in which dissenters were persuaded to change their minds.[149]

Since the vast majority of eighteenth-century trials ended in an extremely brief and highly public petty jury meeting, protracted discussions of any sort were rare, and deadlocks, whether they resulted in illegal practices or not, were wholly untypical. How then were decisions made and what impact did the growing presence of substantial numbers of experienced jurors have on these processes? The importance of the foreman in jury decision making, implied in Hutton's skeptical observation that "juries are chiefly conducted by *one* of their own body," has recently been stressed by Beattie.[150] However, the basis on which foremen were selected remains unclear. Modern jurors report a wide variety of methods from bailiff-initiated selection

146. *Gentleman's Magazine* 61 (1791): 1059.

147. Burn, *Justice of the Peace,* 2:485.

148. Cottu, *Criminal Justice in England*, 54, 143; Beattie, *Crime and the Courts*, 397.

149. *Constitution and effects of a petty jury,* 15–16. Unanimity not being required of grand juries, such processes may have been unnecessary, although the privacy enjoyed by grand jurors may have encouraged debate.

150. Hutton, *Dissertation on juries*, 16; Beattie, *Crime and the Courts,* 397–98. Hutton, who was trying to justify procedures involving adjudicating bodies that were much smaller than petty juries, had a vested interest in making this assertion.

of the best-dressed man or random choices based on seating arrangements to more considered decisions by the jurors themselves on the basis of previous jury service, personal willingness, or other criteria.[151] A similarly mixed set of selection processes appears to have been used at the late-eighteenth-century assizes. Random selection or pre-trial manipulation cannot be entirely discounted. Sometimes the person whose name appeared first on the petty jury panel, drawn up well before the assizes, was later sworn as the foreman—a process that implies that the jurors themselves may have had little influence on the selection in these cases.[152] However, most foremen were not chosen in this way, and the tendency for foremen to be slightly older, wealthier, and marginally more experienced than the average juror suggests that in the majority of cases, some sort of considered decision was made, although it is not clear how far the jurors were directed or channeled by court officials during the process.

The policies juries employed in selecting foremen showed very little consistency, and many foremen do not appear to qualify on any of the measurable criteria. The aggregate tendencies seen in Tables 9.1–9.4 disguise the fact that on the majority of juries the foreman was not the wealthiest, oldest, or most experienced man. Thomas Saward, foreman in the summer of 1777, and Robert Mosebury, foreman three years later, were in both cases the sixth oldest and fourth wealthiest members of their juries. Neither of them was the first person named on the original panel, and neither had any previous experience of sitting on an assize petty jury, although in both cases men with that kind of experience were available within the relevant jury. In all, twelve of the seventeen foremen appointed between 1790 and 1796 were sitting with men of greater experience than themselves.[153] The post of grand jury foreman at the assizes may have been coveted for the status it carried, but on the lesser juries it seems to have been sufficient to find someone of reasonable capacities who was willing to serve. On the

151. D. Barber and G. Gordon, *Members of the Jury* (1976), 15–16, 41, 98, 105.

152. About 30 percent of those who headed the original panel were made foremen in the 1760s. Between 1795 and 1803 the figure was 21 percent. There seems to be no way of ascertaining whether the impaneling officers deliberately selected which freeholder would be put at the top of the list.

153. Only four of the seventeen had previous experience as foremen despite the fact that the triennial system had been operating for more than a decade. Although a quarter of the foremen had estates that were valued at £100 or more, which made it extremely unlikely that anyone wealthier would be on their jury, an equally large proportion were drawn from the lowest estate levels, which meant that most of their fellow jurors would have been wealthier than they were.

few occasions when a man labeled as a "gentleman" found himself on an assize petty jury, he stood a much greater than average chance of being selected as the foreman, but gentlemen also sat under foremen who were yeomen, tradesmen, or clothiers.

In assessing the impact of foremen on jury decision making, their status, age, and experience are probably less important than the personal attitudes and predilections of the individuals concerned. These are rarely susceptible of historical analysis, but it is possible to trace just over 10 percent of the foremen who served between 1775 and 1802 in the membership lists of Essex prosecution associations, and further links of this kind might have been possible if every association had published regular listings.[154] However, membership in a prosecution association does not necessarily imply any particular view of the way the criminal law should be administered, and a roughly similar proportion of all Essex farmers and commercial men belonged to an association in these years.[155] In some cases, serving as a foreman may have stimulated an individual to start an association. Less than two years after his first service as an assize petty jury foreman, Thomas Stuck's name appeared at the top of a long subscription list for the newly formed Halstead Association, but there is no direct evidence that his experience as the chairman of a jury induced him to take part in this initiative.[156]

Service as a foreman on one triennial visit did not necessarily mean that the individual concerned would hold the same position the next time he was impaneled. More than 80 percent of the foremen who served between 1790 and 1796 were also impaneled three years later, but less than two-thirds actually served on a jury, and only one-third took a second term as a foreman.[157] The selection system may have been tightened around 1800,[158] but a limited amount of interchangeability in relation to the foreman's position seems to have continued throughout the first twenty-five years of the triennial system. John

154. See King, "Crime, Law and Society," 193–236, for a detailed discussion of the development of these associations. Many of them produced no membership lists. Others produced only one, so members joining later cannot be traced.

155. Ibid.

156. ERO, D/P 96/8/3. Stuck's name was second out of seventy-odd subscribers.

157. Nearly a quarter were impaneled but did not serve. The institutionalized foreman found in seventeenth-century Kent (see above, text at n. 70) had no parallels in Essex between 1740 and 1800.

158. The proportion of foremen with previous experience as foremen suddenly increased after 1800. See Table 9.4.

Briant, for example, who had been foreman over John Freeborn of Great Maplestead in 1781, found himself under the latter's leadership in 1784 and once again foreman of a jury containing Freeborn in 1787. Similarly, in March 1797 William Hummerston served under the foremanship of the Great Coggeshall clothier Thomas Powell, and in 1800 the positions were reversed. It is therefore possible that the triennial system devalued the position of the foreman to some extent. In juries that contained several experienced men well acquainted with each others' views, the technical leadership could probably have changed hands several times over the years without damaging the decision-making ability of the triennial caucus. Foreman interchangeability was not necessarily a common phenomenon but it raises important questions about the degree to which juries' decision-making processes can be portrayed as revolving around one individual.

In many respects, Beattie's model, which stresses acquiescence by the bulk of the jurors in the verdict arrived at by one or two dominant figures, led normally by the foreman,[159] is a highly convincing one in view of the brief nature of jury deliberations. However, the available evidence is so thin that, in relation to acquittals at least, an alternative model is worth detailed consideration. The unanimity rule may well have posed considerable problems for potential jury leaders. If any juror or group of jurors with previous experience or with a sufficient measure of personal confidence strongly advocated an acquittal, the foreman might find it difficult to dissuade them. To override a minority in favor of a guilty verdict would probably have been easy,[160] but those who held out for a more merciful solution may have had important strategic advantages. By the eighteenth century there seems to have been a tendency to favor leniency in cases where there was any disagreement.[161] Adam Smith, for example, implied this in commenting that

> The laws of England with regard to juries are only defective in one point . . . the whole jury must be unanimous, which renders the office of a juryman a very disagreeable service. A case

159. Beattie, *Crime and the Courts*, 397–98.

160. This would be true apart from exceptional circumstances, such as the prosecution of excise officers or their helpers, when the social groups from which the jurors were drawn were highly antagonistic toward the accused.

161. This tendency may, indeed, help to explain why acquittal rates were so high despite the fact that very few defendants seem to have mounted an effective defense. However, strict evidentiary rules, the nature of judge-jury relations, and general notions about the evaluation of guilt or innocence were more central King, "Crime, Law and Society," 330–33.

> may appear to you more clear than it does to me . . . and yet there is a necessity that one of us should swear contrary to our conscience. In criminal cases there is little danger, people are generally disposed to favour innocence and to preserve life. But in civil cases people are not so much troubled, they are not so much disposed to favour.[162]

Paley clearly felt that the unanimity rule increased acquittals: "the effects of this rule are not so detrimental, as the rule itself is unreasonable" he concluded, "in criminal prosecutions it operates considerably in favour of the prisoner; for if a juror find it necessary to surrender to the obstinacy of others, he will much more readily resign his opinion on the side of mercy than of condemnation."[163]

The frequency with which foremen found it necessary to "surrender to the obstinacy of others" and to avoid time-consuming deliberations by agreeing to an acquittal despite their own less merciful inclinations may also have been increased by the fact that these decisions were made in open court. Before they were rebuilt in the late eighteenth century, the Essex courtrooms were small and were often packed with people of every description, including those whom the *Chelmsford Chronicle* described as "improper company."[164] If Hawkins was correct in asserting that in the eighteenth-century courtroom "everyone interests himself on the side of the prisoner, and hopes, by his zeal on his behalf, to be distinguished as a man of more than ordinary humanity," merciful jurors would usually have had much of the courtroom audience behind them and would often have been sustained by a sense that they were "sure to gain the applause of vulgar hearers."[165] By contrast, the jury leaders opposing them, "fearing the censure that others have incurred by a contrary treatment of prisoners," might be constrained to relinquish their advocacy of a conviction or go for a quick compromise in the form of a partial verdict.[166]

Did the jury have any defensible space in the courtroom that they could call their own? Madan depicted late-eighteenth-century courtroom crowds as noisy and disorderly, and suggested that although they

162. *Lectures*, 52.

163. W. Paley, *The principles of moral and political philosophy* (1785), in *The Works of W. Paley*, ed. E. Paley (1825), 4:422–23.

164. *Chelmsford Chronicle*, 7 Mar. 1788.

165. J. Hawkins, *Life of Samuel Johnson* (1787), 521–23, quoted in L. Radzinowicz, *A History of English Criminal Law* (1948), 1:27.

166. Ibid.

were mainly composed of "the low rabble,"[167] they were hardly restrainable and were in the habit of satisfying their curiosity "by forcing themselves into and about the courtroom."[168] Far too little is known about the layout of eighteenth-century courtrooms, about the extent to which jurors' decision-making processes were visible to, or influenced by, the surrounding audience, about the composition and attitudes of that audience, or about the countervailing influence the judge's close proximity might have had to draw any final conclusions about this issue. However, eighteenth-century courtroom crowds may have had both their own notions of justice and a basic understanding of how to put pressure on the key decision makers at the trial. After the capital conviction of a young boy at Chelmsford in 1800, even the judge, who was usually protected from such pressures to some extent because reprieves were decided in private after the court had been disbanded, was subjected to a considerable degree of popular disapproval. "The scene was so dreadful on passing sentence," he recorded, "to pacify the feelings of a most crowded court, who all expressed their horror by their looks and manners, after stating the necessity of the prosecution . . . I hinted something slightly of its still being . . . open to clemency."[169]

Not every juror, whether he was experienced or not, took an active part in the proceedings. Some, through reticence or laziness, were in effect sleeping partners—sometimes literally so! Madan complained that "the heat of the court joined to the fumes of the liquor, has laid many an honest juryman into a calm and profound sleep and sometimes it has been no small trouble for his fellows to jog him into the verdict."[170] It is also possible, although I have found no direct evidence of this, that court officials sometimes weeded out troublesome or overscrupulous jurors either by dropping them from the jury during the assizes or by simply not recalling them three years later.[171] However, while the active participation of all long-serving jurors cannot be

167. *Thoughts on executive justice*, 145.

168. Ibid., 146. For a rare depiction of the jury and a crowded courtroom, see J. A. Sharpe, ed., *Crime and Law in English Satirical Prints, 1600–1832* (1986), 236–37.

169. Radzinowicz, *History of English Criminal Law*, 1:13, quotes this case.

170. *Thoughts on executive justice*, 143–44.

171. One or two jurors were sometimes released halfway through the life of a jury and a substitute sworn. However, some of those dropped in this way were impaneled again three years later, implying that they were let off for personal reasons rather than in order to remove unwanted elements. One correspondent of *The Times* of 14 July 1791, was convinced "that if a juryman takes down notes or asks any questions that may seem to indicate a mind that means to be directed by its own reason—he is never troubled again with a summons as a juryman."

assumed, it seems likely that the advent of more experienced jurors in the later eighteenth century increased the number of occasions when initiatives not arising from the foreman or one or two jury leaders had an impact on trial outcomes. In the majority of trials the evidence was either overwhelming or obviously weak, and here the foreman or informal jury leader would merely have obtained the nod from the rest of the jury. In a significant minority of cases, however, the desire not to hold up the court or to be seen in the wrong light may have led the foreman to capitulate almost immediately when faced with a group of jurors who indicated that they were in favor of a more lenient approach.[172]

Experience levels were not necessarily the most important aspect of the relationship between jury composition and behavior in this period. The dominance among jurors of men in their forties and fifties may have had a significant impact on the kinds of offender they favored with a partial verdict. Most jurors knew what it was like to bring up a family, and many had adolescent children of their own. Their tendency to give more lenient verdicts to very young offenders and to married men with families to support probably reflected, in some measure, their ability to empathize with these types of offenders.[173] As farmers, tradesmen, or artisans whose wealth was usually, if not always, substantial enough to enable them to employ servants in husbandry or apprentices, they were well aware of the need to keep these young adults under control. Most servants were in their late teens and early twenties, and this was also the age group most harshly treated by juries and judges alike.[174] Although minor pilfering by servants was usually dealt with informally, young adults who refused to adopt a settled way of life would probably have been seen by most jurors as a potentially threatening group toward whom leniency would be ill-advised and misplaced.[175]

Although these verdict patterns are very fragile and incomplete indicators of the jurors' underlying attitudes, it is clear that as business-

172. It remains possible that a rough poll was sometimes taken. Cottu, in attempting to explain why the unanimity requirement did not lead to extended jury deliberations, suggested three possibilities: "that they scarcely ever have to pronounce upon any other than manifest crimes . . . that they are determined never to bring in a verdict of guilty, except on accusations established on the most incontestable proofs, or that the minority make it a sort of duty to join themselves to the majority." Cottu, *Criminal Justice in England*, 55.

173. King, "Decision-makers," 37–38.

174. Ibid., 34–42.

175. For a discussion of patterns of crime and young adult life styles, see King, "Crime, Law and Society," 94–127.

men and parish officers, jurors had many opportunities to develop skills that would be useful in assessing the character and credit of both witnesses and accused. Such judgments were central to the outcome of a large number of eighteenth-century trials, but the underlying criteria on which they were based remain obscure. Jurors had their own particular interests, attitudes, and fears. Farmer-dominated juries had a tendency to convict sheep thieves on the slimmest of pretexts,[176] and in a study of Essex juries during the 1820s, Janet Gyford has suggested that juries composed mainly of farmers were generally more willing to convict. The counsel for the defense in a well-publicized Essex arson trial during that decade certainly worked on that premise. He challenged and removed every farmer on the petty jury, and the resultant collection of tradesmen duly acquitted the prisoner.[177] Commercial men may well have been perceived by many contemporaries as less likely to be swayed by this kind of partiality. Nearly two-thirds of the assize petty jury foremen whose occupations can be traced were tradesmen or artisans, and only about a quarter were farmers (Table 9.2). This was clearly the view of one eighteenth-century pamphleteer, who was sure that "of all the kinds of men capable of being on a petty jury from county squire to £5 farmer there are none, generally speaking, so rational or conscientious as the merchants."[178]

Given the wide range of wealth levels from which jurors might be drawn and the possible differences between the major occupational groups, it would be unwise to suggest that jurors on the three non-elite juries necessarily represented the views of a coherent social group. However, in unraveling the meaning of the contemporary discourse about juries and jurors' abilities, it is helpful to think in terms of three groups: the elite commentators, the jurors of the three non-elite juries, and the laboring poor.

The pamphlets, newspaper articles, and *Gentleman's Magazine* correspondence that attacked the jurors' status and abilities were mainly written by wealthy members of the eighteenth-century elite. Labels such as "plebeian" or "low country people" are relative terms, their meaning depending mainly on the viewpoint and social standing

176 Ibid., 328.

177. J. Gyford, "Men of Bad Character: Property Crime in Essex in the 1820s" (M.A. thesis, Univ. of Essex, 1982), 6–8, 84.

178 *Constitution and effects of a petty jury*, 18. The occupational figures for foremen, like those for jurors in general, may be slightly distorted by the fact that a larger proportion of farmers were not given an occupation in these records. This could not, however, entirely explain the very wide difference in foreman selection patterns.

of the writer. Many commentators used terms such as "ignorant" or "illiterate" somewhat indiscriminately when referring to those whom they considered to be their social inferiors. The jurors' views would have been very different. They did not describe themselves as plebeians, a term defined by a dictionary published in 1774 as "of the common or lower people."[179] Their letters to the *Chelmsford Chronicle* use phrases with a very different resonance: "the substantial farmers," "the principal inhabitants," "the great body of freeholders," or as one correspondent put it, "middling farmers . . . the most useful set of people in the kingdom."[180] Jurors were virtually never drawn from the bottom half of the population in terms of wealth. As local officeholders, ratepayers and sometimes substantial employers, they had long since differentiated themselves in lifestyle and attitudes from the laboring poor.[181] The vicar of Ardleigh might argue, as he did in his assize sermon in 1795, that the accused faced "a jury of his peers . . . not strange to him, but of his own vicinage, whose habits of life corresponded with his own."[182] But although in many parishes the ranks of jurors included small owner-occupiers well outside the top quarter of the local income structure, few farmers or substantial tradesmen were tried for felonies. The great majority of the accused were laboring men.[183]

Late-eighteenth-century Essex witnessed many disputes between the laboring poor and the ratepayers, farmers, and tradesmen who exercised so much day-to-day authority at the parish level. Conflicts over gleaning rights, wages, and poor-relief payments were often intense, and they suggest a fundamental division in interests and "habits of life" between these two groups,[184] a division that may well have been growing wider in the late eighteenth century.[185] Nor can the jurors' actions be easily interpreted as reflecting the attitudes or inter-

179. J. Barclay, *Dictionary* (1774).

180. *Chelmsford Chronicle*, 7 May 1773; and King, "Crime, Law and Society," 401–2.

181. K. Wrightson and D. Levine, *Poverty and Piety in an English Village: Terling, 1525–1700* (New York, 1979), 173–85, K. Wrightson, "Aspects of Social Differentiation in Rural England, c. 1580–1660," *Journal of Peasant Studies* 5 (1977). 33–47.

182. *Chelmsford Chronicle*, 13 Mar. 1795.

183. King, "Decision-makers," 30.

184. King, "Crime, Law and Society," 271–90.

185. For a debate about this using Essex material, see R. Wells, "The Development of the English Rural Proletariat and Social Protest, 1700–1850," *Journal of Peasant Studies* 6 (1978–79): 115–39; A. Charlesworth, "The Development of the English Rural Proletariat and Social Protest, 1700–1850: A comment," *Journal of Peasant Studies* 8 (1980–81): 101–11.

ests of the gentry elite. When account is taken of the literacy levels, social backgrounds, office-holding, and jury-related experience of many eighteenth-century jurors, the derogatory language of the elite commentators appears less as a description than as a cry of frustration. When the Surrey justice of the peace Richard Wyatt recorded that an accused man had been "acquitted by an ignorant jury," he was not making an observation about the jurors' educational backgrounds but venting his anger that jurors did not always follow the paths committing magistrates felt that they should.[186] The passage in which Madan labels jurors as "low and ignorant" follows a detailed discussion of their tendency to produce verdicts "according to their feelings but against their oath."[187] To Madan the acquittals of these merciful jurors not only undermined the deterrent effect of the criminal law, they also threatened gentry interests more directly. These "feelings" could not be relied on. "This may be a very dangerous business," he wrote, "for if a jury can give a false verdict in favour of a prisoner in one case, they may also give a false verdict, in another, in prejudice to the party accused." He went on to discuss the case of "a person of fortune" who was "malicously indicted . . . and as malicously convicted" at the Southwark quarter sessions. This "venerable . . . gentleman" was "a good deal disliked in his neighbourhood," and the petty jurors convicted him "against law as well as fact contrary . . . to the direction of the court" despite being sent out a second time to reconsider their verdict.[188] A correspondent of the *Gentleman's Magazine* writing in 1777 made a similar link. Worried by the fact that a dragoon called out to assist some customs officers had been indicted and initially found guilty under the Black Acts for accidentally shooting at a suspected smuggler, he advocated raising the property qualification considerably and described "the bulk of our juries" as "composed of men in every way unfit for the task, and who, though sworn to give their verdict according to the evidence have often been known to find a verdict in direct opposition thereto."[189]

Eighteenth-century jurors showed considerable independence of mind in certain specific types of cases (in some treason and sedition trials, for example, or in disputes involving game, excise officers, or dissenters). Various categories of civil cases also reveal the jurors tak-

186. E. Silverthorne, ed., *Deposition Book of Richard Wyatt, J.P., 1767–1776*, Surrey Record Society, 30 (1978), no. 13.

187. *Thoughts on executive justice*, 139.

188. Ibid., 139–40.

189. *Gentleman's Magazine* 47 (1777): 214.

ing a stand for the tenant farmer against the landowner.[190] In Essex in 1754 a civil jury humiliated the gentry-dominated game association by finding in favor of three young men from substantial farming or artisan backgrounds who were accused of poaching. A large crowd of farmers then gathered outside the court to celebrate, and similar rejoicings were reported all over Essex.[191] Jury independence is not as easy to exemplify in run-of-the-mill property-crime cases, where policies were less polarized and jury attitudes more opaque. A full analysis of the complexities of judge-jury relations in such cases lies outside the scope of this article,[192] but there are many signs that the jurors were not necessarily any more tied to the attitudes of the elite than they were to those of the laboring poor. The grand jury at the assizes obviously reflected gentry interests, but the approaches of the other three criminal trial juries reflected both the fissures and the solidarities of what may broadly be called, for want of a better term, the middling sort. This was not a monolithic group, but there were growing signs in Essex during the second half of the eighteenth century that they saw their interests as often very separate from those of the gentry.[193] The gap between the elite's frequent characterizations of the jurors as illiterate, easily led plebeians and the reality of literate, office-holding jurors of some wealth and considerable decision-making experience may have been less an error of judgment than an expression of a deep, if only partly perceived, conflict of interest.

Acknowledgments

I would like to thank Middlesex Polytechnic for its support during the period I was writing this paper.

190. For the jury and seditious libel, see Green, *Verdict According to Conscience*, 318–55. For civil cases and a more general discussion, see King, "Crime, Law and Society," 322–26.

191. *Norwich Mercury*, 24 Aug. 1754.

192. For further analysis, see King, "Crime, Law and Society," 321–33. See also Green, *Verdict According to Conscience*, 356–83.

193. This theme will be developed in King, *Crime, Justice and Discretion*.

Ten

The Class Composition of the Palladium of Liberty: Trial Jurors in the Eighteenth Century

Douglas Hay

In 1789 William Hutton described the English jury in most unflattering terms:

> What *was* and what *is* a Jury? It *was* instituted by Alfred, one of the best of kings, who appointed, that a number of people should be summoned, all men of property, equal at least, in that day to two or three thousand pounds in this; and as knowledge is often attendant upon property, they were justly supposed to be tolerable judges, who, by deciding the interest of others decided their own. . . . But time, that great corrupter of things, which is every moment working changes, has wrought a thorough alteration in that palladium of British liberty, *the Jury*. The foundation of this grand building is yet perfectly sound, but the superstructure is rotten, and when the fabric totters, it calls loudly for repairs. The better informed and more opulent persons, to whom this duty of attendance belongs, escape through private avenues, such as pride, business, interest, pretended sickness, secret fees, etc. The weight, therefore, of this important concern falls upon the lower class, who are utterly unable to sustain it. The bailiff finds it difficult to procure the number wanted, even without the requisite qualifications, and may at last be said to have mustered twelve bodies without a head! This officer has been so distressed for a Jury, that I have seen him pick up idle people in rags, while loitering in the open Hall, at Warwick.[1]

Hutton's attack ran very much against the stream of published comment in the eighteenth century. Praise for the English jury resounded

1. William Hutton, *A dissertation on juries; with a description of the hundred court: as an appendix to the Court of Requests* (Birmingham, 1789), 22–23.

in England and America, and in much of Europe. Blackstone, as well as Tory and then Whig critics of executive power and many visitors from countries that knew only the closed courtrooms and fact-finding judges of inquisitorial systems, all celebrated this most characteristic institution of the common law, perhaps especially in criminal trials. And as many historians have remarked, the enthusiasm so widely expressed by the rich and the learned who published their praises also extended down the social scale, so that it was entirely characteristic (to take one instance of many) for the artisans alarmed by the Combination Act of 1799,[2] which provided for summary conviction of trade unionists, to demand the protection of "the grand palladium of English liberty."[3] It seems certain that the trades addressed Parliament with arguments calculated to appeal to it.[4] What also seems certain, however, is that the cumulative tradition of such rhetoric, and even recent practical experience in political trials, made the protection of the jury trial and instances of jury nullification of the exact letter of the law known and valued to artisans.[5] Indeed, because many poorer men and women knew the weak version of that tradition, sanitized and institutionalized in the form of "pious perjury" (finding the prisoner guilty of a reduced charge), the jury often did not show as hostile a face even to laborers and paupers as they may have feared.[6] Judges quite often addressed such grateful defendants with the words, "Prisoner, you have had a merciful jury."

Nonetheless, contemporary criticisms of the jury are not impossible to find. Hutton was anxious to defend a jurisdiction where juries were not used, the Court of Requests, and therefore attacked their deficiencies in the competing county and hundred courts. Other critics

2. 39 Geo. III, c. 81; *Commons Journals* 55 (1799–1800), 645–46, 665, 672, 706, 712 [*sic*].

3. The quotation is a reference to Blackstone, who had castigated the spread of summary jurisdiction some forty years earlier: *Commentaries*, 3:380–81, 4:350.

4. I. Prothero, *Artisans and Politics in Early Nineteenth-Century London* (1981), 43, J. V. Orth, "English Combination Acts of the Eighteenth Century," *Law and History Review* 5 (1987): 175–211, at p. 200.

5. Notably the acquittals of Hardy and others in the 1790s, cases in recent and vivid memory for many artisans. See F. K. Prochaska, "English State Trials of the 1790s: A Case Study," *Journal of British Studies* 13 (1973): 63–82; Clive Emsley, "An Aspect of Pitt's 'Terror': Prosecuting for Sedition during the 1790s," *Social History* 6 (1981): 155–84; E. P. Thompson, *The Making of the English Working Class* (1964), 135–36.

6. For the law, and frequency, of partial verdicts, see Beattie, *Crime and the Courts*, 424–30; D. Hay, "War, Dearth and Theft: The Record of the English Courts," *Past and Present* 95 (1982): 154–56; idem, "Crime, Authority and the Criminal Law: Staffordshire, 1750–1800" (Ph.D. diss., Warwick Univ., 1975), 408, 477–81.

had a host of complaints.[7] Writers suspicious of judicial dominance deplored compliant juries, but judges confronted with verdicts of which they disapproved regretted that the jurors had taken their constitutional independence seriously. From time to time, enthusiasts of a harsher enforcement of the criminal law condemned partial verdicts, suspiciously high acquittal rates, or acquittals or convictions in particular cases known to them personally or notorious from press accounts. But despite their various concerns, most of these critics brandished one explanation for the acts of such wayward juries: their members were unfit men who were not of the standard required by the letter or spirit of the law. The standard most often invoked was that of social class, which was measured by real property and was equated with intelligence or education. The charge was that "substantial" men too often did not serve when they should have, due to favoritism or corruption, and that the poor and ignorant were sworn instead.

William Hutton's remarks were typical of this kind of argument, identifying jurors "narrow in understanding" as men "of the lowest class." Near the beginning of the century a very popular pamphlet on legal reform argued that the members of "a mean Jury, that is a common Jury, (for they throughout *England* are mean Men)" were "very ignorant" and hence the lackeys of judges. He called for a jury of gentlemen in all cases.[8] Martin Madan, who thought that too many acquittals occurred in the 1780s, attributed much of the problem to the fact that trial juries in the provinces were too often composed of "low and ignorant country people."[9] Thurlow, the solicitor general in 1770, predicted the results if "the wisdom of petty juries, country assizes, and untutored mechanics" were to decide the law as well as the facts of a case: "Adieu to precision, adieu to consistency, adieu to decorum." Adieu also, in this case, to convictions, for Thurlow's principal concern at the time was the possible refusal of juries to accept judicial doctrine in prosecutions for seditious libel.[10] And Perceval,

7. See below.

8. [An Attorney], *Proposals Humbly offer'd to the Parliament, For Remedying the Great Charge and Delay of Suits at Law, and in Equity*, 2d ed. (1707), 15. In the fifth edition (1725) a qualification of £50 was suggested. See below, n. 49. For the distinction between a "common" and a "special" jury, see below. Hutton, too, deplored compliant jurors. See below, n. 12.

9. *Thoughts on Executive Justice, with Respect to the Criminal Laws, Particularly on the Circuits*, 2d ed. (1785), 148.

10. *Parliamentary History*, vol. 16 (1813), col. 1146 (27 Nov. 1770). Thurlow was defending Mansfield's position on seditious libel: that juries decided fact, not law, and that whether a writing was a libel was a question of law. To decide otherwise, said Thurlow, was to reduce precedent to "confusion, contradiction and absurdity." For the

the prime minister, in defending the powers of the bench in 1810, said of juries that, considering "what description of persons" composed them, it was obvious they were more prey to popular passions.[11]

Observers, of course, were not likely to complain of "untutored mechanics" when they agreed with their verdicts. The sources thus present us not only with endless panegyrics of the jury but also with many denunciations of the low station of the ordinary trial juror. Moreover, both the celebratory rhetoric and the criticism concerned an institution that appeared in many forms, and this fact alone makes historical judgments about both the praise and the blame difficult. The plethora of juries, the variety of administrative means used to create them, and the significant differences between counties as well as courts were virtually never discussed by critics and commentators.[12]

Juries were an extremely important aspect of civil life in the eighteenth century. At the center of the common-law world, in Westminster Hall, the courts of King's Bench, Common Pleas, and Exchequer all functioned continuously with jurors in term time. The verdicts of those jurors decided great issues in the glare of metropolitan publicity. But juries were also important in England because they were ubiquitous. In many of the thousands of manors throughout the country, the manorial court jury, or homage, was still active, particularly where open-field agriculture was still practiced. Such jurors made detailed regulations for the agrarian regime of their villages, levied fines on offenders, and confirmed the property rights of copyhold tenants. Coroners' juries, also ancient in origin, probably sat with greater frequency than before in the eighteenth century as a result of legislation of 1752 that encouraged coroners to seek out corpses for the sake of

contemporary argument that juries in some sense could or should decide law as well as fact, see Green, *Verdict According to Conscience*, pt. 3.

11. *Parliamentary Debates*, vol. 15 (1810), cols. 373–74.

12. Hutton's principal target was the jury of the county court (and perhaps the hundred court), which heard civil cases and whose members he described as "of the lowest class, collected from the shop, the street, and the alehouse, who, having no character to keep, have none to lose; equally narrow in understanding, and in fortune; humbly submitting to direction, and, by echoing back the words of the Judge, become the magpies of the Court." Hutton, *Dissertation on juries*, 43. The passage quoted at the beginning of the paper appears to be a general comment on all juries, however, as it is followed by an example from a common-law trial at *nisi prius* (where a petty jury was ignorant) and a criminal trial at either quarter sessions or assizes (where a grand jury was vigilant) Ibid., 24–25, 26–29. But the very mixture of examples from very different courts and with different outcomes suggests that Hutton's criticisms, like those of so many others, can hardly be taken as reliable evidence unless the author makes clear exactly what he means to criticize and how commonly he finds the fault to exist. This almost no critic bothered to do.

the fee, if they were not already moved to do so for the public interest.[13] Under statutes of Henry VI and Henry VII, other juries could be summoned to inquire into the concealments of other inquests, of forcible entry and detainer, and of riots. Juries of county and hundred courts continued to hear and determine lesser civil suits in many areas where they were not yet moribund. Important civil actions were heard by juries at assizes (on the *nisi prius* side of the court) twice a year in most counties of England.

The most important and public presence of juries, however, was at criminal trials, where petty or trial juries, and usually grand or presenting juries, were impaneled many times every year in every corner of the kingdom in the principal criminal courts of quarter sessions and assizes, as well as in the supreme court of King's Bench at Westminster.[14] Most criminal prosecutions led, in fact, to full jury trials, an immense contrast to their relative rarity today. Of the thousands of men who sat on these juries (for being male was, until 1919, one of the necessary legal qualifications for service)[15] we know relatively little. Ignorance can lead to incorrect conclusions about the social composition of eighteenth-century juries, especially if we rely on scattered contemporary references of the kind already cited.[16] The most dubious account suggests that criminal trial jurors came from "every segment of the community," including day laborers, which was the poorest group but for paupers. If this were indeed the case, the jury would have been a broadly democratic (albeit sexist) institution a remarkable two centuries before most men had won the vote from a notably reluctant propertied ruling class. The argument also ignores the significance of statutory property qualifications for jurors, the most

13. *Wiltshire Coroners' Bills, 1752–1796*, ed. R. F. Hunnisett, Wiltshire Record Society, 36 (Devizes, 1981); idem, "The Importance of Eighteenth-Century Coroners' Bills," in *Law, Litigants and the Legal Profession*, ed. E. W. Ives and A. H Manchester (1983), 126–39.

14. A grand jury, which heard the prosecution evidence *in camera* in order to decide whether to send the accused for trial before a petty jury, was required for all prosecutions on indictment. When proceedings were by criminal information in King's Bench, no grand jury was struck, and prosecution for murder could be begun on a coroner's inquest without a finding by a grand jury. Such prosecutions without indictment were, however, few in number in most counties.

15. Sex Disqualification (Removal) Act, 1919, s. 1. The one exception was the jury of matrons who investigated for pregnancy on the writ *de ventre inspiciendo*. See J. C. Oldham, "On Pleading the Belly: A History of the Jury of Matrons," *Criminal Justice History* 6 (1985): 1–64.

16. Henceforth, the term *jury* without qualification can be taken to mean the ordinary petty (trial) jury hearing criminal cases at courts of quarter sessions or assizes.

important of which was a 1692 requirement of freehold land rated at £10 per annum.[17]

Such qualifications had existed for centuries, since at least 1414, when the sum had been forty shillings.[18] Of course, a statutory qualification may not represent actual practice. Two problems in particular were mentioned by contemporaries: that such laws were not enforced, and that the stated sums were eroded by inflation. One scholar has suggested that the property qualification declined from the sixteenth century and that by 1692 the new standard of £10 was in fact worth only 25 percent of the forty shillings in 1414.[19] The next change was not enacted until 1825, and we might conclude that in the eighteenth century the qualification was further reduced in real value, especially during the pronounced inflation after mid century. Certainly this appears to have been the belief of Hutton.[20] If even the eroded qualification was unenforceable because of the great need the courts had for jurors, the suggestion that many were relatively poor men becomes more plausible.[21]

In what follows I argue that this was emphatically not the case. The social standing of the actual and potential jurors in the counties of Northampton and Stafford suggests that whatever the nature of juries in the sixteenth and seventeenth centuries, they were certainly not

17. J. H. Langbein, "Albion's Fatal Flaws," *Past and Present* 98 (1983): 107–8, a critique of my description of the "sharp" property qualification and its probable effects in D. Hay et al., *Albion's Fatal Tree: Crime and Society in Eighteenth-Century England* (1975), 38–39. Langbein's assertions about eighteenth-century jurors rest entirely on one quotation from Martin Madan (above, n. 9), an Elizabethan reference (including the quotation, taken from J. B. Samaha, "Hanging for Felony: The Rule of Law in Elizabethan Colchester," *Historical Journal* 21 [1978]: 763, 781–82), and an equally irrelevant eulogy of the moral probity of modern American jurors. He cites but does not discuss the statutory qualification, and he entirely ignores the extensive late-seventeenth- and early-eighteenth-century legislation designed to ensure that the qualification was enforced, for which see below. Indeed, Langbein offers no relevant evidence about the status of the eighteenth-century jury. See also below, nn. 134, 147.

18. For a chronology of the qualification statutes, see J. C. Oldham's very useful appendix to his article "The Origins of the Special Jury," *University of Chicago Law Review* 50 (1983): 214–21.

19. Oldham, "Origins of the Special Jury," 149–50.

20. Quoted at the beginning of this chapter.

21. Writing of the period to 1730, and citing sixteenth- and seventeenth-century evidence, especially the effect of the frequent use of talesmen, Oldham concludes that "Overall, the freehold requirements were, if not a complete failure as a method to ensure honest and intelligent jurymen, of very limited value." "Origins of the Special Jury," 146–47. It is not clear why men without sufficient freehold must be presumed unintelligent or incapable of dealing with what was a wholly oral procedure. (The fear that they might be more easily corrupted, a separate argument, undoubtedly has weight and is considered below.) On talesmen in the eighteenth century, see below.

composed of the poor or even men of average wealth after 1730, when legislation was passed to strengthen the qualification statutes. Jurors were of much higher social standing than most of the men and women whom they tried, or indeed, than the general population. The "common" jury was possibly becoming more rather than less exclusive in the course of the eighteenth century. Ideology, in the sense of class-specific beliefs about the social order, is in fact the source of the contempt that, as we have seen, many literate contemporaries expressed for the jury. The prisoners tried by those jurors were faced with a different reality.

Moreover, the creation of a socially unrepresentative trial jury was a deliberate, conscious policy. In addition to legislation to raise the status of the common jury, Parliament provided for "special" juries, whose members, outside London, were usually from the highest ranks of county society. Taken together, the law ensured that by the second half of the eighteenth century, jury trials were to the advantage of wealthy defendants, propertied prosecutors, and (what was not foreseen in 1730) the state. For the great majority of defendants and the few prosecutors who were poorer than their adversaries, the carefully structured social inequalities of jury trial were manifest and dangerous. They could believe that an unrepresentative jury was better than no jury at all, but they could have no doubt that the jury was a site of significant class power in the legal system rather than a neutral institution broadly representative of all of English society. By the mid-nineteenth century, even some judges realized that such views were commonly held, and they worried about the consequences for the legitimacy of English justice.

The Law: The Property Qualification

The question of who appeared on criminal-court-trial juries[22] was determined by both their qualifications as required by law and the law's implementation (or its negation) by administrative officers, notably the undersheriff, the clerk of the peace at quarter sessions, and the high and petty constables of the county.

The requirements of the law were embodied in common-law rulings but also in a mass of statutes. Peel informed Parliament in 1825 that there were about sixty statutes in force dealing with the qualifi-

22. I.e., "common" juries. On grand juries, see below, text accompanying Table 10.8. On special trial juries, see below, text at n. 55.

cations of assize jurors and another twenty dealing with the impaneling of juries.[23] There were a number of exemptions and disqualifications of particular kinds,[24] but the central policy of legislation was to set a minimum property qualification. In corporate towns, cities, and boroughs, inhabitants worth £40 in personal property were liable by legislation of 1531; for the City of London it was 100 marks in lands, tenements, and goods by an act of 1512, but the eroded value of the qualification was raised in 1730 to £100 in real or personal property, and jurors had to be householders.[25] In the county of Middlesex, because there were small numbers of freeholders and because many jurors were needed for the common-law courts at Westminster and the many criminal trials at the Old Bailey, it was enacted in 1731 that all leaseholders of £50 in that county were also liable to jury service.[26]

For most of the country, however, the general county property qualification was the one that mattered. A qualification act of 1664, requiring £20 annual value in real property, apparently was allowed to lapse some years later.[27] New legislation in 1692 set the requirement at £10 annual value of land or rents for the freeholders or copyholders whose names were included in the panel of possible jurors that the sheriff returned to the writ of *venire facias*.[28] In 1730, tenants of £20

23. *Parliamentary Debates*, 2d ser., vol. 13 (1825), col. 798. See also vol. 12 (1825), col. 966, when he referred to eighty-five statutes dealing with the impaneling of juries.

24. On the latter, see below, text at n. 66.

25. 3 Geo. II, c. 25, s. 19.

26. 4 Geo. II, c. 7, s. 3.

27. 16 & 17 Chas. II, c. 3 (1664). The statute was in force not until 1677, as stated in Oldham, "Origins of the Special Jury," 145–46, 220, but rather for three years "and to the end of the next session of Parliament," probably 1668. (I am grateful to Professor Oldham for pointing out his error.) Michael Dalton, *Officium Vicecomitum. The Office and Authority of Sheriffs* (1670), 87, cites the older qualifications, suggesting that the attempt to rely on the 1664 act in the 1680 case of *AG.* v. *Blood, Christian et al.* (see below, n. 148) was without foundation. The 1664 act's qualification of £20 in freehold lands (£8 in Wales) was applicable to all jurors, including talesmen, at the central common-law courts, assizes, nisi prius, gaol delivery, and quarter sessions. The statute provided a penalty of £5 for sheriffs returning unqualified jurors and £10 for sheriffs excusing jurors from appearing, and it required the return by sheriffs of names of qualified jurors to Easter sessions for review by the justices. The act appears not to have been renewed when it lapsed in 1667. In its general terms it anticipates the later, more elaborate legislation described below.

28. 4 & 5 W. & M. c. 24, ss. 15, 18; in in Wales, £b. If the sheriff, coroner, or "other ministers" included names of people without this property qualification on the panels of jurors returned, the substantial penalty of £5 applied. The practice in cities, boroughs, and corporate towns was unaffected by s. 17. (The legislation was further continued by 9 Geo. I, c. 8, s. 2.) Although copyholders are named in the act and certain

value of land on long leases of five hundred years or for terms on lives were also made eligible.[29] When not enough such jurors attended court, or when challenges or exemptions reduced their numbers, statutes had long provided the alternative of talesmen—that is, sheriffs could select jurors from the crowd in open court, a *tales de circumstantibus*.[30] Decisions in the seventeenth century disallowed talesmen in the courts of corporate towns, cities, and boroughs,[31] and a tales could only be had when judges were acting under certain commissions.[32] But where talesmen were allowed, the 1692 statute set a property qualification of £5.[33]

The property qualification was the most important of the legal tests as to who could be a juror, since (if it were enforced and if the sums prescribed were actual rather than nominal) it would exclude a large proportion of the population.[34] The property qualification raises the three main questions about the class composition of the trial jury considered in this chapter. First, what position in the social hierarchy of wealth did those with freeholds of at least £10, or with long leases of £20, occupy? Second, did practical exigency or systematic corruption result in the swearing of jurors of lower property qualifications—either from the panel, or talesmen—and if so, how often? Third, can the class significance of juries be "read" from their composition, or were juries distinctive in other ways that might be important in determining whether they performed as unbiased judges (in the eyes of the law or of the accused) of their fellow citizens?

Jurors and the Social Structure

A freeholder or copyholder who in the mid eighteenth century owned land assessed at an annual rental value of £10 had, in a county like Northampton, an average of about 35 acres, depending on the kind of

tenants were qualified by a later statute (3 Geo. II, c. 25, s. 18), the legislation was usually referred to as the freehold qualification.

29. 3 Geo. II, c. 25, s. 18.

30. Talesmen were provided for in civil cases by 35 Hen. VIII, c. 6, and extended to criminal trials and actions on penal statutes in 1557 by 4 & 5 P. & M. c. 7, s. 3. On their history after the 1696 statute, see below, text at n. 46.

31. *Basely* v. *Basely* (1647), Sty. 16; *Ball* v. *Knight* (1731), Fitz-G. 274.

32. See below, n. 86.

33. 4 & 5 W & M. c. 24, ss. 18, 19. In Wales, £3. See below, n. 74.

34. The other legal qualifications are best treated in the context of the administration of the law. See below.

land and the history of assessment in the parish.[35] This last point is crucial, for it explains why inflation ceased to reduce the jury qualification in the eighteenth century. Before the 1690s the freehold qualification appears to have been interpreted as the yearly revenue, or the value of the rents.[36] From 1692 the newly assessed land tax provided a ready record of values, although it also assessed some offices and other property and varied somewhat in its weight between counties. In 1730 Parliament enacted that the land tax returns (with poor rates) were to be the test of jurors' qualifications.[37] Comparison of land tax returns with jury lists in the late eighteenth and early nineteenth centuries shows that this continued to be the procedure.[38] But, as is well known, land-tax assessments remained fixed at those of 1692 throughout the eighteenth century. An assessment more or less equal to a rack-rent in 1692 declined to a third or a quarter of actual rental value by the end of the century. Thus the Northamptonshire freeholder assessed at £10, holding perhaps thirty-five acres, had land renting between £17 and £35 a year or more in the 1790s, when rents were from 10*s*. to 20*s*. an acre and higher. The great rise in rents in the second half of the century did not result in higher assessments, with the result that a fixed assessment (such as the jury qualification) selected men with higher and higher rental values. It could even select men of greater relative wealth if the rise in rents exceeded that of other sources of income.[39]

The relative status of the £10 freeholder can only be estimated by making a number of assumptions. The produce of arable land was about four times the rental, or (for this example) between £70 and

35. This estimate is based on the land tax sample described below, nn. 97, 98.

36. See the quotations from the 1560s and 1660s in Oldham, "Origins of the Special Jury," 149.

37. 3 Geo II, c. 25, s. 1.

38. But see below, text at n 102, for evidence that different counties made different use of the assessments in order to achieve the same results.

39. A rise in income shares of the top 35 percent of society between 1759 and 1801 was probably in large measure due to the increased income of freeholders and landlords. P. H. Lindert and J. G. Williamson, "Reinterpreting Britain's Social Tables, 1688–1913," *Explorations in Economic History* 20 (1983): 94–109, Tables 2 and 3; and "Revising England's Social Tables, 1688–1812," ibid. 19 (1982): 398 The drop in the relative position of "lesser freeholders" (see text at n. 43), if the estimates are accurate, applies to the minimally qualified juror; wealthier freeholders moved from the ninety-third percentile in 1759 (the average of Massie's two higher categories of freeholder) to the ninety-fifth in 1801–3, suggesting that wealthier jurors shared in the increased income of landed society, a fact also suggested by much contemporary comment on the marked increase in the wealth of farmers, particularly during the French wars. "Farmer" was the single most common occupational designation of Staffordshire jurors, accounting for over half their number (see below, Table 10.1).

£140.[40] Such a freeholder was very commonly also a tenant on other lands and hence was likely to have greater revenues than this estimate. Given the mixed nature of agriculture in the county, it would nonetheless appear that the minimally qualified £10 juror in Northamptonshire stood above the median of the social group that Patrick Colquhoun, in an estimate for 1801–3, termed "lesser freeholders," with an average annual family "income or expenses" estimated at £90.[41] The corresponding group in Joseph Massie's estimate of 1759 had an annual income of about £50, and in the 1780s, the decade considered in detail below, the average for the group was therefore perhaps £70.[42]

Using this lowest estimate of the average income of the barely qualified juror, we can make a first approximation of his relative importance in the whole social order. Reducing the category estimates of Massie and Colquhoun for all occupational and status groups to continuous distribution curves (Lorenz curves), "lesser freeholders" fall at about the eighty-fifth percentile in 1759 and at the seventy-fourth in 1801–3.[43] That is, three-quarters of the adult males, by these figures, were too poor, even if their entire wealth were in land, to qualify as jurors.[44]

The crudity of such estimates is evident, and closer study of actual populations of jurors is essential. We know that from the beginning the land tax was a formal assessment that had a varying relationship to current land values in different counties.[45] A more serious short-

40. William Pitt, *General View of the Agriculture of the County of Northampton* (1809), 34, citing Donaldson's figures for 1794 and Arthur Young's of 1791.

41. Lindert and Williamson, "Revising England's Social Tables," Table 4. This is also Colquhoun's original, unrevised figure.

42. Massie used three categories rather than Colquhoun's two, and the average of the two lowest gives £57, using the revised estimates in Lindert and Williamson. To make a conservative assumption about the distribution between these two groups, £50 is chosen as the equivalent to Colquhoun's "lesser freeholder." Massie's original figures, averaged, give £38. See also n. 43 below.

43. If Massie and Colquhoun's original figures are used, the standings are the seventy-first and seventy-fourth percentiles. Lindert and Williamson make a convincing case that Massie omitted building craftsmen, miners, and paupers from his table, a consequence of which was to understate greatly the numbers of the laboring poor. "Revising England's Social Tables," 394–95. Therefore, in the text I have given the results of the Lorenz curve based on their revisions.

44. Of course, a much smaller proportion of the population actually qualified, because many masters, tradesmen, and professionals in the higher income categories did not own enough (or any) freehold, copyhold, or land on long leases, or were disqualified on other grounds described below.

45. For the use of the land tax and poor rates in compiling lists of eligible jurors, see below, and see below, text at n. 102, for differences between counties.

coming is that administrative practice in compiling lists of eligible jurors may have been haphazard, corrupt, or changing.

Finding the Qualified Juror: The Statutory Procedure

Inefficiency and abuse had certainly been common in the recent past. The short-lived act of 1664 had been directed at the "abuses in Sheriffes and other Ministers, who for reward doe oftentimes spare the ablest and sufficientest, and returne the poorer and simpler Freeholders lesse able to descerne the Causes in question, and to beare the charges of appearance and attendance thereon . . . ."[46] The act of 1692, which set new qualifications, and one of 1696, which provided for better lists of the qualified, were clearly directed to the same problems. The latter referred to the "partiality and favour of sheriffs, the corruption of officers, and many other evil practices" that had made jury duty a grievous burden for honest jurors and had "very frequently" caused "unfit persons," taken as talesmen, to serve as jurors. The judges themselves had decided a few decades earlier that talesmen could not be allowed in inferior courts of corporations, as such persons would likely be "both profligate and unfit."[47] And King's Bench allowed the exemplary procedure of a criminal information to be exhibited by private individuals against defendants who had conspired to get a verdict for a defendant in another trial by being chosen talesmen on his jury.[48]

Such recurrent concerns were expressed again in a popular pamphlet of 1725, whose author denounced "the Meanness and Corruption of Jurors, and . . . the accursed Knavery practised in returning of them, which is Poison at the fountain of Justice, and Rottenness in the very Heart of our Laws, and by which many Men have unjustly lost their Lives and Estates." He particularly blamed undersheriffs, arguing that even high penalties (such as had been enacted as part of the 1692 qualification statute and increased by acts of 1696 and 1704) could not deter them from "the Crimes they have been so long and so

46. 16 & 17 Chas. II, c. 3, s. 1. Oldham notes that the language is almost identical to that of 27 Eliz. I, c. 6 (1584–85), which had set a qualification of £4. "The Origins of the Special Jury," 145 n. 34. For other complaints from the seventeenth century and earlier, see ibid., 142–43, 144 n. 31; Cockburn, *Assizes*, 112, 118; Cockburn, *Assize Introduction*, chap. 6.

47. 7 & 8 Wm. III, c. 32; *Halsbury's Laws of England*, 2d ed. (1935), 19:309 note e, above, n. 31.

48. *R.* v. *Opie, Dodge et al.* (1670), Wm. Saund. 300.

gainfully accustomed to, and can so secretly commit in the corrupt returning the Juries . . . ." The solution suggested by the anonymous author was a higher qualification (£50), but one that could be enforced. To that end he suggested "a general Regulation made of the Freeholders Books," and the use of ballots to select both veniremen and actual jurors. Walpole's Tory opponents probably originated these proposals.[49]

Such a statute was enacted five years later, and its terms and even its wording suggest that the pamphlet was part of a concerted opposition effort to prevent political convictions.[50] The preamble of "An Act for the Better Regulation of Juries" referred to "many evil practices . . . used in corrupting of jurors" and "many neglects and abuses . . . in making up the lists of freeholders, who ought to serve on such trials, and many persons being lawfully summoned to serve on juries have neglected to appear, to the great injury of many persons in their properties and estates . . . ."[51] Both political parties took credit for the statute, praised by the historian Nicholas Tindal as "a most excellent act":

> Before this time, it was a reproach to the English law, that no provision was made to oblige men of substance effectually to serve as jurymen . . . . There have been many great and notorious corruptions in the trials and causes in courts of justice, for want of proper persons to serve upon juries; arising sometimes from the neglect of persons of good substance and credit, who shifting off from themselves the trouble of attending at those courts to serve as jurymen, made it necessary often to make use of indigent men for that service, who were easy to be drawn in to serve an ill cause; and sometimes from the practice of knavish lawyers, who would often find means to pack a jury by concert, with those who were concerned in returning persons for that service . . . . But this act remedies all those inconveniences.[52]

49. [An Attorney], *Proposals*, 5th ed (1725), 29ff. Nathaniel Mist, the leading Tory publicist, published this, and the 3rd and 4th editions (both 1724). *The Eighteenth-Century Short Title Catalogue* (computer file as of August 1986) lists ten editions of the pamphlet: two of 1707 (London and Norwich), six in the 1720s, and two in 1730. The 1707 London text (I have not been able to examine the Norwich imprint) does not contain the jury proposals found in the later editions and embodied in the legislation.

50. See below, text at n. 144.

51. 3 Geo. II, c. 25 (1730), made perpetual by 6 Geo. II, c. 37.

52. Nicholas Tindal, *The continuation of Mr Rapin's History of England, from the revolution to the present times* (1759–63), 74–75 and note b. The bill was carried through Parliament by Edward Harley, later the third earl of Oxford, leader of the

The statute was also referred to as "An Act Against Jury Packing." The language of Tindal and the preamble, as well as the Tory inspiration of the legislation, suggests that both private corruption and government manipulation of jury panels concerned Parliament. When panels were very large (as in political cases), the defense was at a disadvantage because of its limited number of peremptory challenges. It also became difficult to investigate the background and standing of potential jurors. The issue had dominated the beginning of Christopher Layer's trial for high treason eight years before, when a large number of prospective jurors were revealed to have "no freehold." In fact, the new jury qualifications enacted in 1692, which the act of 1730 sought to enforce, had also been brought forward in the context of political trials. The requirement for £10 of freehold land had originally been part of a 1689 bill for "the trial of peers." After much dispute between the Lords and Commons over the rights of peers, most of the bill eventually became the Treason Act of 1696. During the deadlock in Parliament, the jury qualification was enacted as a separate measure because it was not an issue in contention.[53]

The 1730 act also guaranteed and regularized the "special" jury in misdemeanor cases, which afforded additional protection to those able to take advantage of it.[54] The special jury existed in a number of forms, but almost always its members were of much higher social status than the common jury. In the counties it was composed of wealthy landed gentlemen, many of them justices of the peace.[55] In short, like

Tory country gentlemen opposed to Walpole, with the assistance of William Lacon Childe, a Tory country gentleman from Shropshire, and Thomas Bramston, a Tory lawyer who was instrumental two years later in the enactment of the £100 property qualification for justices of the peace. Romney Sedgwick, *The History of Parliament: The House of Commons, 1715–54*, 2 vols. (1970), passim; Linda Colley, *In Defiance of Oligarchy: The Tory Party, 1714–60* (Cambridge, 1982), 73. Sir William Yonge was also on the committee. The bill was accepted, with a few amendments, by the Lords. *Commons Journals*, vol. 21 (13, 26 March; 3, 8, 10, 11, 15, 20 April, and 12, 13, 15 May 1730); *Lords Journals*, vol 23 (21, 24, 28, 29 April; and 6, 7, 8, 9, 11, 12 May 1730).

53. 16 *State Trials*, 129–38 (21 Nov. 1722). See also the trial of Francis Francia, 15 *State Trials*, 898 (1717), where a *voir dire* as to the £10 qualification was requested by the Crown and granted. The origins of the £10 qualifications in a draft of the Treason Act (1696) can be traced in HMC, *Twelfth Report*, appendix, pt. 6, ser. 17, House of Lords (1889), p. 31, no. 18, 26 February 1689, "Trial of Peers Bill," and ibid., *Thirteenth Report*, appendix, pt. 5, ser. 17, House of Lords (1892), p. 278, no. 417, 6 November 1691, "Trials for Treason, etc. Bill" These drafts proposed a qualification of £20 freehold for treason trials, £10 for felony, or £400 and £200 in "clear personal estate" in cities and corporate towns.

54. Section 15. This applied only to misdemeanor cases tried in King's Bench or at *nisi prius*, but many such cases tried at quarter sessions or assizes could be removed there on writ of certiorari, albeit at great expense.

55. Oldham, "Origins of the Special Jury," esp. 176–96, and idem, "Special Juries: Nineteenth-Century Usage and Reform," *Journal of Legal History*, Dec. 1986.

the property qualification for common jurors, it was perhaps expected to be an additional guarantee against the government corruption possible with common juries. If so, it would be of particular interest to high Tories, since seditious libel, a misdemeanor, was the most common political charge. As will be seen, the Tories were mistaken about the independence of special juries. But the special jury did guarantee that any gentleman faced with most misdemeanor charges (the only kind he was likely to face) would be judged by his peers in the sociological as well as the legal sense. Both Whig and Tory gentlemen saw the sense in that.

There is some evidence that the new act was not always enforced. Certainly evidence that propertied men escaped service continued to surface from time to time. One notorious case was that of John Whitaker, who was summoning bailiff to the sheriff of Middlesex and who was convicted and fined £200 by King's Bench in 1778 for demanding money from those wishing to be excused service (an offense punishable by the 1730 act) and for summoning unfairly often those prospective jurors who refused to pay the bribe. He claimed that the payments were customary and that he had not acted partially. In 1774 there were similar complaints in Staffordshire that constables exempted the wealthy.[56] It may be the case that jury lists were manipulated more often in this way in Middlesex; certainly Bentham's strictures on the special jury lists in the court of King's Bench itself in the early nineteenth century suggest an ill-regulated (or too well regulated) procedure.[57]

On the face of it, the opposite problem—unqualified jurors—should have been solved by the legislation. The 1730 statute, as the 1725 pamphlet had suggested, enacted a "general regulation" of the administrative details involved in the drawing up of freeholders lists from which jurors were chosen under the 1696 legislation.[58] It attempted to provide, at last, an accurate and enforceable means of ensuring that all jurors met the property qualification set in 1692. The net result of the 1692, 1696, 1704, and 1730 acts was to provide that every year constables would make up, for each parish or jurisdiction, lists of qualified men, using the poor rate and land tax returns in order to identify those who were eligible. These lists were posted on church doors for at least three weeks to allow for notice of omissions and mistakes, which could be appealed. The names were certified by a local justice

56. *R. v. Whitaker* (1778), 2 Cowp. 752 (98 ER, 1343); Aris' *Birmingham Gazette*, 26 Dec. 1774.

57. Jeremy Bentham, *The Elements of the Art of Packing as Applied to Special Juries* (1821, although written in 1808).

58. See 4 & 5 W. & M., c. 24; 7 & 8 Wm. III, c. 32, 3 & 4 Anne, c. 18.

for forwarding by the high constable (or taken directly by the petty constable) to Michaelmas quarter sessions. They were then entered by the clerk of the peace in the freeholders book,[59] and a duplicate was sent to the sheriff for use at assizes. This list served for the ensuing calendar year. Jury service gave the juror a certificate of exemption for two years in most counties (including Staffordshire and Northamptonshire). The names on the panels returned by the sheriff (or rather, the undersheriff) at assizes and by the clerk at quarter sessions had to be drawn from the freeholders book, in which details of service and other exemptions were also to be entered. At each step, provision was made for stiff penalties for negligence or corruption that would admit unqualified persons.[60] The aim, clearly, was to end the abuses so often mentioned in the sixteenth century and in the legislation, and to provide "a competent number of sensible and upright jurymen, chosen by lot from the middle rank," whom Blackstone considered "the best investigators of truth, and the surest guardians of public justice."[61]

Parliament considered the freeholders books to be the key. They survive for different periods of time for different counties and in somewhat different forms.[62] In Staffordshire the surviving books for 1782–89 each contain about 1,700 names.[63] The parish lists for Northamptonshire apparently were not copied into books, but the lists themselves are extant for many years. Those for 1777 contain 1,118 names, and probably over 1,400 men qualified in the whole county.[64] The in-

59. Sometimes the practice was simply to keep the original returns (see the evidence for Northamptonshire below).

60. Among others, this included a fine of from £2 to £10 for summoning an unlisted person to assize service. See s. 3. The act also provided that in smaller jurisdictions (counties of towns and cities), the county qualification was to apply in all capital cases. To counter corruption at the last stage, the 1730 act also provided for a ballot, subject to the usual challenges, to select actual jurors from the panel of those returned by the undersheriff (s. 11). The 1725 pamphlet had recommended such a ballot, but also another in the making up of the original panel from the freeholders book. This latter suggestion was not enacted, perhaps because Parliament was unwilling to cut back so greatly the government's power to pack juries in state cases. The ballot was used in Middlesex by 1731 (*Gentleman's Magazine* 1 [1731]. 28) and to pick talesmen for special juries (e.g. in *R.* v. *Horne,* ibid., 47 [1777]: 307) but it appears not to have been available to most defendants, at least by 1820. See below, nn. 139, 141, text at n. 144

61. *Commentaries,* 3:380.

62. A complete census and detailed comparison of extant books and lists is clearly required.

63. They are located in the William Salt Library (hereafter WSL), HM 31/18. Those for 1782, 1786, and 1789 are damaged, and that for 1788 lacks a page. The volume for 1784 has been published with some editorial additions. S.A H Burne, "The Jurors' Book of 1784," *Staffordshire Historical Society Collections* (1948), 71. Burne's transcription of the 1784 volume has been used in the calculations that follow.

64. Lists survive for 1777 for the parishes of the hundreds of Chipping War-

habitants of corporate towns, cities, and boroughs do not appear in them, by the terms of the legislation.[65] Also excluded were freeholders with insufficient property and a number of other groups. Women, peers, judges, some apothecaries, London surgeons, Anglican clergy, lawyers, Quakers and dissenting teacher-clerics, and registered seamen, visitors of workhouses, army officers, Roman Catholic Priests, coroners, gaolers, keepers of houses of correction, and a variety of other public officials were all either exempt or disqualified. So too were men younger than twenty-one or older than seventy and those who were either sick or who had served within the preceding two years.[66] Finally, tenant farmers, even very wealthy ones, did not qualify for jury service if they held only annual leases. A more troublesome category of men supposedly liable for service were the leaseholders of £20 above the reserved rent on leases of five hundred years or more, or ninety-nine years, or for a term determinable on lives.[67] Because of the difficulty of investigating title, it has been suggested that the constables ignored them altogether.[68] After all the exemptions, qualifications, and other decisions (including, possibly, corrupt ones) were taken into account, Staffordshire in the 1780s and Northamptonshire in the 1770s registered 8.5 and 10.4 jurors per thousand population, respectively. By 1823 they had 3,382 and 1,745 jurors enumerated, or 9.4 and 10.5 per thousand.[69] However, the survival of free-

den, Cleyley, Greens Norton, Guilsborough, Hamfordshoe, Higham Ferrers, Huxloe, King Sutton, Navisford, Nobottle Grove, Orlingbury, Polebrook, Rothwell, Spelhoe, Towcester, Willybrook, and Wymersley. Corby, Fawsley, and Nassaburgh Hundred are missing for that year. On the basis of the 1801 census, the number of names should therefore be increased by 30 percent. I am very grateful to Mr. P. I. King, the county archivist of Northampton, and his staff, for providing me with photocopies of this and other material at short notice.

65. A parliamentary return of 1836 noted that the inhabitants of the Staffordshire towns of Burton, Kingswinford, Newcastle, and Walsall were exempted by their charters from jury service. *Parliamentary Papers*, 1836, 43 (336), p. 155. The city of Lichfield held its own courts of quarter sessions and assizes, and its inhabitants do not appear in the county freeholders book, nor do inhabitants of Stafford, which also was exempt by the terms of the legislation. Burne, "Jurors Book of 1784," introduction.

66. Although the 1784 book lists seven men as "infirm," and several Quakers, it appears likely either that this was added after the book was compiled, perhaps when such jurors were called and successfully pleaded infirmity, or that only some constables bothered to return such names at all. Most parishes, including the largest, record no "infirm" or Quakers at all, suggesting that most constables recorded only those they believed to be qualified. The statutes exempting men of particular descriptions are summarized in J. Chitty, *A Practical Treatise on the Criminal Law*, 4 vols. (1816), 1:309.

67. 3 Geo. II, c. 25, s. 18.

68. This was the opinion of the editor of the 1784 volume. Burne, "Jurors Book of 1784," introduction.

69. The numbers of eligible freeholders are taken from the sources listed in

holders books, and the consistent restriction of those named to about 1 percent of the county population, does not in itself prove that jurors were qualified. Two possibilities are suggested by the legislative history. One is that the books were corrupt in their origins or were ignored in practice. The fact that there was repeated legislation on the subject at the end of the seventeenth century is perhaps a sign that the burden of service, and the wide opportunities for local corruption and favoritism, could not easily be put right by legislation, even with more severe penalties. Perhaps Parliament simply abandoned the attempt at reform after the act of 1730. If that was the case, however, the legislature returned to the problem again in the early nineteenth century, a period, like the late seventeenth, of extensive criticism and reform in the criminal law. The state trials of Lord George Gordon (1780), John Horne Tooke (1794), and William Stone (1796) all began with *voir dire* hearings that showed that many veniremen were not freeholders. At Stone's trial Lord Kenyon deplored the evident deficiencies in the freeholders book.[70] In 1819 a bill was introduced into Parliament for "An Act to remove Doubts and Inconveniences arising from Neglect in making out and returning Lists or Books of Persons qualified to serve on Juries," which proposed to make lawful those juries that had to be struck from out-of-date or defective books.[71] And Peel, in introducing his reform statute of 1825, denounced the shortcomings of the petty constable, who was responsible under the act of 1730 for returning the lists of qualified men in each parish. Peel described him as

> an individual who was frequently unable to read or write, and too often open to seduction. Thus he had ascertained that the

notes 63 and 64, and from "An Account of the Number of Persons, in each County of England and Wales, returned and entered on the Freeholders Book, as qualified to serve on Juries; in 1823," *Parliamentary Papers*, 1824, 19 (202), p. 129. Rates are calculated using the population estimates and returns of Phyllis Deane and W. A. Cole, *British Economic Growth, 1688–1959: Trends and Structure* (Cambridge, 1969), 103, and B. R. Mitchell, *Abstract of British Historical Statistics* (Cambridge, 1962), 20. The rates of freeholders per thousand in 1823 ranged from 38.6 in Surrey to 5.8 in Northumberland; most counties fell in the range of 8 to 12 per thousand.

70. 21 *State Trials*, 496–98; 25 *State Trials*, 15–21, 1155–57. See also 27 *State Trials*, 654. Dr. Ruth Paley, to whom I am indebted for pointing this out, has discovered that the home secretary (under pressure from the sheriffs) wrote to the Metropolitan Police offices and to the chairman of the bench in 1804 and 1805 stressing the need for the magistrates to check the lists parish by parish and revealing that no Westminster freeholders book had been received by the sheriffs since 1795–96. PRO, HO 43/15, fols. 55, 256; HO 65/1, circular, 5 Oct. 1804 and 6 Sept. 1805; MEPO 1/64, Hawkesbury, 6 Oct. 1804 and enclosures.

71. *House of Lords Sessional Papers*, 1819, 97 (153), pp. 887–88. It did not become law.

> petty constable, in consideration of some trifling gratuity, often omitted the names of persons who were best qualified to serve on juries, and inserted the names of others who were less qualified to discharge that duty.

The 1825 act therefore turned the responsibility over to the churchwardens and overseers of the poor, whose "respectability" would ensure their honesty.[72] In short, an illiterate and corrupt parish constabulary was perhaps producing misleading lists throughout the eighteenth century as well, or increasingly so. The inaction of Parliament for almost a century may have been the mark of complacency or despair.

The legislative history can, however, be read another way. The fact that Parliament enacted comprehensive statutes in the late seventeenth and early eighteenth centuries to ensure a sufficient supply of qualified jurors may mean that effective controls were put in place, and this interpretation may be strengthened by the fact that no further legislation was enacted until the early nineteenth century. Although it may be dangerous to read much into negative evidence, there was a great deal of other criminal legislation in the eighteenth century, including encouragements to prosecutors. The absence of further jury legislation therefore may mean that the problem of unqualified jurors, apparently so troubling to seventeenth-century members of Parliament, had been solved by the several statutes enacted between 1692 and 1730, or by the effects on the jury of contemporaneous social developments.[73] Peel's remarks, if they were accurate, perhaps apply only to the early nineteenth century, when an enormous increase in the number of indictments must have led to much pressure on constables to excuse jurors from increasingly onerous duties, and when the constable, too, may have been more often chosen from the poor and illiterate rather than from respectable householders.[74] The prob-

72. *Hansard*, 2d ser., vol. 12, col. 968; 6 Geo. IV, c. 50, s. 8.

73. As suggested by Beattie, who argues that the elevation of the social status of the grand jury had a knock-on effect on the petty jury, with middling men, no longer able to sit as the "Body of the County," prepared to appear instead on the petty (trial) juries. Beattie, *Crime and the Courts*, 320–24, 389.

74. Ironically, one clause of Peel's consolidating statute may have reduced the qualification for some jurors. The 1692 statute (4 & 5 W. & M., c. 24, ss. 18, 19) had provided that talesmen be qualified at £5 freehold (£3 in Wales), but in April 1825, in *R. v. Hill* (1 Car. & P. 667) it was decided that the 1696 statute (7 & 8 Wm. III, c. 32, s. 3) prohibited the taking of talesmen except from other jury panels (the case concerned a special jury on an information *quo warranto*, but the headnote states the point generally: "talesmen can only be taken from the panel of the jury summoned to try the other causes, and not from the bystanders"). Peel's statute, enacted the following month, pro-

lem of unqualified jurors may also have been confined to London and to the later years of the century, as the cases in *State Trials* suggest.[75] To judge the success of the legislation of 1692 to 1730 in the eighteenth century, it is therefore necessary to identify the jurors in any given jurisdiction. We must also reconstruct, as far as possible, the administrative processes by which trial jurors were chosen from freeholders books and by which the books themselves were first compiled.

The two counties for which this is done here, Stafford and Northampton, were undergoing some of the most rapid social and economic change in the period, and hence perhaps are jurisdictions in which the legislative scheme of 1730 may have become inadequate in the later eighteenth century. Staffordshire was notable for industrialization and population growth by the 1780s, as what were becoming the Black Country and the Potteries emerged as distinctive high-wage regions. Such changes may have brought new kinds of men to the jury box if the legislation was not being strictly enforced. Northamptonshire, with a mixed agriculture and much rural industry, including extensive growth in shoemaking late in the century, saw relatively little population growth but was one of the counties most affected by parliamentary enclosure in the later eighteenth century. It is not clear whether that would have increased the property standing of jurymen or tended to erode it; as lesser freeholders declined in numbers through this and other causes, either might result. But in both counties rapid demographic and economic change might be expected to have increased the difficulty in keeping track of qualified men or in finding enough of them. The pressure on the administrative machinery almost certainly increased (as Peel's later remarks suggested that it did in the 1820s) because the 1780s saw a great increase in the level of indictable crime, one not matched until the next great wave, which began in 1816 and continued through the 1820s. If jurymen wanted to evade the pressure of heavy duties, if constables and sheriffs faced difficulty in keeping lists up to date and in resisting inducements, the later part of the century, especially the 1780s, is the period in which

vided again that talesmen could be called but described them only as "such other Able men of the county then present," and "such men duly qualified as shall be present or can be found," omitting any explicit requirement that they meet a specified sum or be taken from the freeholders book (6 Geo. IV, c. 50, s. 37). Apparently the practice subsequently became lax: ". . . it is not unusual to requisition any person, whatever his residence or qualification." 18 Halsbury (1911), 252.

75. The cases cited in n. 70 above are the only eighteenth-century cases in *State Trials* after that of Christopher Layer (above, n. 53) to mention veniremen without freehold.

the administrative scheme initiated in the England of the 1730s might be expected to have weakened. A comparison of the sources suggests that it had not.

Finding the Qualified Juror: The System in Practice

The form in which freeholders books and lists were compiled shows that the constables and other officials responsible under the legislation were well aware of their responsibilities. The Staffordshire books are carefully organized by hundred and parish on the same plan year after year, they were written in a clear hand, and they reflect the exemptions gained by service. The original lists from which they were compiled are missing, but in the case of Northamptonshire, where the original constables' lists survive, the headings of many show an acquaintance with the details of the legislation, employing such terms as "ten pound men," and "freeholders qualified to serve on juries." Without exception they had been examined and verified on oath before a justice of the peace. But the meaning of the books and lists can only be tested by considering their place in the whole process by which jurors were chosen. To do this we must make three comparisons. The first works back from the names of jurors actually sworn at trials to the panels of those called for possible jury service, from which they were selected. The second compares the panels to the books (or lists) of those recorded as qualified. Finally, in order to evaluate the freeholders books themselves, we must look to other sources for the actual wealth and social standing of those who were listed there as men of sufficient property to serve as jurors.[76]

Providing jurors was a considerable administrative undertaking.[77]

76. The books for Staffordshire have been compared to the land tax returns on which they were supposed to be based and to rates set in Wolverhampton, the largest town. They have also been compared to the names on the panels of possible jurors summoned to assizes and quarter sessions in the years 1782 to 1787 and also to the actual jurors who were picked from the panels to be sworn. In Northamptonshire we cannot make this last comparison, because we lack the names of most jurors. That county, however, has better sources than almost any other from which to judge the accuracy of the freeholders lists themselves. (For the sources used, see below nn. 77, 97, 98, 113.) An implicit assumption in what follows is that accuracy in either the use or the composition of the freeholders lists strongly suggests accuracy in the other. This assumption may be strengthened or weakened by work in other jurisdictions.

77. The Staffordshire jury lists used here are the panels of those called and the lists of those actually sworn in PRO, ASSI 5/102–20, and Staffordshire Record Office (hereafter SRO), Q/SO, vols. 18ff. I am extremely grateful to Dr Ruth Paley and Ms. Muriel Fielding for their invaluable assistance in preparing the extensive lists of assize

In Staffordshire in the years 1782 to 1787 (the years for which all the kinds of sources noted above are most complete), 531 men were called to assizes on the sheriff's panels for possible service on trial juries, and 193 actually served.[78] Another 288 served at quarter sessions, for a total of 481 men sworn.[79] When we compare these jurors with the panels of those called for service, we can test for the presence of talesmen—those unqualified bystanders, "idle people in rags . . . loitering about the Hall," the "profligate and unfit" who were the bane of the seventeenth- and eighteenth-century critics and a prime concern of the legislators. If names appear in lists of sworn jurors which are not to be found in jury panels, then they are talesmen, and if they do not appear in freeholders books either, then they are possibly unqualified talesmen of the kind that the legislative scheme was designed to exclude.[80]

It is abundantly clear that at the most important court, assizes, the sheriff was having no difficulty in securing the attendance of sufficient numbers of qualified jurors. It was rare that even half the panel (usually of forty-eight) was gone through before all petty juries were struck (there were often two and sometimes three).[81] At only *one* assizes of the fifteen held between 1782 and 1789 did the sheriff have the slightest difficulty supplying jurors. The Lent sitting of 1787 was the busiest of the entire eighteenth century. More than forty defendants were tried, and an extraordinary number of jurors—twenty-seven in all—were sworn on four separate juries, presumably to ease the burden on individual jurymen, or because of illness or challenges. In these circumstances the sheriff exhausted the panel of forty-eight qualified men whom he had summoned to the assizes. He had to find one more man. That man, John Thomas of Cannock, was the only talesman to appear at assizes out of 251 jurors sworn in these years. (The sheriff took steps to avoid even this minor inconvenience at the next meeting of the court; he called fifty-two men to the Summer as-

and QS jurors' names for the computer. J. Bookbinder and R. Rusonik helped with data entry.

78. The minimum number under the legislation, forty-eight, was called in all years except 1787. See below, text at n. 81.

79. We have no extant panels for quarter sessions, only the names of those actually sworn to juries. Although this is a shortcoming, it should be noted that quarter sessions is the less important court.

80. I say possibly here because it is possible that new residents known to be qualified might be called as talesmen although their names were not entered in the freeholders book compiled the last Michaelmas sessions.

81. It is assumed that the clerk called jurors' names in the order listed on the panel returned to the venire, an assumption supported by the fact that jurors actually sworn are numbered in that order.

sizes.) John Thomas was not a ragged lout picked from the crowd; he was a registered, qualified freeholder.[82]

The 1780s were the busiest decade at Stafford assizes, a period when jurors may have been most anxious to avoid the onerous duties of many trials. On the other hand, the press of business may have caused a tightening of the administrative structure. In order to judge whether talesmen and the unqualified juror were indeed rare throughout the eighteenth century, jurors who actually served have been similarly compared with the panels of those called for the 1750s and for the 1720s. The latter period is particularly important as a comparison, for it falls immediately before the act of 1730, which reformed the administrative machinery for finding qualified jurors.

In the extant records for twelve assizes for the 1750s, talesmen were called at only one meeting of the court, Summer 1753, when four appeared.[83] That session was the busiest of the decade, and presumably the sheriff made the same miscalculation as in 1787. Those were the only talesmen called during a period when 205 jurors were sworn on petty juries.[84] They may, as in the 1780s, all have been qualified men, but the sources do not survive to tell us. In the 1720s even jury lists often do not survive for the county, but at the six assizes for which they do, three of the seventy-five jurors appear to be talesmen, the highest proportion of all three periods. On a number of occasions in the 1720s defaulters were fined.[85]

Thus, over the century talesmen accounted for 4 percent, 2 percent, and less than 1 percent of jurors sworn at assizes in each successive period. In the last period, the 1780s, the sole talesman was a qualified freeholder, and that may also have been the case in the earlier periods. The rarity of even qualified talesmen at Stafford assizes was probably not untypical. Charles Cottu, a French barrister who traveled the Northern circuit in 1819, said he had never seen an instance of it.[86]

82. WSL, HM 3/18, freeholders book for 1786, entry under "Cannock." See also n. 86 for the few talesmen in the 1790s. These, too, may have been qualified men, but the freeholders books are not extant.

83. In addition, three names were added to the panel itself at the same assizes, and a name was also added to the panel in Lent 1752. These may be names added by the sheriff after the beginning of the assizes, and hence talesmen in a sense, or simply corrections to the original list. For the possibility that names were sometimes added in lieu of talesmen, see below, n. 86.

84. Another twenty-four appeared on what were probably special juries, with separate panels, in Lent 1753 and Lent 1758.

85. See Lent 1724 O.S., when fines were levied. In Summer 1727 three names were also added to the panel in a later hand.

86. Charles Cottu, *On the Administration of Criminal Justice in England* (1822), 85.

We cannot be as sure about the practice at quarter sessions, since for Staffordshire we have the names of those sworn, not the panels of those called for possible service. However, in only one session of the twenty-four in the period 1782–87, that of Translation 1787, are talesmen noted, three in all, and they are clearly distinguished from the other jurors.[87] All three of them were nonetheless qualified men whose names appeared in the freeholders book for 1786.[88] In short, it appears likely that only 4 out of 480 trial jurors at quarter sessions and assizes between 1782 and 1787 were talesmen, or less than 1 percent. All of them were called in the exceptional spring and early summer of 1787, and all four were registered as men who met all the property and other qualifications. Poor bystanders in court never appeared on Staffordshire juries in this period and probably had not done so since at least 1730.

The second test of the sources is a comparison between the panels of jurors summoned to attend the courts and the names in the freeholders books. This test will reveal whether all the jurors, not just the talesmen, were qualified men. Virtually all of them were, if a few years are representative. At the four assizes held in 1784 and 1785, 192 petty jurors were summoned, and only one (who did not actually serve

(The work is a translation of *De l'Administration de la Justice Criminelle en Angleterre* [Paris, 1820], where the passages quoted agree.) Cottu was told that talesmen had been more common when only twenty-four men were impaneled instead of forty-eight, a practice that had long since disappeared in Staffordshire. There were also legal reasons for the rarity of the tales at assizes, because there were doubts about the power of justices of gaol delivery to award it; Chitty, *Practical Treatise*, 1:520. Chitty explained that justices, when acting under the commission of gaol delivery, may always order a larger panel without any writ but the general precept by which they command the sheriff to have a sufficient number of jurymen ready for the assizes. Elsewhere Chitty remarked that on the trial of an indictment under the commission of gaol delivery, there is no tales, but there must be a new panel, and that under oyer and terminer a fresh panel should also be chosen (p. 517). He also noted that justices of oyer and terminer did have the power to grant it (p. 520). The leading case he cited apparently justified the practice of justices calling talesmen when acting under other commissions—for example, when trying defendants who had been bailed, or who were traversing misdemeanors, or who had been indicted before a grand jury without preliminary proceedings before a magistrate, and hence were not in the gaoler's care. There were few such cases at assizes. An examination of assize jurors and panels for the years from 1788 to 1800 shows four possible talesmen (Lent assizes 1790, 1791, 1796), and five names added to panels (Lent assizes 1790, 1793, 1798, 1800, and Summer 1800).

87. Since the records of the court were kept in the same form throughout this period and—with the exception of Epiphany 1783—in the same hand, the minutes strongly suggest that the talesmen explicitly mentioned in 1787 are the only ones to appear at quarter sessions in these six years. SRO, Q/SO, vols. 18, 19.

88. WSL, HM 31/18 (1786). They were Abraham Ward of Forbridge, Thomas Hammersley of Haughton, and John Keen of Eccleshall.

as a juror) does not appear in the freeholders books.[89] Panels do not survive for quarter sessions, but all the fifty-four jurors who actually served in 1785 are also found in the freeholders book.[90]

The conclusion from all the evidence examined is that in striking juries the undersheriff followed the legislation of 1730 to the letter. He drew up panels of prospective jurors entirely from the official freeholders books, in sufficient numbers virtually to eliminate talesmen, and, as far as we can tell, ensured that those few talesmen who had to be called were all qualified men too.

We come, then, to the last (and crucial) question: whether the freeholders lists themselves were the product of conscientious constables, headboroughs, justices of the peace, and sheriffs, or whether inattention, ignorance, and corruption allowed the rich to disappear from the freeholders list and the poor to invade it. Since Parliament in 1730 and the Home Secretary in 1825 stated that such abuses existed, the lists must be tested against the sources that the constables themselves were supposed to use: tax rolls. It is worth considering also the somewhat impressionistic evidence of social status and occupation available to us from other sources, if only because historians have relied so heavily upon it in the past. In both cases we cannot, given the multiplicity of legitimate exemptions, discover whether qualified men were left off the lists. We can, however, make an assessment of the central proposition of the critics: that all the abuses combined to debase the social standing of the jury below the level required by law.

The Social Standing of County Freeholders

Eighteenth-century occupational designations are suggestive, although by no means conclusive. Although petty jurors in the 1750s were indiscriminately described as "gent," it seems likely that this was simply common form and bore little relation to reality.[91] By the 1780s occupational descriptions are various and consistent with other

89. John Ottway of Brockton (Lent 1784). PRO, ASSI 5/104, pts. 1–3; 5/105, pt. 1; Burne, "Jurors Book of 1784"; and 1783 and 1785 freeholders books. Other years were not checked, given the labor of finding 96 names among approximately 1,700 listed as qualified each year. Ottway may have been resident too short a time to have been enumerated; there are other instances of jurors appearing in freeholders books closely adjacent in time, but not for the year of service itself.

90. This was the only year checked, for the same reason given in n. 89, but there is no reason to believe that it is unrepresentative.

91. King finds the same pattern in Essex and interprets it in the same way. See above, chap. 9, text at n. 42.

information about social status. From those given in the Staffordshire freeholders books and jury lists (Table 10.1), it appears that by the 1780s gentlemen (with one exception) never sat on petty juries in either court; that farmers constituted almost half the jurors at assizes and fully three-fourths at quarter sessions; and that tradesmen and artisans (of unknown status in their trades and occupations) made up the balance, being slightly in the majority at assizes and in a minority at quarter sessions.

The trades and manufactures represented are traditional ones for artisans (tanner, joiner, carpenter, blacksmith), or dealers in foodstuffs and services (innkeeper, victualer, grocer, baker), or workers in the specialized trades so important in Staffordshire (locksmith, brazier, cutler, brassfounder, potter, japanner). It is well known that such occupational descriptions, especially among tradesmen and manufacturers, offer a very imprecise guide to social status, covering the income range from at least the poorest journeyman to a wealthy master. The words *farmer* or *yeoman* also had no certain meaning throughout the century and throughout England. There was one true exotic: a laborer said to be qualified.[92] Moreover, the number of unknowns is large, and since we cannot know that they are evenly distributed by social class (and we might plausibly suspect that wealthier jurors are more likely to have had their occupations recorded), it is imperative

Table 10.1. Occupations of Those Qualified and Serving as Jurors in Staffordshire in the 1780s

	1784 Freeholders Book		Assizes, 1782–87		QS, 1785	
	No.	%	Sworn	%	Sworn*	%
Gentlemen	122	15	1	1	0	0
Farmers and yeomen	336	42	28	42	24	75
Tradesmen and manufacturers	346	43	38	57	8	25
Unknown	941	54			20	38

SOURCES: WSL, HM 31/18 (1784); PRO, ASSI 5/102–7; SRO, Q/SO (1785).
NOTE: Percentages are of total occupations given, except for the figures for Unknown, which is the proportion of all names.
* Panels of jurors called to quarter sessions are not extant. Occupations were taken from the 1784 freeholders book.

92. King found thirty-three in the Essex jury book of 1815 See above, chap. 9, text at n. 44.

to look for other information about these individuals. The sources used here are land tax records for Staffordshire and Northamptonshire (the source, with poor rates, for the juror lists, according to the 1696 statute); militia lists for Northamptonshire; and, for the Staffordshire industrial town of Wolverhampton, the rates assessed in 1781 under an improvement act.

The freeholders named in eleven parishes of the 1784 book have been compared with the Staffordshire land tax returns for the same year.[93] If a man was at all wealthy, his estates were very likely to be found in more than one parish, and therefore for seven parishes the contiguous parishes and townships were also checked for holdings.[94] (In the other four only the parish of residence was checked.)[95] For the total of eleven parishes, in which 113 men were listed in the freeholders book, 35 percent held more than enough land in their parish of residence to qualify. Another 12 percent held within £5 of what they needed, but over half the total of 113 needed at least £5 more of either owned or rented land, and nine men paid no tax on land at all. Of the seven parishes for which holdings were also checked in neighboring parishes, the percentages in the parish of residence (of 45 named men) are similar: 40 percent qualified, 11 percent were within £5, 36 percent held less than that, and 13 percent paid no land tax. Checking immediately contiguous parishes raises the number of certainly qualified men by only three, from 18 to 21 out of the total of 45.

Two explanations are possible: that constables were contravening

93. In the cases of Alton and Okeover (the latter is found in Ilam's return) the land tax returns for 1784 are missing, so those for 1781, the nearest year, are used instead. Returns were sometimes made quarterly and sometimes semiannually or yearly, and in each case the last available return before August (when the jury lists might be in preparation) was used. In each case the assessed value of the land has been calculated from the tax paid, at the rate of four shillings in the pound, and eligibility has been based on £10 of owned land or a tenancy of £20. SRO, land tax returns.

94. Grindon town and parish (and Butterton, Onecote, Waterfall, Wetton, and Ilam were also checked); Ilam and Okeover (and Mayfield, Blore, Calton, Waterfall, Grindon, Wetton, and Alstonfield were also checked), Cauldon (and Waterfall, Cotton [in Alton], and Calton); Ellastone, including Wootton and Stanton (and Mayfield, Blore, Swinscoe, Calton, Caulton, Cotton, Alton, Denstone, Rocester); Blithfield and Newton (and Kingstone, Abbots Bromley, Bagots Bromley, Bromley Hurst, Colton, and Colwich [except Wolseley]); Rudgley (and Colwich [except Wolseley], Cotton, Mavesyn Ridware, Armitage, Longdon, Cannock [except Hednesford, Cannock Wood, and Great Wyrley, Brockton]); and Hatherton (and Shareshill, Great and Little Saredon, Great Wyrley, Cannock [but not Hednesford or Cannock Wood], Huntington, Penkridge, Pillaton, Otherton, Rodbaston, Water Eaton, Whiston, and Bickford, Kinvaston).

95. Brewood (and Coven); Penkridge (and Levedale, Drayton, Pillaton, Otherton, Rodbaston, Water Eaton, Whiston and Bickford, Coppenhall, Dunston, Stretton, and Kinvaston); Cheddleton (and Basford, Consall), and Abbots Bromley (and Bagots Bromley and Bromley Hurst).

the law by listing men without the freehold or leasehold qualification, or that they added in lands held in more distant parishes. Work done on wills in the county suggests that "landholding could extend well beyond immediately contiguous parishes."[96] Also, the small number of parishes examined may be unrepresentative, because of the sixty men with little or no land listed, 42 percent were listed by the constable of the large border parish of Brewood. In short, the low percentage of legal qualification may be caused either by one lax constable or by landownership over the border in Shropshire.

The labor involved in searching the voluminous land tax lists for men known to be jurors suggests the value of using an established computerized tax file and merging with it the much shorter lists of those eligible for jury service. The result is an analysis based on edited land tax records for nineteen Northamptonshire parishes between the years 1774 and 1807, in each case for two years, thus constituting a sample of thirty-eight profiles of a parish in a given year.[97] In each case a list of freeholders returned by the constables as men qualified to sit on juries has been added.[98] For some 1,500 landowners and landhold-

96. This information is from Miles Kingston, to whom I am indebted also for the time-consuming collection of all the Staffordshire tax information from the original returns in the Staffordshire Record Office. A third explanation, I think the correct one, is suggested below.

97. I am most grateful to Dr. J. M. Neeson, who made the analysis possible by generously making available her large computer file. Her original sample was composed of two tax years for each of twenty-two parishes (one with two divisions), but freeholders lists are available for both years in only nineteen. For the editing decisions made in compiling the computer file and the rationale for using land tax records in this way, see J. M. Neeson, "Common Right and Enclosure in Eighteenth-Century Northamptonshire" (Ph.D. diss., Warwick Univ., 1977), appendixes A, B, and C; and idem, "Parliamentary Enclosure and the Disappearance of the English Peasantry, Revisited," in *Agrarian Organization during Industrialization: Europe, Russia and America in the Nineteenth Century*, ed. George Grantham and Carol Leonard, forthcoming. The technical difficulties associated with the land tax—their volume and the ambiguities involved in identifying individuals—have deterred historians from making full use of the records, but recent research has removed many of the doubts about their reliability. As the source becomes better known, comparative work becomes possible. For other assessments of land tax records that support the use made of them here, see J. M. Martin, "Landownership and the Land Tax Returns," *Agricultural History Review* 14 (1966). 96–103; and Michael Turner and Dennis Mills, *Land and Property: The English Land Tax 1692 to 1832* (Gloucester, 1986).

98. The parishes are Rushden, 1774 and 1783; Bugbrook, 1774 and 1784, Wollaston, 1783 and 1793; Wadenhoe, 1788 and 1798, Whitfield, 1791 and 1801, Raunds, 1791 and 1802; Whittlebury, 1794 and 1804; Greens Norton, 1794 and 1804; Islip, 1795 and 1805; Newton Bromswold, 1795 and 1805; Chelveston, 1796 and 1806; Hargrave, 1797 and 1807, Hannington, 1794 and 1804; Sutton Bassett, 1797 and 1807; Weston by Welland, 1797 and 1807; Roade, 1786 and 1796; Naseby, 1806 and 1814; Abthorpe, 1794 and 1804; and Stanwick, 1790 and 1800. Fifteen were enclosed during this period, and four remained open. The sample contains no old-enclosed parishes.

ers (as the land tax records include certain tenancies as well) sampled over thirty years, it is possible to determine the relationship of such eligibility to the tax records on which it was supposed to be based.

Figures 10.1 through 10.4 summarize the jury qualifications of those owning land, and also of those holding land (through either ownership or tenancy). Only 156 men were qualified to be listed as jurors and did not enjoy exemptions from jury service. Figure 10.1 shows that 49 percent of them owned enough land (£10 assessed value or more) in one parish to qualify.[99] Of the 80 others, 33 owned less than £10 freehold but rented over £20 in one parish, thus meeting the tenancy qualification. Either ownership or tenancy thus qualified 109 of the 156, or 70 percent, on the basis of their landholdings in a single parish. Landholding in contiguous or separate parishes was common, however, and it is therefore likely that the other 30 percent of the men listed as eligible were in fact qualified for that reason. The Northamptonshire constables were almost certainly following the statutory requirements to the letter.[100]

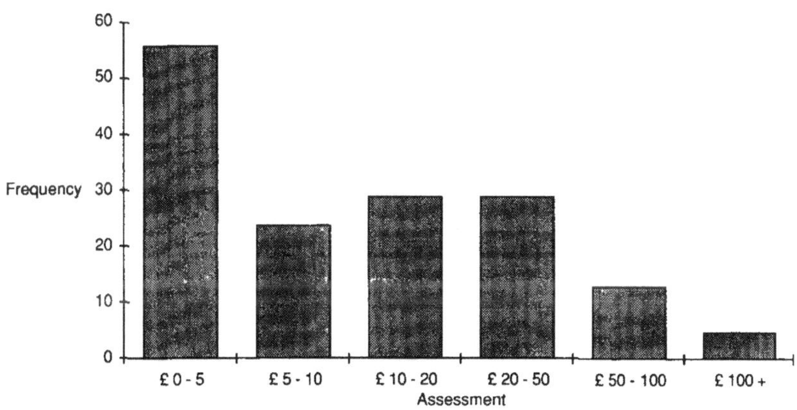

Figure 10.1. Assessments of Land Owned by Taxpayers Eligible for Jury Service, Northamptonshire, 1774–1807.

99. Because the computer file consists of land tax holdings in thirty-eight separate parishes, aggregated, the holdings of each identified eligible freeholder are limited to those found in a single parish.

100. We cannot be sure, however, that they were not exempting qualified men of property who should have been included, which was one of the persistent complaints in the nineteenth century and earlier. The justices who certified the lists of freeholders were empowered to grant exemptions for illness, infirmity, and other causes, and it is probably in this way, as much as through the corruption of constables, that propertied and qualified men escaped listing. The omission of qualified men, however, is not germane to the argument presented here unless a consequence was that unquali-

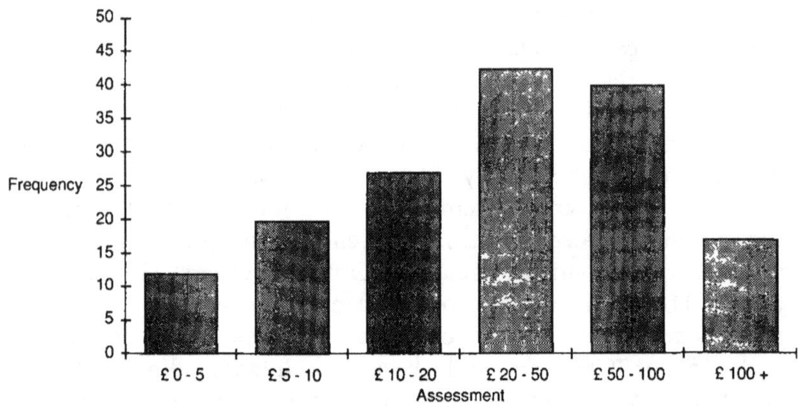

Figure 10.2. Assessments of Total Land Owned and Rented by Taxpayers Eligible for Jury Service, Northamptonshire, 1774–1807.

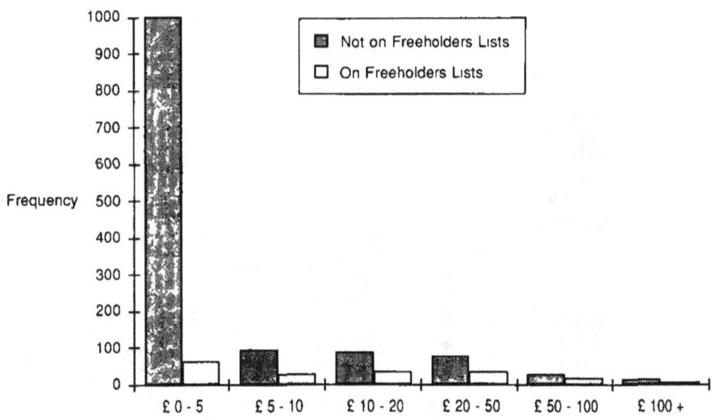

Figure 10.3. Assessments of Land Owned by Taxpayers, by Eligibility for Jury Service, Northamptonshire, 1774–1807.

That men on the freeholders lists were also much wealthier than other taxpayers can be seen from Figure 10.3, which compares them on the basis, again, of land owned in one parish only. Figure 10.4 compares them on the basis of the total amount of land they owned and rented in one parish. In both cases the exclusion of the very large number of poorer taxpayers can be clearly seen. (The exclusion of some

fied men served, and it is clear that they did not. Some critics, of course, would have been happy to see an even wealthier jury than the one specified by legislation.

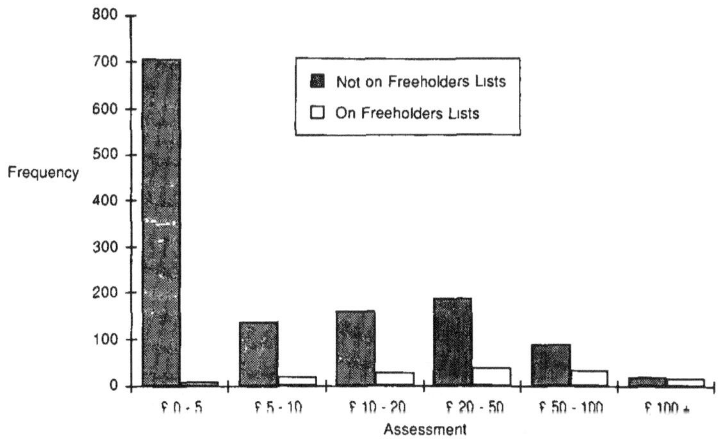

Figure 10.4. Assessments of Total Land Owned and Rented by Taxpayers, by Eligibility for Jury Service, Northamptonshire, 1774–1807.

men with more than enough land to qualify is undoubtedly attributable to exemptions on the basis of recent service, age, office, or profession.) Figure 10.2 shows that when both owned and rented land is taken into account, qualified men were predominantly from the upper end of the property scale.[101]

Although the deficiencies of the Staffordshire land tax sample may account for the difference between the two counties, it is likely that the justices there interpreted the statutory freehold qualification to take account of a notorious fact about the land tax. The total assessments of the counties were unequally fixed in the 1690s and never changed. The result was that while Northamptonshire men paid a rate of tax corresponding to the rental value of their land in the 1690s, it was estimated that Staffordshire lands were assessed at half the fair rate. The certain result was that prosperous freeholders would escape jury service in Staffordshire if raw assessment figures were used. That an adjustment was in use is suggested by the fact that about 1 percent of the population in each county was listed.[102] Evidence about those excluded from jury service also supports this conclusion.

101. For the same reason, if the sample took account of holdings in more than one parish (which this does not), the wealthier end of the graph would shift substantially toward higher values. The fact that few below £10 are identified as jurors suggests that the effect would almost entirely occur above that point.

102. See above, text at n. 69. For the burden of the land tax in Northamptonshire and Staffordshire, see W. R. Ward, *The English Land Tax in the Eighteenth Century* (Oxford, 1953), chap. 1, esp. pp. 6–11, and G. E. Mingay, "The Land Tax Assess-

In the Northamptonshire sample, a large proportion of landholders and landowners were disqualified from jury service because of insufficient property.[103] Of course, a much larger proportion of the total male population was excluded, since only a minority held any land. Here the crucial question is not only how many more men but also what social groups were barred from jury service. An estimate can be made from the Northamptonshire militia lists, which recorded for a number of years for most parishes in the county the total male population between the ages of eighteen and forty-five, with occupations. They therefore record a great number of laborers, servants, and other poorer men who never appear on the land tax. The lists are the best county-wide occupational census for the eighteenth century.[104]

Taking one of the few parishes from the land tax analysis that has an extant militia list for the same year, the parish of Rushden in 1774, we find that 9 men were liable for jury service in 1774, a maximum of 23 men had holdings that would meet the property qualification, and a minimum of 87 other adult men did not (Table 10.2).[105] The militia

ments and the Small Landowner," *Economic History Review*, 2d ser., 17 (1964): 382, quoting a pamphlet of 1732.

103. The exact percentage cannot be calculated, because an unknown proportion of the 90 percent of holdings not identified as those of qualified men were held by men resident in other parishes and perhaps qualified there. Moreover, the sample of parishes is biased in two ways. First, it was selected for other purposes (see Neeson's thesis, cited in n. 97 above). All were late-enclosed parishes, that is, they were not enclosed by the early nineteenth century. Such parishes typically had a great many small landholders, probably above the county average. The second bias runs in the other direction. Many inhabitants, of course, held no land, or so little that it was not recorded on the land tax (the poor with land assessed under 20 shillings were excused). Hence the percentage of the adult male population excluded by the property qualification may have been larger; see below.

104. As a guide to possible jurymen, militia lists are not perfect, since they include males between the ages of eighteen and twenty, who were not eligible for jury service, and exclude those between the ages of forty-five and seventy, who were. For the purposes of the following analysis, the assumption is made that these categories balance out. The assumption almost certainly gives us a conservative estimate of the total male population.

105. In addition to the 9 men listed as eligible freeholders in 1774, all of whom appear on the land tax, another 12 held sufficient freehold land, and 2 sufficient leasehold, to qualify. (Not all of these fourteen were necessarily resident, and hence qualified, in Rushden, it is therefore a maximum number.) Another 87 men known to be resident because they appear on the 1774 militia list could not have qualified as jurors because they held no land in the parish, or so little that they paid no land tax at all. (Some may have held land in neighboring parishes, but the information in Table 10.2 shows that this is extremely unlikely for most of them.) Moreover, another 60 men who paid tax on land in the parish did not own nearly enough there to qualify. (Clerics, peers, Quakers, and other disqualified men have been excluded from these calculations.) Northamptonshire Record Office (hereafter NRO), 1774 militia list, 1774 land tax return, and 1774 freeholders list for Rushden.

list makes clear that those excluded were not simply propertied men who did not happen to have their wealth in the form of freehold land. Those on the militia list who did qualify as jurors included three farmers and a butcher,[106] but those who did not were overwhelmingly artisans, servants, laborers and "poor men." In Rushden in 1774, jury service was a privilege reserved for, at the very most, a quarter of the adult male population. Table 10.2 also shows that the great majority were excluded not only because they held insufficient land but because they were too poor ever to do so.[107] The avowed intention of Parliament to restrict jury service to propertied men was being fully realized in Rushden.

Table 10.2. Militia Men in Rushden Not Listed as Possible Jurors in 1774

	Paid Land Tax	Paid No Tax	Total
Farmers	5	2	7
Artisans and tradesmen	2	23	25
Servants	1	16	17
Laborers	2	21	23
"Poor men"	7	25	32

SOURCES: NRO, 1774 militia list, 1774 land tax return, and 1774 freeholders list for Rushden.
NOTE: The total male population aged 18 to 45 was 110 A total of 62 more men paid land tax in the parish, an unknown porportion of whom were resident but over the age of 45. It is unlikely that the 7 farmers were too young to be qualified as jurymen; it is possible that two held their land in such quantities of freehold and rented that they could not qualify. Of course, any of these men may have not appeared because of earlier service or other exemptions.

106. Five were not traced on the tax rolls, but three of these had the same surname as wealthy farmers and possibly were sons or other male relatives.

107. Mobility upward occurred with age, notably from the status of servants to that of smallholders. Thus a larger proportion of men could, at some time in their lives, inherit enough land to achieve the status of freeholder eligible for jury service. The Rushden militia list names ten farmers, but farmers were disproportionately older men, and an unknown number are therefore omitted from the militia lists (which count only men between eighteen and forty-five). Peter King's figures suggest that 60 percent of eligible men in Essex, where ages are given, were over the age of forty-five (above, Table 9.1). Making the largest possible estimate of eligible farmers in the parish from those able to pay the tax (not all of whom would be resident) and those known to be eligible farmers from the militia gives an absolute maximum of twenty-five. If all of these had eligible adult sons between the ages of eighteen and forty-five who lived in the parish and who would inherit the holding, a maximum of 25 percent of the men not eligible at this date might become so at some time in their lives. It should be stressed that the actual number of residents who were in this category was almost certainly less, since not all the holdings that would confer qualification were held by residents.

Unfortunately, there are few intersections of so many sources. Assessing the typicality of Rushden must therefore be approached by comparing the freeholders lists separately with the militia lists and the land tax. Table 10.3 shows the results of doing this for one tenth of the parishes for which Northamptonshire militia lists and freeholders lists survive for 1777, and for the thirty-eight parishes in the tax file for which freeholders lists also exist.[108] If we make a number of assumptions about the unknown numbers of nonresidents, and about freeholders and others over the age of forty-five,[109] the percentages for both samples rise to a qualification rate of only 18 percent and 16 percent of the adult male population. This demonstrates that in Northamptonshire as a whole (if the samples are representative) eligibility for jury service was no greater than it was in the parish of Rushden, and that it was possibly less.

Finally, the striking class bias in the social composition of Rushden men qualified for jury service is also seen in the 10 percent sample of

Table 10.3. Estimates of the Proportion of Adult Males Qualified for Juries, Northamptonshire

10 Percent Sample of Parishes, 1777 (N = 25)		Land Tax Parishes, 1774–1807 (N = 38)	
Qualified freeholders[a]	108	Qualified freeholders[a]	157
Males ages 18 to 45[b]	1,393	Landholders named[c]	1,463
Percent qualified	7.8	Percent qualified	10.7

SOURCES: See nn. 64, 97, 108.
NOTE: Both freeholders and militia lists exclude the infirm. See also n. 104, concerning the assumption for comparing ages.
[a] From freeholders lists.
[b] From militia lists.
[c] Named on land tax but not necessarily resident.

108. The 10 percent militia sample was chosen from V. A. Hatley, ed., *Northamptonshire Militia Lists, 1777*, Northamptonshire Record Society (1973). The parishes chosen were Aston-le-Walls, Barnwell All Saints, Brixworth, Cogenhoe, Coton, East Farndon, Gayton, Glapthorn, Great Brington, Harleston, Kettering, King's Sutton, Kingsthorpe, Lamport, Luddington, Maidford, Mears Ashby, Milton, Newton Bromswold, Old Brackley, Roade, Rothwell, Stanford, Warkworth, and Woodford.

109. This assumes that there were twice as many qualified freeholders as were listed (on the grounds that some may have served and were excused, others were ill, infirm, or over the age of seventy and had served); that there was no greater number of other males over the age of forty-five; and that only two-thirds of the men listed on the land tax were actually resident. These assumptions are sufficiently conservative to make the revised estimates in the text almost certainly maximum ones.

parishes with militia lists (Table 10.4 and Figure 10.5). In short, gentlemen were eighteen times as likely to appear among the qualified, and farmers were more than three times as likely, as their numbers in the population warranted. Tradesmen and artisans, a widely varying group of different social standings, had a little better than even chance of being rich enough to qualify. The great majority of

Table 10.4. Occupational Distribution of Jury and Militia Lists, Northamptonshire, 1777[a]

	Jury List		Militia List	
Occupation/Status	No.	%	No.	%
Gentlemen and higher	20	18.5	14	1.0
Farmers, yeomen	40	37.0	156	11.2
Artisans[b], tradesmen	47	43.5	442	31.7
Weavers	0	0.0	235	16.9
Laborers	0	0.0	254	18.2
Servants	1	0.9	274	19.7
Apprentices, "poor"	0	0.0	18	1.3
Total	108	99.9	1,393	100.0

SOURCES: See nn. 64, 108.
[a] Using a random sample of every tenth parish in the 1777 militia list.
[b] Excluding weavers but including other textile workers.

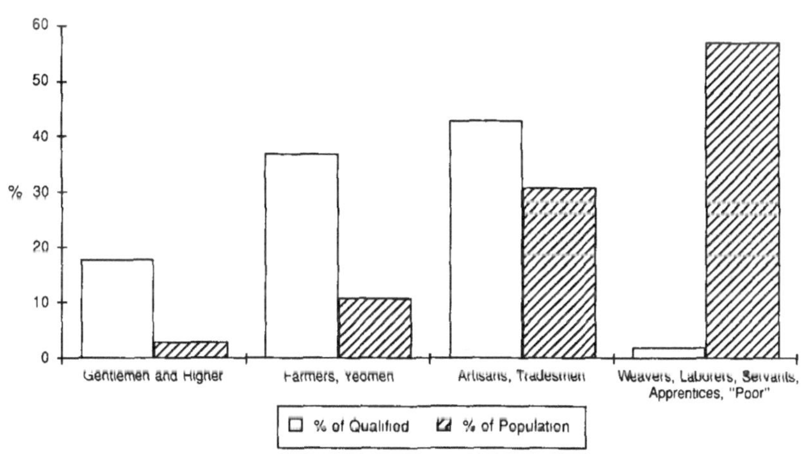

Figure 10.5. Qualified Jurors, by Occupation, Northamptonshire, 1777.
SOURCE: Table 10.4.

weavers, laborers, and servants, 55 percent of the population, could never hope to be called to apply the law to their fellow citizens.[110]

It is abundantly clear that at least half the adult male population was excluded from jury service on grounds of poverty, but we have seen that Massie and Colquhoun's estimates of national income distribution actually suggest that the number may be higher, nearer 75 percent.[111] The Northamptonshire estimates may, in fact, underestimate exclusion by 25 percent, if only because 32 percent of the population whose occupations we know fall into the problematic category of artisans and tradesmen, where status is very mixed but where undoubtedly many poorer citizens were to be found.

This problem, and the possibility that Northamptonshire may be atypical, excluding more people from jury service than other parts of the country, suggests the need to examine the jury eligibility of populations that were composed to a greater extent of tradesmen and artisans. Many parts of the country, such as the industrial areas of Staffordshire, were growing very rapidly in the later eighteenth century, spawning many sprawling villages and high-wage populations as industrial output grew and diversified. Perhaps the jurymen of Northampton continued to represent a propertied agrarian base long after other counties had admitted a wider range of jurymen, and even perhaps the poor, the ignorant, and the disrespectful, whom critics so often thought they saw subverting the social status of the jury. If fully qualified freeholders were difficult to find in Staffordshire because of the under-assessment of the land tax, this might be even more likely. Testing the jury eligibility of such a population will allow an estimate to be made of the maximum proportion of these lesser members of the middling ranks that might have made their way onto juries.

Wolverhampton is the ideal test case. It was growing rapidly in the later eighteenth century as a host of small masters and journeymen, and a few large industrialists, met a vastly increased demand for the products of their metalworking skills. The town, and indeed the whole parish, was characterized by a great many small shops, an egalitarian social ethos, and a social structure that was in many ways the antithesis of that stable hierarchy that was the ideal model of landed society. It was the most populous industrial parish in an industrializing county, and it was also the parish from which most prosecutions at Stafford assizes and quarter sessions originated. It also contributed the most names to the Staffordshire freeholders book of 1782: 141, or

110. See above, n. 107.

111. See above, text at n. 44.

8 percent of the total. For all these reasons, it is an excellent contrasting case to the experience of more rural parishes and counties. If those serving on juries in the eighteenth century were often—or increasingly—plebeian, or if the property qualifications were being evaded, Wolverhampton should have provided the most democratic juries, those most broadly representative of the whole social order.

In 1777 Wolverhampton obtained an improvement act that provided for rate assessments based on the yearly rent or value of most real property.[112] Property under £4 was exempt, rates were calculated on a sliding scale according to the assessed value, and the tax was paid by the tenant or occupant. Because the original assessment had been made so recently, values given in the 1780 returns under the Act are almost certainly reliable, rather than being conventional ones.[113] Appeals were not uncommon, and this is another reason for believing that the assessments reflected real values. The distribution of assessments, and the distribution of the assessments of those who qualified for jury service and were not exempt from it, is given in Table 10.5. It shows that 83 percent of those who qualified as jurors were among the wealthiest third of those assessed under the act, those with property worth more than £10. But even the 17 percent of qualified men who were assessed between £4 and £10, and even those assessed at the lowest rate, £4, were not necessarily men of modest property. Those who appear in the 1784 jury book, which also provides occupations, include three gentlemen and two yeomen.[114] In other words, even the poorest category of assessment included men of substantial social standing. The reason for this becomes clearer when we estimate the proportion of the population who owned or rented enough property to pay even the minimum assessment of £4. Although we do not have accurate figures for the population of the town in the early 1780s, it was probably about 12,000. On the assumption that adult males con-

112. 17 Geo. III, c. 25 (1777): "An Act for Widening, Cleansing and Lighting the Several Streets, Lanes, Alleys, Ways and other Public Passages within the Town of Wolverhampton in the County of Stafford and for taking Down, Altering or Rebuilding certain Buildings therein mentioned, and for removing all other Nuisances and Incroachments, and for regulating Carts and other Carriages within the Said Town." Orchards, pastures, money, stock, and personal property were exempt. If a taxpayer had more than one piece of property, assessments were consolidated for the purposes of the sliding scale. There was a provision for appeals.

113. SRO, D257/M3: "A Rate or Assessment on all Houses, Garden and Buildings within the Limits of the Town of Wolverhampton . . . for One Year Com mencing the 24th day of June 1780 & ending the 24th of June 1781."

114. Indeed, a gentleman and a yeoman are among the three qualified men assessed the lowest amount, £4.

Table 10.5. Assessments for 1780 of Those Eligible for Jury Service in 1782 Compared to All Assessments for 1780, Wolverhampton

1780 Assessment (in pounds)	A Those Eligible*		B All Assessments		C % of Assessed Who Qualified (A/B)
	%	N	%	N	
4 to 10	17.4	16	67.3	710	2.3
Over 10 to 20	50.0	46	25.1	265	17.4
Over 20	32.6	30	7.6	80	37.5
Ambiguous	—	13			
Not found	—	36			
Total	100.0	141	100.0	1,055	

SOURCES. SRO, D257/M3 (assessment for 1780); WSL, HM 31/18 (jury book for 1782).

* Those who can be unambiguously traced in the freeholders book compiled in 1782, a total of 92. Another 13 are names that occur more than once and hence give a range of values, and 36 are not found in the tax roll.

stituted about 25 percent, or 3,000 men, then the 141 named in the jury book represented 4.7 percent of the adult male population,[115] and a minimum of 87.5 percent of the town's adult males were excluded simply because they were too poor.[116] In short, probably a higher proportion of jurors were excluded in industrial populations than in more agrarian ones, if Wolverhampton is representative.

115. Based on the figure of 7,454 in 1750 (see Isaac Taylor's *Plan of Wolverhampton,* surveyed in that year) and William Pitt, *General View of the Agriculture of Staffordshire* (1796), 174, for the figure of 18,500 in about the year 1790. The 1801 census gives a figure of 12,565 for the town and over 23,000 for the entire parish.

116. The 87.5 percent figure was derived as follows. Some men were not listed for reasons other than poverty—age, infirmity, profession, recent service, religious disqualification (see above, text at n. 66), and perhaps corrupt avoidance. About 62 percent of the highest income group are not listed, presumably for these reasons. Assuming that these causes operated equally in all social classes probably produces a conservative bias for the argument, because the most propertied group was the group most likely to be spared service in any given year due to previous service, particularly on grand juries, and because they may also have avoided service, as Peel suggested, through the bribing of constables. (The only disqualification or exemption possibly of greater importance in lower-income groups, religious disqualification of Quakers and of Catholics, would not affect enough men to alter the results significantly.) Subtracting that percentage from the total of those who were assessed between £4 and £10, 266 should have qualified if income was irrelevant. Since only 16 did so, the percentage excluded from juries because of the property qualification was 94 percent in that category. When the same reasoning is extended to the estimated total adult male population of 3,000, the exclusion rate of 87.5 percent results.

Our general conclusions about the effect of the property qualification must be considered tentative, given the inadequate coverage of the sources, but the results are consistent. The militia and tax sources for Northamptonshire tell us that even if all artisans and tradesmen (a third of the population, if weavers are excluded) met the property qualification, over half the population did not. If only half of the artisans and tradesmen were qualified (probably a generous estimate), 72 percent of the population was excluded. In Wolverhampton, well over 80 percent of the population was excluded. And using Massie and Colquhoun's estimates of the distribution of national income, the average income of the social group to which the minimally qualified juror belonged exceeded that of 75 percent of the population. These results from different sources are sufficiently consistent to suggest that the policy legislated between 1692 and 1730 proscribed three-quarters of the adult males of England outside London from jury service. Analysis of actual juries, and of panels and jury books, shows that the statutes were followed in the counties studied, and this may have been generally the case outside London. Charles Cottu, after describing the terms of the qualification statutes, reported in 1820 that "these minutiae are attended to with the greatest exactness." It thus seems likely that the deficiencies in jurors denounced by Peel in 1825 may well have been confined to London.[117] Why particular jurors were chosen to serve is more difficult to ascertain.

Constructing the Eighteenth-Century Criminal Trial Jury

The legislation had little to say on the matter (although the little it did say, as we shall see, is significant). We must consider whether the practices of those who chose jurors from the freeholders books selected men of a distinctive character. The jurors' geographic origins, occupational structure, service on different juries, and experience of jury service can be examined; their other characteristics are a matter of conjecture.

When the freeholders books in Staffordshire are compared to the lists of jurors who were called by the sheriff and those who actually tried cases, it appears that for the most part jury service was distributed in roughly even rotation throughout the county. The assize panels almost always contain proportionate numbers from each of the hundreds, and there is no evidence of a heavy concentration near Staf-

117. Cottu, *Criminal Justice in England*, 61; above, text at n. 72.

ford (the assize town) or any other area.[118] In terms of occupation, a slight bias may have been shown for farmers, but the numbers are too small to be certain (Table 10.6). The reason gentlemen were so seldom summoned for ordinary trial juries, and so rarely served, was that they were reserved by the undersheriff for service on special juries (either civil or criminal). In any event, most of them were doubtless considered to be more than meeting their obligations by frequently repeated service on grand juries.

The patterns of repeated service, in fact, are one of the most distinctive features of the juries struck in these years. Table 10.7 shows the aggregate frequency of repeated service on all four juries taken together: grand juries and trial juries in both quarter sessions and assizes. About one-quarter of the jurors had served before.[119] But Table 10.8 shows that repeated service was most common by far on the as-

Table 10.6. Trial Jury Composition Compared to Freeholders Listed, Staffordshire, 1784–1785

	Assize Panels[a]		Jurors Sworn[b]		Freeholders Book[c]	
Occupations	No.	%	No.	%	No.	%
Gentlemen, Esquires	6	6.3	0	0	122	15.2
Farmers, yeomen	54	56.3	26	60	336	41.8
Tradesmen, manufacturers	36	37.5	17	40	346	43.0
Unknown	93	—	34	—	941	—
Total	189	100.1	77	100	1,745	100.0

SOURCES. WSL, HM 31/18 (jury book for 1784); PRO, ASSI 5/104–5, SRO, Q/SO, vol. 18.
[a] 1784, 1785.
[b] 1784 assizes and quarter sessions.
[c] Compiled Michaelmas 1784.

118. Beattie, *Crime and the Courts*, 382–85, found a very different pattern in Surrey, where jurors came disproportionately from the assize town. In Staffordshire, the undersheriff seems to have been anxious to ensure that no jury could be challenged for want of "hundredors," the necessity of whom was unclear in law, see Chitty, *Practical Treatise*, 1:501

119. Comparisons between periods and jurisdictions are still difficult, because different measures of the phenomenon have been employed. That used here, repeated actual service, corresponds most closely to that of Beattie, but the much greater frequency of courts in the City of London greatly affects the comparison. See Table 8.4. Table 10.7 is also not strictly comparable with his figures because of the lack of overlap between different juries, an overlap that Beattie finds characteristic of London. See above, chap. 8, text at n. 31 and Table 8.4.

Table 10.7. Patterns of Repeated Service on Staffordshire Grand and Petty Juries Combined, 1782–1787

No. of Sessions Sworn At	Men	Appearances
1	684	684
2	90	180
3	12	36
4	6	24
5	5	25
6	6	36
7	1	7
8	2	16
9	2	18
12	1	12
Total	809	1,038
First-time attenders	809	
Jurors with previous experience	229	
Proportion of experienced jurors	$\frac{229}{809} = .28$	

SOURCES: See n. 77.

Table 10.8. Distribution between Juries of Experienced Jurors, Staffordshire, 1782–1787

Jury Service	Assizes Only	Petty QS	Grand QS	Both QS	Total
QS only	—	15	9	20	44
Petty assizes	5	12	18	0	35
Grand assizes	46	0	0	0	46
Both assizes	0	0	0	0	0
Total	51	27	27	20	125

SOURCES: See n. 77.

size grand jury, and that none of that experience was put to use on trial juries. Grand jurymen at assizes, all gentlemen and half of them magistrates, probably attended as a matter of course if they were in town. Experienced trial jurors were most likely to turn up at the less important court of quarter sessions. But the most striking fact of Tables 10.7 and 10.8 taken together is the large number of apparently wholly inexperienced jurors who served only once.

The essays in this volume and earlier work by John Beattie and James Cockburn all show that some of the most important points in the evolution of jury trial from the sixteenth century onward were determined by shifts, at those times or in those localities in which there was much pressure on the courts, from the use of many, inexperienced jurors to relatively few, experienced men who heard many more cases at any one assizes and who returned to court year after year. The decade of the 1780s (in which the number of trials in Staffordshire and elsewhere reached new heights for the eighteenth century) does not at first sight appear to present such a pattern. Thus Table 10.9 shows that there were remarkably few repeaters on trial juries in Staffordshire in the 1780s. Service gave an exemption for two years. Over a period of six years the men in the first two years would be liable, in theory, to three jury calls, and those in the third and fourth years to two. Yet only thirty-three men ever served twice, and no one served more than twice, so that in the whole sample the proportion of experienced jurors was 7 percent, compared to Beattie's 47 percent for the late seventeenth century in London. A more significant figure, however, would be the proportion of experienced jurors at the end of the sample period, when repeaters are most likely to be present.[120] In 1786 and 1787[121] (the fifth and sixth years of the sample), the total rose to

Table 10.9. Patterns of Repeated Service on Staffordshire Petty Juries, 1782–1787

No. of Sessions Sworn At	Men	"Appearances"
1	415	415
2	33	66
Total	448	481
First-time attenders	448	
Jurors with previous experience	33	
Proportion of experienced jurors	$\frac{33}{481} = .07$	

SOURCES: See n. 77.

120. This is because Beattie finds considerable exchange between grand and petty juries in the City of London. See above, chap. 8, text at n. 31 and Table 8.3. In Staffordshire, as in Surrey and Sussex, grand jurors were a race apart. Because they were often repeat servers, they also distort the estimate of experience on trial juries. They have therefore been excluded from Table 10.9.

121. Actually, Michaelmas 1785 to Translation 1787, plus both assizes in 1786 and 1787.

only 15 percent, and over the whole period 1792–1800 it was 18.6 percent.[122]

This pattern is similar to those of Surrey in the 1790s and Essex in the 1770s and early 1780s.[123] There is also a shift, as in Essex, in the later 1780s toward regular recalling of a core of experienced jurors. This happened at Summer assizes and Translation sessions in 1787, that is, immediately after the experience of Lent assizes, which were the busiest in the entire period since 1742 and when there had been an unprecedented use of talesmen.[124] For the Summer assizes the sheriff called four more men than usual, and apparently he deliberately constructed a jury with more experience: it included four repeaters, instead of the usual one or two. The pattern was seen at Translation sessions too, where five of thirteen jurors were already experienced. Unlike Essex, however, that pattern did not continue once indictment levels fell again in 1788. Staffordshire juries again came to be composed almost entirely of inexperienced men. There was an average of only 1.8 repeaters per jury over the whole period from 1782 to 1800.

The significance of repeated service is not wholly clear. Experienced jurors could probably help to speed deliberations; certainly the unusual burden of business in Lent 1787, requiring four juries, was an incentive to try for efficient trials at the next sessions and assizes. Whether this was on local initiative or at the suggestion of the assize judges is not known.[125] For the defendant, however, there may have been another, related consequence. Modern research suggests that the experienced juror is more likely to convict.[126] There are reasons why this may be particularly so today, including the fact that exclusionary rules now protect the inexperienced juror from evidence of past convictions and bad character, but once experienced, he or she is more likely to suspect the presence of such features behind the accused. Such evidence was not withheld from the eighteenth-century juror.

122. For 1782–1800, 1,163 men served once, 212 served twice, 40 served three times, 9 served four times, and 4 appeared five times.

123. See above, chap. 9, Table 9.4 and accompanying text; Beattie, *Crime and the Courts*, 386. The Staffordshire ratio of repeaters to total individuals sworn, at 18.6 percent, is greater than Beattie's rate of 14.8 percent for Surrey in 1792–1801, but seventy-six Staffordshire sessions (both assizes and QS) were examined, compared to Beattie's twenty assize sessions.

124. See above, chap. 6, nn. 75, 93.

125. That has been the burden of the argument to date, coupled with the argument that inexperienced jurors were passive in the face of either judges or experienced foremen. See above, chap. 9.

126. D. W. Broeder, "Previous Jury Trial Service affecting Juror Behavior," *Insurance Law Journal* 506 (1965): 138–43; R. C. Dillehay and M. T. Nietzel, "Juror Experience and Jury Verdicts," *Law and Human Behavior* 9 (1985): 179–91.

But in the longer term it seems likely that even the eighteenth-century juror was likely to become more disposed to the prosecution after extended exposure to stories of villainy in court. Moreover, it is a reasonable hypothesis that undersheriffs, if they chose more experienced jurors in the late 1780s, were choosing men who would not prove to be too exacting of the prosecution case, or too independent of judges. In a system of jury unanimity, a few jurors who are unwilling to convict, too scrupulous of the evidence, or too inclined to insist on the right to jury nullification are more dangerous than many jurors who are too inclined to convict. Judges undoubtedly did not like juries who convicted innocent men, but in that case the harm could be readily undone through a royal pardon. Unjustified acquittals could not be remedied by the bench. The issue may have been particularly acute at this time, because the period from 1785 to 1787 saw the largest number of capital prosecutions in living memory. It also saw the largest number of executions, as the judges apparently carried out a deliberate policy of leaving for execution a higher proportion of convicts. The wisdom of the bench in exercising discretion had become a contentious issue in the previous year; the selection of tested and "reliable" jurors would help to ensure that discretion was not pre-empted by the verdict.[127] Whether or not such vetting of jurors, or packing of juries, took place in 1787 cannot be established. What is more striking is that for most of the period there was so little pressure to find experienced jurors. Certainly they were far rarer in Staffordshire than in London, and this difference is still unexplained. Perhaps there was a greater complacency about acquittals in the provinces; or perhaps the sheer frequency of trials at the Old Bailey forced reliance on a core of experienced men. Whether ordinary trial jurors at the Old Bailey were somehow rewarded (as were the repeaters on special juries in King's Bench) must also be investigated, as so many other aspects of London justice are known to have been permeated with corruption, fees, and rewards that often were not authorized by statute.

The Social Significance of the Qualification

At one level the meaning of the property qualification for criminal trial juries in the eighteenth century is clear. It was intended to ensure

127. See Hay, "Crime, Authority and the Criminal Law," 520–23. I give a fuller analysis of capital punishment statistics for the eighteenth and early nineteenth centuries in my forthcoming book.

that jurors would be respectable property holders of at least middling rank, not those called (by the respectable) "the labouring poor" or "the mob." But where the line fell between "the labouring poor" and "the middling sort" is a problem for social historians. Some have estimated that it lay as high as the eightieth percentile of the population, while others have drawn it farther down the social scale.[128] All agree, however, that its social and political significance was great. Those with property, even property that was very modest in the eyes of a gentleman, might be considered to have enough stake in the status quo to wield power in the constitution. Since jury service was considered to be of great constitutional importance as the guarantee of both individual and collective liberty, the evidence that the jury statutes effectively excluded three-fourths of all adult males strongly supports those historians who argue that the eighteenth-century dichotomy between the "people" and the "poor" was fixed at a high point in the distribution of wealth and income.

In assessing the meaning of the jury qualification, however, both in terms of social consciousness and social structure, we must deal with those contemporary assertions that the jury was composed of poor, "mean" men. One relevant comparison is with other statutory property qualifications that were important in social life and social consciousness. Three qualifications familiar to gentlemen (and gentlemen were the critics of juries) stand out: those for hunting game, for acting as a justice of the peace, and for sitting in the House of Commons. To be a justice of the peace or to hunt required an annual income of £100 in freehold or an equivalent, a sum that excluded about 97 percent of the population. To be a member of Parliament, one was supposed to have an income from land of £300 or its equivalent.

Seen from this highly distorted perspective, the £10 jury was indeed, therefore, a most popular part of the constitution. From the perspective of a ruling class perched on the pinnacle of the pyramid of wealth and income, it may even have seemed at times virtually a plebeian one. Like the privileged in most societies, many of the eighteenth-century ruling class lived in blissful ignorance of how tiny a group they constituted. Robert Owen recounted the reaction of the dukes of York and Sussex to a model of the social pyramid in which a tiny cube at the top represented the royal family and the peerage. It was

128. For the argument that it was drawn at a high point, and that the "middling ranks" were consequently numerically much less significant, see R. W. Malcolmson, *Life and Labour in England, 1700–1780* (1981), esp. chap. 1.

> so strikingly insignificant, compared with all below, and especially when compared with the cubes representing the working and pauper classes, that the Duke of Sussex impulsively pushed the elbow of his royal brother, saying—"Edward, do you see that?" And the whole party for the moment seemed confused.[129]

Not all gentlemen were as ignorant of their nation as the royal family, of course, but both ignorance and the belief in an aristocratic social order led to a radical foreshortening of social perspective. Comments on juries are such an instance. Moreover, the social standing of juries aroused concern because the institution represented such an unusual degree of participation by "middling men" in the affairs of the nation. Although the franchise allowed perhaps one adult male in six to vote, some boroughs had virtual adult male suffrage, and the county qualification to vote was only a £2 freehold. Nonetheless, elections were so rare, and were becoming more so, that courting the people and the mob was a prospect that bothered relatively few gentlemen, only those who chose to be bothered.[130] But juries tried those accused of criminal offenses six times a year in most counties—much more often in London—and they wielded real power. The question of who could be a juror was of concern to every gentleman who ever imagined, or found himself, a prosecutor or defendant in a courtroom. Thus upper-class comment, and the many who wrote in its idiom, often tended to treat what was in fact a relatively privileged institution as if it were far more democratic than it was. Historians relying on such biased testimony will make the same mistake.

It is unlikely that similar distorting judgments were made by those most acquainted with the courts themselves in the eighteenth century. There, both differentials of power and the social identity of the jury were of acute concern to both the man or woman in the dock and the prosecutor who claimed to be the victim of the crime. Identifying the social standing of both prosecutors and accused is even more complicated than placing that of the juror, but the jury lists themselves offer a quick estimate. Thus in one sample year in Staffordshire in the 1780s a mere 2 percent of the accused were men who were qualified to be jurors (Table 10.10), and their crimes, all misdemeanors, were those of propertied men: contempt by an overseer (for ignoring a judicial order), an assault, and two charges of perjury against gentlemen

129. Robert Owen, *The Life of Robert Owen* (1920), 209.

130. J. Cannon, *Parliamentary Reform, 1640–1832* (Cambridge, 1973), 30, 41, and passim.

Table 10.10. Accused and Prosecutors Qualified to Be Jurors, Staffordshire, 1783

	Accused			Prosecutor		
Charge	Qualified	Unqualified	Percent Qualified	Qualified	Unqualified	Percent Qualified
All Offenses	4	177	2.2	33	124	21.0
Thefts	0	85	0.0	27	55	32.9

SOURCES: SRO, all QS series for Michaelmas 1782, and Epiphany, Easter, and Translation 1783; PRO, all ASSI series for Lent and Summer 1783; WSL, HM 31/18 (jury book for 1783).
NOTE: Women were not counted. Each combination of accused and prosecutor counted as one charge. Thefts include receiving.

in connection with other litigation. None of those accused of the most common and serious crime, theft, were qualified to be jurors. In contrast, 21 percent of all prosecutors in that year appear on the freeholders lists.[131] In theft cases, one-third of all prosecutors were qualified and eligible to be jurors. Since most of the exemptions from jury service (apart from poverty) were enjoyed by professionals and gentlemen, the number of prosecutors who could have sat on juries was undoubtedly higher.[132] And if we make the most conservative assumption, that all jurors were barely qualified and that all accused had the median income of laboring men, the social tables of Massie and Colquhoun show that jurors had three times the income of accused men and, of course, far greater wealth.[133]

One legal historian has argued that because the differential of wealth between jurors and gentlemen was probably greater than that between jurors and accused, the social perspective of a juror was more likely to be that of the accused than that of a judge or other gentleman.[134] I think this is profoundly to misunderstand the social percep-

131. Michaelmas 1782 and Epiphany, Easter, Translation, Lent, and Summer 1783. Each combination of accused and prosecutor has been counted separately; no women have been counted. One bias is the fact that prosecutors were likely to be older than accused, and some accused were below the minimum age for jury service.

132. Some other implications of the different social status of prosecutors and accused are discussed in D. Hay, "Prosecution and Power: Malice in the English Courts, 1750–1850," in *Policing and Prosecution 1750–1850*, ed. D. Hay and F. Snyder.

133. This estimate uses the revised tables of Lindert and Williamson (see above, n. 39) and takes into account the median income of those immediately below £38 in Massie's account and below £45 in Colquhoun's.

134. Langbein, "Albion's Fatal Flaws," although the exact thesis is unclear. He criticizes my earlier account for "assimilating" men of great wealth and £10 free-

tions of the eighteenth century, and perhaps any century. I have suggested elsewhere that the middling ranks, from which jurors were primarily chosen, had distinctive interests in the criminal law not shared to the same degree by gentlemen, notably efficient, cheap prosecution and certain, rather than discretionary, punishment.[135] But there can be little doubt that enforcement of the criminal law, the maintenance of discipline among the poor, and the punishment of theft were the common interests of both; that each recognized the place of the other in the constitution; and that they concurred in the exclusion of all laboring men from all parts of it, including the jury box.

Those with modest or great wealth sought to exclude the poor on the grounds that poor jurymen had been and would be corruptible, but as we have seen they also argued that poor men must also be ignorant men, that those of mean degree were of mean understanding. The argument that poor men are corruptible is unanswerable and is a leitmotif of the constitutional thought of propertied Englishmen. But the pervasiveness of references to ignorance and inconsistency as the inevitable traits of poor jurymen suggests that the propertied had an acute distrust of juries who might take a different view of the matters before them than they would themselves. A brief review of the scope of legislation in effect after 1730 makes the clearest case that this was so, and it shows that juries were intended to distinguish between classes of Englishmen, classes defined not only in economic and status terms but also in terms of the consciousness of separate identities.

It has been remarked that the vetting or packing of juries was a principal concern of those who passed the 1730 act but also that it nonetheless remained possible for undersheriffs to choose experienced or pro-conviction veniremen for common juries if they so wished.[136] Packing and vetting in state trials was undoubtedly a refined, recondite art. In most cases its details are still to be recovered, for both the

holders, although my major thesis in 1975 was instead the distinctive interests of each (see below, n. 135). Langbein's associated assumption, that there was a moral consensus across all social classes regarding theft, is too large to address here, but see some comments in Hay, "Crime and Justice in Eighteenth- and Nineteeth-Century England," in *Crime and Justice: An Annual Review of Research*, ed. N. Morris and M. Tonry (Chicago, 1980), 45–84. The idea that there is not, and that there has not always been, a virtually unanimous social consensus as to what is culpable may be disturbing to some of those whose calling is to make an existing framework of law work. See D. Hay, "Controlling the English Prosecutor," *Modern Law Review* 47 (1984): 1–29, esp. pp. 16ff.

135. Hay, "Property, Authority and the Criminal Law," esp. pp. 59–60.

136. See above, text at n. 52.

historical record and the present practice remain formidably obscure in England.[137] But my point here is that the practice of constructing juries in order to try to ensure a particular verdict was only possible in certain kinds of trials.

In civil suits, by far the most common kind of court proceedings in which gentlemen in Parliament might find themselves to be defendants, provision was made in 1730 for juries at nisi prius to be drawn by lot.[138] Defendants in criminal trials—including those on trial for their lives on ordinary capital statutes, and even those tried for sedition and treason—had no such guarantee. A century later, in 1825, Peel announced to the applause of Parliament that the ballot would also be introduced in criminal trials. But Parliament was doubtless not surprised to hear that it would only be available for special juries.[139]

Special juries were in themselves a striking restriction of popular participation on the jury. In the counties such juries were composed of the very wealthiest freeholders—that is, until 1825, esquires. The social exclusiveness of special juries is staggering; Peel mentioned the fact that at the trial of John Cartwright at Warwick in 1820 only 54 men could be found in the whole county to make up the panel, and in Staffordshire only 68 are listed in the 1784 jury book out of the total of about 1,700 names.[140] Moreover, special juries could only be had in trials for misdemeanors and only on the payment of a fee of a guinea a juror. Again, misdemeanor charges were the only kind of criminal proceedings that gentlemen and the propertied middling sort were likely to face.

There were yet other protections for the propertied. For juries in civil trials at assizes, talesmen had to be drawn from the original panels, and talesmen for special juries were picked by lot from the panel

137. But see E. P. Thompson, "The Jury—An Endangered Species" The Meiklejohn Lecture, Brown University, 14 Apr. 1980, some parts of which appear in Thompson, "Subduing the Jury," *London Review of Books*, 4 and 18 Dec. 1986, and Oldham, "Special Juries: Nineteenth-Century Usage and Reform."

138. 3 Geo. II, c. 25, ss. 11, 12.

139. *Parliamentary Debates*, 2d ser., vol. 12 (1825), cols. 969–70; 6 Geo. IV, c. 50, ss. 32, 33. Although mandatory for what Peel called "political cases," i.e., criminal misdemeanors, in civil proceedings with special juries the parties could agree to proceed without a ballot. Cottu had noted in 1820 (*Criminal Justice in England*, 74–75) that the 1730 statutory requirement for a ballot was not being followed in criminal cases; see above, n. 60.

140. *Parliamentary Debates*, 2d ser., vol 12 (1825), cols. 968–69. See also above, text at n. 23.

of common jurors, which greatly hindered packing.[141] Moreover, according to the 1730 legislation, special juries were struck in such a way that the prosecution could not enjoy the benefit of virtually unlimited challenges.[142] None of these requirements applied to felony trials, which were the majority of cases and which typically had the poorest defendants.

In short, the law, both before and after Peel's act of 1825, ensured that three broad social distinctions were drawn in the selecting of juries. As we have seen from both the legislation and the archival record, probably 75 percent of the population was rigorously excluded from common juries. They were virtually only seen in court as defendants. Their jurors were men of comparatively substantial property, even if the very wealthy, on whose testimony we rely so much, often denigrated such jurors. Thus women and men accused of theft were tried by juries deliberately composed of the class that prosecuted most often for theft. No statutory protections existed to prevent the packing of panels with conviction-prone experienced jurors. Conversely, such middling-rank prosecutors were protected from the chance that a single poor man on a jury might force acquittals (either from conviction or because of corruption) in the way that poor jurymen had apparently done two hundred years before. Finally, for the benefit of gentlemen, who were likely to find themselves in court only on misdemeanor charges or in civil suits, control of talesmen and the guarantee of a special jury was enacted by 1730, ensuring that they, like middling men, enjoyed a jury of peers in not only the legal but also the sociological sense, the kind of jury so strenuously denied the poor. Gentlemen were thereby protected from the ignominy of judgment by their social inferiors and from the possible hostility of jurors of the middling rank in cases where a prosecutor might be of that class.

And, as Bentham so caustically reminds us, in the early nineteenth century, juries that favored the propertied were also very useful to the state. There is an irony here, because the qualifications established in 1692 for jury service and the penalties enacted to enforce them in 1730 were probably intended in part to protect defendants in political trials.[143] The qualified freeholder would be less open to corruption; a

141. 7 & 8 Wm. III, c. 32, s. 3. See above, n. 60

142. See Oldham, "Origins of the Special Jury," 176–96, for the practice by which counsel helped select a panel of forty-eight. In state trials for felony and treason, very large panels were of great assistance to the prosecution. But see below, text at n. 144.

143. See above, text at n. 55.

special jury of Tory country gentlemen would know how to treat a malicious Whig prosecution for seditious libel. But the opposition appears to have mistaken the way in which the act would work. They were soon enlightened. The 1729 trial of Richard Francklin, publisher of the *Craftsman,* had resulted in an acquittal, almost certainly because the panel had been chosen by a high Tory. Francklin's conviction in his second trial, in 1731, was attributed to the negation of such influences by the impaneling of a special jury made up of Whigs. The government lawyers had shown that the construction of special juries under the 1730 act would help ensure convictions in state trials. The dismay of the opposition was acute. Their afterthoughts surfaced in an exchange between the *Craftsman* and the ministerial *Free Briton* in January 1732. The *Free Briton* had hailed the act as "a more national Act than the *Habeas Corpus* Act, and most properly a *Court Law.*" The *Craftsman* retorted that it was indeed a "Court" measure in respect to special juries, which it had never expected to be used in state prosecutions. Francklin's conviction showed that the great innovation, the ballot, did not apply to special juries, "which are no more exempt from Corruption, than if this Bill never passed; nor has the Court *put it out of their Power, to practice upon Juries.*"[144]

Moreover, in the state trials of the 1790s and later, when the defendant was likely to be a democrat—an artisan or a tradesman of little property—it was the Crown that was anxious to ensure that jurymen were men of greater property.[145] The jury qualification statutes now assisted the state to make political convictions, and they would do so until well into the twentieth century. Further, the terms of the early legislation that were designed to prevent the packing of juries with the poor did nothing to prevent packing them with the wealthy, the compliant, the socially conservative, and the paid.

The social history of the English jury from 1730 to 1825 is a history of carefully structured inequality. It is also a history of the perceptions and fears that Englishmen with wealth and power had about the greater number who had much less, and especially the vast majority

144. L. Hanson, *Government and the Press, 1695–1763* (Oxford, 1936), 19, 23, 67–68; *Craftsman,* 1 Jan 1732, no. 287, *Free Briton,* 5 Jan. 1732, no. 110, reprinted in part in *Gentleman's Magazine* 2 (1732): 554–55. Hence the significance of Peel's introduction of the ballot to special juries in 1825 (above, p. 353 and n. 60).

145. The aim was not always achieved. One problem was the deficiencies of some freeholders books by the early nineteenth century (see above, n. 70). Dr. Ruth Paley has found that in *R.* v. *Stone* (25 *State Trials,* 1155) the treasury solicitor's papers include a vetted jury panel together with a covering letter (Joseph Burchell, 17 Sept. 1795) drawing explicit attention to the difficulty of knowing whether those on the panel were in fact qualified (TS 11/547/1777).

who, in their eyes, properly had little or none at all. In short, it embodies part of the history of class in England. The eighteenth-century ruling class admitted men of moderate property to the jury box but protected itself from the decisions of such men.[146] In the interest of the enforcement of the criminal law, gentlemen also ensured that moderate property would be protected against any participation by the laboring poor in the forging of unanimous verdicts. The whole was concealed in a cloud of rhetorical effusions about liberty and justice, made somewhat plausible by the role that courageous jurymen had played in resisting the executive in state trials.

The fact that the English jury was molded to sustain the structure of power in eighteenth-century England through a complex of still imperfectly understood decisions under the terms of a very complicated body of law has helped to obscure from historians the extent of the inequality it protected and embodied. The evident independence of jurymen to decide, without appeal, to acquit the accused, as well as to convict, has seemed to some a powerful argument against the portrayal of juries as expressions of class power.[147] It is, of course, no such thing. Probably jurors rarely decided entirely against the evidence, rarely perverted the course of English justice in overtly class-biased ways in the eighteenth century. They had no need to do so. The criminal law of England also shaped, and was shaped by, carefully structured class inequality. The juries so carefully created by Parliament, sheriffs, constables, and wealth were the procedural corollary to the inequality embodied in the substantive criminal law and in English society itself.

The judges necessarily ignored such issues when they concluded, in a decision in 1680, " 'Tis for the advantage of the defendant to have a substantial jury." Their reasoning was based on a false analogy between civil and criminal process, but the conclusion was repeated from time to time as a self-evident truth.[148] Whatever the relevance of

146. This held except in the case of murder, the only felony a gentleman was likely to be accused of, but even here structured inequality existed, in that peers were tried by peers.

147. Langbein, "Albion's Fatal Flaws," 107, citing acquittal rates as evidence against a crude conspiracy thesis he attributes to me. I have argued against such a thesis ("Property, Authority and the Criminal Law," 52–54), explicitly citing, among other things, those same acquittal rates as evidence (p. 60) that the criminal law was administered within a framework of political, constitutional, and social assumptions that gentlemen and judges could accept, although middling men often criticized it. Langbein's misunderstanding of my entire account of the criminal law is fairly complete, and the empirical evidence in his article is misleading on many other matters besides jury qualifications and their effects.

148. *AG.* v. *Blood, Christian et al.* (1680), 1 Raymond 417. In this case, an information for conspiring to indict the duke of Buckingham for buggery, it was moved in

the dictum to a political case in the seventeenth century, it is highly unlikely that the host of poor women and men convicted of larcenies in the century after 1730 would have been convinced by it. It seems certain that they would have preferred to appeal to the wisdom or compassion or openness to corruption of a jury of "idle people in rags."[149] Parliament, by excluding the poorest three-quarters of the adult male population from juries, and all women, ensured that they never had a chance to try the experiment.

Acknowledgments

I am grateful for comments and suggestions from John Beattie, Peter King, Jeanette Neeson, James Oldham, Ruth Paley, Paul Romney, and Michael Sonenscher. The research for this paper was made possible by the Social Sciences and Humanities Research Council of Canada, the Economic and Social Research Council of Great Britain, and York University, Toronto.

arrest of judgment that the venire mentioned a qualification of £20, whereas the statute of 1664 (see above, n. 27) had expired. The argument that an unnecessarily highly qualified jury might be an advantage to the defendant was taken from two *civil* cases cited by the attorney general. Three judges accepted the argument, but Raymond J. expressed the fear that it might allow a court to require an impossibly high qualification, thereby causing the prisoner to be detained for want of jurors to that value.

Blood was dead; Christian was sentenced to two hours in the pillory, a fine of one hundred marks, and prison until the fine was paid.

149. See above, n. 1.

Eleven

A Retrospective on the Criminal Trial Jury, 1200–1800

Thomas A. Green

My recent book[1] provided an overview of the history of the institutional aspects of the English criminal trial jury upon which all of the contributors to this volume have, tacitly or otherwise, commented. That tentative institutional background was intended both to stand on its own terms and to provide a framework for the studies on the relationship between law and society and on the history of ideas regarding the jury that made up the larger part of the volume.[2] The two aspects of my book were joined: the socio-legal analysis and the history of ideas were to a large extent founded upon my arguments about the institutional setting of the jury. The relatively brief institutional overview thus played a crucial role. The preceding essays present new information that supersedes both my own tentative soundings on institutional matters and my syntheses of existing scholarship in that area. Little of my earlier work on institutional problems—jury composition and the like—remains exactly as it was before. Parts of that foundation have been shattered; here and there beams sag; some walls have, I am glad to say, actually been reinforced. In this essay I shall assess the present shape of the structure, following a roughly chronological approach, and, as I did in the conclusion to my earlier work, I shall indicate some matters that particularly require further investigation. My task is to provide an overview of the preceding essays, perhaps even to bring some unity to them, as I view them in relation to my own work. In particular, I shall emphasize the implications of these studies of jury composition for three problems central not only

1. Green, *Verdict According to Conscience.*

2. For the institutional background, see chaps. 1, 4, and 7 (sec. 1); for a social and legal analysis and the history of ideas, see chaps 2, 3, 5, 6, 7 (secs. 2–4), and 8

to the history of the English criminal trial jury but also to the history of the administration of the English criminal law generally. These problems involve (1) the way in which the medieval jury was informed and reached its verdict; (2) the degree and the form of the independence that the early-modern jury enjoyed at a time when the powers of the bench were very great; and (3) the role of the eighteenth-century trial jury, which, although clearly independent, was, by virtue of the status and experiences of its members, arguably a mere extension of the bench.

First, a precis of the institutional side of my published history of the jury. My earlier work suggested that the criminal trial jury emerged somewhat accidentally in about the year 1220, toward the end of what I have called the Angevin transformation of the criminal law and its administration. That transformation involved a shift from private to public prosecution and from predominantly private resolution through monetary compensation to predominantly capital punishment at the hands of the Crown. The presenting jury, dating from at least as early as the latter half of the twelfth century, exercised some significant discretion as it determined who must undergo the ordeal, the existing means of providing the proof normally required for conviction. In so doing, it reflected, broadly, communal attitudes about the sorts of persons who ought to suffer capital punishment or the sorts of offenses for which persons ought to suffer such punishment. After 1220 the trial jury, reflecting similar attitudes and diverging from standards set by the Crown—standards that the bench stood ready to enforce—played a similar role.

The trial jury's power to implement that role derived mainly from the fact that the bench was dependent upon the jury for information regarding the circumstances of presented offenses and the credibility of persons presented. I stressed the jury's role in the offense of homicide, but I also extrapolated outward to theft. I did not deal with the rarer offenses of treason, counterfeiting, rape, and arson. Implicitly, I excluded appeals, which were still mainly private prosecutions that continued to come into the royal courts, although in relatively small numbers.

In my interpretive overview of the administration of the criminal law in the medieval period, I argued that the centerpiece of the trial was the colloquy between judge and defendant. I left little room for other prosecution or defense testimony at the trial. The jury, I suggested, was influenced by the demeanor and responses of the defendant, which provided in-court evidence that it viewed in the context of what it already knew, or suspected, about the defendant, the alleged offense, and the community's view of just deserts in the case at hand. The bench must have been aware that the jury departed from the strict rules of law in many cases involving homicide and theft. There is some evidence that judges occasionally questioned jurors, even pushed them hard, but little evidence that the bench succeeded in overturning jury domination of the resolution of most cases. At least in the law of homicide, legal change appears to have taken account of jury practices, and such change, along with the obvious willingness of juries to apply the law strictly in cases that the bench deemed most serious, encouraged judicial acquiescence in—and sympathy with—jury-based mercy in the less serious felonies. Over time, then, the bench assimilated popular attitudes even while it sought greater control over a system that it could not yet effectively monitor, much less definitively control.

As I formerly viewed the matter, the Tudor period witnessed developments that dramatically shifted the balance of power in the courtroom. Although some of these developments began in the later Middle Ages—most significantly the expansion of benefit of clergy and the investigative activity of the justices of the peace—the confluence of legal, political, and social change made for a great leap forward during the middle to late decades of the sixteenth century. These changes involved, *inter alia*, the long-term decline of the self-informing jury; the taking of depositions from the accuser, prosecution witnesses, and the accused; alterations in substantive law that reduced the distance between formal legal rules and social attitudes; and recourse to the Court of Star Chamber, or to fining by the assize judges themselves, to discourage jury recalcitrance. The resulting shift of control to the bench, I argued, nonetheless had limits. Had the bench not adhered to the application of legal rules in a manner that at least roughly met with approbation on the part of much of society, it might have failed to have its way. Considerations of time and bureaucratic capacities, as well as uncertainty about gaining convictions in some cases, underlay a judicial willingness to compromise, perhaps in return for a guilty plea. Moreover, the perception on the part of jurors and the wider community may well have been that the community shared with the bench the power of mitigation and absolute condemnation. A significant reduction in the number of acquittals and verdicts of self-defense was complemented by an increase in the number of convictions on charges that left the defendant eligible for benefit of clergy, a punishment that was sufficiently modest (branding and, after 1576, the possibility of one year's imprisonment) for jurors to consider themselves merciful and for the bench occasionally to resort to withholding the privilege from those who in fact could satisfy the reading test.

By the eighteenth century, a much more substantial punishment had come to replace the sanction of branding in many cases: transportation. Although I did not explain the process in detail, I suggested that by then the jury had largely been "tamed," albeit in part because of the increasingly evident concurrence of the bench with what I termed "widespread community-based attitudes." Even the rule in Bushel's Case (1671) that the bench could not punish or threaten to punish jurors (except where true criminal fraud, contempt, or breach of administrative rules had been proved) did not often put the bench on the defensive. Judge and jury operated in tandem, efficiently and within a context wherein they conditioned each other's responses. Not that the system suited the needs of all parties at all times. There were cases—"political" in nature—where the bench sought tighter control of juries but found that the everyday practices in which the bench acquiesced provided an argument against that control. Moreover, there were critics of both capital sanctions and of a multi-level system of discretion who argued that certainty and proportionality of punishment were vital for deterrence. Reform of the law of sanctions in the nineteenth century not only greatly reduced recourse to the device of reprieve and pardon, it also reduced much of the by then highly "managed" jury law-finding that was, I argued, traceable ultimately to the early thirteenth century.

It has long been conventional to date the criminal trial jury from about 1220. In recent years we have learned a good deal about the proto-juries of the period 1166–1220 that gave medial verdicts, the defendant who was thereby "convicted" being ordered to undergo the ordeal, to abjure the realm, or to face his accuser in combat. No one has contributed more to our learning in this regard than Roger Groot.[3] Groot has now analyzed the process by which, in the course of several years, such proto-juries paved the way for a criminal trial jury that gave final verdicts, the defendant thereby convicted being condemned to death on the gallows.[4] His work allows us to draw some important—albeit tentative—inferences regarding the relationship between

3. R. D. Groot, "The Jury of Presentment before 1215," *AJLH* 26 (1982): 1–24; idem, "The Jury in Private Criminal Prosecutions before 1215," *AJLH* 27 (1983): 113–41.

4. See above, chap. 1.

jury composition, the setting of the earliest criminal jury trials, and the manner in which "self-informing" came to be a natural aspect of trial jury process.

Groot takes the view that practically from the outset of the trial jury period the bench accepted final verdicts with little question. He does not attempt directly to explain why such great power was thus posited in the hands of the lay community. He certainly does not invoke the traditional view that the jury was in some sense, like its immediate predecessor the ordeal, a surrogate for the voice of God. One level of implicit explanation seems to be that proto-juries had given untrammeled verdicts when merely medial issues were involved, and this practice was then generalized to final verdicts in some natural fashion. At another level, the explanation may be that the post-1220 trial jury was an administrative expedient for which, in theory, the actual consent of the suspect was required. The bench conditioned "consent" by requiring a choice between jury trial and harsh imprisonment (what became the infamous *peine*—not *prisone—forte et dure*) and then induced consent to trial by hundredors and members of the four neighboring vills by forcing nonconsenting suspects to be tried by the hundredors and a body of knights. Thus the authorities achieved nearly universal consent to trial by jury by establishing the more attractive local jury as the common means of proof. It was, in fact, the most logical candidate, for its members—at least those from the vills—were the best informed both about the offense charged and about the suspect's reputation generally. Presumably the hundredors, who had presented the suspect in the first place and who were men of higher standing with less investment in the interests—and prejudices—of the local community, would minimize the possibility of frivolous acquittal or conviction.

From the evidence Groot has marshaled, it appears that at the very outset the jury was forced on persons who were strongly suspected of serious offenses: the use of the jury, Groot shows, must be seen in relation to the extraordinary royal order of 1219.[5] A substantial number of the first persons to be tried by jury, being among the most serious offenders, were thus convicted, a circumstance that may have made jury trial all the more attractive to the authorities. As jury trial came to be the standard method of trial, however, defendants of all sorts put their lives upon the country, with—we might now think—predictable results. Jury trial very soon became a test of popular views on life and death that imperfectly mirrored the more abstract "letter of the law."

5. See above, chap. 1, text at n. 21.

To the extent that Groot distinguishes knights, substantial hundredors, the vill reeve, and men from the vill, he writes about jury composition and the relationship between that composition and the nature of trial. Representatives of the vill came to play a crucial role: their assent was typically required for a conviction. This should not blind us to the fact that such persons had long played a significant role in providing the evidence upon which presentments were based; doubtless, hundred jurors (presenters) did not translate the general suspicion they were bound to report into their own strong suspicion (which was required for trial to proceed, whether by ordeal or, later, by trial jury) without some confirmation from representatives of the locale of the offense. The importance of the local community in the administration of the criminal law thus pre-dated the trial jury, the adoption of which ought to be understood as a continuation and enhancement of traditional practices, not as a revolutionary step.[6]

How well was the bench positioned to see what lay behind a trial jury conviction or acquittal, and to what extent did the jury dominate the production of evidence? My own account of the way juries dominated trials in the Middle Ages probably overstates the matter.[7] There must have been some, perhaps many, cases in which inculpatory evidence came forward during proceedings at the eyre. Local officials were present, including the vill reeves, who subsequently served on early trial juries. But their main duty was to report to hundred juries, who were in turn questioned by the bench, and the hundredors were in a position to relate who was suspected and then to confirm or to cast doubt on the charges. It is difficult to see how central authorities could have prevented local coloration of the facts presented either at the presentment or at the trial stage—how, on their own motion, they could have prevented either unjust conviction or false exoneration.

6. Green, *Verdict According to Conscience*, 4–13. Recent scholarship suggests that the pre-1220 origins of the criminal trial jury deserve greater emphasis than I have given them. Susan Reynolds has demonstrated that group decision making had long been the norm in England. *Kingdoms and Communities in Western Europe, 900–1300* (Oxford, 1984). The trial jury was a natural outgrowth of this fundamental aspect of English political life, as was the jury of presentment itself. I have probably understated the significance of the evidence regarding the use of presentment in the century preceding what I have referred to as the "Angevin transformation" of the criminal law. Robert C. Palmer has suggested that the ordeal was employed largely to determine a suspect's "present moral standing," not simply to ascertain whether specific charges regarding past acts were true. The trial jury carried this tradition forward: nullification of the strict letter of the law, Palmer argues, had relatively ancient roots. "Conscience and the Law: The English Criminal Jury," *Michigan Law Review* 84 (Feb.–Apr. 1986): 792–94.

7. Green, *Verdict According to Conscience*, 16–20.

From our perspective this may seem intolerable, but it bears remembering that representatives of the vills, whether they spoke for themselves or through the hundredors, were rightly reckoned to be the best informed. Moreover, they could usually be counted on to condemn the worst offenders, the suspects who *at the outset* constituted most of the persons who underwent trial by jury.[8]

We still know very little about the transition from the earliest use of trial juries that Groot has explored to their later use in increasing numbers of cases both at the eyre and more specifically at trials on commissions of gaol delivery, oyer and terminer, and trailbaston.[9] Of these, gaol delivery was by far the most common, and significant, context for trials upon felony charges. I have emphasized the fact that those tried at gaol delivery had earlier been presented, taken, and held for trial (or bailed).[10] Many local officials attended the sessions of which gaol delivery was a part, but there was nothing like the general administrative process that characterized the eyre. Defendants were brought forward and the charges against them were read; the opportunity for testing these charges seems to have been meager, at least before the late fourteenth century. As before, much must have depended upon the views of the most knowledgeable of those summoned as trial jurors. But who were these persons, and how were they informed? And what does the sparse information we have on these points suggest about the nature of the trial and the judge-jury relationship from the late thirteenth to the late fourteenth centuries?

The cumbersome two-part trial jury of the early eyres (hundredors and members of the four vills) soon became a jury simply of twelve from the hundred in which the offense was committed. In practice it became more and more infrequent for those who served to have been among the original presenters;[11] although they were not representatives of the neighboring vills in any formal sense, some probably did come from the locale. What little we know about trial jury composition suggests that the jury of the later eyres and at gaol delivery was dominated by members of the village elites. These persons were typically members of the hundred in which the offense had been committed, but they were not necessarily its leading members. They constituted a kind of compromise produced by the interests of the

8. See above, chap. 1.

9. Green, *Verdict According to Conscience*, 20–21 nn. 64–67 and sources cited therein.

10. Ibid., 21–22.

11. Ibid.

authorities, who wanted upstanding yet informed jurors, and the interests of laymen, the most substantial of whom had, to be blunt, better things to do.

Bernard McLane's focus on the special trailbaston proceedings of 1328 allows a glimpse into community processes that research into the gaol delivery records usually does not.[12] The 1328 proceedings involved both an elaborate presentment stage and the trials of those presented persons who volunteered themselves or were taken by force. Because the sessions were ad hoc and were held to deal with what was thought to be a crisis in public order, the presentments focused on common malefactors, persons whose misdeeds were numerous and notorious. McLane concludes that many offenses were thus strained out—settled at the local level. If so, this sheds important light on the latitude that presenters had. As to those charges that did go forward, McLane's comment that presentment was itself a form of punishment is apt, for it helps to explain the high rate of acquittal by trial juries.[13]

By 1328 the separation between presenters (the later grand jury) and trial jurors was well advanced but by no means completed. The former were of decidedly higher status than the latter. The trial jurors, however, included a sufficient number of members of the gentry or of public officials (approximately 25 percent) to allow the inference that most trial jurors were at least substantial freemen; that is, they were drawn from the groups that came to be called the yeomanry. John Post confirms the fact that at late-fourteenth-century gaol deliveries most jurors "came from a broad band in the middle classes of society."[14]

More important, however, is the finding that trial jurors did not often come from the "scene" of the offense, a finding echoed in Post's and Edward Powell's essays. McLane locates those jurors he has been able to trace as living anywhere from at the scene of the crime to ten or more miles distant. A very large number lived from five to nine miles away. But most juries included at least two persons who came from the scene or from no more than three miles away, and most jurors came from within the administrative unit and were, I would venture, people with access to the local officials responsible for hearing complaints and taking preliminary steps toward the final stage of presentment. I shall explore this last point presently. For the moment it is im-

12. See above, chap. 2.

13. See above, chap. 2, text at n. 76. Edward Powell makes a related point in chap. 4, text at nn. 75, 110.

14. See above, chap. 3, text at n. 5.

portant to remember that McLane is dealing with the unusual context of trailbaston proceedings, at which presentment and trial were tandem events. His trial jurors can hardly have been in the dark about the suspicions that grounded the presentments. The opportunities for self-informing were probably at least as great for them as for the presenters. Moreover, for both presentment and trial the nature of the proceedings put a premium on the role of notoriety— most defendants were persons whom local communities wanted to bring under some degree of embarrassment or actual punishment.

The nature of the proceedings also dictated the kinds of defendants who were tried and the considerations that determined the trial jurors' verdicts. Defendants in felony cases probably fell mainly into two classes: a few very serious offenders who stood a strong chance of conviction and who were already under guard at the time of presentment; and a far greater number of suspects who, upon presentment, allowed themselves to be taken, believing that they would not be convicted because they were innocent or because, although they were guilty, the evidence against them was slight or the community viewed them as persons who, all considered, did not deserve to be hanged. Trailbaston proceedings thus generated a communal sorting-out process that began as soon as the order for the sessions was announced. McLane's account of trial jury behavior bears significant relation to the pretrial stages he has investigated. I shall suggest presently that at most proceedings the category of persons acquitted literally for "lack of evidence" against them was smaller than might be assumed. In the case of trailbaston proceedings, it must indeed have been small if the process that generated presentments took the form that McLane outlines, as I believe it did. Even notorious felons and common malefactors were sometimes acquitted for a true lack of evidence in a specific case, but more often they were acquitted, as McLane suggests, for agreeing to appear and to put their lives on the country—and, I would say, for thus implicitly reuniting themselves with the local community. Bishop Brinton (whom McLane quotes) took a less charitable view; he stood at the head of a long line of observers who decried the "wrongheaded" mercy of the criminal trial jury.[15]

Nor were the judges who presided at these and other fourteenth-century felony trials wrong in their own assessment that many guilty persons were granted acquittals. They, too, heard the presentments and must have assumed that those named represented a bad lot. So far

15. For McLane's quote from Bishop Brinton see above, chap. 2, text at n. 1. See also below, text at nn. 51, 52; Green, *Verdict According to Conscience*, 288–310.

as we can tell, however, presentments were mainly conclusory statements regarding suspicions, not presentations of discrete bits of evidence that were tested before the bench. The "test" still resided in trial jury verdicts in those cases for which defendants appeared. Although, given the nature of the proceedings, many of those who appeared must in fact have been guilty, some were either not guilty or were not clearly proved to be, and over this determination, it seems to me, the bench possessed relatively little leverage. Judicial doubts in specific cases led, as McLane and Post have shown, to placing some acquitted persons under guarantors,[16] but not to refusals to accept the verdict of the community on the question of life or death. Whether the judges thought they were most often faced with honest acquittals, misconceived mercy, or outright corruption we cannot say.

If McLane examines an atypical setting, we must not assume that more common settings conformed to a single type. Post's conclusion that "no single or simple hypothesis" can be formulated regarding "the functions of the criminal trial jury" is timely[17]—although I remain convinced that real trends can nonetheless be identified. Post himself finds a mainly hundredal jury, so the system that Powell concludes had largely broken down by the early fifteenth century remains intact in Post's records of the preceding decades. Jurors did not often come from the specific locale of the offense, however, and the process of self-informing must have admitted of many and varied forms. In some cases, Post conjectures, witnesses came forward to testify in court. Although their presence, when it can be detected, as often as not has to do with the "good fame" proceedings that precluded an actual trial,[18] the era of witness testimony was already under way, with eventual revolutionary implications for trial by jury. Post's exhumation of late-fourteenth-century trial jurors suggests a transitional era, but one in which the older traditions nevertheless affected most cases. Jurors of the hundred, well positioned to know of defendants' reputations and often of the weight that the local community placed on specific charges, may well have dominated proceedings. The variety of exceptions to this rule is well marked in Post's essay. I think an extended discussion of Powell's essay will show, however, that the tradition of the community-based determination of just deserts remained the rule even in the early fifteenth century.

Edward Powell's essay focusing on the early fifteenth century sug-

16. See above, chap 2, text at n. 79, and chap. 3, text at n. 53.

17. See above, chap. 3, text at n. 57.

18. See above, chap. 3, text at n. 47.

gests the need for far-reaching reinterpretation of the nature of the late medieval trial and of the role of the criminal trial jury.[19] Powell's research also cautions against the view that there was an early-modern transformation in the administration of the law; the situation in late Tudor times, it is suggested, differed little from that of two centuries before. The thrust of the argument is that by the early fifteenth century, juries were no longer mainly self-informing but instead heard and assessed evidence set forth by private accusers and government officials. By that date, if not before, the bench had the independent source of evidence that I have argued made the Tudor bench more powerful than its predecessors. There is some suggestion that the medieval trial had always possessed an active prosecution, even in the early days, when the trial jury was also, in fact, self-informed. In such a view, jurors originally had two main sources of evidence, and the judge had a check on the jury; acquittals in homicide and theft and verdicts of pardonable homicide were owing in many cases to a lack of sufficient evidence against the defendant (especially in cases where no accuser came forward) and in many others to merciful attitudes in which the bench actively concurred.

Although the evidence for an active prosecution, either by private prosecutor or by local officials, is still very sparse, Powell's speculations are plausible and could lead to a new view of the trial, at least as it was in the early fifteenth century. We should note at the outset that Powell is inclined to give substantial weight to the little evidence for an independent prosecution that has thus far surfaced, on the grounds that the early-fifteenth-century juries he has studied were no longer mainly drawn from the locale in which the alleged offense had been committed. This is an important finding, the significance of which must be assessed with care. First, and most significantly, some juries had no members from the relevant hundred, although on Powell's evidence this was the case for only 15 percent of the offenses. How were the jurors informed in these cases? Did the trial reduce itself to an assessment of the credibility of the defendant, who was closely questioned by the judge, and was this assessment influenced by the nature of the charge? Was the trial likely to lead to an acquittal on grounds of insufficient evidence? We do not know. But whatever we conclude regarding this subset of cases, we are not driven to conclude that there must *typically* have been an active and independent prosecution.

In most cases, county-wide juries carried at least a few members

19. See above, chap. 4.

from the relevant hundred.[20] On some occasions there was only one, a third of the time there were two, and in another third of the time there were from three to six. Powell has shown that jurors were most often well-established persons. Many were hundred officials, and most of the others were persons who had ready access to such officials. Although occasionally jurors were signed on at the assizes at the last moment, typically they had some warning of their impending duty. Two-thirds of the time, jurors went off to a delivery at which only one or two persons from their hundred were due to stand trial; the rest of the time there were three to five suspects under lock and key. Many of these suspects had surrendered themselves to await the delivery well knowing how the community viewed them. Here Powell's data suggest a degree of preformed opinion about suspects to which prospective jurors had easy access. None of this is to say that those jurors who were from the defendant's hundred must necessarily have come to court ready to inform their fellow jurors of the community's view (or views) regarding the appropriate resolution; it is merely to say that they could easily have done so. All the more was this true for the slightly earlier, more heavily local juries whose composition Post has studied. Even if some members of most juries did come to court armed with knowledge of the community's view of the case and of the defendant's reputation generally, might the entire jury nevertheless have received more evidence in court? Surely, as I have suggested, the statements and demeanor of the defendant were very significant, and sometimes the judge must have elicited an all-too-candid response or otherwise incriminating behavior.[21] Should one suppose as well that a private accuser or local official typically testified against the defendant?

For the early period, some evidence takes a form that we would not expect it to take if formal testimony in court against the accused was common.[22] Thereafter, as stated, there is occasional evidence of a pri-

20. See above, Figure 4.2.

21. Green, *Verdict According to Conscience*, 67.

22. *Bracton on the Laws and Customs of England*, ed. S. E. Thorne (Cambridge, Mass., 1968), 2.404–6. Post correctly observes that justices interrogated "defendants and their accusers to elicit claims and statements well outside the formal needs of appeal and exception" (citing *Placita Corone*, ed. J. M. Kaye, Selden Society Supplementary Series, 4 [1966], 8–9, 15–22). See above, chap. 3, text at n. 40. It is important to emphasize that the instances in which this occurred were cases brought on appeal, not on indictment. In the latter cases, the bench interrogated the defendant before seeking the verdict of a jury, but no principal accuser or witnesses are mentioned. No doubt the procedure used in appeals (a small minority of cases) was a significant source of the procedure that eventually emerged in trials upon indictment (the great

vate accuser, but not much more. Altogether, there is too little yet for us to say very much. But, admittedly, this is mainly due to the state of the extant record. It is perhaps unsound to conclude in either direction. Rather, let us accept, for the sake of argument, the possibility of in-court prosecution testimony in the later Middle Ages and hypothesize about its nature and its likely effects. Our central question is, of course, how far does the presence of in-court testimony require a revision of the view that the medieval criminal trial jury typically exercised very substantial power over the resolution of cases?

It is important to keep in mind that the opportunity for self-informing was always present in the Middle Ages. We are not discussing a mythical beast. Powell himself asserts that as late as the early fifteenth century some jurors in some cases were still self-informed. The question he seems to be asking is whether they were still (or ever had been) *solely* self-informed. The evidence set forth by Groot, McLane, and Post is not, I suppose, inconsistent with the possibility of in-court prosecution testimony alongside self-informing, but that evidence—and the evidence adduced by Powell as well—does make it appear that self-informing was at the very least one inevitable and significant aspect of the medieval trial. In many instances, trial jurors simply could not have avoided knowing something about the community's view of events, parties, and appropriate results, and even of the credibility of specific claims. Many trial jurors in the early period had served as presenters in the same case; moreover, throughout the entire period jurors who were leading community figures (including officials) were bound to know a good deal about offenders held for trial. There was no requirement that jurors banish such things from their minds—quite the opposite. Jury self-informing was a lawful fact of legal life.

How ought one to think about testimony for the prosecution in the later Middle Ages *alongside* self-informing? To begin with, it is not yet certain that local officials were called upon to testify in court, beyond stating what formal charges had been laid against the accused. With the exception of some coroners' rolls, their rolls and memoranda rarely record the results of investigations, over and above the formal charges made before them, charges that were the basis for presentments and that remained a check on the level and kind of offense for which a defendant had been held for trial. This is not to say that such local officials (constables, hundred-bailiffs, coroners) did not possess

majority of cases). But there are few, if any, signs that this latter development had taken place as of the time of *Placita Corone* (the mid to late thirteenth century).

useful information. By the time of the trial they probably knew a fair amount. But what they knew may have been, for example, the fact that the accusing parties were still furious or, conversely, that they were prepared to make a settlement; it may have been mainly a matter of the suspect's reputation generally and of the community's view about the "appropriate" resolution of a trial for life or death. It is my guess that if local officials testified, it was this kind of knowledge that structured their testimony. If they served as jurors, they gave their verdicts on a similar basis. Powell has suggested that one reason for the high acquittal rate even as late as the fifteenth century was the large number of cases in which there was insufficient evidence.[23] No doubt that is true. But it might well be the case that much of the time the conclusion "insufficient evidence" was a *result* of communal processes and not, as it were, an objective fact. If local officials did testify, what they said they "knew"—how certain they said they were about the truth of charges—was a reflection of the kind of filtering process that would be hidden from the bench and that I have attributed to verdicts rendered by jurors.[24] If such officials did testify, that is, they probably behaved largely as they did when they served—and Post and Powell show they did serve—as jurors.

We should not, however, overlook the possibility that local officials sometimes spoke with candor in court, even in cases where that candor required setting forth testimony that threatened the outcome that the local community had, through informal processes, agreed upon. Especially from the late fourteenth century on, increasing investigatorial activities by justices of the peace and their inferior officers probably created a relatively non-local source of pressure that placed the local official, in the courtroom, in a bind between his duties to the Crown and his role in the community.[25] Ultimately, it may have been

23. See above, chap. 4, text at nn. 118–19.

24. Green, *Verdict According to Conscience,* chap. 2.

25. The tension I am referring to is, of course, not merely a function of the pressure brought to bear by a "relatively non-local" justice of the peace upon "relatively local" village officials. Within most local areas there probably were significant differences of opinion between social groups—and even within such groups—regarding the resolution of disputes involving criminal offenses. It is important to recognize, however, that I am not denying that local communities were frequently divided on all sorts of questions, that for many purposes there was simply no "community" in the sense of a unified, or even general, community of opinion. What I am suggesting is that there was relatively widespread consensus *regarding the question of life or death,* that at the least there were some cases so serious (or offenders so nasty or untrustworthy) that death was generally deemed to be deserved and others so trivial (though capital under the law) that death was generally deemed unwarranted In some cases, perhaps many, there were conflicting views. In some of these cases, the conflicts were worked

a recognition of the pressures of localism that led the Crown to place so much emphasis upon early intervention by the justices of the peace and upon the recording of statements from all the parties concerned. This practice, combined with the real decline of the local, self-informed jury (whenever it ultimately came about), constituted the transformation of early-modern criminal administration. Its source, but not its mature manifestation, is plainly visible by the early fifteenth century.

Even in Smith's day (1560s) the vitality of the system of prosecution seems to have depended upon in-court testimony of the accuser-victim and his supporting witnesses, not of officials—at least, so far as one can tell from either Sir Thomas's perhaps muddled account or from later depictions of felony trials.[26] What made the system so relatively powerful by Smith's day was the writing down of both the charges and the evidence (circumstances, reasons for beliefs, and other evidence), immediately after the commission of an offense, and the accused's story, probably given as soon as he was taken and before he had heard his accuser's account. This is the kind of information that allowed the Tudor bench a substantial advantage vis-à-vis what was by then clearly a non-local, non–self-informed jury.[27]

Assuming that by the late fourteenth and early fifteenth centuries accusers did often testify in court, their testimony may have constituted a relatively weak form of the prosecution that was common by late Tudor times. The accused's sang-froid in denying complicity, when it was in fact a dishonest denial, must have been much greater when he or she faced a local jury (or even a jury upon which only one or two local persons of substance sat) and knew that the local community took a relatively benign view of the case. (This last point—the defendant's knowledge of the community's view—is significant and not unfairly posited, for it is, quite reasonably, one of Powell's assumptions concerning the reasons why many defendants made them-

out before trial, but in others they were not. I am conjecturing that pressure from "above" and outside the local community (in the form of the activities of justices of the peace) may sometimes have induced local officials to behave as though there were no consensus in the defendant's favor when in fact there was and, a fortiori, not to lean in the defendant's favor when there was no such consensus. I have consistently retreated to general tendencies, even though in particular cases the specific facts were of great importance, because I have sought to identify those trends that were sufficiently strong that they had an impact on, for example, typical jury behavior, dominant judicial perceptions of that behavior, and the "community's" general understanding of what it was appropriate for jurors to do.

26. T. Smith, *De Republica Anglorum*, ed. M. Dewar (Cambridge, 1982), 110–16; *Old Bailey Sessions Papers*, passim.

27. Green, *Verdict According to Conscience*, chap. 4.

selves available for trial at gaol delivery.)[28] And even an accusation that carried some force and was parried by only the weakest kind of denial was still a matter for the jury to resolve. So long as even a subset of the jury was composed of substantial local people on oath to sort out the weak accusations from the strong, the well-meant but "mistaken" ones from the convincing ones ("insufficient evidence" again), there was, more than just in theory, a body of "evidence" on credibility and the like dominated by jurors. Their manipulation of that evidence to exonerate those who were guilty but who ought not (in their view) to be hanged, could remain hidden from the bench. These were facts of life that were themselves instrumental in determining when victims would appeal, or appear to prosecute upon a presentment or indictment. I believe Powell would agree that one corollary of a relatively high conviction rate in appeals was a relatively low appearance rate by victims in the kinds of offenses for which the community rarely hanged offenders.[29]

The result of all this may well have been relatively little candid and forceful prosecution testimony in that great range of offenses for which society was typically reluctant to have recourse to the gallows, even in the later Middle Ages. And I would posit that in many cases there was therefore a continuation of older traditions of hidden, jury-based manipulation or suppression of evidence. This is not to deny, however, that as the bench's views came to accord with those of the community—or were seen to—more and more candid testimony may have come forward, whether from the prosecution, the defendant, or the jurors. Especially in homicide, jury-based rejection of those coroner's inquisition details that inculpated a defendant but did not establish a case for which the community would have him or her hanged was no longer critical. An "understanding" bench did not have to be kept in the dark. Powell's suggestion that by the early fifteenth century the judge and jury openly agreed on mercy seems plausible.[30] If Powell's surmise is correct that by the early fifteenth century there was more of a real prosecution, it may be that these developments were interrelated. That is, we might expect to find both an increase in prosecution by victim-accusers in the most serious cases, where the community was ready to apply the law to the fullest, and greater candor on the part of local officials and others (as jurors) in the least serious ones, where even the bench considered hanging inappropriate.

28. See above, chap. 4, text at n. 115.

29. See above, chap. 4, text at nn. 76, 77.

30. See above, chap. 4, text at n. 123.

But all this remains a matter of conjecture. On the main point that Powell has raised, one must concede the possibility of a different kind of trial in a substantial number of cases by at least the later Middle Ages from the one I posited in my book as nearly universal virtually until Tudor times.[31] One must grant, too, that the "transformation" of the trial began earlier and moved more glacially than I suggested. Indeed, having earlier put my case in the strongest terms, I should now restate it in the weakest form, giving the new evidence both proper respect and room for growth and according the unknowable the caution that is its due.

Throughout much of the medieval period, we ought to conclude, the jury was at least in large part self-informing, and it frequently dominated the gathering and setting forth of evidence, especially in simple homicide and nonaggravated theft. There was a *sufficiently large body of such cases* for a tradition of nullification of the law by juries to develop, one that the bench recognized but was typically unable to prevent in specific cases. Over time the distance between judge and jury lessened with regard to the treatment of such cases, if, indeed, there ever had been real disagreement rather than a community-based fear of disagreement that conditioned the jurors' manipulation of the facts, lack of candor, or reliance upon "insufficiency of evidence." Judicial concurrence in such cases was to some extent the result of legal change that took account of jury behavior, but it also reflected the bench's realization that the jury acted with severity in many of the most serious cases. Nonetheless, it was the authorities' attempts to ensure even more convictions in the latter that led to the increased activity of royal officials and the greater frequency of the submission of a real case for the prosecution. This, in turn, allowed for more careful monitoring of jury verdicts, in the less as well as in the more serious cases. Combined as it was with the ascent of a county-based jury that included virtually no truly local and self-informed persons, the greatly enhanced prosecution augured a new age in the history of the criminal trial. Ultimately, more pliant jurors and the use of Star Chamber also contributed crucially to the power of the Tudor bench.[32] But it is also true that this transformation (if I may still employ that word) owed something significant to changes in the sixteenth century in substantive law that lessened the distance between official and popular attitudes regarding the use of capital punishment.

The truth of the matter, of course, probably lies somewhere be-

31. Green, *Verdict According to Conscience*, 26–27.

32. Ibid., 140–43.

tween the two positions I have delineated. Over the long term, judicial control of proceedings probably increased faster than I have suggested but not so dramatically as to preclude an early period of relatively strong domination by the jury. Trials were probably more complicated affairs than I have suggested. As Post concludes, at least implicitly, sometimes the bench monitored and steered the outcome, sometimes it was overwhelmed. The working out of a judge-jury agreement, especially in homicide, may well have taken place in the context of trials that presented only a partially "hidden" defense. The bench may have acceded to a merciful view of the matter even though if it had pressed, it could have established the "truth" and determined the outcome mainly on its own terms. Trials were not only more complex from the point of view of the presentation of evidence and the options exercised by the bench; they were probably also more complex psychologically or, as it were, socially. All sorts of factors determined how each side would behave, and in this setting, as these studies on the composition of medieval criminal trial juries suggest, there prevailed an even more flexible understanding of the law—and of the appropriate application of legal standards—than the one depicted in my earlier work.

When James Cockburn termed my book "one of the most uninhibited works" of recent legal history, he may have meant uninhibited by lack of hard evidence.[33] Cockburn and I have long differed in our views concerning the subject about which he knows most and I know least: judge-jury relations at criminal assizes between 1560 and 1660. In a lengthy footnote I cautiously suggested that Cockburn had overstated the degree to which the extant evidence suggests that judges controlled juries at assizes, particularly between 1570 and 1625.[34] More significantly, I attempted to shift the terms of the debate by suggesting that the exercise of judicial authority was itself contingent upon some substantial degree of judicial acquiescence in the "standards" that had long been applied by the community, or at least that part of it represented by the trial jury.[35] Of course, Cockburn and I agree that the bench was very powerful during this period. For the reasons stated above, I do believe that in the late Tudor period the constraints upon the jury were more powerful than at most other times and that the

33. Ibid., dust jacket.

34. Ibid., 150–52 n. 179.

35. Ibid., chap. 4, sec. 2.

second half of the sixteenth century marks a culmination in the growth of the authority of the bench, as that authority was exercised in criminal trials at assizes. The issue between us has been, as is often the case, a matter of degree—but a matter of degree that matters.

Cockburn has now both strengthened the argument for the relative passivity of juries in the period 1560–1590 and conceded an increase in jury initiative thereafter. He has also made an important contribution to the history of the criminal law through his demonstration that jury composition, and probably judge-jury relations, underwent crucial changes in the middle of the seventeenth century.[36] I believe that there is much to the view afforded by the essays in this volume that the maturation of the judge-controlled trial was gradual, spanning the years from 1350 to 1550; that it reached a higher peak than I had hitherto supposed, perhaps in the very late sixteenth century; and that a modern era of greater sharing of power between judge and jury emerged fairly suddenly—rather than simply evolving out of a similarly textured past—in the several decades preceding the Restoration. Nevertheless, much as there is to this view, and in the face perhaps of other "jurors" who may be called upon to resolve this question, I should like to hold out a bit longer before reaching a final verdict. I am not fully convinced that jury passivity was ever anything like absolute. I am still inclined to the view that the "community" constituted a significant constraint upon judicial authority with respect to the administration of the criminal law even during the half century (roughly 1550 to 1600) still in dispute.

In part Cockburn and I view the late Tudor period with differing perspectives on what counts as the exercise of authority, and in part we are asking different questions. Where the bench prevented jury control of the outcome through a form of overruling of the verdict, Cockburn rightly sees judicial power and jury ineffectuality. But I see jury process as less than fully controlled and wonder whether the lesson learned is that the jury must not disagree with the bench, or that jury disagreement, although "allowed," may sometimes be subsequently frustrated by the bench. Where Cockburn rightly sees judicial avoidance of the use of the jury, I infer a living awareness, and fear, of potential jury independence. Where Cockburn rightly sees judicial steering of jury resolutions that do not strictly accord with the letter of the law, I wonder whether one result might have been the jurors' self-interested assumption that they shared the power of discretion.[37] In-

36. See above, chap. 6.

37. See above, chap 6, text at n. 93. Cockburn, *Assize Introduction*, 131–33.

deed, I suspect that the bench fostered that very assumption, so far as it believed that doing so would enhance the administration of the law without undermining ultimate judicial control. I do not know how often the bench lost its bet on this risky device, but I doubt that it always won it.

We are only now coming to understand the nature of jury composition in the middle period, especially in the late sixteenth and early seventeenth centuries. Peter Lawson's work, which roughly complements the assumptions about jury composition of some other scholars, notably Cynthia Herrup, suggests that the later-Elizabethan and Jacobean trial juries drew heavily upon the yeomanry at the assizes and (here there is general agreement with Stephen Roberts) upon lesser yeomen and even husbandmen at quarter sessions.[38] Lawson rightly emphasizes that, in the main, jurors were drawn from the elites of England's villages. These were men who, in national terms, may be described as of the middling sort, but they stood closer to the top of society than that term suggests (certainly closer than I earlier suggested).[39] As Lawson admits, the evidence he has been able to muster with respect to the wealth of jurors is sparse, and our conclusions on the recruitment of jurors from the upper reaches of the yeoman class must remain tentative. Jurors were propertied, but they were not all farmers; men of small commerce—artisans and tradesmen—were among their ranks. From a local perspective they were, of course, of high status. Although they were not county leaders, they were nonetheless leaders of village society, persons upon whom much of English governance had devolved. Beholden in a sense to the sheriff, the justices of the peace, and others who exercised the power of selection, these men were, I would suggest, beholden also to the hundreds in which they dwelled and which they helped to govern.

Keith Wrightson has shown how this order both governed the base of the population and mediated between it and higher orders.[40] They had to live among those whose disputes they helped to resolve, and the resolution through jury verdicts at assizes was only one of many forms of intercession they were called upon to practice. It would be

38 See above, chap. 5; Cynthia B. Herrup, *The Common Peace: Participation and the Criminal Law in Seventeenth-Century England* (Cambridge, 1987), chap. 6. On Roberts, see above, chap. 7.

39. Green, *Verdict According to Conscience*, 133 and n. 111.

40. Keith Wrightson, "Two Concepts of Order: Justices, Constables, and Jurymen in Seventeenth-Century England," in *An Ungovernable People: The English and Their Law in the Seventeenth and Eighteenth Centuries*, ed. J. Brewer and J. Styles (1980), 21–46.

incautious to view this order as being able with impunity to impose standards for which communal support was lacking upon the local community—or, if in some sense able to do so, as being so inclined. Lawson rightly calls attention to the instrumental role the yeomanry played in many aspects of local governance,[41] a role that—I would conjecture—conditioned them to understand and acquiesce in the standards of the respectable poor, who were frequently the victims of theft or physical assault.

It was this yeoman class that inherited the duties of the local constables and hundred elites whom Powell found serving on early-fifteenth-century juries. Their circumstances differed, however, from those of their medieval ancestors. As central authority reached down more pervasively into local life, the village elites came under greater pressure from above. Over the course of the seventeenth century, the gulf between rich and poor widened,[42] local elites identified more commonly with the county leadership, and the central authorities sought to rest governance, including assize jury duty, upon the more substantial of these yeomen, even upon some from among the gentry itself. Our glimpse into this world through Lawson's and Cockburn's research suggests that the resettlement of jury duty had begun to take place in the decades before the Puritan Revolution; the sharp increase in serial service and the regularization of the "office" of foreman allow us to identify a kind of watershed in the years around 1650.[43] Throughout this period the yeomanry remained dominant, and even its lesser figures occasionally played a prominent role. At the same time, however, authorities were severely limiting the number of persons who would be called to serve, thereby making it possible to secure jurors of higher status and greater experience—and perhaps ones who better understood, and more readily accepted, the judicial perspective.

Cockburn and Lawson nonetheless see the world of pre-Revolution criminal administration differently. For Cockburn, lesser men—especially less experienced men—meant greater judicial control, and a less regularized system of jury service meant far more frequent recourse to the *tales*.[44] Lawson depicts Elizabethan and Jacobean Hertfordshire jurors as accustomed to governance in their locales, even if they were less experienced as assize jurors than their later counter-

41. See above, chap. 5, text at nn. 80–85.

42. J. A. Sharpe, *Crime in Early Modern England, 1550–1750* (1984), 91.

43. See above, chap. 6, text at nn. 47–76.

44. See above, chap. 6, text at nn. 16–24.

parts. He finds little evidence of the use of the tales.[45] Moreover, Lawson emphasizes the independence jurors retained in this period, although he would agree that their natural inclinations led jurors to be severe where the bench, too, would have been so. Cockburn, Lawson, and I are all in agreement on this last point, and I would stress the importance of the fact that much of society—even England's husbandmen and laborers—was prepared to have done with truly nasty offenders. It was this community of agreement on the most serious cases that had from earliest times, I argued in my book, made reliance upon local elites—a middling class in national terms—both possible and desirable.[46]

It remains unclear just how far assize judges bothered to steer jurors in cases on which general social agreement was less firm. Cockburn's case is persuasive to a point, but the pattern of verdicts suggests a degree of jury-based resolution, which is a body of evidence that Lawson emphasizes.[47] It remains my view that judges were aware of and assimilated these standards, so that even when they led juries they were often moving toward goals jurors saw as their own, and that the process of steering was thereby partly invisible to jurors and the observing public. That "public," moreover, must be viewed as wider than that in attendance at assizes; it included as well persons from the local communities to which those offenders who were not singled out for the most severe—and exemplary—punishment returned.[48] We shall probably never know for certain whether their neighbors attributed their narrow escape to judge or jury, or both. But I am inclined to think that some semblance prevailed of a tradition (that is, a community-based impression) of the jury's right to share in the power of mitigation.

Finally, Lawson's point that we ought not to make too much of the concept of mercy is important.[49] Juries could, in the first place, exercise great severity. And often where they acquitted or rendered partial verdicts they were responding to the degree of seriousness of an offense in a matter-of-fact way. Whether they had a subjective sense of acting out of mercy is more difficult to say. Lawson gives weight to the high standard of proof required by both the bench and the jurors (at least in cases where rank prejudice did not intervene), although he

45. See above, chap. 5, text at n. 43.

46. Green, *Verdict According to Conscience*, 99, 102.

47. See above, chap. 5, text at nn. 151–65.

48. See above, chap. 5, text at n. 95.

49. See above, chap. 5, text at nn. 163–65.

pays greater attention to the influence upon bench and jurors of the character of the offender and the nature of the offense.[50] These were not, of course, entirely separate phenomena: where the offense was capital but of a less serious variety (or where the offender was a recidivist) the standard was higher, and vice versa. Whether jurors thought in terms of the offense, as such, rather than self-deludingly in terms of a constant standard of proof, we cannot say. I shall return to this important point.

The selection process that Lawson describes—and that links his work to much of the scholarship on the late-seventeenth- and eighteenth-century criminal trial jury—may well have appeared differently to different observers. Some eighteenth-century legal writers characterized jurors as too merciful;[51] so, too, did Lambard in the period with which Lawson is concerned.[52] Moreover, the view from below may have been more complicated than the several essays on the early modern period in this volume suggest. Accusers and defendants, as well as the laboring poor of the local communities from which these participants came, no doubt internalized the message of the gallows ritual. Property was, after all, sacrosanct. But they also formed some understanding of the process by which defendants were spared: lives, too, held value, and the ritual of correction might involve forgiveness and reacceptance into the community of the living. From one perspective, as Lawson suggests, the law might not have been modified by jurors, whose independence expressed itself in the application of rules as they were meant to be applied.[53] Indeed, that is the view I have taken.[54] But this seems to me to redefine the law in a way that allowed it to be understood as a law of mercy.

One particular feature of Cockburn's perspective on the Elizabethan and early Jacobean period that I do not entirely share is its implicit message of the triumph of central authorities over the forces of localism. My use of the word *community* with reference to the jury and the people and interests it represented has been too casual. In my conclusion I belatedly pointed out that jury independence relative to the central authorities may sometimes have reflected jury dependence upon local ones.[55] This is a point that Stephen Roberts, writing

50. See above, chap. 5, text following n 165.

51. Green, *Verdict According to Conscience*, 288–310.

52. See above, chap. 6, text at n. 99.

53. See above, chap. 5, text at n. 165.

54. Green, *Verdict According to Conscience*, 314.

55. Ibid., 370.

about the Interregnum, makes with some force.[56] His focus is on quarter sessions, which were decidedly more local proceedings than those held before a predominantly royal bench. It remains to be seen whether gentry influence over quarter sessions jurors (to the extent that Roberts has been able to establish that influence) implies that there was a similar lack of jury independence at the assizes. For the moment, we might doubt that the local gentry surrendered the determination of life-or-death issues to royal judges. Why should we not suppose that the corollary of some manipulation by hundred or county potentates at quarter sessions was jury manipulation by the same local powers at the assizes? Cockburn's depiction of the assizes—the ritual and accoutrements of the presence of royal surrogates—is powerful, and his argument must be read in light of the theater that the assizes represented.[57] It was a moment of intrusion into county affairs that saw county gentry look to the source of power and preferment that was the Crown. But court and country relations were reciprocal. Royal policy always countenanced a sharing of power and discretion with county gentry and yeomanry, so long as it was implemented in appropriate fashion and did not function, as central authorities saw it, as a disparagement of royal authority.[58]

The jury, then, even in decline, was an extension of both central and local interests. Its power, particularly its recourse to discretion, sometimes reflected the limits of royal influence on local politics. I do not mean to suggest that the jury often overtly signaled a tension between central and local power; I do believe, however, that the relationship between central authorities and local interests naturally implied some limits upon judicial manipulation of the criminal assize jury. I suspect that the reorganization of the jury in the mid seventeenth century that Cockburn has convincingly depicted reflected a new era in central coordination of local matters. It both recognized the relatively mild degree of royal control (or the high costs of manifesting control) that had characterized the preceding era of court-country relations and prefigured later central dominance through more sophisticated forms of the cooptation of local elites, forms that, ironically, as I shall later suggest, maintained and even increased the local sharing of power with the central authorities.

Roberts's work on Devonshire reminds us of the diversity of local

56. See above, chap. 7.

57. Cockburn, *Assizes*, chaps. 4, 6.

58. See D. Hirst, *Authority and Conflict: England, 1603–1658* (Cambridge, Mass., 1986), 31.

conditions in seventeenth-century England and of the element of group (or class) interest that informed peacekeeping in the domains of England's local but "godly" magistrates.[59] Not surprisingly, Roberts finds the world of Leveller jury theory a far cry from the reality of everyday practice.[60] At the same time, his study of practices in Devon helps to put the radical jury rhetoric into perspective, because one glimpses therein the source of the frustration felt by those who idealized the legal practices of the original "free" Anglo-Saxon community.

Here one must recognize that the Levellers and some other contemporaries overstated the power of the central authorities. They portrayed those authorities as able to exert themselves almost without limits in the provinces. In this way the local gentry, even when acting on its own interests, was deemed to be in active collusion with royal officials and to be an enemy of the lesser propertied yeomanry and husbandmen whose autonomy had vanished, so the theory ran, with the Conquest.[61] Lilburne's was a view from the center, where the most important local figures sat in the Parliament that, in alliance with Cromwell, sought to stamp out political dissension in the counties and to maintain a tight grip on political representation and social and economic preferment. Digger opposition to the jury, an opposition that I have perhaps underestimated,[62] reflected a more accurate understanding of the interests that controlled provincial civil and criminal trial proceedings.

The Diggers, too, opposed the central government, but they had no illusions about the prospects for local democracy. Roberts's focus on the problem of nonconformity further exposes the absence of total overlap between central and local perspectives and the relatively free hand of local potentates on their own turf.[63] Such cases may have been particularly attractive—and misleading—to Leveller leaders, whose unyielding opposition to the central authorities may once again have diverted their attention from the undemocratic local conditions that paradoxically guaranteed effective resistance by the provinces. But the main point, as I have suggested, is that no matter how great the

59. See above, chap. 7.

60. See above, chap. 7, text at nn. 46–49.

61. Green, *Verdict According to Conscience*, 177–86. Cockburn's discovery that, at least on the Home circuit, 1650 was an important watershed is relevant here: Leveller complaints that jurors were being handpicked by the authorities may well have been influenced by the commencement of the practice of serial service.

62. Ibid., 190 n. 122.

63. See above, chap. 7, text at nn. 70–78.

distance between Leveller law-finding theory and daily community-based practice, Leveller views—precisely because those views were expressed in the rhetoric of local democratic self-government—could nonetheless have great force within a certain restricted corner of the revolution.[64]

The inferences for assize jury independence that I have drawn from Roberts's evidence make more understandable the collision between such royal justices as Hyde, Twysden, and Kelyng and gentry-controlled grand and trial jurors, both in nonconformity cases and in routine felonies.[65] In the early 1660s at least, royal judges occasionally vied with local men of power, and I see no reason to suppose that this was a novel or exceptional event (although the lengths to which the Restoration bench went in order to resolve the tension probably were novel). The episode perhaps highlighted the need for greater central control over local juries and the limits that continued to present themselves to central authorities even into the era of the reform of jury selection and service. I have stressed Vaughan's detachment in Bushel's Case, a case that arose from Quaker preaching and that was at least in part colored by the exhortations of Penn and others to jurors. According to these exhortations, jurors were to "find the law," a theory that Vaughan clearly opposed but seemed not to want to confront openly.[66] A second form of detachment appears to characterize Vaughan's language—if, that is, one reads jury resolutions against the background of local interests and control. Vaughan would have us believe that the issue was, at base, freedom of conscience, presumably freedom from *all* "foreign" influences, local or central. We should not be surprised, however, to discover that all parties found such "freedom" a convenient rationalization for the self-interested resolutions that they sought to protect from other, alien interests. In the face of royal authorities, local men appealed not to their own interests but to principles of justice. Those principles soon took on some semblance of a life of their own.

The history of the jury in the sixteenth and seventeenth centuries, then, is the history of a struggle for control of an institution that stood in the front lines of many kinds of political struggle. Rhetorical declamations passed easily from one context to another; as I have suggested, some opponents of the later Stuarts employed the rhetoric of

64. Green, *Verdict According to Conscience*, 186.

65. Ibid., chap. 6, sec. 2.

66. Ibid., chap. 6, sec. 3, 4.

Lilburne, although they felt little kinship with leveling ideas.[67] Perhaps that rhetoric also drew upon the claims made by selfish local men who put their right to determine local cases of life and death in the most high-minded terms. Whatever the role of central-local tensions in the episode that brought embarrassment to Kelyng, the parliamentary censure of that royal judge came to be understood in terms of a true right of non-coercion.[68] These essays, and similar work recently completed or in progress, have begun to establish the distance between rhetoric and reality in seventeenth-century politics and legal practice.[69] Moreover, this body of scholarship also holds the potential for exposing the relationship—that is, the exchange—between rhetoric and reality, and thus for allowing us to produce an informed history of contemporary ideas about the jury, particularly about the influence of those ideas on ongoing practices at all levels.

The three essays on the jury from the Restoration to the late eighteenth century situate the members of the assize criminal trial jury among the upper orders of English society. I have pointed to the emergence by the seventeenth century of a gulf between the few relatively wealthy and the many poor or downright destitute Englishmen. In this context it will hardly do to speak of jurors simply as middling men, for those groups were nonetheless among the more exalted of English society. Moreover, as these three essays conclusively demonstrate, the authorities strove persistently and successfully to ensure that jurors came from that class of persons who were the cities' and the countryside's natural, though local, governors, men who in almost all aspects of political, social, and economic life dominated the everyday affairs of most of society. Not only were jurors experienced in the affairs of local government and drawn from groups that were used to working together, but they also came from elements that, in many matters, looked for leadership from, and alliance with, England's most exalted rulers. How much a part of, or bound to, this highest order were they? As jurors, to what extent did they, for all their relatively high status, nonetheless reflect the interests and attitudes of the numerically greater part of society? What can one say about the

67. Ibid., 252–60.

68. Ibid., 220.

69. See, for example, J. A. Phillips and T. C. Thompson, "Jurors v. Judges in Later Stuart England: The Penn-Mead Trial and *Bushel's Case*," *Law and Inequality* 4 (1986). 189ff.

class aspect of the administration of the criminal law? Our essays, and work related to them, have begun to answer these questions, but we have not yet achieved a fully unified view.[70]

At least two fairly distinct emphases now characterize scholarship on the political and social role of the criminal trial jury. Peter King identifies the assize trial jurors as men of the middling sort, members of a class or group of classes that stood in the top third of English society but, he significantly emphasizes, below and apart from the gentry in wealth, office, outlook, and manners.[71] King views the middling order as having its own interests. Nevertheless, to some extent he sees its members as reflecting attitudes shared by those below as well as above them, depending upon the issue at hand. Douglas Hay, in the essay published here (more distinctly perhaps than in his earlier work), situates the jurors about where King does in terms of wealth and background, but portrays them as more prosecution-oriented, as less prone to empathize with those below them who were tried at the assizes.[72] Beattie's detailed essay on the trial jurors of late-seventeenth-century London demonstrates that the economic status of these jurors was substantially higher than that of persons who served on the provincial (Surrey and Sussex) juries he studied earlier.[73] He characterizes the status of provincial jurors in terms that accord with King's evidence, but he emphasizes the broad agreement between judge and jury. It appears to be his view that the justice meted out at provincial assizes reflected the attitudes of at least the top third of society. Beattie draws no conclusions about the justice meted out at London trials, but his characterization of London trial jurors suggests that it reflected the views of persons immediately below the small aristocratic elite.[74] Although in Beattie's view London emerges as an exception, it is an exception of great importance, both because of London's influence on the development of English criminal administra-

70. For a review of the literature on the eighteenth century generally, see Joanna Innes and John Styles, "The Crime Wave: Recent Writing on Crime and Criminal Justice in Eighteenth-Century England," *Journal of British Studies* 25 (1986): 380–435.

71. See above, chap. 9.

72. See above, chap. 10, and D. Hay, "Property, Authority and the Criminal Law," in *Albion's Fatal Tree: Crime and Society in Eighteenth-Century England*, ed. Hay et al. (Harmondsworth, 1975), 17–63.

73. See above, chap. 8, and Beattie, *Crime and the Courts*, 378–89.

74. Beattie shows, however, that London jurors were far less wealthy than London's wealthiest persons. Moreover, he points out that the groups that served as trial jurors in London were as involved as rural jurors in all aspects of local governance and were thus involved with a wide range of people

tion and because of the place London trials held in the minds of contemporaries, that is, in what was coming to be the prevailing idea of the jury in trials for felony. In the end, each of these views about the jury possesses its own kind of truth.

I previously maintained that the jury functioned throughout its long history to effect an accommodation between ruling authorities and a substantial part of English society.[75] In this sense, I suggested, the jury was both an elitist and a democratizing institution, although I also cautioned that too much ought not to be made of the latter notion: one man's democratizing institution is another's coopted extension of aristocratic rule. Here Hay and I have disagreed, at least in emphasis, and in my view his present essay strengthens his position considerably. Quite obviously, juries did not represent the entire population; in some times and places, and with regard to some kinds of offenses, they represented a relatively small part of society. We are perhaps reduced to deciding how often jurors had to represent (in terms of their perspective, not their status) how many people and in what kinds of cases in order to be of the larger community, as opposed to being above it. Do we not also need to know the subjective state of jurors as they went about their work? Surely we do, but is even that knowledge sufficient?

Here I would resist an affirmative answer, and my reasons for resisting may help explain my own preference for what I (and I alone) have termed the communitarian view. It will not do to define the jury solely in terms of the class ties of its members, or of their politics in the simple sense of their conscious identification with, or rejection of, authority. We need to know the constraints within which juries acted, even when they were not cognizant of those constraints, and we need to know the psychology that jurors typically possessed when reaching determinations of life or death, even when they were unaware of those feelings. There were instances of people and offenses—the two were not always related, as King's work makes clear[76]—for which the decision to end a life was easy; there were others for which it was unthinkable; and there were still other instances, perhaps very many, in which, whether one took a life or spared a life, some translation into a special language of justification was necessary. Herein lay the potentially competing claims of just retribution and mercy; the latter claim was sometimes (but only sometimes) so broadly defined as to be equivalent to a claim of simple humanity. Our study of that language

75 Green, *Verdict According to Conscience*, 374–75.

76. See above, chap. 9, text at nn. 174–75.

of humanity is primitive, and its inaccessibility to us may lead us to underestimate its pervasiveness and importance.

It is equally possible, however, to overstate the role of mercy, which was, in any case, only one of several significant and conflicting aspects of the administration of the criminal law. We must assess that role in the context of a harsh penal law that claimed the lives of many Englishmen whose crimes were produced by the rigors and injustices of economic life. The mitigation practiced at eighteenth-century assizes was itself often mitigated: the principal alternative sanction to execution was transportation for seven or fourteen years or for life.[77] Indeed, from one perspective the capital sanction was instrumental not only because it induced terror but also because it allowed higher orders to conceive of themselves as merciful even as they sent thousands into long and often cruel exile. Moreover, as had always been the case, it was the widespread agreement that the nastiest offenders ought to suffer the extreme rigors of the law that made even the modest form of mitigation that was commonly practiced an acceptable feature of the law.

Whatever the actual degree of mitigation, and whatever were the conditions that made it common, the manner in which the various orders of English society viewed the abundant recourse to it remains a complex matter. The juror class, for its part, was a law-enforcing class that spent much of its time and energy arranging for its own physical security. But at the moment of trial, and especially at the moment of judgment—that is, of rendering verdict—its perspective may often have been shaped by other inclinations and concerns as well. The courtroom was not a meeting room for an association for the prevention of crime. Its doors may have been open to people and attitudes whose presence caused jurors to see themselves and their role in a more broadly representative fashion. In many cases the moment of verdict may well have been a moment in which, in an important sense, Englishmen acted against their "better" judgment.

In his essay on London jurors, as in his previous work, Beattie seeks the roots of the fundamental changes in the administration of the criminal law that occurred early in the eighteenth century. Emblematic of those changes was the legislative adoption of the lesser sanction of transportation. First and foremost the crime problem was a problem of penology, the tail of the system that, some hoped, might wag the dog.[78] Important, too, however, was the regularization of jury

77. Beattie, *Crime and the Courts*, 450–519.

78. Ibid., 500–513.

service and its settlement upon people whose judgment could be trusted and whose interests made them, if not outright dependent, at least relatively dependable. Beattie here rightly accords great importance to the conscious policy changes of 1650, which constituted a turning point in the history of criminal trial jury composition. In Beattie's view, the London jury system of the 1690s both represented a maturation of mid-seventeenth-century experiments and became, at least in some respects, the model for the experiments of the eighteenth century.[79] And it brought into the everyday practice of the London courts the men who would help frame and inaugurate those latter experiments. Beattie's instinct for the accidents that create new practice and policy—and in short order, ideology—led him to investigate the circumstances that, in London, first delayed and then produced in-court deliberation.[80] It would appear that even as central authorities were rationalizing, streamlining, and taming the potentially erratic impulses of the criminal law and criminal trial procedure, they were, unintentionally to be sure, creating conditions within which competing influences could continue to exert themselves. We can be certain that London jurors worked quickly, often guided by their foremen, and usually decided in accordance with the interests and prejudices of their caste. But, like jurors in the provinces, they also came to do their work in the heated and constraining atmosphere of the public domain.[81]

Placing the status and experience of London jurors is of particular importance. If the typical trial jury was as exalted in the mid eighteenth century as it had been in the early 1690s, what, we are led to wonder, must have been the composition of the special juries that were sometimes employed in London in seditious libel and other political cases?[82] Surely the special jury cannot have been of a much higher class; perhaps it was more dependable in the sense that it was purged of people well known for their dissident views. If so, this tells us something about the less-than-perfect overlap in interests of authorities and the upper middling classes that typically served the London courts. And even special juries could find against the Crown, so there were quite evidently limits even to their dependability, at least

79. See above, chap. 8, text at nn. 5, 15, 50.

80. See above, chap. 8, text at nn. 13, 14.

81. For King's important speculation regarding the impact of in-court deliberation see above, chap. 9, text at nn. 164–69.

82. J. C. Oldham, "The Origins of the Special Jury," *University of Chicago Law Review* 50 (1983): 137–221.

in a specific range of cases.[83] Yet another point: In the pamphlets that debated the law regarding criminal libel, much is made of the question of London jurors' ability. Can this criticism of jurors be well informed, given their position and experience?[84] If all that is meant is that no layman possesses the judge's knowledge of the law, the argument is understandable. Otherwise, it rings quite false. Moreover, jury proponents sometimes wrote about jurors as though the latter took part in common political discourse. Although extremely well off, jurors were—or were alleged to be—fairly common by class standards, part of the large middle class from which Wilkites and others of a similar cast of mind came.[85] In London, as in the provinces, England's ruling elites saw the groups that yielded jurors as a class apart—indeed, as without "class."[86]

More curious still is the role that English jurors in general played in applying the law in routine cases of property crime. Here they cannot have been very far from the bench's point of view. Hay's argument is persuasive.[87] Jurors were the employers of those who were accused of routine felonies, not their co-workers. They owned property or capital and were set apart from the masses of laborers who were called before them to be judged. Jurors may well have identified with England's highest elites insofar as they were part of the natural governing and property-owning classes. They were an important extension of those elites, whose members made law in Parliament or on the bench. And in some respects that law was, as Hay emphasizes, a "class" law that reflected existing gross inequalities of wealth.[88] From one perspective, then, jurors represented an instrument of centrally monitored propertied-class power.

But provincial jurors, perhaps more than their London counterparts, were at the same time members of local elites who had to live with, if not precisely among, lesser farmers, artisans, and tradesmen, if not the laboring poor. They were, it would seem, people whose power over the less well off depended on a mixture of authority and empathy. The groups from which Essex and Surrey jurors—and even Staffordshire and Northamptonshire jurors—were drawn could not separate themselves entirely from their social and economic inferiors, particularly,

83. Green, *Verdict According to Conscience*, chap. 8.

84. Ibid.

85. Ibid.

86. Ibid.

87. See above, chap. 10.

88. See above, chap. 10, text at n. 147.

I would venture, from the attitudes of the more substantial of the latter on life-and-death questions. To a significant degree, they were held in check by groups below them in the social hierarchy, and they were both inclined and *required* to satisfy the instincts of those groups for mercy as well as for retribution, or perhaps more accurately, they were bound to act in accordance with widespread expectations concerning an appropriate regard for the value of a human life. Jurors, then, were part of a set of institutions that created a fit—albeit only an approximate one—between widespread social attitudes and the attitudes of England's natural rulers. One would do well to pause at this point to ask about this fit. Why should we suppose there was one at all? Why was it not closer? What were the "rules" of governing that made the perspective of the ruling groups diverge from those of much of society, if one assumes, as I do, that in a special sense the latter both legitimated and determined the power of the former?[89]

Society in general was not captured, as the legal elites were, by a notion of the rule of law in which a *formal* theory of consistency loomed very large. Communal judgment had always been a complex process in which ad hoc decisions arose from conditions that made them seem natural, appropriate, of a piece. Royal authorities who came to manage that process in serious cases of crime instinctively (some would say, manipulatively) sought to purge that process of the arbitrary and the incidental. Although authorities in fact accommodated a system of justice built largely upon exceptions to firmly expressed rules, they nonetheless created means for articulating fairly precisely the conditions in which those exceptions would apply. Social resistance to capital punishment created pressures, for example, for legal rules justifying mitigation or outright acquittal on technical grounds, so that rough agreement on outcome was achieved even while the larger community and the bench regarded individual cases from very different perspectives. Doubtless, society came to view many cases on the authorities' terms: the indictment was "defective"; the high standard

89. By determined I mean limited, in the specific sense that the assize juror classes drew their views regarding the appropriate use of the gallows at least in part from groups below them economically and socially, perhaps from something like the middle third of English society. As suggested in this paragraph of the text, I do not mean simply that jurors (or those among the highest ruling elites) feared that extensive recourse to the gallows would lead to political conflict but that a more subtle assimilation of attitudes from below resulted from informal contact such as that involved in the carrying out of local governance. Although such influences, of course, worked downward as well as upward, I have emphasized the often-neglected upward side of the process. I have also tried to make clear that the influences from below were partly responsible not only for upper-class notions about when mercy was appropriate but also for upper-class notions about when it was not.

of proof had not been met. In the same way, the authorities perhaps unconsciously adopted social standards regarding merciful treatment of many specific offenders. But the differing perspectives remained, each side thinking in its own terms about the resolution of very many cases. This should come as no surprise. The needs of governors have always embodied their own special rules and forms.

King's research offers a significant vantage point from which to survey some of the issues I have raised. His conclusions, even when they are not startling, are indeed penetrating. Although they are based on a study of a county that was represented by solid middling, rather than distinctly upper-middling, jurors,[90] they seem to me to hold true even for areas that produced jurors of the latter description. King himself makes little claim for a true communitarian approach. Essex jurors were from the local elites, and although only some of them played significant roles in local government, they held together as a class—or set of sub-classes—as persons with a variety of life styles and attitudes that set them apart from both the gentry and the laboring poor.[91] If anything, they were farmer-dominated, quick to condemn sheep stealers, used to employing farm as well as household servants, and ready to discipline them. This was a breed that well knew the temptations to which the young were vulnerable and that could conclude as quickly to remove a threat to their order as to be lenient with a young man understandably (although not excusably) gone astray. One has the sense of a *potentially* arbitrary system, the defendant in many cases owing his life to the happenstance of a few understanding father-figures on the jury. But King argues that jury decisions were in fact "principled," however they may have appeared to some outside observers.[92] King's study makes clear the strength of the claim to good character, in the sense of widespread acceptance of the rules of the game, that the leading local orders, broadly defined, exacted.

For whatever reason, Essex jurors came to be even more experienced, although not necessarily more exalted in rank, after 1784. In a move reminiscent of mid-seventeenth-century attempts to rationalize jury service and to place the responsibility of judgment in the hands of those who understood the parameters of judicial expectations, Essex jurors came to serve once in three years, as members of ongoing entities made up very largely of the same people.[93] In this the

90. See above, chap. 9, text at nn. 18–74.

91. See above, chap. 9, text at nn. 190–93.

92. See above, chap. 9, text at n. 5.

93. See above, chap. 9, text at nn. 114–17.

Essex jury system was, as far as we know, unique, but the reform may prove to be an accurate measure of what the national government hoped generally to achieve. There may have been a parallel in at least one of the counties Hay has studied.[94] By the late eighteenth century, criticism of arbitrariness had become common, and crime rates were (or were thought to be) once again on the rise.[95] The government perhaps hoped to safeguard the existing system by reducing the occasions on which jurors might exercise leniency foolishly, thus maximizing the degree to which measured, selective non-enforcement was applied in a consistent fashion and blunting the charge of inexperience.[96] How far any of this went toward reducing actual arbitrariness we are unable to say, but it hardly brought the charges of arbitrariness to a halt or disguised the fact that the root of the problem lay not with the mechanisms for selection among offenders but with the process of selection itself.[97]

In King's essay we sense that the critical juncture had been reached: no group of jurors could lend credibility to a system of blanket capital sanctions to which, given prevailing social attitudes, recourse could not be had in more than about 10 percent of the cases that came to trial. The criticism of the system was simply too far advanced and too plausible. King and Hay note that elite commentators often derided jurors as illiterate, inexperienced, and of low status, and the two authors rightly suggest that this perspective says more about the critics than about the jurors.[98] King takes this point yet a step further; he suggests that England's highest classes had not so much misgauged the composition of trial juries as they had come to see the groups that yielded jurors as representing a force of their own.[99] Although it may be that jurors' occasional recalcitrance in political cases was partly responsible for this view, much of the criticism was aimed at jury be-

94. See above, chap. 10, text at nn. 122–24 (Staffordshire).

95. See above, chap. 10, text at n. 127. See also D. Hay, "War, Dearth and Theft in the Eighteenth Century: The Record of the English Courts," *Past and Present* 95 (1982): 139, 145, 156.

96. Hay notes that, with regard to Staffordshire in 1787, it is not known whether recourse to experienced jurors "was on local initiative or at the suggestion of the assize judges." See above, chap. 10, text at n. 125.

97. Green, *Verdict According to Conscience*, 356–63.

98. See above, chap. 9, text at nn. 179, 193, and chap. 10, text at nn. 2, 8, 10, 11, 129. It remains unclear why contemporaries not only viewed jurors as ignorant (perhaps a class perspective) but also thought that they came from groups far lower in the economic hierarchy than was the case, and that officials were not enforcing the relevant statutes when they were in fact doing so.

99. See above, chap. 9, text at nn. 184–93.

havior in routine felony cases, and in this context the problem of class was perhaps of less significance. Indeed, the most persuasive and telling criticism came, I believe, not from those who thought that jurors were not up to the task set for them, but from those who objected to the task itself.[100] These latter publicists were the new breed of reformers, who both criticized jurors for being too merciful and conceded that, given the prevailing law of sanctions, simple humanity inevitably would, and probably ought to, govern jury reactions.[101] There is little suggestion that these critics—or any critics when they truly confronted this problem—thought that even the highest-born were significantly less susceptible to the impulse to be merciful. Even the bench and the Crown were said to share in the only-too-human "poor judgment" that allegedly characterized the system.

The system held on for a time despite the onslaught. In his earlier work Hay perceptively argued that the ruling elites were blinded to this particular criticism (or persuaded to weather it) by the advantages they saw in the power of selective enforcement.[102] This was, no doubt, one aspect of the mind-set of many late-eighteenth-century propertied Englishmen. I have myself suggested that at the same time the tradition of jury-based mercy drew its strength from other sources as well, and that those who were less well placed than the authorities but able nonetheless to play a role in various stages of criminal administration may have viewed the institution of jury trial in quite different terms.[103] The leaders of local communities had always possessed the "right" to apply the prevailing law regarding life and death; the jury class held that right not only from the beneficence of the ruling elite that presided over criminal trials but also as an aspect of its prerogative of local governance, which involved managing the affairs of those who were, among many other things, commonly the victims, as well as the neighbors, of local bullies and thieves. Moreover, from the perspective of many of these middling men in their role as jurors (I am conjecturing), this process of judgment was not arbitrary and did not have to be defended against the new reformers; it was, because it was socially based, a natural and predictable process. Only when faith in the efficacy of this process broke down, especially among London

100. Green, *Verdict According to Conscience*, chap. 7, sec. 3. This was particularly true, I believe, of Blackstone, Eden, and Romilly, whose writings were widely circulated and accorded great importance.

101. Green, *Verdict According to Conscience*, chap. 7, sec. 3.

102. Hay, "Property, Authority and the Criminal Law."

103. Green, *Verdict According to Conscience*, 310–15 and n. 156.

men of commerce in the early nineteenth century, was the system brought to the brink of reform.[104]

Of course, as long as the government could restrict the selection process to those with substantial property, the highest elite's own perspective might emerge as the stronger of the two perspectives that vied for dominance in the minds of those who served as jurors. Hay's definitive analysis of Staffordshire and Northamptonshire jury panels suggests that in some times and some places, something close to aristocratic control could result. He locates those who served as close to the very apex of English society. But again, those who served held places in a relatively local society and had local responsibilities and sensibilities. Their views on most matters can hardly be taken to be those of society at large, but their behavior on life-and-death questions in England's close and crowded courtrooms may have reflected not only elite notions but also the attitudes of much of village society. We must proceed here with caution, but it may well be that the dynamics of the courtroom—especially when deliberation was undertaken in open court—combined with the tendencies produced by the unanimity rule further to ensure that even the most exalted jurors often applied the capital law according to well-understood, widespread, and—where much of society deemed it appropriate—distinctly merciful standards.[105] I must concede I have overstated the degree of agreement within the community that characterized English criminal administration regarding the imposition of the capital sanction,[106] but just how far I have overstated the case I am still not sure. Much searching work remains to be done, though it will have to be impressionistic, for, as I have emphasized, we are dealing here with a matter of psychology and of constraints barely felt, or felt but misinterpreted by those who sensed them.

One clue to the distorted perspective of these eighteenth-century jurors—and earlier ones, no doubt—lies in the importance they all accorded to a very high threshold of proof.[107] This is itself a difficult concept. I have suggested at a number of points that from medieval times onward the conclusion that there was "insufficient evidence" was the

104. Ibid., 361; L. Radzinowicz, *History of English Criminal Law* (1948), 1:727–32.

105. For King's discussion of the impact of the unanimity rule, see chap. 9, text at nn. 160–64, 172; for his discussion of courtroom dynamics, see ibid., at nn. 164–69. My own discussion is speculative and, in its invocation of "widespread" views, goes beyond the conclusions that King draws.

106. Green, *Verdict According to Conscience*. See also above, n. 25.

107 Green, *Verdict According to Conscience*, 274.

result of a variety of factors, only some of which we would identify as strictly a matter of the quantity of proof. Critics saw the "high standard" as irrational, too high by far, and they correctly explained its existence in terms of resistance to the use of the gallows,[108] but they often underestimated its importance to the administration of the criminal law. The high standard of proof and the *sense* often experienced in close and crowded courtrooms that it had not been reached were crucial to the system of trial by jury as it worked for centuries. They allowed jurors to conceal from themselves the extent to which myriad other concerns determined the outcome of their deliberations. Perhaps the most significant of these other concerns was the reputation of the defendant, and reputation had to do not only with the likelihood that the defendant had indeed acted as charged but also with more open-ended matters of just deserts that jurors could not easily confront as such.[109] The high standard was a powerful legal and psychological force. It was, to be sure, an instrument of justice, indeed of circumspection and delicacy,[110] a pervasive rationalization that held people of all orders fixed in their respect for the system and their place in it. It was also, however, a surrogate for the implicit understanding, which the bench shared, that general social attitudes regarding the value of human life could not—indeed, should not—be breached. It tended to deceive the English about the nature of their law, their legal system, and their biases. It produced a powerful ethic of supposed legal certainty and consistency, but its true sources lay in an uneasy combination of responses to the needs, both downward-projecting and upward-flowing, of politics and social existence.

Research on trial jury composition, as it now stands, suggests that the English criminal trial jury, especially in cases of felony, was dominated by local elites, men who played a significant governing role in everyday life at the level of the ward, parish, or hundred. The assize criminal trial jury forged a connection between the central authorities

108. Ibid., chap. 7, sec. 3.

109. Ibid., 282–85. See also P.J.R. King, "Decision-Makers and Decision-Making in English Criminal Law, 1750–1820," *Historical Journal* 27 (1984): 25–28. I reserve for another occasion discussion of a closely related phenomenon that I believe played a significant role in the resolution of capital cases in the eighteenth century (and since): the tendency of jurors to take into account—consciously or otherwise—the degree to which, as jurors perceived the matter, offenders had acted under the influence of circumstances beyond their control. I allude to this point in *Verdict According to Conscience*, 301–2, 316, 383.

110. Hay, "Property, Authority and the Criminal Law," 49.

and the level of government below county leadership, a level with which county officials always had to deal. When the hundredal requirement broke down, or was jettisoned, county officials turned to persons of the same class as those who had served earlier, taking them from wherever in the county they might be obtained. If the persons to whom they turned were therefore not dependent upon the politics of the specific locales of the cases they heard, they nonetheless reflected the needs and interests of similarly situated local elites elsewhere in the county. The tie between Crown and countryside reflected in the jury was an important instrument that gave thrust to central initiatives and prestige to local middle-class men. Central authorities both coopted the latter and were, I believe, coopted by them. We are little closer than we were at the outset to being able to describe the power relationship in which judge and jury were locked. But that is as much because that relationship was two-sided and contradictory as because the evidence has been lost.[111]

We are, however, better able to identify the main turning points in the history of trial jury composition. The partial outline of events I formulated elsewhere has been significantly modified and elaborated to produce a revised version that can be summarized as follows. At the outset, jury service was aimed at knights and very substantial freeholders, who were expected to draw upon the knowledge of those lesser landholders whom they trusted or whom they could coerce into cooperating with them. Presentment was the crucial stage, and when a second, final resolution came to be made by jury, it proved to be dominated by those who had served as presenters. To encourage acceptance of this ultimate verdict, the Crown allied with the presenters the more substantial men of the vills nearest to the location of the offense. Thus began the history of a trial jury that, although elitist in the most local context, was composed of men who sometimes ranked below the elites at the hundredal level and nearly always ranked below those who governed the county. The structure of the eyre allowed for continued domination by hundredal leadership, and this under the eye of county potentates at gaol delivery. Hundred representatives were less constrained from above, but their position within the local elites was mixed. The county and hundred officials who supplied the panels increasingly relied on local officials—village constables, coro-

111. Joan R. Kent has approached the problem of the relationship between the central government and village communities in early modern England in *The English Village Constable, 1580–1642: A Social and Administrative Study* (1987). Kent's study provides an excellent context for understanding the role of the administration of the criminal law in the development of the English state.

ners, and the like. By the later Middle Ages, not only was the jury less likely to come from the hundred wherein the offense had been committed, but it was also more likely to contain members of merely village elites rather than the grandest men of the hundred. With the increase of small farmers who laid claim to a place among these local elites, the jury came to be identified squarely with the yeoman class. By the late sixteenth and early seventeenth centuries there were rarely many gentry on the trial jury even at the assizes. For the gentry, powerful representation upon, and direct domination of, the grand jury had become standard. Ultimately, an important social distinction between service on the two juries, grand and petty, became fixed; by the late seventeenth century there was a firm upper limit on the status of persons eligible (in social, not legal, terms) for trial jury service.

The middling groups, then, constituted the trial jury class. In national terms its ranks were small, and it sometimes included quite substantial farmers, and artisans and tradesmen of independent standing in commerce, although these latter groups shaded off more gradually into the ranks of the lesser artisanry and craftsmen, who were themselves above, but not entirely separate from, the better off of the laboring poor. From the perspective of the authorities, jury service by this middling class was appropriate as long as those who served were trustworthy, experienced, and inclined to follow the advice and inclinations of their betters. In a sense, the authorities settled for a "yeoman" jury that seemed to embody gentry instincts. Reforms during the middle and late decades of the seventeenth century stressed both formal property qualifications and a regularization of service, and they began—but only began—to undermine the dependence of the juror class upon local rather than national interests. As the rich and poor separated, jurors increasingly represented groups that were well above the great majority of defendants yet still far below England's wealthiest elite. The late-seventeenth- and eighteenth-century jury remained, to an important extent, a mediating body that was at once drawn from the higher ranks and still (although decreasingly) hemmed in by its involvement in local life. It was, as always, drawn from the propertied classes, and property was more and more a "statement" as well as an economic and political resource. There were perhaps differences from county to county regarding the sheer representation of wealth deciles on assize trial juries. Most often, jurors came from the top third or quarter of society; if some ranged into the highest decile, some others came from below the top third, although rarely if ever from the bottom half of society. This much we now know of the pre-Victorian criminal assize trial jury's economic status.

To an important degree, jury composition remained fairly stable while other aspects of criminal administration changed around it. Although some of these changes were themselves direct responses to the jury, most of them were responses to factors that implicated the jury only indirectly if at all. Historians have associated the rise of an independent prosecution with the decline in late medieval England of a social organization that made self-informing possible. Probably one ought to reconsider this view. There was, perhaps, a potential for an independent prosecution at a very early date, and victims may have pushed themselves forward rather than having been impelled by the breakdown of self-informing. As I have suggested, it was concern with serious crime that governed the decisions of Crown and bench; their treatment of lesser, nominally capital offenses emerged as a byproduct of new capacities for control rather than evolving as a consciously designed policy. Once effected, however, the elaboration of the prosecution allowed in turn for the control of juries in ways that may not have been intended. At the same time, enhanced royal control threatened an imbalance between the state and the individual that threw the jury's role into a special kind of relief. As self-protective and sincerely believed rationalizations of its own position and authority, the state emphasized what had long been mainly the case: that conviction at a capital level required virtually absolute proof, and that the bench stood ready as counsel to the accused. The practice of reprieve for an "unsafe" verdict partially nullified jury convictions against the evidence, an ironic response to the growth of an independent prosecution. Thus jury powers and their limits and the place of the jury in the constitution and in historical myth all owed their existence to the tensions created by the growth of government capacity as it pressed upon the once largely open-ended power of governance by local community elites. The idea of a prophylactic against government overreach—the principle of noncoercion—cannot be entirely separated from that of a safeguard against jury-based lynching or simple error. The struggle for control of jury ideology involved a more two-sided, rhetorical invocation of the right of the defendant than is sometimes recognized.

In such a climate it was inevitable that multiple perspectives on the jury would compete for a place in the English culture's idea of the criminal trial jury. Further regularization and control of the jury would proceed upon an argument for consistency and fairness. Even as late as the eighteenth century, appeals to a right to find the law would lay claim to the notion of a simple law evident to all men of conscience. To some, the jury would seem an unlearned and rustic mob; to others it would appear so much an arm of landed elites as to be a perversion of the very notion of communal judgment. Both of these perspectives were, of course, true. That is what made the jury so powerful an institution, one fluid enough in the impressions society had of it to weather all attacks. It was both the cutting edge of reform and the bastion of the status quo, and those who reviled it in one context lauded it in another. In that climate, one might ask, did subtle changes in composition matter very much?

Of course, changes in composition did matter. They affected actual behavior as well as perceptions of that behavior. The essays presented here not only help to establish who served in the capacity of criminal trial jurors, noting some substantial differences over time and place, they also link composition to behavior in ways that suggest how, both at the micro and the macro level, who sat could mean who lived and who died. There were, however, limits to this compositional effect. These limits inhered not only in the idea or ideas about the jury that prevailed in society at large; they resided also, and perhaps more significantly, in the ideas that jurors—representing the jury as an institution—had of themselves. Behavior was not solely a function of class or status or interest in any narrow, material sense; it was crucially a function of self-image and of one's own perceived role in national governance, in local society, and in the constitution. As jury composition altered, so too did ideas about the jury, but given ongoing traditions of thought, this process of change was necessarily gradual, and its impact on jurors within the age-old context of the ritual of determining life or death must have been all the more subject to ideological friction. Perhaps even highly placed jurors unconsciously acted out a kind of mediatory role on a basis far different from that on which the authorities intended them to proceed. It is even possible that the higher the central authorities raised jurors, the further those authorities expanded the process by which England's national elites gained experience in seeing human behavior from the perspective of society's wide and troubled base.

Acknowledgments

I am grateful to my co-editor, James Cockburn, and to the other contributors for their thoughtful comments on an early draft of this essay.

I would also like to thank Kate Gilbert, Sarah Harrison, and Susan Reynolds. Much of the work on this essay was undertaken during my fellowship year at the Center for Advanced Study in the Behavioral Sciences, Stanford, California. I am indebted to the Center and to the Andrew W. Mellon Fund for their generous support.

Notes on Contributors

J. M. Beattie, a professor of history at the University of Toronto, is the author of *The English Court in the Reign of George I* (1967) and *Crime and the Courts in England, 1660–1800* (1986).

J. S. Cockburn, a professor of history at the University of Maryland, is the author of *A History of English Assizes, 1558–1714* (1972) and the editor of *Crime in England, 1550–1800* (1977) and the multivolume *Calendar of Assize Records*.

Thomas A. Green is a professor of law and history at the University of Michigan. He is the author of several articles on the history of the English criminal trial jury and of *Verdict According to Conscience: Perspectives on the English Criminal Trial Jury, 1200–1800* (1985).

Roger D. Groot is a professor of law at Washington and Lee University. His work on the history of the criminal trial jury has appeared in the *American Journal of Legal History*. He is currently studying the law of suicide in thirteenth-century England and is examining the descriptions of legal proceedings in the Tristan stories.

Douglas Hay teaches at Osgoode Hall Law School and York University, Toronto. He helped edit and contributed to *Albion's Fatal Tree: Crime and Society in Eighteenth-Century England* (1975) and has published articles in both law and history journals on the subjects of legal history and the social history of law and their relationship.

P. J. R. King, a graduate of the universities of Kent, Exeter, and Cambridge, is a research fellow at the University of Liverpool. He is currently expanding his doctoral thesis for publication as *Crime, Justice and Discretion, 1740–1820.*

P. G. Lawson, a visiting assistant professor of history at the University of Toronto, received his doctorate from Oxford University in 1982. At present he is writing a book on theft in Tudor and Stuart England.

Bernard William McLane is an associate professor of history at the University of Rochester. He also holds commissioned rank in the Marine Corps Reserve and serves as a field historian. He is currently engaged in a study of the interrelationship between disorder and legal change in late-thirteenth- and early-fourteenth-century Lincolnshire.

J. B. Post, a graduate of Oxford University, is currently head of the Modern Records Department of the Public Record Office, London. He is the author of numerous articles on the sources of medieval English history, especially on the interpretation and limitations of the criminal records.

Edward Powell, a graduate of Oxford University, is a fellow and the Director of Studies in History at Downing College, Cambridge. He has published several articles on the legal history of the medieval period and is currently working on a study of the administration of criminal justice in later medieval England.

Stephen K. Roberts is a graduate of the universities of Sussex and Exeter and a former research fellow at the University of London Institute of Historical Research. Since 1982 he has worked in continuing education in Warwickshire. He is the author of several articles on seventeenth-century administrative and social history and of *Recovery and Restoration in an English County: Devon Local Administration, 1646–1670* (1985).

Index

Library of Congress Cataloging-in-Publication Data

Twelve good men and true.

Includes index.

1. Jury—Great Britain—History. 2. Criminal law—Great Britain—History. I. Cockburn, J. S. II. Green, Thomas Andrew.

KD8400.A75T94 1988 345.42'075 87–29118
344.20575

ISBN 0–691–05511–4 (alk. paper)

James S. Cockburn is Professor of History at the University of Maryland.

Thomas A. Green is Professor of History at the University of Michigan.

www.ingramcontent.com/pod-product-compliance
Lightning Source LLC
LaVergne TN
LVHW082346011026
849160LV00024B/1159